AF380632

History of English Literature

History of English Literature

Volume 8
Book 1
From the Late Inter-War Years to 2010

Franco Marucci

Translated from the Italian by Alexander Gillan

PETER LANG

Oxford • Bern • Berlin • Bruxelles • New York • Wien

Bibliographic information published by Die Deutsche Nationalbibliothek. Die Deutsche Nationalbibliothek lists this publication in the Deutsche National-bibliografie; detailed bibliographic data is available on the Internet at http://dnb.d-nb.de.

A catalogue record for this book is available from the British Library.

Library of Congress Cataloging-in-Publication Data

Names: Marucci, Franco, 1949- author.
Title: From the late inter-war years to 2010 / Franco Marucci.
Other titles: Storia della letteratura inglese. Dal 1922 al 2000. English
Description: Oxford ; New York : Peter Lang AG, [2019] | Series: History of
   English literature ; volume 8 | Translation of Storia della letteratura
   inglese - Volume V, Tomo II, dal 1922 al 2000 : dal secondo anteguerra al
   2000. | Includes bibliographical references and index.
Identifiers: LCCN 2018032661 | ISBN 9781789974010 (alk. paper)
Subjects: LCSH: English literature--20th century--History and criticism. |
   English literature--21st century--History and criticism.
Classification: LCC PR97 .M3713 2018 | DDC 820.9/0091--dc23 LC record available at
https://lccn.loc.gov/2018032661

Originally published in Italian as *Storia della letteratura inglese – Dal secondo anteguerra al 2000* by Casa Editrice Le Lettere (2011).

Cover image: Graham Sutherland, *Devastation, 1941: An East End Street* (1941).

Cover design by Brian Melville.

ISBN 978-1-78997-402-7 (print) • ISBN 978-1-78874-126-2 (ePDF)
ISBN 978-1-78874-127-9 (ePub) • ISBN 978-1-78874-128-6 (mobi)

© Peter Lang AG 2019

Published by Peter Lang Ltd, International Academic Publishers,
52 St Giles, Oxford, OX1 3LU, United Kingdom
oxford@peterlang.com, www.peterlang.com

Contents

The *Index of names* and *Thematic index* for Volume 8 can be found at the end of Book 2.

List of abbreviations

AAA	J. R. Taylor, *Anger and After: A Guide to the New British Drama*, Harmondsworth 1963.
ATD	W. Allen, *Tradition and Dream: The English and American Novel from the Twenties to Our Time*, London 1986.
BAUGH	*A Literary History of England*, ed. A. C. Baugh, 4 vols, London 1967.
BRM	*Modernism: A Guide to European Literature 1890–1930*, ed. M. Bradbury and J. McFarlane, Harmondsworth 1991 (1st edn 1976).
CAB	*I contemporanei – Letteratura inglese*, ed. V. Amoruso and F. Binni, 2 vols, Roma 1982.
CLA	M. Praz, *Cronache letterarie anglosassoni*, 4 vols, Roma 1951 and 1966.
CMM	*Modernismo / Modernismi. Dall'avanguardia storica agli anni Trenta e oltre*, ed. G. Cianci, Milano 1991.
CRHE	*The Critical Heritage* of individual authors, London, with editors and publication years indicated in the bibliographies.
DES	V. De Sola Pinto, *Crisis in English Poetry 1880–1940*, London 1963 (1st edn 1951).
DUN	D. Dunn, 'Language and Liberty', Introduction to *The Faber Book of Twentieth-Century Scottish Poetry*, ed. D. Dunn, London 1992.
HAP	*Hopkins Among the Poets*, ed. R. F. Giles, Hamilton 1985.
HYN	S. Hynes, *The Auden Generation: Literature and Politics in England in the 1930s*, London 1976.
IDM	F. Marucci, *L'inchiostro del mago. Saggi di letteratura inglese dell'Ottocento*, Pisa 2009.
IZZO	C. Izzo, *Storia della letteratura inglese*, 2 vols, Milano 1961 and 1963.
KET	A. Kettle, *An Introduction to the English Novel*, vol. II, London 1972 (1st edn London 1953).
KPE	F. Kermode, *Puzzles and Epiphanies: Essays and Reviews 1958–1961*, London 1962.

KRG	F. R. Karl, *A Reader's Guide to the Contemporary English Novel*, London 1968.
LET	*Letture. Libro e spettacolo. Mensile di studi e rassegne.*
LRB	*The London Review of Books.*
MAR	*Storia della civiltà letteraria inglese*, ed. F. Marenco, 4 vols, Torino 1996.
MEF	G. Melchiori, *I funamboli. Il manierismo nella letteratura inglese da Joyce ai giovani arrabbiati*, It. trans., Torino 1974 (1st Eng. edn *The Tightrope Walkers*, London 1956).
MIT	L. Mittner, *Storia della letteratura tedesca*, 3 vols in 4 tomes, Torino 1964–1977.
MPR	J. H. Miller, *Poets of Reality: Six Twentieth-Century Writers*, Cambridge, MA 1965.
OCE	G. Orwell, *Collected Essays, Journalism and Letters*, ed. S. Orwell and I. Angus, 4 vols, Harmondsworth 1970.
PGU	*The Pelican Guide to English Literature*, ed. B. Ford, 7 vols, Harmondsworth 1966 (1st edn 1954).
PSL	M. Praz, *Storia della letteratura inglese*, Firenze 1968.
SSI	M. Praz, *Studi e svaghi inglesi*, 2 vols, Milano 1983 (1st edn 1937).
TLS	*The Times Literary Supplement.*
WAR	A. C. Ward, *20th Century English Literature 1901–1960*, London 1964 (1st edn 1928).

Volume 1	F. Marucci, *History of English Literature*, vol. 1, Oxford 2018.
Volume 2	F. Marucci, *History of English Literature*, vol. 2, Oxford 2018.
Volume 3	F. Marucci, *History of English Literature*, vol. 3, Oxford 2018.
Volume 4	F. Marucci, *History of English Literature*, vol. 4, Oxford 2019.
Volume 5	F. Marucci, *History of English Literature*, vol. 5, Oxford 2019.
Volume 6	F. Marucci, *History of English Literature*, vol. 6, Oxford 2019.
Volume 7	F. Marucci, *History of English Literature*, vol. 7, Oxford 2019.

Note. Except for the above abbreviations, full publication information of cited works will be found in the bibliographies for each author.

§ 1. *English literature from the late inter-war years to 2010*

Setting out on this Volume 8 of my work, my observations need to go back to a good fifteen years before 1945, to introduce and contextualize figures, movements and literary experiences parallel to Modernism, or merely touched by it or decidedly and contentiously outside its area. Without this, late twentieth-century literature would not be complete, precisely because in their various transformations they announce developments well beyond the watershed of the War. In the main I have selected the following criteria for inclusion, in ascending hierarchical order: 1) by date of birth, with the automatic *sine qua non* that authors should debut after 1921–1922, and therefore that they should be born after 1900 (with some slight exceptions, nonetheless); 2) formal. As early as the late 1920s, the updated formula of the traditional novel began to re-enter fiction: we have seen that modernist fiction looked back to the eighteenth-century variety of Sterne, Smollett and Fielding, although in that tradition there lay other competing seeds destined to blossom in the long term. In poetry, save for clamorous exceptions, we witness the repudiation of Eliot's poetics of fragmentation, of the mythical method and of every kind of neo-Romanticism, and a greater adherence to daily life; 3) semiotic: that is, a much more polarized attention to the addressee, somewhat more present than previously in literary communication, and more targeted, more directly brought into play. A greater interaction is also sought, instead of adjusting the product to coteries or eliminating the reader *tout court* by opting for self-communication; 4) one consequence is the decline of the supremacy of the signifier, of linguistic playfulness, of parody and generally speaking also of the technical and tightrope experiment; every uncouth emphasis on content over form is avoided, but an emphasis on, and imbalance towards, the formal tend to be reduced; 5) commitment: an undertaking to reform society, to approve and appropriate a poetics and practice of intervention which led writers off to the war fronts wherever freedom was being violated; a concretely socialist and communist commitment. As I mentioned in the previous volume, D. H. Lawrence too emphasized content over form, but fought for a cultural and sexual revolution, not one first and foremost political; 6) the inverse of the above: religious and spiritual commitment, with an expressly Catholic literature, the photographic negative of Bolshevism, also because human beings are portrayed as being in a vertical relationship with the absolute in the first instance, rather than as members of a horizontal community from which they are separated. In certain cases, the two groups intermingle since they are fighting for the same objective, but this merger arises more in the passage of Bolshevist sympathizers to forms of spiritualism than the contrary. This scenario will lead to borderline cases, and up to 1945, and also a little beyond, it will prove impossible to clearly separate epigonal Modernism from commitment, notably in Henry Green, or other experiences that dilute it or make it instrumental to political intervention, as in early Auden, in the Orwell of *Coming Up for Air* and others. One can foresee incorporating likewise the final backlashes of Modernism itself, with the last 'tightrope walkers', the last *pasticheurs*, and all of the postmodern up to the threshold of the third millennium. At this point we must introduce, postulate and register a second interstice, those writers who emerged during the first half of the century, in the inter-war years, and were active afterwards as well, in some cases with fifty- and sixty-year-long careers (such as Graham Greene). In what follows the points listed briefly above will be expanded upon, while other later transitions will be anticipated in the form of general coordinates, the subject of the six parts that make up this volume.

2. In the chronology of twentieth-century English literature it is possible, and indeed essential, to establish the decade as the unit of measure, not the twenty-five-year generation; or even the discriminating factor of the year of birth. Being born in the early 1890s had a quasi-mathematical effect: taking part as adults in the First World War. Being born in the first years of the new century meant eschewing it, and not even living it as witnesses or as combatants, while growing up in the atmosphere of decay and disillusionment of the early post-war years. Being born in the early 1920s or 1930s was something totally different again. And so, to repeat, twentieth-century English literature can also be divided up generally speaking by date of birth. As 1844 was for the Victorians, so the years from 1903 to 1907 were of grace for the new generation. Common traits can be found among those born in those years, in Waugh, Greene, Green, Powell, Beckett, and Snow, who read one another even if they were not really close, and who had mostly followed the Eton-Oxford scholastic model, exhibited a note of Modernism that was not that of Joyce, and were brought together under the sign of

the burlesque and the dialogic fantasy. Having arrived too late for the First World War they fought, some of them, in the Second; but first they had to face the crossroads or triple crossroads between Protestantism, Catholicism, and humanist agnosticism or Bolshevism. In the 1920s, apathy, disaffection and irresponsibility reigned, as shown by the small turnout for the 1919 elections, with Prime Minister Baldwin gaining success because his was not a politics of principles. The Great Strike of 1926 called urgently to public responsibility a young intelligentsia that believed they could burn themselves out before the age of thirty, and whose daredevil capricious vicissitudes are described impassively in the early novels of Huxley, Waugh and Powell. It is no coincidence that the main alternative to Modernism is the Auden generation of the 1930s, taking its cue therefore from the similar characters of a group of writer-friends animated by common purposes and objectives in that decade. The task of every historian of this decade-long literary movement has been made easier by Samuel Hynes's book, *The Auden Generation* (1976), an extremely useful spectrogram of the politicized, socialist and Marxist literature that recognized Auden as its leader. In fact, into this network were gathered, tangentially or directly, all the great and less great writers with few exceptions, and exceptions that are signally the whole of historical Modernism, which is unquestionably not insignificant. Hynes's book is also a calendar that measures and categorizes – taking the pulse, as it were, of the literary community year after year and even month after month – the development of the aesthetic and ideological debate, as well as the curve of simple moods, against the convulsive background of the major historical events. Above all, Hynes reconstructs the mixed sentiment of the generations of university graduates born during the first decade of the century, who felt envious of those who had gone to war, and regretted not being of an age to fight. Their vision of the First World War was substantially filtered through the poetry of Owen, who, in his most famous aesthetic definition, disavowed blind and fanatical heroism: 'the poetry is in the pity'. This notwithstanding, an alternative myth of the war was being formed. In the wake of the panorama of futility and destruction in *The Waste Land*, two groups were born: Waugh's 'bright young things', and the political activists who gathered around Auden, who himself nevertheless held the most ambiguous and indecisive political ideology of them all.

At the end of the 1920s, the *Oxford Poetry* series began to appear, which, in anthologies edited also by Auden, gathered together the compositions of that university's aspiring poets. Each yearly issue opened with a preface, and these prefaces represent a gradual becoming aware of the relationship between art and society. Already in 1930, nostalgia for the myth of the First World War, with its repercussions and deformations, confused itself and overlapped with the fear of a second war, which even translated into a search for a hero to invest in, who could be a fascist and communist at one and the same time: in concrete terms, the two Lawrences, D. H. and T. E. Room was made for the dream or reality of a revolution, which, however, had to lead to the basically Georgian goal of a primitive, rural, uncontaminated England: 'Merrie Olde England'. Apart from the poetry magazines and those of a miscellaneous nature,[1] politicized publishing was born by merit of Victor Gollancz, whose first work, which appeared in 1933, was a catalogue of victims of Nazism, and who in 1936 founded the Left Book Club with the goal of politically educating the masses. The emergency caused new and more politically committed literary genres to open like a fan, such as the documentary, in film as well as in print, and reportage, since, in certain cases, writing was synonymous with informing; another fortunate repertoire was the travel book, aimed at restoring to the reading public the sense of an enlarged world, and at once a surrogate for exploration and heroic adventure. In 1936, when the first warnings came of the intercontinental storm brewing, the committed writer had gradually to repudiate the traditional pacifism of left-wing writers. But the distressing outcome of the Spanish experience was retraction, apathy, and resignation. The farewell to the 1930s was meted out in the most ferocious terms of indifference and abjuration by Malcolm Muggeridge in his *The Thirties*

---

1   Many of those just born, which distinguished themselves in editorial programmes and policies from the modernist magazines, included in their title the adjective 'new', as in *New Signatures*, brought to life in 1932 by Michael Roberts, where the politicized writers of the 1930s espoused the idea of literature as an instrument of change; or *New Country*, edited by Roberts again since 1933, or John Lehmann's *New Writing*. That same year *The Cambridge Left* was born. Grigson's *New Verse*, from 1933 to 1939, reinstated the criterion of quality, toning down the political content.

(1939). But a debunking had already come from Auden, who defined the political experience, which he himself had originated, a 'low dishonest' decade, virtually the same words as in Christopher Caudwell's verdict. The protagonists accused themselves of having taken their stance too much on the heat of the moment, of having abandoned themselves to gross error and spontaneous gestures, and above all of having cultivated so many ambiguities, and been prone to a great deal of indecision and uncertainty of aims. Orwell and Caudwell had been right: the courage to become out-and-out politicized writers had been lacking. The essay by Virginia Woolf, 'The Leaning Tower', written in 1940, annihilated a generation roosting as on a Tower of Pisa, leaning and above all of ivory, a generation that founded its subsistence on the alienation of the masses but felt threatened by the world's revolution: one therefore that propelled whoever lived on the tower downwards towards the masses. For others, the Oxfordians' obvious sense of guilt was due to the privilege of living off and exploiting the workers as well as the wealth coming from the Empire, were it not for the fact that this warmth towards the workers was romantic, mythical, and sentimental, rather than being a coherent political vision. Reams have been written to say and remind us that, in the final analysis, Marx was adopted by the Thirties poets as a convenient tool to act more freely, and to write poetry undisturbed, with no real intention of repudiating the middle classes.

3. Socialism and communism immediately after the War, and Anglicanism and Catholicism, alternatively or also consecutively offered themselves as an anchor to which to cling in a world in decline to those born in the early years of the twentieth century, who had escaped the glory and ignominy of the First World War by dint of their age (and this is largely Orwell's diagnosis, as we shall see, in 'Inside the Whale'). Viewed statistically, Catholicism was more tempting and won out over communism: the writers of the 1920s were almost all communists, convicted or potential, and if some continued heatedly to be so, others crossed to the opposite pole. What was it that these writers found in Catholicism? Waugh converted from atheist nihilism, apolitical and therefore not socialist, and did so as a form of interpreting and normalizing the contemporary world. The Catholicism of the last decade of the nineteenth century, aesthetic and decadent, imbued with mysticism and sensuality, and as such a compromise,

fascinated him. It was no coincidence that Waugh became Catholic after studying Rossetti and the Pre-Raphaelites and the ambiguous cult of the saints, especially the female ones. Greene too let himself become infected, since his Catholicism – which, he would always maintain, was not emotional, but abstract and intellectual – was an upturned *gradus ad Parnassum*, that is, a mystique of sin and hell. These two writers, in particular, conceive human life as a Baroque, Counter-Reformation agon, contextualized in everyday life, between the sinning man and the pursuing God (above all Greene). But, we come to realize, this is a representation, and the representation of Nineties Catholicism – that of Johnson, Dowson, and Francis Thompson – which dated back to Hopkins. Ford Madox Ford, too, who was benevolently prefaced by Greene, depicted himself as a damned soul incapable of defeating the seductions of sin, particularly of the sexual kind, cultivated and caressed satanism and had it fight with the instinct of purification. It was only a short step to another Catholic *sui generis* with daring ideas on sexual morality, born only a decade and a half later: Muriel Spark. The polarity between the Catholic generation and the politicized poetry of the 1930s is highlighted by one fact: Auden's affiliates could not live alone, while Waugh and Greene could not but live alone.[2] At the same time, it is an implicit result that while Auden and his group were poets, the Catholic generation, and in any case another contemporary generation outside Auden's, were novelists and prose writers operating on two radically divergent aesthetics: serialism and indeterminateness. Some of them built coordinated, closed and interrelated oeuvres, and were authors of sagas and sequels, or novels modelled on one another and obedient to a fixed formula as regards setting, layout, time and place (Powell, Snow, even Beckett), whom we might even call classicists or neoclassicists. Others – Angus Wilson, among many others – did not write even one novel the same as another; they reject any principle of internal order, surprise and faze the reader, each novel representing a new beginning.

2   See in Couto 1988 (bibliography of Greene, § 49.1), the conclusive interview with the novelist, and his irony concerning that 'gang' to which he glories in not having belonged, and his approval, as a general rule, of writing in isolation.

4. Poetry, the novel and the theatre came to operate over the last half-century against a background formed by the added parameters of the sociology of mass communication, of the literary market and of the huge broadening of the field of English language literature, but *ipso facto* no longer English or even British. New elements, factors and phenomena of the scenario to take into account are the increased leisure time, which made further room available for reading and entertainment; it was radio, cinema, and above all television that emptied the theatres where musicals and the commercial repertoire had always held sway. Poetry, from the time of Larkin and the Movement, has tried desperately to find a remedy for its intrinsically elite nature, by means of a relative lowering of its formal and lexical difficulty, while at the same time attempting to produce texts that can be recited, performed, even sung, or serve as a vehicle of protest and a festival event. The novel has lately become torn between the trap of market demand and absolute inspiration, a market gone mad and turned savage due to the profound crisis of publishing, the advent of the Internet and a disaffection with quality reading, a market conditioned by the predominance of the escapist, sensationalist, instant sale variety. Is a compromise possible? The media maintains the exact opposite and often persuades even the most cautious and presumably objective and unswayable of critics that this or that novel will pass into history, that it is the masterpiece of the current century and will continue to be so into the next. Indeed, the typical novelist of our times appears tyrannized and obsessed by the market, and when an author has debuted with a successful novel, which may even be deeply felt, he or she is pestered by the publishers and obliged, while the iron is still hot, to come out immediately and fatally with a less polished and convincing product. With the aid of advertising, writers therefore dissimulate their collusion with the bookshop system. It is also true that they often make the risky wager of lampooning mass culture, perhaps like Amis in *Money*, simply by describing it and exploiting its expressive means and idiolects. The most questionable aspect is that many novels written by wily authors are already designed to be transposed for the cinema or as television series. And in any case the highest accolade for a novel is to be transposed for these media, whilst the digital encyclopaedias rush to say, as if it were a certificate of guarantee, that it has been filmed by and

with whom, listing also the book prizes won, which, it is easily intended, are obtained by a sapient hype. As things stand, various contemporary novelists who have just passed on have remained the authors of a single book, having then produced in series largely forgotten works, as in the case of Anthony Burgess.

5. Flexibly, as many do following a formula of compromise, I too shall imply as 'English literature' that of the British Isles including Ireland. The term 'English literature' has now become notoriously improper, but is retained here in this unquestionably imprecise sub-significance. As a result African, Indian, Australian, Canadian and Caribbean writers in English will be excluded. Pending are cases such as those of writers who were born and grew up in Commonwealth countries and moved to England as adolescents, youths, or young adults: these are situations to be resolved case by case using common sense, without splitting hairs, and according to the variable extent to which they have become part of the literary establishment centred in England and in particular in London. I am no less perfectly aware of the error or impropriety committed in separating and splitting up a literary universe in the English language like today's, that is, globalized and hence cemented by strong internal ties; aware, in short, of the myopia that hinders conceiving it and considering it as such, in place of the literature of 'little old England'. They are both undoubtedly overlapping universes, separate and independent yet sutured together by the English language in which the literary works are written. A second problem concerns the inclusion and exclusion of living and hence still active writers. It would have been a transgression against the principles underlying this work to aim at exhaustiveness. This is of course a mirage, found in many cadastral surveys of twentieth-century literature that are repeatedly unleashed onto the market, since there is barely the time to write about and interpret in a makeshift way a work that has just come out that another takes its place. According to Eliot's well-known criterion, each new work alters the provisional vision of even a single writer, when it does not render it completely obsolete. I for my part will not fall victim here to encyclopaedic ambitions, and have resisted the temptation, or rather the unrealistic ambition of the card index or *catalogue raisonné*. My objective is not to level off and set everything on substantially the same

plane, but to map the geography and dig deep, highlighting the differences and eminences, passing quickly over that which stands out the least and over the flatter surfaces. The second reason is that history is not a news commentary, and I believe that, by and large, for up to at least two thirds of a writer's career it is not possible to draft a credible, objective summary that is not arbitrary and subjective, or still conjectural. The panorama of English letters in the last twenty-thirty years remains indecipherable, too fragmented, too cacophonous, too fleeting, eluding intelligible classification and even semi-definitive evaluation. This means that dozens and dozens of the latest authors, or even those on everyone's lips, will not be found included here. Talking about this work of mine with friends and colleagues I have often heard glowingly recommended the name of this or that writer to be dealt with *indispensably* over any other – entirely unjustified enthusiasms for a historian. To these invitations I reply that it is still too early, and that prudence is wanted, elicited by writers who were alive thirty years ago, on whom incautious critics decided to write overly premature books that now have very little or no value, since they have become obsolete or have been superseded by later works of this or that poet or playwright, whose developments were unforeseen. Hence, readers of this volume should by no means be surprised if, assuming the voice of Jiminy Cricket, I shall complain to the point of tedium about these cases of precipitousness concerning writers such as Durrell, Golding, Spark, Angus Wilson and others. This is to say that literary events, writers and their works should be and will be seen in perspective, a word that implies fully realized detachment from the experience in question, and presupposes, above all, the coming into being and the availability of a literary experience in its totality or virtual totality, and not in mid-stream. Similarly, amongst the late twentieth-century writers open to historical analysis, and whose production is closed by now, some only have been singled out for attention. Living writers at the height of their powers will not be dealt with save for a few exceptions; but others will, such as Geoffrey Hill and Doris Lessing,[3] since they are so advanced in years that

---

3   Lessing and Hill were living when this Volume 8 was first published [translator's note].

it is difficult to think that their further productions can radically alter an estimation that has already been well defined and delineated as their work developed. In taking this decision – no living writers, save for the documented exceptions – I automatically exclude not only promising authors in their thirties and forties, but also some writers now in their sixties of undoubted and already proven importance, certain of whom are conceivably on their way to becoming in twenty or thirty years the most representative of their generation. This I readily concede.

§ 2. *From reconstruction to desocialization*

It was the very historians and sociologists of the second half of the twentieth century who suggested to compress these fifty years according to these two antithetical terms and concepts, reconstruction and desocialization, which are also two poles that never come close by their very nature. And they cannot, given that, since 1945, politics and society have been travelling on two asymptotic, or better divergent, roads, progressively deaf and mute to one another, as it were. Politics may rebuild houses destroyed by the war, in concrete terms, and return to filling citizens' wallets; but re-establishing society needs educators and inspirers. It is easy to notice that with the Second World War the *maîtres à penser* or even just the cultural mediators disappear, the last being Orwell and T. S. Eliot, who, in updated horizons, covered the function carried out by Ruskin, Matthew Arnold and, in his small way, Hopkins in the nineteenth century. Other potential educators, such as Marcuse, denied that they were so, with their implicitly disintegrating message. But there were also fewer charismatic leaders and even the reference point of the monarchy faded out. British politics has only counted two important figures from 1945 until today, if Churchill's last cabinet is excluded, and two figures who, with their name and antonomasia could leave their mark on an epoch or, at least, on a segment of an epoch, and thus faintly comparable to a Peel or Disraeli in the most recent past: and they are Margaret Thatcher and Tony Blair. The sufficiently marked character of these premierships can be gathered from the fact that terms have been created from them that have become part of the political lexicon, such as 'Thatcherism' or 'Blairism', whereas in the period 1945–1970 the two main parties were not excessively distinguishable in terms of differences of opinion, and were somewhat camouflaged, so much so that it was common to speak of 'Butskellism'.[1] And as I shall explain, a distinctive or more distinctive programmatic objective of Thatcher and Blair's mandate was precisely that of the reconstitution of the community, or at least of a community (desocialization means nothing less than the collapse of Matthew Arnold's organic social unity). With all of her tact and discretion, or precisely in virtue of this, Queen Elizabeth II, whose reign has now surpassed in length that of Victoria and her namesake Elizabeth I, could not aspire to define these sixty years as 'Elizabethan' without running into an unfortunate equivocation. However, to return to my opening assertion, there could not be any mediator or educating agency in the late twentieth century precisely because the battle against the principle of authority had been won, and continues to be won daily hands down. This could prove to be a very general key to understanding this recently ended half-century as well as the one that has just begun. The components and proofs are various, as are the phenomena. After 1945, there was an explosion of anarchic and individual freedoms after an unconscious, century-long repression; and oppression was something that British society, the grandchild of its Victorian ancestors, knew well. A kind of domino effect rapidly began, which led to questioning and destroying everything that had been acquired and become time-encrusted. Above all, there was a desire to re-dictate history *ipso facto* and one that until then had been identified with violence, extermination and war. Immediately after 1945, Britain was very far from embracing a radical disarmament, in fact it launched and financed research into the H-bomb, and was ready to intervene militarily worldwide to support any armed revolt against communism, to keep under control various strategic areas and points on the globe, such as Gibraltar and Singapore, and to preserve precious bridgeheads. The British protests and marches of the 1950s against nuclear arms and the atomic threat were not aggressions, since an apparently contradictory culture had begun to spread

---

1   From a combination of the names of the politicians Butler, Tory, and Gaitskell, Labour (M. Fforde, *Storia della Gran Bretagna*, Bari 2002, 345). Neither of them, repeatedly predicted to become Prime Minister, would ever be elected.

from America, one of good graces, gentleness, flowers, and respect for the environment. The 'beat' root covered a multitude of semes, among which the two most significant were the 'beaten' and the 'blessed'. The so-called 'generation gap', which is actually an eternal sociological fact and a constant in history, became radicalized in this half-century. The young moved to the assault and arrived in the front line in the name of the revenge of fantasy, and in the name of fantasy wanted to eradicate everything old and gangrenous.[2] The ideal of eternal youth seems a typically contemporary, modern myth, with the young who must remain young, attractive and without an ounce of adipose tissue, and who attend the gym daily to have a body that is slim, lithe and muscular; but the adults go too, to become young again, while the ladies subject themselves to lifting and plastic surgery. In reality, this was a Faustian dream, an eternal myth, which thirty years earlier had been expressed by Waugh's 'bright young things', for whom there was no tomorrow, and even if there was, it did not count. The boomerang of repression is permissiveness. In the early 1960s, the use of contraceptives was no longer clandestine or prohibited, surrounded by an air of scandal and demonized. The myth of virginity and feminine purity was superseded and demolished from one day to the next, like that of the family nucleus as the basis of society. In an unstoppable vortex one by one the myths of respectability collapsed, while those that until yesterday had seemed insurmountable barriers of ethics and morals were shattered. The revolution in the world of fashion consists in the fact that its only constriction is freedom, the freedom to mate garments, mix colours, upset traditional combinations of dress and occasion – in a nutshell, to write new rules for the system; and this principle extended also to hairstyles and hairdos. The 'informal' was not merely an exquisitely artistic phenomenon, which had to do with pop art or Ian Fleming and Le Carré who had staggering sales while the purely literary-cultural limped onwards; or with cinema that, with Reisz, Richardson and Loach accompanied and often prevailed over

---

2   Along with the protagonists of the plays and novels of the 'angry generation', which I shall be studying, we might recall here another document of the sudden exaltation of anarchic freedom and the ascent to national fame of the teenage class, the in-itself mediocre novel *Absolute Beginners* (1959) by C. MacInnes.

the literary communication, by making it more flowing, while broadening youthful rage and feminine protest. On the contrary the 'informal' also means a social behaviour that can be observed in the fashions of first-name terms at first sight, of walking barefoot around the house or removing your shoes on the train and putting your feet on the seat being tolerated by ticket inspectors. But this fancy is also prone to abandon past fetishisms simply to adopt others, picking up fleeting, infectious, plagiarized fashions one after another, such as toe nails lacquered now with pale diaphanous varnishes and now with gaudy ones. As a penultimate, tangible symptom, or even as an allegory of the clash between the repressive Crown and individual freedom, some have interpreted the otherwise inexplicable national grief over the death of Princess Diana.

2. The country in debt, the state coffers dried up, 600,000 war casualties, its prestige as a pre-war superpower, above all else, faded and gone: for Britain in 1945 this was in short the balance of the aftermath on the cessation of the conflict, despite its having been won. For the first time in its recent history, Britain needed help to rebuild, and it asked for loans.[3] The paradox pointed out by Eric Hobsbawm is that this post-war Britain, reduced to admitting defeat, underdeveloped, without industries, with a galloping deficit and recourse to rationing, which according to other historians was entering the 'great British economic disaster' between 1945 and 1992,[4] was nevertheless, and remained, 'a golden age'. As Macmillan proudly said in 1957: 'Let us be frank about it – most of our people have never had it so good'. And the history of manners comes to our aid in noting the counterpart of a London that for the whole world was 'Swinging London'. An impartial solution to this difference of opinion could be that Britain was coming out of a period of fatted calves, that all European countries had to cope with reconstruction after six years of war, and that Britain had to adapt and tighten its belt a little, and more than the others since, willing or not, it was on the point of carrying out a vast decolonization, with all the

---

3　　Planned to last for four years starting from 1947, the Marshall Plan offered various forms of aid to Europe for a total of 12.5 billion dollars.

4　　M. Fforde, *Storia della Gran Bretagna*, chapter XIII.

economic repercussions that this would bring.[5] The ignominious result of the 1956 Suez crisis was judged by some as proof that Britain wished to re-establish its old imperialism, and with the failures and upsets that Britain met in Cyprus and above all in Ireland; but then it was France that bluntly imposed a veto twice on Britain's agonized requests to join the EEC, a road that would not end until 1973 when the UK finally entered. The crisis, or a crisis, intervened at the end of the 1960s and the early 1970s; tangibly in 1973, with a rise in the price of oil made by the producing countries, or perhaps two years earlier with the devaluation of the pound. Attlee's Labour party, in power after the end of the war, had meanwhile launched a nationalization policy (the Bank of England, electricity, civil aviation) and support for council housing; but the real feather in its cap was the Welfare State which ensured a free health service for families. Under Macmillan decriminalization of homosexuality between consenting adults began its path through Parliament; but ironically, his government slipped on a banana skin of Meredithian memory, the Profumo Affair.[6] The course of literature, the dramatic one at least, was unexpectedly derailed by a new university legislation, with the political decision to opt for a mass university system that would flank – not substitute for! – that of the elite of Cambridge, Oxford, or London, and new-built, decentralized campuses which took the name of 'red brick universities'. But those who live by the sword die by the sword: the university for the masses assimilated subversive contents that backfired on those who had supplied the tools to acquire that culture. Literary 'anger' was born in the mid-1950s as a protest that was genuinely and solely British against the university education system, fifteen years earlier than the Parisian protest of 1968; but this emerged also as an indefinable

5   As a fruit of its decolonization the United Kingdom became multiracial; against this Britain the right-wing extremist Enoch Powell used to thunder with his slogans advocating the return of all non-English citizens to their homelands.

6   This a tangible example of the contradiction between politics and society, out of phase with each other: unmasked, Profumo denied a flirt with the call-girl Christine Keeler, who was splendidly immortalized by the photographer Lewis Morley, nude and sitting backwards on a chair, in an obvious citation of Marlene Dietrich in *The Blue Angel*.

and indefinite malaise, which evidently eluded Macmillan when he uttered that celebrated sentence – 'You never had it so good' – thinking exclusively of the wallet. Harold Wilson became Prime Minister for the first time in 1964 with a programme of industrial and technological modernizations and above all the opening of credit for the younger class; however, during his second, minority, mandate in 1974, he backtracked and withdrew daring new modernizing projects, focusing instead on a return to stability and the 'quiet life' – to traditional British values, therefore. When the Tories returned to power, Mrs Thatcher not only launched severe measures against deflation that impacted on the currency's purchasing power and provoked a wave of protests and strikes, but also resuscitated the imperialistic spirit with the reconquering of the Argentine Falklands. With this she hammered on about restoring the old individualist Britain, healthy, isolated, proud, tenacious; she actually wanted, in a way, to re-Victorianize Britain.[7] Blair won the elections in 1997 focusing on the co-responsibility of the individual in managing the community: if, in other words, the individual prospers then the community benefits, which is an updating of Matthew Arnold's organicism. To close on the note I began with, we need to see if and where an evident attempt to further Europeanize Britain will lead, tangible in the rail tunnel under the Channel opened in 1994. In 1993, Europe became a federation, but significantly Britain remained outside the Euro.[8] A short time from now it will be necessary to weigh up a new social mediation, that is, the network of total, non-stop communication for groups of users on the 'Web'.

---

7   See the eloquent excerpt of a speech quoted in M. Fforde, *Storia della Gran Bretagna*, 357. Fforde also goes into a detailed description (362) of the economic and ideological foundations underlying Thatcherism, those of the Austrian, naturalized English economist F. Hayek and of the philosopher K. Popper, both contrary to large-scale state economic interventions, and, as already noticed, into the Tories' assimilation of the right-wing extremist pseudo-ideology of Enoch Powell.

8   As this volume was being translated, Britain voted to leave the European Union in the referendum of 24 June 2016 [translator's note].

PART I

Writers against Totalitarian Regimes

§ 3. *Auden* I: The burnt-out meteor. Militancy and disengagement in the leader of the poets of the 1930s*

The literary decade of 1930–1940 is dominated by Wystan Hugh Auden (1907–1973), who was head and shoulders above any other figure working in England in the dramatic and poetic field – without turning to the novel, therefore – with the sole and possible exception of Dylan Thomas, who

* *The Complete Works of W. H. Auden*, 8 vols, ed. E. Mendelson, Princeton, NJ 1988–2015 (*Plays and Other Dramatic Writings, 1928–1938*, 1988; *Libretti and Other Dramatic Writings, 1939–1973*, 1993; *Prose and Travel Books in Prose and Verse 1926–1938*, 1997; *Prose 1939–1948*, 2002; *Prose 1949–1955*, 2008; *Prose 1956–1962*, 2011; *Prose 1963–1968*, and *Prose 1969–1973*, 2015). The poetic editions here referred to are *Collected Poems*, ed. E. Mendelson, London 1976, 1991, 2007, which contains Auden's final revisions, and *The English Auden: Poems, Essays, and Dramatic Writings, 1927–1939*, ed. E. Mendelson, London 1977, which reprints the poems included in the first published edition. *Juvenilia: Poems 1922–1928*, ed. K. Bucknell, Princeton, NJ 2003.

 Life. C. Osborne, *W. H. Auden: The Life of a Poet*, London 1980; H. Carpenter, *W. H. Auden: A Biography*, London 1981; T. Clark, *Wystan and Chester: A Personal Memoir of W. H. Auden and Chester Kallman*, London 1995.

 Criticism. F. Scarfe, *Auden and After: The Liberation of Poetry 1930–1941*, London 1942, and *W. H. Auden*, Munich 1949; R. Hoggart, *Auden: An Introductory Essay*, London 1951; J. Warren Beach, *The Making of the Auden Canon*, Minneapolis, MN 1957; M. K. Spears, *The Poetry of W. H. Auden: The Disenchanted Island*, New York and Oxford 1963, 1968, and, as editor, *Auden: A Collection of Critical Essays*, Englewood Cliffs, NJ 1964; B. Everett, *Auden*, Edinburgh and London 1964, J. G. Blair, *The Poetic Art of W. H. Auden*, Princeton, NJ 1965; F. Binni, *Saggio su Auden*, Milano 1967, and 'Wystan Hugh Auden', in CAB, vol. II, 235–321 (the second essay, which is a reprint of the first with some additions, is muddled and repetitive, albeit rich in useful information and critical comment); J. Replogle, *Auden's Poetry*, London 1969 (focused on the discontinuities in contents, style, voice and genre, connected with an alleged antithesis between 'Poet' and 'Anti-poet'); A. Serpieri, 'Lo specchio e il caos', in *Hopkins-Eliot-Auden. Saggi sul parallelismo poetico*, Bologna 1969, 165–208 (an excellent general survey); G. W. Bahlke, *The Later Auden: From 'New Year Letter' to 'About the House'*, New Brunswick, NJ 1970, and, as editor, *Critical Essays on W. H. Auden*, Boston, MA 1991; J. Fuller, *A Reader's Guide to W. H. Auden*, London 1970, and *W. H. Auden: A Commentary*, London 1998; F. Duchêne, *The Case of the Helmeted Airman: A Study of W. H. Auden's Poetry*, London 1972; F. Buell, *W. H. Auden as a Social Poet*, Ithaca, NY and London 1973; *Auden: A Tribute*, ed. S. Spender, London 1975; E. Mendelson, *Early Auden*, New York 1981, 1983, and *Later*

emerged even more precociously in that decade, and of D. H. Lawrence. This supremacy could be slightly reassessed if we think that, at the beginning of the 1930s, Yeats was publishing his last collections, that Eliot was entering a delicate phase of reconsideration of his art, that Beckett the playwright was not yet born, and that Beckett the novelist and poet was still in gestation. In fact, before going into detail on the intrinsic and individual significance of Auden's literary advent, we need to look at the historical and collective issues surrounding it. With his charismatic personality, Auden gave life to a movement and a generation that can be designated as Thirties poetry and be divided into four main aspects and concepts. After repeated and chronic isolationisms, or fanciful and ephemeral fellowships, a form of associated culture was reborn in Britain, with a close-knit group of poets and intellectuals with common intentions – and yet objectively critical of one another – of a kind that had no longer existed since the early Romantic period: a circle that felt the joyful and fruitful sense of composing together rising forth, like Wordsworth and Coleridge,

---

Auden, New York 1999 (studies by the most authoritative critic and connoisseur of Auden, indebted to the transversal approach of J. Hillis Miller); D. Mitchell, *Britten and Auden in the Thirties: The Year 1936*, London 1981; G. T. Wright, *W. H. Auden*, Boston, MA 1981; E. Callan, *Auden: A Carnival of Intellect*, New York and Oxford 1983; CRHE, ed. J. Haffenden, London 1983; S. Smith, *W. H. Auden*, Oxford 1985, and *Auden*, Plymouth 1997, also editor of *The Cambridge Companion to W. H. Auden*, Cambridge 2004; L. McDiarmid, *Auden's Apologies for Poetry*, Princeton, NJ 1990; J. R. Boly, *Reading Auden: The Returns of Caliban*, Ithaca, NY 1991; M. O'Neill and G. Reeves, *Auden, MacNeice, Spender: The Thirties Poetry*, Houndmills 1992, 6–34, 85–115, 145–80 and *passim*; A. Hecht, *The Hidden Law: The Poetry of W. H. Auden*, Cambridge 1993; C. Dell'Aversano, *The Silent Passage: itinerario poetico di W. H. Auden*, Pisa 1994; R. Davenport-Hines, *Auden*, London 1995; M. Bryant, *Auden and Documentary in the 1930s*, Charlottesville, VA and London 1997; A. Jacobs, *What Became of Wystan: Change and Continuity in Auden's Poetry*, Fayetteville, NC 1998; R. Emig, *W. H. Auden: Towards a Postmodern Poetics*, London 1999; A. Myers and R. Forsythe, *W. H. Auden: Pennine Poet*, Nenthead 1999; *The Poetry of W. H. Auden: A Reader's Guide to Essential Criticism*, ed. P. Hendon, Cambridge 2000; P. E. Firchow, *W. H. Auden: Contexts for Poetry*, Newark, DE 2002; A. Kirsch, *Auden and Christianity*, New Haven, CT 2005; T. Sharpe, *W. H. Auden*, London 2007, and, as editor, *W. H. Auden in Context*, Cambridge 2013.

and who cultivated the ancient custom of the dedication, of compositions written 'to' or 'for'.[1] In that decade, around the brightest star, Auden, gravitated in particular three satellite writers, Christopher Isherwood, Stephen Spender and Louis MacNeice; and following a slightly wider orbit, Cecil Day Lewis and Edward Upward. This platoon constituted a totally and deeply English formation and mode of literary expression, and this can be well noted in the fact that they were educated in public schools and then Oxford University. At Oxford, Auden had impressed his fellows with his pontifical behaviour, inexhaustible eloquence, Wilde-like poses and volubility. The group was then the product, the final one, of the extremely prolific British educational system, where the immediately previous literary scene could boast only very bland and tardy fellowships like that of Eliot, Pound and Joyce, the writers of the moment being either American emigrants (Eliot, Pound), or Irishmen bearing historical and extraneous racial and even anti-British marks (Yeats, Joyce), a spasmodic and rootless writer like Lawrence, or another isolated phenomenon like Virginia Woolf. The second and third data are that Auden's generation proposed itself as yet another re-founding of the literary art and intended art as a revolutionary tool; the fourth is homosexuality that, along with the literary passion, bound this group together, and had to be long hidden or at least camouflaged by all of its members.[2]

2. Like many of his peers, Auden came under the spell of Mosley's fascist propaganda, and believed in the messianic advent of a strong man. This is a myth, and a self-projection, that surface throughout his work with real and imaginary references, the first of which is certainly that charismatic saviour who answered to the name of T. E. Lawrence. As with many poets working in the early years of the century – suffice to

---

1   HYN, 85. This compactness should not be exaggerated, and one reads at times 'negationist' *boutades* like that of Press 1965, 24 (the book on MacNeice cited in this poet's bibliography, § 17.1), that is, that there is no evidence that all four poets ever got together and sat down for a discussion in the same room. It is true that MacNeice was systematically excluded from the basic quartet.

2   Auden and Isherwood were lovers until 1939; only MacNeice was not homosexual; Spender was, despite marrying twice.

think of Dylan Thomas's declaration of intent[3] – Freud was attributed a revolutionary value that could complement that of Marx. Auden wished above all for a purely psychic revolution, the liberation of the personality, especially of the senses, and from religious repression, the liberation of the id, that is to say. Only after his trip to Berlin in 1929, did he understand revolution in its exquisitely political sense, without ever forgetting the Freudian sub-sense, however. The *trait d'union*, up to a certain confused point, was also the philosophy of the subconscious, only partially Freudian, of the other Lawrence, D. H. But Auden and company eventually chose the antidote to fascism. In 1922, Auden remembered losing faith and at the same time to have begun writing poetry thanks to the incitement of an old school friend, Robert Medley.[4] During the 1926 General Strike, he took the side of the unions and gave proof of political commitment for the first time. In certain moments, Auden's early poetry describes, without symbolic filters and allusive networks, the desolation of the poor and the 1929 Depression; his plays provocatively illustrate the futility of bourgeois existence, the confusion of the modern world, with all its conventions and prejudices. His work in drama and cinema was espoused as a vehicle for political engagement and an impulse to transform society. The ever juvenilely intellectual and fanciful Marxism of the poetry of the 1930s nevertheless definitively faded away with the signing of the Russo-German pact in 1939, and would be more tangibly retracted after Auden's move to America. Auden and the other poets of his circle failed in other words to challenge Orwell's position as the only real socialist writer, albeit dissident, before the war. Coherent with his ideological support for the republican cause, Auden had gone to Spain in 1937 with the idea of becoming an

---

3   'My poetry [...] is the record of my individual struggle from darkness towards some
      measure of light' (quoted in Fitzgibbon's 1970 biography of Thomas, 151–2, listed
      in the bibliography in § 69.1).
4   Medley, who became a painter, was the first to arouse Auden's homosexual inclination.
      Auden attributed it to his father's long absence from home, in the war between 1914
      and 1918, just as his weakness for smoking was linked to a too premature weaning at
      his mother's breast (Osborne 1980, 44).

ambulance driver,[5] but after witnessing the spectacle of churches in ruins he returned home disillusioned, having nonetheless written what was judged to be the most intense English poem inspired by that conflict. The reverse side of militancy was resistance and indecision, dissimulated by self-incitement. Auden was never a card-carrying member of the English communist party, whilst in 1938 Orwell described him and Spender as 'parlour Bolsheviks'[6] – his *bêtes noires* – and Auden in particular as a 'gutless Kipling'.[7] The English Marxist Auden already aspired, almost like Yeats, to the restoration of a patriarchal, humanistic and enlightened order. The ultimate litmus test of his cautious ideological stance is an extremely late questionnaire addressed to a few poets concerning the war in Vietnam: Auden objected that poets knew less than the ordinary citizen, since they also found out about political events from the newspapers. In fact, his response was anti-communist, in favour of a negotiated peace, requiring the Americans to remain in Vietnam until this was stipulated. He also wrote a poem against the Soviet invasion of Prague. The fact is that political engagement had never invalidated art for art's sake. The early Auden was a poet's poet who blended together echoes and provenances of the most disparate and stratified kind. His apprenticeship was a period of transition, as he imbibed doses that had to be metabolized: distinct phases of absorption which were swallowed up and, as it were, spat out again. A native of York, he was the third born in the family of a doctor and an ex-nurse, the family relocating to Birmingham when his father became a functionary of the military medical school and a professor of hygiene at the university. Therefore the first scenes to impress themselves on his mind were the mining districts of the ill-famed central zones of England. As a child he read avidly brief treatises and publications dealing with science, geology and mining and, until the age of sixteen, wanted to become a mining engineer. His family library nonetheless also abounded in books of fairy tales and facetious poems. He said that the impulse to write poetry

5   In reality, his duties were reduced to that of a radio announcer for programmes in English destined only for compatriot combatants.
6   OCE, vol. I, 347.
7   A judgement later retracted.

came first from de la Mare's anthology, *Come Hither*, in 1923. Hopkins had been revealed to the wider reading public in 1918, hence at a time when Auden was particularly receptive. But no less influential were Owen and his experiments in pararhyme, Hardy and his formal and stanzaic variety, Anglo-Saxon alliterative poetry and, on the opposite pole, the rhythm of the vaudeville and the blues. At Oxford he discovered Eliot, who displaced Hardy and Edward Thomas in his sympathies. At that time he held that poetry should be clinical and austere, far from the passions of the average man. In another short manifesto, he sustained the idea of art as the disposition of words in a pattern, with sentiment and idea relegated to the sole function of the occasional. Discussing the 1930 and 1933 collections, MacNeice drew attention to the chameleon-like quality of the writing, deriving from the Metaphysicals and Eliot's 'music of ideas', and underlined the extreme variety of rhythm, measure and tone: solemn and light-hearted, dramatic and humorous. It immediately became common practice to exalt or deprecate Auden's obscurity, complaining that his authentic gifts did not come to fruition in a finished work and that he obstinately pursued an odd kind of associationism. The insidiousness of early Auden derives naturally from the absence of contextualization, in itself a vice common to practically all the poets of his time, and also from the vice of empty deixis – here, this, that, but where and how and when? – and moreover from the use of abbreviations or kenning ('the children of the sea', or rather fish) and from the intentional and necessarily encoded references to homosexual love,[8] and the Oxford student jargon. Evaluation in the heat of the moment took the usual British form, that

8   Auden's sexual habits suggest a controlled, in reality somewhat disconcerting hiatus between irresistible starvation and the self-control of artistic work: two spheres incommunicado. The promiscuous Auden was a hunter of muscular boys, and he gathered a collection of conquests in the most diverse locations on disparate occasions. As the psychiatrist Layard stated (cited in Carpenter 1981, 90), 'Wystan liked being beaten up a bit'. This reciprocal separation between body and mind was dated back (by Mendelson 1983, 65 and 216–17) to the nine months spent by Auden in Berlin in 1929. In 1983, an examination of notebooks and letters not yet published at the time, allowed Mendelson, who made extensive use of them, to discover and cast light on some links within the lyric poems. Auden, in particular, detailed the inner

which, influenced by taste, confined itself to cataloguing as efficacious, vigorous and successful certain lines extrapolated from texts to the disadvantage of others, treating the poet as a musician who can be lauded or rebuked for the pure sounds he produces. A fragmentation such as this could be justified because it came about from the way in which Auden's poems were put together, composed at times of material discarded from others submitted to his friends and pruned by them.

3. The ongoing diatribe regards late Auden. If I have defined Auden as the poet who got a decade underway, this is implicitly because the decades that followed where no longer dominated by him. After such a promising start the community of readers and scholars expected something new and more from him. He is the far from rare example of a poet who reaches his peak, in quantity and quality, extremely precociously; in terms of a wider estimation, Auden dried up in 1957, leaving afterwards minimal, insignificant remains. His friends were fully aware that he knew how to dress everything in poetry, understood as a metrical and prosodic involucrum of extremely beautiful, moulded rhyming and assonantal lines, but that left to himself he had not much to say. Hence the fault in Auden is his not having found along the way his own definite, marked, personal conceptual universe, transfused into unprecedented metaphors and symbols, entirely his own. It is undoubtedly a bit of an anticlimax to say that Auden is the champion of spiritualized love set against hate (one overly rhetorical line proclaims that 'we must love one another or die'),[9] that his poetry is a criticism of hubris and a eulogy of humility, or that his leitmotiv is that art 'makes nothing happen'. His 'vice', therefore, is conceptual

---

torment of his homosexuality, and in fact up to 1933 his poems also conceal this fatigue.

9   This is the closing line of a repudiated stanza in one of Auden's repudiated poems, 'September, 1, 1939', the date of the outbreak of the war (this contortionism is habitual in Auden, as we shall see). Another brief repudiated poem, to be found nonetheless in the anthologies, 'Petition', from 1929, between the comic and the pathetic calls on God for a universal palingenesis, summarized however in an easy, Dickensian formula as 'a change of heart'.

weakness, a scarcity of ideas.[10] What ideas there are, are often of little interest, and yet developed with suffocating prolixity.[11] Until the infatuation with Kierkegaard, Auden borrowed these ideas from minor thinkers, both marginal and little accredited, and justly so, excluding himself thus from the general circle of fruition.[12] In the end, leaving aside the enormous promise of the golden decade, the successive reflective poetry is anything but fascinating,[13] whilst the long poems are almost a fiasco. We must therefore search for Auden's more native vein in the songs or in the short poems, witty though also vigilant and bare as regards the imagery, often slightly absurd and incongruous, where his imagination and flair in blending are kept under control and the line of thought is neither dominant nor overly cerebral, and unhindered by erudite digressions. The sudden loss of invention transpires undeniably from the long poems written after 1940, to the degree that Auden fails to hide the need to rely on pre-existing ideas, original ones having dried up (his beginnings were not like this, indeed quite the contrary). In 1939 he had celebrated the deceased Yeats, but there continued to be denied him, as an anti-Romantic, Yeats's visionary, apocalyptic and prophetic scope, hence visionary poetry. He did not have a personal myth derived from a figure of antiquity, such as Helen or Ulysses.[14]

10   The 'lack' in Auden of a 'settled ideology' was noted by T. S. Eliot, adding that if a writer lacked 'ethical and religious beliefs' the technique, too, is damaged (quoted in Carpenter 1981, 137).

11   The reviewer R. Mayne (CRHE, 449) rightly noticed that Auden at times 'complexifi[es] simplicity'.

12   Apart from Freud, Lawrence, Marx and Groddeck, Auden, as shall be seen, was influenced by Layard and Gerald Heard.

13   Indeed, the word 'bore' and the adjective 'boring' appear with independent regularity in the judgements of some more or less famous historical readers: Edith Sitwell, E. A. White, Evelyn Waugh and P. Dickinson (quoted in Carpenter 1981, 137, 189, 247, 348). Auden himself, in the poem 'The Cave of Making' (1964), hoped to become, or already believed he was, 'a minor atlantic Goethe', silly like all poets, and 'at times a bore'. In recent times, Derek Walcott alone has insistently emphasized the 'tremendous intelligence behind the poetry' of Auden (quoted in Jenkins's article discussed below in n. 33).

14   As Serpieri 1969 also notes, 168–9 and 170, where he mentions Auden's 'repugnance for personal myths'.

As a child he had been enthralled by the Old Norse myths,[15] without them appearing on the page however, if not very superficially. He moved to America in 1939 with Isherwood and was enrolled in the American strategic services with the purely fictitious rank of major. In the autumn of 1945 he was already on his way back to America from Germany and in 1946 took out American citizenship, taking the opposite path to that of James and Eliot.[16] This decision was judged emblematic of an ideological surrender, of cowardly political disengagement, and Orwell rebuked Auden again in 1943, saying that he was 'watching his navel in America'. A short while before he had reflected himself in the *alter ego* M. F. Ransom in the drama *The Ascent of F 6*. This hero, who fails and succumbs, is a mystic divided between solipsistic hubris and socially worthwhile activity; but he is also one who has failed to dominate a devouring Oedipus complex. One should thus disassemble Auden and read him through a series of dualisms. The first is nationality, the rift between the English and the American Auden. The watershed falls in the year 1939, almost exactly halfway through his life, if not his career. This date also demarcates the atheist, communist Auden before 1939, and the religious and spiritual Auden afterwards. As a young man, he had cherished a project that comes to an end with his departure – the project of an active, communist and revolutionary literature which at the same time claimed to be absolute and artistic. If one moves down a level, one can perceive other dualisms within the writing. Auden is a poet and dramatist, and as a poet writes poems which he himself collected in two volumes containing respectively the long and the short. As a dramatist he wrote alone or in collaboration, either autonomous works or serving other artists as a librettist. One should not forget his mediation in this field of music and opera, including his collaboration with Britten, or his translation into English of some of Mozart's libretti and the service done in two of the operatic masterpieces of the twentieth century, by Stravinsky and Henze.

15   Auden believed that he had Norse ancestors, and that his surname, in truth uncommon in England, was the corruption of a Scandinavian one.
16   Auden looks to the island, or many islands, and opposes them to the Continent, a constant theme both in the work and the biography.

4. Alongside the Auden in the making, who wrote and published, another Auden was revising his work from a distance to form a parallel canon, while subdividing his short poetry into four phases that doubled the afore-mentioned dualism.[17] Labelling the two editions of his poems, both short and long, as 'collected', in 1947 and 1957, he showed he was prematurely ready for disarmament. In 1956 he returned to England to take up the post of Professor of Poetry at Oxford, which he held until 1961. In the last decade of his life he lived between New York and Europe (Italy, Ischia, and Austria)[18] following a rhythm similar to that of the great wealthy Victorians – winter at work in Austria, summers in the agreeable south of Italy. By now, for the general public, he had acquired the unmistakable features of a large wrinkled elephant, or of a small Buddha with creased skin and yellowed fingers, his nails black and bitten to the quick, who cared little for clothes and personal hygiene, and would appear in public wearing tattered felt slippers. Having officially joined the Anglican Church, he went to church regularly on Sundays in the Austrian village where he had settled, making a virtue out of necessity and attending the Catholic churches, but going to Masses that were celebrated without a sermon. His faith was elastic and irenic, one that notably did not consider his practised homosexuality, condemned at that time by the Church, either as an obstacle or a reason for guilty feelings. An inveterate smoker, he was found dead after a heart attack at the Kirchstetten summerhouse. The year of his rediscovered faith is 1940, but the process was gradual and his acceptance remained mostly hypothetical – often merely the recovery and employment of a series of parallel myths as a vehicle for particular emotions. Faith was born from the repudiation of that liberal humanism that also elicited Eliot's distaste,

17   Replogle 1969, chapter II, maintains that Auden is discontinuous and contradictory, Poet and Anti-Poet, an antithesis that is far from apt and is applied too mechanically. They are the two faces of the same poet, the first sublimating, the second satirical, making a joke of everything. The discontinuity is between solemnity and self-parody. Auden's prose, too, is supposed to reveal the rift between the Poet and the Anti-Poet (*ibid.*, 176).

18   The Kirchstetten farmhouse was bought in 1958 with the Feltrinelli prize money, purchase of a house in Ischia proving too expensive.

and left Auden disappointed. The concept of 'anxiety', the hinge of his personal theology, was explained by Auden both in a psychoanalytical and an existential sense, through Freud (anxiety with regard to the past and one's parents) and through Kierkegaard (anxiety as the feeling of the relationship between the self and God).[19] Anxiety changes nature, from illness to unease, leading to choice and hence it means man's insecurity in a period of crisis presaging an outcome.[20] The complement to anxiety is a triad of conflicting theological concepts, Eros, Logos and Agape. Following Yeats, Agape does not deny the flesh, but places it in equilibrium with the body, opposing it to Logos which is pure spirit. But St Augustine at this stage comes to his aid, in the case study of the city, simultaneously healthy and unhealthy, a city that may be agapic or egotistical. This series of ideological and theological concerns is elaborated in abstract and heuristic terms, rather than deriving from a powerful personal intuition, from an intimate and dramatic conflict, articulated nonetheless in tranquillity. Auden was aware of this, and made it known that he was not attracted by the mystical manner of Eliot and Hopkins, who rattled off their troubles dauntlessly.[21] He had never been a heated and anguished poet. One never hears him scream or see him tear his clothes, not even in his youthful poetry. His stance is neither lyric nor symbolist.[22] According to Spender,[23] he lacked the real 'experience from which to write'. In this poetry of ideas, the corollaries are the discourse on the limits of art faced with life and the eventual inefficacy of art in changing the destiny of the world, a leitmotiv

19   Auden edited the works of Kierkegaard. Replogle 1969 attempts too casually to demonstrate that the progress from Marx to Kierkegaard was consequential and painless: the latter shared the analysis of human alienation, but added God.

20   The spiritual and religious sense of the concept of the 'frontier' is hence re-semanticized (Spears 1963, 185), as I shall discuss further on.

21   Quoted in Spears 1963, 334.

22   Serpieri 1969 insists that Auden operates in the area of allegory, rather than in that of symbol and symbolism, or in that of Modernism or the archetypical method. He notices in the second, converted Auden, the advent of 'a new allegorical manner', as in Eliot.

23   CRHE, 342, echoed by Duchêne 1972, 14, who argues that Auden is a poet constantly withdrawing from experience.

that is common to the many obituary poems, whose outcome is the negation of the thaumaturgic magic of art. Man's loss of status as lord of creation does not receive the apocalyptic treatment found for instance in Beckett; rather the animate and the inanimate proceed in asymptotic progression without ever meeting, indeed in reciprocal indifference, a theme which stands out in the odes on the great dead, whose death nature attends impassively.[24] Albeit less anguished and tormented, Auden shares with Matthew Arnold a tolerant, liberal, pro-European message, which therefore exalts love conceived not as egocentric romanticism, but rather as a synonym for friendship. In conclusion, the two contemporary major writers, Auden and Beckett, shared inverted destinies, the latter moving from Baroque turgidity to a naked, telegraphic dryness, whilst the former moves from the bare, paratactic poetry of the early years to the overloaded, sumptuous verse – it, too, and above all, Baroque – of the years following 1939. Gradually the expansive and discursive Auden comes to resemble late Browning, as he is by no means alien to an erudite, peculiar mental viewpoint, in the form of fragments picked up here and there in a somewhat casual manner. Had not Browning investigated the relationship between human and divine love, between body and spirit, between sex and sublimation? Like him, Auden always knew, in exceptional moments, how to write the immaculate lyric, the little tardy masterpiece.[25] His ideal climate, his period of election after 1940 was, apart from metrical experimentation, the Augustan one. This is proclaimed by his predilection for wit, for brachilogical form, for the absence, albeit not uniform, of diffusion. Auden loves the aphorism, the acrobatics of allusive, hence obscure, thought; he is fond of the epitaph and writes encomia like the greats of the eighteenth century. It is clearly easy to locate this ascendancy, mixed and entirely irreconcilable with others, because Auden is the great transformer and blender of disparate experiences. Praz hit the mark when, after adhering to Bates's opinion that he is our Keats, our Pope, our Donne,[26] he observed that the more accurate

24   Bahlke 1970, 18.
25   Browning is rarely evoked with regard to Auden. Herbert Read does so in his tribute
     to him in CRHE, 272–3.
26   PSL, 683.

alter ego was Pope. With Auden, the pseudo-eighteenth-century vein of the verse essay was heard again, a reflective vein confirmed by his mature and senile loves, Goethe, German philosophy and Byron. So the sign of late Auden is that of an extremely elevated poetry of occasions. He is the great jester who knows how to dress everything in poetry as long as he is given an occasion: to find an Italian equivalent one must turn to a poet such as Monti. Or he is a King Midas who turns everything he touches into gold, that is, verse of high workmanship and formal variety.[27]

5. It is understandable that the first critical monographs, written when Auden was still alive, were exegeses and commentaries. As a result they are arid, catalogue-like, in their 'crude paraphrasing'[28] of poem after poem. This type of approach is instructive: books such as those of Spears from 1963, Fuller from 1970, and Mendelson from 1981, prove indispensable for the quantity of information, for their resolution of small enigmas and the elucidation of cultured and erudite references; however, they also show how straw-clutching and nagging, inventive and irritating the search for presumed, arcane and subtle concepts in Auden is. The challenge of the poetry of ideas[29] is hard to meet, and if Auden's poetry after 1939 is reduced to prose, one simply collects from each example a series of contorted axioms that are not easy to verify and are above all of little originality. Or one notices a discrepancy between their meagreness, or superficiality, and the ability of the verse, the sparkle of the words, periphrases and tropes. Faced with the unrelenting paraphrasing of the commentators one is left in doubt as to whether it was the critic or the poet who wrote this barrage of repetitive sophisms, and receives the impression and experiences the evocation of that 'critic's critic' whose analysis, Auden himself found, 'is so much more complicated and difficult than the work itself'.[30] As said by Desmond MacCarthy,[31] in

27   This ability was recognized by C. James (quoted in Carpenter 1981, 421).

28   Spears 1963, 223.

29   Replogle 1969, in chapter I, analyses Auden's poetry as a 'source of ideas' (90).

30   *The Dyer's Hand*, 49. Even Mendelson 1983, who usually explains and paraphrases everything, must hoist the white flag in some cases, and attribute his explanatory helplessness to the poet's confusion (cf. 139–40 n. †).

31   CRHE, 336.

Auden one perceives 'the suggestion of some portentous significance which melts when examined'. Above all the late, or second American Auden of the long poems, has been thus either exalted to the point of delirium or murderously slated. For instance, the disagreement on *The Age of Anxiety* is irreconcilable: John Bayley judges it a masterpiece and Randall Jarrell the worst work written by Auden in about twenty years. Thom Gunn shifted the target to *Homage to Clio*.[32] In 1969, Auden was already a distant classic over whom hovered what had become by then an academic debate. Hence, the poet's death certificates followed each other in constant rhythm, that is to say, with every new work coming out after 1939. Recently, however, Auden has become the representative poet of a coterie, that of the homosexuals. Auden's homosexuality is a suppressed chapter, by Auden himself who never flaunted it,[33] and one which the scholars of gender are reopening with the usual deformation of taking it as the keystone, unique and revealing, of the world of the poet. He is undoubtedly the poet of reference of this international micro-community.[34] Auden in America and for America lends himself, however, to a more variegated balance. The third and fourth phases of

32   Spears 1963, 327.

33   Uninformed or ingenuous readers proved the universality of Auden's love and erotic poetry also thanks to the English language's possibility to make no difference among the genders of adjectives, or dissolve any male-female ambiguity or ambivalence. In fact, Auden's love poems were born and thought of after homosexual experiences, and as revealed by Carpenter 1981, 76 n. 1, Auden appended the name of the inspirers and dedicatees of his love songs in the 1934 copy of his poems given to Chester Kallman. N. Jenkins, 'Historical as Munich: Auden at 100: Who Is He Now?', *TLS*, 9 February 2007, 12–15, brilliantly reveals that the poem 'Lay your sleeping head, my love' camouflages the name of his 'love', Michael Yates, a thirteen-year-old pupil whom the twenty-six-year-old Auden fell in love with, in a web of echoes and borrowings from Yeats's poem 'A Prayer for My Son', playing on the homophony of Yates and Yeats, on the fact that also Yeats's son was called Michael, as well as the paternal affection he felt for the youth.

34   Auden returned to public favour thanks to the recital of an amusing composition of his, praising a dead friend, in the British comedy film *Four Weddings and a Funeral*. We cannot predict whether the constant widespread presence of Auden in today's pop and synthpop music scene is an index of universality, as discussed in the aforementioned article by Jenkins.

his career invent a small poetic genre without any true precedent, which was studied and adopted enthusiastically by the younger American poets: the verse conversation or rather that poetic style halfway between the prose and the poetic register, imbued with highly formalized self-irony and conscious carelessness – the voice of a Berryman or a Lowell.[35] This *sprezzatura* style, which for Auden always works quite well, is nevertheless prolix and most of all full to the brim with private and incidental references which can be neither enjoyed nor shared, and at times, if not always, it ends up in digressions that are an end in themselves.

§ 4. *Auden II: Cabaret theatre*

Regarding early Auden and his compositional and constructive method, two observations can be made and must be set down preliminarily. Auden makes parody of parody, insofar as he accepts the juxtapositional method, based on temporal and above all contextual hiatuses, of Eliot's *The Waste Land*, but composes collages and puzzles which, as such, empty Eliot's analogous method of its seriousness and its tragic spirit. Those of Auden are more horizontal than Eliot's mostly vertical ones. In a musical sense the internal segmentation of Auden's first dramas, undoubtedly in a progressive decrescendo, responds not to criteria of linkage or chromatism between the various movements, but rather to diatonism and the staccato. The reader must either despair of finding a clue linking the episodes and sections or strive to find one, ending by admitting that it does not exist or that 'the absence of a clue is the clue itself'.[36] This diagnosis is especially valid for *The Orators*. The other factor is the interchangeable nature of separate pieces, which often come together and insert themselves in radically different textual frameworks. Auden had composed them previously. The possible explanations are the following: either chaos reigns in these alternative frameworks or else all the textual material deriving from the ferment of

35   Mendelson 1983, 202, instead identifies another idiosyncrasy that was transferred to American poetry for a couple of decades, from the 1930s to the 1950s: the connection of 'aspects of the world of the emotions with heterogeneous aspects of the world of cities and armies', in practice, similes of the type of the 'talent like a uniform'.
36   Mendelson 1983, 10.

the late 1920s and early 1930s descends from a mysterious but profound unity of inspiration, and it speaks of a single theme. Auden demonstrates that the 'land' was still a wasteland even ten years afterwards, or only six, and that it is a wasteland for the precise reason diagnosed by Eliot, the absence of true love. The imagery is that of war, the *topos* of the opposition between two sides, but it is also an extension of a sporting competition. One should note, in fact, that the two 'sides' in *Paid on Both Sides*, either winners or losers, are indicated by different colours, and by a species of shirt or jersey which distinguishes them on stage; and in the interstices of the drama there is talk of rugby, sport commentary and sporting events. In the dramas the mother is always the driving force, often vengeful and sanguinary, of the protagonist, and it is enough just to name her to unchain it. A psychic dependency on the mother, therefore, is paramount for Nower, for Ransom and for Grimm's killer in three of Auden's dramas. Where Eliot is ritual, solemn, liturgical, prophetic and mystical, Auden is only half serious, playful, joking or jokingly tragic. The dominant isotopy which runs through these dramas has always been found as that of an alarm, of preparation for an attack, for an imminent conflict – that of spying, of the ambush. Nevertheless, that was a filtered climate, not one experienced in the first person and as a professional: a species of youthful epic, of cops and robbers or a war of buttons, or a remake or an echo of the Mortmere myth, discussed below, or of contemporary heroic feats, of war books, or soldiers' memories, or *mutatis mutandis* of the Brontës' Gondal and Angria sagas taken together. Love, said Auden, is victim of an 'ancestral curse' which amounts also to the burden of the dead. It is existential love divided against itself, repeating the sexual act but without union. It can reach its catharsis only in death, but without the overtones of the religious poetry of Eliot, that is without any mystical or otherworldly regeneration.

2. In parallel with poetry, Auden's first steps were in the area of drama and of the communicated, acted and shared word. His main ambition at the beginning of the 1930s was that of restoring the prevalent social dimension of drama and that of ritual, too, enabling the writer to affect the spectator and the ordinary man more efficaciously. Drama is indeed Auden's first vocation, if not his vocation *tout court*, throughout the decade 1930–1940 and beyond, at least judging from his last, at least semi-dramatic, evolution.

I will hence devote my attention first to his drama in my chronological examination, for the further reason that editions of his poems were made by Auden uprooting from the dramatic context, in which they have a precise function discussed further on, some if not many songs or jingles entrusted to characters internal to the dramas, and which, read as decontextualized poetry, present an even greater obscurity. Auden's activity in this field, initially conducted in collaboration with Isherwood, was intense and feverish, and it produced a few polished and finished dramas which are now rarely staged, and which nonetheless bubble with a vein of effervescent linguistic gusto and bring into play the freshest of scenic inventions. The rapid sequence of these works revealed a masterful dramatist exhibiting all his talent. Indeed some perceptive readers noticed in real time that Auden's prose – in which parts of the dramas and all of *The Orators* are written – surpasses Auden's poetry.[37] However, the dramatic urge petered out in less than a decade. Having used up all his ammunition by the early 1930s, Auden was to dilute his innovative, sacrilegious vein in servile librettos for operas. Some of his solutions lead directly to Beckett, who may have developed them independently, but twenty years later. Auden's drama could be defined as immature, and 'negligible' in the history of modern theatre,[38] only because this was a time when Beckett's explosion had not yet occurred. Conceived and launched at the end of the 1920s, it entered a vacuum or a concentric vortex of a conservative kind. Auden himself summed up the drama of his times in three types, the 'romantic sham-Tudor', with which he perhaps meant the historical drama with characters in regal clothes; the 'cosmic-philosophical' and 'high-brow chamber-music drama', equivalent in short to the drawing room comedy. The theatre he himself tried to build was one of charade in a zigzagging of stylistic variations that can range from the serious to the comic to the grotesque, and in a chain of spurious forms such as mime, pantomime, dance, musical numbers, and from there trespass on the eccentric and hence the absurd. T. S. Eliot worked along the same lines with the one-off Aristophanesque fragment *Sweeney Agonistes*. This ferment can be understood and ranked within the broad definition of verse drama: but

37   CRHE, 161–2, and 164.
38   Hoggart 1951, 74.

nothing could be further, for its derisive burlesque tone, from the still-living grand author of 'poetic' theatre, Yeats, or the future Eliot (and Auden remains immune to the temptations of Noh theatre). Auden's playwriting is indeed radically English, and brings onto the stage the grotesque of the Victorian cartoon and caricature tradition, while frankly overdoing the perversions and foolhardiness of the well-heeled bourgeoisie. As a result, behind it we can recognize and trace the operetta tradition of Gilbert and Sullivan, especially when the characters speak or sing in apparently facile euphonic verse, with funny or playful rhyming couplets, and on eccentric or ludic turns of phrases. Auden is their direct descendant and imitator, merely exacerbating a political satire that was already active in the source, albeit camouflaged.[39]

3. However, this dramatic technique was also by a fortunate coincidence almost the same, while having a rather greater estranging function, as Brecht's epic theatre, which in 1928 had been absorbed first hand by the two young Englishmen, Auden and Isherwood, in Berlin. The fragmentation of the play into unrelated scenes and self-enclosed episodes was inspired by Brecht's lesson, the one prescribing that 'every scene exists for itself'. To the extent that some of these plays were aborted, not published or remained incomplete or still as manuscripts, Auden could include whole parts or entire subplots within other plays, in a sort of permanent remaking and reshuffling. His dramaturgy is a kind of single text in progress, with a basic, unchanging scenario with decisive integrations along the way. For example, the 'reformatory scene' reappears several times – suggesting that it was deeply felt – with its farcical comedy and fulsome exhibition of educational hypocrisies; so does the world of mining, the workers, the protests, the strikes and the mine-owner exploiters, who are also adulterous lovers of their employees' wives. There is even enough on the plate, since Auden gathers on the same stage the symbolic spaces he most cares about: his drama has to be set in a mining area, where the workers live in conditions of hunger; but this scenario interacts with that of the school and institutions, in order to target the middle classes that support it. However, the powers

39   Volume 6, § 286.

that be, and the public figures, exhibit on stage their slimy, disgusting and obscene private life: high-ranking, lisping officials seduce boys from whom they demand depraved services; headmasters take a fancy to girls who are actually transvestite schoolboys. Even the justice system is corrupt, and by a fortunate coincidence moral integrity is incarnate in a bishop who is arrested because he is believed to be a seducer of young girls. Auden worked on his dramatic projects as if they were cinema scripts, and in this way he was also to conceive some of his long poems, re-using, for example, a voice off stage. They all have a sequence of tableaus with an invisible camera that moves from one to another. A similar dramatic construction may have been influenced by the episodic style popular at the peak of silent cinema, or by the serial Victorian novel in instalments. It develops in fact from totally disconnected narrative poles and layers, which with Dickensian skill are gradually brought closer and stitched together. A second thematic saga concerns the political fantasy of the armed confrontation between Ostia and Westland, alias Austria and Germany, the former ruled by an emperor, the latter by a 'Leader' who, Auden vainly wished to disavow, is Hitler, then already on a war footing. Behind this can then be perceived the echo of late G. B. Shaw.

4. The imaginative and highly suggestive afflatus of *Paid on Both Sides*, which appeared in 1930 in Eliot's *Criterion*, would be transmitted and transfused to Eliot himself who had, *in pectore*, *The Rock* and above all *Four Quartets*. Eliot probably appreciated the freely associative flow of the choruses and monologues, the airs that seem suspended and only vaguely and distantly linked to the stage action, and all significantly hinging on the relationship between past and present, on the irredeemable, and at the same time hopefully redeemable, weight of the atavistic malediction. This hypothesis of absorption and echoing on Eliot's part is not a random one, bearing in mind Eliot's ability to metabolize wide-ranging and momentary influences, and the programme of his poetry as a mosaic of echoes. On the other hand, the cabaret content of Auden's play is close to that employed by Eliot in his unfinished dramatic fragments of *Sweeney Agonistes*.[40] The

---

40 In Auden's Christmas interlude, which in any case is a dream, as I shall explain in
    the following sub-section, the grunts of a spy are 'produced by jazz instruments',
    and the beat is also that of a popular song rhyme. Eliot camouflaged an evident

transfusion or simple contact between this charade and Auden's early poems could be better verified since both featured in the same edition from 1930. This edition was the first, provocative testing ground for the novice poet and playwright, as well as indirectly being a verification of the courageous or faint-hearted tendencies of contemporary criticism. Empson's favourable judgement[41] was countered by Leavis's firm dissent, since, he said, the relationship of trust between addresser and addressee had been betrayed, poetry having ceased with Auden to communicate with the average reader, by becoming a private experience.[42] *Paid on Both Sides* is really Auden's first, sensational exploit, in face of which the commentator and the interpreter must at several points declare themselves beaten and throw in the towel: in other words, it is possible to square off the text in a broad summary, but the detail both tantalizes and remains elusive. It is an inexhaustible kaleidoscopic and also cacophonous deflagration of dramatic sequences that succeed one another with violent hiatuses in the scenic and dramatic texture. These are introduced by invariably ironic, schematic captions, often also deceptive or perversely elliptical, since they are intended to increase the reader's embarrassment in trying to decipher the scenic diegesis. The register covers almost the entire range of dramatic possibilities: the dialogues can be of a brutal brisk concreteness, immediately relational and communicative, and conform directly to the action, hence flashes of pure 'veristic' theatre; but these alternate not only with the soliloquy, or the intervention of the chorus revived from classical theatre, therefore static and evocative, solemn and declaimed, but also with the whirligigs of pantomime, with bickerings, with

---

infatuation, if not Eureka moment, with Auden's work with attitudes of ambiguous or else contradictory caution; but despite his 'reluctance' (see the entire n.* by Mendelson 1983, 32) he published *Paid on Both Sides* in the journal of which he was editor.

41   CRHE, 78–80.

42   CRHE, 88–91 and 100–1. A third contribution by Leavis, elicited by the 1934 reprint of Auden's poems, was blander, but even more polemical towards Empson (CRHE, 140–3). In 1936, too, Leavis pitted himself against the immaturity, the uncertainty of purpose and 'irresponsibility' of Auden (CRHE, 222–5). This accusation was to be repeated by Edmund Wilson (CRHE, 232–5), who, however, noted in 1937 the loss of the personal stamp and vigour of the early poems in the collection *Look, Stranger!* Wilson was later to embrace Auden's cause in toto (cf. CRHE, 406–11).

burlesque and word play. In the passages in verse Auden, at this early stage, is already a tightrope walker, whether they are in free verse, half rhyme or pararhyme. Here the syntax is dislocated, the logical and contextual thread zigzagging, the very grammar defective, even erroneous, in fact intentionally primitive.[43] The glaring oscillations of this text are due to the fact that Auden, at only twenty-one, on the one hand knew how to objectify and render absolute his existential ferment, but on the other did not. The drama is thus touched by clear naivety alternating with supreme moments of distancing. Wide-ranging sources, suggestions and ruminations, gleaned from chaotic reading, are heaped and fused together without lending themselves to coherent meaning, albeit being poetically compact. Auden was going through a period of tempestuous upheaval which miraculously, although intermittently, he could objectify and cool down on the page. He was committed to ridding himself of an Oedipus complex which he had brought to a level of awareness alone and through psychoanalytical therapy. He aimed to correct Freud because he saw in the mother figure the transmission of hate and hence the impediment to gaining love, love *tout court* and heterosexual love; he corrected Freud above all because he did not believe in the therapeutic capacity of anamnesis, rather in the cancellation of the past, convinced that overcoming hate and 'healing' derived instead from satiety.

5. This private geography is transcoded into the action of *Paid on Both Sides*. The extremely brief charade stages, in a surreal and one may say pre-absurd climate, two factions which go into battle, and not only in words; they follow each other, spy on each other and lie in ambush to kill, revenge and eliminate each other. The term 'absurd' is employed because the scene is divided if not divisionist, anticipating the reduction of the scenic apparatus and the stylization of the characters that Beckett was to achieve some twenty years later. This divisionism is close for example to Beckett's repudiated first drama, where in any case the conflict is between one, the son, and many, the family and society.[44] The two hostile factions can be recognized in Auden by the colours of their armbands, and the two minor

---

43 Cf. Mendelson 1983, 42 n. †, on the paraphrasing of l. 1305 of *Beowulf* in the play's title.

44 § 110.3 and n. 97.

characters bear names adumbrating Beckett, Bo and Po. This anti-drama puts the chorus on stage. But Auden in reality exploits the contrastive nature of the line, the characters knowing how to pass from practical, operative language, from the order and from the intention to act, to oases of reflection from which, in a visible leap, phrases of poetical loftiness, suggestive and elliptical, come *ex abrupto* to their lips.[45] On the other hand, in the sphere of operative language the characters speak in the tone of the despatch or telegram, not only the reader but also the actors on stage themselves struggling to understand. The care with which daily speech is constructed, and the *tour de force* of the verse passages, prove the extent to which this is a prevalently formal experiment. The sense of suspense comes to nothing and its exact nature is unknown, forming an absolutely inexplicable metaphysical climate. Auden wishes to create an atmosphere, that of the unreal detective story of the kind of Buchan's classic, *The Thirty-Nine Steps*. The verbal skirmishes of the two groups, borrowing terms from espionage and guerrilla warfare, explain the parallel recourse to analogous terms and situations in Auden's early poetry, the protracted sign of which is the half-serious recourse to military metaphors, drawn from war stories still fresh in the mind and from the experience of a British school system informed by that spirit. *Paid on Both Sides* fictionalizes and hence renders more comprehensible the drier anecdotes in the poetry. The internal symbolic plot is the impossibility of overcoming the ancestral laws of revenge and likewise the impossible advent of the jurisdiction of love, even if from the emergency, intolerable in the long term, and from the sense of rivalry, springs an invocation for peace (a member of the two factions decides in fact to leave for the colonies).[46] The climax is the ambush laid for the leader of one faction

---

45   The opening 'aria' of John Nower's mother is furthermore an echo of Hopkins's 'The Leaden Echo and the Golden Echo'.

46   Mendelson 1983, 47, unconsciously imposes the scheme active in Eliot's far later *Four Quartets* on Auden's work when he states that Auden's theme is the 'entrapment in time' and the 'psychological restraints transmitted as if genetically from the past' (cf. in Eliot the 'enchainment of past and future' and 'the release from the inner / And the outer compulsion' in the first quartet). The two poets agree on the diagnosis, even if they give a different meaning to the therapy, that the curse is overcome by love.

by the opposing one. Having made a date with a woman he escapes, but
he is eventually found and killed. A spy is captured and summarily killed
by the protagonist Nower, who having committed the act suddenly feels
the need to escape from the determinism of revenge. The trial of the spy is
humorous and surreal, the judge being Father Christmas and the defend-
ant miraculously coming back to life, albeit wounded, so that a farcical
doctor is needed on stage. In the published text, Auden excluded a stage-
direction which warned that the Christmas scene was to be intended as
Nower's dreaming after falling asleep, a dream which could and should
have been interpreted as his acceptance of the laws of love winning over
hate and revenge.[47] What then is this interlude? It is a dream of public and
private worth, or rather a nightmare in which the exorcism of the war is
acted out. *Paid on Both Sides* is hence the exorcism of war *tout court* and of
the Great War in particular. It is hardly casual that the right-wing faction's
German name is Lintzgarth and that its fellow soldiers number a Kurt and
a Zeppel, to which one only needs to add an -in to evoke the terror of aerial
bombing. One could emerge from the nightmare of the war by means of
tabula rasa, starting over from zero, with the total cancellation or removal
of the past. First, however, or simultaneously, Auden is rebuked through
the hermaphrodite Man-Woman for possessing only sick love, that love
he will likewise ascribe to himself in *The Orators*, sick because its object is
ambiguous if not double-natured, of undecided gender and hence sterile
and inconclusive. After scene shifts of meteoric suddenness, the minor
conflict, sedated by the wedding of the rivals' children (a parody of *Romeo
and Juliet* in cabaret style), is reopened by the murder of the bridegroom.
The epilogue suggests the failure both on a personal and individual level,

47   Mendelson 1983, 49–53. The tirade of the Man-Woman is an abstruse rebuke for a
      sterile and mistaken sexuality that Auden may have addressed to himself, identifying
      with Nower; what becomes clearer during this dream is the symbolic, hence therapeu-
      tic value of the extraction of a huge tooth from the body of the spy, who immediately
      afterwards fraternizes with Nower, planting a tree with him; after which Nower,
      apparently healed, strides a horse to go and ask the hand of the enemy's daughter.
      Therefore, on a private level, Auden admitted and hoped for the recomposition of
      his personality, which was to start from the cutting off, or psychoanalytically from
      the repression, of the past.

of Auden the man reflected in Nower (whose name indicates or alludes confusedly to something new),[48] and on a historical one. In other words the malediction of hate was rife in 1928–1930 still, at home and abroad.

6. In *The Enemies of a Bishop, or Die When I Say When* (written by Auden and Isherwood in 1929 and never published or staged, revised the following year without being completed, although all the poetic interludes of the 'spectre' were included in the 1930 poems),[49] the various dramatic pawns, whose moves exude an explosively repressed and unhealthy eroticism,[50] are made to converge on a concentric plot or on a web of reciprocal relationships mostly woven inside a hotel. A mine manager, Robert Bicknell, struggling with his double and thus clearly with hints from Stevenson[51] (to the extent that he believes he can destroy the spectre, but instead kills himself), is wildly in love with the wife of his deputy, while his brother, a Dickensian satirical target in his sinister greasiness,[52] directs a reformatory and has lost his head for a girl who is revealed to be one of his schoolboys, who has disappeared disguised as a female. In the hotel two slave traders working for the American market attempt to kidnap the boy, while a colonel tries to induce another man to whip him. A female detective unravels the situation, arresting, however, the only innocent character. This moral hero is a bishop named Law, who incarnates Homer Lane, a psychiatrist whom Auden considered a prophet and healer, and who was actually the head of a reformatory and a pedagogue with advanced ideas, such as that

48   Mendelson 1983, 49, links the name of the protagonist with 'now', surmising that Nower wants to live *now* and no longer in the past, being the man of the here and now who is ready to operate and transform society; but the suggestion of the name does not change. If one prefers this idea, the pronunciation of the name, which could be either ['nowə] or ['nawə], is the second.

49   This spectre was to become Nick Shadow in Auden's and Stravinsky's *The Rake's Progress*.

50   The same one denounced in *The Orators*.

51   Even if the idea may have been taken more directly from a 1926 German film (Mendelson, introduction to *Plays and Other Dramatic Writings 1928–1938*, xviii).

52   The words used make it possible to identify the reformatory director as the voice speaking to the assembled students in the first part of *The Orators*: both harangue against the 'rotters' and the 'slackers'.

of 'liberating' the sick by giving free rein to their instincts.[53] The internal allegorical conflict is expressed by the allusiveness of the two names, Law, the bishop, and Wright, the detective. *The Dance of Death*, commissioned by Rupert Doone for the Group Theatre[54] and performed in 1934 and 1935, though lauded as groundbreaking in its demolition of the barrier between stage and audience, does bring members of the public on stage, but is little more than a dramatic sketch. It is an allegory of the death of the bourgeoisie in the form of cabaret and pantomime.

7. *The Chase* (1934), written by Auden alone, and later revised with Isherwood as *The Dog Beneath the Skin*,[55] became in the latter form the first of Auden's two best and most famous plays. The starting point sounds like material from playful poetry or ballads. The old moneybags from a mining village, where workers are fired having been substituted by machines whilst the owners live in the lap of luxury, at his death has left his property to his son, who after falling out with him has disappeared without trace. These prior events are communicated in the form of a press conference given by the local vicar to three journalists. Right from the start the rhyming couplets turn into operetta-like, curtain-raiser ditties, gradually merging with parts in prose. There is a continuous passing from one metre, and hence from one register to another, with lightning-quick entrances of small choruses intoning limericks and nursery rhymes. In its first part, *The Chase* incorporates, entirely or almost, the reformatory plot of *The Enemies of a Bishop*, but with more estranging solutions, such as that of the prompter who informs the audience of a most unwelcome delay in the change of scene. In the presence

53　Lane was a pupil of John Layard, whose idea was that man's desires were natural and should be indulged, sin being only disobedience to the 'interior nature', and that sickness had a psychosomatic origin.

54　Certainly not a little, semi-amateur London theatrical troupe as it is sometimes defined, but rather an initiative of notable importance, born to stage and make known the dramatic ferment in England in the 1930s.

55　The title echoes, with variations, a line from Eliot's 'Whispers of Immortality'. The parts in prose are normally attributed to Isherwood, those in verse to Auden. The play had a number of finales, how many we cannot know, due to a vivacious exchange of ideas between the two co-authors, as we can read in Mendelson 1983, 277–80. I refer here to the text given in the volume of the plays edited by Mendelson.

of the entire village community, a performance anticipates the development of the play, the search for the absent heir by land and sea. Alan Norman, who has taken on the task with the promise of having the heir's sister as his bride, first stops off at the hotel of *The Enemies of the Bishop*, where there is some objection to the dog accompanying him. In the background the workers' unrest rises, in two subplots which are combined precariously and artificially, the one fantastic, the other pseudo-realist. In the latter there is doubt on the part of both workers and owners as to whether the repression of the workers or concession to their claims can resolve the issue. The case of the miners in agitation is followed intermittently, as if in a series of episodes. In the first version the heir dies on the operating table in the hands of a distracted medical team, and it is left to Alan to give the funereal news to his sister and the community, whilst on the other hand blood is spilt in the brutal repression of the miners' strike. In the second version, *The Dog Beneath the Skin*, the plot is more Gilbertian, indeed preposterously so. The action turns more concentrically on the denouement of Francis Crewe, completely eliminating the subplots of the miners and the reformatory, substituted by other episodes. Hence the material is spread over a less dispersive and more unitary storyline, which assumes the semblance of the picaresque, both dramatic and fantastic at the same time, and accumulates grotesque and salacious numbers along the way. The episode of the hotel survives and is indeed amplified, Alan falling in love temporarily with the buxom Miss Vipond; it is, however, postponed to that of the burlesque surgical operation. Greater prominence is given to the role of the dog, beneath whose skin is hidden the missing heir, who therefore has never left the village: the scoundrel of a dog, thirsting for whisky on the boat on which Alan is voyaging to the reign of Ostnia. In this imaginary, largely Ruritanian court, everything comes up for the worse, whilst the unreal king and queen are made of cardboard, even if the rioters really are executed, and they are handsome, muscular boys, the object of pity, to whose widows the queen doles out gifts. The entire world is a jocund carnival, as in a story by Firbank – 'nothing but a racket'.[56] In this scene religion looms in Marxist terms as a

---

56   Alan Norman, the pronunciation of whose name sounds like both 'no man' and 'normal', is the traditional *naïf* character, or better an 'innocent', that is the only normal

distraction from the problem of the division of society into the rich and the poor. In Ostnia, Francis is hunted down in the red light district; in Westland, the voice of the Führer blares from a loudspeaker in the lunatic asylum where Alan has finished up, from which he is freed by the dog with the aid of two journalists.[57] In a farcical mode the corrupt levers manoeuvring the world are exposed: in one of the many kaleidoscopic numbers the son of a high financier is a *poète maudit*, the target for satire of a well-defined literary individual. But why has Francis hidden himself in the dog's skin for ten years? In order to scrutinize with an even more estranged eye and with Swiftian malice – an old artifice used by Ouida, in the dog Puck in the novel bearing the same name (though Auden may not have known it!) – the hypocrisy and immoral cowardice of the little village. The vicar, far worse than in the preceding drama, is found guilty of having immobilized the community with aberrant reactionary ideology. Hence Francis is the unheeded benefactor of the community which, leaving the farce behind, issues a serious invitation and warning to overcome apathy, thus acquiring the faculty of choice and revolutionary awareness. But as soon as he is revealed Francis is not unexpectedly lynched, his corpse stitched up again in the dog skin so that the murder will not be unearthed and punished.

8. *The Ascent of F 6* (1936),[58] written in collaboration with Isherwood, and staged to reasonable public acclaim in the West End, is instead a brand

---

person in an entirely sick society, whose codes he contravenes with gaffe after gaffe. In fact he is a poet, romantic in his own way, who concludes his mission conceding to himself only some human gratifications, and in this he is the representative of art, above all literature, which power (in this case, the financier whose dirty trafficking could be easily unmasked) attempts vainly to purchase.

57 Auden conceals Hitler's identity without preventing it from being guessed. The speech is a long tirade which illustrates the lies of Nazi rhetoric, which presented Germany as the custodian of world peace when it was about to launch the slaughter of the Jews, 'men of science, obscurantists and Marxist traitors' who had published 'enormous books', including *Das Kapital*. The depiction of Nazi Germany as a lunatic asylum state is glaring.

58 Ransom, the name of the main character, speaks for itself, even though he is in part modelled on T. E. Lawrence. The title role was played by Alec Guinness in a revival at the Old Vic in 1939.

new play. It is far from the hitherto repetitive grooves and rehashings, even if the mixture of prose and verse, singable and prosaic though extremely refined, and the figure of the solitary climber – implicated nonetheless, as he believes, in strange magic rituals – might lead one to think on the one hand of the influence of Brecht (who frequently has his characters sing) and on the other of the nonsensical Shaw after *Methuselah*. At the same time the oscillation between urban and social realism and esotericism – with the legend of the demon who reigns over the mountain peak, beheading its profaners – and the climate of half-serious or decidedly comic badinage recall Rider Haggard's *She*. The play opens with a soliloquy delivered by a Dantesque, Ulyssean adventurer, Ransom, who thirsts not so much for 'virtute e canoscenza' ['virtue and knowledge'] as for power, and individualistic power. All the rest of the plot illustrates the burden of some infantile traumas, that is the privation of maternal affection in favour of the other brother, which is the transferred target of Ransom's quest. The latter develops John Nower from *Paid on Both Sides*,[59] even if it seems that the subject of the play was suggested to Auden by Isherwood.[60] However, it is also true that the classic theme of early Auden returns, the formation of a palingenetic group, made up chiefly of reckless and fanatical followers who adoringly congregate around a charismatic leader whose status to lead and command is weakened and entirely destroyed by unresolved childhood or psychotic complexes. Ransom's dilemma is whether he should become a man of action or a mystic, a leader or a cloistered monk. The former desire is impure but retreating into isolation is another form of sin. The ascent of the mountain to satiate the thirst for power gives off a Christological and demonic reflection: Ransom wishes to save humanity and feels himself to be invested by a messianic mission not disjoined from profound egotism. Close to the slopes of the mountain he falls prey to the renewed temptation of power and succumbs. It is also impossible not to note that the play foreshadows Auden's theory of the sea, of the ship and the symbolic crossing expounded in *The Enchafèd Flood*: it is not actually a sea voyage, but nevertheless a crew is engaged in a mission under a guide obsessed

59   As appears also to Fuller 1970, 90.
60   Fuller 1970, 90.

by the mirage of reaching a destination. Under the sign of Kierkegaard's 'desperation of temerity', for Ransom the peak is like Ahab's white whale. According to the categories in Auden's book I have just cited, Ransom is an aesthetic hero, a superior being or almost a demigod undermined and corroded by pride. However, the drama is not only metaphysical and absolute, but also impregnated with a fantastic and grotesque realism. Indeed, it is a political parable, or more precisely a political fantasy, which rests on the counterpoint to the major plot represented by a petit bourgeois couple who follow world events mainly by radio in their home and also the evolution of Ransom's F 6 mission. Further scenic effects are the radio bulletins heard at length on stage, over which are superimposed the various reactions of the couple. Auden again does not forget the function of newspapers and communication media: a news magnate, a synecdoche in Brechtian style, appears on stage to give his version of the events and exploit them to his own benefit. In this subplot the whole of politics is summed up by the tag of a 'political racket'. The couple feels uprooted and alienated from the national community and gives voice to the embittered resignation of a class devoid of horizons, while international politics bets all on colonial enterprises providing merely surface lustre and translating into scarce benefit for the population, or none at all. In the climate of this political fiction, in fact, Britain disputes with Ostnia the peak of a strategic and above all magic mountain, a species of Thomas Mann's 'enchanted mountain' therefore, possession of which ensures talismanic control of the colonial populations threatening to rebel and only to be repressed in this way. Two rival expeditions compete for the peak to secure the real and magic powers linked to it. The spasmodic Prometheus, Ransom, lends himself to being used as a man of public utility only because he 'sees' his mother pleading on stage, which leads him to intuit that this could be a figurative expedition, designed to eliminate his brother, hence ritual and at the same time Oedipal.[61] In a euphoric fit, even the little couple overcome their resignation and find themselves emotionally involved, such is the electrifying and aggregating

---

61   One more reason to convince Ransom to accept his mission is his mother's revelation that his brother is the spitting image of their father. This dialogue takes place in a scene played out between realism and hallucination.

power of the expedition. Act II is marked by the inexorable elimination one by one of the expedition members, as they gradually work their way towards the peak. On the realistic plane, the danger unmasks human meanness, whilst on the metaphysical plane Ransom has seen in a magic crystal the final conflict which awaits him, still isolated in his heroic aura.[62] Only in the finale does the drama deteriorate, as Ransom sees the image of his mother superimposed on the demon of the mountain.[63]

9. *On the Frontier*[64] (1937–1938), again co-authored and inspired by the echo of the preparatory phases of the world war, is set close to the confines of two powers, Westland and Ostnia, which end up declaring war on each other. These two countries, respectively a dictatorship and an absolute monarchy, are and are not Germany and Russia.[65] The drama is a demonstrative fable, a piece of fantastic embroidery that is also easily predictive, on the discontent of factory workers in the late 1930s, on

62   In an overly contorted dialogue, the Abbot reveals to Ransom the secret reason for the climb, which Ransom has already read in the crystal ball: the demonstrable proof of his will power and the aspiration to become the saviour of humanity; however, this a Schopenhauer-style *Wille zur Macht*, which is hence self-destructive. In fact the Abbot, unheeded, advises him 'to completely abdicate his will'. The Oedipal and the heroic thus overlap.

63   Ransom kills his brother or lets him die and the mother reveals herself as the reason behind this dream-like murder, lulling her son, returned a baby, and lavishing him with her undivided love; and Ransom dies having concluded his heroic mission. This finale seems to have been designed mostly by Isherwood, who laboriously attempted to liberate himself from maternal tyranny (§ 13.2). Three alternative endings were discarded: the British win, and their flag flutters on the peak, but Ransom is spiritually defeated; in the second, the expedition is lost in the snowstorm and Ransom is spiritually and physically maimed. In the third, the last word is given to the petit bourgeois couple, with a marked sense of the extinguishment of the heroic hubris.

64   Classified as a melodrama and dedicated to Britten, who had set it to music, the play was so topical that a brief delay in staging – Cambridge, November 1938, with the collaboration of the economist Keynes – was enough to bring out its obsolescence, since at that date Hitler had already annexed Austria and invaded the Sudetenland. In a 1939 staging at the Globe it was performed with Eliot's *Sweeney Agonistes*.

65   In the course of the play, the two bordering powers stipulate a pact of non-aggression, but the proper and geographical names suggest a compound, merry, carnivalesque chaos, in a vaguely Central European setting.

the warmongering fanaticism of Europe's nationalist bourgeoisie, on the profiteer cynicism of the arms manufacturers, who had every reason to procrastinate the outbreak of the conflict, on the romanticism of a dictator who had emerged from the midst of the throng, and finally on the underhand manipulation of the press and media to the detriment of the proletariat. The play's dictator, as the two authors warn in some very detailed, extravagant and even humorous captions, was not supposed to resemble living figures and should wear a beard rather than a moustache, but naturally this is an instruction to be ignored. Both humanized and caricatured, this Hitlerian puppet has barely time to solemnly declaim disarmament and a vocation for peace before a border upheaval drives him into a declaration of war. Contrapuntally – in a scene divided into two non-communicating sections following the cases of two families of both nationalities – love, acknowledging no frontiers, springs between two of their members, but is no less romantically doomed to die. The use of the radio – which in one effective episode emits alternately the slogans of the king and of the dictator – is joined to the cunning artifice of different lighting: the two young lovers, tender pacifists, meet in a utopian dream-like circle while the rest of the stage is in darkness.[66] Despite verging on sentimentalism in its treatment of love on stage, the play has Eric and Anna launch an unheeded appeal that is tantamount to a recipe for saving the world by now devastated by the storms of war: that of the 'good place' and the 'garden', the earlier Eden, that is, one of the centres and conceptual axes of Auden's later art.[67]

---

66   A surreal, oneiric interlude, and a dramatic stratagem dear to Auden ever since *Paid on Both Sides*.

67   Auden then takes up again, from *Paid on Both Sides*, and just as pessimistically, the aspiration to pure, idealistic love between two young lovers from enemy families or nationalities, who aspire to a world of dedication but succumb. Eric, a conscientious objector, is wounded in the civil war at the side of the workers, whilst Anna, a nurse, dies from an infection. A further scenic division in the drama is the see-saw between the families of the Thorvalds and the Vrodnys on one hand, and on the other the cases of the languid but astute Valerian, the warmonger, similar to a Firbank puppet or a Wildean aesthete, who believes he can acrobatically keep his head above water with any regime, but who is shot down by a soldier. Auden reckoned that the war would finish almost immediately with a proletarian *coup d'état* and the mutiny of

§ 5. *Auden III: Solipsism shaken by the call to action*

A collection of Auden's early poems, totalling thirty-six printed pages, was published privately in a limited edition by Stephen Spender in 1928, immediately after Eliot's refusal on behalf of Faber and Faber, though with words of cautious admiration.[68] However, in 1930 Eliot did consent to publishing *Poems*, not entirely identical to its predecessor. A second edition in 1933 incorporated *Paid on Both Sides*, an anthology of the poems from previous editions to which were added some unpublished ones. Wedged between the two editions was the publication in 1932 of a second exploit, *The Orators*. Since Auden's debut, therefore, an extremely intricate philological and textual question had arisen, which reverberates and indeed aggravates to the point of insolubility throughout his career as a writer. In 1945, at barely forty years of age, Auden felt himself obliged, or sufficiently immortal, to compile his own definitive poetic canon, which each successive collection was to render semi-definitive. In 1957 he included all his 'short' poems in another comprehensive edition without respecting the collections previously published singly; not only that, he also intervened on the text, pruning, correcting, re-titling, and above all excluding, particularly poems which he confessed were 'dishonest', written without real feeling, or born from repudiated sentiments. At that distance of time he himself divided his canon *a posteriori* into four phases, demarcated by the years 1933, 1939 and 1948. An entire book, by J. Warren Beach,[69] was written to read into this editing an ideological intention, the devious desire to inter Auden's communist past. Beach and many others like him were akin to new versions of Charles Kingsley, the well-known Victorian polemicist who charged Newman with being a Catholic prior to his official announcement of his conversion. In other words, Auden would have been a Christian and a believer even when he was proclaiming himself a Marxist. Every objective

------

the armies on both sides, and that the Führer would end up being assassinated. With the exemplary parable of Valerian, *On the Frontier* is still one of Auden's best studies of power, and Valerian is a camouflaged and grotesque version of Ransom.

68   Cf. also above, § 4.4 n. 40.

69   Cf. Spears 1963, 202–4, for a discussion, prevalently negative, of the book by Beach 1957.

examination of Auden's poetry should be both conducted or remade bearing in mind the real sequence of the poetry collections, making these the basic text and therefore recovering the expunged poems, in a by no means easy zigzagging between the editions available today, including the critical and official ones.[70] The omitted poems even constituted a 'counter-canon' of favourites for the contemporary public.[71] It has often been noted that Auden, having read only scientific, medical and geological treatises since enrolling at university, was unfamiliar with poetry, and had to start from scratch; hence the chaotic shortlist of poets who have been associated with him and who had an influence on him in not always simultaneous phases. For instance, the derivation from Hardy, corroborated by Auden himself, seems remote and of little importance on closer examination. It is true that Hardy, also because he was a highly prolific poet, devised and practised an impressive myriad of stanzaic forms and metrical solutions, but his poetry is perspicuous and most of all narrative, that which Auden immediately rules out. The breathless discovery of Eliot at Oxford was described by his tutor, and was accompanied by the repudiation of Wordsworth. Graves and Riding had already written and published poetry in that staccato register which was to become the mark of the decade, and of Auden above all.[72] By 'Nordic mask' one intends the legendary, lapidary terseness of Auden's language, which frequently does without articles, and his epic rhythm. By 1933 the poetry, taken as a whole, is an alternation of many measures, in

70   In particular, Mendelson's 1976 edition should be combined with the 1977 *The English Auden*, as is done in his edition of Auden's poetry in the complete works. In each single case I shall keep the titles of the poems according to the 1976 edn.

71   Duchêne 1972, 12. The compositions excluded from the complete and definitive collections are the highlight of the anthologies, and, thanks to this, continue to be amply present and proverbial in the mind of English readers.

72   As Hoggart 1951, 88–9, demonstrates with some unequivocal examples. Emily Dickinson too – who, Hoggart reminds us, had been anthologized in England in 1924 – contributes her own in terms of a fragmented parataxis of the verse. Mendelson 1983, 44 n. *, in turn points out the influence that the syncopated, Skelton- and Dickinson-like diction of Laura Riding exercised for a year, 1928, on Auden. This very new style also infected an older poet, Robert Graves, who at the time was living with Riding. On Auden's use of syntax and the lack of visual images, cf. also CRHE, 85.

which rhyme is either absent or is felt to be absent, since it is either not there, is imperceptible or turns to assonance or consonance, or rather is impure (as learnt from Owen). At Oxford, Auden would reiterate to his friends his faith in a minimalist aesthetic which, in only three adjectives, summarized correctly the significance of Eliot's, or even Pound's revolution: poetry should be classical, clinical and austere, adding that it should also be impersonal and detached,[73] though he stopped short at the mythical method.[74] In his early poetry there is no evidence of the contrapuntal lesson of *The Waste Land*, no confrontation of the present with the past, only the present. Neither is there poetry as a collage of quotations and orchestration of fragments and echoes. However, Eliot's lesson resurfaces with variations, because when Auden redressed, re-accommodated and patched up his poems with lines that his friends had saved from compositions he submitted to them, then was his poetic practice similar to that of Eliot. And when he stated that what he held most dear was the pattern of poetry, he was following in the wake of his predecessor. The esoteric, private and highly allusive system of imagery in Auden's poems and texts before 1933, which for each new reader is obscure and decidedly difficult to grasp, becomes notably clearer when one considers its links to the university Mortmere myth.[75] This myth was launched by Isherwood and Edward Upward at public school, and had a circulation that was above all oral; it was then transplanted from grammar school to Cambridge, and when Auden and Isherwood met up again was superimposed onto the Nordic myth, whose fascination arose in Auden – or was increased – hearing Tolkien recite *Beowulf*. The Mortmere myth acts in Auden in the guise of a small group of new warriors preparing for war or an imaginary mission. Such a student scenario

73   From the very beginning Auden could not see himself as the torn poet who transfers his torture onto the page (Hoggart 1951, 29). The 'clinical' concept had to do with his studies as the son of a doctor, and his familiarity with the sphere of psychology.

74   As such can also be considered, however, the disguising of the contemporary quest in the linguistic forms of the Anglo-Saxon epic. Mendelson 1983, 42–6, analyses the phenomenon in relation to Pound, but without referring to the mythical method.

75   The best reconstructions, above all concerning the repercussions on Auden, are those of Replogle 1969, 16–18, and of HYN, 35–7.

was functional to the concept and image of the voyage and of the frontier to cross (a 'frontier' which appears not only in Auden but also and more conspicuously in Rex Warner, for whom it had mainly a political meaning, as the frontier that the bourgeoisie had to cross to gain access to reality and Marxist awareness). The Mortmere movement constituted in essence an innocuous student unrest with reduced political potential, above all in relation to the highly conscious revolutionary spirit of the avant-garde.[76] Auden's political awakening did not occur until his visit to Berlin in 1928–1929, during which he discovered German Expressionism, which was extremely politicized, and above all Brecht, whom he saw performed.

2. Of indefinable, poetic, prose-like and semi-dramatic genre, *The Orators: An English Study* (1932, revised in 1934 and with a new preface in 1966) is maybe the closest Auden came to the European avant-garde. An obscure, initiatory operetta of an astonishingly suggestive fascination, and the most creative in Auden's career, it unleashes an inexhaustible goliardic gusto and a matchless facility in the use of words for their own sake, so much so that the content is at times eclipsed by the dazzling but gratuitous feat of the imagination. Auden's Foreword, added later (1966), is the best key for reading the piece and confirms just how fleeting in the British intelligentsia in the 1920s were the boundaries between fascism and communism – as in Orwell, Eliot and Yeats. The climate in which it arose was that of the cold war between the ruling class and the proletariat, of the echoes of the European communist insurrections, of Italian fascism and of German repression; also that of a possible, second British fear of an English revolution after 1870 and the Paris Commune. But Auden reveals nothing, in the Foreword, of sampling this real scenario as a pure game. In the author's re-reading of the work, the 'central theme' is to be traced to Carlyle's hero worship, and, he added, 'we all know what that can lead to politically', to fascism that is, as seemed to emerge from the examination of the great Scottish writer then under way amongst the critics.[77] The Auden of 1966 was being the psychoanalyst of himself, and attributed the work to an unconscious need to exorcize

76   Buell 1973, 68–9.
77   Volume 4, § 12.

insidious and dangerous tendencies – the same as those of the alleged disciples of Carlyle, such as D. H. Lawrence in his novels *Kangaroo* and *The Plumed Serpent* – giving them free and capricious fantastical vent. The polyvalence of third-person pronouns in the various sections masks the distinct facets of a unique paradigm, as well as the frenzy of the young Englishman to acquire a heroic and prophetic stature for a community in danger. This need is also investigated at a psychic level, that of power rela-tionships between those in command and those who obey. At twenty-five years of age, Auden was skilful at transfusing the suspense of social warfare into burlesque, with his marked taste for razzmatazz and that cabaret style or even that pre-absurd feel he had acquired in Germany. The emergency is underplayed, relativized and distanced and thus objectified: the cast of the Anglo-Saxon epic also operates in Auden's coeval poetry, as anticipated, as witness its frequent situations of play, which is also the play of and at war.

3. Some early readers were ready to see *The Orators* as a recasting, by no means slavish, of *The Waste Land* a full ten years later, that is a diagnosis of the spiritual tone of an epoch,[78] and the denouncement of a disintegrat-ing society in its alternation of sociological reflection, allegorical hints and parody. Auden's 'English study' is like *The Waste Land* a kind of orchestration in separate frames; it is a collage, a web of unrelated and mimetic fragments of a disassociated and disordered reality: genuine chaos basically, albeit entirely horizontal, and lacking in mythic depth and any co-implication of past and present. The obscurity of the poem derives in equal part from the fact that its constituent sections were pre-existing and sewn together, as often is the case with him, without any visible reciprocal congruency, Auden not knowing whether to parody or second its content.[79] If the general theme, in mock-heroic and deforming tones and disguises, is the quest for a saviour;

---

78   CRHE, 124.
79   Mendelson 1983, 147. In his long and in many respects indispensable exegesis (93–116), Mendelson can only limit himself to taking note of the mental confusion and mud-dled positions the poem came from, the shortlist of indiscriminate suggestions, its reworking of the strangest ideological fragments and second rate sources (see below, n. 88).

if the poem is a ritual conducive to the formation of a group, a failed rite and some unfinished magic, because the leader succumbs and Auden, emerging from his solipsism, must watch the group's degeneration, its non-aggregation and reduction to a mush: then logically we are not far distant from the ideological horizons of *The Waste Land*.[80] Like the latter, Auden's operetta is evidently, if not glaringly, disjointed, in truth a jumble of reciprocally isolated and monadic fragments, in which the reader who does not want to accept the complete freedom of design will end by discovering a partial, albeit acrobatic connection. Moving through the sub-sections of the first part, the thematic nexus which emerges is the absence of love and the hope that it will return and be won again. 'This country of ours where nobody is well', this is the apocalyptic and palingenetic motif, which rather than being trumpeted out, is masked and distorted in lampoon. If nobody is well, then the country is sick and absent love is a consequence of the national sickness. One self-enclosed episode is that of a love letter conceived on two planes of ambiguity, the most hidden of which is the 'letter to a wound'. Another form of linkage is that the single pieces are delivered each by a different type of orator-addresser and that each is in the first person: a public speech, one that is more interiorized, a letter, a diary, some odes. For the whole of the first half the rough suturing of the discourse, once the absence of love is established, is the investiture of modern apostles who follow Christ as far as Gethsemane and then go forth into the world;[81] the second detaches itself, parodying heroism through a satirical and self-satirical portrait of a fanatical airman preparing himself for an unreal, imaginary war about to break out.

4. *The Orators* consists of five parts, with a prologue, three sections divided in turn into sub-sections, and an epilogue. The absence of perceptible connections, or the existence of only very vague ones, stands as the image of the impossibility of keeping together the components of a society or of a micro-society. Auden cultivated the ambition of being a guide but objectifies and dismantles himself as ridiculous and cowardly one, and makes

80   This religious metaphor of the leader was shared by the other poets of the 1930s.
81   Regarding the young students' self-mythologizing as modern romantic knights, see
     Fraser in Spears 1964, 83.

him the victim of a prank.[82] This is still a pessimistic document therefore, despite its goliardic patina, and in the end it sketches a land that is still a wasteland. In itself it is a mixture of verse, prose, exhortation, epistle, diary and ode, which evinces a dauntless desire to find a new form. The title alludes to the vocal nature of the work, to the multiplicity of oral emissions and to the ambition to persuade. A work for voices, single speakers and conceivably even choruses, it is therefore semi-dramatic in the broadest sense. The general design is the failed quest for a leader of a group, or maybe the satirical dismantling of the figure of the leader, particularly those on the horizon at the time. But all of this is done with a sweeping, fleeting game, both sibylline and ambiguous, and in a desecrating and mock-heroic vein: Auden believed in what he was parodying, in part at least, and at a later stage recognized the work as a means of venting and healing vain desires for command, by giving free rein to the imagination. The beginning in prose is the delirious harangue of a ringleader who is little more than a neo-graduate, like Auden himself, and who fuels a game of revolution, starting from the fantasy of a commission of angels descending to earth to draft a report on the condition of the English state. Love is absent, or overly noxious towards its neighbour, or scant towards God. The angels return to heaven with a report which is a catalogue of neuroses, tics, Dickensian manias or psychoanalytical symptomatologies. However, a final contortion of the sermons exhorts the boys to exterminate these categories of individuals. The English public school was the traditional forge of managers, as Auden had verified in his recent experience as a teacher at a Scottish school. This beginning is a cloyingly carnivalesque version of the typically English genre of the school farce. The group, whipped up and catechized, is thus formed, and in the second part of *The Orators* the members speak as a chorus or individually, but this is a group that fantasizes, a group of unprepared and deluded jokesters, invoking imaginary guides in tongue-twisters and nursery rhymes or parodies of the Marian litanies, rendered chaotic and unhinged as if it were nonsense poetry. The shaken and disoriented initiates nostalgically remember their leader. A sect of fanatics has been born, deifying their guide and making

82   Mendelson 1983, 97.

him into a god. But, in the meantime, the leader has disappeared and passed away.[83] Thus this is a metamorphic phantasmagoria of Gethsemane, from which the Apostles emerge 'reborn', and from which, in the end, a burlesque prayer, yet a prayer nonetheless, arises, indeed a supplication for salvation from an 'irate' and vengeful He. They are still apostles, in a highly twisted and contorted story or parable, who follow the footsteps of a Christological figure to a Gethsemane, at the end of which a crucifixion is staged. But the new Apostles have to face once again a catalogue of sickness, neuroses and human malaise. Their litanies end up by arousing in the reader's memory the alternative geneses à la Blake. The 'Letter to a Wound' is, in one aspect, a letter sent to the absent hero, but it is written in the elegant and feminine style of two betrothed from other times, secret and distant. This umpteenth disciple is an immature, fatuous fop who writes, in a hazy epistolary language of the eighteenth century, a parody of maudlin, weak, scarcely masculine love, hence apolitical and conceivably homosexual, too.[84] The Journal of an Airman is not a war diary to be taken seriously, as the airman above all fantasizes, and one should remember Auden's declaring in the 1966 Foreword that it was modelled on 'a very dotty semi-autobiographical book', that of General Ludendorff. Indeed, Auden's playfulness overflows, as in the airman's delicious alphabet based on those of Victorian poetry for children, as well as in the description of the physical appearance of the 'enemy'. The diary opens with semi-parodic disquisitions that denote the hand of an imaginative expert in psychological theory, such as that of an enemy who seeks to sabotage a secure psychic system. The erudite psychological disquisition is based on military metaphors and rests on geometrical diagrams.[85] The

83 Conceivably, behind this was a summer trip to Scotland of a group of fanatical young schoolboys who invoke cartoon and detective story heroes in a parody of liturgical litanies and chants; similarly, Clough had narrated in Homeric, hence parodic casts, a study holiday in Scotland in the poem *The Bothie* (Volume 4, §§ 138–139).

84 Or even real: Auden was suffering from a rectal fissure, maybe as a result of homosexual intercourse (Carpenter 1981, 121).

85 It is singular to note that the diagram of 'self-regard', with its centre and circumference, recalls one of the dominant images of Eliot's *Four Quartets* (Volume 7, § 100.3).

point is how the human being can pursue and obtain undisturbed the old aesthetic, and also decadent dream of the cultivation of his or her own distance and unique personality without external interference. Hence the enemy is as much a psychic hypostasis as a social reality. The airman draws up an accurate, shrewd, festive and extravagant taxonomy and phenomenology of the enemy, but this is as much an enemy in flesh and blood as and above all an endogenous one. The journal, therefore, represents the transferral of the psychosis of war onto the plane of personal obsession.[86] The therapy is a Eureka moment *in extremis*, that of not combating the enemy in guerrilla warfare without quarter, but of offering no resistance, thereby removing the 'friction' it provokes, namely war. Victory is a paradoxical absorption of the conquered by the victorious. The point of view is therefore close to that of the kamikaze, that is death as supreme self-realization. Behind all this lies the obscure teaching of an uncle who attempted suicide but survived, a photo of whom bears the inscription 'I have crossed it'. The airman is thus one of Auden's *alter egos* and the first study for Ransom, the climber in *The Ascent of F 6*,[87] and in this perspective the enemy is the projection of subconscious internal aggressiveness, of his *Wille zur Macht*. In front of the mirror the airman symbolically confesses: 'Thoughts suitable for a sanatorium'.[88] The final odes ironically desublimate, even liquidate in

86   Mobile, fluctuating with a change of horizon and register at every step, made up of short phrasal verbs closed by a full stop, notably similar to the stream of consciousness.

87   It is due to this that the airman is seen as a doppelganger of Lawrence of Arabia (Spears 1963, 50, and Binni in CAB, vol. II, 293–4, who draws attention to Lawrence's technical manual for use by RAF staff, written, he says, in a 'magnetically inventive' style). There is also most possibly a reminiscence of Yeats's 'An Irish Airman Foresees his Death'. Buell 1973, 21–2, calls the airman a figure of the popular imagination, linking him to the exploits of Lindbergh, Amy Johnson and T. E. Lawrence, without mentioning the most automatic choice, Yeats's airman.

88   The Journal unleashes far richer and more impenetrable suggestions than this précis of mine. Mendelson 1983, 93–116, partly clarifies, on the basis of one of Auden's letters, that the esoteric key is to be traced to an anthropological essay by John Layard, the psychiatrist Auden met in Berlin in 1929, on the shamans of the island of Malekula in the New Hebrides (contemporary Vanuatu). This is the peak of Auden's acrobatics in 1932, and of the exclusion of the collective fruition of the poetic word, oriented solely at initiates.

humour the quest for a hero or for a present-day guide who can liberate and save the homeland, as is evident in the third in particular, which salutes this figure, preposterously and playfully, in the new-born son of Auden's friend Rex Warner. The other side of the coin is Auden's pessimism, aware as he was that the proletariat and the privileged classes would remain quite distinct and distant, and that the saviour was not actually on the horizon.

5. Various poems from the 1933 edition, which contains some of the odes and interlinear verse compositions from *The Orators* and also several choruses from the dramatic script in preparation which was to become *The Dog Beneath the Skin*, must be enjoyed for the sheer suggestive power of the images and situations, as well as for the combination of words and often assonantal rhymes, without attempting to localize the more precise underlying content. The initial self-mythologizing is that of the wanderer,[89] catapulted into the present from a far off primordial epoch, and who moves in a stylized, unreal, hallucinatory environment distorted by the imaginative heredity of the Anglo-Saxon poems, which is difficult to recognize as English with its glaciers, the whirling winds, the heavy snowfalls and hailstorms and the distinguishing marks of a volcanic landscape. Britain is transfigured as a kind of Iceland. Only in stretches does this visionary trance dissipate, for example in the poem 'The Watershed', which contains undistorted stills of a desolate, macerated area, waterlogged and miry, of abandoned machinery and an exhausted human work force, like that of the mining district where Auden grew up. The Mortmere sampler traces a visible internal link to the images of war and guerrilla warfare, of conspiracy and preparation for an assault at times described in slightly ironic and playful terms (as in 'Let History Be My Judge') or familiar ones (as in 'Have a Good Time'), with mountain passes to cross, maps to decipher and follow, preparations, expeditions, campsites and bivouacs, and various records of military life. Poem after poem, a climate of palpable danger is formed, which nonetheless provokes fear and even anguish in the supposed heroes.

89   This is a title that takes up that of 'The Wanderer', one of the most famous Anglo-Saxon poems. Auden's wanderer is often an observer, from the height of a hill or from a window.

From the band of the fanciful an *alter ego* detaches himself who must 'depart and face / Danger and sorrow' having 'abandoned most of his friends'. A third chord, which takes Auden back into the literary climate and grooves of 1920s alienation and disorientation, is that of the solitary poet attempting to get the better of the private and public wear of the sentiments. Love is transient, but nature deludes one into believing that its cyclic route could begin again every time. Love 'remains', 'infinite', beyond all consumption, and everything spins incessantly and is renewed after 'love's worn circuit'; meanwhile, a thirst for the immutable arises, such as the spectacles of nature, or the imperturbable gelid moon at night. The dialectic and argumentative contrast is marked by the median caesura of a 'but' which recurs in these poems with singular regularity.[90] Not always, however, because in some rare cases – 'Too Dear, Too Vague' – the diction purifies itself into exquisite Elizabethan variations, into movements of light verse and delicate and shrewdly constructed tongue twisters and word play. '1929' is the only poem with a clear political and revolutionary afflatus, and, outside the groove of the mock-serious, leaning towards the militant. This ode stands out from the others for its tone and grandeur, being an evocative and descriptive memorial which occasionally bears touches of Yeats's concreteness and symbolic penchant, and which soars in a passionate, muddled peroration which fatally overpasses the canon of calligraphic sobriety observed in the rest of the collection. Conceived and planned at Easter during the workers' insurrection in Berlin, it first argues religion's inefficacy in saving and regenerating the world, on the very day that that promise is celebrated. The first of the four scenes depicts the frogs croaking in the pond and above all the clouds crossing the sky 'without anxiety'. The euphoria of the lovers clinging to a nature permeated with spasms of renewal is violently contrasted with a 'solitary man' sitting afflicted on a bench who, resembling an embryo chicken, is a grotesque parody of the risen Christ. Life and death are interwoven throughout the first scene in the memory of the evoking poet, without the offer of renewal

90   It will recur again in the later poems 'of the islands' (Mendelson 1983, 341–2), where it indicates a change in theme, the impossibility of reaching the destination.

dissipating the funereal mementoes. Auden suddenly presents himself as a public man with a mature civil and political conscience. However, the medicine invoked, or heard, in front of the spectacles of desolation in Berlin, is of this world: he is ambiguously a 'strong man' capable of deciding, even at the risk of being mistaken. In the second scene, the port's ducks are particularly Yeatsian in their estrangement from human pain. Like Yeats's swans, they 'paddle', and from the fresh contrast between their imperturbability and the glaring excitement of urban warfare arises a diagnostic recapitulation of the biological, psychological and social history of man, who, from the embryonic state onwards is cast into an adventure of alienation, uselessness and aggression.[91] The historical present lies under the aegis of Thanatos rather than of Eros. The more demanding third scene again fractures faith in political or spiritual intervention and, by wondering whether history is teleological, a 'wonderful fructification', or rather, the 'infectiousness of a disease', sketches the pessimistic portrait of the soul shutting itself in and glimpses a desolate and fatalistic approach to death. This said, the fourth and last scene suddenly blares like an apocalypse in transforming the distressing perspective into an unhoped-for cry of Easter expectancy. Yeats cedes to Eliot in the invocation of the 'dragon' and above all of the 'devourer' that descends expectedly in the sign of a 'terrible calm' preceding cataclysm. Religion's salvific capacity seems to be re-affirmed with a supreme appeal to the real love of the risen Christ,[92] a love that is total and mysterious and implies a destructive and at the same time constructive revolution, that is a cosmic bonfire of all that is old and worn out.

§ 6. Auden IV: Poetry until 1939

Auden's uncollected poems written before 1939 appeared in *Look, Stranger!* (1936, entitled *On This Island* in the 1937 American edition

---

91   To speed up a line of reasoning which could become too heavily theoretical, in this phase Auden does away with the definite article, resorting to his typically telegraphic and note style.

92   As his vision I interpret 'lolling bridegroom' in the 'clear lake', the image that closes the ode.

dedicated to Erika Mann),[93] *Letters from Iceland* (1937),[94] and *Journey to a War* (1939). The titles alone of these collections reveal some keywords together with equally evident thematic signals. The 'stranger' is one who is not or is no longer within an organic community, or who reaches a new land from outside that is not his homeland; thus we see emerging the myth or the motif of the journey, and a journey, in at least one case, towards an island. The poem in sestets 'Paysage Moralisé' hesitantly opposes the quivering *Sehnsucht* of the islands on the part of indomitable sailors, to whom a shipwreck looms large, with the stagnancy and frustration of a secure life in 'starving' cities.[95] This voyaging is the symptom of a varied aetiology: Auden began to travel out of a desire for knowledge, or to puncture his isolationism, or to obey an urge to flee from a model that was too unbearable, or even attracted by the mirage of earnings. A tourist guide of Iceland and a reportage were commissioned to him, for which services he received payment. It was a sentimental and romantic notion that prompted Auden to make this journey to Iceland, which was linked to the family myth of the origins of his name and ancestry. In two of the three journeys, to the lands mentioned by the title or implicit in it, the destination was a theatre of war. *Journey to a War* refers to the Sino-Japanese conflict, where he was sent as a correspondent.[96] In reality, it is not easy, taking a close look at this diagram

93   Erika Mann, daughter of the novelist, married Auden in 1935 but purely out of convenience, in order to hide Auden's homosexuality, and also because Erika, deprived of her German citizenship, needed an English passport. They almost never lived together. In reality, this marriage was accepted by Auden because of a wish to regularize his sexuality, as was a later flirt with the American Rhoda Jaffe.

94   A 'heterogeneous parable', of the same mixed structure as *The Orators* (HYN, 288). Mendelson 1983, 94 note *, says instead that this structure is repeated in *The Sea and the Mirror*.

95   The flight from the city to the island can certainly be transformed into a new estranging solipsism, and the islands become 'Islands of self'. Iceland is called a 'refuge' where 'Europe is absent'. Much more beneficial were the sensations felt on landing in *On This Island*. In fact, in the first poem of *A Voyage*, the island is the proof of the existence of the 'Good Place'.

96   The further outcome were twenty-one sonnets 'from China', which, with too much generosity, were hailed as a great breakthrough, in fact the most significant short poems of the decade, on a par even with Elizabethan collections. Vaguely indebted to

derived in skeletal and intuitive terms from the titles of the collections, to find further coherence. The poet, who had been accused by the academic intelligentsia of not communicating with the average reader, now wrote some rather plain 'letters' and responded with the offer of a historically more anodyne genre, travel poetry. Which is to say, he definitively left the hermetic solipsism of his beginnings. However, the biographical events clash with the letter of the poems, and also with the theatre that Auden had written up until 1939 with so much objective passion, giving for granted that it was really politically convinced. In fact, while the war was breaking out or was about to break out all over the world, his poetry speaks of a poet and intellectual who on the one hand discovers the inefficacy of predicating universal love,[97] belied and trodden on everywhere, and on the other seeks to obtain a decentring, and yearns for a form of protective exorcism.

2. 'Spain' is an ode or better a tripartite oration and peroration, in unrhymed quatrains, on the three historical-symbolic moments of yesterday, today and tomorrow, with the measuring criterion, and watershed – rediscovered, passionately and solemnly declaimed – in the Spanish War, according to the recurrent appearance of the refrain 'to-day the struggle'. The past, the path of civilization from the origins until today in a planetary radius – even the 'absolute value of Greek' – is relativized and subsumed by the Spanish War. Thus ended a historical cycle of death, tyranny, class and social divisions, while another opened up of life, in the 'heart' of the world, Spain and Madrid. Battalions of a heterogeneous but transfixed

---

Rilke, for a good half they unimpressively trace an imaginative story of the symbolic phases of the creation and evolution of a wild primordial man who has not yet discovered the advent of consciousness; but by discovering it one day he becomes a natural poet who may be taken for a Homeric double, since he is blind. With a centuries-long leap this primordially Romantic poet feels the pressure of the Enlightenment. The second half, too long drawn out, gives us, in an unsuitable metric module, a panoramic vision of the war in progress, with the appropriate accents of denouncement. These sonnets inaugurate in Auden a type of poetry of historical summary that is often rather unsuccessful.

97   During an alleged 'mystical experience' in 1933, reflected in the poem 'A Summer Night', Auden had found out what it meant to love others for themselves, from which was born the extremely fertile idea of Agape.

humanity are hastening there by a free and decisive choice, rather than waiting vaguely for life and history to become the protagonists of change. The last third of the ode exhorts the addressee not to become distracted from the immediate tasks of the libertarian war by prematurely cradling dreams of a hopefully rosy and democratic tomorrow. This was also the routine stuff of today, whilst the war imposed that 'necessary murder' which made Orwell rise up against Auden's amorality and his *de facto* non-involvement in the life of the Party. Auden modified this expression in a reprint, but the reason why he suppressed the poem forever was on account of the last lines in which he sang the praises of history as the prize that always smiles upon the victors. The fascination of the composition lies in the imaginative, synecdochic, often extravagant and apparently random cataloguing of the phenomena chosen to define the turning points of the past civilization and those of a life reborn. However, the intimate lack of conviction in this warlike song and anthem is suggested by the conscious choice of 'metaphors of unconscious nature',[98] by the concealment of doubt, by the enthusiastic incitement, and even by the subtle case-histories of motivations that drove so many foreigners to Spain, among whom the 'suicide pact, the romantic / Death'. In other words, the escalation of the war provoked in Auden a reduction, not an increase, in his civic commitment and passion; almost an irritation, not a fervour. The poet becomes more private, closes the door to the public, ceases caring, and feels no guilt. This drifting is expressed through the idealization of places protected from the tumult, closed and walled in, medieval citadels that kept afar the uproar of the world outside, or else islands, which faintly incarnate Auden's myth of Arcadia or Eden. The future professor of poetry, a successor to Arnold, writes a 'Dover Beach' in which one can overhear some even literal echoes of Arnold's celebrated rhapsody, albeit in verse which in itself is somewhat insignificant.[99]

3. The salute to a worn out period, of ancient codes and deeply rooted habits, is pronounced under the pressing threat of war in 'Danse Macabre'.

98   Cf. the discussion by Mendelson 1983, 316–23.

99   Dover is, ambiguously, the port the emigrants set sail from, as well as the one at which those coming home disembark.

The renunciation is also expressed in a mild, resigned pessimism, because given the unheeded wish for universal love in a world consecrated to pain, and in view of the corruption of man and history, only innocent animality can be idealized. A poem composed, so to speak, of a series of captions, like 'Night Mail', although commissioned Auden by the producers of a state film,[100] does not render the effect of a poem of impending war, rather pours out a trusting optimism more suitable for prosperous times of peace, and oozes a sense of the poet's whole-hearted adhesion to the community he describes, a compact and healthy one struggling for the good things in life, and anxiously pulsating. This is not the sole symptom of giving in to a range of *démodé* popular poetic forms, such as, in addition to the travel album in verse, the ballad, the nursery rhyme, the ditty, and the fantasia. Auden is objective in observing the tenacious daily battle, vain as it was, against *tempus edax rerum*, in his peers who have not given up but are strong-willed, feisty and lucid combatants ('As I walked out one evening'). *Twelve Songs* contains snapshots of the surrounding reality, stories and anecdotes of the common man and woman – almost, we might say, emblems of the paradigmatic figure of 1930s literature, the tramp – caught in the ugly anonymity of their routine, yet in gestures and sudden movements that are really or fantastically reactive. The highs and lows of life are presented and sweetened in the easiest and most approachable poetic genre ever, the ballad; that is to say, examined within the sphere of the pathetic and therefore of the non-political. The two excessively lengthy and rambling ones, 'Miss Gee' and 'Victor', constitute the surprise of an Auden who in Tennysonian vein ventures into the brisk stylistic traits of the ballad in quatrains, to show the fatal consequences of moral weakness in a poor defenceless humanity. The second tackles the odyssey of the careless worker duped by an ambitious prostitute, an age-old naturalistic scenario, because in fact the unprepared and immature man murders the woman who has betrayed him, like Wilde's convict. The suppression of lyric poetry in favour of objectification ultimately leads to seeing art as catharsis, impassibility, and balance. The scrutiny of the mechanisms and the functions of

---

100   After teaching in primary schools from 1930 to 1935, Auden worked for a government-run film company, the GPO Film Unit.

art and its relationship with life begins with the collections from the end of the 1930s, a relationship of objective reflection,[101] but at the same time of the exorcism of suffering. Auden compares his poetics, and his being an artist, with other historical or possible artistic records. He reflects himself in *alter egos* – Rimbaud, Housman, Lear – and discovers himself and them the victims of varieties of psychic illness, of repression, and of psychoanalytical complexes. In two programmatic poems, 'The Novelist' and 'The Composer', the novelist is like an old master who knows how to come close to the human spectacles that he witnesses; only the musician leaps over the barriers, unconstrained by the moralistic or consolatory functions of poetry. 'Musée des Beaux Arts' was inspired by Bruegel's *Icarus* to exemplify art's transfiguring and sublimating capacity in relation to experience – even the painful variety – and the sovereign, downplaying hierarchical levelling out of the various human spheres in a balanced light and shade background. The poem is also an example of a new genre in Auden, that of the poetic ekphrasis following in the wake of Keats's ode on a Grecian urn, but in a poetic style of an indiscernibly conversational vein.[102]

101   Bayley, quoted in Spears 1964, 67, points to a technique of a cinematographic type, and the use of close-ups, in Auden's impassive look at the pure phenomenon.

102   The poem imperceptibly cites Ruskin's idea of the 'old masters', but to overturn and improve on it. The old masters, all told, rather shared, for Auden, that sense of 'gaiety', serenity and detachment that Yeats attributed to the artist – and to the simulacrum of the artist, or even to his counterpart, the tragic player impersonating, with dry eyes and masculine stoicism, Hamlet and/or King Lear – in the almost contemporary 'Lapis Lazuli' (see Volume 7, § 84.2). In Auden one can certainly read a similar justification of the artist's *ataraxia* in times of war, or the threat of war. The ontological frame is in fact alarming, since the composition reveals in the background a sceptical spoliation of every divine attribute – and therefore every divine vestige – in man, or in the 'human position'. The old men reverently await the miraculous ostension of the Child, but other children keep their distance without participating, busy with their games. More seriously, and improperly, the dogs continue to ferret about undisturbed while the horses scratch their rumps. All of this sounds like a cynical reduction, Shakespeare or Swift style, of man to a Calibanesque, semi-bestial being, only absorbed in his biological reality. For Auden, Bruegel is the disenchanted painter who portrayed a reality from which the signs of the divine and the miraculous have disappeared, or of people who no longer perceive or care about them, by

4. In *Letter to Lord Byron*[103] (1937, revised in 1966), annexed to the letters from Iceland, Auden the parodist mimics Byron's *Don Juan*, adopting and imitating his mannerisms, his procedural devices, his leaps in register, his formal twists and idiosyncrasies. He even reuses that form of metapoetry which consists in declaring in rhyme that there is no other rhyme but that one, or that a certain line is 'the flattest one' ever written. In Iceland, Auden wandered around consciously following in the footsteps of august predecessors, including Morris, and the choice of Byron as recipient of this letter was considered, as Byron himself wrote in the opening of his own poem, after evaluating other heroes and finding them wanting in heroism. This 'letter' is not written in *ottava rima* but in the rhyme royal composed of seven rhymed lines *ababbcc*; but this modification is barely perceptible to the reader. The discourse struggles to get going simply because it must; that is, it must be made up of small bathetic, paradoxical, surprising observations (we write better poetry when we have a running nose from a cold ...). In the first canto Auden, beating about the bush, imagines himself in the company of the quick-witted poets of the eighteenth century, a Bradford, a Cottam, a Dyer, a Prior. The task of the second canto is to update Byron in the afterlife on today's England and on the habits and customs of the common folk. Auden confirms his investiture as impartial observer of life's events. His gaze is unreactive, from a position that gives rise to political apathy and the nostalgia for 'things that used to be better'. Technological inventions leave him cold, he draws back in the face of the discoveries of what was then modernity; and in looking at society he perceives the profound rift between the rich and poor and a false concept of democracy, united to the acute perception of British isolationism now on the wane. This is then a letter on the state of the union, disguised under this pretext. The second canto also insists in unargued flashes on the manias, the unbearable superficiality and snobbery of well-heeled society, and has fun

---

now become a workforce of mercantile civilization, or belonging to that 'semantic' and no longer 'symbolic' cultural type theorized by Yuri Lotman. The ship has its commerce to attend to and sets sail. Icarus is the image of a man being sucked into the depths, no longer rising to the skies.

103   For Auden's essay dedicated to Byron's poem, see below, § 10.3.

quoting as if on the stock exchange the writers who count, as Orwell did in those same years in more orderly prose essays. After high society a mass of repressed and subdued beings is described on the point of exploding. In the third canto Byron is hailed as the sane poet who taught how to live a normal life, or, more precisely, one of action and courage – albeit criticized by the moralists – in a comical-humorous, non-educational vein. In contrast, arrows are let fly against Wordsworth and Milton. In the fourth canto Auden presents himself as a Ulyssean adventurer invigorated by his journey, or, simply aware of the path taken, rereading his story and humorously sketching out his life in indulgent reminiscences. The refusal of a merely artistic art is disdainful; art ought to be subjected to the imperatives of life, to love and purity of the heart. Byron is a fleeting *alter ego* on the way to Auden's second manner, the 'airy'.

§ 7. *Auden V: An emigrant from the islands*

A collection that is already amorphous, without high notes, but merely professional, is that of Auden's poems entitled *Another Time* (1940). In 1939 he had demonstrated to himself that the project pursued over the previous decade had failed or had finished. He had in fact believed that poetry could achieve a twofold goal, objectifying his personal angst while at the same time being a political weapon; his departure from and the abandonment of his homeland represented the dissolution of the balance between private and public. The shadow of the war looms over these compositions albeit not much; for example over the confused and pretentiously phantasmagorical 'The Dark Years', ending in a prayer for a metaphysical Light that will descend from above, or over the equally turbid rhapsody 'In Sickness and in Health'. Nor can it be said that they bear the mark of the sense of place, even if a long ode does half-heartedly discuss, with forced humour, the new state-controlled tendencies of pre-war American culture.[104] One waits patiently for the poetic masterwork, but in the end remains convinced that this was a moment of stagnation or minor urgency in inspiration, or

104 'Under Which Lyre', a stinging satire against a mass utilitarian culture in universities. The American 'unknown citizen' obeys the rules, but at the price of an empty, automatic and mechanical existence of routine.

of the priority of a certain randomness which is the symptom of a dearth of content.[105] The best results still arise in poems in a minor vein, songs in several cases, unfurling from the euphoria of erotic gratification; and from those resolved in the humorous or relieved register of *boutades*, or by others in which the theological or philosophical question or quandary is posed in the form of witty parables, anecdotes and allegorical fantasies,[106] or still others such as brief, cadenced, anaphoric ballads in long or short stanzas with refrains. Amidst the occasional pieces, there are little sermons like those for children's birthdays, recited by a kind of wise, silver-tongued grandfather, openly outdated and nineteenth century, and repeating by now obsolete formulae.[107] Where and when Auden philosophizes without images, and complicates the argumentative thread, he becomes abstruse, falters and even irritates. To a large extent, what predominates is a specious and tortuous discourse that does not justify the outlay of words and the labour of interpretation. It is the triumph of the discursive vein, subtly ratiocinative, or worse, quibbling. And there are also other various, in fact numerous, poetic examples that are completely out of place, sound a strident note and leave us speechless by their hair-brained nature.[108]

2. This segment of Auden's poetic itinerary opens with a tribute to Yeats under the sign of commemorative poetry. From the very first stanza the ode hinges on the friction between the desensitizing, numbing cold of the wintertime of death, and the live, inexhaustible flame of the deceased: the instruments to measure the temperature are precise, but the loss is not registered, that is, the world in general does not realize that a great poet has died. But the hiatus is filled by the fact that though the man is dead his poetry survives. This public disgrace for poetry is a metaphor for art and

---

105   In a purely descriptive, albeit sumptuous, vein is the anthem narrating the invention of music by St Cecilia, later set to music by Britten.

106   Like 'The Maze', on the doubts of the man who finds difficulty in orientating himself in the world.

107   Travel experiences are reflected in 'Pleasure Island', where the tropical climate invites swooning and the lowering of one's intellectual and moral vigilance.

108   'Lady Weeping at the Crossroads' is a heraldic imitation that seems to parody Keats, or even Morris, about a woman who betrays a knight and is gnawed by remorse.

the artist: after his death and disappearance, the poet survives through his art, a theme that is eminently Yeatsian. The poet lives on in his admirers, he does not die, he is a metempsychosis; hence the dictum 'poetry makes nothing happen' is ironically rebutted. And yet Auden has to admit that by then poetry was an elite phenomenon, since if Yeats is art, he survived only because of the 'few thousand' who, on that day in January 1939, found themselves doing 'something slightly unusual'. Poetry no longer finds space, and the scientific mentality is deaf to it, like humanity floundering in veritable physical survival: it is therefore true that as a weapon of civil progress poetry is dead. Auden closes his commemoration by recalling that every true art issues a message of optimism and civilizing joy; but the barking of the dogs is a metaphor for war at the gates, and the announcement of the unheeded message of the joy of poetry, and the unchallenged reign of hatred.[109] In 'In Memory of Sigmund Freud', written just a short while later, Auden demarcated in 1939 a turning point, that of the war, but at the same time that of the synchronized loss of great and elect spirits who sought to organize human life according to more just and liberating laws, demiurges and benefactors cut down in the supreme moment of their meritorious philanthropic work. Freud was the avant-garde of a human phalanx of love, and among the leading heroes who, by dying, had left the field open to universal hatred. Conceivably, Voltaire is evoked for the only reason that, like Yeats, he acted ideally close to another historical upheaval, that of 1789, and to a cataclysm similar to the one gathering in the skies of Europe, he battling for a better life, open to joy ('only his verse could stop them',[110] thereby reconfirming art's civilizing function). Looking back over his biographical span, Auden confirmed that he had reached a mature condition of balance and wisdom, had sought and found, and had at least come very close to the utopias he had been pursuing.

3. In 'The Prophets', a face that is perhaps the divine one responds, without entrenching and hiding itself; Auden grants the children paternal wishes, pointing to the necessity for humility. And he hails the superseding

---

109　Cf. HYN, 349–53, for the gestation of this elegy, and the reasons for the inclusion of the second of its three sections.

110　'them' refers to the forces of obscurantism.

of every Manichaean or narrowly Protestant vision, having escaped the Calvinistic torture of the obsession with evil and the struggle against it. It was Melville who had discovered good late in life, and at the same time the normality of evil, its familiarity with the other passions man lives with.[111] Love as a spiritual and physical flame, the impetus of union and the overcoming of every separateness, are sung in poems that are addressed to an unidentified interlocutor ('my dear', f., or even 'my dear', m.), and which, if they were not so cerebral as they sometimes are, would seem to be miming a Marvell, since they come close to the seventeenth-century philosophy of the spiritual and physical union of lovers (even if in one case Auden quotes Blake). This isolating love is praised – in the twelve songs, often also intoxicated by such unison – against the background routine of automatized society. 'The Quest' is a 'Rilkean' series of around a score of sonnets, some of them metrically impure, which form a sibylline prophecy laboriously realized, without proper names and only indefinite pronouns that leave a halo of doubt on the true nature of the hero and the evident allegory of the things that happen to him. It is also a mystery distantly modelled on the Grail scenario, with, in the centre, a sort of Gawain or Percival; or a mix of various allusions to other stories, last but not least Browning's 'Childe Roland', albeit the free derivation from the adventures of Carroll's Alice is literal and declared at the start. Because it is in fantasy mode, 'Atlantis' develops much better, and with somewhat greater poetic afflatus, its theme of the search for a utopian place (here we are living in the world of mirages, and the destination is reached only if and when one has completely forgotten seeking it).

§ 8. *Auden VI: The post-war age of anxiety*

Between 1941 and 1947, Auden seems to have wanted to challenge his critics, who insistently and with perplexity reproached him for only being capable of writing short poems. The four 'long poems', whose aim was an attempt to leave a more enduring and memorable mark of his poetic experience in mid-century, are also unmistakeable exemplifications of the

---

111   At other times, the sense of the presence of the devil and therefore sin and looming punishment cast a shadow over the sunshine of love.

religious and spiritual change that that his move to America brought about. Objectively speaking they fall under the aegis of Kierkegaard's dialectic between being and becoming, and as a passage, or more properly a leap between phases, from the aesthetic to the ethical and in due time to the religious.[112] However, this frame of thought is not a weight, nor is it slavishly pursued. In both cases Auden emulates T. S. Eliot above all.[113] Since there are four of them, they are deliberately Auden's 'four quartets',[114] or to be more precise a quadriptych that probes a single or correlated question, the function of art in the contemporary world, definitively subordinate to ethics and religion. That challenge, which in the heat of the moment seemed to many brilliantly victorious and a triumphal achievement of Auden's art, was in reality lost. In all four poems, Auden is pointlessly conceptual, but not because the profundity is so arcane as to require an analogous and mimetic difficulty in the poetic discourse; on the contrary, if one tries – following Goethe's dictum – to pare the concept or concepts to the bone, what remains are extremely simple, if not simplistic assertions. The conceptual objective is no more than an excuse to flaunt a real tightrope walker's ability in rotating ever changing stanzaic and prose forms, particular sound patterns and the most varied discursive registers. The domain is that of parody, a parody so superficial that it appears to be an end in itself; while above all else the characters of these pageants chatter and entertain. What prevails everywhere is a kind of discursive superfetation that may recall the verbal smokescreens of late Browning, who likewise worked on 'continuations' and 'contaminations' of others' themes, such as the extremely obscure poem *Fifine at the Fair* modelled on Molière, or the Aristophanic diatribe *Aristophanes' Apology*. This is true above all for

112   Auden was struck down on the road to Damascus due to his reading of the theological works of Charles Williams (who had edited the second edition of Hopkins's poems in 1930), and in particular of his *The Descent of the Dove*, which insists on the operations of the Holy Ghost in history and on the function of the Church as a divine incarnation. In turn, Williams was the *trait d'union* with Kierkegaard.

113   Eliot was hailed in 1948 with a very personal tribute on his sixtieth birthday. For Auden, Eliot was a poet who, with a measured language in the face of historical emergencies, 'did much to / prevent a panic'.

114   As Serpieri 1969, 202, observes.

that ambitious failure, namely, Auden's 'comment' on Shakespeare's *The Tempest*, *The Sea and the Mirror*.

2. *New Year Letter*[115] (1941, republished in 1967), an epistle in octosyllabic lines in rhyming couplets, returns to the measures of a philosophizing didactic art in indicating the medicines that can save the world from the ongoing threat of its dissolution. These include a new intersocial compactness on the axis of uniting love, acknowledgement of guilt, suffering and collective atonement. It is a *construens* message entailing the condemnation of the current cultural and ideological tendencies, the consequence of some distortions of distant origin, more exactly the economically based cultures and those exalting the unrestrained ego, averse to equilibrium and the control of 'blind desires' and impulsiveness. Disrupting the discursive order, Auden demonizes far too many historical enemies, pernicious philosophers, aberrant ideologies and messages; so that the poem, formally in the manner and metre of Pope and the Augustans, turns into a chaotic and repetitive flux that obstinately reduplicates its thrusts. From the concrete New York scenario below the window, from the Manhattan climate at the end of the year, evoked in familiar terms, and barely formalized in versification, the letter takes a plurality of directions that range from phantasmagoria to the fragmentary and flickering reconstruction of human history, from invective to condemnation, from diatribe to prophecy and prayer. A metric and conceptual analogy with Browning's *Christmas Day* has been found;[116] for me the strongest resemblance is with the late nineteenth-century apocalypses of the 'lost city'. And indeed the main, underlying allegorical model is the Dantesque journey, the ascent from the world as infernal abyss to a Purgatory, and to Eliot's 'fire that refines'. Thus, Auden's *New Year Letter* is his response to *Four Quartets*, a meditation on time and eternity and the possible redemption of history, as well as on the paradoxes of purgation and

---

115 Entitled *The Double Man* in the American edition, to indicate more visibly the reason for the division and the necessary psychic integration. The first edition of the poem contained eighty-odd pages of notes, mostly superfluous and of the erudite type, and was closed by 'The Quest', shifted to the short poems in the later collected editions.

116 Hoggart 1951, 160.

the purgatorial path.[117] Like Eliot, Auden concludes with a prayer to the 'unicorn among the cedars', a divine symbol that can transform the desert into a city. The beginning dwells on the strangeness of a world which is splitting and breaking apart in the summer of 1939, and on the climate of the '*civitas*', that is, of harmony and oneness and a fusion of sense, intellect and affections that is being established on a distant soil – American – between two cultured people, the poet and his female interlocutor, in virtue of music, that is, human art seen as a Beethovenian pledge of unity and fraternity,[118] beyond any political, racial or ideological barrier. The philosophical or speculative point that Auden sets out to investigate is order as the goal of the converging erotic and artistic impulses. Indeed art points toward order and is order; it encourages, urges on, comforts, but man must then make his contribution in daily reality, disciplining the anarchy of the will. The first visionary flash of light is the image of all responsible artists, who feel the binding and in some aspects demoralizing example of their great predecessors sitting in judgement, and artists devoted to serving human-ity, once they have tamed their savage egos and hence their egotism. From Dante begins a phantasmagoria of the afterlife, a subterranean journey into a modern limbo populated by the shadows of great spirits, a family that Auden evokes to exemplify the necessary liberation from every superhuman and Promethean urge in the artist and the rediscovery and valorization of their function of serving the public good and man's psychophysical order. In Auden's vision, the site of the disaster and the cataclysm virtually coin-cides with the whole planet. In the second part, the Dantesque allegory is more explicit since the world has sunk into the abyss and man is prey to an angelic-diabolical duality, 'Half angel and half *petite bête*', hence a man 'divided' as frequently in Victorian poetry, and a Cloughian 'dipsychus'.

117   Auden, as mentioned, had by then entrusted himself to Kierkegaard and Protestant theology decreeing the need to overcome the Freudian and Marxist medicine to build a 'Just City'; however, Replogle 1969, 57 n. 73, does well to contest E. Callan, according to whom the three parts of the poem mime Kierkegaard's three phases of life: aesthetic, ethic, and religious.

118   In reality, this sense of unity and psychic order is evoked by the performance of chorales by Buxtehude.

The Devil, a hypostasis internal to every human being, induces him or her to systematic negation and resignation; but this is a *felix* duplicity, since, in virtue of a Browninguesque casuistry, the continuous insinuation of doubt produces a tension toward truth, and the awareness that human freedom is never total, but bound by necessity. Since original sin the devil is also blamed for the intellectualistic tendency to separate intellect, intuition and instinct, typical of the modern world – Auden's form of the 'dissociation of sensibility' – which involves the contrary impulse of the *ordre du cœur*. Satan in Eden and Luther in history give one another a hand in backing this dualism; conversely, 'if the monist view be right, / How is it possible to fight?'. Throughout this part, Auden breathlessly tries to review and underline the negative forms with which satanic dualism has wrought damage in history. In the phantasmagoric fresco there is room for a comment on Marx's 'heroic charity', Marx being the first of the band of those pointing out the necessity for humanity to unite in cooperation. The epilogue hammers home the necessity to leave the inferno of being to enter the purgatory of becoming. Here the recipes for healing are clearly laid out: always ascend the purgatorial hill, always climb upwards, wandering on sight towards the goal albeit in the haze and uncertainty, gropingly.[119] The inner life is vindicated against the public one marked by mechanistic depersonalization, hence a 'fully alienated land'.[120] In the last visionary section, filled with bitter verdicts, Auden attacks the foundations of the economic man dating back to Renaissance individualism and before that to Plato, who generated the current 'industrial man'.

3. An oratorio *in memoriam* of his mother, *For the Time Being* (1944) is a recital of the Christmas story that seeks to breathe new life into its topicality and eternity. The cyclical historical frame, barely conspicuous, is Kierkegaard's succession of the three phases: historically from the world of Roman ethics, worn out, and from the by now archived Greek aesthetic

---

119   This is the resolution or metamorphosis of Ransom's image of Prometheus' ascent, hence disavowed, in *The Ascent of F 6*.

120   Here we have the first evocation of the calcareous landscapes of infancy as a symbol of humility.

phase,[121] up to the religious, having verified the falseness and insufficiency of all the preceding stages of existence. These three states were synchronous and rival in the present age. What works better in this voice drama, which as a whole is somewhat limp and at various points gives the impression of merely token versification and of a libretto for music,[122] is the suspension of dramatic sympathy, a trick that Auden knew well as an astute user of the stratagems of epic Brechtian theatre. The narrator always speaks according to two discursive planes, as the voice of late Roman culture awaiting the event that changed history, the Incarnation, whilst at the same time connoting the cyclical repetition of that time in the present, hence a time of a new waiting. The historical characters wear contemporary clothing, and leave the past and enter the present and vice versa in an efficiently estranging pendular rhythm. The choral opening is on a wintry world and a sense of desolation in which the symbolic community is shattered and dispersed. The wait must overturn the existent or be its oxymoron. Following one another on stage are frames of the metaphysical moment of loss, of evanescence and the void. The miraculous advent of the humanized divine requires a Baroque-style set of examples that all play on paradox and contradiction, as always in religious poetry that attempts to define the essence of faith. After the prologue the parable follows the pattern of the Genesis creation story, that is, the birth of man who, with his free will, decides to give in to temptation and weakness,[123] so that Mary is required to atone for Eve's error and dress love with flesh. The historical cause of the Incarnation is seen once again in a sin of man's desire or freedom. Man believes that he can 'choose his own necessity' – a 'hubris of every tainted will' – rather than submitting, and this is a sin of intellectual pride that was repeated and has echoed on up to the present. In contrast, Mary needs to be warned that being the mother of Jesus was the Child's choice, not

121   Witnessed to and hinted at in the figure of a by then tired Hercules in some withered garden.
122   Above all in the choruses of the angels and shepherds in the manger scene.
123   The Edenic monism, the indivisible oneness of man, is shattered by original sin, and the 'four faculties', intuition, sentiment, sensation and intellect, come into play thanks to the 'error', that is, sin. They sing in short *naïf* verses in the first scene.

hers. Following the thread of estrangement, Joseph is presented in well-pressed trousers and newly shined shoes, as a dull, faint-hearted country oaf unable to come to terms with what has happened. The choruses that greet Mary and Joseph, and pray to them, converge on the theme of a 'middle way' to salvation, since only this will allow 'common ungifted natures' to believe that 'their normal vision' can 'walk to perfection'. As proof, the Magi, who have come to Bethlehem guided by the star 'against their will', are humanized and trivialized, though they remain symbolic of the three purely human approaches to the incomprehensible divine event.[124] Simeon is a contemporary thinker who reflects – in prose – on the divine plan of redemption, but who ends up losing the thread of his own theological quibbles, which would aim translate into human words the ineffable and inexpressible paradox of Incarnation. An estranged Herod, who soliloquizes like a politicking reformer aware of his successes, dedicated to progress, to the advancement of reason, and by now horrified by the irrational, is a fine theatrical success of the Browning type and nature, those of the monologues of Karshish and Cleon.

4. A touch of Browning may also be found in *The Sea and the Mirror* (1944), since it demonstrates even more tangibly Auden's need for a kind of pre-existing text to develop and vary; and because Auden is more than ever a poet's poet in his capturing of literary scenarios and in letting them inspire him. This is indeed a posterior paraphrase, a series of resuscitations, echoes and variations on the theme of what was for Auden Shakespeare's most magnetic and intriguing play, *The Tempest*, a springboard that raises subtle and more often convoluted questions of dramatic aesthetics, just as late Browning had brought Euripides and Aristophanes together on stage in a night-time agon on tragedy and comedy.[125] Prospero is the hypostasis of the divine demiurge who grants unconditional freedom to Ariel, and

---

124 The end of the Magi scene marks the return of the narrator, whose voice summarizes, in that witty and appealing way so congenial to Auden, the propaganda of a certain brand of positivism and contemporary pragmatism that believes all the problems of the civil community to have been solved, except for the most important one, the spiritual condition.

125 Volume 6, §§ 17–18.

who literally 'unleashes' him, giving the spirit total control over the use of his freedom – a grave danger according to Auden. Thus, in the background, is the contrast between imaginative poetic art, which generates evanescent dreams and phantasms, and concrete reality. Magic art, that is, has a value in the circumscribed jurisdiction of the island, but outside it is nothing. Each of the numerous characters in Shakespeare's drama hence lets himself be heard in the form of the repercussions, often of regret and self-correction, which the experience on the island has had on him. All feel regenerated, with the sole exception of Antonio, who incarnates one of the most heartfelt inquiries of late Auden, the danger of the unrestrained rebellious will, left to itself, Antonio being the sole unredeemed character, the ego that chooses and in doing so offers the will an unlimited range of action. The fact that Auden did not admire Prospero and stood on Caliban's side had been admitted and clarified in his essay on drama in *The Dyer's Hand*. Browning too had written one of his most celebrated monologues on the same figure, but from a totally different, 'mimetic' perspective. In his prose intervention on the proscenium, which occupies half the space of Auden's entire work, the functional and estranging ambiguity is that Caliban is both the character and the actor impersonating him. Being the negative of Ariel, he can only make a case for his dramatic admissibility, and he does so by remonstrating against the breach of the rules and the banning of the monstrous. Caliban's speech is unquestionably a parodic pastiche that is so complacent and self-referential that we might think it sprung only from Joyce's pen in the twentieth century;[126]

---

126   Auden, rather oddly, said he had parodied Henry James. The use of rhyming couplets, which is the metre of *New Year Letter*, is successfully exploited in Sarastro's imaginary address to the audience ('Metalogue to the Magic Flute', from 1956), the fruit of Auden's enormous interest in Mozart's opera, whose libretto he translated. However, the genre is that of Caliban's monologue, an essay-writing operation if not one of criticism, rather more balanced and successful, which merges Auden's ideas on Mozart, a musician read in every era following different affiliations. This 'metalogue' is at the same time a witty speech on the staging of the *Magic Flute*, already at that time anachronistic and audacious, and a ferocious but amusing satire on the custom of belcanto. In both pastiches, it is above all the Auden of *Letter to Lord Byron* who is speaking.

and precisely because of this it scarcely repays the efforts and patience of the interpreter wishing to untangle his circumlocutions and his *exempla* spreading for line after line, a mountain that often gives birth to a measly conceptual mouse.[127]

5. *The Age of Anxiety*[128] (1947) is subtitled 'A Baroque eclogue', since from time to time its four orators feel like modern Virgilian shepherds who sing, indulge in regret, and together formulate schemes and hopes for the future (and perhaps it was MacNeice who gave Auden the idea, as we shall see). However, 'Baroque' is a term for which in closing I will have to find a more essential and precise analogy. A mixture of prose and verse, it has the appearance and the initial captions of a spectral drama and scenic action, or more exactly a dramatic script or screenplay. And given that the characters live their daily life – but leave it to enter a dream-like adventure in which they discover they are different, or live possible extensions of their life, and are fatally thrust back into the daily grind – it recalls as much Shaw's *Heartbreak House* as Barrie's *Dear Brutus*; however, the disorientation of the characters in those dramas was that of the aftermath of the Great War. The scarcely realistic setting is that of a New York bar where four habitués, who are human abstractions and therefore four 'everymen',[129] meet to recall, forget and fantasize, while the symbolic time is the eve of All Saints' Day in a time of war. Quant is a widower clerk looking at himself melancholically in the mirror behind the counter; Malin is a Canadian medical officer who thinks back over a failed scientific career; Rosetta a well-off single woman nostalgic for a clean family past in the country; Emble a young man who is also dissatisfied and frustrated. The emblem and the symptom of anxiety are the mirror double of Quant, who is the most psychologically

---

127 Replogle 1969, 155, observes that Caliban's theses, once reduced to homiletic prose, would cover half a page.

128 The term anxiety is rooted in Kierkegaard's 'terror' and Kafka's Angst. But the poem, as I am saying, is evocative, rather than philosophical or existentialist.

129 Behind the four characters allegories have been seen of Jung's four faculties of the 'ectopsychic' sphere: Malin Thought, Quant Intuition, Emble Sensation, and Rosetta Sentiment. It seems to me entirely misguided to find the genesis of the name of Rosetta in the Egyptian Rosetta Stone.

disturbed having undergone an infantile trauma, and who feels hunted, under accusation, spied on, and visited by guilt. The four strangers grow closer after the first speeches, which must confirm the psychic data and the representation of the opening stage directions. In turn the preliminary single interventions give out an Orwellian atmosphere of meetings between world powers planning a future of 'sedatives, soft drinks', and a 'moral planet / tamed by terror'. Visionary glimpses of the present and the desolation of the war alternate with others of an uncertain, and equally precarious, future. The succession of monologues and then of dialogues is interspersed with short linking captions, while voices off stage are radio headlines which, as in Auden's dramas of the 1930s, issue war bulletins or regurgitate its commercials. The body of the poem is a survey that leads the quartet to cross or re-cross the seven ages of creation modelled on Jaques's soliloquy in Shakespeare; these are dreamed episodes, brimming with regret, and at the same time protests against the depersonalization of contemporary life and harangues against the slaveries of the economic system, the routine of work, the crushing produced by the system, 'this stupid world where / Gadgets are gods and we go on talking'. There is then a symmetrical transit through the seven phases of purgation, a regressive journey towards 'prehistoric happiness', which, being an ascent, is a redu-plication of the purgatorial one of *New Year Letter*, as well as, naturally, an inversion of the metaphorical voluntaristic hubris of Ransom, the hero of *The Ascent of F 6*. In separate pairs, or together, the four heroes cross through the atemporal symbolic and allegorical archetypes of the lacustrine land, the city of vice, the cemetery, the enchanted garden, the forest and the labyrinth. The dream-like journey ends with a bang, and the return to the present is accompanied by an undertone of thunder, lightning and rend-ing sounds. This, the revisiting of the 'hollow men' in 1947, is not the only citation of Eliot. *The Age of Anxiety* can in fact be defined and understood as a 'comment' and a gloss to *Four Quartets* because of its meditation of time and on time, and because of its nostalgia for lost times of innocence, particularly in the character of Rosetta, though Emble, too, regrets having lost the key 'to the garden gate'. The seventh age of Man flashes upon Malin like Gerontion's old age, with a loss of muscle tone, the advent of mental torpor, along with the invocation of a divine 'sign' in 'inert afternoons'.

The closing scenes, closer to the concrete reality of the time, see the four characters accept time as the time of waiting, and the story has become that of suffering creation preserved from destruction, but still waiting to be 'adopted'. However, the end of the 'dream' is also accompanied by the words of the barman who announces that it is 'closing time'. This caption reveals that Auden's poem is an unmistakable variation of the pub scene in the second section of *The Waste Land*, by imagining that the patrons will end the evening at one of their homes. This is what Auden attempts to add, without the sudden solidarity having a continuation, so that the allegorical parable ends up back at square one, with the four strangers becoming strangers again, and splitting up after a temporary intimacy, without any appreciable human and affective results.[130] It is therefore no coincidence that *The Age of Anxiety* was greeted on its appearance as a pendant to Eliot's *Waste Land* for the children of Eliot's peers, who emerged from the Second rather than the First World War, and as the voice of the mood of disillusion and alienation of an entire generation. This flattering judgement was attenuated and overturned over time, and the poem gradually lost any aura of a masterpiece.[131] The reasons for this *défaillance* lie in the fact that the four heroes do not manage to attain or maintain their archetypical stature, and to fill up the gap between their private lives and their universal dimension,[132] and that the allegorical progress does not follow a clear and obvious pattern in its various correspondences. The conceptual weakness of the work is the obverse of a metrical *tour de force* visible in a sometimes very strict observance of the Anglo-Saxon alliterative model, which demands

130   It is ironic that Emble, to whom Rosetta feels attracted, falls asleep on the sofa, making any possible, even physical union impossible.

131   Among the authoritative supporters of its paradigmatic value was Praz, who chose the title of Auden's short poem for the concluding chapter XXI, on the twentieth century, in his PSL. *The Age of Anxiety* has indeed become proverbial for its abstruseness, like Browning's *Sordello* in the nineteenth century. Philip Larkin (CRHE, 417) said with a *boutade* that he had never finished the poem, nor met anyone else who had.

132   Rosetta is Jewish, and an emblem of the Holocaust, but this racial cipher, which only emerges in the final words of her last intervention with a verse from the Bible in Hebrew, is overall artificial.

continuous virtuosic exploits to maintain the series of alliterations. This does not alter the fact that, above all in the short stanzas sung during the crossing of the seven phases, Auden's imagination occasionally runs free in fresh surreal visions of a well-nigh Carrollian taste in certain unpredictable and outlandish associations. The purely evocative vein, or even the metrical challenge, predominate over the texture of meanings, and the poem excels in pure variations that are an end in themselves, like the arias of an opera which embellish the plot without carrying it forward. This resolving and dissolving into a collection of short and long arias out of context – of musical gems, delicate in their images, but closed in themselves, multiplications of visual sensations and spectacles, rather than authentic alterations of mood – is typical of the librettist, and of that novel Metastasio into which Auden was by now transforming his physiognomy and role as a poet. This is the reason why the eclogue is 'Baroque'; and also why the poem is singularly static, and nothing or very little happens.

§ 9. *Auden VII: Uncollected poems until 1957*

The final phase of Auden's work, and the last that he himself edited and supervised, continues to offer poems for the most part pleasing, smooth and distended, witty and beguiling, though occasionally clotted, and tending to be overloaded and enveloped in a patina of erudition, somewhat pretentious and overly informed, and prone to the curious anecdote and to the encyclopaedic digression. Their material is sometimes drawn from case histories or from the curiosities of the tour guide, and thus they are always endearingly prolix. For Auden, and for history, the time of tension was over, and it has been appropriate to speak of this as a relieved neo-Horatian vein due to the recurrent parallelism between the decadence of imperial Rome and the aftermath to the Second World War in the twentieth century. 'Memorial for the City' is the last, pompous, inflated vatic ode on historical becoming, traced out in stanzas each chosen as a chapter to illustrate the slippery slope, taking in Luther and the French Revolution, after the dissolution of Graeco-Roman compactness. The barbed wire still dominates obsessively, and the city and the City are destroyed. The fourth section perhaps wishes to wittily highlight the claim that humankind has never been irresponsible in history, and is instead responsible for what happened before him, too. 'The Shield of Achilles', arguably the single most beautiful poem Auden ever wrote, is so because of the immediacy without comments and glosses of its contrast between the reality sublimated in the imaginary Achilles' shield forged by Hephaestus and the desolation and destruction appearing to Thetis. Auden never enters the fray, and speaks preferring the pronoun 'we', silently making himself a spokesperson for the community of the cultured. 'Precious Five' is a decidedly anti-lyric poem since it begins by lauding the nose, followed by the other sensory organs. From this point on we hear in the poem the witty lament for a world inexorably changed: the nose once smelt odours that no longer exist. The ideal shift that occurred in Auden's spiritual biography is that from the city, again, to the island, a contrary motion, therefore, from that of Auden running away from England over a decade earlier. He delights in this apparent lull from which an Eden is recreated in the islands, and which is not only spatial: he is therefore a poet who has once more become detached from his social role, who thinks and reflects cut off from society, in a void. The interferences of actual history are muffled, or are but small intimations: from afar he realizes from time to time that there is a city and a mass conformist society that has lost its capacity to believe in pretence, and expects only real, verifiable things. This is the theme of the variations 'The Truest Poetry Is the Most Feigning'. One lived in the Forsterian era of telegrams, which for Auden was the era of statistics, of 'reducing to figures / What is the matter, what is to be done'.[133] The archetypal island had materialized in Ischia, visited for the first time in 1948. Places like Ischia inspired and reinvigorated Auden, but there is something picture-postcardish, an anonymous impression of a journey lacking in authentic personal resonances, and hence a touch of superficiality and of the merely workmanlike in these glazed, expert compositions. The last poem in the 1957 canon is a diorama of the spectacles of southern Italy, a collage of small frames, some vivid, some dull, and also of witticisms (like keeping the volume of the radio high, as a challenge of the pagan to the Parcae). And

---

133   This proud but also ironic and humorous separateness is at the centre of 'We Too Had Known Golden Hours'.

yet there is an inner chord, that of Auden's dialogue with the landscape, a landscape that can always be evocative, and more often teach humankind, by reprimanding, correcting, and adjusting its perspectives.

2. 'In Praise of Limestone' studies the associative correlations between Auden's idea of humankind and the, or a, landscape: limestone is more or less one of T. S. Eliot's objective correlatives,[134] with links that are all clarified and explored, and hence it becomes something close to symbol or allegory. The landscape is in fact anthropomorphic, it has human features and morphology, skin-deep but also profound; it is gibbous, rotund, and hence maternal, while also being a little infantile kingdom in which the law of pardon and indulgence reigns. It incarnates tangibility, closeness, familiarity, far from the *Sehnsucht*, the sublime or the untouchably nebulous, or 'immoderate', of Romanticism. This calcareous nature is contrasted with the indestructible granite with its defined and indestructible confines. Indeed it is the anthropomorphic granite that urges the 'calcareous' youth to immerse himself in the romantic enchantment of the sea and venture down the road towards self-glorification. The poet is not so deluded as to be unable to weigh the simplistic and overly defeatist message of the limestone: lifting the veil of nostalgia, he cannot, however, avoid recognizing that 'it disturbs our rights', and is a constant admonition: an admonition to metamorphic availability, to the darting revision of thought, to the odourless immateriality of music, a hint from which issues a light, Swift-like revulsion of man, and of every divinized man.[135] The modifications of matter are a forewarning of the resurrection of the dead, hence from the landscape also emanates a sense of the corruptibility and at the same time of the eternal renewability and metamorphic nature of creation from an otherworldly perspective. The poem is punctuated by addresses to a silent interlocutor, as in a dramatic monologue, but is substantially a dialogue of the poet with himself. The dialogue with the landscape continues in 'Bucolics', reflections, always between the

134 And yet Auden 'had never exactly understood what the objective correlative is' (quoted in Carpenter 1981, 114).

135 *Horae Canonicae*, modelled on the 'hours' of the breviary, shows that Auden is neither a religious poet nor a mystic, since the liturgical occasion is the inspiration for external digressions that are hardly absorbing.

rambling, the anthropological and the didactic, on atmospheric phenomena and the spectacles of nature such as the winds, the woods, the mountains, the lakes, the islands and the plains. One of these is the digression on the islands, famous islands that have been the theatre of celebrated historical events. In 'Woods' nature is the seabed of human evolution and accompanies it through its phases. Auden is an aquatic poet because he identifies the metamorphic flux of water, which can make a calcified, rigid being liquid, that is, gladly mutable and ready to change. Going back over the associations that, linked to woods, have occurred in human history, Auden closes pithily the poem with: 'A culture is no better than its woods'.

§ 10. *Auden VIII: The critic*

The Enchafèd Flood[136] (1950), a fascinating fresco for its audacious, debatable and at times erroneous theories, and for its indomitable cavalcade amongst far-off and unrelated texts, consists of three chapters that broadly deal with sea literature, with the symbol of the sea and the symbolic adventure of a ship cleaving the waves and often sinking, a metaphor for a historical and existential journey. Unquestionably, this literary and symbolic scenario was almost *ipso facto* a property of Romanticism. For Auden the sea is a symbol of disorder and of the undifferentiated primordial element, from which civilization emerged but into which it can always slip back. In this ideal journey, or iconography or symbolic *Weltanschauung*, it follows that we venture onto the sea in situations of danger, since without danger we remain in a city which is at one and the same time, and precisely because of this, a garden. Auden emphasizes his simple vision of history as a departure from an Eden towards the disorder of future civilizations. To show the peril of the sea he sketches a patchwork of places and citations from seafaring works that were dear to him and came to his mind instinctively. From the very first chapter the book is designed as a survey of examples, sometimes read autonomously, and given in their entirety. For Auden there is no distinction between high and ludic literature, and a useful scenario he often turns to is Carroll's *The Hunting of the Snark*; other confirmations or exemplifications come from

---

136   A quotation from Shakespeare's *Othello*, with the subtitle *The Romantic Iconography of the Sea*.

a similar 'low class' repertoire, opera librettos. One of the supporting texts, the protagonist being an antecedent of Romantic navigators, is the passage from Dante in which Ulysses summons his sailors for his last daredevil, even outright demonic, journey (a hubris that had already been evoked literally by Ransom's opening speech in *The Ascent of F 6*). Shakespeare himself was a dualist who contrasted the world of the tempest, hence of atmospheric chaos, with order, the tempest being the 'enchafèd' sea. However, in his last dramas the sea is the purgatorial place in which one comes to his senses. The result is the same, because the symbolic context is the rebuilding of a city that is suddenly prey to chaos, through a perilous sea crossing. But for Auden Romanticism seems to violate this scheme, at least partially: the Romantic seafarer wishes to be daring, and thus also wishes to abandon order since it is banal; hence the ambiguity or amphibious character of the sea. Turning his gaze on the Romantics, Auden reads the double nature of the symbols, which have the value of the less, and at the same time, of the more. When he introduces the desert as the counterpart of the sea, he also reproduces the structure of the poems of *Bucolics*, as he reviews the urge by which the citizen feels the need to head for the desert, including the intention to restore order to the city left behind in a gesture of symbolic heroism. In the 'negative' sea and desert, the happy island or oasis can rise, they too emblems of a terrestrial paradise where 'there is no conflict between natural desire and moral duty'.

2. A slight flaw is in *The Enchafèd Flood* the absence of any reference to Conrad and his symbolic sea yarns, highly relevant to this argument. In addition, midway through the first chapter, the reader looking for orientation might wonder what type of book this is, and seek to situate it better. It is in fact a kind of rhapsodic, symbolic and archetypal criticism. Very quickly it begins to focus on the anthropological tasks and on the symbolic resonances of the journey of a hero, a 'wanderer' over land and sea. The critic of reference may be individuated in Northrop Frye, since these shared symbols, which are repeated and echo down the ages, from the Bible on and in western culture, are, though in their transformations, collective archetypes of the Jungian variety. With these multiple keys the book is a criticism of Romanticism in the broadest sense, and of its relation to the sea and voyaging. Except that – the last suggestion – the haphazard mosaic of citations, to which are appended sober comments, or even none at all, may evoke the procedural style of a Mario Praz: not coincidentally the book is, all in all,

the study of a disease. The first chapter closes with an examination of the Romantic struggle against the banal city and with the breakup of the organic community – which is why Conrad could have been useful – in a massed western society after the Industrial Revolution. In the second chapter the objective of founding or re-founding the real city, based on fraternity and a universally recognized truth, is reaffirmed. Romanticism is reread, starting above all from Blake, as the overturning of the Newtonian concept of God as a rational architect separated from the created: instead, God is rediscovered as immanent to and present in the cosmos. *The Enchafèd Flood* could, however, be identified, in the final analysis, as an *escamotage* to discuss and fathom *Moby Dick*, thus supporting the original thesis with other sporadic examples. The *Pequod* in the middle of the ocean represents human society moving through time, and struggling with its destiny; Melville's delirious and noxious Puritanism superimposes on these data the values of the Bible, such as the Fall, sin and redemption, or even transforms Ahab's mission into a simple parable of metaphysical liberation from the restrictive obligations of city life. The third chapter enucleates three types of literary hero, the aesthetic, the ethical and the religious; through a deliberate combination or superimposition this terminology owes much, of course, to Kierkegaard. The religious hero can become a demon, an Iago, through a dedication contrary to love. Auden discusses these types in the figures of the biblical and Melvillian Ishmael and in Don Quixote, the latter a type of religious hero, romantic and hence solitary and unhappy, and such because deluding himself he wishes to restore the golden age. The final part traces too many symmetries in *Moby Dick*, reading allegorical and symbolic meanings into the characters of the crew.

3. The eight internal sections of *The Dyer's Hand*[137] (1962 in America), Auden's key work as essayist, photograph the entire gamut of the poet's main interests: theory and aesthetics, Shakespeare,[138] and music. At the same time, they give the idea of a stylistic stamp in twentieth-century essay writing. Auden's manner is not self-reflective, a peculiar personal style

---

137   This too is a citation, from Shakespeare's Sonnet 111.
138   *Lectures on Shakespeare* is apocryphal, since the lectures were gathered together from students' notes. Auden the professor taught off the cuff, and the notes of these and other lectures have been lost.

that imposes itself as his, not therefore belletristic in short; it is rather an essayism of ideas, vehicular, demonstrative, and argumentative, as much as his poetic style is prevalently Baroque and decorative. Its usual measure is the aphorism, and several aphorisms combined can even resemble private annotations, a skeleton to be clad and fleshed out later on. Every now and again schematic assertions, declared without any possibility of reply, come to the fore; and when a lemma or a definition or an apodictic assertion urgently needs an example, what sallies forth is that English vein of the commonplace, or the curious, or a convoluted comparison as support. This procedure recalls on the one hand Bacon, and on the other the frill-free pragmatism of a Bertrand Russell. However, Auden wishes to theorize more than he should, and he often gets stuck, readily throwing himself into bizarre daredevil digressions which are of little interest. He had matured ahead of any juvenile Modernism, and he wrote as a critic with his feet firmly planted on the ground; not a post-Joyce or Beckett-influenced Irishman, he was firmly anchored in tradition, eccentric maybe, but tradition nonetheless. His budding aesthetic starts from the principle that the writer's material is 'life in general'; and the poetic art does not deal with things, like science, but with people and personal relationships. One of poetry's goals is heralded in the answer to the questions: Who am I?, and: What are the differences between me and other creatures? And: What is the state of man in the universe? Auden's adherence to a vague Freudian scheme of personality led him to say that a conscious being is active in the writer, who is, however, subject to interference from a muse or an angel that must be courted or fought. Auden's conservative critical enlightenment is unmasked when he tackles the question of poetic language. The poet uses a language spoken by others, subject to the constant danger of being corrupted and deteriorating; however, he is against the poetic purification of language and against any asemantic species of poetry. On the contrary, every word of every poem must be found in the dictionary, and this helps make poetry significant, communicative, and intelligible, at least to a certain degree. It is heresy to deem possible that poetry could 'come close to music', and Mallarmé and Rilke are lambasted as lovers of poetry's magic and to an even greater extent because of their indifference to the material universe. Poetry is of equal value to prose as a 'medium for the lucid exposition of ideas', and its function is to tell the truth, to disenchant and detoxify. Such aesthetic sanity is proven by the fact that, although Auden is hugely indebted to psychoanalysis, the end result of *poiein* is in fact 'due to subconscious activity over which [the poet] has no control', while at the same time one of its components is 'due to conscious artifice'.[139] Every poem is a 'verbal contraction' which must have or present a notion of a 'beautiful life' or of a 'happy place' in a post-lapsarian, fallen, evil, but redeemable world. The systematic contrast between a really sullied world and an Edenic lost world (as in *The Merchant of Venice* that between Venice and Belmont) is the unifying element in Shakespeare's Venetian dramas, all intimately hinging on the notion of an Eden as a world where one *is* – hence outside time – rather than *becomes*. In the nostalgia for Eden (which Auden distinguishes from the prefiguration of the New Jerusalem, where 'contradictions' have been resolved) lies Auden's highly original interpretation, as I noted in a previous volume,[140] of the world of Dickens's *Pickwick* and of the Pickwickians themselves, atemporal beings that never grow. Apart from Shakespeare, Auden dedicates himself to a brilliant, albeit disconcerting, reinterpretation of the myth of the hero in modern literature: Don Quixote, Faust, and Don Juan. The latter is for Auden an erotic arithmetician striving to expand his list of conquests, and a record man who might as well be collecting stamps! The presupposition of the monographic essay dedicated to Byron's *Don Juan* is that the poem is comical, rather than satirical, and that the contradictions of human beings are all amiably accepted. Reviewing his experience as a librettist, Auden indirectly formulates equally eccentric and often debatable opinions on eighteenth- and nineteenth-century melodrama; for example, he maintains that Rossini's Figaro is a greater creation than Mozart's due to his lesser rational powers, or that the purely instrumental pieces inserted

139   A thesis reconfirmed in *The Enchafèd Flood*, in which Auden asserts that there is a 'conscious side' in artistic creation, whereas Romanticism had privileged 'imagination and vision'. However, this assumption had been present to Auden since 1935 (HYN, 167).
140   Volume 5, § 29.1.

into operas are boring, or that the character of melodrama must be feisty and hence cannot sing arias of resignation on stage.

§ 11. *Auden IX: The songbook of the passé intellectual*

In terms of sheer proportions, the late Auden is remarkable, as his output in the period 1959–1974 includes the collections *About the House* (1965), *City Without Walls and Other Poems* (1969), *Academic Graffiti* (1971), *Epistle to a Godson and Other Poems* (1972), *Thank You, Fog* (1974). Taken as a whole, this is a massive but unfiltered production, having the effect of a notebook or even a hotchpotch in which not only the measures, but also the content itself amounts to a disjointed shortlist of abysmal discrepancies, and where it is increasingly unthinkable to expect the poem that stands out, the ambitious composition, the touch of magic. The tenor and regime are deliberately kept to a minimum. The variation and excursion of the forms comprise the short lyric poem in bare and tightly organized stanzaic measures imitating the *haiku* and *tanka* modules, directly after other opulent, Baroque ones, in a prose that is only just rhymed and unrhymed, spreading across almost the whole printed page. The formal extremes are also the aphorism of the 'shorts', small sabre thrusts on human deeds and observations of behavioural phenomenology, and letters and rhapsodies in long lines, of a mock-sloppy type, and extremely rambling. In the era of permissiveness the veil of modesty and reserve is rent, and some openly sexual and homosexual poems bob to the surface. Unlike the norm of the ageing poet, Auden does not dry up, does not economize nor mute his voice, but throws down everything that comes to him, in an indiscriminate disbursement and without restraint. In this poetic stream of consciousness there is no scrimping on parentheses, digressions, lengthy comparisons, logical leaps; and the text is stuffed with every possible neologism and with words drawn from the most disparate, specific, specialist fields, to the extent that Kermode suggested the wise precaution of always keeping the OED or the Webster dictionary to hand.[141] Without exception each poem carries out an argument or linked

141   CRHE, 471.

arguments, with a tendency to cavil and capitalize on microscopic aspects and predicaments of life. These also originate from provocative data and sayings that lead to twisted, audacious, unintelligible discussions. Pages and pages are filled with unrhymed aphorisms that must subsist and justify themselves by merit of their abrupt sharpness or provocativeness. In *About the House* the poet celebrates an up-dated Biedermeier (he himself speaks of 'egocentric monologues'). The subsection 'Thanksgiving for a Habitat' vibrates with an irrepressible digressional erethism, testified by the throng of terms drawn from the most varied fields. It unwinds as a visit to Auden's Austrian house, but is ready to deviate towards extemporaneous digressions, some cutting, some benevolent, on an impressive quantity of subjects and curiosities that incarnate the poet's intellectual mobility, no longer at his ease in the modern world, as he remembers and benignly denounces. Almost in parenthesis he does nothing to hide his caprices, his irrational fears, his behavioural tics; he craves indulgence, and always measures himself *en passant* against the society and customs that surround him. These evolutions range from the sacred to the profane, from the sublime to the excremental. Surrounding this are the amiable, extemporaneous, unrhymed lyrics of the traveller, of the conference speaker or the re-visitor, with passages of humour and self-deprecation. The *graffiti* are playful quatrains that portray in fantastic humorous poses, as if they were new limericks, figures of writers and cultural personalities; organized alphabetically, they follow the initials of their surnames. In the final collections reverberations of the world outside include Kennedy's assassination, the campaigns against drugs, flower children, and the moon landing; public facts alternate with private history, including the deaths of his last friends, who are commemorated. The last poems voice the moods of the by then passé intellectual gazing at the modern world in which he lives. The obsolescence, befuddlement and hesitations of the old man are pathetically and humorously acknowledged in one of the few poems that stand out, 'Epistle to a Godson', who is Spender's little boy; or in the tighter 'Doggerel by a Senior Citizen'. A *démodé* scent can be sensed, or better a *rétro* taste, in an Auden who entitles a poem, in Wordsworth's style, 'Lines to Dr. Walter Birk on his Retiring from General Practice', or writes a 'Short Ode to the Cuckoo'.

§ 12. *Auden X: Opera librettos*

Auden and Kallman's opera librettos must historically be considered one of the most successful modern attempts to bring back equal dignity to the opera libretto compared to the musical score, and to restore that admirable symbiosis which had existed between librettist and musician in the times of Mozart and Gluck (with Metastasio, Da Ponte, and Calzabigi). This symbiosis had ceased with the purely servile libretto, often inferior as literature, which had taken over with Romantic and 'verista' melodramas. Auden's pre-existing passion for melodrama was sharpened by his meeting and collaborating with Chester Kallman, a real opera enthusiast. This pairing created four fundamental librettos set to music by three composers, Britten, Stravinsky and Henze. On Auden's introductory page to the libretto for the operetta *Paul Bunyan* (1941), and written for the *New York Times*, myth is defined as a historical episode fictionalized as poetry, a collective creation of an era in which individuation and division of labour had not yet come to dominate the world. America had a historical delay that allowed it, almost uniquely, to create modern, post Industrial Revolution myths. Auden grasps the sense, or a sense, of the American myth of man's struggle against the forces of nature, only recently won: the paradigm is repeated of the subjugation and domestication of nature, which, being mythical, is threatening and demoniacal. Paul Bunyan is an incarnation of human tenaciousness subjugating nature, and veils a transition process of civilization, namely, when that domestication was made possible by passing from the use of pure human force to that of the machine. Like any mythical poet, versed in the myths which, à la Jung, had been deposited in the collective unconscious, Auden feigns not to be able to explain the blue ox, which perhaps stands for the soul of the woodman; nor why Bunyan's marriage founders. Other characters have an allegorical value. But at the same time, this is a personal parable: mankind, initially subjugated, taps the goal of choice, the 'life of election', after having dwelt in the cocoon of unawareness; weaned and vaccinated, he becomes *faber suae fortunae*. America was created and born through a fusion of ethnic groups gathered on the virgin soil, with the acceptance of the tasks assigned them, and thanks also to the population's tenaciousness and abnegation. Bunyan bids his farewell as the benign genius, the *deus ex machina*, the intermediary in realizing the American Dream in the nation of America, which for a Briton who had grown up in a monarchic system could seem like the coming true of the democratic dream ('America is you and me'). Which is to say, Auden wrote a panegyric of the positive forces discovered on the new continent, having fled from the old in disgust.[142] At the same time, Bunyan is a humorous and mythical version of the leader who appoints proselytizes who are later dispersed, the very fulcrum of 1930s dramaturgy.

142 Auden's collaboration with Britten (cf. Mitchell 1981) lasted a good five years, and took form, in addition to this opera, in the composition of the text for *Night Mail* (1936) and *Our Hunting Fathers* for soprano or tenor and orchestra. *Paul Bunyan* ran for just one week after its première on 5 May 1941 at a student theatre in New York. More than twenty years later, Britten, after a heart operation in 1973, took the score in hand, and the opera is heard today in the revised version from 1976. Commissioned for schools, and hence with pedagogical and educational aims, it is a little gem of sparkling lightness, in many ways quite delicious. The text was due to an Auden who did not merely provide an instrumental service, but also prepared a libretto that was traditional yet with many personal elements. He improvised himself as the author of ballads and nursery rhymes devoid of any apparent existentialist elements, working within the timeless genre of nonsense and playful English poetry, light verse, or even semi-fantastic fairy-tales, in which geese and trees are gifted with song and speech. Auden speaks for Britten when in the foreword to the text he describes the Wagnerian difficulties of showing a giant on stage, as he must only be audible as a voice, but not visible. Musically, Britten is, as he always is, a sophisticated blender of echoes and manners, and a musical polyglot. Nor can it be doubted that at many points there is an explicit attempt at emulation – Auden and Britten like Gilbert and Sullivan. The operetta is born in this vein, and Auden in no way makes one regret Gilbert, even though the latter remained the peerless pioneer. For his part, Britten is a melodramatic humorist like Sullivan, indeed more than Sullivan. Hence the verbal and musical texts are enriched by numerous comic or feignedly plaintive numbers, including arias, ballads and recitatives, which always make one smile. The three or four linking ballads that bring the plot forward, and in which a storyteller sings in a natural voice accompanied by guitar or banjo, are further pioneering examples, laying the basis for the later successful genre known as Country Music. But, as a temporary American, Britten absorbs the popular song, the blues, the black spiritual, and of course the cinema musical, American opera and Gershwin; yet he also parodies the belcanto tradition and nineteenth-century opera, from Donizetti to Wagner. In short, this is a harlequinesque *tour de force*, free from points of reference and filled with non-stop parodies and twists. The epilogue is a Christmas party interwoven with refined comical numbers pulled out of the hat, and continuous changes in register, from lyrical to plaintive, to comic and cabaret. And Britten even pokes fun at himself!

2. The matchmaking occasion for *The Rake's Progress* (1951, almost half of which was written by Kallman) was a visit paid by Stravinsky to an exhibition in Chicago in 1947 at which he saw eight Hogarth paintings depicting the 'Rake's Progress', dated 1732. Aldous Huxley was the 'godfather' of the resulting opera, since he recommended Auden to Stravinsky, the former co-opting Kallman, at the time the best Anglophone librettist. From two temperaments that could not be more different in terms of background, culture and ideology, came a miraculous marriage of intentions and an admirable pairing of text and music. The score for *The Rake* is a mixture of two centuries of European melodrama, the only absence being that of Romantic melodrama, which comes back into play in Stravinsky, however, under the guise of the very late, neoclassical Verdi.[143] The terms of reference are Mozart, and, before him, Handel and the Italian opera composers who had the *castrati* warbling coldly and stonily.[144] This is an opera of extreme concision, without patches of colour, or *grand opéra* sections, fleeing from any musical pathos as soon as it starts to mount. There is no *daccapo*, the music moves in an atmosphere of swift, even tyrannical dryness, without concessions to the audience and belcanto, that is to easy listening. Auden and Kallman's libretto is written in the ideal spirit of Augustan poetry and satire, pithy, slim, terse, often in rhyming couplets, cutting and sober, its movements precise, limpid and clean-cut. The polish of its verse makes it

143   In the final scene at the asylum, Anne, who is forced to present herself as Venus, sends Tom (who believes he is Adonis) to sleep with a mournful lullaby in which we can hear almost imperceptible echoes of Verdi's 'willow song' in *Otello*. I cannot therefore agree with E. W. White, according to whom (*Stravinsky*, It. trans., Milano 1983), 'There is nothing [in *The Rake*] that shows any influence of operas after Donizetti and Verdi's middle period' (554).

144   The model of the libretto is therefore the Metastasian drama for music, and it obsequiously follows the classical divisions of recitative, aria and cabaletta, but arranged in emblematic frames. It has often been said that the opera which is musically closest in spirit is Mozart's *Così fan tutte*, but it is difficult to deem the overture (lasting just thirty seconds, and played by the fanfare) as Mozartian, nor the very frequent preludes and orchestral interludes for wind and strings, or the dreamy trumpet melody that introduces Anne's aria in the second act. This instrumentation owes more to Handel's celebrated circumstantial music. As I shall say below, at certain points of the libretto and the music, *The Rake* comes close to *Don Giovanni*, if anything.

by unanimous consensus one of the finest opera librettos ever written in English. Auden bore Hogarth's allegory in mind, but modified it, above all because Tom is a rather Voltaire- or Fielding-like *ingénu*, when not a squanderer; while the seduced Sarah is replaced by Anne, who, as we can understand from her surname Truelove, is ready for sacrifice and dedication (and in Auden, the name Anne always augurs well). Shadow, again absent in Hogarth, is the diabolical *alter ego* of the main character, and is called Nick, a popular sobriquet for the devil.[145] Auden enriches therefore the scenario he has accepted, and makes one extreme variation, amalgamating, far from originally, the two main western myths, those of Faust and of Don Juan, extreme because this is the ultimate link in a long history of literary-musical reworkings. Rakewell is a pale, disciplined Don Juan,[146] and above all a dreamier Faust who wishes, stubbornly, to transform stones into bread. Was it possible to glimpse and found an age of gold, or was the myth of the Earth's renewability over for good? The answer is negative, and mankind is the prey, and punished victim, of its palingenetic and self-deifying impulses. And there is more: the satanic challenger combats theological predestination, and trusts in the whims of fortune, in fact, courts it. Auden was not to abandon this motif, and would retrace it (but with unthinkable half-serious and parodic twists, more subterranean than here) a dozen years later in Euripides' myth of Pentheus vainly trying to eradicate the cult of Dionysus. Reaching London, Rakewell tackles again the problem of freedom, distorted in a paradoxical manner: the marriage with Baba, the monster, is presented as an extreme gesture of severing the knots of desire and conscience, hence as a revolt against determinism and predestination.[147] America likewise, in the previous libretto, was the symbolic

---

145 In Auden's dramaturgy it is easy to work back to the figure of Robert, the hero of *The Enemies of the Bishop*, who, as we have seen, is obsessed by a double (§ 4.6).

146 On the contrary, Anne, but only in her libretto role, recalls Micaela from *Carmen*, coming on stage to restore his wits to her bewitched lover, as noted by R. Vlad, *Strawinsky*, Torino 1983, 219 (1st [Italian] edn 1958). Vlad also recalls, along with many others, the precedent of Gounod's Marguérite. Shadow is in turn Mephistopheles, Leporello and Iago fused into a single character, above all in the second act.

147 An echo of the vogue for Gide's *acte gratuit*. The career both outlines and encloses a biblical 'fall' from Eden, which is the Arcadian country residence, with its garden,

and emblematic place of 'choice'. Rakewell wants to withdraw, to flee from the three temptations like Christ in the desert, but ends up capitulating. Tom's hesitation in following his 'progress' is associatively caused by the question he is asked regarding the definition of love, and unconsciously by the thought of Anne who has left him. This crucial experience takes place in a London brothel, which metaphorically represents the character's sexual initiation. At the same time the brothel-keeper's three questions build a bridge to the cemetery scene, when Tom, after one year and one day, will undergo a much more dramatic interrogation by Shadow, who will ask him to pick three cards on pain of damnation. The link is corroborated by the fact that Shadow, at the brothel, cheated Tom by setting the clock back, and thus proposing a possible postponement of repentance *sine die*, and telling him that 'time is his' and Rakewell is its master. Marlowe's Faustus also pronounces his final monologue under the urging of the hands of the clock or time, whose inexorability he had attempted to resist. Rakewell is again imprisoned, despite having 'chosen'. He had therefore deluded himself. But he does redeem himself, rising up from his indolence and fantasizing that he can benefit humanity with his invention, and re-establish Eden on Earth.[148] For the cemetery scene Stravinsky composed a lugubrious, quartet-style prelude to the *redde rationem* and the epiphany of Satan. The harpsichord alone provides a background to the spectral ritual of the card game. The female figure of the redeemer saves the sinner from damnation, but the devil, defrauded, obtains in compensation Rakewell's madness. He ends his days in an asylum, where, despite being saved, he cannot bear the vision of his loved one. In the cynical epilogue all the characters in chorus, without their wigs, declare that the salvation of Rakewell is exceptional; in fact they proclaim that 'all men are mad' and 'everything they say is theatre'. The agon between conscience and the devil is always ready to begin or be resumed. Except that, overturning *Don Giovanni*, it is not the punished

---

  perfumed spring and pergola, plus the Edenic lovers who sing of their imminent, purest Hymen, in the opening scene.

148 The pantomime of Shadow who pretends to turn stones into bread in his 'Baroque machine' can also be taken as Rakewell's dream, and it is that oneiric episode in the form of an interlude, and a dream that was at the same time precursory, which Auden had been fond of ever since *Paid on Both Sides*.

dissolute to be sucked into the flames of hell, but the satanic Shadow, who plunges into his tomb.

3. *The Bassarids*[149] (first performed in Salzburg in 1966) offers instead an example of a conflict between words and music; if anything we may surmise that the music responds to the libretto's intentions with dissonance, tragic dissonance, however, and not exactly as entertaining and parodic as it is in the text; or with the eclecticism of the echoes and of the borrowings, which do not create a real parody, except in the Intermezzo.[150] The librettists perform the reworking of a myth that this time is handed down by tradition, but is a version of it that is iconoclastic and even postmodern in its striking anachronisms (rhymed verse is abandoned for the rhythmic, again except for the Intermezzo); and anyone coming to the music after the libretto would expect something else, perhaps the polystylistic Britten of *Paul Bunyan*.[151] Indeed the libretto once again banalizes, empties and parodies the high tragedy through the costumes, through the reduction to caricature of some venerable figured, and through stage directions that had never been so ample. The stage directions are in fact little masterpieces of an imaginative, iconoclastic and anachronistic costume designer, and

149 The name designates worshippers of Dionysus, both male and female; therefore it includes Bacchae and Maenads.

150 That this Intermezzo remains alien to the spirit of the music, and therefore to the opera as Henze conceived it, can be verified by Mendelson's assertion (in a short review from 1990 which can be read at <http://audensociety.org/06newsletter.html>), that Henze encouraged its omission in performances of *The Bassarids*.

151 Henze worked mostly in the wake of Schönberg's *Moses und Aaron* and Berg's *Wozzeck*, even if the atonalism is intermittent, often interspersed with tonal episodes and even traditional patterns in both the vocals and the accompaniment, as is to be expected from a composer whose virtuosity and eclecticism are proverbial. Agave's and Dionysus' remarkable arias in the first part of the opera, in particular, teeter on the brink between tonal and atonal. Pentheus is not only Amfortas, he is also and above all Tristan, as underlined by a doleful and plaintive leitmotif on the oboe, of a classic Wagnerian stamp. The twelve-tone component is exemplified by music of bewilderment and panic that is too often used for apocalyptic and catastrophic emphasis under the form of sudden loud clashing of broken glass or metal scratching that chafe and disturb the ears; or by dithyrambic interludes in which the instrumentation is enriched by harps, chimes, bells, drums, castanets, triangles and sundry other rare instruments.

this is arguably the tastiest and most creative area of a libretto that is not as fortunate as that given to Stravinsky. In the midst of the mass stands as an extra, so to speak, an enigmatic, nameless mother, as if hypnotically guided by a small daughter clasping an enormous doll; with an absurdist effect the final curtain falls on this little girl as she smashes up her doll and begins to jump for joy. Auden dresses and disguises his characters according to the future ideology of which they are the spiritual fathers and progenitors. Tiresias enters as an Anglican archdeacon wearing dark glasses and having an androgynous corpulence; deprived of T. S. Eliot's sapient voice, he tumbles from his pedestal, and is the most ardent among those who have hastened to pay homage to the revealed god. The peak of the droll and carnivalesque estrangement is Dionysus' appearance. When he comes on, he is a kind of Byronic bully, his shirt open to the waist, in clothing that Byron might have worn, says Auden, at a picnic in the Roman countryside. Pentheus too is reread and interpreted in line with later codes, made more precisely proleptic; he is a medieval, monastic, ascetic monarch, preluding Wagner's Amfortas. The Intermezzo is set ahead in time in a Rococo atmosphere, and is acted by mythical characters in later dress. 'Calliope's judgement', presented as a game of Chinese boxes, is the farce of mythology. This Intermezzo, or masque, which, as one can intuit, takes up from that in *Paid on Both Sides*, once again has a psychic and dream-like value, and it is what Pentheus 'sees' in the mirror that Dionysus offers him, realizing and above all liberating his sexual repressions. Pentheus heads for the mountain dressed as a woman, as if 'for a stroll in the *Bois*', and without being recognized takes part in Dionysus' vigil. In the score, Pentheus' lament is both Verdian and Wagnerian (he is prostrate Othello and Tristan), the oboe ornamenting in the background. But the stage directions take another amusing liberty with the Bacchae and Bassarids entering, the former with hair '*à la* Brigitte Bardot', and the latter with the long hair of American flower children. The mother and the aunt have killed Pentheus at Dionysus' behest, in a Dionysian fit, no less.[152] For the moment it is vain to struggle against demanding gods who subjugate human freedom. Dionysus triumphs and inflicts exile and punishment on the survivors, but his dethroning is nigh.

152   Once again, in Auden's libretto pride of place goes to the ancestral enmity between mother and son, even if Dionysus does rehabilitate his own mother Semele, summoning her from beyond the grave.

§ 13. *Isherwood* I: The Berlin sagas*

Historically, Christopher Isherwood (1904–1986) has suffered from Auden's superior stature, and is sometimes spoken of as being merely the right-hand man of that dramatist and precocious poet, his shadow and double.[1] He has instead his own independent calibre, which rests on three or four highly personal novels accompanied by travel journals, some autobiographical memoirs and various essays that document his late conversion to Hinduism. He is also the first great exponent of twentieth-century western homosexual fiction. The first concrete step in his narrative, perhaps the only one, to have had uncommon importance in the period spanning the Second World War, which is also the first scenario of his fiction, derived from his stay in Berlin from the late 1920s to the early 1930s. There he began a series of rather short sketches, which were sober, chiselled without any excess, so precise and clean to the point of seeming cameos. They were city tales therefore, and this city was the capital of a nation in a crucial and tragic decade, when communism squared up to Nazism and

---

*   C. G. Heilbrun, *Christopher Isherwood*, New York 1970; A. Wilde, *Christopher Isherwood*, New York 1971; F. King, *Christopher Isherwood*, ed. I. Scott-Kilvert, Harlow 1976; J. Fryer, *Isherwood: A Biography*, London 1977, rev. ed. *Eye of the Camera: A Life of Christopher Isherwood*, London 1993; P. Piazza, *Christopher Isherwood: Myth and Anti-Myth*, New York 1978; B. Finney, *Christopher Isherwood: A Critical Biography*, London and New York 1979; C. J. Summers, *Christopher Isherwood*, New York 1980; L. M. Schwerdt, *Isherwood's Fiction: The Self and Technique*, Houndmills 1989 (very informed and thorough PhD thesis, though based on a somewhat pedantic application of the theories of the psychologist E. H. Erikson); S. Wade, *Christopher Isherwood*, Houndmills 1991; N. Page, *Auden and Isherwood: The Berlin Years*, Basingstoke 1998; *The Isherwood Century: Essays on the Life and Work of Christopher Isherwood*, ed. J. J. Berg and C. Freeman, Madison, WI 1999; P. Parker, *Isherwood: A Life*, London 2004.

1   For the plays from the late 1930s, written in collaboration with Auden – *The Dog Beneath the Skin* (1935), *The Ascent of F 6* (1936), and *On the Frontier* (1939) – see above, § 4. Isherwood travelled with Auden to China in 1938 in view of a book on the Sino-Japanese War that came out under the title of *Journey to a War* (1939; cf. § 6.1). Isherwood emigrated with Auden to the United States on the outbreak of war, arousing scandal among his interventionist compatriots. Without Auden, he soon went to live in Hollywood, where he worked as a scriptwriter and taught creative writing at the University of California.

the inexorable rise of Hitlerism was looming. This is a space-time dimension which was to be Isherwood's thematic reservoir of situations up to
the Second World War. Only for an instant can we compare Isherwood to
Durrell, almost contemporaries. Isherwood is deaf to any myth, does not
explore the city's or any city's fatal glamour, despite it being centuries old.
Nor did Durrell's expressionistic and visionary streak burn within him;
everything in his writing is the representation of daily life, attention to
its idiosyncrasies and hence often humorous sides, too. Yet both were in
a way apocalyptic writers viewing an immediate future ready to swallow
up life and proceed to extermination of the human race; in such a plight
it was then just as well to eat, love, fornicate, and live it up.[2] Apart from
two immature but promising first novels, Isherwood wrote with no care
for fashions, and he lent no ear to the experimentalists, oriented as he was
towards the *côté* of Waugh, Powell, Greene, that is objective and rootedly
English novelists. The study of moral laxity or indifference, of weakness
of character, of vices and foibles, is carried out without pointing a finger.[3]
The background of the rise of Nazism in Berlin lent itself to Isherwood's
overview, as I have mentioned, but he could smile at this too: people desired
more than anything to satisfy the pleasures of the palate, to make money,
enjoy life; and changing colours was no problem ('these people could be
made to believe in anybody or anything'). His adherence to the communist
Left, shared by almost all the writers who were in their twenties in the 1920s,
was phoney, unbelieving, superficial. Isherwood must have been almost
immediately disillusioned, and we can gather this from the fact that half of
his doubles declare rather quickly that they are ex-communists. His is not
an engagé fiction, politics becoming a pretext for humorous, comical or
detached descriptions of rather fanatical assemblies, noisy political meetings, and of the unheroic figure of the political and intellectualized writer.
He is more interested in human curiosities, delightful contradictions, the

2   Like Durrell in the same years, Isherwood emigrated with his lover Heinz and others
     to a Greek island in 1933, an experience reflected in *Down There on a Visit* (§ 14.2).
3   This is the conscious diagnosis in *Prater Violet* (§ 13.5): that of a writer who 'has imagi-
     nation, can invent dialogues, knows how to develop a character', and can 'describe
     almost everything'.

raw ferment of passions, pagan, wild, cowardly even. Candidly, Isherwood says of himself in *Prater Violet*: 'for all my parlour socialism, I was a snob'. The implications of the Berlin sketches are that Isherwood hides himself, withdraws, puts himself aside, even abolishes himself. He resigned himself to a fiction of objectivity, declining to write the novel of the soul with all its introspection and laceration. He himself figures on the page, and enters the scene, as Christopher Isherwood, writing in the first person like one who in life has just debuted as a writer. But his passions, both hetero- and homosexual, are tepid, occluded and suffocated, as if vibrating under a veil of noble platonic friendship. He is a controlled, wary confidant, a support for others, frequently coming to the aid of whosoever is in difficulty. In the opening words of *Goodbye to Berlin* such neutrality, and such an attitude of expectation, were given an aesthetic formulation borrowed from cinema technique: the observation of phenomena as if through a camera that registers them impassively and without any apparent selective filter. Isherwood honestly closed his Berlin narratives when he had to, without unnecessary exploitation. Unfortunately he did not truly exchange it with a second setting yielding equally juicy fruit. The three or four American novels left no trace, rapidly disappeared and today are largely forgotten. Isherwood got nearer and nearer to the confessional, subjective, no longer purely representative novel, hence homosexual, in concentric circles and in a progressive silencing of narrative scruples and euphemisms. At first, a constant in Isherwood is the narrative device of an *alter ego* who, dried up and disappointed, vainly seeks an authentic relationship and an existential amalgam, breaking out of isolation, with another, female, more often male, figure. The transition from the solitary life to the fulfilling partnership seems not of this world and, rarely happening, vanishes almost at once.[4]

---

4   See what Patrick confesses to himself in chapter V of *A Meeting by the River* (§ 14.4–5): 'What I want is a life beyond their taboos, in which two men learn to trust each other so completely that there's no fear left and they experience and share everything together in the flesh and in the spirit. I don't believe such closeness is possible between a man and a woman—deep down they are natural enemies—and how

2. Isherwood's father, an army officer of artistic temperament, died as a war hero when Isherwood was still at a tender age, and Isherwood grew up with the nightmare, largely shared by his generation, of unwarlike cowardice. His mother, a domineering woman, harboured dreams of glory for her son and wanted to make of him a respectable university professor with a family; whence a second nightmare, maternal oppression provoking a reaction in the form of a nascent and then explosive need for liberation, if not his homosexual inclinations. In Isherwood's narrative, as a consequence, there abound figures of vicarious fathers and of kindly and beneficent mothers. At St Edmund's public school in Hindhead he met Auden, whilst at that of Repton he met his lifelong friend Edward Upward, with whom he wrote the extravagant 'Mortmere stories'.[5] In 1925, at Cambridge, he took up again the association with Auden, whose first poems he read and commented, writing himself some in the nonsense genre. His first novel, *All the Conspirators* (1928), is stylistically a pastiche of a number of modernists. It seems above all to accept or rather anticipate the practice of a Henry Green, suppressing as much as possible the descriptive passages in favour of purely skeletal dialogue, timidly nearing therefore Green's particular type of laconic Modernism.[6] *The Memorial* (1932) goes to the heart of Isherwood's anamnesis depicting a spasmodic relationship between a mother and a son,[7] the latter, however, transfused or projected into a vicarious character or one parallel to the protagonist, a double drawn from the mythology of the epoch: the mentally maimed survivor, a vagabond, real and symbolic at the same time, who leaves a false and sterile heterosexual love affair to take up a homosexual relationship with a Berlin 'boy'. The temporal dislocation, in four inconsecutive time

---

many men ever find it together? Only a very few even glimpse the possibility of it, and only a very few out of that few dare to try to find it'.

5   Cf. § 5.1 and n. 75.

6   Cf. Schwerdt 1989, 29, for a later statement of Isherwood, to the effect that he considered himself at the time 'an experimental novelist'.

7   Also reflected in the hero of *The Ascent of F 6* when he reaches culmination on the peak and discovers that it is his mother (§ 4.8).

phases, is reminiscent of Faulkner.[8] Isherwood began to study medicine in 1928, but gave it up to join Auden in Berlin, the one and the other to satisfy without hindrance or scandal homosexual passion in a notoriously disinhibited capital.

3. *Mr Norris Changes Trains* (1935) is the first of Isherwood's books of which one can and should speak more at length. At first sight it is a novel in the old style, a chain of sketches corresponding to as many chapters which sustain a plot of moderate tension. Isherwood had by then conquered a detachment from his materials, so convulsive in the previous novels, which were of an impetuous subjectivism. The result is an amiable, pleasant and polished book, mainly written in short sentences and consisting of theatrical dialogues veined with just a minimum of rhetoric and pomposity. The background is Germany in the early 1930s and Berlin under the dense and threatening shadow of Hitler. This scenario is observed during the period of almost two years from two points of view, that of Isherwood's *alter ego* William Bradshaw,[9] who makes a living by giving English lessons to rich Jews, and that of the mysterious Arthur Norris, a supposed commercial agent who simply gets along, and substantially works as a spy or rather double-crosses the Bolsheviks and the Nazis. However, the political plot is not so dominant as the daily events of the two characters in Berlin, who become friends on the border between Holland and Germany from the moment when the trembling Norris, on the point of being recognized and arrested by the customs officers, saves his skin in a train under the eyes of his young compatriot, whom he has just met. Very little is concretely known about the commercial activity of Mr Norris; we learn much more of his dissipated and extravagant lifestyle. Isherwood camouflages and eclipses himself, keeping his eye on that character and his idiosyncrasies. Norris loves acting, pronouncing rotund and rhetorical tirades, listening to himself talk. He is a big eater, a squanderer and a host who offers meals and drinking bouts. His teeth are horribly rotten, but his nails are manicured and his hands well cared for. He always wears a wig and is not ashamed of admitting it. One sees him later in certain sybarite rituals,

8   Wade 1991, 25. For Kermode (KPE, 125), the time-scheme is instead 'Conradian'.
9   The first names of Isherwood himself.

such as covering his face with tan cream, having a hot bath every morning, or the perverted Sadistic performance of himself being whipped in front of the whores of the up-market Berlin brothels, prostrate and in the act of polishing shoes (a scene which in itself is a parody of the distant Decadent and pornographic novel *Teleny*). Norris is in a way a twentieth-century Micawber with a thousand resources, always getting back up or falling on his feet. Basically he is a romantic character, contradictory, impulsive, voluble, and easily depressed and exalted. The Nazis are not to be under-rated, but the communists are opportunists. However, politics is all told conspicuous for its absence and there is no upcoming tragedy, because the key to the story is humour. Such a Victorian, humorous narrative approach, both amiable and 'phatic', is rounded off with the portraits of the minor characters, with the mass of Berlin revellers, the left-wing political agita-tors, the occult fascists and many homosexuals who swell out their chests and show off the size of their biceps. One of these, a baron, attempts to pick up Bradshaw, but the scene comes to nothing.

4. *Goodbye to Berlin* (1939) is unquestionably Isherwood's masterpiece. It is composed of six stories linked by the passive presence, only or almost only with the function of an observing filter, of an internal narrator who bears the name of the author himself, but is a fictitious version of him and a double ('a ventriloquist's dummy'). They are stories reciprocally imbricated, since to the original nucleus of characters others are added, progressively widening the circle. This collection was meant to be called *The Lost*, an explicit title indicative of a link with the preceding novel about Mr Norris, were it not that the style is more impressionistic, slightly more estranged, more cutting and less benevolent. The good humour has been dissipated or lost. There are not exactly the same types of characters as previously, rather they have turned around and undergone some change. In the first piece, which is explicitly a diary like the last, the story moves ahead from the boarding-house of the landlady Fräulein Schroeder, in which live German and English guests. The eye is focused on the depiction of character, on the conflict of positions and the skirmishes, more than on the advancement of the plot. The touch is light in catching the subtle anti-Semitism in this setting, the veiled calendar of Nazi events in the background, the natural-ness of promiscuous relations or the economic need which leads men and

women gaily to prostitution. In the world of Berlin, as described also by Maugham and Katherine Mansfield and earlier by Thackeray, one is bound by and stuck in the material, the crass and the alimentary. The student Hippi provokes the English tutor, offering him fruit and food, and also with her prurient erotic curiosity. The rejected or replaced title, *The Lost*, groups together a cross-section of humanity given up to a desperate *carpe diem* behind the outbursts of folly. One lives for the moment, lucidly aware that this time will pass and *après nous le déluge*. The diagnosis and at the same time the framework is 'the neurotic post-War life of the German people'. One does one's best, but everyone is uprooted, suffering and disadvantaged. Sally Bowles, the young dancer from the variety,[10] lives also in a dimension of precariousness and disorder. She passes hopefully, and even enthusiastically, from one love story to another, always deluded but ever famished. Crazy and incoherent, she has to forsake the child of a man who has left her, which gives us an idea of how ungrateful human love can be. She has an abortion, but romantically has a fit of remorse immediately afterwards. Solemnly weighed down by her thoughts, she gets into every kind of trouble, confirming that the world is in decline and horizon-less. In a ravenous human universe the narrator hides his sexual diversity in being only the friend of women, shrewdly abstaining from loving or having sexual relations. He is homosexual simply out of not loving women, due to a chastity that is exceptional in the entirely heterosexual panorama. He is not fish, flesh or fowl, often giving non-committal replies, in disappointing and insipid phrases straight from the conversation manual. Not even politically is he a well-defined character, replying to the pertinent question that he is 'not a proper communist'. At times, in his politics and behaviour, he is so 'correct' that he does not seem to be serious.[11] He also acts generically, out of pure circumstance and routine. For example, he changes lodgings, and, leaving Fräulein Schroeder, goes to live with the Novaks. This working-class family demonstrates that in this second Berlin study the moneyed bourgeoisie

10   Sally Bowles is based on a Jean Ross, whom Isherwood met in 1931, whilst Gerald Hamilton was the inspiration for Mr Norris.
11   Isherwood became an American citizen in 1946 and therefore could have been called up, but he managed to have himself recognized as a conscientious objector.

in *Mr Norris* has left the scene. The social extraction is lower, the range of the movements not extending beyond the poor quarters, a half-closed microcosm in which neurosis is at the point of exploding. Here brief, neat, clean and effective scenes follow each other without tension, with well-chosen and recited dialogues. The satire is mainly focused on Herr Novak, always somewhat exaggerated in his behaviour. The Landauers are Jewish and one follows the exploits of the impertinent tomboy Natalia, who is full of complexes, and the probably homosexual Bernhard.

5. *Prater Violet* (1945), which with some qualifications could still be defined as a Berlin tale, remains a little, brief narrative of the self, so brief that it could really be classified as a short story. Isherwood enters again the lists with his own name and surname as the scriptwriter of a film bearing the title of the story, which is being made in England as a reworking of an existing vaudeville show directed by the Austrian Bergmann, just when, in the historical Austro-German scenario, Hitler is launching the first wave of anti-Semitic repression. Its mock-serious vein, which is not, however, dark or macabre, precedes Waugh's *The Loved One*. But Isherwood soon withdraws in order to record the amusing things he sees around him. The first person narrative is never invasive, which is by now a law; rather, his own personal myth of the apathetic, resigned writer without will power, resurfaces: 'I had a will of my own', he says, but this is in fact a perfect denial. On the other hand, he surrounds and gratifies himself with a small dose of narcissism, as his books are mentioned and someone has read them, while others ask him for information. He is also attentive in following a male friendship, genuine and apparently free of homoeroticism, between the German director and the unsuccessful English writer. The episodes and the caricatures are finely managed, whilst rhythmically the echoes of the political escalation in Germany resound. Bergmann is a copy of Norris with a changed nationality, as he is loquacious, expansive, eccentric, generous, subject to mood swings and easily got around;[12] a good heart, all told. After the initial diffidence, a strong friendship with Isherwood ensues, the development of which is followed through dialogic sketches and phases of oratorical, rhetorical and

12   The model was the Jewish Austrian director Berthold Viertel.

frivolous small talk. Politically, Isherwood points up the contradiction of the left-wing writer and intellectual who remains a bourgeois aesthete, having only a 'romantic' transport for the proletariat, and thus is diagnosed as 'declassed', which is more or less the same as Gissing's 'unclassed',[13] an analysis with which Orwell would have probably agreed. During the shooting of the film, a Dickensian comedy takes shape amongst the actors, as their private affairs blend with those that they must act. Bergmann, shocked by the developments in Germany where his family still lives, languishes and gets paralyzed, suffering the same destiny as Mr Norris. The finale is highly surprising, Isherwood or his double coming out into the open to abruptly hymn an authentic, overwhelming and isolating love covering the horrors of the war in a thick veil. The figure of the sexual partner is identified only by the letter, J., and can be taken, due to Isherwood's ability in omitting personal pronouns, either as a male or a female.

§ 14. *Isherwood II: The painful and doubtful awareness of diversity*

Both of Isherwood's long, immediate post-war 'novels' leave much to be desired, or rather decidedly disappoint.[14] The second, in fact, does not even merit this appellative, lying halfway between the invented story and the untransposed diary. *The World in the Evening* (1954)[15] is substantially the first of Isherwood's novels to follow all the rules of the genre, rather than a collection of sketches and episodes. More precisely, and here lies the cause of its failure, it is the first novel where Isherwood, who was by then fifty, does seek a change of material, which however is partial because the Berlin nightmares and fantasies continue to reverberate (in the figure of Gerda, a German deportee or refugee). It represents at the same time an attempt to escape from a first-person narrative referring to a character who bears the name and surname of the real narrator. But, far from Berlin,

---

13   Volume 6, § 123.1.

14   Wade 1991, 115–16, seems to be almost alone in considering these novels an outstanding achievement.

15   The novel was typed by Don Bachardy, whom Isherwood met in 1953 on a beach in Santa Monica; Bachardy was at the time an adolescent, perhaps only sixteen. Their relationship lasted until Isherwood's death.

Isherwood is a fish out of water, and tries to write a novel of which he is basically incapable, the melodramatic and psychological novel, with a complex structure containing also epistolary inserts and organized with a mixed time dimension and leaps back and forward that continually create peculiar optical effects. The autobiographical origins of the unaligned writer and intellectual, now of Quaker extraction, though lapsed, are still there. In fact, in the plot Stephen, an English emigrant in California, constrained, after an accident, to remain for a long period in bed, goes back over his life. From this a mental autobiography arises, starting from the meeting with his first wife, a writer, in London, when he was twenty-two. His memories are stimulated by her letters sent to other people and to himself. Re-adopting the technique of his second novel, Isherwood manufactures a see-saw narrative tempo, which at one moment is in the present and follows the thoughts of the convalescent, while at another it is in the past and goes back to two decades earlier, in narrative episodes that expand the letters of his wife. Insofar as a short period of Stephen's life was spent in Berlin, that framework is updated. Isherwood coquettishly makes the hero's wife the author of a novel having the same title as the one he is composing, which is read and evaluated by Gerda, who hears the protagonist say that the secret of the novelist is to transpose and transfigure the massacring, discrimination and prejudice in the name of a snobbish separation from real life. Isherwood was in timid search of a novel making his homosexuality explicit, but he had not yet closed the circle, merely opened it, and organizes the plot on disguise, exchange of identity and circumlocution. He begins by depicting a pair of happy homosexuals; he then saddles the protagonist with two loveless and uneven marriages. Stephen contracts the first with an older novelist with a heart disease, who only needs a secretary and factotum and writes plaintive letters to her friends. As this woman is named Elizabeth, a reference to the marriage of the Brownings – one between an older temperamental woman and a subjugated and long suffering husband – seems to be plausible.[16] Between the two marriages there is wedged the quite natural

16   It has been said instead that Isherwood wished to hint at two writers he admired, Virginia Woolf and Katherine Mansfield.

friendship between Stephen and a male itinerant English photographer, a love story which is confessed, but also ephemeral, terminated without any apparent trauma.

2. *Down There on a Visit* (1962) encloses four linked tales which rework the Berlin sketches; in fact Isherwood returns to naming himself among the characters. More precisely, they take up again the Berlin experience from an even earlier period. 'Mr Lancaster' repeats the modes and cadences of Isherwood's earlier humorous work – the comic and witty remarks and the little idiosyncrasies of Charles Lamb's etchings, although the precise sense of the exhumation evades comprehension. The voyage on a ship belonging to a distant relative who owns a shipping line, an unwilling stay in a German port, a banquet and the eccentricities of Mr Lancaster: all of this is a bit forced, without structure, the humour no longer fresh, indeed stale. In Lancaster Norris and all his descendants fail to be brought back to life. In 'Ambrose', Isherwood and Waldemar stop off in Athens because the latter has been invited to be cook by a gym teacher of authoritarian and homosexual temperament. The merry crew go to an island picking up new acquaintances and install a male community there, a strange, bizarre idea indeed, and little more than a prank. The scarce interest in the events happening hardly justifies an action that is described and is intended to figure as an expression of protest and disgust: the little group of pederasts reject all social conventions, isolate themselves from history, almost creating a separate existence. The third episode makes it clear that Isherwood is aiming at a hybrid form, that of a short story assuming an amorphous nature, and of a selective diary of a plot concerning public and above all private affairs often concealed and reticent (the love stories are always bisexual). Hence, one is not even sure whether to assign this novel to the category of invention or to that of the memoir, so subtle is the confine. Isherwood takes us back in time to 1937 and 1938, and to his return from China where he had gone as a war reporter with Auden. On the ship on the way back he meets an old female companion from student days, a fervent communist, who has become the fiancée of one of the Germans from the Greek island. The Nazi nightmare fuses or collides with the enthusiasm for the Spanish war. In the fourth episode, Isherwood is in Hollywood as a scriptwriter, infatuated with oriental

mysticism. Acting as a saviour he entrusts a 'male prostitute', suddenly in the grips of a spiritual crisis, to the care of a guru. Paul is enrolled, and then intends to embrace a profession, but the ménage comes to nothing. The story ends just before the time of writing, when Isherwood returns to Berlin and meets one of his old friends.

3. *A Single Man* (1964) has been deemed of historical importance as the founding text of the contemporary homosexual novel along with Forster's *Maurice*. It is the parable of a homosexual, George, who, like Isherwood, feels discriminated and forced to bear the mark of his supposed deviancy. But at the same time it is a protest against the American system of the time: against the lies, the hypocrisy, the utopias, the false security and the cult of efficiency, all witnessed by a college professor, disenchanted, bitter within and lacerated, yet constrained to feign. It is also true that Isherwood sought to write an Americanized novel, both because he wished to reflect a multi-ethnic society and because he mimed a dialogue which is no longer cultured like that of the Berliners – filtered, re-written and hence theatrical – but rather informal, jargon, gathered live, as it were. George is watched, vituperated, emarginated or else tolerated, or more precisely 'interpreted', in an American neighbourhood fraught with aggressiveness and neurosis. Behind him stands of course Isherwood himself, who manufactures the novel from the outset as a psychic diary of estrangement and hallucination, of facts registered phenomenologically in the now deserted and solitary house, hence the present tense of the writing.[17] The novel spans just a day, covering captivatingly and truthfully the stream of consciousness of a professor teaching Aldous Huxley's latest novel. The moments in this day are waking up, breakfast, the lecture, the hospital visit and the session in the gym. The lack of the exceptional amounts to a bitter balance and translates the failed adaptation of the main character to an alien American reality, well described in flashes of observation. In this day other cases of uprooting, of masked existential unease and of frustration are reviewed. There is practically no example, in this human panorama, of a realized and harmonious existence. Here, in this novel, the motif of

---

17   The final application of the metaphor of the camera-eye (Schwerdt 1989, 164).

the ontologically isolated and solitary life reaches its peak, whence the exasperated search for an authentic affective relationship, which once it appears (Jim, George's companion) is immediately subtracted, provoking the quest for other human relationships which in part deceive, and in a lesser part bring satisfaction, but stop always far from the ideal goal, which is therefore just as ontologically inaccessible.[18] One of George's students is a hidden poet who is eyed up by the mature professor in a Californian bar. In this, almost the last, or second last scene, a certain fleeting resemblance between this short novel and the general design of Joyce's *Ulysses* becomes more manifest, because destiny or fatality have put each on the other's path at the end of the day after an unconscious reciprocal search. They are the professor who has just lost his deeply loved and irreplaceable companion, and the young student who is having a dissatisfying relationship with his girlfriend. It is by now repetitive to say that Isherwood, in this imitating Lawrence, leads them, at the end of a finally frank and disinhibited dialogue, to the shores of the ocean and has them dive naked into the nocturnal waves. Isherwood, however, is realistic and pessimistic enough to bring down the curtain on the still yearning George in search of a substitute for Jim.[19]

4. Isherwood embraced the Vedanta faith in the 1940s, after having professed himself an atheist since university. It was the historian Gerald Heard who introduced him to the Swami Prabhavananda, a Hindu monk who had founded a centre for study and prayer in California. The cardinal principle of this mystique is the divinity of man, capable of uniting with the nature of God. The new faith was in agreement with Isherwood's pacifism (against which the right-minded had railed, confusing his flight from England with cowardice) and did not oppress the faithful with the weight of sin, above all homosexual, stigmatized without any possibility of being

---

18   The scene of the evening meal at which George dines with Charlotte is particularly awkward and unsuccessful. Her case mirrors his to the extent that the woman has just been abandoned by her husband and gives over to excessively nostalgic memories, and at the end of the evening she kisses the unyielding George on the lips.

19   According to some, George masturbates at the end of the day (King 1976, 20); to others, he dies during the night.

pardoned by the Anglican Church. Almost a century earlier, the Decadents had identified in Catholicism a fold which it does not seem Isherwood was ever tempted to join. In the Hindu monk Isherwood found a hypostasis of the rejected Christian God and a father figure. He became his 'guru' about whom he wrote a book bearing that epithet in the title, *My Guru and His Disciple* (1980). With him he collaborated on the English translation of some classics of Indian mysticism, and in propaganda initiatives such as the biography *Ramakrishna and his Disciples*. Oliver, one of two brothers who are the protagonists of *A Meeting by the River* (1967), is a monk living in meditation in a monastery on the Ganges, and a disciple of a swami met in Europe and now deceased. This, therefore, is, unequivocally, the imaginary, and indeed partly real continuation of an actual experience and the realization of a missed vocation, since Isherwood had vaguely entertained the idea of following his master into the Californian monastery. In a series of ingenious correspondences, the narrator reflects himself first in an *alter ego* only nominally called Monk (*The World in the Evening*) and then in a real Hindu monk. In *A Meeting by the River*, Patrick, Oliver's brother and a bisexual husband with his feet firmly in the world, is hedonist rather than Hindu. In this way, Isherwood effected a synchronic decomposition of his aporias or rather simply of his irreconcilable drives, aspiring to reconcile them asymptotically. In the end the prodigal son is reconciled with his mother and his brother.

5. The result of Patrick's visit to Oliver in India represents the acceptance of the maternal interference that Isherwood had obscurely recognized as responsible for the direction his life had taken: 'She only did what so many mothers do – she cast her sons for roles in life'. The decomposition under way is that of the two souls of Isherwood: the active life and the contemplative life, heterosexuality, bisexuality (and hence homosexuality), and abstinence, body and soul. Oliver is apparently further ahead than Patrick, because dialectically he has left behind both the erotic practice and the active life. From philanthropic activism, and as a member and functionary of the Red Cross, he embraced abstention, meditation and the exclusive cultivation of the soul ('the Christians believe in action, and that's what he was evidently yearning to give up'). Implicitly Oliver responds to the incessant exhortations previously addressed to other of Isherwood's

protagonists by internal interlocutors, that art should be interventionist and bring about change. He also responds to the objection of Isherwood's far-off compatriots who had branded his behaviour as the cowardice of a defector. In reality Isherwood along the way unexpectedly reveals himself to be equidistant. That is, he downsizes Oliver and re-evaluates Patrick. The latter, in fact, during the brief stay at the monastery, induces his brother to examine his conscience, rendering him more optimistic, indulgent and tolerant, even almost doubtful about the choice he had embraced with such conviction. The Indian meeting had begun with a fair dose of hypocritical fiction, because Oliver the monk could not suppress his atavistic hate for his brother. Isherwood has Patrick himself warmly invite his lover, whom he is about to dump, to meet girls in order to form a family and have children. Isherwood returns to a certain compositional experimentalism and to his belated partiality for the epistolary or mixed form. A story with no authorial linkage whatsoever, and where the extra-diegetic narration is completely inactive, *A Meeting by the River* induces the reader to believe that the material could have been far better treated and developed by an omniscient narrator. The letters that the two brothers exchange from far distant geographical locations – belied, corrected and completed by extracts from the diary – sound on reading artificial, unnatural and overly stiffened in stereotyped formulae.[20]

§ 15. *Spender* I: The imperious question: 'Why do I write?'*

Should we define Stephen Spender (1909–1995) as a poet, and even more as a Thirties poet, there would be two good reasons why we would risk not doing justice to his figure, thereby reducing his stature a great deal. Spender wrote poetry before and after the 1930s, and effectively a

---

20   Those directed by Patrick to his lover Tom, in particular, are marked by a false and verbose pathos.

*   *Collected Poems*, London 1955, and, with a different assortment, London 1985 and 1986, are in reality selections edited by Spender himself, with often conspicuous revisions of the texts compared to the first publication; *New Collected Poems*, ed. M. Brett, London 2004, is also a selective edition. The disconcerting fact is that in

dozen of his compositions, noble, humanitarian and immediate, hence slightly rhetorical, won unanimous acclaim and entered anthologies on a regular basis; however, these were isolated exploits in a more anonymous and, aside from anything else, almost always desultory production. They showed that Spender lacked the congenital instinct of the great poet, let alone a chameleon-like verbal, rhythmic and prosodic capacity, and that their sphere is that of a reflective, gnomic and derivative vein, with few or no symbolic halos and scarcely any nuances. In other terms, Spender's poetry is subsumed by his writing as a whole, and his writing is often theoretically subordinate to concrete action.[1] Spender was a poet, playwright, novelist, literary critic, ideologist, political scientist, even an aesthetician; conscious of the irreducible limits of the written word, after the Second World War he became a cultural promoter, a lecturer, a professor of literature, a cultural ambassador, and an authoritative voice in the support of human rights. He was above all, and will continue to be seen as, a memorialist. His autobiography *World Within World* is dated 1951, and together with his diaries is considered almost unanimously to be his most representative work, and I too will begin with it. The author presents himself condemning any biographer to paraphrase the first half of his life;[2] however, this is a double-faced work which, while attending to the reconstruction of his

---

many cases the titles of the poems change from edition to edition; in citing them, where possible, I follow the 1986 edition, indicating the variants. *Journals 1939–1983*, ed. J. Goldsmith, London and Boston, MA 1985 and 1992. I shall cite the autobiography *World Within World*, London 1951 and 1977, as WWW. S. N. Pandey, *Stephen Spender: A Study in Poetic Growth*, Salzburg 1982; H. David, *Stephen Spender: A Portrait with Background*, London 1992; M. O'Neill and G. Reeves, *Auden, MacNeice, Spender: The Thirties Poetry*, Houndmills 1992, 35–62, 116–44 and 206–42 and *passim*; D. Leeming, *Stephen Spender: A Life in Modernism*, New York 1999; J. Sutherland, *Stephen Spender: The Authorized Biography*, London 2004.

1   A purely vicarious action: he was a simple fire fighter during the London Blitz. After the war he mainly concentrated on editing the magazine *Encounter*, from 1953 to 1967.
2   Apart from the reticence regarding his bisexuality, with the resulting change of name of some lovers, indicated only by initials, and the suppression of some intimate relationships.

private story, also acquires the value of a paradigmatic public testimony. On reading it, we have to agree that Spender is obsessed by self-analysis, intent on explaining himself, placing himself in perspective, as a reflective writer thrown back on himself who can, as a result, appear the victim of unbounded egotism. His is a torn and messed-up personality that attempts to recompose itself, splintered into many egos that are unable to correlate to one another in one larger ego: the poem 'Trigorin' confesses, for example, human weaknesses, even pettiness and slothfulness, and this allegedly larger ego turns out to be small in the sum of its entities (and among these partial egos there is also one that 'excret[es]'). Such existentialism brings him close to Matthew Arnold, from whom he took, for example,[3] the theory of the two selves, one real and one ideal, that battle it out in the theatre of the person.[4] Spender's dualisms, confessed in *World Within World*, are practically infinite, and one that he makes no mystery of is his bisexual nature. However, the general aporia concerns the actual trade, the vocation of the writer, solipsist and escapist or caring and involved, and even optimistically instrumental to the goals of an ideal and in the service of humanity.

2. Born into a liberal family of an inveterate progressive tendency, Spender grew up with an acute sense of his own belatedness with respect to a heroic era that was over and forever superseded. His father, a parliamentary journalist with ties to Lloyd George, seemed straight out of Dickens's novels, or brings to mind the father of Harry Richmond in Meredith's eponymous novel. A man devoid of backbone, misguided, he was also inclined to pompous rhetorical language, and his flourishes and sound bites are evoked with gusto and also a touch of ridicule by his son. With his mother dying when he was twelve, Spender and his three brothers suffered a certain Spartan austerity, despite the family having maids and governesses. His maternal ancestors came from Germany, and he acknowledged that he had a quarter of Jewish blood in his veins. Spender recalls that he became aware of this, and that he always proudly emphasized it, ever since his family was attacked by an anti-Semitic magazine directed by Chesterton and Belloc.

---

3   See WWW, 311.
4   Arnold's name is brought up by Pandey 1982, 204, regarding Spender's recurrent symbol of the island and human solitude.

Before university, Spender had studied in France and in Geneva, with the blooming of his first homosexual passion for a peer referred to only by his initial D. At Oxford, incredibly timid, he immediately got to know Auden and became his friend, despite feeling an insuperable subjugation. Auden seemed icy to him in his character, brutal and caustic in his way of speaking; but Spender ultimately managed to extricate himself from Auden's alchemical poetry, from his distillation of pure words, the poetic content or subject reduced to a simple washing line to 'hang the poetry' on; and therefore remain immune to the primacy of form.[5] For him, poetry meant speaking of experiences he had had and that had actually occurred. It says a lot that, at the age of nine, Spender had discovered his poetic vocation in the Lake District on hearing Wordsworth recited. However, in the beginning, his poetics leant on the overcoming of the poetry of invocation, or of the pure translation into words of a natural sensual image, and on the assumption of the experience and of nature into a 'symbolic inner consciousness'.[6] The poet stands inside time, rather than fleeing from it. In Hamburg and Berlin, at twenty, the stages to approach communism had already been covered under a personal exposure to reality. Nazism had been foreseen by some writers, and a fruit of their art fed by a destructive force.[7]

3. This is, in part, the thesis of Spender's second most famous book, *The Destructive Element* (1935), namely, that the great modernists had written a solipsistic and individualistic art against the background of a world without faith. From the safe haven of individualism art had to burst into the open and face the advance of fascist dictatorships head on, if possible stopping and subverting them. Spender's paradigmatic quality is only partially that of Auden and Isherwood and the other 1930s writers. Instead, his ideological parable is much more similar, and vaguely parallel, to Orwell's; also the style of Spender's autobiography is the self-restrained one of Orwell's essays, free from bragging or back-slapping, albeit sprinkled with some jokey, humorous and satirical little scenes, and the occasional lively portrait. Above all what is true is that the two writers, almost peers, both left the ranks of a

5   WWW, 51.
6   WWW, 95.
7   WWW, 190.

well-to-do, already declining bourgeoisie, and that both queried the nature and purpose of writing, and asked themselves the pressing question, 'Why do I write?', coming up with answers that, at least initially, were not dissimilar. In essence, neither Orwell nor Spender had difficulty in admitting that writing is a solipsistic, self-gratifying act, and that only the historical emergency had inspired them to make it a weapon to change the world on its slippery slide. Orwell admitted that the aesthetic goal was what pulsed most strongly in him; Spender was called to a writing of militant action, abandoning the equivalent of figurative painting in words. Orwell had not had an Auden to extricate himself from and clash with, like some shadow or hypostasis of a father, or the tormenting ambivalence of gender. However, both Spender and Orwell left Spain with their communism having lost its attraction: or to be more accurate, repudiating Stalinism and the demonstrable precept that the Party is always right. Spender's account of the Spanish Civil War and Orwell's *Homage to Catalonia* have *pour cause* many points in common;[8] and both writers precede Doris Lessing's story 'The Day Stalin Died' and the disillusionment she tells of. However, compared to Orwell, Spender retraced his steps to his departure point, and having believed himself able to make the leap away from liberalism,[9] ended up admitting that poetry was 'not the same as action', and a poem 'not the same as a political thesis'.[10] All in all, Orwell could not esteem him, owing to a communism that had not been fully investigated in its foundations, not dialecticized, not analysed in its bases and contradictions. Indeed, from Orwell's essays we have the inevitable confession: that he thought, said and wrote that Spender had been a 'parlour Bolshevik'.[11] Spender was actually linked to nineteenth-century idealisms, was more of a Christian-socialist than a Marxist, and behind him stood Frederick Denison Maurice and above all, yet again, Arnold.

8   This is the sense of the brief parallel sketched by Sutherland 2004, 268–9.

9   *Forward from Liberalism* (1937). F. Binni (in CAB, vol. II, 252–3) maintains that Spender's ideas were not very different from those of the great tradition of British liberalism, of Godwin, Shelley and Mill.

10   Quoted in HYN, 270.

11   Cf. OCE, vol. I, 324 and 347, the latter a conciliatory letter, embarrassed and also clumsy, in which Orwell refrains from commenting on *Trial of a Judge*.

In fact, we can perceive in him more than one streak of ancient German-Jewish pride, the same one that we find acquired, or perhaps inherited, in Arnold, and which harks back to 'Kultur' and to the sacred office of guarding 'Geist';[12] hence Spender's constant reference to German cultural history, his trips to Germany, the affective centre it represented for him, his many books dedicated to Germany, and his attention to its poets and musicians, first and foremost Beethoven. Spender's heroic poetry also includes a tribute to the composer of the *Eroica*, based on the romantic idea of the artistic genius through whom nature speaks, indeed who is the very voice of nature, in unison with it.[13] Ever since the war Spender had defended art as form – and he had earlier denied it – and the rights of the imagination; since the war he had not dodged the classic question of the 1930s, which is in fact timeless: how to preserve art's specific quality and at the same time answer and tackle the crisis of the contemporary world. In other words, it achieves Auden's famous goal of a poetry 'that makes nothing happen'.

§ 16. *Spender II: Romantic heroism between the wars*

Spender is a kind of scapegoat against whom the critics of the Thirties poets railed, for his outbursts, his theories that did not hold up, his ingenuous assertions, and his watered-down communism; and his poetry met a reception that was no different. After the early zeal, after Auden's favour and esteem, and after Eliot's flattering opinions, but also the severe criticisms of the Leavises, Spender the poet ended up leaving most later readers cold and dissatisfied, some of the latter even smirking at his intrinsic limits, his sentimental rhetoric, his intermittent, temporary, plagiaristic Modernism. Spender's heroic or golden age is the decade 1930–1940; he was to live for another sixty years, but he appeared dead on arrival, his mind and feelings all spent in the first thirty years of his life. A cardiac graph would show a very high peak without dips in the two decades from 1930 to 1950, then a kind of flat calm. It was he who cut himself off in 1951, almost having stopped living,

12   On all this, cf. the interesting article by D. Aberbach in *TLS*, 27 February 2009, 14–15.
13   A poem to be read together with page 71 of WWW, where Spender recalls his discovery of the music of Beethoven, introduced to him by Isaiah Berlin.

no longer updating and extending his autobiography, but revising his poetry. And the fact that the editions of his poetry continued to be selective is proof of their limited intrinsic poetic value. Among Italian critics, who paid little attention and showed little interest, Praz was the one who knew him best, and every important later work by Spender, especially in prose, was commented on with fresh savoury reviews, but all, or almost all, negative. Spender then passed significantly untouched through the post-war close examinations of the various critical, structuralist and poststructuralist approaches; nor has there been anything more than cursory deconstructionist scrutinies.

2. In 1985, Spender divided up his work according to a thematic or vaguely musical criterion that was not strictly chronological. The real demarcations are the year 1937, and, even more incisive, 1939, the date after which Spender the poet gradually had almost nothing more to say. Having meanwhile reduced an already lengthy parable in 1965, with an edition of selected poems that does not exceed eighty pages, he gave a testimony of high probity. Looking back over this first ascending section,[14] the poem 'Statistics' reveals that Spender was no stranger to a bubbly sense of humour that was almost that of the spirited Elizabethan song: he contrasts the scientific or even purely technological civilization with the 'poetic' or anti-scientific vision, and humorously takes the side of the ancients. Except that this lightness is gradually submerged by a type of poetry that is increasingly oratorical and resembles a chorus, enriched by the cadenced veins of the hymn or of the biblical sequence, with insistent anaphoric formulae of a pseudo-prophetic slant. 'After They Have Tired' announces the *sic transit gloria mundi* theme and the overthrow of the powers-that-be on the Day of Judgement, when Death will make every-one equal before the Judge. Thanks to this consummation, far-off but hoped-for as it is, the coryphaeus pays tribute to the strength that must deeply unite the poor and subjugated. And so this invitation to love can sound the same as that of Christ's followers, because love stands proud against power, wealth, and the very works of mankind. Therefore, this is

---

14   Consisting therefore of the collections *Poems* (1933) and *The Still Centre* (1939), some lyrics from which were excluded from *Collected Poems*. The third collection of poems by Spender is *Poems of Dedication*, from 1947.

a communist chorus, with the coryphaeus addressing his 'companions' whom he exhorts to engage in an indomitable class struggle that must be handed down to successive generations. This transformative struggle seems to be the natural historical result of chaos and of a breakdown of the current system. Spender evokes three power centres on earth – the banks, the cathedrals and the governments. The invoked revolutionary explosion is, however, the typical dawn of communist and socialist chants since William Morris, that of the tiger[15] or the plant that sprouts new buds. The cult of the revolutionary hero emerges in 'The Prisoners', on the stoic acceptance of suffering, and the uselessness of anger over how creation was created, a creation which is unjust, divided, and not made following criteria of equity by its creator. Spender's two most celebrated poems on heroism are from 1931, and speak in reality of the impotence of the intellectual, whose only form of action is poetry, as spasmodically perfect as it might be. The first, 'The Truly Great', is emblematic of Spender's declarative, stentorian vein and of its incessant, indomitable heroic thirst. 'I think continually of those who were truly great': 'continuous' and 'continually' are terms that recur at every opportunity in Spender and are decidedly the favourite ones of his idiolect. This is a hyperbolic lyric, rich in absolute and frontal contrasts. The epos and above all the pathos of the quest are never levelled off, but assume biblical and romantic formulations and figurations, such as the lips which, touched by the ardent firebrand of prophetic investiture, are announcers of the Spirit incarnate in the song. The biblical prophet is fused with Shelley.[16] Traffic, an emblem of current civilization, is in antithesis with the flower of the spirit, which is suffocated by it. By this time the heroes have risen to a Valhalla of the purest air, while fog shrouds the plain, or in a kind of Elysian field of waving grass. They have been trailblazers, so that the shallow air is also marked by their honour; Icarus figures then, not melted

15   Polemically, not that of Eliot (Volume 7, § 95.2), which is, however, a devourer in 'Gerontion'.
16   The topic of a critical book by Spender, from 1952.

by the sun's rays.[17] The second, 'What I Expected', is devised in line with the Romantic symbolic codes of the fearless ascent towards unclimbed mountain peaks, and draws a surreal landscape like that of the ascension in Browning's 'Prospice'.[18] What is invoked is an athletic exercise, a 'continual straining' that strengthens and tempers. However, the poem takes note of the utopia of heroism, since humans are intrinsically weak, and also brought back to earth by the spectacles of a fallen humanity to be seen all around. And so the poetic 'I' is a discouraged Zarathustra who would like to be a superman but fails. As a non-believer, Spender only registers that corruption of mankind in history which Hopkins, in a sonnet almost literally imitated, complained of, then immediately forgot, hastening to take refuge under the wings of the holy redeeming Spirit. Hopkins is not far off since Spender himself yearns for a regenerated world, one that has gone back to being snow-white and innocent. The conclusion asserts that the poet can for now only contribute a surrogate of action, 'crystalline' poetry.[19] 'My Parents'[20] needs to be reversed in its meaning, and represents the imminence of Spender's crossing of the ditch that separates a bourgeois education spent in clover, and his ideal joining of the proletariat. The brutal, foul-mouthed and even violent ragamuffin brats that little Spender's family protected him from, are tomorrow's 'companions', and they ooze an indomitable energy, an animal-like courage, stripped also literally of those shoes and clothes that were the symbol of the wealthy. They suggest a harmonious and even feline force, and if they are little tigers they are close to the animal which is symbolic of the revolutionary; more exactly they are wolfhounds that bay against 'his world'; and

17   In it these heroes are different from a mysterious other Icarus who accepts the challenge, and is admired, but crashes to the ground ('Icarus').

18   However, the metaphor, even if much richer and broad-spectrum, is also the same as that found in *The Ascent of F 6* by Auden and Isherwood.

19   'The North', also entitled 'Polar Expedition', is about the intellectual who either escapes into the purity of the snows in a dream, and there vents his 'rage', or is induced to return to the alienating world of routine. In fact, it describes a 'continual hypnotized march' through snow. At the end of the exploration there can be a happier civilization with new laws. The poetic 'I' is broken up, lacerated, in crisis.

20   Also entitled, rather more vividly, 'Rough', something like 'Street Children'.

it is wrong, preposterous even, to pardon them. 'The Express' does not abandon the political path, and may constitute an allegory, albeit forced, of revolutionary energy. In itself, this is a late Futurist poem, exalting the anthropomorphic majesty of the train travelling through the night (and if this is so, then it imitates a celebrated and finer poem by Auden).[21] The aeroplane too is treated with the respect and stupor with which the Romantics idealized the hawk or the eagle. But if in the stratosphere fine pure air blows, on the ground there is urban decay and the world of the factory, and poverty and inhumanity.[22] 'Not Palaces' pays tribute to the tautological goal of a man to be a man. The poem is dream-like, but ultimately this is a party anthem, a revolutionary march with echoes of Brecht, like the repeated necessity not to cultivate sweet dreams that weaken, or radiant, totally uncritical utopias.

3. The short poem *Vienna* (1934), a dream-like rhapsody on Dollfuss's repression of the workers and socialist demonstrators, with the arrest and capital execution of the people responsible for the civil unrest, is of an indefinable, composite, multi-style nature, and the only modernist text ever hazarded by Spender. The first of its four parts is a splintered dramatic monologue without links, which in its oscillations and fluctuations echoes early Eliot.[23] Spender masks and unmasks himself as a young Englishman just arrived in Vienna in a *pension* whose vain chattering he reports, but in the frame of a forced thematic antithesis: forms of life that are death, and elsewhere a death that should be life, with the prolepsis of an example of sacrifice and resistance that will produce results. From worldly and frivolous scenarios the monologist shifts to a different, more disturbing reality. As well as a Prufrock who endures sexual temptations, clashing unconfessed impulses, and obscure senses of guilt, this *alter ego* is a kind of spitting image of Clough's Dipsychus. After the repression, the government imposes a false order, gilds the pill, and the unemployed, who also want paganly to live, are remissive and apathetic. The historical reconstruction

21   § 6.3.
22   'The Landscape near an Aerodrome'.
23   The analogies with Eliot were first mooted by W. Y. Tindall, quoted in Pandey 1982, 92 and n. 33.

is pushed, in less blazing and more orderly forms, as far as the flight, capture and execution of the leaders of the insurrection. Spender's absolutely best and most powerful work, *Trial of a Judge*,[24] is not strictly poetic, but a drama for voices. It was written and performed in 1938, but it symbolically referred to possible or probable facts of 1932 in Austria or Germany, and nostalgically commemorated a fatally weak liberalism or bogus conscience that could stand up to Hitler and check Nazism, but had tragically missed the opportunity. Petra, a young Marxist and Polish Jew, is killed by five Black Shirts who appear as condemned men to the judge who has sentenced them, in the form of a mental hearing and a dream-like trial. The judge fights unfailingly for absolute justice that is not a servant of power, and therefore equidistant between communism and fascism; however, after refusing to review the trial, absolve the fascists and condemn other communist suspects, he is overpowered, dismissed, and executed. For its part, the self-styled liberal and civil-libertarian government proclaims its decision to co-opt the head of the fascists into the government, to better control him. The goal of the play is the classic resistance to the perverse axiom 'might is right'. Spender has written a Brecht-like, didactic, overly allegorical *Lehrstück*, in effect a mixture of verse, prose and choruses, with scenes of vigour that are intermittently convincing.

4. Spender's poems on the Spanish Civil War may be added to those of the poets of the Great War, and form a belated chapter of their poetry for the humanitarian and protesting disdain with which the war is depicted. Close on hand are two poets, Owen for the 'pity' its horrors and human losses arouses, but without particular formal innovations; Sassoon, especially, for a poetry that is immediate, gripping, played out on contrasts and denunciation, sarcastic and satirical. Very Sassoon-like is 'Ultima Ratio Regum', with the anaphoras of the anonymous soldier no one could care less about, and with cannons as an expression of destructive power, in turn fuellers of the heavy war industry. Spender's perpetually rhetorical-sentimental vein all comes out in this poor little ignorant soldier who was

---

24   Praz (CLA, vol. II, 87–9) was rather perplexed by this play, particularly because Spender partisanly places the communists among the good, but cannot convince the spectator of what he is showing.

'a better target for a kiss'. The poem's secondary theme is the meditation on war as being inspired by the human thirst for power, which today crushes yesterday's winner in a deterministic chain. A warmongering god is still to blame for the war. After 1939, and when his first wife had left him, the crisis Spender's poetry centred around became all too private; the poems now mirror acrimony, regret and jealousy, but they leave us perplexed since they are too confessional, shapeless and anonymous. After long inactivity, in 1971 Spender published, almost unnoticed, his last collection, *The Generous Days*, of intimate and personal lyric poems, followed by other sparse and occasional ones up until his death.

§ 17. *MacNeice* I: A communist supporter without a party card*

If Spender continually asked himself 'Why do I write?', the question that periodically, if not suffocatingly, reverberates in Louis MacNeice (1907–1963) is: 'Who am I?'.[1] He never answered this question in his poetry, except in illusory, and thus only temporary and sedative forms. The poet turns to his infancy, reanimates it and reconstructs his own story; sex isolates and makes us happy and forgetful; or he rues a circle of 'liberal' humanist poets

---

*   *Collected Poems*, ed. E. R. Dodds, London 1966 and 1979, and, ed. P. McDonald, London 2007 (of whose respective arrangements of the corpus I shall speak below); two editions of *Selected Poems* were edited by Auden (London 1964) and M. Longley (London 1988). *Selected Prose*, ed. A. Heuser, Oxford 1990; *Selected Plays*, ed. A. Heuser and P. McDonald, Oxford 1993; *Letters*, ed. J. Allison, London 2010. J. Press, *Louis MacNeice*, London 1965; E. Smith, *Louis MacNeice*, New York 1970; W. McKinnon, *Apollo's Blended Dream: A Study of the Poetry of Louis MacNeice*, London 1971; D. B. Moore, *The Poetry of Louis MacNeice*, Leicester 1972; *Time Was Away: The World of Louis MacNeice*, ed. T. Brown and A. Reid, Dublin 1974; T. Brown, *Louis MacNeice: Sceptical Vision*, Dublin 1975; R. Marsack, *The Cave of Making: The Poetry of Louis MacNeice*, Oxford 1982, 1985; E. Longley, *Louis MacNeice: A Study*, London 1988; P. McDonald, *Louis MacNeice: The Poet in His Contexts*, Oxford 1991; M. O'Neill and G. Reeves, *Auden, MacNeice, Spender: The Thirties Poetry*, Houndmills 1992, 63–84 and 181–205; J. Stallworthy, *Louis MacNeice*, London 1995; *Louis MacNeice and His Influence*, ed. K. Devine and A. J. Peacock, Gerrards Cross 1998; R. D. Brown, *Louis MacNeice and the Poetry of the 1930s*, Tavistock 2009.

1   Recurring literally in the second section of *Autumn Journal*.

one by one, all decimated or distanced, or the university *bohème*. All that remains is the palingenetic dream of a classless society, and the Bolshevik revolution fought in the 1930s. But sooner or later everything is shattered. MacNeice's alienation is also political and historical, and shared by others especially in that decade; yet what gets the better of him is one that is purely existential, private and personal. His infancy is revisited because MacNeice felt defrauded, robbed of a childhood and adolescent past which, as we shall see, could only be idealized and caressed in virtue of a Paterian 'enchanted-distance fallacy'.[2] If MacNeice pursued redemption he applied, above all to himself, the following Cartesian principle: I remember, *ergo sum*. He felt himself born too late, or too quickly grown up. There was no need for Cyril Connolly to recall the primordial and archetypical situation in which poetry spontaneously bloomed in MacNeice: an imaginative, slightly discontented infancy, lived out in view of the sea ploughed by ships, like the Irish one washing Belfast where MacNeice was born, and watched from the house where he lived as a boy. Like Spender, MacNeice lost his mother at an early age, and had only the surrogate but incomplete affection of servants and tutors; the nightmares, traumas, and acute sensations of these origins would remain fixed in him, but relived in tranquillity. So MacNeice was one of many poets who grew up and was educated in the institution of the parsonage (his father was a Protestant rector of liberal and progressive views, later Bishop of Down), an environment that was not desirable in itself, but a cradle and a natural humus for poetry. It was he himself who several times told of the miasmic fumes, the mirages, the Fata Morganas, the childish phobias; while near the rectory lay a cemetery. At first sight a family air may be found with the Tennysons and the Brontë sisters, but with the obvious transpositions of time and place: around MacNeice's home rose the atavistic signs of the rural, small farms and fields dotted with factories as the symbol of incipient industrialization; and lastly the sea, or the trains of a nearby railway line that opened up a way of escape and an inviting slipway. Every element of this situation had a further auditory identity, so that the first blossoming of MacNeice's poetry is a catalogue

2   Volume 6, § 177.3 n. 78.

of sounds and onomatopoeias,[3] and at the same time a notebook of colour contrasts, between the misty and the sparkling, between the gloom of the house and the glare of the sunlight outside, above all between what MacNeice called the fluid or flow and petrifaction. The most celebrated of his autobiographical poems is 'Carrickfergus', an evocation of his childhood life against the background of invasions and epics of the rulers who landed in Ireland.[4] Amongst many others, this poem exemplifies MacNeice's rejection of the role of the Irish intellectual serviceable to nationalism. His irredentism is bland with respect to a Yeats earlier or a Heaney later.[5] The crepuscular theme and Celtic mythology do not appear intrusively in him, nor do we find poems with a historical background and of explicit militancy. The patriotic responsibility felt by all Irish is substantially evaded; indeed MacNeice even caused a scandal with his repeated yearnings to rid himself of the paralysing trammel of a one-way speech, to escape from a vicious circle and the particularity of Ireland, as issues forth from the sixteenth section of *Autumn Journal*. Like Joyce, he is cosmopolitan, and his first cultural opening is towards England. Joyce's Miss Ivors could have readily called him a West Briton. Before the Second World War he was already a camouflaged Irishman, a lecturer in Classics in English universities; a citizen of the world, a man of the institutions,[6] he directed the British Institute in Athens, was an imperial official in India, and worked

3   Longley 1988 (*A Study*), 6.
4   MacNeice organized his theoretical essay, 'Modern Poetry' (1938), as an autobiography, and another autobiography left interrupted is *The Strings Are False* (1965).
5   For Heaney's negative opinion of MacNeice, cf. N. Corcoran, 'Keeping the Colours New: Louis MacNeice in the Contemporary Poetry of Northern Ireland', in Devine and Peacock 1998, 114–32, in particular 118–20.
6   MacNeice's work as a radio playwright for the BBC has earned controversial opinions, some seeing it as a concession, others as the crowning of his art. Much admired is *The Dark Tower* (1946), a reworking, accompanied by Britten's music, of Browning's 'Childe Roland to the Dark Tower Came', which, like other plays, exploits the symbolism of the 'quest'. In his radio plays MacNeice effectively reworks those Nordic and Anglo-Saxon, Arthurian and above all Irish sagas that stand out by their absence in his poetry; that is, they corroborate and fuel the 'parabolic' turnaround of his last season; more of which later.

for the BBC from 1941 until his death. His communism was like a kind of snowstorm that melted the next day. He accompanied Auden on a trip to Iceland in 1936, out of which came a co-authored goliardic work; Auden esteemed his poetry so much that he edited it after MacNeice's death. But he had not fought in Spain. Compared to Spender, MacNeice is an enemy of every rhetoric and every sublime heroism. In particular, he defended the supreme rights of the imagination over any form of political commitment; and he did not blame excessively those who fled and sought shelter in America on the outbreak of war, because it was their artistic conscience that had the last word. With such ideas he could not possibly idealize the Party even for a moment, and still and suffocate his own individualism in mass assent.[7] And so we must conclude, a truth by now self-evident, that MacNeice was a sufficiently independent poet,[8] and the least associated and associable with, in fact the most tangential to, Auden's group and the Thirties poets.[9]

2. The misunderstanding of MacNeice as a politically committed poet, or Irish in the broadest and most traditional meaning of the word – that is, melancholy and tearful – has weighed not a little on the historical assessment of him.[10] Among his compatriots the question has raged until today about his betrayal of his mission, and the muffling and stifling of his patriotic voice;

7 The classic dichotomy of the Thirties writer – aesthete and pleasure-seeker, on the one hand, and a member of the proletariat and progressive, on the other – is evident, however, in a confession reported by Press 1965, 25.

8 MacNeice was excluded from the two anthologies edited by M. Roberts, *New Signatures* (1932) and *New Country* (1933), which announced the advent of a new social order and of a 'new Lenin'.

9 Longley 1988 (*A Study*), 35, compiles a list of the experiences the poet had in common with them and the more numerous omissions (he had not been in Berlin, he had not been a paid-up communist, etc.), with respect to a sort of usual initiation into the committed poetry of the 1930s. But MacNeice was not only a defector by default. One declaration is very strong: the communist camaraderie replaced bourgeois 'romance', and led to an idealization of homosexuality (quoted in Marsack 1985, 22–3). Homosexuality is an implied requisite of the Thirties poets' mystique which is absent in MacNeice.

10 The prudent and normally impeccably reliable HYN partially falls into this (cf. 334, 369 and *passim*).

and the Irish critics have thrown themselves headlong into this diatribe with their typical self-referential pride, moreover highlighting where and how this exile proclaims and confirms the indestructibility of his roots, with a two-pronged awareness and nostalgia, of an almost Dantesque stamp.[11] Enthusiasm and passion are flagrantly *in absentia* in MacNeice, who built himself an eighteenth-century or neoclassical poetics, one typical of the caustic and ever lukewarm observer, at times apparently even half-hearted and apathetic, able to transfuse memories into rigidly closed, sedate, guarded forms, framed in clean and defined prosodies. All his materials, even while being occasionally presented in free verse, are mostly filtered and swathed in the exquisite and even too dapper and mechanical wrapping of rhyme, and arranged in measures of the classical tradition, including the tercet.[12] When MacNeice is not objectifying his autobiography, he uses the same filter in observing the fragmented, chaotic, stunned reality of the period between the two world wars, and the same empty and insensate daily routine.[13] In this way he becomes a fine classicist poet[14] and an unknowing precursor of the objectives and poetics of the Movement of Davie and Larkin.[15] The first presage is perspicuity, that is, a poetry oriented to the reader,[16] to whom poetry must speak by communicating an emotional experience or an Arnold-style criticism of life; hence the flat language and the preference for

11   Questions touched on in McDonald 1991, 4–9 and 204–29, and of course in Devine and Peacock 1998, with a discussion of MacNeice's influences on later Irish poets.

12   An exemplary observation can be found in 'Modern Poetry', quoted in Longley 1988 (*A Study*), 107: 'the poet's *matter* tends [in free verse] to appear insufficiently digested or distilled; a technical problem often helps the poet to get his own meaning clear to himself'.

13   This attitude, subjective and objective at the same time, was defined by MacNeice as an 'amalgam' in 'Modern Poetry' (cit. in McDonald 1991, 65).

14   For Auden (an uncollected 1939 item quoted in Marsack 1985, 142), MacNeice was 'perhaps the only poet today whose work is directly in the classical tradition'.

15   On Larkin's anticipations in MacNeice, and Larkin's favourable opinion on him, cf. Longley 1988 (*A Study*), xii and 47.

16   Cf. the declaration quoted in Longley 1988 (*A Study*), 96.

the anecdotal tale, naturally graceful, lucid and disillusioned. In his manifestos, MacNeice expounded, without false modesty, a low profile aesthetic, disarmed and even self-destructive: in the poet were fused the skills of the entertainer, the critic and the informer, he said, and making poetry was equivalent to recording a fact 'modified by his own emotional reaction to it'.[17] The essay 'Modern Poetry' (1938), of those that are more sensate and concrete in their premises and objectives, insists on a close correspondence between rhythmic-prosodic signifier and signified, and holds up the primacy of naturalness. The rhythmic accent must fall on the important words, he observes, attacking Hopkins and criticizing his eccentricities and extravagances. He is an ultra-conservative entrenched in rhythmic patterns and rhyme. Eliot was deemed a 'highly sensitive aesthete', and MacNeice's pioneering critical study of Yeats (1941) rests on the thesis that the poet had not managed to reconcile the poles of esotericism and public interest.[18] Since MacNeice had been a university professor poet, and a translator of the classics, his poetic book momentarily suggests a comparison with Housman's; it was MacNeice himself, in his later years, who saluted Horace, who along with Catullus was close to him in scepticism, apathy and disillusionment.[19] As a sensationist philosopher, he stands against abstractions in favour of experiential reality, against monism and the philosophers of being, like Parmenides, rather than becoming. 'The Window' is emblematic when it describes a praxis of tension towards asymptotic objectives; art freezes antitheses to life, a life that lies in always transcending the real to reach the form. In reality in MacNeice, an enemy of every Platonism, and a follower of Aristotle, a little Platonism does survive.

3. Appreciated for his early and final production, a veil of silence is normally drawn over MacNeice's vast median zone. For example, Auden, a friend and admirer, skipped this textual segment in his anthological

17   Quoted in Marsack 1985, 42.
18   Longley 1988 (*A Study*), 99.
19   The lyric 'Epitaph for Liberal Poets' recognizes Catullus as the singer of individuality, and the last of those who were not 'adaptable'; MacNeice's lot was 'no less cold', and he hopes that the 'frozen' words that he and his ilk will leave could melt in the future 'to accentuate a thirst'.

selection, including nothing of *Autumn Sequel*, and implicitly deeming it a false step. This work, and to a certain extent also a great deal of MacNeice's poetry, was taken as arid, didactic and reflective, or simply phenomenological and narrative, copying the Augustan model – verging on gags, the burlesque, the *jeu d'esprit*, the devices of light verse – and the pre-Romantics, and was a type of poetry that was as unfashionable, at the time when MacNeice began, as the dramatic monologues of the Victorians. Recurring significantly in the first appraisals was the disagreeable characteristic for which Eliot had blamed Browning and Tennyson, namely, that MacNeice was a 'ruminator' and had the flaw of a certain freewheeling prolixity. Further dangers were those of transcribing impressions without filters, and a diction that was too prosaic. It is true that MacNeice's Augustanism is not parodic, but natural or involuntary; it is also true that in him there are no radical stylistic upheavals, at least to the extent apparent to a certain group of critics. Once his repertoire of subjects, affections and situations had been established, MacNeice repeated it *ad infinitum*. The collections he published are many, a small *monstrum* of versifying facility and in a career lasting 'only' thirty to thirty-five years. The 1966 edition of the collected poems, partially edited and arranged by MacNeice himself, includes several hundreds of pages and just under half a thousand lyrics without counting those omitted; it also shows that the internal chronology is inconspicuous, and can even take second place because, I repeat, it is not marked by any real turning points. The internal segmentation of this 1966 edition is into fourteen time spans that do not exactly match the published collections. Auden himself overturned the chronology in his selection by not indicating the dates of composition and by bringing forward and postponing single poems as he pleased.[20] I am not saying that MacNeice's last or intermediate works can be readily exchanged for the first ones, and that MacNeice is a poet without internal times and periods. He is, however, the poet of a certain type of lyric whose formulas and emphases are repetitive, and the typical poet of the sequence and the series. If this is the case, it indicates his incapacity to renew himself, or even to fall silent to avoid repeating

20   The demarcations between the collections have been restored in the latest edition from 2007, edited by P. McDonald.

himself. It should therefore be expected that MacNeice wrote periodic poems of revisitation. As late as 1950 came 'Day of Renewal', a bloated, muddled poem of summary and of anniversary, which reviews the stages of his story and with some difficulty discerns a teleology.

§ 18. *MacNeice II: The Autumn calendars*

The abundant mosaic of MacNeice's lyric poetry finds its four vital exceptional moments, which must remain fixed points of twentieth-century poetry, in as many poetic genres ingeniously reinvented and updated from the classics. They are the eclogue, the two cycles of poems in the form of a calendar, *Autumn Journal* and *Autumn Sequel*, and, at the end of his career, the absurd and estranging parables of contemporary alienation. What marked MacNeice's debut (already proleptic in the collection's bizarre title – *Blind Fireworks*, from 1929) is a poetry that is eccentric, skilful and capricious, with picturesque, surreal effects and calligraphic devices (such as the scheme of the rhymes inside each stanza in a small *tour de force*), or sounds, with lists of words developed from a single root in chains of assonance, consonance or phonic similarities, similar to certain items of Hopkins's childhood diary.[21] This was a dead-end, embraced above all in homage to fashion and as a result a poetic attitude that was less than heartfelt. MacNeice then became anchored in the concrete, the here-and-now of the experience in all its spectacles, and already at that stage, as counterbalance, he wrote more conventional poems frankly taking into account the inexorable passing of time. In his second collection, four sweeping 'modern eclogues' are thus entitled because they form scenes to be played out between two real characters or human types at a crossroads. The precedent was not Yeats's early poetry in this form, nor was that of John Davidson who reused the same title;[22] rather, this is the first case of a refined reanimation and re-adaptation of a classical genre. The dialogues staged in these eclogues are often inconclusive, and, precisely because of this,

21   HYN, 332, and McDonald 1991, 49, notice a youthful 'cult of the Sitwells', no doubt
      traceable.
22   Volume 6, § 246.5.

also look ahead from afar to Beckett, an exact peer,[23] and, earlier on, back to Synge. The device and the stylistic traits of the eclogue activate the clash between the transient and the eternal, and maieutically lead to an admission that the renewal of the world at Christmas time is merely nominal ('An Eclogue for Christmas'). At the same time, signs of a Synge- and Beckett-like theatre, as I mentioned, are the encounter on the road of two wayfarers, with voices that are distinct and separate but at the same time facets of a single consciousness. Starting from factual and heartfelt considerations they arrive at a dystopian upcoming future, awaiting a tomorrow that looks to be populated by grotesque fantasies, thus subverting the conventional picture of a palingenetic Christmas full of promises. This fantasizing is also political, painting behind the parodic veil, in a subtly oblique way and with few concrete and many other attenuated metaphorical references to contemporaneity, the absence of perspectives among workers in the early 1930s. More surreal still, and echoing Synge's plays, is the eclogue of the two shepherds met by Death, who mocks them, by a 'five-barred gate';[24] also two motherless orphans rant and rave over the contemporary absence of future prospects.[25]

2. *Poems* (1935) gathers the notebooks and notes in verse of a poet wandering among the urban sights, and it already forms a diorama of city scenes that are not particularly festive, or are more exactly a kaleidoscope of the mechanical, repetitive movements of a humanity that sets itself minimal objectives, stupefied by the rhythm of modern life. When the holiday comes, the people feel free and fling themselves into a giddy vortex, until they become prisoners once more. Poems of urban illusion strike for Italian readers a Leopardi-like chord because of the vain attempt to stop time, and because the possession of things is illusory, since they are only empty shells. 'Snow' is the epiphany of a world that is surprising in its strangeness and unpredictability, as in Hopkins ('I [...] feel / The drunkenness of things being various', a

---

23   On the discovery of Beckett, and MacNeice's admiration for him, cf. Longley 1988 (*A Study*), 150–1.

24   In another poem, not formally titled as an eclogue, ancient Icelandic wayfarers speak with a god.

25   This eclogue – 'between the Motherless' – was written after MacNeice's wife Mary suddenly left him, leaving their son Daniel practically an orphan.

line that could have been penned by the author of the sonnet 'Pied Beauty').
From the expedition to Iceland with Auden an explosion of playful poetry
burst forth that masked a desire for escape and novelty and the boredom of
life back home. This was also a journey made with the aim of political disengagement and as reflection from a distance, unburdened and distracted,
on the troubled, gory facts of Europe (Spain, the first rumblings of war).
Iceland is an alternative myth, a pendant, or even an antidote. Overflowing
with astonished evocations of a civilization that is more dreaming and sensitive to the marvellous is 'The Hebrides', the timeless fairy isles ('the tyrant
time / Has no clock towers'). Virgin lands, 'unspoiled by contact' with the
outside, backward and primitive, they are evoked in an epic-biblical tone, as
a primordial Eden of existences in a community dimension, before alienation. 'Sunday Morning' is one of MacNeice's most celebrated poems, above
all because of the closing image of the bells which, in a nightmare, become
speaking skulls, and for the recollection of the ingrained torment of Sunday
religious practices. In his poems from 1937 and 1938 MacNeice shows himself
to be completely focused on the theme of the ineluctable passing of time,
whose repercussion is nostalgia. From then on he was to write more lyrics
filled with crepuscular, worn-out melancholy, and a touch feminine (such
as 'The Sunlight on the Garden', Elizabethan, Marvellian, or even vaguely
Byronian), or of a slightly more masculine romantic escapism, and envisioning
paradises that must be left to return to the regime of the real. Their prosody
is that of suffused slender quatrains, oozing *Sehnsucht* that peels apart in
the face of the impelling call of life. Among the disillusioned is the delicate,
lazy, voluptuous and remembering poet, tossed into a hostile world. They
are not then powerful and virile poems, but celebrations of individualistic,
hedonistic, oriental indolence, and of an exquisitely private range. 'Christmas
Shopping' yet again recalls Leopardi as a meditation in verse on the empty
euphoria of Christmas, a recurrent theme in MacNeice. And 'Bagpipe Music'
surprises us because the poet abandons elegy for stinging sarcasm, a rich and
exuberant diction and the telegraphic staccato, imitating newspaper headlines , the simplified language of the blacks[26] or the nursery rhyme. This is a

26   In a cultivated and elegant poet like MacNeice, one notices the deliberately marked
anaphora of the slang expression 'it's no go'.

coarse, rough ballad with grotesque, visionary spectacles of contemporary civilization dominated by lucre, avidity, and low sensationalism.

3. *Autumn Journal* (1939), in twenty-four sections, may be considered MacNeice's best, most accomplished and enduring work. With few exceptions it is his most unified and continuous, not merely a series of short independent lyrics; though not exactly original in its configuration, it is also a reanimation and an adaptation. Tennyson's *In Memoriam* had been a calendar illustrating the classic Victorian parable that moves from temptation to non-being, then to the renunciation and negation of life and of a creative plan, and finally to the exhortation to oneself and others to live and live again, and to discover new motives for surviving and continuing to hope. MacNeice, who organized his work in fewer sections which nonetheless mimic Tennyson's quatrains (even vaguely reproducing the changing rhyme scheme), describes the fear of waking up in a world without God and without gods; and craves Nirvana, disappearance, non-being and annihilation – were it not for the symbol of the spider, which, in weaving its web, believes in becoming rather than non-being, and teaches renewal and demonstrates it. The number of MacNeice's sections is that of classic epics; however, in the end the pilgrim comes out, like Dante, to metaphorically see the stars. The basic antithesis is from the beginning that between isolation and communitarian impetus, and that between the meditating poet who asks and the poet who in the end finds an answer. Clough's *Amours de Voyage* is also a journal, and an interweaving and embroidery of private and public which evidently lies behind MacNeice's and echoes it,[27] above all because it is not a wholly lyrical journal, and in fact it often slips into the sarcastic, the purely digressive, the macaronic even. A third lurking presence is the Byron of *Don Juan*, in that, like Byron, MacNeice can readily and breezily range over a variety of registers, including the pedestrian and scurrilous.[28] This is an unmistakable echo when MacNeice, on the one

27   A shrewd critic, albeit often brusque in his exposition, like Marsack 1985, 52, does not
      fail to notice this. Clough is cited by Press 1965, 33, above all, however, for a religious
      creed 'on a razor's edge', as I am arguing.
28   These marked analogies or affinities with Byron, which will also be found in *Autumn
      Sequel*, are not normally recognized by MacNeice's critics.

hand, has no fear of making metapoetic considerations, and on the other of revealing a philosophy of life that admits primordial needs, and ridicules idealisms, scruples and sublimations. From Byron MacNeice took a frank revolt against the soul and the spirit, even if in the end the lyrical register gains the upper hand, with the Christmas snow inviting to sleep and dream, and what is dreamed and expressly hoped for is a better world. However, the political denunciation is enfeebled by the congenital scepticism of a poet who, despite aspiring to a fairer life in the distribution of privileges, is aware of an unbeatable system, in which those at the bottom wish to dominate and enslave those at the top (hence 'victory for one implies another's defeat'), and fears the perils of a depersonalized society or of a popular democracy. This would cause a lowering of the cultural level (but it is a tempting voice, in reality Tennyson-like, and hushed up, and the poet soon shakes himself out of his indolence and irrational fears). Love brings a meaning and an impulse, albeit Catullian, to the waiting for good happy things; however, what the journal increasingly accumulates, more than future prospects, are memories of radiant moments of the past, and the dominant dimension is remembrance, not always devoid of disillusionment in the end. Greek philosophy invited us to *carpe diem*, yet even in the world of Greece there were squalid sides, and slavery was permitted. MacNeice's expectations as a student on arriving in England were not those of Spender, but of a pleasure-seeking, joyful, hedonistic, romantic, anti-platonic life: he did not yearn for forms, but for harmonious conjunctions of body and spirit. The sixteenth section takes an inevitable stance on the controversial relationship between MacNeice and his compatriots, and emphasizes a heated criticism of the perennial climate of vendetta and guerrilla warfare. In the eighteenth there are echoes of Lawrence, with the end of a bucolic, pastoral and Arcadian England, by this time squalidly defaced by factories. MacNeice increasingly confesses himself more tempted by disengagement and by the choice of an ancient Epicurean scepticism; snowy London inspires a flight towards the south and Spain that is a holiday filled with food and love. And yet he never ceases to represent himself 'on the razor's edge', imploring God, should He exist, to smooth the antinomies of a man who feels sure because he denies, or is free. The last section seems like a premonitory song and is therefore hope-filled, and it hails returns, resurrections and signs of renewal.

If nothing else, this is the moment to rest, to recuperate and become strong again to fight, to wake up in a regenerated, harmonious community. In reality, the paean to change sounds forced and false, and a provisional hasty closure dictated only to avoid prolonging the sense of scepticism.

4. The war inspired MacNeice to produce a highly successful and very well-known lyric poem, 'Prayer before Birth', with something of Dylan Thomas in its theme, its vaguely *calligramme* form and unusual linguistic-prosodic acrobatics.[29] A peroration that is certainly humanistic, advocating the maintenance of the gifts of independence, dignity and free will, which the war threatened to quash, it is also, however, a rhetorical poem of a fame greater than its merits; and yet it does express in a memorable formulation MacNeice's frequent yearnings for self-annulment, and his desires to bury himself in subterranean worlds 'of amber', verging on non-being. In other poems he is a man who must begin again from zero after unlearning to be a man and a human being. In fact, he goes against the grain with a poetry that deliberately forgets and exorcizes the war, and turns, for example, to the libertine or the nightclub stripper. 'The Springboard' is the short anecdote of a high diver undecided whether to descend into the world, and diffident since he believes his arrival will not be renewing and regenerating; this is also, in many linguistic clues, a de-automatizing metaphor for the incarnation of a doubting Christ. 'When We Were Children' is a spirited song, nostalgic for a time when multiform reality was associated with colours, and vanished in a time when abstraction prevails. For a long time after 1940, MacNiece published a poetry that was rather automatic and anonymous, following the timidly varied paths and forms of his previous collections. It comes natural to remember once again Tennyson after *In Memoriam*, the author of laboured lyrics and ballads, or even 'novelettes', as flat as those of MacNeice on the crazy gardener, or of sentimental anecdotes. The sudden adoption of a more irregular, even free prosody, seemingly improvised and slovenly, together with an amateurish desire to philosophize, also recalls late Browning. This reflective and discursive poetry unfolds, on the other hand, in massive measures, opulent forms, verses of an uncommon length and

29   Like Dylan Thomas, MacNeice admired George Herbert.

lush arguments. Drifting parentheses predominate over the lyrical impulse, undermining the unit of measurement. MacNeice pays the price of such boundless verbal developments and such hazy smoke-screens, delivering on the whole common truths of a practical and simple philosophy, of modest, even self-evident import, ingenuous and pedestrian despite being presented as oracular. The section of poems from 1950 to 1951, which roughly matches the collection *Ten Burnt Offerings*[30] (1952), moves from an epigraph marked by pessimism, with the poet whose word is a burnt cross or offering, yet burnt so that the word would live. The biographical context is that of the period MacNeice spent in Greece, when, oddly enough, he was unable to take advantage of the propitious occasion, and wrote lyrics that reach one of his nadirs, unbalanced in their measure, frayed and formless, mostly the freewheeling monologues of a 'gabbler' who embellishes the anecdote or key point of the poem with too many inert parentheses. Alongside Homeric reconstructions, such as Ulysses' monologues yearning for return, we find the kitsch elegy to a dead cat in four long sections,[31] the hyperbolic paean to a loved one, various reminiscences inspired by places, including a poor inconclusive rhapsody on Byron's Greek exploits.

5. After various wearisome trials and far from convincing examples of sprawling poetry, *Autumn Sequel* (1954) is again a central work: precise, finished, formally squared off, despite its organizing principle being an associationist memory which is *ipso facto* ungovernable. As a sequence of cantos, numbering twenty-six in total, it could sit under the wing and shadow of Pound and above all Dante, with the further clue of the metre in tercets *aba bcb cdc*, hence with the last syllable of the second line of the tercet propulsively launching the rhyme of the following one in a cast-iron chain. In fact, the work accumulates, from a new and later autumn, that of 1953, evocations of the living and above all the deceased. Original in its conception, it belongs to the periodic British katabases, and is the poet's debt to his retrospective mania, looking ahead – this is often neglected and overlooked – to Heaney's *Station Island*. Unanimous

---

30 Burnt offerings, in fact, in homage 'to a god / Who does not answer to his name'.
31 The accusation of sentimentalism is discussed but not exactly parried in the fourth section.

opinion is customarily perplexed or negative, but only because one expects a poem that is lyrically evocative, emotionally involved and even enraptured, on the part of a poet who instead remains controlled and objective, and who echoes and imitates once again, and above all, Byron. It is also negative for its odd, motiveless English ostracism against *terza rima*, a metre with which it would seem impossible to write fine poetry in this language. My own opinion is rather more Solomonic. The shortcomings are partially due to MacNeice himself, yet they are of the same nature as the qualities or at least the characteristics and idiosyncrasies of the author of *Don Juan*. They include, for example, the cataloguing and listing, the digression and the improvisation, the metanarrative parentheses, the adages on art and aesthetics that can seem pedestrian and facile. What is especially Byronic is the caustic, sceptical humour, never truly cheerful; and also the abrupt transition from the historical to the contemporary register – bathos, in other words. The truth is that *Autumn Sequel* never breaches the boundary of empathy and identification, to the point of even destroying at an early stage any small concession to one or the other. MacNeice, then, who in one canto declares himself little sympathetic to Augustan poetry, is, if anything, Augustan in this collection, which is never coarse and always courteous, elegant, as easy-going and smooth as a poem by Pope. Certain procedural flaws are due to a poetic form without immediate predecessors, remarkably and boldly experimental. The impression soon forms that the poet is protracting and playing for time, that what he says is not fresh, the clichés increasingly frequent, the transitions heavy, and the inlay manufactured: in short, that there is much padding, with extensive stretches lacking diapason, calligraphic interludes of atmosphere, scenes of a London in different colours with the change of season, but in passages that are 'purple', smug and not strictly necessary. In reality, this is a diary deliberately made of any old routine facts, which must not and cannot be related since they serve to illustrate the lack of sense in life and its inertia. No choice is apparent, nor a reduction of life to its emotional climaxes; everything, conversely, is run-of-the-mill;[32] hence a release of tension or stridency between the

---

32   The tenth canto consists mostly of a versification of the news the poet reads in his morning newspaper.

facts and the form cladding them, the ingeniously rhymed tercet. The risk run is very high. Unquestionably, some cantos are mediocre, not to say so modest and poor, tangled and confused, that they can be readily skipped; the text is mottled, discontinuous and irregular, with highs and lows, and it shows its better side when MacNeice does what he does best, namely, recalling clearly and vividly.[33] This does not exclude a highly controlled, skilful, associative swinging between present and past, since what is happening in the historical present is a cyclical repetition and a recourse along the lines of an ironic, even estranged mythical method.[34] The names of his deceased friends are disguised and changed since they have consciously become part of the immortal gallery of Lycidas and Thyrsis.[35] At the end, Dante reappears to support the allegory of a historical pessimism palely open to hope. Bitter in realizing the demobilization of ideals, the vanishing of resounding dreams of glory and the post-war proclamations, MacNeice records a reality that has returned to how it always was. And yet this second diary doubles and repeats the pattern of the first: chronically and cyclically the poet feels the constriction of living in a 'waste land', but must remain strong. MacNeice persists in his eternal wrangling with time, in his attempt to check it, just by describing its inexorable passing. The obligatory passage, the hinge of the grammar of memory, is the revisitation: of Wales, Norwich and Oxford, journeys

33   The seventeenth canto includes one of the freshest memories, though it is a fatally transitory epiphany: that of the Catholic domestic cook and the Irish fairy-tales, and the fears of the winter night.

34   One cyclical internal situation is the spectral dialogue with a 'master', in whom Thucydides is discovered.

35   Gwylim is the name given to Dylan Thomas, who dies during the imaginary time of the collection, and whose figure is long remembered with MacNeice's usual, vigilant pathos (the reason for this pseudonym is explained below in § 73.3). In the second canto, Gwylim-Thomas is the poet who, with his inventions, is able to extract the pincers of the spider that threatens to bite him, that of conventions. MacNeice must resignedly lament his impotence in creating castles in the air and sublime buildings in a daily grind that wilts creative desire, and he owns up to being that poet who, after the war, works for the very institutions he criticizes. As for the other pseudonyms used, Egdon is Auden, and Boyce is the classicist Dodds, the future editor of MacNeice's poems.

back in time that make the poet realize his fatigue and therefore the pain of his living the present, caught unprepared and fallen. MacNeice's humanism again lies in the elegy of an elite, an intellectual collectivity of vigilant, integral and independent beings: it lies in the repetition of the appeal already heard in the poem in favour of 'liberal poets', who are the real humanists.

6. MacNeice emerged from this poem with uncollected lyrics that stand out because, while his anecdotes had always been more often anonymous and second-rate, he suddenly devises or records some others that chill and arrest by their sinister, enigmatic and visionary diversity. The objectifying poet is now a little less objective, and he moulds the event and reduces and tames only *in extremis* a dream-like and ghostly potential that seems ungovernable, as in the burning immediacy of 'Beni Hasan'. The cycle *Visitations* (1957) contains lyrics that recall particular epiphanic moments of a reality that even dazzles the observer, who benefits from it, feels it, and quivers with further prospects. Small transformations and formal rotations, like the lullaby, the nursery rhyme, parallelism, anaphora, and unusual arrangements (such as 'notes', on 'incorrigible' forms and essences in a quadriptych of dandelions, cats, corncrakes and the sea), rub shoulders with other casual ones, in the reign of the curious, the playful, the Biedermeier, alternating with returns to the old chatty manner, occasional ditties and fugacious fillers. Ultimately, MacNeice cannot avoid being garrulous and expansive, never once dry, definitive, and powerful. *Solstices* (1961) is effectively made up of bitter and more acute reflections, and it moves onto urban spectacles caught in their pungency and discretion (such as the solitary, shy little clerk in the park). 'The Blasphemies' is unable to deny a disconsolate nihilism, almost a defeatism which, among the contemporary ideological chaos and disorder, can find no valid substitute for religious faith. *The Burning Perch* (1963) emits an acrid polemical flavour in its collection of nonsense nursery rhymes, glimpses of an estranged urban reality, absurd and even downright weird as in the spectral 'The Taxis', a fourfold burlesque, pantomime-like case of a taxi ride aping the journey of death. The tenuous novelty that transpires from this very last season are the short parables or ballads on urban neuroses and alienation, the eruption of death in the everyday scenario, the

contemptuous and iconoclastic lyric poem, the euphuistic tongue twisters on the disappointment of life.

§ 19. *Day Lewis* I: Anthems and choruses of the marching proletariat*
Some time ago a reviewer teasingly deemed Cecil Day Lewis[1] (1904–1972) to be close to becoming a mere footnote.[2] This could be the consequential nadir of a form of ostracism so livid and obstinate as to seem preconceived. The poet was pigeonholed among the writers whom the British call 'bombastic', that is, braggarts and show-offs; with an ill-concealed xenophobia they evidently equated him with a reanimation of the stage Irishman, a descendant of Barry Lyndon, a quick-change artist with seven lives able to adapt to all reversals (and the poet was also a native of Ireland). Legendary and devoid of half measures are the slatings that were inflicted on him, with the main imputation of being a conformist rebel, that is, a sham, in fact a phony revolutionary. They found him, in addition, an amateur who sought unsuccessfully to excel and vie above all with Auden, over whom he could boast a certain temporal advantage, being three years older and having debuted earlier, at twenty-five, with two small volumes of poetry.[3] A few appraisals even find that his detective novels, written

---

*   *Collected Poems 1954*, London 1954, and *The Complete Poems*, ed. J. Balcon, London 1992. *Selected Poems*, edited by the author, Harmondsworth 1951, 1957, 1969 and 1974 with successive expansions, is organized in reverse, starting from the last collection published. Another selection is edited by I. Parsons, London 1977. C. Dyment, *Cecil Day Lewis*, London 1955 and 1963; S. Day Lewis, *C. Day Lewis: An English Literary Life*, London 1980; A. Gelpi, *Living in Time: The Poetry of C. Day Lewis*, New York and Oxford 1998; P. Stanford, *C. Day Lewis: A Life*, London 2007.

1   A certain confusion, partially caused by Day Lewis himself, surrounds the way of mentioning and writing the poet's surname, which was and remains for some Day-Lewis, or simply Lewis. My spelling is the one the poet himself indicated as the most correct (cf. Gelpi 1998, 11–12), and in this work, including the Indexes, the poet will be mentioned and classified by the initial D.

2   Review of a new *Selected Poems*, by W. Wotten, in *TLS*, 3 June 2005, 6–7.

3   Since 1934, Day Lewis had been the bugbear and sworn enemy of the critic Geoffrey Grigson (Gelpi 1998, 43, 58, 78 and *passim*). Virginia Woolf published, for her

under the pseudonym of Nicholas Blake, are masterpieces of their genre, and far outstrip the value of his poetry. This critical view only holds good, if at all, for the decade of the 1930s. His political poetry is insistent, but rings forced and insincere. It can also be accused of plagiarism, since it is modelled on the classic and archetypical image of the quest, which has become a surreal journey towards a peak and which is therefore a climb, as was memorably told and represented in Auden's *The Ascent of F 6*. The revolutionary march as an approach to an asymptotic yet real destination is an archetype of Thirties political poetry.[4] That this was a false and temporary masking, the contagion of a collective possession, can be seen from an ineradicable traditionalist *côté*. In 1936, Day Lewis joined the Party, but two years later he had already resigned; yet as an 'independent' communist he continued to write for conservative dailies. His ardour spent, he had become, on the eve of the war, integrated; he had accepted public positions of prestige, such as that of Poet Laureate, and had become part of the very system he had attacked. MacNeice had not advanced so far forward, in fact he had stayed behind to watch. Common established opinion agrees that his best came after the political decade, when his capacity to enclose intense emotion in precise formal modules emerged; and it was generally deemed superior to that of Spender and almost even of MacNeice. But this is not a particularly rehabilitating compliment. Having shelved his political poetry, Day Lewis basically revived the Georgian poet 'who has lost his way', forced to embrace a poetry of peroration and revolutionary persuasion, and who fluidly sets down – as soon as he can, at times succumbing to a slapdash attitude – the basic elements of poetry: a soul profoundly sensitive to nature, a genuine poet who sings of frustrated and unrequited, or even fulfilling love, in all its correlatives or contrasts, and therefore in the setting of nature itself; a lyric poet of exquisite Elizabethan and Caroline affiliations, or more precisely Marvellian. In the foreword to his selected poems, which first came out in 1951, Day Lewis had difficulty to find continuity in his poetry, and noted a series of 're-departures from

---

Hogarth Press, six books of poetry by Day Lewis (Gelpi 1998, 79), but distanced herself from him in her well-known essay on the 'leaning tower' (§ 1.2) from 1940.

4   Gelpi 1998, 39.

zero'. He also, contradicting the critics, attributed a progressive refinement to his poetry, a greater variety and flexibility, not a decline. In 1931, he held that poetry should be 'a kind of transmitting station';[5] in his book *A Hope for Poetry* (1934) he specified that the poet should find his own tradition, and that a solid and robust link with tradition is cloaked 'in the language of revolution'.[6] In his 1951 foreword, Day Lewis sounds like T. S. Eliot on a small scale: every critical operation must be above all appreciative, that is, one must sample and enjoy a poem before critically evaluating it, and every poem is unique and at the same time imitative, and its 'place in tradition' must be ascertained (with a manifest paraphrase of the theories in 'Tradition and the Individual Talent'). What is a poem? A remembering, the reliving of an acute experience in order to explain it, first of all to ourselves, and then to others. It is the act of a poet who interprets the meaning of an experience for him- or herself.

2. Day Lewis had originally much in common with MacNeice. They were both born in Ireland but were soon transplanted to England; the son of an ecclesiastical father and master, Day Lewis lost his mother at the age of four. Both followed the path from public school to Oxford University. He too became a classicist and a translator (of Virgil,[7] of Valéry's *Cimetière marin*, of Baudelaire), and like MacNeice, an editor of others' poetry, such as that of Owen, as well as a brilliant, or at any rate productive, literary critic. From the cocoon-like isolation of the parochial environment, the teenage Day Lewis emigrated while still young with his father and maternal aunt to the mining district of Nottingham, where he witnessed the workers' unrest and saw the virgin forest of Robin Hood marred by the slag from the mines. However, during the 1926 strike he was a collaborationist and

---

5   HYN, 96.

6   HYN, 157–8.

7   On the importance and particular meaning of Virgil, and on the Virgilian revival of the 1930s in England, intertwined with that of Hardy, cf. Gelpi 1998, 83–92. The translation of Latin classics is, for example, the antechamber of the classical-style, Virgilian and narcotic poetry of Charles Hubert Sisson (1914–2003), and of the mythological and Arthurian embroideries of John Heath-Stubbs (1918–2006), equally eclectic and somewhat superficial.

handed out a mediation leaflet inspired by the Archbishop of Canterbury.[8] After graduating, he taught in schools, scandalizing the conformists with poems of a communist tendency and above all explicitly sexual. His first collection, *Beechen Vigil* (1925), is a short book, sober in its quantity and measure, and so shy and modest that it does not allow us to identify a physiognomy and a series of personal quirks. If anything, it is distinguished by an elegant and precise, clean but not lavish vein of Georgian ascendancy, with objective anecdotes of a non-urban environment, set in the countryside and on the riverbank, and delicate but not mawkish descriptions of moods and amorous frustration. The poet speaking here is well-bred, languorous, seeking to rouse himself from immobilizing reveries that distance him from concreteness, as in the fairy stories or nursery rhymes of the boy poet in harmony with nature. More exactly, this is an escapist poetry that delights in songs, fantasies, surreality, natural swoons and self-projections into mythical roles, such as the Arcadian shepherd boy or the Arthurian knight as protector of the beauty of the chatelaine maiden. Symptomatically, the appointed place is the forest. *Country Comets* (1928) has a more erotic backdrop, and is marked by disappointment objectivized with serene melancholy, in an impassive nature from which the poet cannot learn to instil in himself a resolute acceptance. But this is a series of moods that are even idealized behind the veil of form, in accordance with the codes of courtly love, rather than immediate and mimetic ejaculations – versifications that are often elegant, imitative of the canon of the great erotic poetry, namely, the seventeenth century (the epigraph is by Marvell), hence moderately concettist.[9] Nature vainly invites the poet, despite his self-control, to react in a manly steadfast way, and this decisive, bold impetus *ad extra* is described and perhaps realized in at least one poem, even if it remains ultimately intermittent: a man leaves his monadic, solipsistic existence, and faces the world to discover the organic nature of creation, and that mankind must contribute by making talents bear fruit. At this precise point the bases and implicit features of Day Lewis's future poetry are cast. The poet is torn,

---

8   R. Duranti, 'Cecil Day Lewis', in CAB, vol. II, 119–38 (121).

9   The swooning of the poem 'Arcadian' also recalls in its diction the suffused world of an O'Shaughnessy (Volume 6, § 151.1).

overcome, awaiting a re-composition, which can come about through the regenerative power of Eros, boasting those thaumaturgic gifts that will pass on to political faith. But Eros by definition is ephemeral.

3. In *Transitional Poem* (1929), Day Lewis revealed unequivocally how dazzling his encounter had been with Auden, with whom he had edited the anthology *Oxford Poetry 1927* writing alternative paragraphs of the foreword.[10] *Transitional Poem*, which was the 'Ur-poem' of the 1930s[11] because it metabolized a repertoire of images of technological civilization,[12] witnessed the existence and subsistence of Auden's circle. After the dusty fogs, the admissions of weakness and feminine languor came a manifesto of virility that Day Lewis himself launched and asserted. The poem celebrates, he wrote in his notes, the 'undivided mind', that is, the mastery that the intellect must exert over the real with a cast-iron power of control; hence this is, in its way, an essay on the human mind that civilizes and exports and imposes order. The poetry of dream, the very primacy of dreaming, abate in favour of a manly, decision-making and ordering activity of the mind, and from the first poem of the collection the poet announces the completion of a rite of passage and the coverage of a stage of the *Bildung*: having left the minority status, he has reached the age of reason, having also swallowed the poison and the pus of a gangrenous reality. This is the first set of strong, even shocking images. A similar 'symmetry' of the mind is not 'fearful' as in Blake, but 'tetragona' ['well squared'] as in Dante. Immediately afterwards comes the first of the symbols of sovereign and dominating reason, the hawk. English poetry after 1929 was to take possession of this

10   Reproduced in Appendix A of HYN, 397–8. For F. Binni (see his profile of Auden in CAB, vol. II, 273), its basic points are the awareness of living in a world that is a chaos of values, and the genesis of a genuine poetry out of the self-same public chaos.

11   HYN, 44, even if this covered and buried under sand a romantic, or perhaps Georgian imagination, as some Marxist critics were not slow to notice. In fact, Hynes states that it is surprising that this poem, basically traditional, was welcomed as a rupture leading towards a new Modernism.

12   As Gelpi 1998, 29, underlines (and this is equally true for Auden), the portrayal of the civilization of machines cuts both ways: on the one hand, it symbolizes the decline of capitalism, and on the other the upbeat perspective of a new political order.

image, immortalized above all others by Hopkins in a sonnet, especially as a symbol of the violent yearning and uncorrupted energy of a nature subtracted to the moral jurisdiction; thus, ultimately, the hawk does not derive in this case from Hopkins, but transforms Blake's tiger (as it was to be in Ted Hughes and Geoffrey Hill). The hawk frames the thirty-four poems in various metres, most often in quatrains with only a pair of rhymes; and it is as much an image of rapacious haughtiness as of a calm panoramic vision of creation, hence a metaphor for the composure of reason.[13] In the closing poem it 'rides' in the sky to better focus on the panorama of the earth, and joins the skylark that stops singing in the evening. After the symbolic and paradigmatic cycle, the poet has sunk into peace. Thus a journey has been described, and with it a dialectic. After the first two poems, Day Lewis dwells, with repetitions or variations, on the necessity for such a still, disillusioned, scratch-resistant[14] gaze, and proclaims it possessed through a series of hyperbolic assertions that attempt to echo, and plagiarize, Zarathustra's supermanism, and were disliked and even torn to shreds by reviewers. The poet, barely twenty-five, issued his own 'Thus Spoke Zarathustra' of Promethean maxims and recommendations interspersed with memories and veiled and foggy autobiographical episodes (such as 'No peace till creature / His Creator has outgrown'). In every field the poet, or his mask, boasts and brags a disdainfully heroic and sarcastic attitude against human pettiness; love is conscious and dominating, the abstract art of 'contemporary Don Quixote-like intellectuals' branded with sarcasm. The poet of the mind is the prophet of a reawakening and an authentic dawn, not that false one mistaken for the deepest night; and he cites his travelling companions, *in primis* Auden with his dishevelled hair, in complicated euphemisms or antonomasias. In reality, the heart of the cycle is made of imaginative rhapsodies, vibrant with surprising turnarounds and departures; it is a kind of freewheeling image-filled trance, fascinating

13   As such – 'his way of looking at life from a very great height' – Auden had taken it from Hardy (Mendelson 1983, 33 [quoted in Auden's bibliography]). Auden's poem 'Missing' opens with the line 'From scars where the kestrel hovers'.

14   The poet plays an infinite number of times, in his poem, on the natural and suggestive homophony between 'metal' and 'mettle'.

but scarcely linked to a perspicuous meaning, and its divisions elude us. Extensive, obscure, private, incomprehensible pronouncements are nonetheless succeeded by poems of a *naïf* stamp, of tender ecstatic admiration for women and love, such as the fifteenth, which rebuffs the general thesis of the poem, and tells how rational steadfastness is merely bluster. Thus the poet must eat his own proclamations and re-admit the strength with which the flesh and the feminine unhinge the authority of reason.

4. *From Feathers to Iron* (1931), slated by early readers as no less chaotic, is instead among Day Lewis's most remarkable and everlasting works. The thirty-odd odes are still astonishing because of their facility and their flowing ecstatic diction, the non-cumbersome use of extended metaphor, and the fanciful images of Elizabethan and Caroline euphuism. These are love songs that can be read one by one, separated and extracted from the context, as examples of that timeless English poetic genre, the lilting song, aerial, rocking and jaunty, slightly varied in other imperious, dry and prescriptive registers that proclaim a newly found, sound, controlled vision of reality. As a whole, the cycle is a prolonged instant of visionary fancy, an overflowing delirium of optimism, both a fluent prothalamion and an epithalamion. A couple of parents about to have a son feel vibrantly part of the procreative motion of creation, and celebrate the regenerative force of love, a theme dear to the Thirties poets.[15] The couple set the pace for a public and prophetically universal renewal. At the start, Day Lewis cockily celebrates the blooming of this transient love, which delights in the here-and-now and does not bother about what is coming, nor about the transience of creation, certain that there is no future scenario. This is an echo of Catullus – love and love now.[16] In other words, the poet is celebrating the fullness, the exultation of intoxication achieved and possessed. The awareness of death would return intermittently, with the reprise of the

15　　This is a transfiguration of Day Lewis's first marriage, in 1928, with the daughter of the headmaster of the Sherborne public school. From the end of the 1930s he had relations with many women of culture and others without culture (he had two children with the wife of a local countryman); in the end he divorced to marry an actress, Jill Balcon.

16　　The famous 'Odi et amo' is translated in Day Lewis's first collection.

hendiadys womb-death, which rhymed (womb-tomb), and highlighted the conceptual and symbolic closeness of life and death in John Donne; so that Day Lewis' poems are also an exorcism of death. The couple's wellbeing translates into public wellbeing, since, overflowing *ad extra*, it can order, rationalize, organize and civilize; and in fact, the poem echoes that same desire for universal renewal that Hopkins sang, that is to favour the re-emergence of a 'freshness deep down things'. It is a joyous, unstoppable natural ferment that the couple is called on to support with their own procreative fertility, and they become one with it on the change of seasons. In this case, Day Lewis sings Hopkins's self-same, inextinguishable Heraclitean fire. This is a lay version of the biblical 'go forth and multiply', just as by a revealing touch the couple tackle an umpteenth 'waste land' and develop and fertilize it, and April is not 'the cruellest month'.[17]

5. The joy that Day Lewis hails and prophesizes in *The Magnetic Mountain*[18] (1933) is linked to the sense of a community of revolutionary intellectuals who feel like electrified operators of a forthcoming – in fact immediate – political regeneration. The symbol evoked in the first line of the first of the thirty-four poems is the hawk of *Transitional Poem*, an image of a force that is curbed but ready to lunge forth in attack, and an unexpressed energy on the point of exploding. This is not then the dove of Jesus' baptism and the Trinitarian emblem of the Holy Ghost, but it symbolizes another spirit that will destroy and pillage, before rebuilding. The second framing image is the one anticipated by the title: revolution as an ascent towards a mountain peak, an ascent dotted with the corpses of those who fell on the climb. But the two sets of images blend in the fact that this peak, not reachable by mapped and travelled paths, is the nest of the hawk which is its emblem. Dedicated to Auden, reproached repeatedly along with Rex Warner, Auden is the hawk that wheels and infects, and therefore in one of its values he is the magnetic mountain itself. The constitutive poems flow like pounding songs and choruses in a march that will be formed by collecting the masses of the discontented, of the exploited, or even the victims

17   Eliot's Phlebas is recalled polemically in the twenty-first poem, a long lecture to his own son on the miserable reality he would be tossed into by being born.

18   This title may also echo and parody that of Thomas Mann's *The Magic Mountain*.

of inept guides. The revolution is awaited and hoped for in exalted meta-phors and strings of images of a psalmic or prophetic and biblical type,[19] but overturned into a revolutionary chant that incites and stirs, creating a myth that takes a distance from concreteness and feasibility, which is to say the myth of the heroic warrior, the fearless combatant, scornful of peril, dedicated to the cause, and ready to die for it.[20] Except that here the countermelody is that of more sarcastic, realistic episodes, devoted to the doubting workers and revolutionaries who are afraid to tackle the climb, that there will be no reward at the peak. The delirious certainty abates, giving rise to a dramatization of the debate of intimate voices and dilemmas, between conservation of the good in the system, hence reformable, and its destruction. On the imaginary stage the voices of four 'defenders' of as many enemies follow one another, in an apparent parody of Eliot's *Murder in the Cathedral*: voices that are falsified and ventriloquial, instigations to a life of routine and revolutionary slumber, or even acceptance of everyday life, in a potpourri of tellingly imitated slang expressions. The worker or even the weak intellectual were being bombarded, according to Day Lewis, by the voices of dreaming quietism or bewitching Decadent escapism, and in addition by the reformism and patriotism that supported the British system as being the best of all possible worlds – and even more, echoing Marx, by a Christian religion which is reconciliatory and compliant on principle.

6. Day Lewis stopped teaching in 1935 to become a full-time writer, compensating for the sparse remuneration from poetry with handsome earnings from his thrillers, where he put his Hyde side to good use. *A Time to Dance* (1935) was the last attempt to link a congenital romanticism to political poetry, mainly because the drive of revolution was vacillating, and the poet, who had dared too much and bragged too long, confessed to being stentorianly torn, facing tomorrow with a fraction of his 'rebel cells', and yes-terday with 'veteran longings of the heart'. He was by now cut off, an exile on

19   Suggestive choruses marked by a Blakean prophesying, on a new, post-Flood world, are woven into 'Noah and the Waters'. The most politically allusive refrain is the vision of arable lands that are a 'graphic of history', since the wheat tries to speak, and this is 'the desperate appeal / Of men who had no other voice'.

20   HYN, 46 and 121–2, recognizes the dawning of this myth, criticized by MacNeice (§ 17.2), in *Transitional Poem*.

the mountain peak, no longer that 'magnetic' one of the previous collection, but an ivory tower – a real, 'enchanted' or 'magic' mountain therefore – from which he no longer uttered comprehensible words, and from which he could throw himself, having discovered his failure. The largely unsuccessful ballad 'Johnny Head-in-Air' restores the revolutionary significance of the mountain, which the class of workers and oppressed will reach by arduous paths after being relieved of the burden of religious gods. In reality, the most surprising note is the difficulty with which Day Lewis spies a rosier tomorrow, and the frequency with which he lingers resignedly over the fatal corruption of the revolutionary objective, or even the ruin and failure that awaits every commitment to improving and righting society. A celebrated song by Marlowe – just as T. S. Eliot had overturned Spenser – is parodied to comment sarcastically on the irremediable flaws in the system. The long, but rather weak verse tale which gives *A Time to Dance* its title celebrates two indomitable Australian aviators, with the aim of demonstrating the poet's envy of constant risky knife-edge challenges, and above all that the heroic example is undying and urges emulation.[21] The standpoint of *Overtures to Death* (1938), written just after the Spanish Civil War, is a flagrant negation of the champing revolutionary optimism of the early 1930s poems. Day Lewis now admits that human rationality is powerless in the face of a 'germ' of violence that holds the world in its grip and is ineluctable. The common man acts through rash and even absurd automatisms, and the intellectual lucidity of the working class is dulled, numbed and flattened by the new tool of consent and falsification exploited by the powers-that-be, namely, the cinema (in the sarcastic 'Newsreel').[22] The resignation progresses in leaps and bounds, the chorus

21   This is an early example in Day Lewis of a story narrated in various steps, having abandoned his favourite genre of the short poem without anecdote. The suspense of the flight and the sense of danger exploit stylistic solutions that recall Hopkins's 'Deutschland', particularly because technical terms of aeronautics make their first appearance in poetry. The objective of the poem is strengthened by the added epicedium, grafted on unconvincingly, on the death of Day Lewis's friend Hedges, who, like Lycidas, or Arnold's Thyrsis, is not dead but 'relives' in the poet singing him. The adoption of these classical modules is in itself discordant.

22   However, the second part of the collection includes poems of a more heroic and emphatic kind, such as 'The Volunteer' and the overly long and muddled ballad 'The Nabara', which tells of the resistance of a Republican ship against a stronger

contradicting the message and its previous refrain, while death, in a series of poems, is the object of the anthem that was earlier devoted to a trusting hope in life; and loss and defeat already feature in the titles, and even love itself is undermined by estrangement.

§ 20. *Day Lewis II: Poems of political disillusion*

For better or worse, Day Lewis remains a Thirties poet, and his later poetry, which covers a good half of his collected works, for our purposes could even be glossed over.[23] The insistent and erratic appreciation that some poems have earned from the critics is a kind of *excusatio non petita*. It is true that Day Lewis replaced the tension between committed art and propaganda with that, less public, between erotic enjoyment and frustration and alienation, managing to absolutize his biography even when it was still pressingly warm. The few war poems in *Word Over All*[24] (1943) feature the slippery slope of history, ineluctable decay and government of the world by the inept. The war over, he returned to a discouraged love poetry, formalized and wearily modulated to the classic theme of transitoriness. The 1943–1947 section (published in 1948) sought to usher in a new vein that was by this time existentialist, starting from the admonishment of two demanding epigraphs, one by Hardy on a man who struggles to stand on his feet and is about to go under, and the other by Valéry on the poet's extreme 'attempt to live', shaken by the wind that 'rises'. The poems in this section insist, starting from the title, on the motif of the self-portrait, and double and multiply a search for identity that had begun when Day Lewis was young, in poems where he repeatedly gazed at himself in mirrors. It could also be said that the poet is psychoanalyzing himself, looking back,

---

    and better armed Franco fleet in the sea off Biscay. Behind all this, the models of Newbolt and Kipling may be sensed, imitated with a rhetoric of libertarian heroism that fails to rise to parody: hence the failure (cf. HYN, 335, who adds Chesterton among the influences).

23   *Pace* Auden (cf. a letter to Day Lewis in Gelpi 1998, 221), who also spoke *pro domo sua*.

24   This collection was dedicated to the novelist Rosamond Lehmann (§ 68.1), for whom Day Lewis divorced his first wife, but whom he left in 1950, after a relationship lasting nine years, in order to marry a second time; hence the tortuous tension, the neuroses, and the 'double life' that the collection reflects.

and from a by now distant vantage point, he finds himself torn; his very teleology and entelechy are incomprehensible to him. The rifts multiply and return, such as that between mind and heart. Camouflaged autobiographical evocations, along with allusions to his affective life, typical of a lyrical poet that was, leave no decisive sign; in fact, some that are a little slovenly come as a surprise from a poet born with a dry, rapid style. The personal vein really has dried up if Day Lewis must shift to encomiastic or elegiac poems. The term 'neo-Georgian' is due to the quantity of anonymous and lifeless descriptions of natural scenery.

2. *An Italian Visit* (1953), in seven parts, is ultimately not, or is only superficially, a kaleidoscopic travel poem; rather a forced, composite pastiche in continual metamorphosis. On the whole, it imitates Browning's poems after 1870, with frequent and specious discursive contortions and philosophizing ballast that lead to few firm and clear points.[25] The poem opens as a debate among three men departing for Italy from an airport; they are unquestionably 'three persons in one man', that is, triplications of the poet's own identity. Through the three parts of his being, Day Lewis confesses to travelling as an escape into oblivion, as liberation and evasion, or as the pure illusion of fleeing from what, with hindsight, will seem like a 'truly virgin place'. Or the journey is a symbol of mankind's presumed freedom from the nooses of some metaphysical entity that binds and hinders it, or the simple possibility of going with the flow. The plane that crosses the Channel is described with the protracted metaphor of a bull, acrobatically replaced by that of the maternal womb, with the intoxication of the velocity that persisted as a revolutionary myth and an ingredient of Thirties poetry. The predilection for allusion can be construed in the letter from Rome, which smilingly protests against the excess of historical memories that throng and overlap before the cultured visitor, and which wink at the Clough of *Amours de Voyage*, while at the same time betraying that typically Browninguesque mixture of morbid curiosity and scorn for the Eternal City and the seat of Catholicism. This the freshest, most fluent episode, varied and eventful in the tradition of the Italian journey in verse,

---

25   The existential metaphor of the journey as self-exploration is, for example, the framing one in Browning's dramatic monologue 'Bishop Blougram's Apology'.

together with the tale of the coach journey to Florence. Here a further *tour de force* is a series of sketches dedicated to the monuments and beauties of the city, written in the manner of other poets, including Yeats and Dylan Thomas. The range of moods and tones widens, from the playful to the humorous and the serious, as in the sixth section inspired by a sunset at Settignano, a Baroque rhapsody on the inexorable vanishing of everything and on the poet's vain, heart-rending epiphanic desire to repossess his lost love. Cyclically the poem closes with another dialogue of the trio as they are about to leave.

3. *Pegasus* (1957), stuffed with cold recreations and reworkings of classical myths – of Baucis and Philemon, and Pegasus and Psyche – looks like an updated version of William Morris's *The Earthly Paradise*. Other poems are casual and some are epicedia; the more personal ones are marked by an overly explicit and bitter confessional vein, or by the flowing of the elegiac memory, lightly sentimental and crepuscular, of Day Lewis's Irish childhood and of his parents, aroused in a poet who seems to be thumbing through a photo album. *The Gate* (1961) gathers examples of meditative, disconsolate poetry in natural correlatives, where a vain waiting can be traced for an afterwards that will perhaps be nothingness, and which inspires certainty in the here-and-now. Poems of phenomenological observation describe helpless confined animals, symbols of a caged energy. The wave of memory is fixed on his son's departure for the unknown. However, the poetic space seems now saturated by unconvincing exercises in the genre of the dramatic monologue, the revealer of hidden unconfessable twists and turns of the psyche. One is told by the brother of a drowned man whom the speaker did not save, or even wished dead; another, very long, is of a Scottish female murderer condemned in America. *The Room* (1965) shows a return to euphuistic and concettist poetry on the repudiation of vagueness in poetry and in love and of the search for the indefinite, and the invocation of clean, precise, circumscribed boundaries; it is therefore yet another liquidation of any residual Romantic Titanism.[26] Included in this

---

26   From a theoretical point of view, after his Thirties commitments, Day Lewis can loom
      as a forerunner of formalism and structuralism preaching a close inter-connection
      of form and content, and the non-restrictive but stimulating function of 'form' (for
      a discussion of this aesthetic, cf. Gelpi 1998, 178–80).

collection are various occasional public poems, for example on the death of Churchill and the assassination of Kennedy. Unusually unified, pervaded by memories of his exile from Ireland, and the figures of his nationalist heroes, is Day Lewis's last collection before his death, bearing the meaningful title of *The Whispering Roots* (1970), hence belatedly crossed by Yeats's shadow.

§ 21. *Orwell* I: The safeguard of intellectual integrity*
A member – to borrow Orwell's own contorted words, which indicate just how oppressive and obsessive an exact definition of his social class was – of that 'lower-upper-middle class' which had covered minor managerial

---

*   *The Complete Works of George Orwell*, ed. P. Davison, 20 vols, London 1986–1998. OCE (for whose bibliographical details see the List of abbreviations) is a selective edition of Orwell's essays and letters, generally but not unanimously praised for its editorial standards (see its microscopic examination by J. Meyers, in CRHE, 373–81). *The War Broadcasts* and *The War Commentaries* are both edited by W. J. West, London 1985. G. Fenwick, *George Orwell: A Bibliography*, Winchester 1998.

Life. P. Stansky and W. Abrahams, *The Unknown Orwell*, London 1972, and *The Transformation*, London 1979; J. Buddicom, *Eric and Us: A Remembrance of George Orwell*, London 1974 (the memories of a childhood female friend, his first platonic relationship); B. Crick, *George Orwell: A Life*, London 1981 (written with a discretion all in all preferable to the penchant for gossip and interpretative embroidering of other biographies, such as that by Shelden listed below); M. Shelden, *Orwell: The Authorized Biography*, London 1991; S. Ingle, *George Orwell: A Political Life*, Manchester and New York 1993; P. Davison, *George Orwell: A Literary Life*, London 1996; G. Bowker, *George Orwell*, London 2003; D. J. Taylor, *Orwell*, London 2003 (on the few new elements of these last two biographies cf. *TLS*, 20 June 2003, 3–6).

Criticism. T. Hopkinson, *George Orwell*, London 1953 (many opinions are to be taken with a pinch of salt); J. Atkins, *George Orwell: A Literary Study*, London 1954 (first survey of Orwell's views); L. Brander, *George Orwell*, London 1954; C. Hollis, *A Study of George Orwell: The Man and his Works*, London 1956; R. Rees, *George Orwell: Fugitive from the Camp of Victory*, London 1961; R. J. Voorhees, *The Paradox of George Orwell*, West Lafayette, IN 1961; S. Greenblatt, 'George Orwell', in *Three Modern Satirists: Waugh, Orwell, and Huxley*, New Haven, CT and London 1965, 35–73; E. M. Thomas, *Orwell*, Edinburgh and London 1965; G. Woodcock, *The Crystal Spirit: A Study of George Orwell*, London 1966, Harmondsworth 1970 and New York 1984; B. T. Oxley, *George Orwell*, London 1967; J. Calder, *Chronicles of Conscience: A Study of George Orwell and Arthur Koestler*, London 1968, and

roles in the British Indian administration, George Orwell[1] (1903–1950) was a pupil at Eton without going on to apply for university. In fact, he was to join the British police in Burma when he was not yet twenty, returning

'Animal Farm' & 'Nineteen Eighty-Four', Milton Keynes and Philadelphia, PA 1987; K. Alldritt, *The Making of George Orwell: An Essay in Literary History*, London 1969 (studies Orwell in his gradual detachment from 1920s symbolism); R. A. Lee, *Orwell's Fiction*, Notre Dame, IN 1969; *The World of George Orwell*, ed. M. Gross, London 1971; R. Williams, *Orwell*, London 1971, 1984 and 1991 (notable *tour de force*, with an examination of Orwell's ideological contradictions) and, as editor, *George Orwell: A Collection of Critical Essays*, Englewood Cliffs, NJ 1974; D. L. Kubal, *Outside the Whale: George Orwell's Art and Politics*, Notre Dame, IN 1972; R. Kalechofsky, *George Orwell*, New York 1973; A. Sandison, *The Last Man in Europe: An Essay on George Orwell*, London and Basingstoke 1974 (presents Orwell, somewhat unconvincingly, as a 'twentieth-century heir of the Protestant tradition' [124]); A. Zwerdling, *Orwell and the Left*, New Haven, CT 1974; CRHE, ed. J. Meyers, London 1975, and, as author, *A Reader's Guide to George Orwell*, London 1975; S. Manferlotti, *George Orwell*, Florence 1979; F. Ferrara, *La lotta contro il Leviatano. L'analisi dei sistemi culturali e dei conflitti fra individuo e potere nell'opera narrativa di George Orwell*, Napoli 1981; *Inside the Myth: Orwell: Views from the Left*, ed. C. Norris, London 1984; D. Patai, *The Orwell Mystique: A Study in Male Ideology*, Amherst, MA 1984 (a densely documented study, of great commitment, which harshly stigmatizes Orwell's prejudices, above all his 'androcentric' ones, and therefore also the connivances of common opinion and criticism); I. Slater, *The Road to Airstrip One*, New York 1985; P. Reilly, *George Orwell: The Age's Adversary*, Houndmills 1986; *Orwell: 1984*, ed. L. Russo, Palermo 1986; *George Orwell*, ed. H. Bloom, New York and Philadelphia, PA 1987 (takes a hard line, including essays that mostly support the editor's idea, which is that Orwell was not a great writer); D. Wykes, *A Preface to Orwell*, New York 1987; G. Bulla, *Il muro di vetro. 'Nineteen Eighty-Four' e l'ultimo Orwell*, Rome 1989; J. Rodden, *The Politics of Literary Reputation: The Making and Claiming of 'St. George' Orwell*, London 1989; V. Meyers, *George Orwell*, Houndmills 1991; C. Pagetti, *Il diario e il microfono: il pianeta di George Orwell*, Torino 1994; R. Fowler, *The Language of George Orwell*, London 1995; A. Gardner, *George Orwell*, Boston, MA 1995; *George Orwell*, ed. G. Holderness, B. Loughrey and N. Yousaf, Houndmills 1999; C. Hitchens, *Orwell's Victory*, London 2002; J. Myers, *Orwell: Life and Art*, Urbana, IL 2010; R. Colls, *George Orwell: English Rebel*, Oxford 2013; P. Marks, *Orwell the Essayist: Literature, Politics and Periodical Culture*, London 2015; M. G. Brennan, *Orwell and Religion*, London 2016.

1   His real name, Eric Arthur Blair, clearly of Scottish origin, was repudiated when he found out that Scotland was the destination of deer hunters, and therefore the playground of the rich. The Orwell is a river in Suffolk.

home five years later after deciding to become a writer; and moved by a sense of compensation for the oppressed, and desirous to take a step back in social class, for a while he joined forces with 'the destitute'.[2] In the 1930s he published four unexceptional novels, and three effective reportages, one of them devoted to his participation as serviceman in the Spanish Civil War. He then went on to collaborate with left-wing journals, wrote essays on various topics, and achieved international fame after the war with an extremely popular anti-Soviet fable, and a no less acclaimed dystopian novel. It is clear from 'Why I Write',[3] the most lucid and reasoned of Orwell's essays, that he had become a half-heartedly committed political writer. From a young age he had cultivated an identity that was separate, secret, and jealous. The absence of his father and solitude, abandonment, and lack of affection had driven him to introversion and to some caprices. The very earliest Orwellian literary vein bloomed under the sign of imitative Romanticism (Blake) and a vacuous, triumphant patriotism; immediately afterwards, he came under the influence of the Georgians. At sixteen, he confessed that he was in love with the pure sound of words, that he had drafted or only planned naturalistic novels abounding in purple passages and terms chosen purely for their sound.[4] Generally speaking, for Orwell there are in this memoir four reasons to write (putting aside the fifth, the need to earn a living). The first is essentially equivalent to vanity and the desire to stand out and be talked about. Orwell refers in passing to his general theory of literature, stating that the writer is among the few in whom the instinct of activism survives, compared to a human mass overwhelmed by passivity. The second reason is beauty, in the world and in the words, a legacy of the aestheticism of the Nineties. The third, 'to see things as they are', a phrase in itself unthinkably Arnold-like, explains his documentary books, such but written with art; the fourth, the political objective, is the reform of society. Similar impulses, sifted in a chronological and ideal sense in a sort of climax, are clearly not

2   Orwell's vision of England is the alienated one of someone returning home: of a foreigner therefore, and partially the same as Kipling's, as underlined by Williams 1971.

3   OCE, vol. I, 23–30.

4   This confession may mask the influence of a writer like Conrad, the early Conrad of the 'heart of darkness', or of the flawless prose of Gissing.

harmonious, but conflictual. Orwell candidly presents himself in 'Why I Write' as an aesthetic writer, because, except for the emergency of his times, the first three reasons, belonging to the private sphere, would have had the better over the fourth; nor does he hide his nostalgia for an 'age of peace' in which one could write solely for the sake of beauty.

2. Consequently, 'Why I Write' describes and recollects the gestation stages of the political writer, who remains that kind of writer 'without sacrificing [his] aesthetic and intellectual integrity'. In this way the art-commitment couple is protected and enacted and comes to be born almost simultaneously. Ultimately the writer's main and pre-eminent gift is political sincerity, and if this is lacking, his books ring false; however, in the seventh paragraph of 'Why I Write', Orwell runs with the hare and hunts with the hounds, and strays frighteningly. He reiterates that a writer's prime impulse is political – standing by anyone who has suffered a wrong, unmasking a falsehood; but then he admits that the objective should be pursued with art. Art is not pure propaganda, but that childhood vision of the world or predisposition to enjoy it and to savour the beauty of the pure word, are inalienable. The enigmatic final admission is that 'every book is a failure', with a disconcerting closing paragraph in which Orwell returns to the language of the romantic genesis of the artistic product, and again adds that writing is an ordeal, that at the bottom of every writer's motives there lies a mystery, and that he is dominated by an almost infantile 'demon' that must be crushed. In 'Why I Write', Orwell basically believes in the vocation of the writer *ab aeterno*, the almost irrevocable divine call of a prophet invested with a mission. The writer is born, not made. This sense of fatal inexorability is a small sign of a narcissistic romanticism becoming intensified: it is useless to resist this summons, just as it is useless for the saints to say no to the Lord who calls. This is a duplicity reflected in the choice of his alias: there was once an Eric Blair who dissociated himself from a George Orwell. Eric Blair lauds the pub with its garden and the ritual of the 'nice cup of tea', and he is not Orwell when he makes Arnold-like distinctions on Dalí, or when he condemns the 'pulp' genre and the new ideology of the Americanized 'thriller'. He has problems reconciling the nostalgic with the socialist who wants to change the world, and accepts with gritted teeth some uncomfortable truths on modernity. The tough,

inflexible socialist is also in his implications the nostalgic of quiet, Eden-like rural England; and nothing is more coessentially English than the 'bygone times' of cricket.[5] Some light is cast on these two souls of Orwell in his late essay on Wilde's 'The Soul of Man Under Socialism'.[6] Orwell was always oddly tender over Wilde – he always defined himself as 'pro-Wilde' – and *pour cause*, because he saw in him a writer that strenuously upheld the otherness of the artist, his escape from the real into the intact realm of beauty and art, which was Orwell's own, unconfessed and unconfessable goal. While contesting some of his utopias, at the end of the day he approved of him since Wilde also glimpsed in socialism a way of allowing the artist to enjoy his separate artistic life.

3. A writer aware of these two *alter egos* was therefore bound to incessantly see their birth and becoming. Orwell was a writer much devoted to self-surveillance. He was able to split himself into the writer who thought and jotted down his first impressions, as well as the critic of that writer, who came back to interpret himself, and put himself into perspective at such a short distance. Yeats did the same but falsified himself more, gratified himself to be more exact; instead, Orwell reread himself at the shortest possible intervals. Each of his novels and many of his essays soon return to his education, to his childhood, to Eton, to his Burmese change in direction, to his choice to live like the vagabonds and the poor, to the Spanish Civil War. His longest and most incisive essay on a writer, the one on Dickens,[7] regardless of its intrinsic value, is an autobiographical cover story. Orwell, masked as Dickens, writes about himself,[8] about a snobbish and patronizing

---

5   OCE, vol. III, 66–8. In an essay on Herbert Read (OCE, vol. IV, 69–73), Orwell maintains that it is difficult to reconcile anarchism with the cult of the machine, and therefore he does not hide his annoyance with a mechanized society, dominated by the technical, which thwarts creativity. In fact, Orwell often had to force himself not to appear backward looking in highlighting (as he did in OCE, vol. III, 102) his view that a constitutional monarchy is the regime that has been best at avoiding and beating fascism.

6   OCE, vol. IV, 483–5.

7   OCE, vol. I, 454–504.

8   Orwell the novelist was a disciple of Dickens, but not to the extent of beginning his autobiographical fiction from memories of childhood: this, as we shall see, would

writer who wishes to dissociate himself from the deprived while upholding their cause; about a writer whose objective is rural idleness, both for himself and his characters, and who does not possess either a sense of community or a revolutionary spirit. The paradox of this essay is that Orwell sets out to criticize Dickens as a political writer, but for reasons that undermine and weaken his own political writing: Orwell too was a snob who had to hold his nose to avoid smelling the stench of the proletariat. A gathering of workers confirmed his theory of a 'physical degeneration' of the race. What else is an Orwellian hero if not someone uprooted from a community, an alien? Is he not perhaps disconnected from all professions, does he not aim for natural peace and tranquillity, a habitat in which to live and work undisturbed, as if he were a Tennyson come again to life in his palace of art, and the poet dreaming of the riverside residence of the Lady of Shalott? All of Orwell's fictional heroes are small or anti-heroes, unexceptional sensual men, weak, often also debauched: depraved, cynical, and profiteering. They do not know what the class struggle is, they have no interest in politics and are proud to be apolitical. And yet Orwell leads them from this position of apathy, which is also political apathy, to the threshold of political awareness. These small bourgeois are touched personally by the system's economic and depersonalizing economic distortions. Indeed, his first hero is a suicide victim; then Orwell hangs some optimistic but sibylline solutions on his plots of unease: Dorothy Hare represents the third response – one socialism, two suicide, three religion – to that nothingness of life which is abnegation and, even worse, the annulment of the self in religious mysticism and philanthropy. She leaves it violently but returns, and becomes re-imprisoned, after wiping the slate clean of previous idolatries, ready to begin again, and, who knows, to go from a faith *tout court* to political activism. George Bowling, who is no saint, feels the threat of the bombs and understands what's cooking. Gordon Comstock, who possesses a smattering of juvenile socialism, is merely a negative existentialist who tries everything, but in vain, to stay afloat, and who only in the end manages to

------

be dealt with by memorialist and re-evocative essays; and none of his novels stars children.

be not only an apocalyptic philosopher and masochist, but also to re-enter the ranks of the bourgeoisie in the meantime.

4. Orwell's novels before 1940 form a provisional and incomplete macrotext that needs to be completed by his essay writing and his actual political militancy; only then can we have an explanation, albeit rather dialectic, of the definition of the writer as a political novelist in the sense given in 'Why I Write'. The two main and dominant themes of Orwell's fiction and essays are, summing up, in this combined light, (1) a definition of the role of the intellectual and writer in the era of advanced capitalism and totalitarian dictatorships up to the aftermath of the Second World War, and (2) the unattainable nature of the socialist revolution. As regards the first point, Orwell wishes to demonstrate the necessity of the post-Romantic writer being overtaken by the committed socialist writer, hence the quashing of the Decadent, Symbolist, Georgian and modernist writer, corresponding to the periods that essentially followed one another from the Nineties onwards and the main literary climates that his path crossed. And yet George Orwell presses an Eric Blair who is rebelling. Essay writing is more advanced than fiction in Orwell because it draws this political writer's photofit, and therefore an incarnation is deemed possible, while the novel lingers over the intellectual, stubborn in protecting his identity, the sacredness of his solipsism, the attraction of those words that 'alone are certain good' (Yeats), and over his balking at following and implementing an awakening of political consciousness. The first four novels hinge on retraction, in other words turn on figures of dreamers, always too weak to be able to head a revolutionary movement. 'Why I Write' thoroughly denudes these ever open conflicts; another essay, 'Inside the Whale', reiterates that Orwell's secret fascination was to close himself inside the whale's belly. But there is more. Also in his essay writing and reportages the transformation of the solipsistic writer into a political activist meets with some setbacks. In part, Orwell is seeking an alibi. It is self-evident that the English writer and intellectual is bourgeois, and that whether he wishes to or not, he could never present himself to the community of workers as a worker, and speak their down-to-earth language, empathize with their horizons, really join forces with them. For a certain period Orwell the political writer and socialist in the making sought real organic communities to join, without

finding any, either because they were short-lived or because they were unworkable. In reality there was a community of socialist and communist writers he could have enlisted in, but here the second hitch comes into play: the socialist and communist intelligentsia of his day were not only disconnected from the masses, whom they did not know nor frequent; they were also damaging that very socialism, in turn alienating the masses from it. Those organized intellectual socialist circles were blind and servile dependencies of Moscow, and were destroying and suffocating the writer's otherness and integrity. Orwell's alibi consisted in the fact that, ultimately, devotion to Art almost seemed to prevail over, and even eclipse, the political objective. The relevant proviso was that socialism itself is unrealistic, since the socialist remains tainted by his ineradicable bourgeois identity. Up to a certain point Orwell's essay writing suggests his conviction that it is possible to achieve the establishment of socialism; however, after the war essay writing and fiction concur. As for the second dominant theme, Orwell was often hopeful that a socialist revolution could occur and a British socialist state be realized, and that even a European socialist federation was not merely a mirage. Even more often he realized he had done his sums incorrectly, and that there were more stumbling blocks than concrete prospects. Above all he was fearful of the bureaucratizing of socialism, of the fatal passage from a list of ideals or an abstract agenda to their translation into political acts. Hence the impossibility of making a revolution permanent, virtually equivalent to an oxymoron.

5. Orwell's three reportages document the search for and actual finding of three communities that establish a road to socialism and that are, for the time being, an effective form of socialism, or if not socialism, authentic brotherhoods. The problem with them was that they were temporary or simply micro-communities. The first was that of the Parisian *bohémiens* of 1928, a circumscribed episode of a goliardic community that established a life of chance, played almost childishly with the contrast between slaves and masters, but slaves that help one another. Also the British tramps treat one another like brothers at the very least. In Orwell's decision to embrace this life is reflected a Scottish, Calvinistic sense of guilt to be atoned for: the guilt of an exploitative class and of British domination in India. This exit from his own class is a torment: his head

tells him to stick to it, his instinct as a snob distances him from it.[9] In fact, the community of miners of the second reportage is an organic one of serious and active workers. In both these cases socialism is applied in its minimal version, corresponding to a spirit of elementary brotherhood among the destitute or exploited. Instead, the establishment of socialism is ephemeral but admirable in the Spanish anti-Franco militia. The peak of a realized socialist utopia on earth is Barcelona in 1936, when a thrilled Orwell noticed so many signs of his dreamed-of socialism: 'the Spanish militias, *while they lasted*, were a sort of microcosm of a classless society', the asymptote come true. *Homage to Catalonia* is an exceptional litmus paper: after a few months, Orwell re-enters Barcelona and notices a changed city, namely, the ongoing Eden-like socialism wiped out, and the former balances of power re-established. From this alone it is easy to understand why Orwell was and was not a Trotskyist: revolution must be permanent, since, by congealing into bureaucracy, deteriorates, is blocked, and degenerates. Even the theoretician of permanent revolution, Trotsky, would have turned into a bureaucrat if he had come to power. Only with a permanent revolution was it possible to prevent its becoming bourgeois and its corruption into totalitarian oligarchism,[10] and into what Orwell called the bureaucratic degeneration of the Party. Revolution, as a result, is an ideal that cannot be translated into practice. The irony is that Orwell never finds this community, which flees from him, wisp-like; some, once found, were sullied by him himself and subsequently left, in disappointment and disillusion. In short, he could not get hitched either downwards or upwards, to either the deprived or the intellectuals, whether left-wing or right-wing. Precisely in this strenuous

---

9   Poverty as a philosophy of life was a choice that Orwell would make again when, famous and rich, but irreparably ill, he voluntarily took refuge on the Scottish island of Jura.

10   According to M. L. Salvadori, 'Democrazie e totalitarismi, la seconda guerra mondiale', in *La storia*, Roma 2004, vol. 13, 24, the adjective 'totalitarian' appeared in 1924 in some anti-fascist articles, to indicate a state in which the party in power destroys the other parties, and violent repression of opposition is used on a large scale, political and civil liberties are quashed and – a fact pertinent to Orwell's standpoint – society is subjected to increasingly rigid control.

struggle against the homogenization and standardization of the intellectual and the common man alike lies the highest civil and human value of Orwell's own historical presence. His work exudes condemnation, protest, disillusion and threat. He is the exemplary bastion against the dulling of one's thoughts in order to support anything unheard, overheard or fanatically believed in. His work and his fiction can be summed up as the safeguarding of man's intellectual sanity and autonomy.[11] Some have called him the missing link between Swift[12] and Kafka.[13] No doubt he explored the exiled and alienated condition of the twentieth-century thinking man, the man abandoned, shipwrecked, devoid of ideological handholds: without, for example, the comforts of the Christian faith or those of its negative and counterpart, Marxism and materialism. A distressing image that recurs twice in his essay writing[14] is that of the wasp sucking jam from a plate even when its body has been cut in half: 'It is the same with modern man', a man then reified, and made an insect, like Kafka's 'monstrous vermin'. Orwell himself held many of his books to be satires, warning us of his art's non-realism, an art that is visionary and distorting and which intensifies the grotesque, the surreal, the demoniacal. He is as much a descendant of Swift as of Defoe, able to switch from meticulous and inventorial descriptions to the apocalyptic snapshot.

11   A revealing question: 'Are there really such things as nations? Are we [English] not forty-six million individuals, all different?' (OCE, vol. II, 75). The whole of the first part of this essay – 'The Lion and the Unicorn' (§ 22.6) – is a demonstration of diversity within the entity of Great Britain, even if only ethnic and regional, and at the same time of the necessity to transcend this in the face of the war emergency.

12   The essay on Swift (OCE, vol. IV, 241–61) is not kindly, however. Swift is judged to be an incognito conservative reactionary, and an anarchist who echoed certain rigid Catholic notions that Orwell found in contemporary ideologies, for example on the function of science. And therefore he was not left-wing, even if he dallied with certain left-wing causes and campaigns. The central point of the argument is the one dear to Orwell, repeatedly declared and hard-fought in his essays: that of a pessimistic Swift who gave in to the irredeemable nature of the world.

13   MIT, 1160, notes that Orwell became well known at the same time as Kafka, in the wake of the fiasco of the war, which ended up overturning previous utopias.

14   OCE, vol. I, 178, and vol. II, 30.

6. Carlyle, Arnold, Ruskin, Morris and Hopkins, more or less 100 years earlier, had postulated the same apocalypse as Orwell, and sought very similar remedies, worried about the plight of the workers and the indigent, but advocating that partial socialism – notably that of Ruskin, and even more so that of Carlyle – which, as Orwell himself was later to realize, resulted in something very close to its contrary, that is in that singular but frequent veering of socialism to fascism. Orwell echoes those predecessors in his yearning for an England that is clean and virgin, one of fresh limpid waters, and in the denunciation against machines and industrialization.[15] Such conservative socialism, which dissociates itself from the mad panegyric of progress, is therefore very far from Morris's corrosive one, much as this latter writer is often compared to Orwell.[16] With respect to the nineteenth-century utopias of Ruskin and of the communist Morris, the working class had to fight for a more restricted and circumscribed objective. Morris, and especially Ruskin, attributed great weight to the spiritual and even the artistic life in order to refine – in reality soften and curb – the masses; to Orwell, it was by now clear, the artistic smattering of the refined masses no longer mattered. Thus there were lesser issues at stake, and this was the simple, decent life, a life of subsistence, and a slightly more comfortable survival: the 'indispensable minimum'. Orwell was by now a combative layman – no longer an apathetic agnostic – who took for granted the end of religious faith in contemporary society, replacing it with an 'earthly realm', based on the awareness that there is no

15   In certain situations and in certain stances we can see in Orwell the extreme incarnation of an Arnoldian conservative humanism: in an article on science (OCE, vol. IV, 26–30), which seems a response to one of Arnold's 'discourses' in America (cf. Volume 6, § 32.2), Orwell defends an organic, related culture, and a scientism tempered and fed by literature and art. This 'culture' is also politically the only liberal, prudent, democratic one: pure scientism only supported fascism in more than one case.

16   Arguably, Orwell's most Morris-like essay ever written is the one entitled 'The Moon under Water' (OCE, vol. III, 63–5), because in it Orwell pretends to describe his own favourite pub, an idyllic oasis with first-class beer to drink, where the barmaids are courteous and affable, the customers sociable, while outside a splendid garden allows customers to breathe pure beneficial air: but halfway through his piece Orwell says that this pub does not exist, it was only imagined.

beyond and that all must be brothers. In one of his last, ebullient reviews, on Graham Greene, he hammered home his attack against the 'Catholic novel', and Greene paid the price: the paradox proposed or supposed by Greene was that it is better to be a Catholic sinner than a virtuous pagan. In fact, in Orwell, there emerges sooner or later a polemic against holiness, against the surrender to faith in an ultra-terrestrial life that even dragged in such a non-Christian saint as Gandhi. This Catholic novel honoured the myth of the distinction and vocation of the damned man and of the sinning priest, while 'Reflections on Gandhi' attacks non-violence, which is a way of escaping from the world and avoiding tackling and resolving its evils.[17] Conversely, Orwell felt himself a member[18] of a transversal school – Silone, Koestler, Borkenau, Serge, Malraux – of semi-inventive writers who rewrote history, hence a counter-history, which was ignored in the official versions. He was to catch up by filling the gap of a literature of disenchantment about the Soviet Union. The denunciation of the cult of power and of the corruption and decadence of revolutions is traced in Koestler. The most famous book of this Anglo-Hungarian writer infected Orwell with its contrasts of dark and light, its leitmotif of detention and torture, its nightmarish atmosphere. Koestler described a hero forced by police torture to confess to crimes he had not committed, save for that of hating the Stalinist regime. Orwell, however, ultimately disagrees with Koestler when he pessimistically proclaims his belief in utopia, and therefore in the establishment of a terrestrial paradise: he is a hedonist, another Orwellian category, derived from Koestler, and hedonist is equivalent to utopian, that is someone who desires a metamorphosis of the here-and-now, as if happiness were possible on this earth, given that

17 The gist of the essay 'The Prevention of Literature' (OCE, vol. IV, 81–95) is that authoritarian regimes kill freedom of literary expression and destroy art itself; and that only poetry – defined, with a Paterian nuance, as a solitary and solipsistic activity – can prosper, since it has less content. Orwell adds the debatable assertion that over the last three centuries Catholicism had not produced novelists of any value.
18 OCE, vol. III, 271.

the Christian beyond does not exist, as Orwell is always heard repeating.[19] At the end of his essay on Koestler,[20] he declares that all revolutions are a failure, but to different degrees. The axiom that the committed writer and the politician must incessantly have before them is that the world to be constructed is not a perfect, but a better one. In 1943, Orwell was to protest precisely against dystopia, and made it clear that his socialism did not mean an aspiration to a perfect society – which would be a utopia in fact – but an aspiration to a perfectible society. Two crucial pages on this issue are in the essay dedicated to Yeats,[21] and the 'As I Please' of February 1944.[22] In the latter, Orwell recalls the fact that reactionaries, above all Catholics, or at least the mystically inclined Catholics, liquidate everything by saying that it is not new, and thereby block the process of renewability and the effective renovation of history. Both Yeats and Chesterton, mutual enemies, at least agreed on the cyclical principle, which precludes any authentic future renewal: if everything must return, everything always remains unvaried, which is to say, injustice and inequality are perpetuated.

7. The agreement with the above-mentioned Victorian thinkers lies in the fact that Orwell was one of the last *maîtres à penser* of the English tradition. Of the *maître* he did possess some fundamental requisites, such as presumption, the spirit of challenge, candour, delirium, folly and instinct. Intellectuals wishing to cover this role must be able to present their own *Weltanschauung* and a series of correlated ramifications: for example, an idea of national literature and of the literary language, their own sociology, political theory, aesthetics. They must have a *tranchant* exhibitive manner, be peremptory and able to reduce to a few assumptions the facts of the culture in which they are operating. Clearly, these intellectuals will

19   A wary essay by Evelyn Waugh (from 1946, reproduced in CRHE, 211–15) for the first time addressed the question of Orwell's position on religion, correcting him when he attributed sectarianly Catholic ideas to Chesterton without taking into account that the 'enemy', that is, Chesterton himself, had often expressed these views before formally becoming Catholic. In fact, the only serious weakness in Orwell's thinking is, for Waugh, to have glossed over the authentically religious dimension of life.

20   OCE, vol. III, 270–82.

21   OCE, vol. II, 311–17.

22   OCE, vol. III, 119–22.

have many enemies, and will earn much criticism for their apodictic way of reasoning and debating.[23] Orwell was all of this. Perhaps he himself intuited it, since he felt some of the earlier presumptuous cultural dictators hovering over him, and he sought to take a personal, negative, and often arbitrary stance against them. In Orwell, there are only summary opinions of Ruskin and Morris; but he showed singular respect for Hopkins, well beyond a celebrated page of luminous linguistic and stylistic analysis of the sonnet 'Felix Randal'. Orwell is a Hopkins in negative, inside out, and Orwell's essay production is a natural pendant to Hopkins's letters. Both were incorrigibly presumptuous, wrote loosely, and received clamorous rejoinders from experts; both formulated their very own organic vision of British history and culture; both were, in their own way, in favour of persuasive literature, persuasive in one case – Orwell – that the war and the victory against the Germans could give rise to a new planetary *ordo*, the same one which, in Hopkins, could come to pass thanks to the reanimation of Catholicism in England and in Europe. Hopkins spat instinctive judgements, but his was a guided instinct, every manifestation of which descended from his ideological frame. Orwell possessed a similar frame, but one more rudimentary, simplistic and pragmatic.[24] He lacked a Duns Scotus; if he had adopted Scotus's ideal negatives – if he had really delved into Marx and Lenin –[25] he might have substantiated his thinking with

23 On Orwell's inconsistencies, or ideological zigzagging, dating back to his service in Burma, one of the keenest retorts remains that of the journalist George Woodcock, the editor of *Now*, honestly included in OCE, vol. II, 257–9.

24 Even if Q. D. Leavis had it right when she said that 'even his enthusiasms [...] turn out to be solid judgements' (CRHE, 189).

25 According to Woodcock (in CRHE, 239), Orwell, like Morris, would never 'have identified himself as Marxist', an objection or prejudice undermined later by Zwerdling's book from 1974 (cf. for example page 20, where he states that Orwell had read Marx and knew him well). The eventuality, in fact necessity, to transform a war against capitalism into a civil and revolutionary war had in any case already been enunciated in letters by Lenin (for Orwell cf. the statement in 'The Lion and the Unicorn', in OCE, vol. II, 119), even if Lenin spoke of imperialistic war, and the war referred to was the First World War. One of his books is entitled *Imperialism, the Highest Stage of Capitalism* (1916). In the meantime, Orwell had understood and

more ideology. But this objection, too, might be answered by the fact that Orwell cannot be taken for an ideologue, and that he faces reality as a writer; and that being a man of few ideas is not actually a limit, but a proof of consistency, if and where those ideas remain the same. As for those on language, Orwell soon understood that power is administrated and consolidated by slogans and propaganda, and that it leverages transparent but also devious means of visual and verbal communication. In his writings of the 1930s he had already understood that radio was the vehicle of propaganda information, and that propaganda was based on the linguistic manipulation of events. Before *Nineteen Eighty-Four*, even in such a confused essay as 'New Words',[26] Orwell had formulated a theory on the life of language: words disappear and others are born, language is an imperfect representational system, unable to express certain spheres of human life, above all psychic and dream life (cinema does this better); language has evolved – it seems a foretaste of Foucault – starting from sound, from the grunt, even, of Neanderthal man, accompanied by gesture, and every deictic referent was first identified, as a substitute, with the utterance that accompanied that gesture. On reaching *Nineteen Eighty-Four* we find propagandistic communication entrusted to newspapers and 'telescreens', audio and video transceivers. The functioning of Newspeak is investigated; new or old as this may be, it is demonstrated that the maintenance of power is also based on the permanent rectification of any past errors. From the telescreens gushes a rhetoric of power that is precisely the aberrant, nefarious use of language and of its resources. Orwell's essay 'Politics and the English Language'[27] discusses and denounces the standardization and superficiality of the modern world, also and above all because everyday speaking is through automatisms and slogans, trite figures of speech, and

---

witnessed the repeatability of history. Lenin himself saw in the Great War the natural outlet of the contradictions of capitalism. In his April Theses, Lenin had preceded Orwell in an analysis of the nature of imperialism as the last stage of capitalism, and theorized an imminent socialist revolution, which was supposed to start by demolishing the bourgeois economic order in Europe.

26   OCE, vol. II, 17–27.
27   OCE, vol. IV, 156–70.

speaking plainly is the *conditio* of political renewal.[28] As a pure theoretical historian of language, Orwell belongs to the group of Victorians – Barnes, Doughty, and Hopkins once again – who dreamed of restoring and revalorize the archaic Anglo-Saxon layer of the English language; and in fact he set himself the objective of erecting a wall against infiltrations from outside that would hybridize it, such as excessive Latinisms used without a reason, or French expressions and American slang. Very frequent was his critical mention of the pretentious, unnatural, highbrow language, incomprehensible to the masses, of newspapers and politicians; and from literature too he requested a simple language, close to the spoken variety. As I have already indicated, in his essays Orwell wrote a history of English literature with gaps, but strong in its idea or bias. The indispensable norm is that literature must be concrete, with the result that Orwell vents his spleen against all writing that is forced, nebulous, exhibitionist, full of linguistic waste. When reviewing Dalí's autobiography,[29] Orwell listed à la Arnold the painter's anomalies, violent perversions, oddities and sexual aberrations. Does an artist have immunity? Can he represent everything including the disgusting in the name of art? Orwell replies in the negative: the artist too has a social responsibility, both as a citizen and human being. The avant-garde movements were reactionary, or at least Hulme's Imagism was – a movement that was pessimistic, Catholic, fascist, pacifist and anarchic.[30] The cultural world of the 1920s was corrupt, with so many sophisticated aristocrats who frequented the European capitals and made themselves patrons of the arts. If we note a certain interest by Orwell in 1944 in eighteenth-century writers such as Smollett, Goldsmith, and Fielding, it may be because he saw in them a psychological realism capable of representing – as in Joyce or Henry Miller – the real whole man, who

28	Cf. George Steiner's reflections in an article included in CRHE, 363–73, and – on Orwell's pioneering intuitions about the domesticated, often perverse, when not antithetic use of language, including the later 'politically correct', that is, euphemism – the essay by G. Hughes, 'Lingua e letteratura nel Novecento', in MAR, 421–56, in particular 448–50.

29	OCE, vol. III, 185–95.

30	OCE, vol. III, 81–4.

acts out of low selfish reasons in an age when moralism was fatally entering the scene, that is, the blunder of having prejudices weigh more, such as the triumph of virtue and the supremacy of the senses.[31]

8. Hopkins and Brecht are the two major absentees when Orwell's critics seek to forge associations; and it is sufficient to browse through the indexes of names in books of criticism to realize that these two writers almost never appear. The parallel with Hopkins is unquestionably far-fetched and acrobatic; the absence of that with Brecht decidedly conspicuous. Orwell was initially associated with a few compatriots of the past, but in order to distinguish him from them in light of his socialism and independence bordering on dissidence, and of his nature as a political writer. He estranged himself from the politicized group of the Thirties writers, who disillusioned by Stalin's purges took refuge in shamefaced isolation. If English political writing of the twentieth century had few takers, it was natural to associate Orwell with other European writers in whom the political passion was fierier. Aside from the transversal family of Silone and Koestler, the sole association at the centre of a book – by A. Besançon – is with the almost unknown Russian intellectual, Vladimir Solovyov. It is very odd, and almost incomprehensible, that Orwell himself never mentioned the true, unique giant of political writing in the first half of the twentieth century, Bertolt Brecht. Let us start from the fact, if we wish to trace this summary parallel, that they were almost coetaneous, that Brecht had a birth *décalage* of five years and died six years later, that they debuted therefore with a small discrepancy, of a *lustrum* or perhaps a decade – Orwell was less precocious – and that their genre options did not precisely coincide. Brecht is one of the greatest twentieth-century playwrights, and a poet, essayist, theoretician, but the

---

31 Orwell even extended his recognition to the very latest literary phenomena, such as paraliterature, literature for children and escapism. The essay 'Raffles and Miss Blandish' (OCE, vol. III, 246–60) discusses how the stereotypes of the thriller evolved from the circumscribed radius of its initial examples – a 'gentlemanly thief', local and quite at home – to a text oozing blood, perversion, and sensationalism, in the wake of American 'pulp magazines'. What is tacit is his harsh criticism of the American fads that were taking root. Additionally, Orwell found in them a tendency towards the worship of power!

author of little prose that is truly inventive; Orwell is a novelist, an engagé essayist, a literary critic and, descending in importance, a student of mass culture, an ideologist, a poet of no account, never a playwright *tout court*, save for the fact that the third part of *Nineteen Eighty-Four* is that trial-play into which Brecht's dramatic art evolves, that is a dream-like surreal theatre, a dramatization and incarnation of Winston Smith's psychic conflict. And Brecht's *Galileo* is at least an equivalent of *Nineteen Eighty-Four* as an 'implicitly anti-atomic play',[32] that is, a drama linked to the dropping of the atom bomb on Hiroshima, and a condemnation of the scientists who had not put science at the service of humanity, but contributed to its destruction. On the ideological plane, Orwell and Brecht find themselves in agreement on several programmatic points, and above all on the function of literature: both declared and dealt with the necessity to understand and explain reality, rather than to communicate vague feelings; hence they were moved by the need to change the existing order, to fight and have the workers fight for a better world, a transformable world (the fourth justification of the writer in 'Why I Write'). And the existing order was that of capitalism and the exploitation of the working class, an exploitation whose roots debuting Brecht traced, in his Anglo-American 'quadriptych' from 1921 to 1928, to the nations and geographical areas where it emerged, namely America and Britain, carrying out his analysis of colonialism from the same point of departure as Orwell, that is, Kipling. It is, however, inevitable to point out that Brecht fought against capitalism like Shaw, in a certain way: by exploding its contradictions in the form of parody, play and provocation, whereas Orwell does not cultivate full-blown farce, save for the forced interlude in *A Clergyman's Daughter*, and chooses the weapons of photographic realism, also because he made no use of drama. However, this coincidence resulted in Marxist orthodoxy once discovered (Brecht); in Marxist socialism perhaps, certainly not Soviet in practice, in Orwell.[33] Ultimately, the dramatic objective most attributed and intrinsic to Brecht, which applies equally to

32   MIT, 1401.
33   Brecht too was a dissident when he settled in the GDR, and from 1956 there is a
      letter to Ulbricht, critical of the regime. But this dissidence 'never went against his
      Marxist convictions' (MIT, 1388).

Orwell, is unmasking: except that the two writers unmask, alongside some common targets, such as capitalism, also others that are not common at all; to be sure Brecht never unmasks Sovietism. Brecht pursues the action of unmasking because he is a playwright, the art form closest to its receiver; Orwell chooses more mediated forms. Upstream, they share the double target of capitalism with its ally, religion. Brecht, too, unwaveringly admits and reminds himself that after this life there is no other. Operatively, they are both in search of a new elect community, though they call it in a different way. Reconsidering the common approach to the written word and to political consciousness, we realize that they were both bourgeois who began 'to saw through the branch' they were sitting on.[34] They finally resembled one another in their deliberately sloppy way of dressing. Brecht had patented his clothing, his own uniform of left-wing intellectual – hair cropped almost to zero, round metal-rimmed glasses, a vaguely Chinese tailcoat or tunic, which perhaps covered a shirt of costly silk, to indicate the two souls, the bourgeois who wishes to fall into the shoes of the prole and imitates him, in disguise. Likewise, we always see Orwell wearing crumpled corduroy jackets, dark shirts with their soft collars, trousers without a crease, and sporting a thin moustache edging his lip, his face furrowed and open in a timid, weary smile, his bushy hair piled high.

9. Those tackling Orwell for the first time or delving into him must admit to a natural and instinctive congeniality, that is recognized in men who are sincere, loyal, in good faith, laudable in their stigmatizing of prejudices, hypocrisies and injustices, firstly and above all their own as well as inherited, congenital to their race and nationality. He was a writer who fought by any means to build a better society and bring about a decorous standard of life and individual freedoms that benefited the less well off, in the classic era of twentieth-century fascist tyrannies. It soon became proverbial to describe him as a lay saint who, on returning from Burma, stripped off his rich lavish clothes like St Francis, donned his sackcloth and embraced Sister Poverty. On the strength of this spontaneous benevolence, a reader who opens the chapter of Orwell's critical reception discovers,

34   For Brecht and this image, cf. MIT, 1356.

wrong-footed, that this esteem is anything but unanimous, and that Orwell was contested, aspersions were cast on him, and he was quite literally torn apart by both the Right and the Left.[35] The right-wing critics and readers could not of course adopt a socialist like him, albeit a non-aligned one; nor the Left an independent dissident thinker, and the contrarian of Marxist and Soviet orthodoxy (Togliatti, for example, the then leader of the Italian Communist Party, deemed *Nineteen Eighty-Four* a 'farce' ['buffonata']). When the critical and ideological Marxist aegis waned[36] things got even worse, and Orwell had practically no residual defenders and the organized critical gangs became his enemies – formo-structuralism with its followers and developments, understandably indifferent to Orwell; feminism because of the scarce weight and importance that women have in his human hierarchies; gender for the presumed repugnance homosexuals aroused in him; postcolonial criticism for his constantly imperfect and ambiguous anti-imperialism. To call him a snob was, for some critics, understating things, and so there was an effort to make him into a Swift-like hater of mankind who joined the workers in spirit, thanks to a 'conscious effort', after which hatred would sprout once more.[37] Every representative of a determined intellectual clique, current, party, ideology, or trend, felt they had to reprimand Orwell for not having expounded and shared his or her ideas. Orwell criticism is, as a result, packed with posthumous suggesters who have complained that Orwell never said exactly what they had in mind and what it was right, even fitting, to expect him to say. The campaigner against every type of bias thus perishes with the same sword with which he did injury; his struggle has turned against him, and his passionate de-automatizing work has been dismantled as a mountain of prejudices. The ostracism against him was dictated precisely by that battle against the English class system, hence defeated and vain, that Orwell had

35   Truly exceptional is the opinion of one reviewer, namely, that Orwell can be defined
      as the greatest English writer who lived entirely within the first half of the twentieth
      century (CRHE, 164).
36   But see the collection of essays edited by Norris 1984, whose 'views from the Left'
      are critical and hostile.
37   Hopkinson 1953, 10–11.

always fought. The question that seems to have obsessed critics is how much Orwell's prophecies had come true by the fateful deadline of 1984; since many of these have not come true, that book, *Nineteen Eighty-Four*, was declared superseded, and was discarded like some period-piece, prophesying that it would no longer be read, as if a real critical parameter were that the greatness of science fiction writers must be gauged by the quantity of their prophecies that have come true. Two or three generalizations seem to echo throughout the critical essays and the books on Orwell: that as a fiction writer he lacked inventiveness, that he was greater as an essayist and literary critic than as a fiction writer, that he was an essayist who had forced himself to become a novelist, something for which he had no natural gift, as Q. D. Leavis accused him of being,[38] while Julian Symons found that he was actually a novelist of ideas, less adept at carrying through stories about people.[39] Orwell himself, in retrospect, had no good opinion of his own fiction: he preferred to gloss over it, repeating that he had written novels to make money or for training; a certain pride transpires only as regards *Animal Farm*. The third, compensatory consideration is that he possessed an admirable prose style, crystal-clear and without artifice.[40]

§ 22. *Orwell II: Evolution of his political and aesthetic thinking*
The four volumes of Orwell's essays give an overall impression of being a disorganized pile, and this is because Orwell could not think of them as parts of an organic corpus, given their largely occasional nature. However, this fragmentary, dispersive mass of letters, literary criticism, standalone sketches[41] and various essays reveals some natural demarcations that form as many thematic re-groupings and let us hear some particularly heartfelt

---

38   CRHE, 188, and in more recent times Bloom, in Bloom 1987, 7.

39   CRHE, 252.

40   Cf. however Alldritt 1969, 109–21, for a severe taking down of Orwell *even* as an essayist and stylist.

41   Both the pieces on the life of a tramp and those on hop picking are trials for episodes found in novels and later reportages. 'Clink' (OCE, vol. I, 109–19) is a prison scene – Orwell gets drunk on purpose and lets himself get arrested – which is the preview of others in *Keep the Aspidistra Flying* and *Nineteen Eighty-Four*: in the cell there is a blocked water closet like the one where Winston is detained in the novel.

chords. The reviews he wrote were far from perfunctory, and we soon understand that the books reviewed contain some kind of provocation, challenging Orwell on his own terrain, and stimulating reflection. What are these fixed points? In the first place, an examination of British society, the discussion of Britain's domestic policies over two decades, 1930–1950, the battle against fascism and the support for non-dogmatic and genuinely revolutionary socialism: the function of literature, therefore, and its relationship with the milieu, with the implicit drawing of a map of English literature in those years and decades. From here arose, pragmatically and empirically, an idea of literature that could photograph life, and, emphatically, the life actually lived by the common people. One often wonders, in surprise, the reason for Orwell's choosing a certain book and writing a certain review, only to discover along the way the far from recondite point of suture or interest (for example, one of those writers fished into the net was Stendhal, exploited as a writer who dealt with class struggle and hatred). The key points of Orwell's essay writing are its polemical obstinacy and its synthetic gift. In one essay-review of no more than a couple of pages, Orwell can often confidently isolate the qualifying import of a book; he is able to grasp its gist, letting us understand more than a long analytical essay would. He almost never wrote simply to fill the allocated space. If many of the more specific questions that absorbed Orwell have by now lost their heat, his remains an engagé essay writing deliciously interspersed with provocative arbitrary pieces, and with others that are totally eccentric and extravagant, like those of a post-Romantic essayist, à la Lamb or Thackeray, whose disciple he was.[42] What are they? For example, that on the saucy postcards, with set caricatures and allusive captions; that on children's literature and on its stereotypes and supposed ideology of faint-hearted reactionism; the cleverly sociological one on the common people's prejudices regarding poetry, precisely caused by a poetry that was abstruse, incomprehensible, and obscure, and on the necessity to attract

---

Also in Orwell's house in Wallington the loo used to become blocked if a too thick toilet paper was used (OCE, vol. I, 392).

42   On Orwell and Lamb cf. Wykes 1987, 111; a parallel between Orwell and Thackeray is insisted on in Brander 1954, 1–2.

people to it through the brand-new support of the radio; or that of Orwell as gourmet, praising the speciality of English cuisine and explaining how to make 'a nice cup of tea', another essay of an eccentric. Are not these and other parenthetical essays, on the nice cup of tea or on English cuisine, or on the variety of flowers recorded by British English, but abolished by American English, in the spirit of Ruskin?

2. At St Cyprian's, in Sussex, Orwell suffered the proverbial toughness and hypocrisies of the British school system, but distinguished himself sufficiently in his studies to win a scholarship to Eton. His evocative auto-biographical essay 'Such, Such Were the Joys'[43] is in line with the Victorian and late Victorian epics of an adolescent's school-day sufferings, and recalls Charlotte Brontë's Lowood (in the poor hygiene and insufficient dietary regime), Thackeray's juvenile sketches, Meredith's *Feverel*, and every other Victorian tract against the inhuman public school systems; except that the hero's first sexual disturbances could not have been described so explicitly by the reticent Victorians.[44] It is a convincing demonstration that, eighty years after Dickens's Dotheboys School, the British school system had changed very little. At the centre of the sketch are two denigrated authoritarian figures, the scowling, masculine Flip, the wife of the headmaster, who is always in riding gear and whirls the whip, the same punishment administered by the headmaster Sambo with amused sadism. In the second section of the sketch the not very secret aim of many second level public schools is unmasked: to attract boys from prominent wealthy families, and let them shine to win scholarships to Eton, bringing reflected glory to the school itself. In this way evident favouritisms in terms of treatment of pupils were created. The curriculum was finalized to seek success in exams; the teaching was fact-based, aged, and in part farcical. A psychosis was soon created in Orwell: win a scholarship or, if not, become a clerk at 40 pounds a year. The poverty of his family, and the fact that he was kept at school in conditions of favour, was brutally rubbed into his face

---

43   From 1947 (OCE, vol. IV, 379–422).

44   In the weekly comics for boys from the 1930s, reviewed in 'Boys' Weeklies', 'Sex [was] completely taboo, especially in the form in which it actually [arose] in public schools' (OCE, vol. I, 509, and cf. below n. 49).

almost daily. This awareness provoked a sense of disesteem and the certainty of being a good-for-nothing, a slacker, and a sinner. Orwell would later never miss the occasion to hold up the reform of the English school as necessary for the advent of socialism. At the same time he thought it urgent to make a sociological analysis that should place the present state of education after the 'ascetic' age of Victorianism, namely, in the early twentieth century, marked by luxury and snobbishness, and the cult of wealth as the supreme value, and by a sense of real, albeit transitory, ease in the high and medium-high middle classes, from which he felt marginalized and estranged. The post-1914 historical moment did present positive signals; nonetheless the memory of vexation at school did not disappear at such a distance, and the memoir closes with the visionary gossip, not denied, of the 'Dickensian' burning of the hated school. At that time, 1947, Orwell was already musing over *Nineteen Eighty-Four*, and it has been easy to connect the two works in the same unconscious and affective genesis, under the mark of a precocious rebellion against an authoritarian system ('I was not a rebel, except by force of circumstances') which, like the Oceanic one embodied in O'Brien, through Flip and Sambo punishes with inflexible, albeit intermittent, sadism, though with sudden flashes of benevolence and capriciousness.

3. In his first literary reviews from 1929 to 1930 Orwell seems to have been suspicious of formalism, in other words of what is tinsel and covers the paucity of the contents under its layers. In the literature of the time he struggled to understand its stylistic sophistication, which seemed to him out of context and mere unjustified bravura pieces. Reviewing a book by Edith Sitwell he criticized its expository haziness, the unnatural English, the excessive length of the words. Anyone overdoing the use of adjectives, embellishments, or rhetoric, like Carlyle, is sniped at. On the other hand, regarding a novel by Priestley, Orwell states that the aim of a fiction writer is to 'be a vehicle of beauty'. Orwell would always hold up and praise the criterion of telling a story 'from the inside' of a character.[45] The novelist's task is to fill the gap dug between the intellectual and the man on the street.

45   OCE, vol. I, 173.

Until Orwell's time, novels had been written by intellectuals for intellectuals, excluding the common people from enjoying them; or they were mere entertainment. Occasionally, he makes attempts at a sociology of literature. For instance, he notices among the general public a disaffection and ignorance of books and good books; he depicts a moment similar to the long Victorian decades, when trashy or crime or women's writing sold like hot cakes; he draws up a list of the titles requested in second-hand bookshops, in order to say that the classics of more than half a century were no longer read. As an expert bookseller, he tells us that long novels are back in fashion, and that the vogue of the short story is over.[46] However, the escapist novel had now been ousted by the emergencies of the present – by Hitler, Mussolini, and the imminent war. 'In Defence of the Novel'[47] is a diagnosis of the decline of the novel, ending, however, with the hope that it would regain vigour thanks to a more honest review procedure, as reviews lowered the standard of excellence with indiscriminate praise. In 1936, the date of this essay, two openly conflictual aesthetics confronted one another in Orwell: the nostalgic residue of art for art's sake and a penchant for the partisan anathema against Catholics and communists. Testing the waters of the publishing world, 'Boys' Weeklies'[48] – a pioneering example of market research – focuses on the English epic of the weekly with stories for boys, through an appraisal of its technique, its ideology, its taboos, and as a sub-product of public school publishing, partially deriving from Kipling and even further back in time from Thackeray and Dickens. These publications had been anachronistic for at least a generation, and over them there reigned a deliberate omission of real references to the world outside, together with a falsification that created prejudices in its audience, and distanced them from a proper assessment of the problems on the table. Orwell fatally recognized in these a right-wing operation, which raised the question not of how left-wing fiction for children might

46   'Bookshop Memories'.
47   OCE, vol. I, 281–7.
48   OCE, vol. I, 505–31.

be possible, but whether it would be possible to make the existing ones more real and credible, and more objective.[49]

4. Orwell's aesthetic is enunciated and articulated in his essays in a progressive way: it is absolute, with unchanging principles and criteria, it is contingent, that is, it becomes slightly more up to date with the passing of the years and the concrete reference to the evolution of contemporary literature. For this reason, many interventions overlap. Orwell found himself debuting as an essayist when the critical fashion, after the 1920s having steered the emphasis onto the technical facts of the literary activity, had begun to insist on the political ones, along with Upton, Henderson, and, to a certain extent, also Caudwell, Marxist critics who expected revolutionary exhortations from committed writers. However, there was a competitive 'revival of Catholicism' in progress that made Orwell curious about Catholic books, or of sociology and history from a Catholic viewpoint. Ultimately, Catholic meant for Orwell 'against capitalism' in the same way that Dickens was; in other terms, for Catholics it was enough that the capitalist should 'behave well'. As a reaction against biased literature cast in ideological terms, Orwell's radio broadcasts midway through 1941 seem to be again defending art for art's sake, for example in the abundant praise of the technique and archaic-style lexicon of Hopkins's sonnet 'Felix Randal', and of the reasons for disinterested apolitical literature. Literature had been invaded too much by politics, or so Orwell found himself forced to maintain; one was living under a threat, and it meant a loss of objectivity. Totalitarianism subjugated and suppressed even thought and freedom of

49   This splendid, easy-read essay aroused, as I mentioned, an equally splendid and sharp rejoinder by the only author – Frank Richards – who for over twenty years had been writing the texts of the little school sagas examined by Orwell. In fact this is a parry even better than Orwell's attack, in its expository clarity, wittiness, and linguistic accuracy, and one that additionally demonstrates Orwell's undocumented apodicticity in various cases. Aside from correcting certain oversights or simple suppositions of Orwell, this reply is a boomerang, since it admits the defensive conservative point of view with which that epic had been written. Other objections are rebutted using remarks that seem to paraphrase the positions of Stevenson, Barrie, and, in part, even Dickens – that it is better not to grow and to remain deluded as long as possible.

thought; moreover, it 'shuts you up in an artificial universe in which you have no standards of comparison'.[50] 'The Rediscovery of Europe'[51] sets a demarcation of the modern at 1917, and in 'Prufrock', and literature prior to 1914 is reviewed to examine what had changed. Before that date writers saw nothing beyond the British borders; after it there were apolitical, 'primitive' writers who were moderate believers, but aesthetically vibrant. Wells is compared with Lawrence to prove the end of utopian interest in science. The war had disillusioned his contemporaries as to the possibilities – nefarious and destructive – of science. In another comparison, between Joyce and Galsworthy, Joyce represents pure technique, and the loss of faith, though with the residual permanence of the mental and cultural frames acquired from Catholicism. These arguments can be traced back to a belated resurgence of the Orwellian myth of the writer's solipsistic avulsion, tending to resistance to standardization, and deaf to the nonsense of progressive slogans: a writer who finds solitary refuge in protest, in the nostalgia for a primitive cosmos that actualized the unison of body and spirit, or in pure technique. 'Writers and Leviathan',[52] late (1948) and recapitulative, again supports the objectivity of critical judgement, hoping it is not conditioned by political ideology, or by occult or blatant propaganda in the book being reviewed or criticized. It is a prodrome of 'doublethink' that Orwell should invite his reader to apply two weights and two measures, or to practise a conscious ambiguity in questions of literary judgement, almost admitting that a book can be beautiful, and artistically successful, even if ideologically and politically reactionary or apolitical. The same, obligatory left-wing collocation of the post-war writer constituted a form of uncomfortable acquiescence to orthodoxy, acceptance of which 'is always to inherit unresolved contradictions': let the writer be an old 'double', acting the propagandist in public squares for his party, but he must be aware that his activity as a writer is 'something apart', even a denial of his public political identity. If 'the invasion of literature by politics' cannot be exorcized, Orwell is the first to make an ideological reading of English literature, attacking his *bêtes*

50   OCE, vol. II, 162.
51   OCE, vol. II, 229–40.
52   OCE, vol. IV, 463–70.

noires, and enthusing over instant idols. Reviewing Eliot's *Four Quartets*, Orwell betrays a hostility and enmity that would later be mitigated. For him, Eliot was better pagan and atemporal in the face of death than forcedly religious, in line with a questionable, arbitrary, functional instinctive aversion to a reactionary, religious, solemn, converted poet, and a preference for a poetry that was despairing but ardent, in Eliot's early manner, against that of a melancholy faith in the second. Yet Eliot's early poems were Decadent, and gave voice to a 'rentier' aristocracy unable to act. On the strength of the principle he had declared, that 'all art is [...] propaganda', behind Eliot, says Orwell, lay an ideology, one that was misguided at that. Eliot, he adds, emerged from his Decadent futility by ageing, and choosing one of the three roads offered to poets, that of joining the or a Church. Orwell always nourished a particular aversion – even if he himself wrote a fable – for authors of fables and books for children. Barrie is excoriated, and Stevenson declared intolerable, perhaps because they were writers of escapism from the real. Galsworthy is not a *bête noire*; however, Orwell loses no occasion to attack him for having become, from a subversive writer, an entertainer. A recurring target, not to say one gradually habitual, is one class or a subspecies: that of the stricter Marxist intelligentsia, which is guilty of approving the Stalinist regime blindly, and which is therefore only ironically 'illuminated', in Orwell's terms. Acrobatic, disparate, clutching at straws of the category of 'good bad poetry', is the eulogy *in extremis* of Kipling, after having stamped him as aesthetically execrable and an apologist of white violence, because he was merely pre-fascist or a sentimental fascist, without counting a gift that ultimately Orwell always praises, his adherence to reality described with seriousness, precision and objectivity, and his poetic realism, often exaggerated in its dialect effects and thus verging on farce. In short, Kipling had celebrated the permanence of the pedestrian, the vulgar, the commonplace, the semi-beautiful, preferable to the foaming of Wilde's epigrams or Shaw's mottoes. Yeats was in turn nostalgic and Decadent, from the same family as Eliot. In itself, nostalgia is not, as we have seen, a distasteful and negative gift for Orwell, quite the opposite; however, it must be nostalgia for the right values. That it was always positive to exaggerate in realism, rather than the contrary, is the premise underlying Orwell's essays praising Henry Miller, who wrote on the side of the concrete and for the man in the street.[53] Miller had 'debased' human nature in the already mature era of the collapse of religion in the modern world, that is, he had avoided the 'mawkishness' and the glamour of sex as represented during the last century of fiction, calling attention to its crude reality. Hence Miller had come close to Swift in conceiving man as a Yahoo. But the vision of nothingness provokes in him open joy and enthusiasm for life, not pessimism.[54]

5. 'Inside the Whale'[55] (1940), an impassioned and engaging essay, contains an in-depth and as never before organic appraisal of every phase of English literature practically from the 1890s to the outbreak of the Second World War. It is the theory and the history of the English literature of that half-century as seen by Orwell, and therefore a partisan, provocative history that naturally only deals with one face of the prism, or sees only one colour of it. The inspiration was Henry Miller's *Tropic of Cancer*, a novel from 1935 on the life of expatriate American artists, largely degenerate and penniless, partially genuine and partially not, in scenarios of a suburban, fishy, shady, dishonest Paris. It was that same city where Orwell, not by chance, had lived 'down and out' at the end of the 1920s, and which he had nevertheless idealized with his indomitable spirit of bawdy sociability. Orwell, in that essay, really does want to clutch at straws, in other words defend the indefensible, that is, a novel, such as Miller's, that studied this environment, and emerged from it, without caring about Hitler and Mussolini and the winds of war. A disengaged novel, then, exactly while an activist, revolutionary, politicized way of writing, inspired by Marxism, was all the rage. Orwell finds that Miller's novel lingered in the mind, that it created its own atmosphere and that, like Joyce's, it had – an apparent miracle – made the familiar and everyday visible and narratable, since for Orwell literature had always verged on the opposite extreme, and had been too falsifying, too poetic, and too

---

53   Cf. in particular his review of *Tropic of Cancer* (OCE, vol. I, 178–80).

54   After the publication of *Black Spring*, Orwell was to keep his distance, however: Miller had escaped at a tangent from depicting the real, towards a 'Mickey Mouse' world where the concepts of time and space had disappeared. Orwell was extremely severe over late Miller, in whom he perceives a 'nihilistic quietism'.

55   OCE, vol. I, 540–78.

filtered. Miller's merit is that of writing on the man in the street, describing credible characters, without a linguistic filter and by means of an immediate contact with reality.[56] As a comparison, Orwell distinguishes Miller's manner from that of Céline, defeatist and apocalyptic, and compares him, in the way he accepted the real, to Whitman. We are disoriented hearing Orwell praise a writer like Miller who seems to passively accept the horrors of 1920s and 1930s civilization, and absolutely everything about it. Yet, in this way, Miller is closer to the 'ordinary man'. Orwell returns therefore to the axiom – one of his most repeated – that humanity is brutalized, faceless, resigned, and passive, save for some highly individual intellectuals. In fact, it can be understood that Miller's defence is paradoxical and provocative – specious to be more precise, because Orwell must, with Miller, rebut a communist literature that is insincere, spoilt, enslaved, a corruption of good, and therefore abysmal. Orwell attends to this repudiation in the second chapter of the essay, a reasoned analysis of English literature practically from the dawn of the century, starting from Housman's naturalistic vogue[57] followed in the decade 1920–1930 by a different group that included Eliot, Pound, Wyndham Lewis, Lawrence, Huxley, and Strachey. The keynote were the pessimistic gaze and the tragic sense of life; almost everyone invoked a return to the past, almost everyone believed in a world without God, and all betrayed a striking political indifference; in fact, for them literature consisted only in the 'manipulation of words'. No one was left-wing, they all leaned towards conservatism and some of them towards Catholicism. Such pessimism could flourish because the writers lived in an era of widespread prosperity. Orwell seems to have found his natural allies in the political poets of the 1930s, but this impression is mistaken. This Marxist-influenced literature was no longer close to the masses, and those poets' siding with communism meant the joining of a movement which, born to fight capitalism, had degenerated into a tool of Russian foreign policy. They had joined communism, as others had Catholicism, as a nest, a barrier and a refuge in the face of the slide in values. But this was the 'patriotism of

---

56 This parameter is closer than it seems to the one applied, in praise, to Hopkins's poetry in the in-depth reading of the sonnet 'Felix Randal'.
57 Cf. Volume 6, § 251.1 and n. 2.

the deracinated', and its members were young writers, irresponsible in their support of violence. The diagnosis, limited to 'Inside the Whale', is that it is better to steer clear of politics, albeit not totally, since we must tackle the dilemma, either keep mum or assent to the Party directive. Orwell always felt his duty to count himself outside of any even hypothetical community that jeopardized the independence, integrity and jealous isolation of the writer. The basic thesis seems clear, namely, disgust for enslaving communism, which authorizes and invites choosing Miller's passivity. The novel, by definition an unimpeachable, free, and Protestant literary form, rather than Catholic-dogmatic – a debatable thesis, naturally, that there are no good Catholic novels – did not enjoy good health *pour cause* in the 1930s. Orwell's constant nightmare is the stamping out of human individuality by new totalitarianisms: on the contrary, it matters to him that mankind continues to survive as consciousness, with the feeling of being individual. Therefore absenteeism and disaffection are merely a justified temporary behaviour, in the historical interval between the end of liberal literature and another literature – it is to be hoped – re-given freedom of movement. The 1930s were not a world and a time for writers, and the writer saw himself as condemned to the belly of the whale waiting for more propitious times.

6. 'The Lion and the Unicorn',[58] from 1941, is dedicated to the defence and safeguarding, in a time of national emergencies, of British sanity, albeit with its pardonable flaws. It must above all acrobatically exonerate, if not approve, patriotism, a value which one might perhaps deem a little, if not totally, anti-socialist.[59] Orwell is no defeatist, in fact his wish is to build, and he praises his compatriots, though he is objective about their hypocrisies (the Empire), their weaknesses and idiosyncrasies. In 1941, the gut hatred of class was less than the need felt by all to defend the homeland; even internationalism took a back seat (save among the left-wing, anti-patriotic intelligentsia). At a time when there was a dread of Hitler's invasion and the conquest of the island, Orwell yelled at the danger and invoked the revolution of the British model and elevated Britain to a bastion of freedom.

---

58   OCE, vol. II, 74–134.
59   Orwell lauds Byron's 'The Isles of Greece' several times because of its patriotic sentiment.

With 'Blimp' and the Blimps, Orwell defines the class of the imperialist military bourgeoisie, and Blimp is a prototype of the demobbed colonel with a pea for a brain. Together with this target, Orwell aims at that of the xenophile red intelligentsia. In his diagnosis of British society he notes how the standard of living had risen for everyone thanks to technology and mechanical progress, but without salaries rising. In the second part he answers the question: why is socialism better than capitalism? Because there is no production surplus in socialism, or any production of goods with the sole aim of personal profit for the producers. Nazism seemed like socialism as an owner of production means, but this was a subterfuge to institute equality and exploitation. In that period of emergency the ruling class had to be changed, and economic inequality to be levelled; it was especially necessary to start a revolution, bloody or not. 'The war and revolution are inseparable', that is, it was not possible to establish socialism without defeating Hitler, nor was it possible to defeat Hitler if society remained ideologically stuck in the eighteenth century. The birth of a revolutionary British socialism could not, however, be entrusted to the Labour Party, linked as it was to capitalists and imperialism. The driving group must be that of workers and the middle class, the latter allied to the workers. Orwell becomes singularly proactive, and formulates a kind of programmatic map of post-war socialist Britain in six qualifying points. Among these was the nationalization of the mining industry. However, income was not to be distributed on a totally equal basis but on a 1–10 range. For the sake of consistency, India would be granted the status of a 'dominion', since it was not possible to proceed to total decolonization overnight. Orwell is hopeful that such a sub-movement could come to life, and that it would put a stop to certain gangrenous ganglions of power. His rejection of pacifists is therefore obvious, and in fact it was soon extended[60] to the figure of Gandhi.

7. In 1938, Orwell was convinced that a revolution, in the context of a victory over fascisms, was possible, but not as a peaceful form of collaboration between the classes, especially between the rich and the poor, who

60   Letter to I. Jones, in OCE, vol. II, 134–6.

would always be the thief and the victim of theft, respectively. A drastic change was needed, 'if necessary also violent', without losing contact, as communism and fascism had done, with the essential values of democracy. 'I am not a Marxist', Orwell had proclaimed,[61] adding that he was not among those who used to state that the Party, or a party, was always right. If it was known that in Russia a process of modernization had already begun before the revolution, the question was: were they better off before or after? Orwell does not do a startling thing after all when he belittles Trotsky, who would have been a Stalin once risen to power. In 1939, the warmongering sentiment of the Left was suspect for him since it would have led to a retraction, and brought a British fascism to life. The year 1940 closed with Orwell's profession as interventionist, having identified what he believed to be the connection between an incipient revolution in Britain and the necessity for armed resistance against Hitler. On the outbreak of the war, in particular on the strength of the Russo-German pact, Orwell reached the conviction that fascism and Stalinism were contrary and the same, that is, two variants of the same totalitarianism, or oligarchic collectivism. The war, seen from Britain and the Left, responded to two combined objectives: beating Hitler and overturning the capitalist regime in force in Britain, and this was felt not only by the proletariat, but by now also by the middle classes, who could find common cause with the former. 'My Country Right or Left',[62] from 1940, summarizes Orwell's evolution from a primitive, almost complacent absenteeism at the time of the Great War to a fashionable pacifism and then to the discovery that it was necessary to defend the homeland from dictatorship and to support it in the war against Hitler. It must, in other words, absolve socialism from patriotism and interventionism. Supporting the war had become a logical consequence for socialists who had given their support to the Spanish Republicans, even if this was Chamberlain's war. In 'The English People',[63] from 1944, Orwell had by this time realized that the impact of the war made patriotism stronger, and observed that the class

---

61   OCE, vol. I, 404.
62   OCE, vol. I, 587–92.
63   OCE, vol. III, 15–55. Its unusually more rosy and official mood, that of an anodyne documentary, was due to its destination (the *England Illustrated* series).

divisions had softened into a more general form of solidarity, even if the proletarians stood out for their scant revolutionary sentiment. Here, for the first time, pops up that congenitally irreligious, in fact pagan, British proletariat, healthily dedicated to the pleasures of life, which is the life-buoy of the totalitarian society in *Nineteen Eighty-Four*. In the final part of the essay there is a timid hint of the way in which a socialist revolution can be started, a peaceful one, without bloodshed; but as for the future, a world divided into three blocks is already dreaded.

§ 23. *Orwell III: The reportages*

A diary-style work in various chapters, *Down and Out in Paris and London* (1933) is an autobiography that is only slightly distanced and retouched, and therefore told in the present tense, almost off the cuff, by a witness – Orwell himself in Paris to teach languages – of anecdotes and slices of life in a slum. Its episodes include instances of involuntary, poetic *camaraderie*, filth (bedbugs are omnipresent), mean tricks to survive, chronic booze-ups, the moral and existential discomfort of abject poverty (on average six francs a day), the humiliating performances at the pawnbroker's. In the sleazy hotels the availability of 're-sellable' clothes is the only guarantee to avoid being evicted from the rented room; with suspected insolvents having to pay a deposit. However, one fact of this cross-section of 1930s Paris is also the desire to enjoy life, to find leisure time, to have fun, namely, wine and sex.[64] The milieu is of the penniless, and like the Victorian London of braggarts, Paris is the city of immigrants, Italians, Brits, Arabs, Hungarians and post-revolution Russians. The narrator's right-hand man soon becomes Boris the waiter, a former Russian fusilier who is fired by optimism on a full stomach, but in reality never gets anywhere. Tasty and salacious anecdotes alternate with jokes, such as the one about the waiter who believed he had prayed to St Eloise, receiving from her the miracle of a few francs, before realizing that the miraculous effigy was only that of a prostitute, and so he owed the saint nothing *ex voto*. In short, this is

---

64   In the first pages, a braggart Charlie is confusedly recounting his experience in a
      luxury brothel (1,000 francs for a mercenary rapport with a reluctant but needy
      virgin).

a small, involuntary Parisian picaresque, its odysseys closed within the urban perimeter, and with the two tramps, one English one Russian, who always believe in cheating others, resorting to a thousand tricks, and are instead cheated themselves, until Orwell is forced to work in a hotel as a dishwasher. In this hotel, a subtle study of hierarchical relationships soon forms. We really come to know all the work rhythm, the positions and the activities, and even the behind-the-scenes secrets of the micro-community of waiters and cooks, as Wesker was later to portray in his play, *The Kitchen*. Orwell's second job is found in a disreputable, ramshackle, never open and ill-equipped Russian restaurant, after having disastrously left the previous one. This long interlude on restaurants destroys the myth of the goodness and impeccability of French and Parisian cuisine. At the time, Orwell, or his double, reveals that he had never been minimally politicized: he knew nothing of the communists, so much so that he agrees to string them along by writing make-believe articles on British politics for a Russian newspaper. This was a prophetic intuition many years early: Orwell rebels against the pure copying of a British conservative rag, with the announcement that it is enough to write the opposite of what they say. Other political murmurings? The *plongeurs* are enslaved, brutalized beasts with no time to think, while they really ought to form and politicize themselves into a union. Moreover, fear of the plebeians induces the upper classes to keep the masses busy to stop them thinking. The second part sees this life of hardships repeated in London, but the dormitory scenes evoke a spine-chilling sense of disgust (stench, coughing, stinks) where the Parisian scene was enjoyably bawdy. The background is England during the depression of the 1930s. The poor souls receive a hand-out of tea and a *brioche* in exchange for taking part in the prayers in the chapel; however, like Buñuel's vagabonds, they are unable to be grateful, offending and spouting blasphemous language. Where the French journal was witty and humorous, the English one accentuates the disgust, degradation and squalor. Like Dickens, Orwell does nothing to hide the snobbery of the poor, in the gestures of authority, in class consciousness and in the aristocracy within the status of the vagabond. The political agenda is the accusation against useless professions and induced luxury. The paradox is that being a beggar is a job like many others, in fact better than many which bring no benefits. If only beggars were wealthy they would be more socially tolerated, therefore being is having. The last chapter deals with the widespread prejudice against socially dangerous tramps, whereas their life is the only outlet for destitution. Here the voice takes on a different tone, is no more homodiegetic but external, and it lucidly and wisely points to the social pathology to be remedied.

2. In *The Road to Wigan Pier*[65] (1937) Orwell observes that many communist miners he had met considered him an educated middle-class person; in the diary from which he had taken this reportage, however, he also noted the effect he had on them, that of an 'honorary proletarian'.[66] He had also approached socialism thanks to the owners of the bookshop where he was an assistant, who were activists in the Independent Labour Party; however, it was the publisher Gollancz who commissioned this reportage on unemployment in the mining districts, and who paid him an advance on sales.[67] *The Road to Wigan Pier* sways continuously between reportage, that is, from facts gathered live, *in loco*, and statistics, political diatribe, interspersed however with personal examples and demonstrative occurrences, and sketches. A documentary part – the life of the worker, especially the miner – serves for the thesis, the necessity of socialism, the socialism that Orwell approved of and supported: with socialism implemented, society would function better and the worker would have a more decorous life. At the end of the reportage Orwell is confident to have precociously shown and argumented some of his strong points, such as an analysis of the middle class that claims to be a socialist champion of the proletariat with its subtle inconsistencies and prejudices, against the

65   The objective of the journey was 'romantic', as Orwell himself revealed: to see a famous wharf – on the muddy canal that runs around the town – which, however, unknown to him, had been demolished in the meantime (cf. OCE, vol. I, 296). In reality, Wigan lies well inland on *terra firma*, equidistant between Liverpool and Manchester, in the upper tip of a triangle whose two lower angles are very obtuse.

66   OCE, vol. I, 221.

67   Orwell stayed in Wigan for just two months to take notes on the conditions of the miners and cotton workers; then he went to Liverpool to meet the dockworkers; then up to Yorkshire, to Sheffield and Leeds. Gollancz, of proven Marxist faith, wrote *ex post* a long memo in which he distanced himself from Orwell's heterodox positions on socialism.

background of an already fairly complete retrospective of the development of British society from just after the war until the time of writing. The opening of the first of the two parts is as much an aseptic dossier on the working conditions of the industrial and mining districts – given by a homo- and heterodiegetic narrator – as a composite satirical and grotesque vignette in whose centre stands out the lodging-house, with adjacent tripe shop, of the Brooker couple. This space-time element, the none-too-clean lodging-house, says a lot about Orwell's literary ancestry. Dickens and Trollope and occasionally Thackeray had made it one of the privileged settings of their fictional universe; Orwell surprises us and wins us over with a satire that is as biting, merciless, and visionary as in Dickens. He wishes to inform and persuade – that was exactly how things were, I witnessed it, believe me – but the scene is also worthwhile as a creative page on its own. The typical Victorian satire of the boarding-house focused on the eccentricity of its inmates, and so does Orwell. The hygienic conditions are scrutinized under a magnifying glass with a finely tuned capacity for isolating the revolting detail: the crumbs on the table in the morning are the same as those of the evening before, and they move imperceptibly across the tablecloth; the buttered bread always bears the black fingerprints of the owner's ever filthy hands; and where does it come from and how often, and so how fresh is it, that tripe in the shop, which is never served for lunch? On the filthy, closely packed beds of the room sleep four guests, each with their own eccentricities. The idiosyncrasies of the Brooker couple, often repellent, receive a masterly treatment. Sociologically, in this historical moment, the 1930s, the conditions of the lower middle class and the suburban proletarians were just as unstable as in the middle Victorian decades. The marriage rate was perhaps still low, and people preferred to live as bachelors in lodgings and simple rooms, since it was already difficult not just to buy a house but even to rent one, which would be, apart from anything else, small and dramatically lacking in even the most basic comforts, such as a bathroom with hot water. As a result, the business of the lodging with meals survived and flourished, meeting the parasitic existence, of pure and passive subsistence, of many unemployed, invalids, or pensioners. With his condemnation of working-class passivity Orwell establishes the key point of his political thinking: the exhortation to the proletariat to give itself a shake, and identify the mysterious power that loomed over it waiting to clip its wings; in short, to join forces. As in Dickens, the worker can be cleaner – this is a fact of personal commitment and will-power – but 'circumstances' do not encourage him.[68] In the long term, Orwell is an observer of poverty who camouflages himself the better to bear witness to it, like Yeats, the gatherer of myths, wandering the Irish countryside. He goes on reconnaissance, pretends to trust extracts from his diary and notes taken along the way. He describes the descent of the miner, the long and difficult road to reach the coal seam on all fours, the phases and procedures of the extraction work, even the belt that carries the coal to the cage that is lifted. The technicalities of the mining work are all there. Then he shows and describes how the miner washes, all black with coal and soot, and the sorry conditions of the dwellings. It should be the State that ensures the miner a more decent life: he is a benefactor of society, which at that time lived off, and hinged on, coal. The quiet, lucid, rigorously informative tone, at times moderately witty, evokes that of the nineteenth-century reports on the European school systems, for example Matthew Arnold's. When Orwell tackles subjects like the miner's personal hygiene, the lowly pay, the risks and the mortality rate – the firedamp! – his typically conservative caution and his suspicion of modernity and mechanization emerge, while the nostalgic eulogy of healthy muscular and manual strength soars. He poses the problem of the slums like Shaw does: what is urgent is a radical solution, not an intervention on the single case or a simple lowering of rents. *The Road to Wigan Pier* is an intertextual book, but not because Arnold or Shaw are surreptitiously cited. Orwell mildly criticizes Lawrence, who had written that the black boundary walls emerging from the snow-covered hills rippled away into the distance 'like muscle'. When he denies that the slums are made to exist by those who live there and not the contrary, he

68   The wellbeing of green nature is unattainable in this black labyrinth with its impenetrable confines; the antithesis produces spontaneous revolts typical of an incognito disciple of Ruskin.

cites Galsworthy, who put this false truth into the mouth of an owner. And how many arrows are shot at Chesterton, author of the *boutade* that coal is not the driving force of civilization and that the slum is poetry. When Orwell tackles head-on the pros and cons of the project to reconstruct council housing, the book reveals its hybrid character even more unmistakeably. In other words, he has come to frankly discuss political measures, and the literary invention is on hold. We can almost witness a new, perceptible regurgitation of Orwell's conservatism when he seems to be defending the right of slum dwellers to enjoy the dirt and degradation, but in freedom at least, whereas life in 'Corporation houses'[69] is oppressive and coercive. The decade of the Depression came from the 1929 crisis, but this one was different from those of the past, and one in which poverty did not give up on pleasures, bragging and splendour. Orwell cites the example of the cheap warehouse clothing that clad these poor like cinema stars. Cinema and fashion had entered the arena, together with other distinguishing marks of a faster civilization that alleviated hunger: such as the telegraph, editions of American newspapers, radio, and the football pools. With Swift, for Orwell too humans are animals that eat, not spirits that think. The stirred sociologist and dietologist notes the damage to the worker's physique caused by a reckless diet that harms both the body's beauty and health, which the lean salary obliges. Orwell is, oddly, in favour of a Ruskin-style life that is 'aesthetic' in its own way, since the worker must also be beautiful in body. The final chord is that progress goes against *mens sana in corpore sano*, and this is announced in the tirade against tinned food, precooked and harmful to health.

3. The second, totally theoretical part of *The Road to Wigan Pier*, builds à la Arnold – and here lies its importance – a theory of British class stratification: the middle class with an income fluctuating between £300 and £2,000 per annum, the 'lower-upper-middle-class' that leans towards the lower limit, possessing the manners of the upper class but not the means, its culture but not its substance. A cross-section is drawn, a theory, a vision of British post-First World War society until the time

---

69   Council housing expressly built by council bodies.

of writing, as in a livelier, less robed *Culture and Anarchy*. Gissing is also central for Orwell since he had coined the figure and the concept of the 'unclassed': 'Here I am, for instance, with a bourgeois upbringing and a working-class income. Which class do I belong to?'. The heart or one of the hearts of the discussion is Orwell's attempt to analyse why the more or less upper class cannot stand the proletarians, and therefore the effort to transcend this prejudice. The middle class – and Gissing's reference is even more pertinent – cannot approach the proletariat because they are unwashed and they stink. The final point is the ineradicable demarcation between bourgeoisie and socialism. Middle-class people remain middle class, they find it hard to mingle with the class they support, and remain on the sidelines. To show this, Orwell resorts to a summary of a British post-war society who had triggered a war of the young against the old and against any form of authority and orthodoxy. The young who had come out of the public schools were both socialist and snobbish at the same time, but in fact theirs was a snobbish socialism. Their acknowledged inconsistency was that on the one hand they had been condemning, at fifteen, the capitalist system, while on the other they had become annoyed with the proletariat. Orwell reveals to us that he had emerged from his experiences in Burma and India as an anti-imperialist, and having felt on his return an impelling need to exonerate himself, which translated into a decision to reinvent himself. This is an instance of dutiful analogy: the poor souls of Britain are the equivalent of the Burmese. In this book, however, Orwell's socialism is rash or fatally partial. The world resembled a raft on which there are provisions for all; which is to say, everyone needed to work for the same remuneration, thereby obtaining the corresponding portion of the provisions. In reply to the question as to why socialism was behind in 1937, and beaten on all sides by fascism, Orwell adduced that the socialist is a middle-class person shunned by the proletariat, whose language he does not speak because of the frequent use of abstractions. Socialism could be reduced to two slogans: 'justice and common decency' for all, or 'justice and liberty'. The final issue concerns the connection between socialism and 'mechanical progress', a link that needs to be debunked, denied, reconsidered, on pain of socialism becoming a losing force. Once again, Orwell echoes Ruskin, though not Morris, formulating a kind of medieval socialism that is natural, idyllic and patriarchal, that of the ancient hard-working communities operating within an industrialized society, but only to the inevitable extent; and a British socialism, scaled to the problems of the nation, independent and separate from Russia. Straight to the point, the machine makes 'a fully human life impossible'. In the repudiation of the myth of utopian socialism, and of its slogan 'a glittering future for all', there is a whiff of *Nineteen Eighty-Four*. Progress points to a goal of luxury that everyone wishes to exorcize, even if it is doubtful that humans do not feel well when they are not working; and mechanization will clip creativity's wings.[70] And fascism? We would expect an Orwell who is furious, dismissive, scandalized. Instead he defines it as a mirror image of socialism, which means fascism without its flaws!

4. Orwell arrived in Spain at the end of December 1936, his sole reason being that of fighting fascism on the side of the Workers' Party of Marxist Unification, or POUM in Spanish. A witness of the unrest in Barcelona, he received a flesh wound and was admitted to hospital. Back home in July 1937, he settled again in Wallington, declining an offer to return as a journalist to India. Because of a pulmonary lesion he then spent almost six months in a sanatorium, whiling away the time by fishing and writing reviews. For the same reason he went to convalesce in Morocco with his wife Eileen for six months. *Homage To Catalonia* (1938) was preceded by various intermediate interventions from the field of action or immediately after his farewell, of which 'Spilling the Spanish Beans', the most articulate one, briefly summarizes the positions. In this precious memo, from 1937, which is also an abbreviated version of *Homage*, Orwell aims to inform his compatriots of the real internal relationships with the Left and with the republican forces during the war, and to polemically condemn the fact that the most serious disinformation and distortion was practised in Britain by the communist or working-class publications, the *Daily Worker*

70   Orwell rails against those, such as Ruskin, Morris, Hopkins and the Victorian medi-evalists, who had been unable to imagine a future society that was not a repetition of a past one, and found, for example, such an unsurpassed or asymptotic model in the Middle Ages: 'there is no need to pretend that [a desirable civilization] has ever existed in space and time'.

and the *Daily Chronicle*. Orwell was writing riskily with the war still in progress, and restricting his sights to Barcelona and Catalonia. The first bitter truth is that the Spanish government, including the semi-autonomous one of Catalonia, was, while Orwell was writing, more frightened of the revolution than of the fascists, having implemented a reign of terror, restricted the freedom of the press, suppressed the parties, and filled the gaols not with fascists but with revolutionaries, whose ideas were not too right-wing, but too left-wing.[71] The true war, or a war, was the one inside the anti-Franco bloc, a war between revolution and counter-revolution. Orwell had left the Spanish government a liberal-communist coalition in which the communists were a counter-revolutionary force, allied with middle-class reformism. His theory of the genesis of the war saw Franco as the head of a coalition of landowners and a parasitical Church. Both the workers and the middle class were fighting against this neo-feudalism; in other respects sworn enemies, they had the common goal of avoiding a penalized economy. The Popular Front, which resulted, was a monstrosity, one side fighting in the long term for capitalism and the other for socialism. In fact, in the early phases of the war, the workers had launched an egalitarian society with compulsory purchases and collectivism, workers' militia in charge of proletarians, but rashly leaving control to the government. This brief interlude had ended with the exit from the government of the anarchists and the entry of communists and right-wing socialists, when the middle classes were allowed to re-emerge and society was allowed to become class conscious again. This seems like an early resolution of the allegory of *Animal Farm*, with a parallelism between Spanish events and those in Russia, because Orwell also identifies a circular process that is the exact breakup of that of the revolution. Paradoxically, Russia had supplied arms to the government with the premise that it would stop the revolution, in order to avoid compromising the Russian-French alliance and good relations with Britain. *Ergo*, communist Russia had become a counter-revolutionary nation! Communist propaganda focused in an

---

71   Among the British, Bob Smillie, the grandson of the leader of the Wigan miners, had been imprisoned merely because he had been found in possession of obsolete bombs and other war souvenirs.

underhand way on the fact that fascism means irrationality, aberration, mania, and horror, but without acknowledging its links with capitalism; in fact fascism could have been fought through middle-class democracy. Anyone who opposed such falsification was accused of being Trotskyite.[72] Indeed, it was the Trotskyists of the Workers' Party of Marxist Unification (POUM) who were imprisoned in Spain at the time, and Orwell was one of them. He was defined as a fascist in disguise, who, by posing as an ultra-revolutionary, intended to break up the left-wing forces. In reality, Orwell shows that the Trotskyists, the authentic and only ones who were still revolutionary communists, supported the objectives that only a short time before the communists were supporting. And paradoxically the authentically fascist government is the liberal-communist one that imprisoned the Trotskyists and therefore imposed a dictatorship: ostensibly fighting fascism, it was actually steering the country towards fascism.

5. In *Homage to Catalonia* the war diary unfolds along the lines of the good-natured mockery of the army's lack of preparation, of its phlegm that is inconceivable to the Briton. It is just as symptomatic that discipline is not repudiated at all by Orwell, while respect for hierarchical relationships is deemed necessary. But this criticism is offset by recognition of the natural goodness and frankness of the comrades in arms. After training, the volunteer was sent to the Aragonese front, where a kind of War of the Buttons was in progress, in an atmosphere of exasperating inaction. Anyone looking for an exhaustive war story is, however, disappointed: in retrospect, in fact, Orwell regretted that he had fought little and had not fulfilled his romantic dream of achieving something concrete against capitalism. Two mythologizings can be attributed to him: he is always the Briton who feels superior, rational, and an organizer, and thus able to teach, and as a result a little know-it-all. His party, the POUM, had been accused of conniving with the fascists, and Orwell really was a little fascist when he added that, at the end of the day, Spanish fascism had a human face. For Orwell, the Barcelona uprising of May 1937 was that of a city by then free from any revolutionary ardour, sunk in its private sphere and solely interested in

---

72   This term is defined, in its three senses, as the champion of a global revolution, a member of that Spanish party, a fascist in disguise.

the internal feud between anarchists and communists, rather than in the outcome of the war. In the crucial eleventh chapter of *Homage* the object is that of exonerating anarchists and Trotskyists from the accusation of having provoked an insurrection to stab the Spanish government in the back. The two factions were therefore accused of secretly conniving with fascism. Orwell brings the backstage to light and defends the anarchists above all, who had been systematically denigrated by the press. He denies that the POUM is Trotskyite, and states that the definition of Trotskyite applies to any dissident who undermines the monolithic and absolutist stance of the Communist Party.

§ 24. *Orwell IV: 'Burmese Days'. Outcasts in Burma*

Orwell's ideological and political growth begins ideally from the edges of the Empire, the first link that counts in his biography; however, the suicide of the protagonist in *Burmese Days*[73] (published in 1934 in America, the following year in Britain) suggests that Orwell objectified and distanced it, understanding the blind alley he would end up in had he remained a policeman in India. The novel comes in the wake of Kipling, because of its British community tossed into an unreal and unnatural geographic and spiritual climate. It does not touch on an area of Conrad, which is merely close; it does, however, borrow and mirror Conrad's irresistible magic – the paralysing magic of the Orient, with its loss of awareness and self-determination. It also repeats, from both, a similar political analysis: the British in Burma are a variegated community, some good-for-nothings like Ellis, who is the voice of sinister reactionism and racism; others are noble, Kipling-like apostles of the white man's burden; others still, exceptions,

---

73   The idea of 'going east' had begun to germinate in Orwell at Eton. On the outbreak of the Great War, his father enlisted and was ordered to Marseilles, and Orwell himself was militarily trained without interrupting his job as a journalist. Having decided not to enrol at Oxford, his family suggested he emigrate to India or Burma, where his grandmother lived. In January 1922 he enrolled in the course for India Office executives and left in October that same year. In the summer of 1926, he came back home on leave and took advantage of this to hand in his notice for unspecified health reasons.

have stripped imperialism of its cloak of falsehood, uncovering the fact that its goal is merely exploitation.[74] Flory, the male protagonist, is an unrecognizable Kurtz, as is Orwell – to anticipate – in his sketch 'Shooting an Elephant', with his division between reason and instinct, institutional and non-institutional functions. There coexist in Flory an instinctive hatred for the 'yellow faces', objectively repulsive, devious, duplicitous, and the rationalized dismantling of the imperial system. As an official, Flory is an oppressor; as a thinking human being he is the opposite, since he supports the locals and sides with them. Politically, the exploiters, who have everything to oppress with, are in some cases themselves oppressed and exploited, and therefore powerless. The majority of the local Burmese are passive parasites: they fight for survival, and pay homage to their lords and masters as a result. For example the British, having a need for servants, provide work for many locals; prostitution thrives and the brothels are crawling, the bazaars overflowing with foodstuffs only because they are staples of the colonizers. This is the locals' retribution on their oppressors. Ultimately, *Burmese Days* ends tragically only because of the extortion of the kept woman against Flory. Technically, it is still a novel of a nineteenth-century type: certain sexual allusions are more explicit and denote the renewal in customs and a slackening in prudery; but the module is frequently that of Victorian satire and Dickensian caricature, and of the variety and eccentricity of the characters within a small closed area, the meeting place of the European Club. Embedded in this setting is the sentimental story of the debauched and lethargic Dickensian hero, who seeks the redemptive little flame in eroticism, without finding it.

2. *Burmese Days* elects as a microcosm of Burma, and of the British imperial domination, Kyauktada, a town of 4,000 natives with seven British

---

74   These wrecks of humanity, who caught by nostalgia for their homeland are awaiting their packet of newspapers and fantasize in a melancholy but paralysed vein, resemble the three, unrealistic wrecked sailors in Stevenson's *The Ebb-Tide*, or in fact the 'outcasts of the islands' of the early Conrad. Orwell was to return to Conrad's motif of the outcast in his last novel, left as a sketch, *A Smoking-Room Story*. Nor is there a lack of thematic and structural analogies with Forster's *A Passage to India*, above all in the friendly relationship between an Indian doctor and an Englishman.

citizens in residence, working in branches of the police, the administration and commerce. The daily rendezvous is at the European Club where the British sunbathe, squabble, and vent their frustrations and neuroses. This could be a theatrical scene in prose, with its cyclical evening rhythm and its conventions taking place in this claustrophobic and explosive atmosphere. The very title suggests a succession of monotonous, arid days without a meaning, an end, or an objective. However, the novel is at the very least bifocal, since its first mainspring is the intrigue devised by the local magistrate U Po Kyin to rise, as a Burmese, through the echelons of imperial power. This native is a rare emblem of the enterprising spirit, as corrupted and revolting as it is, in an otherwise subjugated and apathetic Burmese context. To reach this goal U Po Kyin must undermine the prestige of Doctor Veraswami, who, westernized, is a sincere friend of the British and an admirer of their civilization, and is protected by Flory, who forces himself to see the good in the natives, and, vaguely a communist, denounces to his compatriots, through gritted teeth, the falsehoods and infamies of the Empire, of which against his will he is a tool. The meek Indian doctor is arguably the only positive character in the novel, albeit a poor disenchanted man; all the others are wicked and irredeemable, and show their worst side and their human nullity, above all when in danger. The mark of Dickens emerges in the caricatures of the locals with their frequently disgusting somatic traits, their smells, their life habits; the small British community is in turn a collection of highly disagreeable sketches.[75] If Orwell was in search of an 'organic', authentic community, that of the British in Burma was definitely a 'counter-community'. Flory, who in some ways resembles Clennam in Dickens's *Little Dorrit*, is a thirty-five-year-old whom Orwell describes with an ugly, bluish birthmark on his cheek.[76] The end of the

---

75   Graham Greene, Muggeridge and other reviewers (CRHE, 52, 55, 56) noted exaggerations and imprecisions, and an excessive and unjust satirical swiping at the British and local corruption.

76   This is a probable reminiscence of Dickens (Volume 5, § 35.1), aiming to express obscure implosions and decisive hindrances. On the other hand, confirming the persistent influence of Dickens's novels in Orwell, Elizabeth has the habit of leaving her sentences unfinished, like Rosa Dartle in *David Copperfield* (this comparison is

novel includes an overview of the characters' successive careers, using, like Dickens, the retaliation strategy to show how they were promoted or punished in and for their designs.[77] At the same time, *Burmese Days* is a novel, if not of two nations, of two internally worm-ridden communities. A real mixture is the indigenous one, a racial melting pot of different religions and ethnic types, whose moral fibre, already compromised by racial indolence, is aggravated by the social and political climate: either they have to pay silent obeisance to the powers that be, earning some small favour or other, or they must scheme, pretending to adulate them while actually trying to con them. The perfidious parasite U Po Kyin is the soul of that Burma which wishes to escape from exploitation, but by working shrewdly. He adulates power, aware of the fierce, biased hatred of the British for Orientals; he stays afloat by defamation to the detriment of his compatriots, first of all against the collaborator Doctor Veraswami, who esteems the British in spite of everything, and is popular with the novel's Orwellian *alter ego*. Flory is the only one who tries to free himself from the fatalistic stereotypes of the British dominator in India,[78] and the only one who counts himself out of the reactionary chorus and condemns the degradation of the by-then rotten imperialism. This situation – transplanted British morally adrift, on the slippery slide, and locals who are abject, repulsive and opportunist – is greatly aggravated by imperial domination. Flory is Orwell himself who actually left Burma after five years of service in the police force: but the paths of the two characters diverge as soon as Flory, travelling homewards on leave, is precipitously recalled to Rangoon by his superiors. He is not a policeman like Orwell, but a clerk in a company producing teak,[79] a sinecure. When Flory meets the Indian doctor, Veraswami, Orwell's usual overturning of

---

made by Orwell himself). Greenblatt 1965, 43 and 52, observes that every character in Orwell has an intimate 'birthmark', psychological and therefore not always visible, which stands for and symbolizes his or her separateness from the community.

77   As Alldritt 1969, 23, notes, citing Atkins 1954, 269.

78   This double is exact, to the point of having assigned to himself the exploit of the killing of the elephant (cf. below, § 24.3).

79   Like the French maternal grandfather of Orwell's mother, whose maiden name was Limouzin.

perspectives takes place: the Englishman has thrown overboard the white man's burden, that is, has destroyed any vestige of imperialism in himself, even though he is still a weary ganglion of it; and it is up to the educated westernized doctor to defend British civilization. It is he who – and this seems to paraphrase Kipling – summarizes all the historical civilizing merits of the British, and sings the praises of the investments that have modernized the country to a Flory who jadedly replies that the British are only there to pillage. Flory, this drifter, though not deprived of redemptive desire, wilting as it is,[80] is therefore a re-edition of Conrad's clerk in the 'outposts of the Empire'.[81] While he slashes Kipling's imperialist ideology, the influence of the small and longer sagas of the British in India is oozing from all his pores. A typical character from Kipling, the early Kipling of *Plain Tales from the Hills*, had been the prim Englishman fresh from his studies and having just arrived in India, where he is soon corrupted by inertia, unsatisfied eroticism, the climatic enchantment, becomes bogged down a few steps from the thresholds of the surreal, the nightmare and the hallucination, and is afflicted by loss of memory and control ('Kipling-haunted' is another of Orwell's expressions). By a strange, contagious and enchaining power, once bogged down no one moves any more, in fact wallows masochistically, and India becomes the new homeland. The novel's 'darkness' lies in the lack of actual possibilities of redemption in this moral turpitude: in the end, with all the ways of escape closed off, the main character is forced to kill himself. In fact, Flory had believed, mistakenly, that he could begin again from zero with smarmy Elizabeth, sent to relatives in the Burmese village for the sole purpose of finding herself a husband. The flirting begins at first sight between the young couple, and the awakening of desire is alluded to in the vicarious scene of the native dance, in which a female dancer sways heatedly in front of the couple, until Elizabeth, upset, frees herself from the hypnosis and wooziness into which she threatens to fall, like Adela in Forster's caves in *A Passage to India*. The frenetic and thrilling leopard hunt

---

80   Flory, after all, does not have the courage to dissociate himself from a note drafted at the club, which decrees that no local citizen can be allowed entry: in this way he disappoints the doctor, who feels threatened by the perfidious U Po Kyin.

81   The expression 'outposts of Empire' is used by Orwell in chapter V.

is another approach stage, a trial, and also a new ersatz of the senses that become excited. But the marriage proposal is interrupted midstream, and grotesquely, by a sudden earthquake. The next day, Flory makes himself look ridiculous in front of Elizabeth by falling from a horse while trying to pierce a pole with a lance, an exploit expertly carried out by a young British officer who has just arrived to quell the rebellion that is fermenting among the natives. It is not the appearance of this dandy that makes Flory hateful to Elizabeth; it is her aunt who warns her that Flory is frequenting a Burmese prostitute. Elizabeth, who could have been taken for a young woman who was smart but not wicked, ends up by coming straight to the point, and Flory falls back into his earlier slothful, debauched life, bitterly aware that this life-buoy, of pure regenerating love, has slipped through his hands, and he plunges back into lethargy and fornication. Not even his gesture of bravery during the outbreak of the rebellion lets him win back his woman, since his Burmese prostitute suddenly appears in church and reveals their past together. At this moment, Flory's birthmark becomes an even deeper blue with the shame. He remonstrates, vainly pleads for understanding, and in desperation kills her dog and then himself. U Po Kyin also triumphs over Doctor Veraswami, whose supporter is dead.

3. The highly lauded, short Burmese anecdote 'Shooting an Elephant'[82] is the densest and tautest of Orwell's narrative essays. It is written as if wishing to demonstrate to himself the capacity of drafting those precise, finicky, realistic pieces which he says are his gift in 'Why I Write'; the description of the cadaver of the collie and of the drawn-out death of the elephant is literally extraordinary. Here the puppet master has become the puppet; or the director of a theatrical spectacle is now the actor; or an avid crowd obliges a sissy to become a hero, exercising over him an atavistic, inexplicable influence. An arcane psychological subjection forces him to perform a thaumaturgic propitiatory rite. If the oppressor is a self-styled possessor of a superior civilization – if he is venerated as a god come down to earth, or a simple magician – it is correct, according to the grammar of myth, to demand

---

82   The killing of a mad circus elephant in the village of Bursley, recounted in terms and
      with details very close to Orwell's, forms the background to the death of old Baines
      in Arnold Bennett's novel, *The Old Wives' Tale* (cf. Volume 7, § 20.3).

from him the risky act of slaying and eliminating the cause of the ruin, that is, of being the champion and bringer of rebirth. Orwell becomes the mythical saviour for the locals. However, in the Burmese social geography the exception, always relative, is the enterprising local, who – stripping the carcass of the slain elephant clean of edible flesh and of its tusks – exploits the few chances of promotion offered by the system of exploitation. Like Flory, Orwell was against imperialism as a system, but, at the same time, he was disgusted by the behaviour of the natives; hence an irresolvable uneasiness, a coercion to do the opposite of what he was doing. In the end, the killer is of the elephant silenced and immunized in front of the whole community, having acted according to its frenzied expectations, and even according to English Law; but, even so, he is in a secret inner crisis.

§ 25. *Orwell V: 'A Clergyman's Daughter'*

The discontinuity of *A Clergyman's Daughter*[83] (1935) is striking. Its setting is Suffolk, in a geographical and social milieu of the apparently sleepy but neurotic suburban England; and the main character is a woman who lost her mother, but is not Bolshevik or revolutionary or debauched like Flory. She is the self-sacrificing Dorothy Hare, the daughter of a peevish reverend, rector of a rural parish where religious faith is reduced to a flicker. Right from the start Dorothy is an oppressed and disturbed personality: the morning alarm clangs like an air raid, because the woman is coming out of a dream that has deranged her, and she goes into hiding under the covers, and rises, straining to silently recite a short verse from the Bible, and arranging, at first light, to carry out a long series of domestic and parochial chores. She is a woman destroyed by religion, a particular religion. Having forgone her impulses, and being withered within, she acts for the good

---

83　The creation of Dorothy, who camouflages Orwell, stems from the period Orwell spent in 1932 at 'The Hawthorns' as a teacher at a highly devout school, where his duties included going to the chapel and attending the service, working shoulder to shoulder with the vicar and following and directing the pupils' theatricals, spending a great deal of time preparing cardboard armour (OCE, vol. I, 130). Having contracted pulmonitis from overwork, he left teaching and returned to his parents' in Southwold, then on to London to work part-time in a bookshop.

of the others without really understanding why. An automaton-woman, obsessive in scolding herself for small oversights, for her insufficient charity, for desultory malignity against her neighbours, slothful and also bad but fleeting thoughts, she pricks herself with a pin every time she 'falls'. Politically, Orwell has drawn in his claws; all he wants to do is to present a character clouded by faith, and thus propound the thesis that religious faith is a useless, long surpassed medicine for the individual and for society. The first part of the novel ends with Dorothy who, exhausted, is collapsing from sleep after a fatiguing day. We thus have the initial impression of a tidy, clear-cut, clean progression of facts: the novel of a day, and a kind of *Ulysses* in a smaller format, which slavishly follows the memo Dorothy herself has written before lying down. This stenographic list of jobs has a twofold value: it anticipates what is actually happening and at the same time, with efficacious irony, the violent breakdown that will happen the next day, when Dorothy will be afflicted by memory loss and will run away from home. The running away and the memory loss are a metaphorical reaction to oppression, and therefore a cry of rebellion towards freedom and against religion.

2. From the point of view of the social and temporal scenario, the morning liturgical service reveals that things have not greatly changed with respect to Victorian novels 'of the parsonage': the world-weary, absent-minded, hurried reverend; the beguines, pressing economic problems, expenses to restore the church; the tense relationships with other local religious communities. In all of this we recognize a deliberate wink at the 'scenes of clerical life' of Eliot and Trollope, and until her escape Dorothy is part Eliot and part Trollope with some expected Lawrence-style modernizations or imitations.[84] On the other hand, Hardy comes to mind in the bells that are causing cracks in the paving of the bell tower and in the urgent restorations for which, however, there are no funds.[85] This drama of the liberation of the senses and of the sense of self, of the autonomy and

---

84   Alldritt 1969, 27–8. Equally significant of this climate of retracing, even of citing the great Victorian novels, is that Dorothy should be reading Gissing's feminist novel of loss of religious faith, *The Odd Women*.
85   A rector's daughter is Elfride in *A Pair of Blue Eyes*.

independence of the persona, grows against the recognizable background of the state of employment in the 1930s. The 2,000 souls of the village are mostly workers at a sugar refinery who no longer attend church, and whom Dorothy the missionary tries to bring back to faith. The petite bourgeoisie attends, deafly, to its weekly rites; the local magnate is elected to Parliament among the conservatives. The historical moment is that of the crusade of conservative believers against the ideological Modernism of a Bertrand Russell and a Huxley; thus there is a hale and hearty Anglicanism very different from any Romanism, though sworn enemy – the usual intricacies of the English faith – of every Lutheran and Calvinist Protestantism. Victor, the local schoolmaster, is a kind of last Newmanite Tractarian who believes that the answer to the rampant disaffection is an intensified ritualism. However, the novel begins to come off the rails verging on the improbable when it seeks to bring in the ideological weakness of Dorothy, who, in that first morning, bumps into the much maligned Warburton, a dandy with artistic leanings who has had three bastards with a woman, and who invites her to his house in the evening to meet a writer of pornographic novels. Dorothy accepts, but it is only a pretext, and there is to be no novelist at Warburton's house. In short, this is an unconscious payback for her need for rebellion. Before this *clou* meeting, Dorothy is Orwell in women's clothing who wishes to testify to and describe the poverty of the neighbourhood: to write a second, Orwellian reportage, therefore. The workers' resignation seems to underwrite the Marxist concept of religion as the opiate of the masses: the poor woman whom Dorothy goes to visit complains that nothing can be changed in this world, and her hope lies in the next one. Dorothy massaging the old lady's rheumatic legs symbolizes the inefficacy of religion as a cure for social ills. Warburton is the satanic temptation, the Lucifer who wants to make her doubt her beliefs and also sexually capitulate; like Christ she resists, but their rendezvous has been espied by the village gossip.

3. The second half of the novel is even more dissatisfying. The long intermezzo of the hop picking in Kent has a very feeble structural motivation. Orwell wanted to describe first hand this task of the poor, and had a reportage ready with the aim of explaining a microcosm of outcasts who get by, work hard and never grumble, and who help one another, substantially

happy with little. When she has recovered her memory, Dorothy tackles the dilemma of Dickens's Harmon in *Our Mutual Friend* and of all the Mattia Pascals of late nineteenth-century literature: is it really such a good idea, she asks, to go back to my previous identity? She would like to, but conjectures that her father will refuse to welcome her back since her repeated letters never receive an answer; and so she emigrates to London, where, after wandering around in vain, she eventually finds a lurid and stinking boarding-house – more smells! – which is, in reality, a den of prostitutes. Her search for a job is fruitless, paradoxically, because she has no luggage and speaks too correctly, like an educated woman. Also the London market of small trades and odd jobs is described in a brief sociological chapter, under the form of statistical data that only later are referred to the main character's situation. The real surprise of *A Clergyman's Daughter* is an interlude in a rigorously dramatic form, enlivened by some homeless during a night outdoors in Trafalgar Square, which, in its virtuosity and parody, is openly imitative of Joyce, and even of future Beckett in its plan.[86] Naturally, they all talk to themselves, and what reigns between these tramps, one of whom is a defrocked canon who sings sacrilegious songs under his breath, is a perfect lack of communication. In her internal psychological parable, Dorothy no longer prays, does not even feel the need to do so, and the novel has become one of disillusion from a quietist, out-of-context religion, almost practised out of challenge or instinctive repulsion, like that of the reverend her father. The job that Dorothy finally finds as a teacher is also instrumental to condemning the state – largely still Victorian – of British private schools, a Dickensian affair. The polemical objective is to be found between the lines, mixed with the character's actual vicissitudes. Even in his essay writing, Orwell hoped that school programmes would open up to sex education and the humanities, removing the primacy of practical know-how. The Donjuanesque Warburton is the reborn Perseus who arrives onstage to free Dorothy and make clear to her that her loss of

86   In 'Inside the Whale' Orwell had recently written of Joyce who, so much loved, made him feel like a eunuch with a squeaky voice who would like to be taken as a bass. Pagetti 1994, 29, is among the few, regarding this interlude, who opportunely mention Shaw, too, as an influence or an imitation.

memory was only an unconscious stratagem to flee from an unbearable life. But she cannot find the courage to break the chains. The novel ends on an Arnold-like or high Victorian intellectual compromise, that of an 'honest doubter', with Dorothy who has lost her faith but not its need. Which is to say, it ends in a *pis aller*, with acceptance of faith to avoid the difficulty of reflecting on it. This circularity makes us suspect – recalling the beginning of the novel, and that Dorothy is psychically unstable – that the whole London adventure has been, very likely as in George Eliot's *Silas Marner*, only a nightmare or a bad dream.

§ 26. Orwell VI: 'Keep the Aspidistra Flying'

Keep the Aspidistra Flying[87] (1936) is the most Gissing-like, and therefore bitterest, of Orwell's novels. It in fact rewrites and updates the sociological analysis of *New Grub Street*, seeing in action the grip of money that not only squeezes society but conditions and hinders the career of the writer, who is left with the unique and ultimate perspective of survival which is that of prostituting his talent with words, and his very literary art, to commercial imperatives. It is also Orwell's most political and socialist novel, albeit more problematically so. The iconoclastic epigraph is a parody and a little pastiche of St Paul's First Letter to the Corinthians, on the primacy of charity, a word that Orwell replaces with 'money'. The passage, turned upside down, announces that all human life turns around money, on the haves and have-nots, and that on wellbeing depend the ease and aesthetics of life: a writer does not produce if he cannot at least live decorously. Such a writer is Gordon Comstock,[88] a poet in love with nature, which offers him a refuge from the urban squalor of London, and who is trying to become known and in the meantime makes ends meet as an assistant

---

87   The sickly, dying, but still surviving aspidistra, is a symbol, at the beginning, of the writer's tenaciousness, but, in the end, of the ineradicable tenaciousness of the bourgeoisie and of the writer's bourgeois temptation. An aspidistra plant is also in the Sissons' living room in Lawrence's *Aaron's Rod*.

88   Gardner 1995, 47, highlights the rarity of the surname and dubiously opines that Orwell had taken it from 'Comstockery', a society to suppress vice founded by one Anthony Comstock. Bulla 1989, 46, suggests 'common stock'.

in a bookshop that also works as a circulating library. The novel begins at a meticulous pace, registering the protagonist's minimal heartbeat and his secret thoughts, while it gives us gradually his anamnesis, which is exactly that of Orwell. The son of an average middle-class, shabby-genteel family, Comstock was educated as a poor pupil at a prestigious public school, where he shared Orwell's own first, rebellious socialist fanaticism, which later vanished. This opening presents, at one and the same time, an age-old, tried and tested British *topos*, that of the small second-hand bookshops, often untidy chaotic mounds of cheap knick-knacks of every kind, with little boxes of books at even more laughable prices arranged on the pavement in front of the window. In the shop, Gordon has under his gaze a living cross-section of the literary market of the 1930s, just as Gissing's Reardon traced that of the 1890s. The books are like females of different ages and brazenness: non-deflowered virgins, young widows, spinsters already shrivelled up offer their graces to the voyeur. On those shelves one can find *feuilletons* that are selling like hot cakes, or the masterpiece that attracts because it is indecent, such as Lawrence's; there are even books that are hard-earned and intimate – poetry – but do not sell. Orwell himself speaks, like Gissing, of an inanimate 'Darwinian struggle'[89] on the part of the books, to ensure, as living beings, the most prominent places to offer themselves to readers: concretely, to ensure an 'eye-level', to win the shelf from which they can most easily be eyed by buyers, without raising or lowering their gaze. The commercially 'competitive' books, most attractive, sold and read, are alive and are at eye-level; others – well-known strategies of the vendor – end up lower and lower or high up on the shelves. This is an indirect way of telling us that the Victorian's best-sellers had, by 1936, ended up in oblivion; that by now at the top, that is, not even too visible, were the biographies of the nobles and royalty, and just before them religious literature. At eye height were the fashionable novels with a few exceptions, such as Hemingway and Virginia Woolf. Gordon Comstock, who looks at this epitome of the literature that attracts, is naturally paralysed by a sense of his own sterility and uselessness. If only he had money he could join the literary circles

89   Volume 6, § 122.3.

that counted, and find the opportunity to publish, and more money: since money produces money, it brings sap and courage, energy and the desire to do. However, it is equally clear that by now the market demands a standard product that is as a minimum a compromise that the writer's purest authenticity must endure. Gordon's moments in the shop are given rhythm by mentally composed verses on the wind ruffling poppies, an ugly and inane poem as he himself realizes, and whose composition is in the making. But he is also surrounded, outside in the street, by advertising posters that show how it is possible to use the word in a different and commercially more efficacious way – the slogan – as well as exemplifying in their messages a kind of vital *élan*, of the joy of living, of keenness, of easy and phony publicizing optimism for a life that is bursting with energy and health, and thus continues, and is therefore also an indirect encouragement to desist, and partially also, in a precocious foretaste, to forget.

2. At the boarding-house where Gordon Comstock lives, only a clerk, Flaxman, indulges in little vices, pinching the bar women's bottoms, scraping by also quite nicely, and shows him a trouble-free life. He, Gordon, has his own rigid, inflexible Spartan code; and not for nothing is there a Scottish *côté* in his family. What is Gordon cultivating, what does he aspire to, when all is said and done? Wallowing in the ivory tower of poetry, like Orwell when he was young. He cherishes the aesthetics of the aristocratic writer, believes that inspiration is proportionate to wellbeing and leisure, that to write takes a heated house, good friendships, tobacco, and a full stomach. Virginia Woolf theorized the same thing in *A Room of One's Own*. At the literary reception of a leading critic, to which he has been invited, he expects to meet an outdated intellectual class, and ladies who still speak of Swinburne and Pater; but he is let down when only he, who counts so little, has not been told that the party has been postponed. All roads close, and some of them are cut off by himself out of pure inflexible masochism. His poems are refused by a publisher, he discovers on returning from a long stroll after the postponement of the literary party. In Ravelston, the socialist editor of a poetry magazine, Orwell seeks to represent, contrary to Gordon, a bourgeois who would like to take the proletariat's side, but remains an incurable snob. His life is studded by concessions to a series of habits and lifestyles that are unconsciously aristocratic, and he lives in a

poor quarter, above all for the image. The disagreement between the two friends, on the meaning and role of British writers of the 1930s, confirms the passive and apocalyptic – and therefore politically incorrect – attitude, because of being apolitical, of Gordon, a *post litteram* Decadent, though without approving the sympathizer with the full pockets who trusts in the healing of the world through socialism. At the end of this clash, Gordon discovers his similarity to Gissing's 'unclassed': he is of middle-class culture, but according to the cash in his (empty) pockets, a proletarian; on his part the rich socialist leaves, disgusted, the pub that stinks of the common man.[90] Gordon cannot afford it, and being the only pub within his means is forced to rub shoulders with the foul-smelling workers.

3. The alternative to money and to the driving force of writing and inspiration is sex. Gordon experiences this illusion under the form of a Rosemary whom he had fleetingly met when he was working – symptomatically – as an advertising agent, that is, a creator of slogans. And yet he ends up realizing the vicious circle: marrying costs, and with no money even sex can be squalid. Rosemary is forced to agree with him – that not even love is possible, that it is not even possible to gratify oneself through free love – when they are trying to have sex in a clearing, one Sunday, during a trip that had been happy up until then, because Gordon has not brought a contraceptive. This scene of the trip – well-known or expected, at least in the sketch about the waiter who tries to have the two diners order dishes that are too expensive in the phony luxury restaurant, with Gordon in a cold sweat, as he does the sums in his head – is also mindful of the ballads of the London workers' carefree oblivion as described by Thomson B. V. and Davidson, the latter the author of 'Thirty Bob a Week'.[91] It is a liberating trip until the failed intimate moment. Afterwards Gordon is defeated; it is natural that when a cheque arrives from a magazine that has accepted his poetry, he squanders it by getting drunk, ending up in jail after offending

90   In the next scene he goes to a restaurant by taxi with his fiancée, who continues to observe that the workers stink; and at the restaurant, a little effortlessly, she nibbles a succulent steak in contrast to the poor starving workers from the industrial estates.
91   Volume 6, § 246.3. This is a literal quotation, being thirty shillings the salary Gordon lives with, in his second job at a second-hand bookseller's.

a policeman. Overcome by the desire to disappear, Orwell attributes to him Gissing's metaphor of the insect and the larva. The other Gissing, that of *Ryecroft*, pops up in his wish for segregation far from the throng and in his desire to sink into anonymity and the amorphous. He recovers and perks up thanks to Rosemary's comforting and support, but he has shelved his dream of becoming a poet, and since Rosemary has become pregnant he decides to marry her and keep the child, and is taken on by the advertising firm, where he will be able to exploit his abilities as a poet, but selling himself short. Orwell could not have devised a more indeterminate ending, since he disowns the solipsist and escapist, Decadent or Georgian writer who has lost heart – a poet, not even a novelist – without converting him to a combative constructive socialism. His poverty and awareness of the omnipotence of money are not shared in a community where they are more bearable, but they implode in London's alienation. All that awaits him is a middle-class marriage and above all the reduction of his art to an advertising slogan, hence that subjugation of the artist's autonomy, which is the threat that Orwell always wards off. I mentioned that this novel is his most political before the final ones, because in it he condemns the socialism of the middle-class intelligentsia even without an alternative suggestion. Comstock's socialism is a hazy, in fact by now a spent youthful memory, but that of Ravelston is theoretical and abstract, and steeped in a jargon that was suspect to the workers to whom it was presented. The socialist remained bourgeois, and for both it was necessary to make a symbolic journey to Wigan, to mingle as equals among the workers' community.

§ 27. *Orwell VII: 'Coming Up for Air'. Petit bourgeois hedonism gains awareness*

George Bowling, the main character in *Coming Up for Air*[92] (1939), fat, red-faced, his teeth remade,[93] is an average ugly and unpleasant

---

92   On the occasion of a 1947 reprint, Orwell revealed (OCE, vol. IV, 436) that he had never used a semicolon throughout the entire novel.

93   Orwell's teeth had been remade (OCE, vol. IV, 495), and so this at least is an identification mark of his double.

forty-five-year-old who smokes, drinks, and cheats on his acid wife Hilda, who is obsessed by price increases and fearful of the future, and he only just puts up with his children.[94] All these vices are mixed, however, with a seeming sensibility and a fine, acute, unsuspected spirit of observation. Orwell regularly insists on some misdirecting detail, giving his *alter egos* marks similar to his own together with other antithetic ones to differentiate them from him; nonetheless, this time he builds a double who is the most distant from him, both physically and ideally.[95] Through a filter like this, the objective is an anamnesis of the British milieu on the eve of war from the perspective of the trading middle class of average affluence. The widespread sentiment that Orwell attributes to Bowling, believing to be objective, is discontent with life; it is also that – a valid paradigm for the average British citizen, in whom the author himself is camouflaged – of a progressive, inevitable public awareness after having cultivated memory, nostalgia, and immersion in private affairs. If in the sky can be heard the premonitory rumble of the bombers, on the ground there are scenes of war among the poor at the shops, and one constantly verifies a deterioration in living conditions. Yet the merit of the book lies this time in its voice, the voice of colloquialism with no literary starch, kneaded together with dialect expressions, jargon, syntactic contractions in speech, and a crude and brutal metaphorism. But this is a literary voice in its own right, and a mental babbling that apes the stream of consciousness. And naturally, only a stream of consciousness technique could be used to give expression to a character who clings to his private world and is deaf to any form of public awareness. The literary family of this intimist novel, whose register lies between what is really said and what is thought, and of this mental flow, was soon to be that of American novels 'of speech': certain interjections we find in *Coming Up for Air*, together with others, will recur, for example, in Salinger's *The Catcher in the Rye*.

2. Orwell therefore set himself the tricky task of creating a low character, rather than a product of the universities: an ignoble scoundrel without

94   'kids aren't in any way poetic, they're merely savage little animals'.
95   As for Bowling's profession, Orwell made use of tales from an insurance-broker friend (Wykes 1987, 109).

flights of fancy who does not mince matters. In this way he makes him impermeable to the various nationalistic, religious, and cultural forms of rhetoric, yet to ultimately let us discover in him a secretly romantic character, a hasty, politically apathetic person who says he never wants to be moved and is never moved himself, and who is instead and above all a sentimentalist. His voice corrodes all rhetoric and pomp, until he turns into a rhetorician of anti-rhetoric. This autobiography, or memoir, unfolds with all the marks of non-bookish orality, and becomes a book but according to the declared plan that it has no wish to be a book: that is, it creates a writing of anti-writing and recounts everything as if it were 'real', not yet 'that kind of thing [that] only happens in books'. George Bowling imagines the spectacle of the ruins of the near future, and as an antidote takes refuge in the idyll of childhood. Hence an impossible imitation of Joyce and Proust,[96] in the form of a recollection of pre-war childhood in the Oxfordshire rural, pastoral and archaic countryside, a life of simple pleasures now fallen away, including that inebriating one of fishing, one of the many distinguishing marks of a superseded world now at its last tremor, and at the same time, and symptomatically, probably the most solipsistic recreation that exists. George was forced to leave school to become a shop assistant, given the pre-war crisis; but these 'were good times', people died and people suffered, there were no comforts but one had certainties for the future, and everyone knew that life would go on. The Great War had made a clear-cut collective historical demarcation, suddenly making even things of the other day seem remote. *Coming Up for Air* is a revisitation of a world that was not all roses, but was happy, and that is lost; it exudes the perception of a gulf between the past and now, and the terrible deterioration in the conditions of life that had been reached.

3. However, the third part propels the novel towards another dimension. Because of an instant of worry, or a presentiment, George decides after the long spurt of memories to go and listen to a speaker talking of the menace of fascism. He becomes annoyed, incredulous, distracted, and attacks the

---

96   Without forgetting Henry Miller, recently read and admired, and also some echoes of Bernard in Woolf's *The Waves*, above all in the lengthy monologue in which Bowling brings himself to calmly accepting life.

speaker with his biting, politically apathetic irony; however, a spark has been struck. Immediately afterwards, another instructive and symbolic emblem appears: the Oxfordian shut up in an ivory tower, a kind of Podsnap who decrees what he does not think as inexistent, and therefore escapes the present by clinging to classical culture. Emerging from these experiences, by now George has a mental vision of the war and of the post-war period. After the lecture, travelling by car, he stops in a flowering meadow and smells the fragrant primroses; then, struck by a shiver, he decides to 'search for lost time' and to revisit the town of his birth, to relive and revel in the past. Naturally, the birthplace of his memory no longer exists, nor the people he knew. Once again we have landed in that no-man's-land between reality and dream that Silas Marner also experiences in Eliot's novel when he returns to Lantern Yard, and no longer recognizes it. Above the rural village has risen, in Lower Binfield, a fairly industrialized town, buried and rendered unrecognizable by the bricks of the new constructions.[97] Above all, the older small industries have been converted into bomb factories, and through the village parade brigades of young combatants; a bomb is even dropped on the village, by mistake. George wanders like a Dantesque ghost through this limbo. Even the pleasure of fishing has been sullied: the sites are no longer all there just for him, but have been turned into commercial meeting points. In an incisive epilogue, George, who is in the village without having told his wife, believes he hears an SOS on the radio that announces that she is dying, and so he returns home. When he arrives he is in torment, because ultimately some gleam of conjugal affection has remained in him. He learns of the misunderstanding, that the SOS referred to someone with the same name; but in the meantime Hilda has discovered everything. In the comedy of errors she believes that George has been with a woman and has had an adventure; he that she really is ill or even dead. There are no concrete decisive outcomes on the political plane, but we can guess that George, not unlike

97   On his embarrassed statement of being George Bowling the hotel receptionist does not turn a hair – in other words, she does not recognize or does not really know him. Other pitch-perfect scenes are his failed courting of a widow who is a hotel guest, and, even more effective, his meeting with Elsie, an old flame, who is now fat and tawdry, and to whom George does not reveal himself.

Dorothy with her religion, will again subjugate himself to the oppressive conjugal routine. Even his penchant for socialism is a big question mark.

§ 28. *Orwell VIII: 'Animal Farm'. Stalinism unmasked*

After 1939 and *Coming Up for Air* until *Animal Farm* (1945) no new novels were written by Orwell, and the six years of silence are partially explained by the necessity of action, and partially because literature was everywhere in a phase of stall since paper was scarce, and the short length was back in vogue.[98] As an interventionist, and thus a renegade from the Independent Labour Party, Orwell did not take part in the war, having been declared unfit because of his pulmonary illness; until 1943, however, he was a member of the Home Guard, a subsidiary defence body ready to face a German invasion. Later he found 'essential war work' in the BBC's India Service, which he left in 1943, when he was taken on by *The Tribune*; then from 1942 he began his collaboration with *The Observer*. The serial letters to the American *Partisan Review* sounded British life practically hour by hour during the war years. Without changing subject matter they mainly play on the accusation against right-wing and left-wing pacifism, 'objectively pro-fascist'. All the essay writing of the war years, in the absence of novels, is actually an accumulation of data, notes and ideas for the upcoming last two. Their main sources of inspiration had taken shape some time past, and had then consolidated after Orwell's experiences as a combatant in Spain. These novels were to be, naturally, a reflection on the true nature of Stalinism, a degenerate form of state capitalism, combined with the awareness that to be anti-Stalinist did not mean being anti-socialist; and the nightmare of the falsehood forever consigned to history, that is, the impossibility of measuring the present against the past, aggravated by the gradual disappearance of eyewitnesses. In the last retrospective of the Spanish Civil War,[99] from 1942, we can read the forecast of a leader or

98   In reality, Orwell was contemplating a 'huge novel', perhaps a trilogy of which *Animal Farm* would be the second part, preceded by a book never written on Winston Smith's ancestors.

99   OCE, vol. II, 286–306.

some clique who, once in power, would control not only the future but also the past (and the example is given of a two plus two that makes five).

2. Orwell's intention in *Animal Farm*, repeated more than once, was to explode the mythus of Russia, a despotic regime that deprived its subjects of freedom and perpetrated the same misdeeds as Nazism. A form of justificationism prevailed in Britain, too,[100] and therefore it was even more necessary to clarify for the British just what Russia was, and the extent of its degeneration in 1945 compared to 1917: 'the destruction of the Soviet myth was essential if we wanted a revival of the Socialist movement'.[101] There is a flagrant lack of an 'Orwell figure' in *Animal Farm*,[102] which therefore constitutes a temporary variation on the autobiographical model towards a purely political diatribe.[103] By 1945, the fable was a *démodé* literary style, the weapon of Swiftian literary Illuminism,[104] often if not always criticized by Orwell in its Victorian fans such as Kingsley, Barrie, Stevenson and Kipling.[105] Nevertheless Orwell resorted to it to transpose the long story of Stalinist degenerations into statism, that is, from acquired freedom to dictatorship and the repression of freedom. Major's initial dream is the

100   OCE, vol. III, 443.

101   In the Preface to the Ukrainian edition of the novel (OCE, vol. III, 455–9).

102   As Williams 1991, 69, points out, adding that disillusionment and defeat persist, being, however, those of a community and not of an individual.

103   If the biographical context has some influence on the genesis of Orwell's fable this is due, as often and specifically in the case of Kingsley and Carroll, to the need to entertain Richard, his adopted son who, fairly gifted in manual operations but little in intellectual ones, began to speak late and showed no interest in reading. Orwell wanted a son and his wife Eileen, who died in 1945 after an operation for fertility, refused to adopt one. The animal farm is precisely the one that Orwell himself looked after at his house in Wallington: one goat was called Muriel, and Orwell took care not to leave the animals to their own devices when he was absent.

104   The variant with respect to the classical animal fable and to the animal types is that the horses are not intelligent but obtuse, only brute force and blind to the service of the cause.

105   Woodcock, in CRHE, 243, astutely calls it the negative of *The Island of Doctor Moreau*, in which men are turned into beasts (cf. also Meyers 1991, 39). In turn Pagetti 1994, 41, draws attention to *The Fox*, an adaptation for the BBC of a story by Ignazio Silone, edited by Orwell around 1942.

condemnation of the exploitation the workers are subject to. This is Marx speaking to the masses of the whole world,[106] but the farm is British. These two plans – the past Russian revolution and the possible British revolution, with its mementoes and corrections of the model – are kept in constant fusion. Mankind, the animalesque counterpart, is, outside the allegory, the boss, or the aristocratic class in power: the exploiter, the owner of the means of production; but also historically the Russian Tsar. Major preaches non-collusion with the tyrant, postulating any form of alliance and collaboration between revolution and capitalism as impossible. A trio of farm's pigs, since they are more intelligent, take the reins after the owner has been chased away; and from Major's speech a philosophy and ideology of animalism are formed, that is, a certain collectivism, even though among the various gut reactions appear apathy, hedonism, vanity, even the old mirage of a sugar candy mountain that is paradise, that is, the opiate religion of the people and sleeping draft for the masses, even if the working class lets itself be gripped by some nostalgia for at least some of the privileges of the past jurisdiction (ribbons, sugar itself). Above all else, unanimity of viewpoint turns out to be impossible. The farm's heptalogue eliminates luxury and alcohol, but almost immediately theft, avidity, the sense of appropriation return in favour – milk disappears, some are sly, that is, they do not share the product of the work. In a short time democracy – the power in the hands of all the people – gives way to a dictatorial and tyrannical oligarchy that dramatically changes the cards on the table, deforms the truth and the very story of the revolution.

3. The first living confutation of the possibility of a socialist democratic state, or the first danger, is the political bureaucracy, that is, the leadership and hence the officials of the apparatus and the apparatus itself. Those who direct and plan, and lead and guide, cannot work at the same time, and so it is in the nature of things that a situation arises of small and then ever greater privileges. The pigs invent, and become, a sub-caste, that of

---

106   Many critics have observed (cf. for example Zwerdling 1974, 90–1 for the reasons) that Lenin is the 'missing link'. Instead, for many other commentators the pig Major is a mixture of Marx and Lenin. It seems unquestionable that Major's speech at the beginning of the novel is an unveiled parody of Lenin's so-called December Testament of 1922.

functionaries, party leaders, ideologists. Meanwhile the revolution is spreading, or is trying to do so, to the neighbouring farms. The attack by Jones and the other owners is successfully repelled, but shortly afterwards the tensions inside the leaders' triad explode: Snowball is for the modernization and mechanization of the state; Napoleon opposes this. Orwell never ceases to highlight the immense ability of the slogan to fanatically conquer and control the masses. The purging of Snowball is carried out with the contribution of the dogs, the guards of the regime that barbarously chase away the dissident. Napoleon, the uncontested dictator, begins to resemble Jones more and more, that is, the former master. Thus begins the demolition of the revolutionary system, passed off as its consolidation; and now a police regime takes over that hunts down any form of dissidence, and even abolishes freedom of speech and thought. It is, however, an unavoidable necessity to re-establish relations with humans, something forbidden by the heptalogue, in order to advance the standard of life and stop recession: which is to say, how the revolution will make pacts, agree and sign collaborative alliances with capitalist countries. One strategy designed to curb and avoid mass protests, and to blind them, is slander, that is, the defamation of the traitor Snowball, who is blamed for disasters that are simply natural, while hate is kept alive by evoking his possible, in fact allegedly certain, clandestine re-entry into the farm. When, given the many signs of unrest and hardship, the community can no longer hide the fact that things are deteriorating, purges begin with the physical elimination of dissidents, who are also and above all those who seek to remain immune to the party propaganda. This is the historical and paradigmatic climax of the revolutionary degeneration, that is the satrapical dictatorship of a Roman emperor who nurtures the cult of personality, the *divus* emperor who bases his ascendency on a few phantom public appearances, so that the legends about his persona and prowess flourish, and art prospers in his celebration.[107] On the historical plane, Orwell intended to show how objective hindrances mean that a revolution, so late in history – the western history of a millennium

---

107   Big Brother and Emmanuel Goldstein in *Nineteen Eighty-Four* are stand-ins for Stalin and Trotsky; they are also two figments, that is, two pure bogeymen without an equivalent in flesh and blood, idols and therefore myths.

of capitalism – must represent, if agreements cannot be reached with the very capitalism it repudiates, an objective return to more primitive conditions of life. Also, to tackle the need for a decent life for all, nature does not spontaneously offer its products, which need to be either extracted or processed or conserved; as a consequence one must either produce the machines to facilitate progress or import their parts. On the parallel plane of contemporary political history, after this phase the breakdown in the Franco-Russian pact, the war against Germany, and the post-war Soviet regime are in sight. The regime inside the farm becomes gangrenous, the customs forbidden by the seven commandments are reintroduced, the visible privileges of the pigs have increased; old Boxer, wounded, is sent to heal in a hospital far from the farm – in short, sent to the knackers' yard. Over the course of time, what has been established is not a structure in which one master does not work and receive the profits, but an entire caste of bureaucrats who merely program. For the masses, the socialist goal of a more decent life has not been reached; more precisely, everything has remained unchanged, and an exact assessment of what has happened is hindered by memory lapses, by those facts being remote and therefore interpretable in a different way.[108] It is the business of the humans, invited as guests of honour to the farm, to note that the same repressive measures towards the 'lower animals' that they use against the 'lower classes' are adopted. The curtain comes down on a mirage offered to the animal's eyes: an excited and rowdy card game, but without it being possible to understand who are the pigs and who the men, so similar have the pigs become, in every way, to humans.

§ 29. *Orwell IX: 'Nineteen Eighty-Four'. The last man, the last humanist*
Written between August 1946 and November 1948, and published in 1949,[109] *Nineteen Eighty-Four* had been conceived in terms of its

---

108 Save for a privileged witness, the mule Benjamin, which lived before and after the rebellion.

109 After Eileen's death, Orwell sought a second wife, also to give a mother to his adopted son, and he proposed to Sonia Brownell, but without success. In February 1946, he suffered a haemorrhage, and in May he left for Barnhill, on the Scottish island of Jura, accompanied by a governess and by his sister Avril. However, at the end of 1947

ideological, politological and prophetic contents back in 1943, when it seemed to Orwell that, with the imminent conclusion of the war, a division of the world into three blocks or areas of influence was forthcoming, a perspective confirmed in 1944 with the outcome of the Teheran Conference.[110] He believed that the A-bomb danger could not change the planetary balance,[111] for the simple reason that it was too costly to produce the bombs, and because of the sheer terror of mutual extermination; hence the permanent Cold War of the three blocks, without winners or losers, carried out while avoiding the use of atomic weapons, with power concentrated in few hands and a significant deterioration of the conditions of life for the peoples subject to it. Indeed, he had seen, before the end of the conflict, that degeneration of politics that he defines as 'power politics' establish itself, a politics whose objective is to hold and maintain power for an oligarchy.[112] Power politics was synonymous with the breakdown of socialism into despotism, totalitarianism, oligarchic collectivism, and was therefore the hidden maggot inside unrealized socialism. *Animal Farm* had just allegorized the irreparable breakdowns of the failed socialist revolution. In the review of a book on life in contemporary Russia, Orwell configured that regime in the same terms as the society of *Nineteen Eighty-Four*, with the internal Party at the top, and, below, a proletarian mass devoid of elementary rights, the victim of a police regime in which it is the children who condemn their fathers for being Trotskyite,

---

he was admitted to a sanatorium in Glasgow where his TB slightly improved thanks to streptomycin; in July 1948 he left the hospital feeling anything but better, and typed three copies of the novel all by himself, with unbelievable strength of will. At Christmas he was again admitted to a sanatorium in Gloucestershire. He hoped to get better or to become a 'good chronic invalid'. He married Sonia on 13 October 1949, arranging to leave all his belongings to her and his friend Richard Rees in his will.

110   OCE, vol. IV, 520. A democratic block, headed by the USA, Britain and France, had already been seen as a far from strange idea in a book by C. K. Streit reviewed in 1939 (OCE, vol. I, 436); however, this union was criticized by Orwell, as it was a union of powerful democracies that were exploiters of the weakest states.

111   OCE, vol. IV, 23.

112   The idea began to flash through his mind in the essay, which I discussed above (§ 22.7), 'The English People', in the section on the future of England.

while Stalin the invisible is adored Nero-style, like Big Brother. The present historical *impasse*, defined as 'depressing', is that capitalism leads straight to the queues for bread and to wars, and collectivism to the concentration camps. In a more contingent sense, Orwell received a further impulse for the novel during the general election in 1945, which brought to victory Bevan's Labourites and marked the end of the Churchill era. Orwell, who had been looking forward to this moment, had grown aware that the new government was facing an incredibly difficult task, whether it was to be right- or left-wing. *Nineteen Eighty-Four* is at the same time an extension of the British war emergency. Orwell transposes in the novel the climate of wartime Britain without changes, with its rationing and scarcity of basic necessities, such as razor blades.[113] More specifically, in a letter to the *Partisan Review* of December 1944, he admits some errors of his in the light of the war victory, and above all the glaring one that war could be revolutionary, and that war and revolution formed an inseparable pair. The war was won, but socialism had not arrived;[114] in fact everything had remained unchanged. Europe was coming apart and there was Russia which annexed to the east and west; back home, a socialist Labour government had come to power but was unable to cope with the gravity of the situation, unable above all to ensure that famous, merely decent standard of life for the mass of workers. It seemed self-evident, but if socialism had risen to power then Britain should give up India, and in doing so the standard of life would be lowered, not increased. The difficulty therefore also lay in trying to convince the proletariat to swallow the bitter truth that socialism is a better form of life, 'but not necessarily, in its first phases, a more comfortable one'.[115] But there was more: a complete, Copernican revision of Orwell's historical thinking, carried out without clamour, that can be dated to early 1945, and that consists in the awareness of the intrinsic failure of every revolution. Under the German blitz Orwell had believed a British or perhaps global

---

113   It is puerile to place the blame on Orwell, at least in the light of this novel – as Hopkinson 1953, 9, does – because it describes the future as the present.
114   A refrain that begins to appear in OCE, vol. III, 336.
115   OCE, vol. III, 450.

revolution possible. In an essay on Koestler[116] he attributes to this writer an aphorism that bitterly became his own: that revolutions always end badly. This was to become true for Orwell in a specific sense and gradually also in an absolute one. For some time, he would be able to find the alibi that past revolutions had always ended badly, and that perhaps a future one could be successful. In his essay 'Toward European Unity'[117] the failure of the implementation of socialist society is admitted, yet Orwell does not give up outlining the imminent formation of a European socialist federation to save a world gone awry. The obstacles were the Russian and American opposition, and the ending of colonialism with a lowering in the standard of life for the average citizen, in addition to the usual opposition of the obscurantist Catholic Church. Orwell then specifies, in a close-knit review of Wilde's 'The Soul of Man Under Socialism',[118] that the problem which has not been perceived is the increase in production; that the abolition of private property does not mean more food on the workers' tables; and lastly that machines do not solve the problem of disagreeable work, as Ruskin and Morris had clearly prophesized.

2. For all of this the books and theories of the American politologist James Burnham were a dialectic test bench for *Nineteen Eighty-Four*, not its slavishly followed foundation.[119] Orwell feared what Burnham had anticipated, that socialism had not taken root, on the contrary that the world was veering towards a division among super-powers united in a coalition, with a generalized tendency to totalitarianism: with the fall of Hitler, De Gaulle was to appear, Stalin would remain and the American millionaires, that is, overseas capitalism. Everywhere an authoritarian Fuehrer was to be seen on the horizon.[120] In reality, it seems that from the 1945 essays

---

116   OCE, vol. III, 270–82.

117   OCE, vol. IV, 423–9.

118   OCE, vol. IV, 483–5.

119   Burnham's prophecy had already been formulated and summarized by Orwell, in particular in OCE, vol. IV, 25.

120   In *Nineteen Eighty-Four* a London square is overlooked by a statue of Cromwell since that dictator provided the best analogy of Stalin (OCE, vol. IV, 34). Nonetheless, that a little of Mussolini had ended up in Big Brother is hinted in a review of a book on the *Duce*: those who attacked him were the same ones who had praised him for

onwards, Orwell was flipping a coin to decide whether the future global scheme would be of two or three super-states. This American scholar, Burnham, saw on the horizon a planned society with the manager class at its head; these would eventually eliminate the capitalist class and crush the working class. Pessimistically, Burnham maintained that a democratic society had never existed nor ever would, and that every successive class in command after revolutions is always seeking power. Therefore, Burnham is the Goldstein of the novel. In Orwell's wide-ranging discussions in his essays, the American writer and politologist is harshly attacked; however, his detailed objections prove his interest. Orwell feared above that the Americans would remain indifferent to the geographic cancellation of Britain or would colonize it. Burnham is also criticized for believing in the old myth of class relations being unmodifiable, based on the principle that something can be changed *now*. Burnham's second book, anti-Soviet and pro American, and dictated by this fear   a book by this time late, with respect to the prophecy of *Nineteen Eighty-Four* – had been written on the basis of the concrete atomic danger, and did not avoid speaking of only two blocks, American and Soviet, the latter a block in expansion, dominated by an oligarchy that would extirpate any dissidence (since it was probable that only America and Russia could avail themselves of atomic weapons). According to Burnham, the answer to Soviet expansionism could only be an American expansionism, which would include the swallowing of Britain and its dominions. War, a third world war, was, in his opinion, a matter of days away. Contesting Burnham's conservative and reactionary design, Orwell puts forward his own utopia, the socialist United States of Western Europe and Africa. Ultimately, Burnham fell back into that renunciatory pessimism that is always stigmatized by Orwell: something could be done, even though it never had been.

---

the things they now accused him of (OCE, vol. II, 364). In the 1940 review of *Mein Kampf* (OCE, vol. II, 27–9), Orwell also believed Hitler capable of radiating the same fascination and the same hypnotic effect as Big Brother, and confessed that he had never hated him; only on 'reflecting' would he have wanted to kill him given the possibility, as he says of Winston in the novel. Orwell places the 'three great dictators' on the same plane, therefore.

3. The inspiration for *Nineteen Eighty-Four* came not only from Burnham but also from the utopian and dystopian writings of the late nineteenth and early twentieth century. Orwell never hid this. Jack London's *The Iron Heel* imagines an oligarchic American revolution countered by capitalists, with the elimination of dissenters. In Zamyatin's *We*[121] the people of the twenty-sixth century are monitored in their daily life, and condemned to live in a glass cage (and, it is added, 'before television was invented'). In that future world it is hypothesized that people would eat synthetic food and that sex would be regulated. Zamyatin's dictator is called the Benefactor and in the novel there is the description of an amorous affair between a kind of predecessor of Winston Smith, an engineer, and a woman affiliated to a resistance movement. The rebellion wanes because the 'nerve-centre responsible for imagination' gets burnt out, and the man goes back to being an obsequious speaker for the regime. It is highly significant that Orwell defined this novel as not anti-Russian or anti-Stalinist, but against the 'drift' of industrialized society: a 'study of the Machine', in particular, by a primitivist. Orwell's essay on Swift[122] contains in turn some passages that at least suggest an influence. Swift had prognosticated the police regime of totalitarian states, and the war hysteria into which the reasons for discontent are diverted. This is in fact a crucial essay, since Orwell affirms the necessity for construction, but is unable to check the coming of the Apocalypse. He had also recently read, in order to review it, Gissing's oeuvre, and *New Grub Street* once again looms in the background. *Nineteen Eighty-Four* is about an isolated man in an inferno. Both Gissing and Reardon of that Gissing novel are *alter egos* into whom Orwell projects himself. There is the common problem of sudden sterility, the temptation to write without inspiration for the dough, the selling short of genius; along with the awareness of the cruelty and emptiness of the society surrounding him. Even Gandhi enters the fray, indirectly, because of the mystique of renunciation and of sexual abstinence, the same one instilled unconsciously by the Party, since sex must only be procreative.

121   OCE, vol. IV, 95–9.
122   Cf. § 21.5 and n. 12.

4. Winston Smith[123] is a brother of Orwell's heroes of the first four novels; in particular of John Flory, George Bowling and Gordon Comstock, propelled into a future very similar to the present, even though a notably worse version. On the one hand, this future year 1984 resembles in quality, if not in quantity, the 1935 of *Keep the Aspidistra Flying*. It is connoted with the same vulgarity, degradation, squalor, poverty among the working class, and with the same overwhelming commercialism. On the other hand, Winston is like him a writer, or someone in charge of a particular form of verbal message; and both John and Gordon, and in some ways also George Bowling, are amateur or wishful writers and poets.[124] Is not Winston's assignment that of rectifying, and hence recreating, slogans, those same advertising slogans, but in a sphere that belongs more to commerce, which Gordon invents when he becomes middle class again? Is not Winston once again the solitary individual, the man apart, who seeks his own room for dreaming, for thinking, for cultivating his own ego – according to the axiom that every writer's impulse is to 'keep out of politics'[125] – in a depersonalized world and a regime of loss of individual identity?[126] His plight is unquestionably aggravated because while the previous two heroes were allowed room to be alone, Winston is precluded, directly engaged as he is in that system which spies on him and imprisons and monitors every other human being. *Nineteen Eighty-Four*'s political discourse on the future order of the world following the post-war threat overlaps that on the individual being standardized, an individual who must relinquish

123   Perhaps named after Virginia Woolf's Septimus Warren Smith.
124   Once again, Orwell shows that he always needs to be objectified in an unattractive main character, in fact ungainly, bony, with some physical defect and some illness. The always itchy varicose veins and the five false teeth – the same number as Bowling in *Coming Up for Air* – reveal Orwell's relationship with this character. However, Bowling's corpulence – Winston is skin and bone – is transferred to the farcical and always filthy Parsons, who, like Bowling, has two unruly children, to put it mildly.
125   OCE, vol. I, 373.
126   One more recent reference to the danger of the loss of individuality can be found in 'The Prevention of Literature' (OCE, vol. IV, 81–95), where Orwell looks forward to a literature that is not in the service of the state, and not aligned with it.

his or her particularity, and undergo frustrations and renunciations in the field of the free expansion of personality, including the affective and sexual spheres. Winston is as much an apocalyptic visionary as Gordon had been; he is also an existentialist dissident, not a political party member, and he wishes to safeguard the values of civilization. For page after page, he is a pure nostalgic, only intent on showing himself, against the evidence and the general blindness, that things were better before and that the quality of life has worsened; he is a seeker of 'useless' knick-knacks that are the tokens of a bygone era, among them even pure and authentic sex life, not aimed at procreation. The opening shows in Winston a character who, typically in Orwell, is returning from work – not going to work – and significantly from unpleasant work. He comes home for a break and to find private refuge, ever jealous of a vital space all his own, and which is increasingly restricted. Even his visit to the proletarian district, to find certainties on the past, is a transgressive impetus and the abandonment of a communal activity to meet the need for solitude, individualism, and eccentricity. London, the capital of Airstrip One, the third most populous of the provinces of Oceania, is home to four main Ministries, that deal in part with the opposite of their name.[127] That of Love is supposed to keep order and safeguard the law; in reality, it is a place of torture. The 'telescreen', or monitor, is multi-purpose, a transceiver that spouts propagandistic news, images of parades and victories; above all, it spies.

5. The obsession with forgery, that is, the counterfeiting of history, and of the consequent addiction, was born in Orwell, as will be recalled, at the time of the Spanish Civil War with the noted distortions of the British communist press regarding the events of the war and the operations of the POUM in particular: the justification of that party is an objective rather too present in Orwell and a wound that always reopens. The real subject of the novel is the loss of memory and of the possibility of confrontation. The interim essay writing, between *Animal Farm* and *Nineteen Eighty-Four*,

---

127   It seems confirmed that, still in the area of Orwell's transpositions of elements and aspects of the present or the immediate future, the Ministry of Truth was modelled, in its architecture and in its journalistic practices, on the BBC London headquarters, where Orwell worked in the India Service from 1941 to 1943.

opaque and often occasional, not coincidentally lingers on memories, on fleeting moments and the good times of childhood, or even the yearnings for liaisons now lost.[128] Right from his first appearance, Winston is busy keeping memory alive, that is, not to forget: forgetting whether things were better before the advent of the regime in power. He forces himself to keep the contact alive, and to keep taut the umbilical cord of the past. It is the usual nostalgia of Orwell's main character. And the token and the sign, the tangible point of contact between past and present, is the old notebook with its smooth paper in which he notes his memories. The Orwellian writer is now, at least, a diary keeper. At the same time, with his small testimony, Winston wishes to transmit memory to the future generations. For the last time, Orwell's double is searching for a community, that phantom Brotherhood of rebels headed by the 'traitor' Goldstein; careful in revealing himself as an opponent of the regime, he scrutinizes the faces of his colleagues at work to identify affiliates. On the one hand, this Brotherhood does not exist; on the other, Winston is playing for time as a conspirator and, fatalistically, he believes he can recognize several small signs of a bad end awaiting him. His unblocking of the kitchen sink of his neighbour, whose young children are already fanatical young members of the regime, contains a sinister prophecy: the two young children, like aspiring policemen, pounce on Winston accusing him of being a traitor. In the surreal scene of Winston's meeting with the proletarian at the pub, an old customer protests that they call the pint a litre, and demands an old pint. At the second-hand dealer's Winston finds another token of the past, coral encapsulated in crystal, a paperweight he buys for its sheer beauty and associative power. A return, a re-emergence from the past is the nursery rhyme being sung by the woman hanging out laundry in the shop courtyard. Winston is also writing his diary for the adored and idealized O'Brien, whom he believes to be a dissident like himself, and who turns out to be his gaoler, in fact the head of the Thought Police.[129] He verifies

---

128 Orwell was criticized for an essay on the 'common toad' (OCE, vol. IV, 171–5), in which he celebrated a middle-class preoccupation, the return of spring.

129 Alldritt 1969, 156, formulates the interesting conjecture that his name evokes Irish and therefore Catholic origins, which fits this inquisitor figure. Cf. Hollis 1956, 179–80, too, who deduces Orwell's scant sympathy for Irish nationalism.

himself the doubt over the alteration of the past as his work consists in rectifying erroneous estimates of Big Brother regarding the wellbeing of the nation and the provisions adopted, since the dictator is always right.[130] There is an ongoing alteration of the entire written legacy of the past – even of literature, therefore – having a political content. But Winston ultimately rectifies castles of words: the true and the false find no correspondence in reality, since what reigns is a total separation of *res* and *verba*, and it is all a game and all virtual. The work at the Ministry of Telecommunications – of Truth – focuses on supplying ideologically cleansed literature that fosters and cements fanatical membership of the Party. A new language is being elaborated – Newspeak – that economizes on words, and destroys useless ones, and is therefore giving birth to a means in the service of a political end. The complete obsolescence of English by the year 2050 is all part of the impoverishment of the future. Significantly Winston is reluctant to turn old English into Newspeak. In the affective sphere there is a distant relationship between the regime and conjugal unhappiness and the impossibility of living an authentic life of the senses, also as a consequence of a studied political measure: removing pleasure from the sexual act, making it a mere means of procreation. The strange thing is that no form of religion seems to have survived in the novel's universe. In fact, 'religion' is among the many words destroyed in Newspeak, since the corresponding thing no longer exists. Orwell's Newspeak is a tardy answer to William Empson, since it eliminates ambiguities, above all politically heretical ones. It allows people to think well, that is, 'doublethink'. It is a gradually impoverished language, since some words, in fact many, fall into disuse by not having any longer – like political freedom – a referent. Therefore its main guideline is economy: a lemma has a double use and purpose, as a verb, noun and adjective. One of the good effects of Newspeak is rationalizing – that is, standardizing – the well-known irregularities of English, especially the verbs, and also its plurals and comparatives. Hence this becomes a planned decimation of words: 'whole batteries' of them are destroyed – consigned to obsolescence. In reality, a certain verbal ambiguity or ambivalence survives:

---

130   Agreed: but how is it possible to alter and 'rectify' copies of newspapers in the possession of single readers?

there are words that have one semantics for the Party and another for its enemies. In this way the universal linguistic process is turned upside down, the one that moves and progresses from primitive forms of expression to other increasingly sophisticated ones, rich in resonance and nuances: and it is the shades of meaning that are the first effect to be abolished. The final phase of this operation is the destruction of the universal library, and of English letters in particular: the task of a sector of employees is to 'translate' the works of the great authors into Newspeak, and by the time this task has been accomplished the originals 'would be destroyed'.

6. Utopia and dystopia work on leaps forwards and backwards, and the arrival point can be in a worse or better order of things, perfected or degenerate. The model that works for Orwell, and is also closest to him, is that of Morris and *News from Nowhere*. Morris imagined, a century away from his present, a revolution of the subjugated, in which the harassed workers would re-establish a communist-style order relying on redistribution of wealth and an archaic hierarchical system of values. The essence of Orwell's variant can be reduced to this, that the temporal gap is incalculably shorter, and the revolution is imagined to have begun after the war, in the early 1960s, precisely when Morris wanted it; and that the main character, thirty-nine in 1984, has two fundamental disadvantages compared to Morris's William Guest. He is not a time traveller, as also Butler is in his diptych, and so the time of the novel, or even the place, is not binary.[131] Secondly, and decisively, Winston is deprived of the possibility of a confrontation. At a certain point of the extract from Goldstein's book, it is noted that the masses cannot rebel 'so long as they are not permitted to have standards of comparison'. Consequently, Orwell reworks his favourite theme – from *A Clergyman's Daughter* onwards – of the loss of memory, both collective and individual. The confrontation might be between life before and after the revolution, but those who could be vigilant, or merely able to remember, have been overwhelmed and rendered oblivious by addiction: on one exemplary page of Goldstein's

---

131   This and other rules of the utopian genre, accepted and violated, are discussed by V. Fortunati, '"It Makes No Difference": A Utopia of Simulation and Transparency', in Bloom 1987, 139–50.

book it is explained how the regime, with its expert tactics of mass psychology, has managed to engender in the individual the forgetfulness of having forgotten.[132] Winston was young when the revolution began, and his memory is now fuzzy; he has only a vague feeling that things are worse and not better. Also the elderly, like the proletarian interrogated at the inn, have lost, not so much the capacity to remember, as that of connecting memory fragments into a continuum. Orwell dramatically insists on the lack of testimony about that past which the regime is either destroying or falsifying: a hundred years earlier, with that same feeling of lacerating swoon, Browning and Arnold had complained of the absence of ocular and auditory witnesses to the words of Christ, and to Christ's actual passage in Galilee. Orwell is in *Nineteen Eighty-Four* a memorial writer who clings to the capacity to remember, desperately wishes not to forget and tries to preserve the integrity of his own awareness; in short, he foresees the future theoreticians of a weak consciousness that crumbles and thus becomes unconsciousness.

7. The extracts from the imaginary book by Goldstein, the new, true Emanuel, the rejected saviour and *nemo propheta in patria*, which Winston has found and reads in secret, summarize the historical process that led to the American and Russian blocks, with Japan as an inconvenient third. War is in progress, but less lethal and destructive (the atomic bombs, many of them dropped in the 1940s, are still produced but not used, and serve as a deterrent), because, substantially, the ideologies behind the super-powers have only slight differences. Permanent war is also due to the geographical extension of the three blocks and the technological parity of the armaments, in addition to self-sufficiency when it comes to raw materials, and therefore a lack of need to find markets. Guerrilla wars, not full-scale ones, are fought for possession of small strips of land. Borders fluctuate. As for the standard of life, Goldstein also attributes its deterioration to mechanization. The problem for the oligarchies in power had been how to prevent the lower classes from becoming aware, that is from rebelling. Answer: by

---

132   Also active in Morris, but in a rather different way, is the oppositional dynamic between forgetting and remembering, applied to the transformation of the Decadent, sheltered writer into a committed one (cf. Volume 6, § 143.1).

not distributing production surplus, but using it for the ends of war. If you slake the workers' hunger they become aware and rebel, if you keep them hungry they remain subdued. In particular, the members of the Inner Party adopt 'doublethinking', that is, they know that everything is unreal and false but act as if it were real. Their object is to 'extinguish once and for all the possibility of independent thought'. In Goldstein's book, Winston even reads about a cyclical pattern, that of a blocked three-part structure, of high, middle and low without a possible harmony: the low want to fight for a society in which all are equal, the high occasionally become half-hearted and are undermined and beaten by the middle, allied by promises to the low being chased back down as soon as the objective has been reached, so that the middle become high in turn. And yet in all these upheavals there has never been in history any real progress in wellbeing, nor steps forward towards equality. And socialism, over the course of the twentieth century, had gradually and increasingly abandoned the goal of equality. What happened during the twentieth century? That equality really seemed possible even if it was necessary to subdivide the functions and tasks in the field of work. Yet this goal became discredited right at the moment when it was within reach. There had been a swing towards forms of authoritarianism, favoured by the development of communication technology. Later authoritarianism was more rigorous and scientific than historical fascism and communism in repressing freedom and controlling every moment of existence for individuals and potential dissidents. The new system that the high decide to impose everywhere is oligarchic collectivism: it is the Party that possesses everything. The capitalistic expropriation wanted by the socialists has been done, but has been translated into permanent inequality. Seeing that it is necessary to make this Party anthropomorphic, use is made of the effigy of an inexistent Big Brother, a fetish in which to invest the potential of identification of the masses, and a 'focusing point'. 2 per cent of the population of Oceania is in the Inner Party, the Outer one is 13 per cent, while 85 per cent are 'proles'; of the latter, the potential rebels are eliminated by the Thought Police.[133]

---

133   Naturally, such a concept of the Party as a fiction that links some high, that is, exploiters and supporters of inequality, collides with that of the Party among the orthodox

8. Sex becomes the ersatz of a revolutionary act, and prohibited intercourse is the first step to corroding the purism and Puritanism which are one of the tools the regime stands on, exploiting sexual frustration to channel it as warlike hatred for the enemy. Julia offers Winston an alternative, that of collaboration for mere survival; she too is apolitical, yearning to live her own life, sceptical of the existence of the Brotherhood, and not interested in righting the existing order with a second revolution. Therefore she is not really the ideal companion of fortune for Winston. A presage of the tragic end is the broken-nosed face of an old dissident who has been beaten and lobotomized, seen unequivocally to be going soft in a café; it will be discovered as a prefiguration of Winston himself after his 'memory' treatment. In the love nest, rats emerge from the wardrobe provoking unspeakable terror in Winston, who will be tortured, with rats ready to maul him, in the final scene of the novel. In the prison cell others like him have ended in the net, and Parsons, stupid Parsons, is the first to suffer retaliation: he, the hunter of heretics, is in the guardhouse, his good conscience having betrayed him: in his sleep he yelled 'down with Big Brother!'.[134] The paperweight, a sliver of coral swimming in a little sea – a foetus wallowing in amniotic fluid –is also a foretaste of the apnoea that Winston will feel during the interrogation. In the arrest scene the paperweight shatters after being dropped by the perfidious Charrington, who had sold it to him, and who therefore felt scorn for this token of the past, making it something functional out of something only 'useless', and functional to let Winston fall into the trap. Winston is not 'vaporized' – and this is a mystery or an incongruence – but is subjected to the therapy that cancels memory and awareness, in order to provoke proper doublethink, that is knowing that something is as it is, but consciously believing in its opposite. Thanks to the torture he is led to believe that truth is not objective but is only the truth of the Party. On the historical plane, the

Marxists, for example the one praised by Brecht in 'Wir sind Sie', that is, 'We are the Party', a song proudly sung by the workers who willingly accept to be submerged and annulled beneath the protective wing of the party itself.

134   Another link: from the blocked sink, with its filthy clot of hair, almost at the beginning, to the blocked foul-smelling loo of this cell.

stage reached is not yet that of an imminent possibility of a proletarian revolution, but of the very distant and perhaps inexistent probability of one. Meanwhile, the Party holds the power for its own sake, not for other ends, or only for the goal of establishing an oligarchic dictatorship. In the final, or almost final scene, there is a parody of Satan's temptation of Christ in the desert: O'Brien is Satan – and is also Faust-like for this very reason – expressing the human aspiration to possess the others' mind; previously, O'Brien had appeared to Winston a paternal and divine hypostasis whose mind contained his own, while Goldstein was the satanic 'primal traitor' through a heretical and apocryphal Bible, namely a 'book' without a title and by definition. Controlling reality means controlling the mind, because it is the mind – Berkeley – that confers existence on things: 'nothing exists except through human consciousness'.[135] The world created and staged by the Party is the opposite of the hedonistic utopias of the old reformers: it is sadistic power that reveals itself by making the victim suffer and by cancelling love, also of the sexual kind. Winston, who does not believe in God, is the last man, or at any rate the last to believe in man's spirit; therefore he is also, in a literal sense, the last humanist.[136]

135   There is a current and widespread idea that Orwell had simply and imaginatively amplified the tortures and policing systems of his school days at St Cyprian (cf. § 22.1) and that his bitter pessimism was due to the tribulations and catastrophes of his last years of life. With good reasons, Woodcock 1966, 55, denies this. Orwell's letters a few days and minutes from his death are Senecan in their steadfast, conscious dignity.

136   Orwell admired James Hanley (1897–1985), one of the classic loose cannons of twentieth-century fiction, and the striking, fluent Welsh writer of numerous novels of effervescent, raw seamen's life, who had recently found other, occasional illustrious admirers, principally in America where he emigrated as part of the vicissitudes of a somewhat turbulent life. However, his brother Gerald Hanley (1916–1992) is more of an Orwell double. A native of Liverpool, a Catholic, the son of a poor family of Irish extraction, Gerald Hanley emigrated to Kenya to work as a farmer until the war, and lived for a long time in India and Pakistan before relocating to Ireland in 1954. His novels, among which *The Journey Homeward* (1961) stands out, reflect his African and Indian experiences from an anti-colonial perspective.

§ 30. *Caudwell*

It is not unjustified to agree with some scholars[1] in saying that Christopher Caudwell (born Christopher St John Sprigg, 1907–1937) is the greatest British Marxist theoretician and literary critic of the twentieth century, *pace* Herbert Read, Raymond Williams and Terry Eagleton. One would have to say, ultimately *pace* George Orwell, too. Orwell was a splendid journalist, an almost infallible critic, and the author of two wonderful novels of political fiction, but objectively he does not possess an in-depth articulate political theory with a related aesthetics; rather, as we have just seen, merely a vague, broad albeit very noble liberal humanism, and an elementary ideological pragmatism that is averse to excessive subtleties.[2] Let it be clear: Caudwell is not Gramsci, nor is he Lukács; however, his two main books, *Illusion and Reality and Studies in a Dying Culture*, are mature fruits and not merely unripe promises, and they exhibit an acquired technical idiolect all his own, a distinct and confident dialectic sophistication, a non-slavish critical assimilation plus an astounding capacity to move around the contemporary cultural map and fearlessly jot down original, idiosyncratic, inevitably arbitrary sketches of political history. They are still striking today for the wide range of references and the degree of updating on the state of knowledge in his times. Let us say more, and remember and recognize that these two books were written almost on impulse by a veritable *enfant prodige* of British and even European culture. A genuine and rare monstrum of precocity and versatility, Caudwell died just thirty years old during the Spanish Civil War, which he could not help joining, as I shall explain, through a sort of consequential ethical and ideological equation. However, in those few years of activity he had already written a small library, displaying an astonishing unfamiliar eclecticism: poems of a

---

1   For example HYN, 189 and 256.
2   Orwell himself, who mentions Caudwell very few times, showed that he did not consider him a leading light but a somewhat anonymous thinker along the lines of Edward Upward. And somewhat oddly, given Caudwell's opposing or divergent ideas on communism, he does not debate with him. Which is to say, Caudwell remained classified as a maverick, immature, easily attacked, dissociated, isolated, and a dissident. On this marginalization in orthodox Marxist criticism, cf. HYN, 260 and 267.

'metaphysical' and Jacobean bent, characterized by a very sober caustic wit, drained of any conventional lyricism; and, to pay his keep, a good six or seven thrillers and other works of a more heuristic and serious kind, such as four theoretical books, one of them on the relationship between quantum physics, science therefore, and society.[3] Everyone is free to conjecture what he might have pulled out of the hat had he not died so young: other theoretical books, even more pondered and deeply rooted, other works of applied Marxism; and perhaps even, like Orwell, practical translations of his ideas into novels and poems – given the irremediable shortcomings of contemporary socialist art – of a left-wing bent and supportive of the proletarian revolution.[4] Or perhaps none of this, others have supposed, since Caudwell himself did not know and would not have known how to overcome the *impasse* he himself stigmatized, that of a middle-class artist who remained unable, as Spender said, 'to transfer [himself] to the working class'.[5]

2. Caudwell would have scornfully refuted to be classified under the label of the insurgence of utopianism, since socialist utopianism was one of his main targets, without however realizing he was a victim of it and therefore an adept of that utopianism. At precise historical moments the apocalyptic utopians had diagnosed the end of their culture, and surprised the world by pointing out that, behind the facile complacent optimism, in reality everything was going to rack and ruin. Society, at the peak of health, was subtly diseased. And no one had realized this. In relatively recent times,

3   He also wrote no less than five aeronautics manuals. Just recently, some of his summary forays into the relationship between society and the cinema have aroused interest, cinema being a means that began to accompany literature as an art for the masses. Perhaps, he said, cinema was the socialist art of the future in view of the ineluctable corruption of literature, in the wake of Lenin who considered it the most important art for socialism, because of its potential ability to represent life for the spectator, almost without verbal filters.

4   This is because, according to Hynes in one of his most severe assessments, his poems and thrillers, and his only serious novel, had had no 'political content' (HYN, 260).

5   Quoted in HYN, 261. Caudwell, who had been a member of the English Communist Party since 1934, had nonetheless handed out communist leaflets, been an agitator, and in the London suburb of Poplar he had frequented the dockworkers.

this overused physiological metaphor had had its main, masterly illustrator in Carlyle (in his essay 'Characteristics'); after him it was applied by the great Victorian *maîtres à penser*, from Arnold to Hopkins and Ruskin. Caudwell flaunts the same diagnoses even if he changes the sign to the factors at stake – yet only slightly after all, since the liberation of the worker was a matter of concern to those predecessors, who cherished a socialism that was certainly imperfect, 'Christian' as it had been officially baptized, but still socialism. It is absolutely true that in the early 1930s a planetary and international malaise had become more acute (financial crises, the rise of right-wing dictatorships, threats of a new war, discontented workers), and that this was reflected in the domestic British scene by unrest and strikes. And the intellectuals had no wish to sit on their hands. To Caudwell it seemed that a paradoxical contradiction was occurring: that an undeniable scientific *progress* in physics, chemistry and applied sciences was synchronous with a *regression* or a dangerous involution of the associated forms of living. His ideological system rests on some very simple premises, and for him modern history had two fundamental key points, feudalism and capitalism. The destruction of feudalism in the name of freedom emerged, however, in the replacement of the feudal system with an equally non-liberal social regime, even if this 'liberator' could be justified, and was excusable, since it was not aware of founding anything less than western capitalism. The result of capitalism had been, through organized work, an increase in productivity and therefore also a rise in the standard of life and the civilizing of the ill educated worker, by abolishing the regime of the jungle; however, it had also brought with it the creation of a new servitude (Caudwell's keyword, from beginning to end, is coercion). Caudwell's Marxism becomes Freudian when he argues that both the capitalist, and above all the worker, are not conscious of this imprisonment and this new form of lack and trampling of freedom. The search for agreements between Freud and Marx was so fashionable, and tyrannical, in the early 1930s – Auden and the Thirties poets, Dylan Thomas – that there is no reason to underline once again this fascination. The therapy? The writer, a Freudian agent, must superficially psychoanalyse the unconscious workers so that they become aware of their slavery, not individually, obviously, but by forming coalitions, cooperating, and joining other workers in the struggle. For Caudwell, art is a ritual and a tool of participation and cementing of the community as a whole, and cannot therefore be an asocial art. And only art that prompts collaboration within the revolutionary class is 'good' art. The second cornerstone of Caudwell's aesthetic is freedom. An art that is sick and false, non-liberating, or a promoter of a false awareness, is bourgeois art for the bourgeoisie, even the art of those who criticize capitalism. The middle-class illusion is that of an individualistic and solipsistic art, and only proletarian art is liberating; but it does not exist as yet and never has existed. It is the task of the critic to goad middle-class artists towards a radically different art.

3. *Illusion and Reality* and *Studies in a Dying Culture* form a pair of posthumous books, and, both published in 1937, complement one another. The first one, only partially heuristic as we shall see, is a sweeping, sometimes long-winded Marxist theoretical foundation of western art, but seen as an integrated activity according to British eclecticism, and thus welcoming and re-elaborating, in its twelve chapters, cues from ethnology, anthropology, psychology of art, psychoanalysis, even Russian formalism and the most recent home-grown linguistic criticism of Richards and Empson, plus epistemology and logical positivism.[6] On the one hand, it seems to foreshadow Arnold Hauser, while on the other, at least in the first two or three chapters, Caudwell sounds like a William Golding abstractly theorizing a prehistoric and primitive perception of reality, as recreated in his much later novel, *The Inheritors*.[7] The aetiology of poetry is also distinguished in its specific key points in relation to the birth of the novel, and in a series of oppositions such as those between the primitive and the evolved, the subjective and the objective, and particularly – in as much as the novel is a reflection of reality – the immediate and the mediate. Except that reality

---

6   The procedure is therefore irregular, since after six diachronic chapters dedicated to the development of poetry from the primitives to modern times, there comes an abrupt break, and the following five are synchronic and ahistorical, while one of them surprisingly switches to a taxonomy of the so-called physical-technical facts of poetic language, echoing Tynjanov, Brik, Jakobson and even early Lotman. The academic and scholarly nature of the book, which covers nearly 300 pages, is proved by a rich bibliography and even by a thematic index.

7   § 141.1.

is, or rather, historically, becomes, a function and a variable of the division of labour; it becomes the economic. After the primitive historical phase, art was no longer a collective ritual, but was precociously appropriated, if not expropriated, by the middle classes: it thus became capitalist art. The central chapters are devoted to a second survey of English literature according to the litmus test of a disillusioned middle-class artist, that is, one unconsciously tending to conserve his middle-class privilege by passing it off as progressive, revolutionary, even proletarian; a privilege that means precisely the renewed, strengthened possibility, through his art, of attending to the free, out-of-context cultivation of his ego. Thus, for Caudwell, the history of English literature, from the Elizabethans to the Romantics, to the Victorians and the Decadents, is a chain of 'withdrawals' from the frays on the part of single artists after having loitered awhile on the fringes: in fact, middle-class artists did not know they were keeping alive the very enemy they had declared war upon. For our purposes, what counts is the *in cauda venenum* of the penultimate page. In a sudden regurgitation of militancy, Caudwell assumes the falsetto of a 'conscious proletarian' and reproaches contemporary artists, famously accusing Auden and his group of being bourgeois artists, not only deluded but also dishonest. Their aporia was to live as proletarians but remain bourgeois artists; basically to fight for the old immunity of a life without social responsibilities, solipsist and ultimately anarchic, as 'lone wolves'.

4. *Studies in a Dying Culture* is in turn a selective radiography of committed contemporary British fiction. Caudwell is severe and impossible to please, unhappy above all with a little circle of writers who were even by and large socialist and palingenetic. But this was not enough, they were not authentically socialist enough, above all they were abstentionists, individualists, not prone to taking risks and to say consistently uncompromising truths. Caudwell looked around him and, disillusioned, was unable to recognize any authentic political hero, that is, any bourgeois willing to make sacrifices and even give his or her life for the people and freedom. It is paradoxical, as I shall explain immediately below apropos his criticism of T. E. Lawrence, that his first step in the book is the same as Byron's at the beginning of *Don Juan*: that modern history did not offer any hero, that there had been no real ones since Napoleon's times, and that, *a fortiori*, the

First World War had been devoid of heroes universally recognized as such by the collective imagination. Caudwell himself wished to be a modern hero for the people, and he left for Spain in 1936 foreseeing that he would almost certainly die; almost seeking death, he had submitted the manuscript of his book to the publisher giving precise instructions regarding its publication.[8] Caudwell says nothing here of the modernists,[9] but his silence amounts to a disqualification: they were too dedicated to individualism, solipsism, the cult of the abstract word; they did not even think, even at the risk of making mistakes, about how to refound history, society and art. The ideological background is the stubborn, renewed and ever necessary attack on the middle classes and against their awareness, a false awareness. Everything originates from this presupposition and converges on it. The bourgeoisie, he says, effects a 'coercive control' over the proletarian class, so that the freedom of the one equals the coercion of the other. The secret and the cure-all is no less than utopia, an integrated society without social classes. In his analytical essays, Shaw is simply a contemplative adept of utopian socialism that does not become concrete in action: he is one of the many playwrights who, conscious of the bourgeois illusion, do nothing to proceed to action, lacking the courage. D. H. Lawrence almost seems like the hero Caudwell needs, since he is palingenetic; but his primitivism is ultimately like that of the other Lawrence, that is, unconscious; he certainly wanted to change the world, but in a fascist sense. Consequently, the two Lawrences were not so distant from one another, and both idealized Sicily, Sardinia, ancient Etruria, Mexico, and Australia, but intended to do away with intellectualism, but in a conscious way. They fought for freedom, not in social relationships, but despite them, that is, they too ultimately

---

8   HYN, 245, who, however, on a previous page (188) declares totally apolitical the interest in a book on the non-stop flight from England to Australia of the Parer-McIntosh couple, which also formed the subject of a poem by Day Lewis (§ 19.6); instead, Caudwell celebrated pure heroism, for the moment not yet politically indexed.

9   The uncompromising criticism of the Decadent and solipsistic ideologies of the modernists, with T. S. Eliot in the lead, had been carried out the previous year, in the 1936 book *Romance and Realism*.

preached an isolationist art. Against Wells, the petit bourgeois wishing to be self-promoted, Caudwell launches a veritable, closing tirade.

§ 31. *T. E. Lawrence*

One of the questionable axioms introduced by Christopher Caudwell in his essay on Thomas Edward Lawrence (1888–1935), contained in *Studies in a Dying Culture* – whose subtitle is 'Study of Heroism' – is that the hero is often as unconscious as a Siegfried, and the more unconscious he is, the more able he is to transform the world and reshape the surrounding environment on the wings of an original, limitless freedom. The objective of this rudimentary theory of the heroic is *sub rosa* to establish the absence of true heroes spawned by the Great War and modern times with respect to the distant and recent past, and above all the canonization of Lenin over the numerous 'charlatans' who had appeared on the scene, and who, like Mussolini and Hitler, were then inexorably swept away from their era, after having speciously featured and presented themselves as genuine heroes. For Caudwell, Lawrence was anything but a charlatan; in fact ever since he was young Lawrence had vibrated with nostalgia for human relationships based on the fascination for the elected leader and for archaic loyalty, and above all with hate for the 'present middle class', polluted by capitalistic profit. Inevitably, however, his ideal faded, his project withered, and he lost his messianic power, so that ironically Lawrence ended up bequeathing the Arabs a middle-class organization, thereby westernizing them. From a potential communist hero he was reduced to a middle-class pseudo-hero or a 'bourgeois hero who miscarried'.[1] In reality, these pages of Caudwell only celebrate and exalt, in the form of denegation or simply disillusionment, the fascination and myth of the last great British man of action, who, in spite of Caudwell, for the collective imagination exhibited all the marks of the exceptional and superhuman. And his magnetism, as we have seen repeatedly, also pulsated among the higher levels of the intelligentsia, which long lamented his premature death. Welsh, an Oxfordian, and

---

1   A verdict that substantially matches the rather laconic ones of Orwell, who defined Lawrence as a right-wing intellectual (see OCE, vol. II, 94).

an archaeologist from 1910 to 1914 in Mesopotamia, after 1916 Lawrence joined the British military contingent stationed in the Middle East, and as an ardent supporter coordinated the various Arab factions, uniting them to systematically sabotage the Turks and ending up being instrumental in the fall of the Ottoman Empire. A delegate at the Peace Conference of 1919, his pan-Arabic dream was bitterly quashed by diplomatic games when, with the Sykes-Picot agreements, France obtained the creation of a Syrian state under its aegis, and Britain received a mandate on Palestine, Transjordan and Iraq. Lawrence emerged from this disenchantment by again becoming a simple airman for the RAF, a kind of polemical retreat resulting in him moulding a new personal identity (a precocious, doubting existentialism that is intriguing as much as the previous mystique of his daring).[2] He was to die after having practically lent the poet Thom Gunn, and later youth culture, another myth, that of the motorized centaur and of the inebriation with speed on a motorbike.

2. *Seven Pillars of Wisdom*,[3] the long-drawn-out memorial of his guerrilla actions in Arabia, which to avoid misunderstandings and by definition was soon attributed to 'Lawrence of Arabia', was first published in a limited edition of eight copies in 1922, then in a commercial edition, but still numbered, in 1926; the edition normally read now is the posthumous one of 1935. This is a clear pendant to those memoirs that the British infantrymen wrote (often, like him, students of Oxford) from the Western Front, and

2   Cf. HYN, 190–1, for eloquent opinions of the Marxist Ralph Fox, Churchill, Isherwood, and Auden. It remains, however, rather enigmatic and unsettling that despatches and documents at that time not in the public domain, and made known later, have revealed that Lawrence was instrumental in the design to break up the Ottoman Empire to reduce the Arab populations under British control. At the Peace Conference, Lawrence supported a solution of equidistance between safeguarding British interests and the expectations of the Arabs.

3   Without the article *The*, which, however, normally appears when the book is mentioned by critics and scholars. The unsatisfactory, abridged version of 1927, *Revolt in the Desert*, was planned to reduce the costs of the complete edition. Lawrence's purely literary art glows even more in his letters, published posthumously (1938) and edited by D. Garnett. Lawrence also translated the *Odyssey* into prose, and was the author of another memoir on his enrolment as an airman.

it may be compared, in terms of volume, date of publication, though not genre, with the visionary epic of David Jones, *In Parenthesis*. At the time, Lawrence was much older (twenty-eight in 1916), and he was a professional diplomat, not a sour university employee tossed into the fray who sent his relatives back home weary, visionary, or sarcastic lyric poems. The general title, taken from Proverbs, and the subheading, 'a triumph', create expectations of rhetoric and magniloquence that are not followed up and verified. On the contrary, the style is diary-like, paratactic, with only some parenthetic or passing observations, which occasionally become more incisive and at times even venomous. To call it a masterpiece of the modern epic, or even a romantic epic, is therefore slightly misleading, just as it would be erroneous to take it for the scrupulous chronicle of a professional historian. In a broader sense, it has been called a 'novel' and therefore exactly a romance, with all of its arbitrary falsifications and idealizations. Nothing is over-described or merits exceptional treatment: the facts of blood, violence and brutality, are reabsorbed into the daily routine with a sort of twentieth-century *nihil admirari*. And yet Lawrence did have a handle on the Eureka effect, and was able to suddenly take flight, without notice, from the arid phenomenology of the desert march and sabotage, and from the general description, to impressions of landscapes, to the vivid discreet detail, to little caricatural scenes, to the curious and humorous anecdote, to the narrative oasis and the sketch (Feisal in the field with his foibles; the dressing of Lawrence in Arab robes,[4] the pederastic advances of the Bey rejected by the unbending and stoic Lawrence). But in the end we can apply to *Seven Pillars* the usual adage of the least read books amongst those which are most spoken about. It should be anthologized and pecked at, unless one is among the specialists and experts on the theory of war; the fine pages of portraits and cameos need to be extracted, otherwise the desert routine is too much for 700 pages, and is wearying.

3. Lawrence's objective was emphatically that of forging 20 million Semites into a single nationality, and to achieve the palingenesis of one

---

4   In this scene there is a Carlylean criticism of symbols hidden in clothing: the western-style military cap with a peak is a barrier between the human and the divine, something that the Arabs do not notice.

part of the inhabited world. Not for nothing had he studied as a young man the 'Crusader Castles', but ironically he did not possess the physique for the role, and, too low in stature to be enlisted as a soldier on the outbreak of the Great War, he could only be taken on as an officer for the ground troops in the Middle East. Unquestionably, he shared with Yeats and Joyce and many others of his time a cyclical, Gibbon-inspired concept of history, mixed with some Protestant myths of sexuality: the Turkish Empire was by now broken, infected and degenerate, also, if not above all, due to sexual promiscuity. Conversely, the Arabs represented lifeblood that was still fresh, healthy and virginal. Lawrence applied a clear sexual metaphor in the dominant opposition between Turkish impotence and Semitic fecundity.

PART II

The Novel after Modernism

§ 32. *Huxley* I: The retaliation of evolutionism*

In Aristotelian terms, ignoring 'accidents' and looking at 'substance', two basic questions are debated in the work of Aldous Huxley (1894–1963): resistance to the genetic and historical legacy and the affirmation of individual freedom. With Huxley we are induced to admit that nineteenth-century

*   *Collected Works*, London 1949–1975; *Collected Essays*, ed. R. S. Baker and J. Sexton, 6 vols, Chicago 2000–2002. *Letters*, ed. G. Smith, London 1969. A. Henderson, *Aldous Huxley*, London 1935; T. Brunius, *Aldous Huxley*, Stockholm 1947; A. Gérard, *A la rencontre de Aldous Huxley*, Paris 1947; P. Jouguelet, *Aldous Huxley*, Paris 1948; J. Brooke, *Aldous Huxley*, London 1954, 1972; J. Atkins, *Aldous Huxley: A Literary Study*, London 1956, 1957, and, rev. edn, 1967; S. K. Ghose, *Aldous Huxley: A Cynical Salvationist*, Bombay 1961, London 1962; S. Greenblatt, *Three Modern Satirists: Waugh, Orwell, and Huxley*, New Haven, CT 1965; *Aldous Huxley 1894–1963: A Memorial Volume*, ed. J. Huxley, London 1965; P. Bowering, *Aldous Huxley: A Study of the Major Novels*, London 1968; H. H. Watts, *Aldous Huxley*, New York 1969; L. Archera Huxley, *The Timeless Moment: A Personal View of Aldous Huxley*, London 1969 (memoir by his second wife); A. Scurani, 'Il sincretismo religioso di Aldous Huxley', *LET*, XXIV (1969), 551–68, and XXV (1970), 263–82; L. Brander, *Aldous Huxley: A Critical Study*, London 1970; C. M. Holmes, *Aldous Huxley and the Way to Reality*, Bloomington, IN 1970; M. Birnbaum, *Aldous Huxley's Quest for Values*, Knoxville 1971; J. Meckier, *Aldous Huxley: Satire and Structure*, London 1971; P. E. Firchow, *Aldous Huxley: Satirist and Novelist*, Minneapolis, MN 1972, and *The End of Utopia: A Study of Aldous Huxley's 'Brave New World'*, Lewisburg, PA 1984; K. M. May, *Aldous Huxley*, London 1972; G. Woodcock, *Dawn and the Darkest Hour: A Study of Aldous Huxley*, London 1972, 2007; S. Bedford, *Aldous Huxley*, 2 vols, London 1973–1974, 1979; P. Thody, *Huxley: A Biographical Introduction*, London 1973; *Aldous Huxley: A Collection of Critical Essays*, ed. R. Kuehn, Englewood Cliffs, NJ 1974; CRHE, ed. D. Watt, London and Boston, MA 1975; C. S. Ferns, *Aldous Huxley: Novelist*, London 1980; S. Manferlotti, *Anti-utopia: Huxley Orwell Burgess*, Palermo 1984, and *Invito alla lettura di Aldous Huxley*, Milan 1987 (with a useful panorama of the critical fortune); G. Nance, *Aldous Huxley*, New York 1988; D. K. Dunaway, *Huxley in Hollywood*, New York 1989, and *Aldous Huxley Recollected: An Oral History*, Walnut Creek, CA 1998; D. Guardamagna, *La narrativa di Aldous Huxley*, Bari 1989; R. Baker, *Brave New World: History, Science, and Dystopia*, Boston, MA 1990; *Readings on 'Brave New World'*, ed. K. de Koster, San Diego, CA 1999; N. Murray, *Aldous Huxley: An English Intellectual*, London 2002; D. Sawyer, *Aldous Huxley: A Biography*, New York 2002; *Aldous Huxley*, ed. H. Bloom, New York 2010; D. Watt, *Aldous Huxley*, London 2015.

and Darwinian evolutionism, and heredity, really do exist and are not a genetic fantasy. Huxley may in fact have considered himself the first victim of that form of programmed descent on which *Brave New World* hinges, where he describes a threat to the freedom not only of the future state of the world but also and above all to the present, as *Brave New World Revisited* shows. He rebels against genetic conditioning and stands out as an uncompromising critic of science and scientism; his final intellectual stance repudiates history, which he calls an 'immediate evil'.[1] If all of this is true, Huxley authored a work that is highly unified in its various stages, for all its vastness and apparent dispersion. I will attempt to see how those two access keys can be found deductively rather than inductively. This also implies that Huxley, mainly known today for *Brave New World* while almost all the rest of his production has become archaeological material for specialists, is a first-rate author worth salvaging. His ancestry was illustrious and eminent – a kind of horoscope that predicted a bright future for him that he felt obliged to attain. Amongst his paternal ancestors was T. H. Huxley, the biologist and the strenuous popularizer of Darwin, and, by transverse maternal lines, Matthew Arnold. His beginnings in poetry, almost contemporary with those of T. S. Eliot (who shared his infectious admiration for Laforgue), marked the provisional assertion of his maternal *côté*, as through Arnold he also harked back to Keats – to the proverbially sensuous Keats. His youthful poetry may therefore appear anachronistic, redolent of the sensibility of the Nineties, yet not without the influence of the early Yeats's crepuscular mode – the swooning atmospheres, the wandering heroes lost in thought in the midst of pastoral scenery also smacking of pre-Romanticism. Huxley translated Mallarmé's *L'Après-midi d'un Faune*, while *Leda* from 1920 is a medium-length mythological verse tale that, in its prodigiously glossy fluidity, may represent the opposite of the dramatic sonnet version of the same theme by Yeats. A series of prose tales from 1920, *Limbo* exhibits a burlesque and indeed decidedly comic vein that reminded some contemporaries of Beerbohm and Anatole France,[2]

---

1   CRHE, 290.

2   In the most successful of these stories, the main character Richard Greenow presents collusions with female transvestism that were in the air, since for the general public

but it explores both the immaturity of its hero and the friction between reason and passion. By 1921 Huxley had in fact practically exhausted the hereditary repercussion of his maternal genealogy. Or rather, he was ready to re-enact the same change of skin as his ancestor Matthew Arnold, a sensuous Keatsian poet with feverish moods who eventually became a balanced and detached essayist. In this way his paternal *côté*, the scientific side of T. H. Huxley, gained the upper hand.

2. To close this 'genetic' introduction, Huxley's compromise is the discussion of strictly heuristic questions in an inventive form, that is, in novels defined as 'of ideas'. Having set aside poetry and drama, he was left with the essay, and in fact, after 1921, Huxley authored various collections of cultured, crystalline, urbane essays, whose prose was judged not inferior to that of the best English essayists by many historical readers and critics who deprecated the hybrid form of the 'novel of ideas'.[3] Huxley the novelist remains an essayist because even in his novels he has a *Weltanschauung* to expound. Nothing human *a se alienum putat*. His omniscience still has the nineteenth-century stamp of an 'eminent Victorian'. His first gift is then eclecticism: he is a poet, playwright, short-story writer, novelist, sociologist, philosopher, historian, politologist, epistemologist. However, in boasting too many skills he runs the risk of not having any really deep ones. At this distance in time, his place among the thinkers is reduced to a footnote, at most. The most obvious *trait d'union* with the late nineteenth-century cultural climate lies in the fact that he questions the determinism of evolution, weighs up whether it is worth while to encourage all the proposals of evolutionism, and encourages human resistance to it. Linked to this is the age-old question of the ultimate relationships between science, art and life. Positing a *callida junctura* between art and science, he is the advocate of an integrated and integral humanism.[4] He is the encyclopaedic 'grammarian' who has read every book – a pedant in the worst sense, an erudite

---

he is the anti-war intellectual while he secretly writes novelettes supporting philistine patriotism under a female pseudonym.

3   Maugham compared him with Hazlitt, for example (CRHE, 343). But see P. N. Furbank's slating of Huxley as an essayist in *TLS*, 9 March 2001, 4.

4   This is also C. P. Snow's definition (CRHE, 222).

of former times, with universal knowledge at his fingertips.[5] He can also effortlessly step from one sphere of this knowledge to another; and he is therefore the last 'Metaphysical' or neo-Metaphysical. More exactly, he is the twentieth-century writer who can embody and exemplify Eliot's re-association of sensibility, and for whom Spinoza and the scent of a rose are one and the same perceptive and intellectual experience.[6] Hence the transfusion of Huxley himself into the figure of a sage churning out speeches that seem off-the-cuff, and are instead structured, polished, finished and argued like essays of a Montaigne. However, the predecessor he most resembles is Burton, Burton of the *Anatomy of Melancholy*, the 'cadastral' collector of clippings and citations.

   3. The novel of ideas is theorized by Huxley's *alter ego* Philip Quarles in *Point Counter Point*, where it is defined as the literary mode of novelists who are not 'congenital' and write instead novels 'with a plot'. Huxley recognizes that a novel of ideas is a 'made-up affair', and that in it human types speak who are 'slightly monstrous' and know how to 'reel off formulated notions'. Consequently, in all of Huxley's novels, the plot is flimsy and evanescent and the characters, or one at least, are mainly chatterboxes, and often stop what they are doing to present and debate at length ideas, theories and opinions, and, more often than not, irrational fixations. Huxley's period of grace as a novelist was the 1920s. The four novels that came out a short distance apart at this time were his most representative and homogeneous. The first one came immediately before, the other three immediately after, *Ulysses*; but technically and formally this landmark passed unnoticed, because they were parodies and reworkings that looked back to the most solid, autochthonous insular tradition, that of Sterne and of the more erratic eighteenth-century writers, and to the Romantic eccentrics

5   It is no *boutade* but true that Huxley carried the Encyclopaedia Britannica with him on his travels when he was young (Atkins 1967, 19; cf. also Huxley's essay 'Books for the Journey'). Ford Madox Ford's Tietjens was an encyclopaedic man, too (Volume 7, § 127.2).

6   The ability to 'invest [a scientific fact] with poetry', as in Donne, was noted by D. MacCarthy (CRHE, 49) and by L. P. Hartley (CRHE, 151). To T. S. Eliot's opinion on Huxley I shall return below.

like Peacock: the same ones inspiring Meredith, who is therefore another predecessor. Just a few years earlier, this tradition had been re-launched by Norman Douglas in his supreme and only masterpiece, *South Wind*.[7]

7   Norman Douglas (1868–1952), whose *South Wind* was published in 1917 when he was forty-nine, therefore belongs, save for a few other later writings, to a literary period that I have already dealt with in the preceding volume; but he needs to be introduced here as a forerunner of an infectious fictional mode and of an equally widespread post-Decadent sensibility. Of a noble lineage, born in Austria to a British, more precisely Scottish father and a German mother, he became a diplomat in 1894, but was dismissed because of a probable sex scandal, and in a backlash became infatuated with Southern Italy and its supposedly greater freedom of habits and moral laxity. Having bought a villa on Capri, he lived there almost permanently. Douglas thus shares some traits with other British twentieth-century self-mythologizing expatriates. Two of the latter that spring immediately to mind are Lawrence Durrell and Lowry. Durrell chose to live in historical metropolises and above all necropolises of the imagination; Lowry created and lived the late Romantic myth of the *maudit*. Both myths implied the abandonment of a waning civilization suffering from a breakdown of authentic values, to which one could only react by 'shoring' Eliot's 'fragments'. The self-chosen metaphor of these writers is that of the spectator of the Flood or Empedocles' ascent to the edge of the volcano (in the imaginary geography of Douglas's novel there really is a volcano, and one magnificent surreal scene is an ash-storm that darkens the island). In *South Wind*, which is Forster's *A Room with a View* unrecognizably transposed (and many of Forster's stories are also about 'panic', in a precise meaning of the term, as defined in Volume 7, § 29.4), a British bishop undergoes the positive, beneficial influences of the Mediterranean landscape on an island, Nepenthe, which camouflages Capri. This he does by overcoming any intransigence and all superfluous intellectual and moral rigidness, and adopting a more bland and tolerant philosophy of life. Browning, too, had celebrated a thousand times similar spiritual 'recoveries' under the Italian sun; and if the 'south wind' is the Sirocco, this is the same wind that blows in Browning's 'The Englishman in Italy'. Douglas's novel is like a magnified evocation of the kaleidoscope of that poem. Suffice to say that bishops tread the boards in their dozens in Browning, beginning with Bishop Blougram, and that Douglas is able to perfectly redo Browning's pedants in the numerous, painstaking, last 'grammarians' who throng the island. Thomas Mann's *Death in Venice* preceded Douglas's novel, but Settembrini and Naphta from *The Magic Mountain* seem to be irresistibly derived from the various Mr Keiths, Mr Eames and Count Caloveglia, estranged apocalyptics, epicureans and plain odd fellows who duel and hold court with the most eccentric theories in a similarly soundproofed limbo, unaware that elsewhere the bloodiest of wars was being fought. At home, the authentic English

In their structure, Huxley's novels do not then respond to the formula of realism or of post-Victorian comedy and satire; and the sole, feeble modern or modernistic element is the recourse to the burlesque and the mock-heroic. The first two belong to the genre of Firbank's playful, surreal, even pre-absurdist fantasy, and never radiate, for example, the 'high seriousness' of D. H. Lawrence's contemporary novels – his spasmodic temperament, inebriation and delirium. However, Huxley's second novel, appearing one year before *The Waste Land*, showed that he had assimilated Eliot's mosaic technique with its patchwork, stubs and fragments of the literary tradition.[8] And taking a closer look at Huxley's second novel, we discover that the theme, too, vaguely resembles Eliot's: the corruption of love intended as *agape*, and sex reduced and degraded to copulation without achieving spiritual unison, a merely carnal experience, as shown in the 'typist's scene' in Eliot's poem; therefore, even the general atmosphere is that of Eliot's 'waste land' immediately after the war. The key character in these initial novels, moving gradually from periphery to centre stage, is the Elizabethan 'humour'. This eccentric, however, after his first verbal fireworks becomes repetitive, in fact unbearable, and seems called on stage merely to present a series of conceits or common truths never before noticed, or to exhibit

---

Protestants – who, by definition, were silenced as hypocrites by the enlightened – could in turn but execrate Douglas as the latest of the unctuous eulogists of Catholic and papist hypocrisy, and of collusions with the Italian mixture of faith, superstition and paganism. The judgement of those who unwaveringly believe in a realist fiction and a non-ambiguous commitment, has always been unfavourable on Douglas, verging in some cases on the scandalized and Puritan anathema against filth; on the contrary, those who cherish the fantasy, the out-of-context or even complacent, cynical and amoral digression, and recognize themselves in an epigonic Decadentism, have been mad keen: for these Douglas is a writer *de chevet*, superlative and indispensable. To return to the question of the novel of ideas, the Peacock-like 'conversation piece' had had its followers and experimenters in the late nineteenth century and then had died; Douglas brought it back into favour before Huxley. However, the wake of this fascinating type of novel is the long one that reaches even as far as John Fowles; and an Italian reader finds in it a foretaste of the pastiches of a Carlo Emilio Gadda.

8   Many of Huxley's novels, and indisputably the second, the third and the fifth, sixth, seventh and eighth, have literary quotations as titles, to vouch for the author's wit, as well as his emulative ambitions.

some Sterne-like hobbyhorses. After 1930, Huxley found this formula worn out and wrote his most famous and lasting novel by making a detour towards sensationalism, a transition that was latent in the previous works. *Brave New World* is an indisputable landmark in the history of dystopia; however, Huxley is never apocalyptic, or is only so when facing particular moments and phases of historical emergency. In that little masterpiece of twentieth-century essay writing, *Brave New World Revisited*, and in his underestimated novel, *Island*, Huxley in fact disowns *Brave New World* when he supports suggestibility 'where necessary', or approves of the primitiveness, albeit partially evolved, of the island's social organization. After *Brave New World*, he gradually freed himself 'of the embarrassment of a story',[9] skirting the boundaries of fiction towards a hybrid form and a purely historical, though fictionalized discourse – ideological, philosophical, prophetic or esoteric, it, too, germinating from the previous novels. However, he never freed himself from the embarrassment of history. If the nightmare that weighs on Huxley is that of self-damaging progress, and of a science that foreshadows or causes appalling catastrophes, the deposing of history remains his foremost and ultimate theme. In his post-war writings, also post A-bomb accompanying the possible drift towards a third planetary conflict, Huxley frequently invoked for himself and for humanity the Swift-like figure of the ascetic and recluse after the experiences described in the fourth part of *Gulliver*, for whom the body is an 'ape' and mankind's task is to rise by meditative degrees to the apprehension of 'essence'.[10] Huxley's last *alter ego* rejects history, embraces contemplation, renunciation and abstraction from the world's vortex, and enters eternity.[11]

9   B. Ifor Evans, *A Short History of English Literature*, Harmondsworth 1940, 179.

10   CRHE, 416.

11   Huxley's physical stature (he was among the tallest of all British writers, almost six and a half feet), and the fact that he was almost blind, his sight having been damaged before he was twenty, have often been taken as an existential metaphor, that of an exile from the world, which he therefore 'did not know' and had no links with. His blindness forms an inner pedal note since the book *The Art of Seeing* (1942) and the novel *Eyeless in Gaza*. A review by S. Collini in *TLS*, 10 May 2002, 3, still harps somewhat derisively over all of this, confirming that Huxley has not yet come back to life, in fact continues to be unfashionable.

4. The critical attention commanded by Huxley was conspicuous in his lifetime, and his provocative capacity is attested by the heated discussions in the press on the appearance of each new novel, and by the monographs that studied him and were published before his death. Later, his fame was largely linked to his dystopian masterpiece, which belongs to a genre that never fails to make the news and cause sensation. And yet today Huxley is forgotten and, if anything, a niche author on whom only a few cursory lines can be found in literary surveys and textbooks. Dissensions are focused on one single shortcoming: that ultimately he is not a pure novelist, and therefore that the choice of the novel of ideas is wrong. As a result, Huxley has never had a champion or a major apologist. He was ripped asunder by T. S. Eliot as a novelist who 'must perpetrate [*sic*] thirty failed novels before writing a good one';[12] and no critical favour did he enjoy from Q. D. Leavis and the *Scrutiny* group. Edmund Wilson deemed him inferior to Waugh and even Firbank, who were destined to survive much longer.[13] Other critics, notably Kermode, were even more clamorously frank.[14] Not even his most illustrious peers appreciated him. Wyndham Lewis declassed the dialogue of his novels to that of the serials published in the dailies and of the 'penny novelettes'; mixed, when not perplexed, recognition was granted by Thomas Mann and Hesse. It is crystal clear that Huxley, who debuted almost at the same time as Auden, was not even minimally attracted, even as a young man, by the mirage of Marxism, although, when elderly, he inclined towards spiritualist positions not too dissimilar to Auden's.[15] Orwell, who always treated Huxley with ill-concealed sufficiency, imposed a reading of him

12   CRHE, 145.

13   CRHE, 349.

14   Huxley, as some have been inclined to do with H. G. Wells, has been even struck off the histories of twentieth-century fiction and moved to essay writing, as in D. Daiches's book *The Novel and the Modern World*, Chicago 1939.

15   Huxley emigrated to America, accompanied by Gerald Heard, in 1937, just two years before Auden did with Isherwood, and, like Auden, on the first winds of war and at any rate following the disillusionment of many British intellectuals after the Spanish Civil War. Auden's first American poetic works were not dissimilar to Huxley's pacifist, meditative and mystical proposals.

that gradually became hegemonic, that of a writer espousing pacifism, therefore political inertia, having passed through 'Life-Worship'.[16]

§ 33. *Huxley II: The wasted youth of the 1920s*

Huxley's first four novels, which came out close to one another from 1921 to 1928, form a unified discourse, and take stock of Britain's educated well-off society observed in the years immediately after the war. The space that Huxley cut for himself was that of the essayistic or digressionistic novel. The intrigues and vicissitudes of characters decline in significance; the presentation and discussion of ideas gains ground. The novelistic form is even specious – a mere cover – save perhaps for the first of these four novels, in which the formula and combination of the two elements are implemented in a way that is still fresh, spontaneous and successful; subsequently, the balance goes awry and the mechanism of the novel disintegrates. From the very first moment, Huxley aims, within a tenuous traditional framework (like that of the immature poet leafing through the daisy chain of his loves), to sketch out a free tribunal of debating sessions between supporters and opponents regarding a series of issues. He does this faking the naturalness of these discussions, and after summoning a representative delegation of English society into a closed space. In that historical moment of post-war darkness and apocalyptic desolation, the gist of these arguments is a reflection on the present, and therefore also on the past and the future of the world and of the nation. Thus a 'dialogue' is camouflaged, as in Neo-Platonic symposia in which all the relevant material is debated without anxiety, rather with calm and detached objectivity, with participants having an infallible summary of it at their fingertips. In *Those Barren Leaves*, Chelifer, one of the characters, aptly describes these gatherings as of people willing 'to discuss the problems of the universe [...] to dogmatize about the nature of God and to draw up plans for the future'. This is more or less the standard situation in these novels. There is always a blabbermouth who poses as a sage, the voice of truth and of the critical conscience, the Socratic dispenser of knowledge, and who, as a result, must

16   OCE, vol. I, 558.

indoctrinate the onlookers and stir their torpid intellects. A second, inevitable character is the historian of his own genealogy. Cardan is one of the prototypes in *Crome Yellow*, because he has 'views on life, on literature', and 'he knows a thing or two [...] about all these subjects'. In the same novel, Sir Henry Wimbush recounts two anecdotes on the history of his family, that of his dwarf ancestor and that of his apparently bulimic grandmother, anecdotes that are delightful in themselves and stand out for their clarity and the vividness and curiosity of clean-cut eighteenth-century cameos.

2. The first confrontation of these novels, substantiated by the very freshest historical references, is, however, the ancient one of the good teleology of the cosmos against random and therefore probably negative mechanism. Huxley the historian cannot avoid his characters speaking of history, a history in which until the other day *tout se tenait* and is now more unintelligible, and seems to have been diverted into a new epistemology. A distant descendant of the other Huxley, the nineteenth-century evolutionist, Aldous Huxley fights until the bitter end against the positive optimistic Darwinism of Spencer and Shaw, even if, on the basis of the novels alone, these two versions of Darwinism are a pure sounding board of contrasting hypotheses. In a certain sense, the inconvenience of Huxley's novels is that their characters gradually dwindle, right from their entry, into mere mouthpieces from which words freely explode. The memories of bygone habits and customs, and therefore the sense of the inexorable passing of time, arise as something too automatic, and are recaptured in often purely erudite digressions. The distance separating the four novels from *Brave New World*, which may appear a clamorous *saltus*, is less than it might seem, however. The most superficial reason is that in the interminable, orgiastic banquets of ideas held by the internal orators and erudite characters, a future scheme is being tested, one in which unhappiness and pain will have been abolished, and humanity afflicted by boredom will sigh for its previous condition. Among the many topics discussed, there is an agreement that the perfect state advocated by Wells and the utopians is not viable, and merely induces boredom; and therefore this is precisely where the root of *Brave New World* lies. The modern or at least innovative feature of these four novels is actually the leave-taking from western mimesis and from nineteenth-century plausibility and realism. They belong, if

not already to science fiction, to fantastic realism. In them Huxley invents and practises a largely absurd farce. In real life no one speaks at such length on abstract topics without being interrupted. Because essentially we see them living and not studying, Huxley's characters are instead inexplicably a walking encyclopedia and can recite by heart entire passages from poems and novels – even the most recent – and have a universal, humanistic and scientific culture at their fingertips. This is only in part the normal loaning of the author's ideas to his creations and an act of substitution. A further step forward in technique is more deliberate, more carefully planned, when it becomes apparent that the four novels are virtual constructions, or better, farces and burlesques of the absurd. *Antic Hay* still plays on the subtle dividing line between reality and improbability, with its clique of wishful and amateurish pseudo-aesthetes, one of whom dreams of making his fortune by patenting padded trousers. *Those Barren Leaves* is improbable from beginning to end: a string of odd events right from its inception. Seeing that Huxley is so fond of using musical metaphors, we may call these novels his quartets, in fact his four quartets (perhaps the title was fashionable, even before T. S. Eliot). Each novel is a quartet in its internal musical structure, in its analogies with the sonata form, the agogics of its motifs and timbres, and the overlapping of the themes. If this is indeed the case, these are imperfect quartets, since they are based on trios, quartets, quintets and even sextets of male characters.

3. *Crome Yellow*[17] (1921) superficially exhumes Peacock's 'conversation piece', but is actually mostly indebted to Sterne. Huxley distinguishes himself with a writing style that is elliptical, exuberant, and empathic but

17   This is the first of Huxley's intertextual titles, and it contains a punning reference to a shade of the colour yellow and to the place name of the Crome estate where the novel takes place. Many explanations have been mooted for the adjective 'yellow': 'the euphoric heat of the summer' for one anonymous reviewer (CRHE, 58); a range of shades, as the novelist Scott Fitzgerald found (the yellow mist of the smile, the 'canary' characters, the saffron-coloured springs, the pale yellow sun, etc. [CRHE, 73]). Manferlotti 1987, 44, relates it to 'pale colouring'. Personally, I sense the colour of old age, the absence of freshness, of withering, as the adjective 'barren' in the title of Huxley's third novel would confirm.

with some reserve; sentences are largely paratactic, short but sophisticated, suggestive, never conventional. The slight plot features an immature poet and young intellectual, plunged into a symbolic ordeal, and therefore into a potential *Bildung*. This objective is pursued in the traditional *ad hoc* setting, an ancient country residence surrounded by nature, where a handful of aptly chosen characters find themselves in explosive coexistence in a concentrated lapse of time: no more than a few days, but just enough to finish their portraits and launch their verbal fencing. The eruption that ensues is mostly of an affective nature, but in some characters it is purely intellectual. The novel's third objective is to make these guests emblematic, and the ambitious aim that of sketching out an allegory. *Crome Yellow* is an enquiry into the continuity of time and, *ipso facto*, a reflection on change and the very turning points of history. It is a study of its heavy or light burden, and of Britain's unknown future. In its unity of place and time, and even in a ceremony staged at the end, it is extraordinarily prophetic of another later historical allegory, *Between the Acts* by Virginia Woolf.[18] Initially, Denis Stone is about to arrive at the Crome estate; like Eliot's Prufrock, he is a poet and timid lover who, alone but internally soliloquizing, 'goes to make his visit', feeling awkward and frustrated.[19] Like Prufrock, he has 'hundreds of hours' in front of him, but does not know how to make them bear fruit, and wastes them.[20] The following morning he looks at himself in the mirror, and adjusts his clothes; he wishes to please and make an impression. The novel opens with his arrival and closes with his departure from the estate, and within this symbolic arc of time he learns something about himself.[21]

18   In the next novel, *Antic Hay*, the main character declares: 'Most of one's life is an entr'acte'.

19   In reality, Huxley compares him on one occasion to the extenuated poet Ernest Dowson.

20   The first ideological contrast regarding time is a disagreement with the station manager: the impatient Denis insists on having immediately the bicycle he brought with him, but the official answers him by almost echoing Eliot's 'there will be time ...' (Volume 7, § 93.3).

21   This spiritual journey corresponds to the plot of a novel that Denis has planned and is actually writing, and which was revealed to him, in fact intuited, by the blabbermouth Mr Scogan. Naturally, this plot is the same as that of the novel.

Denis cycles to the estate through sinuous hills evoking in him the curves of a woman's body; he resembles Tennyson who, when he felt obliged to be moved would ladle out a citation, as Verlaine complained. Sensually atrophied, he lives off words.[22] Over the short span of this July holiday, he will only manage to make a clumsy declaration of his intentions to Anne, the niece of the estate's owner, while being unaware of the passion he has aroused in another guest, a young deaf girl whose love he discovers when secretly reading her diary. He will suddenly depart on the advice of a third female figure. The human repertoire of guests at the estate is completed by an ex-Cubist painter who now paints 'formalised nature', and by a know-it-all, a kind of Jimmy Cricket who needlessly keeps lecturing on all the branches of knowledge.[23] The group is almost immediately introduced, and painted in its staticity, at the traditional occasion of tea time; and here the verbal fencing smacks subtly of a bygone residual world like Jane Austen's. The plot of the loves yearned for beyond anything progresses at a snail's pace, and is interrupted and deferred by the entries of other eccentrics who leave equally meteorically. One of them is a fanatical writer who rambles on about inspiration, mistaking it for a specious, charlatanic, mediumistic practice that sounds very much like a parody of Romantic aesthetics.[24] Ivor is a Don Juan who, like every self-respecting Don Juan, arrives, tempts, seduces, takes what he is looking for and departs for his next adventure. Mary dabbles in Freud and psychoanalyses the repression of her instincts,

22   Of significance is the pause in which the poet tells how he fell in love with the word 'carminative', used for its sound and its echo, while also discovering that the exact meaning is quite the opposite of what he had imagined.

23   In reality, Priscilla Wimbush camouflages Lady Ottoline Morrell, the celebrated patron of the arts and the artists whom she received at her manor in Garsington, near Oxford; and Mary Bracegirdle reflects the painter Dora Carrington. The novel's other characters also have their equivalents in minor figures of that entourage frequented by Huxley during the war, in which he did not enlist because of problems with his eyes. At Garsington, Huxley met his wife Maria Nys, a Flemish woman who had taken refuge in England, becoming her widower in 1955.

24   More precisely, this could be a parody of Trollope, who also, in his autobiography (Volume 5, § 85.2), showed he intended inspiration as conscientious methodical deskwork, and believed that it was measurable and procurable.

and her distress is a gentle satire on timidity and hesitation that keep her from carrying out the sexual act itself. The novel's chapters seem to follow one another erratically, while in fact their order is astutely planned. For instance, one Sunday the company has been chatting idly over breakfast about the decline of religion; in the following scene in church, they hear an apocalyptic sermon on the end of time and the necessity of conversion. This sermon is transcribed in its entirety and provides a crushing proof of Sternian discontinuity; at the same time it is also a parody of Joyce's 'Grace' and of an episode in his *Portrait*.[25] The sermon is an inquiry into the paths and perspectives of the modern world, and the priest is a fanatic who rants and raves about the Second Coming like a spiritual descendant of the visionary, hallucinated, demented Ruskin in his last delirious prophecies.[26] The internal and immediate counterbalance to this apocalypticism is the vacuous and pig-headed evolutionist optimism, à la Spencer and Shaw, of the writer Barbecue-Smith. This inquiry connects the characters of a plot that is otherwise irremediably frayed. The first person Denis meets while wandering through the deserted abode is the chatelaine herself, a horoscope enthusiast; and it is no coincidence that at the fair which is granted to the local working plebeians by the feudal owner of the estate, Mr Scogan should appear disguised as a seer.[27] The divination of the future on the basis of the past is the distinctive mark of *Crome Yellow*. The estate itself is declared a Pompeii that future excavators will have to unearth, thereby triggering the implicit threat of an imminent destruction pro- voked by a volcanic eruption, and the extinction of the self-styled landed gentry. The proprietor, Wimbush, a co-protagonist, is not terrorized by the nightmare of history, but his consciousness is all the same constantly busy on testing its continuity. In Wimbush, a historian by profession, the awareness of origins and the proof of his own genealogy is a comforting mental support, or even an exorcism of time itself, galloping through the past as if swallowing it. When there is a reading of a substantial chapter of the genealogical history of the founders and builders of the estate, starting

25   See Volume 7, §§ 134.4 and 137.3.
26   This preacher is in fact described as seated 'under the Ruskinian window'.
27   A seer who, to confirm Eliot's suggestion, is called *Sesostris*.

from the progenitor, we have a second proof of Huxley's Sternian unpredictability; however, it is also very hard to resist the temptation to consider this novel the spark for Woolf's *Orlando*, since from that story emanates the same curiosity for the habits and customs of past epochs and for the eccentricities of ancient residences. A second story reveals other aspects of an eccentricity that is more grotesque than just comical. This concerns the three sisters, including the grandmother of the chatelain, who gorged themselves in secret to maintain intact their fame as spiritual women. If we exclude the priest and the sermon mentioned above, the perception *en abyme* of a world on the brink of the abyss, and of a cosmic earthquake is mainly amused or even sardonic. The guru, Scogan, predicts a future world in which sex and procreation are dissociated, the latter having become an 'impersonal generation'; this is said in the context of a Swiftian visit to the pigsties, where a sow has just given birth to a litter of piglets. Every now and then this rather caustic character, Scogan, is the voice of truth: in the future it will be necessary to 'canalize' the madness of the world's maniacs 'into proper channels', and bring the rational state into play. In this future state, society will be divided into three classes.[28]

4. *Antic Hay*[29] (1923) is also a novel on the condition of the aestheticizing youth, lucidly aware of having no hopes and addicted to a *carpe diem* that seeks to be joyful and satiating and is instead merely and pitifully melancholy. As a consequence, it unfolds and proceeds in the tones of an absurd and estranged burlesque, whose nature can be exemplified by the main character's extravagant expedient: to make a fortune inventing and patenting 'trousers with pneumatic seats' for everyone who has to sit on hard surfaces for hours on end.[30] Huxley, in other words, veers towards the tangent of the improbable plot, full of surreal and freaky exploits that

---

28　Possibly a satirical echo of Wells's prophecies.

29　A title echoing a line in Marlowe's *Edward II*.

30　The publicity on the new discovery intends to focus on the necessity to protect the 'lumbar ganglion', a veiled thrust at Lawrence's sexual theories (Volume 7, § 122.2). Also targeted against Lawrence may be the fact that the beard is a sign of virility by which women are unfailingly attracted. However, the beard was a distinguishing mark that was equally typical of a Lytton Strachey.

only Meredith, who is here the main inspirer, was capable of: towards a narration, that is, of a kaleidoscopic, rhapsodic, chaotic type, deliberately lacking in backstories, which are alluded to, more than presented for the sake of clarity. The other characters are eccentrics that do not interact with the plot, remain peripheral to it and form a gallery of humours:[31] they are the protagonist's father, a utopian architect; an envious and frustrated painter offended by an offer to produce advertising posters; a Bolshevik and Leninist tailor; the Jewish financier of the padded trousers project. The youth was that of survivors from the Great War, which had left behind a 'waste land' in the form of a collapse of values and an acute sense of the historical watershed. No one knows what tomorrow will bring, and meanwhile life is aimless wandering, enlivened only by sex practised as a game and a distraction. Adventure provides a narcosis in the face of the tragic absence of prospects, making it possible to avoid having to think 'of the past and never for one moment consider the future'. The incidence of the dramatic post-war destitution is limited in the novel: in an effective scene, however, the affected dialogues of the *bon viveurs* are stridently juxtaposed to, and alternate with, those of a couple of poor souls who tell of their hardships. The intertextuality and the erudite allusion being enhanced, the collage structure is even more perceptible. The narrator, in an indistinguishable mimesis with the characters, lets himself go with constant citations, while the characters themselves are a kind of repository of fanciful remembrances, witticisms, and sophisticated mannerisms. All are marionettes, precisely because Huxley has opted for a form of summary psychologism lacking any real depth and breadth, and deliberately refrains from tidily revealing everyone's backstory. The title is a declared quotation from that slightly minor Elizabethan repertoire on which T. S. Eliot – the supreme epigraphic and epigraphist poet – also drew.

5. What emerges and materializes therefore in *Antic Hay* is the erudite association of a bizarre dance, grotesque and not too lucid, in fact almost drunken. The protagonist Theodore Gumbril is a secondary schoolteacher of history who resigns because of a crisis of credibility in his work; hence the

---

31   CRHE, 353.

indelicate idea of making money by launching that new garment onto the market. This idea is hinted at, perhaps even forgotten, in order to follow the inconclusive, often squalid and unpleasant sexual adventures and misadventures of a sample group of young degenerates and wishful thinkers – cultured graduates, scientists, humanists and even artists – whose salient psychic datum is the immature dissociation between the intellect and the senses. This clique of transgressors is the protagonist of a series of Boccaccio-like bawdy erotic adventures that are, however, insipid evolutions also recalling those of Gissing's 'unclassed'.[32] The members of this quintet are all cosmopolitan and super-informed about the latest cultural issues; they have all travelled everywhere in Europe, they have all enjoyed diverse experiences, they are all artistically talented; they go to the theatre, to exhibitions and shows; they are multifaceted geniuses, scientist-humanists. They are above all belated aesthetes, isolated and deaf to the world, and somewhat doubles of Huysmans's Des Esseintes. They are acquaintances, not friends. They are cemented by a fascinating eccentric model called Myra – a mirage in other words, that of the femme fatale, who, being a type, or an archetype, cannot have a story, and 'supposes' she is twenty-five; coveted by all, she refuses everyone; the eternal female, she is called *Mrs* Viveash,[33] and no one knows how or why. Lypiatt is the multiform Wagnerian painter, an erstwhile poet and musician, magniloquent and megalomaniac, rhetorical but mediocre, and imploded. After him come a journalist of the precise word and rather clichéd aloofness; a physiologist who lives distractedly without realizing that his wife is betraying him under his nose; and a sardonic and blasphemous Latinist. It is an odd quintet of people who are fond of hearing themselves talk, rant, rave and weave impertinences and insipid jokes, witticisms and wisecracks, and engaging digressions, almost in a preview of the dialogue of the theatre of the absurd. In the casual conquest made by Gumbril, who dupes the dim-witted young wife of a

---

32   Volume 6, § 123.1.

33   Her incapacity to love, and her self-condemnation to frustration through flirting, is due, however, to the unhappy love for a war victim, mentioned in passing. This fact may suggest that she might be modelled on the extremely 'fatale' Nancy Cunard, for whom Huxley felt a short-lived but intense passion.

friend, a rather distracted scientist[34] (she is seduced by his virile but phoney beard), Huxley stages a recognizable, coarser parody of Eliot's 'typist's scene' in *The Waste Land*. Specifically, he sets out to represent mechanical love emptied of spiritual *agape*.[35] Gumbril might redeem himself, but has little wish to do so, and he lets slip the chance for pure disinterested love and himself sullies this prospect, because at the crossroads he opts for the fascination of the promiscuous, non-spiritual Eros instead of the monogamous *agape* offered to him by the delicate Emily, and feels himself surrounded by 'aridity' and a 'parched desert'.[36] However, the erratic progress of scene after scene is, once again, less erratic than it might appear at first sight, and the novel converges in reality, in concentric circles, on the theme of the future course of the world and the necessity to find prompt solutions, often even imaginative ones, to its crisis. The planner of new urban spaces, proud of his small models of Wren's city – the true utopia – heralds a typical Carlylean 'sartor', a tailor who, while letting Gumbril try the padded trousers, prophesizes the cure-all of the Bolshevik revolution in a tomorrow without social classes. The opening chapters present the inquiry into the sense of history in the form of a teacher, Gumbril himself, who has to correct homework on the Italian Risorgimento, which might arguably be 'the most important event in modern European history', that is, an implicit idea of history as positive evolution, and teleology if not theology – and the reader guesses that Stephen Dedalus at Deasy's school in *Ulysses* is behind him. And through the quintet's flippantly woolly dialogues gleams the nineteenth-century dilemma of a cosmos guided by the

34   Shearwater, the first of Huxley's distracted scientists with their heads in the clouds.
35   Not coincidentally Gumbril, just before the seduction, recalls and associatively mentions Tiresias. The unrealistic, bizarre goings-on increase and really flare up when Rosie, Gumbril's dim-witted lover, is sent by him to another of the *bon viveurs*, and from him to still another, committing an identical adultery with both. The young men pass her around without her husband realizing.
36   On the train journey that takes him, too late, to the meeting with Emily, Gumbril talks with another passenger, and the subject is, once again, the prospect of an overpopulated world, and a Britain that gives refuge to too many Jews. Orwell had this novel in mind, even if he pretended to have forgotten its title, when he accused Huxley of an anti-Semitic vein.

God in whom certain 'deluded' people still believe, or else of a sceptical, amused, sardonic, even blasphemous mechanism. The physiologist and the painter are believers, the other three disbelievers.

6. One feels a certain disappointment in gradually realizing that *Those Barren Leaves*[37] (1925) is an almost exact repetition, in its constructive and demonstrative cornerstones, of *Crome Yellow*. The human types are re-presented, lightly disguised, as are the topics of discussion, with the sole variant of a change of venue: the estate that welcomed the speakers in the English countryside is now an ancient villa of Italian princes and nobles among the hills of the Versilian hinterland.[38] The host in *Crome Yellow* had been a man; now the owner is a Mrs Aldwinkle, an eccentric Englishwoman no longer in her prime, of the typical Forsterian 'Italianate' variety, who dreams of recreating in her villa the atmosphere of Baldassarre Castiglione, and surrounds herself with 'a company of poets, philosophers and artists'. There is the addition of local colour; we hear jokes in Tuscan dialect; a few caricatures appear collected from life and hence are not without some scenic relief; ultimately, however, Huxley is interested in a further gathering of chosen delegates of British society, who can take stock of the state of the nation, with all the nuances demanded by their various ages, and at a time that seems – but in fact is not – far from the disaster of the war. And there is no longer that brio, freshness, or even – everything is relative – the sobriety of the preceding novel; just as the narrator has made himself more irritatingly and strangely erudite, both on his own and when the author is disguised in his *alter egos*. The four parts, each with a title of its own, may suggest a more rigorous structuring, but this is glaringly not so, since this

37 Again a quotation, from Wordsworth. One of the few straightforwardly and happily evocative fictional moments of the poet Chelifer's autobiography is the recollection of his taciturn, introverted father who once suddenly started spouting Wordsworth's poems on the peak of Mount Snowdon. Equally felicitous is the witty bathos that follows, since, on descending to a tavern, the air is filled with the smell of fried onions, and because the adult who is remembering in the present recognizes that those high-sounding, moving lines turned out to be 'useless'. The ineffectiveness of the restorative cult of Wordsworth's nature, applied to the tropical landscape, forms the subject of one of Huxley's most celebrated essays, 'Wordsworth in the Tropics'.

38 Vezza, where the action of the novel takes place, is now called Seravezza.

is Huxley's most casual and least constructed novel – improvised, untidy and fragmentary. In this confused muddle, Huxley's object is the strange representation of a female Donjuanism that the males shun. Some at least of the females, including above all Mrs Aldwinkle, are man-eaters who fail to catch their male prey, representing a cold masculinity whose senses are spent. In one of the four subplots an improbable marriage, sought only for convenience, is foiled by a calamity; and a certain purity, though playful, unreal, ingenuous and totally infantile, smiles only on a down-at-heel lord and on Mrs Aldwinkle's very young niece. Because it is too sudden and unmotivated, the end sourly outlines a negative reaction to the flame of love and the liberation of the soul from the subjugation to the material. There is no character who really stands out in a story that is stereophonic, choral, with several voices alternating in the limelight. The initial phases are mostly narrated from the point of view of the novelist Mary Thriplow, a guest at the villa; this part tackles with economy the reader's need for information on the guests. They arrive at the villa and enter on the scene one by one, their psychologies summarily described, and they are warmed up, so to speak, before being launched into the dialectic arena. Clumsily hiding an emotional fragility due to a burnt-out juvenile passion,[39] the novelist Thriplow strips herself of hypocrisies and social masks; in a still warm September, she welcomes in the owner's stead a gentleman guest arriving at the villa after much journeying, himself with a troubled sentimental story behind him. He is slightly wizened, though of good appearance and manners. Among the guests there is also a timid young slave of her possessive aunt, and an awkward lord of progressive and radical ideas, who surreptitiously courts her. However, it is during dinner that the inevitable *maître à penser* emerges to hold court. He is a Mr Cardan; silencing all the dinner guests, he tosses into the ring the eternal question of the value of the past with respect to the present, and, *ipso facto*, of the continuity or discontinuity of history.

39   The recovery of this backstory seems artificial and forced, even though or perhaps because it is attributed to a psychic associationism borrowed from Proust: the smelling of a bay leaf whose scent triggers the recollection. According to Bowering 1968, 63–4, who also focuses on other relevant details, at the time Huxley had 'absorbed Proust'.

It is of course Huxley who is feeding him ideas, questions and dilemmas, above all the inebriating shortlist of citations and erudite references. As in *Crome Yellow*, eventually all the characters variously contribute to the basic subject: Mrs Aldwinkle romantically keeps alive a superseded ceremonial, Cardan lucidly reflects on where the world is going, the lord is a socialist who believes in the thaumaturgic power of a revolution.

7. The novel's sudden and visible turning point occurs with a second part characterized by a change in register and voice, and therefore also of scenario and time: such is an extract from the written autobiography of Chelifer, one of Mrs Aldwinkle's lovers.[40] The novelty is undeniable but ultimately mystifying: Chelifer's backstory is not communicated to the readers and to the internal characters in the form of lectures during convivial occasions, but Huxley equally provides him with a podium from which to speak freely, without an interlocutor. Which is why this rather pioneering extract is far from enchanting. It is not exactly an interior monologue, although it is 'dramatic' and in prose; it is more of a diary-style memoir that mimetically, and therefore disjointedly, blends evocations, anecdotes and disparate and common opinions. The disconcerting fact is that it revolves around the same ideological fulcrum as that of Mr Cardan – whether human evolution towards a 'brave new world' consisting only of joy and happiness is really feasible, and whether, when it has been realized, it is then 'repellent to humanity'. The anecdotes internal to this autobiography provoke tedium, as they refer to encounters in which the passing of time, and the differences between past and present, are invariably the topic. However, in the most acceptable, more flowing and factual phase of this part, a description of a new erotic initiation of the hero is described; it is recollected as a moment in which he managed to isolate himself from the world and live 'here and now', without thinking of the future. Following a marked confusion of narrative times, the Shelleyan

---

40   Chelifer, who directs the *Rabbit Fanciers' Gazette*, represents, with all the relevant anecdotes, one of those absurd and surreal flashes of inspiration of which Huxley was always capable.

poet Chelifer[41] is about drown in the Tyrrhenian sea near Viareggio; as he says excitedly in his narrative, on being saved he sees in front of him conventional and stereotyped Italian figures, before a whim of providence sucks him back within the radius of the English *grande dame* Mrs Aldwinkle. The reader regrets that this episode comes to a close, since it is more successful than the third-person story that was left temporarily in suspension. The third part follows the sudden birth in Mrs Aldwinkle of a possessive passion for Chelifer – as if he were a Galsworthian *objet d'art*, or more exactly a femme fatale's uncontrolled and instinctive infatuation. Huxley becomes even more imitative and parodic when he stages a minuet in three movements in which the three couples of lovers-to-be exchange vapid simperings in the garden in front of the villa. Owing to their reluctance and lack of conviction, notably all on the part of the males, these loves do not progress, and the story starts to limp and is plumped out by gratuitous and unlikely collateral episodes, to be saved only by the return of the essayistic vein, with Mr Cardan taking again the stage. Later, however, Cardan gets lost in the surroundings during the night, and we follow him in his nocturnal wanderings until two mysterious British tourists, who live locally, run into him. Cardan's loves form a further internal episode modelled on the pattern of the surrealism and weirdness of the erotic vicissitudes in *Antic Hay*. We are informed in a separate flashback that he once robbed his troubled and ruined English brother of a young *naïve* – and mentally retarded – girl, Grace, whom he wanted to kill, as she was the sole heir to a large fortune, though Cardan had promised to marry her for the personal profit of the interest on that fortune.[42] In the fourth and last part, Huxley can do no better than to adapt a travel diary, and to follow the slow advancement of the four plots within the framework of a car journey of the whole company to Rome. This is the cue for interminable, strange and frequently irrelevant digressions on the landscape and on ancient Italian history, offered without any principle of

41   An overused comparison is in fact that between the drowned Shelley, near the bay at Lerici, and the almost drowned Chelifer.

42   With a distant echo of the trick with which Tito persuades Tessa in George Eliot's *Romola*.

selection. The only authentic jolt in the narrative is the death by intoxication, during the journey, of the heiress.[43] The couple formed by Calamy and Mary Thriplow finally proposes the mystical path of cultivation of the soul and detachment from the material to achieve salvation in this life. This does not appear to be a genuine existential choice seriously suggested by Huxley,[44] merely the last of the practically infinite issues of the ongoing debate, almost preparing the ground for Huxley's dystopian novel and extending to the standardization of society, which presages far from positive goals for the mankind of tomorrow.

8. *Point Counter Point*[45] (1928) is Huxley's most ambitious, imposing and structured novel, and his masterpiece. It deserves this primacy because its governing idea fuses with the plot much more naturally; because the characters and their stories incarnate the horns of its basic dilemma, and no longer or not only are they presented in the form of muddled or academic orations; and because it follows the actions of a credible community of contemporary members of the British intelligentsia and aristocracy of the 1920s. This helps to bring Huxley's fiction, always bordering on the unlikely, within the confines of an authentic or a more authentic realism. In fact, the social, political and ideological context makes it a confrontation of current ideas and proposals, typically designed, as is usual in Huxley, to ponder and foresee the immediate future of humanity and of the specifically British societal model. Between fascism and communism, opposing extremisms, Huxley points the needle of the scales towards authentic humanism – even if its nature

43   The funeral ceremony in the Roman church is a remarkable impressionistic flash that is rather unusual for Huxley, and full of bitter, satirical anti-Catholic jibes directed at the priest celebrating the service. Cardan dies by the sword, and having wanted to marry Grace for profit, must pay the funeral bill.

44   Calamy, in the novel's last improbable expedient, has gone into retreat on the mountain like an anchorite, a Buddhist monk, or a follower of Tolstoy, and he explains to the sceptical Cardan and Chelifer the mystical gospel by which he was struck. It is a somewhat abrupt solution, but in hindsight it indicates Huxley's path.

45   This is an enigmatic, whimsical, non-grammatical title, since 'point' is not a musical term, and in English the word is 'counterpoint', without a separation of the two words. Even Praz, who rarely errs, translates it as *Punto contrappunto*, which does not make much sense in Italian and does not correspond to the original title.

remains undecided, and he is uncertain whether a suppression or a liberation of erotic impulses should prevail, and to what extent these should be liberated. Critics have correctly identified a temporary reversal in Huxley's oeuvre. He no longer points to mysticism and the renunciation of the flesh and sex, as suggested by the epilogue to *Those Barren Leaves*; but, echoing Lawrence, he calls for human wholeness and the harmony between body and spirit. The beginning and end of the novel are particularly intriguing for their powerful contrast. The opening plays on the shades of a light, unforced satirical comedy describing the aristocratic ritual of a party, from which the main and subsidiary characters impressionistically emerge. The end is progressively tragic, as it stages another ritual, punitive rather than self-celebratory, involving a scapegoat; here certain premonitions previously left suspended tap into a sudden potency, uncommon in Huxley. In the middle, however, the novel falls back into some of Huxley's narrative defects, such as prolixity and purely adjunctive, inert and pleonastic scenes. One can only agree with the first historical readers, who found that the contrasts between the characters are not fully developed, and that, as a result, the novel is often static.

9. *Point Counter Point* features a totally closed space, London, after *Those Barren Leaves*, an 'open' novel, nine-tenths of which had taken place in Italy. This unity of place is matched by an equally clean division into two narrative moments. The exact internal tempos are concealed, but the plot is divided into a first part occurring entirely on one evening in the first months of a certain year and a second happening in summer but in a multitude of places. Organizing and balancing the novel as the interwoven and overlapping stories and erotic vicissitudes of a sextet of contemporary young intellectuals, Huxley takes two steps back and, with a different degree of maturity, picks up the plot of *Antic Hay*. More sophisticatedly, he also reworks Gissing's *New Grub Street* fifty years on. Four of the main sextet of young men move in the world of magazines and in that of literary and visual art: a journalist, a reviewer, a novelist and a painter, studied as they fluctuate between public and sentimental life.[46] From the very beginning Huxley

---

46   At a certain moment two women poets present themselves to Burlap, an editor. They are the authors of horrific, cheesy poems under a pseudonym, and it is hard not to think of a satire or parody of Michael Field (Volume 6, § 248.3).

manages to find what for him is a miraculous balance between the essayistic urge, kept on a leash, and sheer narrative; the result is a text lightened of ballast, intelligible, even enjoyable. As I mentioned, however, this long novel does not maintain the tension of the first third throughout. It breaks up and crumbles into numbered chapters, in turn subdivided into self-enclosed sub-units separated by asterisks. Various of these splinters, taken out of the continuum, have nothing to do with the basic plot, and seem to be added to obey the length Huxley imposed on himself. Because of this, the male sextet is well delineated, but the figures of other subsidiary characters are overly sketchy and schematic. The patches of dialogue are shorter and no longer erupt into odd and irrelevant quotations in every language. There are many aristocrats on the scene who engage in conversations on various subjects. These factors make this Huxley a kind of more refined Galsworthy.[47] The internal time and the general atmosphere are those of the second Forsyte trilogy. Galsworthy-inspired is the swathe of intellectuals, painters, novelists, journalists, politicians, and officers; as is the range of subjects and predilections, from painting to music. Clearly, this is not a compliment or a total compliment, because it means that *Point Counter Point* is no doubt more likeable, easier to follow, and more natural than the previous works, but also slightly duller. Some early reviewers rightly accused it of being a de luxe *feuilleton*.[48] A melodramatic relationship is that between Walter Bidlake and his lover Marjory, the latter always caught sighing and weeping and in the hysterics of a betrayed woman, the former in his anguished promises of faithfulness and self-emendation while he is enchanted and driven mad by Lucy Tantamount's seductions. The scenes between Walter and Marjorie are as mushy and sentimental as those between Walter and Lucy are disastrous and clumsy. As I mentioned, the novel's central clash is now that, Pauline and also Hardyan, between the flesh and the spirit, Eros and abstinence, body and soul – Baudelaire's agon, too, the agon of whoever knows that 'the flesh is sad' and he/she has sinned all possible sins. The novel's characters are therefore more or less divided between sensualists and spiritualists. The former are all old impenitent immoralists; the young

47   As noticed by one reviewer (CRHE, 154).
48   CRHE, 99.

are more ascetic, but in words and not in deeds, given that the flesh is weak, as well as sad. Senile sensuality, vain, overflowing, and impenitent, is treated with a Balzac-style farce reminiscent of *La Cousine Bette*. John Bidlake, Walter's father, is an old satyr of a painter who sees, paints and appreciates only the female body; the inconclusive Quarles senior has an affair with a typist (again this Eliotian echo) and leaves her pregnant. The arm wrestling is even crueller for the young men. Two of the six main characters are married, and four are single. In all of them the affective bond is ephemeral and tormented. The Quarles couple is veiledly unhappy, disunited, in an open breakdown or on the way there, and the two spouses insensibly gravitate towards unfaithfulness. No conjugal morality code is active, and promiscuity is rising. The essential thing is that Huxley does not take sides. He has his characters' ideal positions fight in turn, without putting his oar in. The polar opposites are libertine polygamous promiscuity and ascetic abstinence. Promiscuity is embodied in old Bidlake and Quarles, in their lovers, and in Lucy Tantamount. Abstinence unfolds in a range of degrees. Among the elderly characters Philip Quarles' mother is a woman of ancient codes, and an inflexible believer in religious marriage. Reviewer Walter Bidlake's lover, Marjorie, belongs to Victorian melodrama with her icon of a 'fallen' girl mother who repents and is converted, begins to pray, acts as a pious woman, and forms an ideal pair with the other authentically religious mother, Mrs Quarles. Spiritual Marjorie represents a sincerely profound vector in Walter, who is overwhelmed by the carnal impulse, a polarity that has come down to him from his sensual father and from his spiritual mother. Eros is suffocated in Spandrell, the Dostoevskyan debauchee, a kind of fanatical, crazed Raskolnikov[49] who is fact a murderer, but through a vortex of delirium and obsessions, including the one of *not* having fallen in war, where his degenerate life might have acquired some sense. The greasy Burlap, the Jesuitical and therefore ambiguous magazine editor, in his hypocrisy supports spiritualism but allows himself 'distractions', and has a 'platonic way of going to bed with women'. In the couple

---

49 J. W. Beach, *The Twentieth Century Novel: Studies in Technique*, New York 1932, 459, has him derived from Gide's Lafcadio; Brooke 1972, 17–18, highlights the biographic trail of Baudelaire.

formed by Walter Bidlake's sister Elinor and the novelist Philip Quarles, Elinor is idealistic and romantic, while Philip has dried up sensuality and lives or would like to live in the monadic dimension, aspiring to exile and peace. Eros is deflected and sublimated in the hubris of Webley, the political demagogue.[50] The conflict is made far more dialectical, however, in the figures of Burlap and Rampion. The former claims to deny Eros in abstinence but ends up falling for it, albeit in an oxymoronic conjunction of the bodies, spiritual and mystical. With Rampion he forms a *coincidentia oppositorum* testified in the novel by their strange mutual empathy and attraction, despite detesting one another. Every time Rampion enters the scene the novel comes back to life, perhaps because his model was closer and more obvious (it was D. H. Lawrence, in fact).[51]

10. The reconstruction of the childhood, adolescence and first steps of the career of Rampion forms a lucid introduction to Lawrence and demonstrates the fascination he exercised over Huxley. Through Rampion, Huxley underlines the education Lawrence had received from his mother, the ineradicable Puritan background that continually rose anew against later ideas, and the open dilemmas of his world-view.[52] The historical, epistemological and cultural targets of this double of Lawrence are asceticism and promiscuity. Burlap is writing a biography of St Francis, whose life he

50   Fond to present himself at public gatherings of his 'Free British' astride a white charger with heraldic trappings, and sympathizing with the colour green, Webley, a double of the historical Oswald Mosley, evokes the later liturgies of Italy's political party 'Lega Nord'. However, Guardamagna 1989, 47 n. 5, points out Huxley's 'clairvoyance', since in 1928 Mosley was still a member of the Labour Party.

51   According to Meckier 1971, who dedicates an entire chapter of his book (78–123) to the controversies and changeable personal and ideological relationships between Huxley and Lawrence, at least four characters are modelled on Lawrence in Huxley's fiction.

52   The quip, attributed to Rampion, that the man of Barrie the playwright seems as if he had pneumatic cushions available, throws light on the image of the pneumatic trousers in *Antic Hay*. However, the adjective 'pneumatic' is often used by Huxley to designate the buxom female form. Once again, this is a connotation he derived from T. S. Eliot (see 'promise of pneumatic bliss', l. 20 of 'Whispers of Immortality'). The expression 'pneumatic bliss' was by then proverbial, and is also cited in chapter I of *A Man Could Stand Up* by Ford Madox Ford.

idolizes. In one scene he buys a few of Rampion's canvases (the Lawrence of this novel is above all the author of the censored paintings); in turn Rampion harshly derides him and attacks his false, hypocritical Christian-Catholic spiritualism. The parallel stories of the various characters close towards the end, some in a gradual fade-out (those of Walter, Marjorie and Lucy), others in clamorous tragedy, others in farce, like Burlap's ever equivocal, spiritual-carnal Franciscan love, in which the lubricious massage gives way to a celestial and ascetic corporeal conjunction. The cruel struggle requires a human sacrifice: the death of a young son and of the two old satyrs. Spandrell, too, commits a murder, though discovering immediately after – crime and punishment – that God exists while listening to Beethoven's Opus 132 quartet movement in the Lydian mode. Music and musical pieces are often referred to in *Point Counter Point* as in every other novel by Huxley. Musical metaphors – more: musical analogies – mark and identify this novel as an image both of its formal construction and of the dialectics of its meanings; they penetrate its most intimate pores as in the novels of Thomas Mann.[53] *Point Counter Point* opens with the musical performance of one of Bach's orchestral suites during an aristocratic party, and closes on the notes of Beethoven's quartet Opus 132, two works that are intimately linked to the internal dialectics of ideas. The Bach suite is a counterpoint of movements, and, as Huxley explains in a, let us say, musical ekphrasis, a reflection and at the same time a sublimation of life; it evokes the sensation of clouds disappearing from the sky in the form of an exceptional rarefaction. However, life is noble but also variegated, as the movements of the suite subjoin, denying one another; and Bach's dialectic musical pattern is of parts that agree and clash, in harmony and discord, though ending up harmoniously. After a superhuman effort of self-repression, a similar symbolic path is discovered by Spandrell, the murderer,[54] in Beethoven's quartet,

---

53   1924 is of course the date of publication of Mann's *The Magic Mountain*.

54   He beat with a club in an ambush the fascist agitator Webley, who had arrived at Elinor Quarles's house to persuade her to betray her husband. This is an obscure, vindictive and jealous action against a woman to whom he has never openly declared his love. Elinor is partially rehabilitated, because she leaves home, before the erotic meeting, to join her young moribund son.

and as such expounded to Rampion, who cannot but coldly reconfirm Beethoven's anti-humanism, and the 'art of a man who has lost his body'. The metaphor of the counterpoint asserts itself as an isotopy acting on various levels. In his science laboratory, Lord Tantamount – the fossil of an immature baby, but with an ultra-developed intelligence[55] – is working on his experiments during the Bach performance; his principle is that 'the life of an animal is a fragment of the global life of the universe'. In practice, he operates on Lavoisier's axiom that everything is transformed and nothing is destroyed. The third meaning or the third implication of the title is that, for the British fascists, the State must also be a musical harmony as the result of a never-quenched tension between the three classes. They fuse in their diversity: a concerto, more precisely, or a Vivaldian 'cimento dell'armonia'. The fourth meaning is precisely the one passionately supported by Rampion-Lawrence: the harmonic, complete man, in whom body and spirit have sought and found the right synchrony, with no prevalence of the one or the other. The novel's historical background is a British political scene in which the polar opposites of fascism and communism are contrasted; but beside these two revolutions a more metaphysical and palingenetic one is sighted, that of Rampion-Lawrence. The musical metaphor in fact needs to be extended, and the narrator is the conductor of an orchestra tackling a score in which leitmotifs and other secondary ones alternate; or, without being a catachresis, this is a choral-symphonic score consisting of various instrumental and vocal sections. Technically, the first half of the novel constitutes a *tour de force* almost without precedent: with only two external flashes, it is a kind of sequence shot narrating in a single and highly concentrated temporal unit (where the writing is almost slower than the action recounted) a series of events taking place from early evening until darkest night. The fictional camera moves among selected groups of diners while the sound registers a subtle bouncing back and forth of topical and absolute issues; the party becomes a *mise en abyme* of the British aristocracy. Well into the book, the musical analogy is that of chapters which alternate as symphonic themes in the various subplots; but within

55   Resembling Gide's 'experimental biologists' for J. W. Beach, *The Twentieth Century Novel, op. cit.*, 458.

the actual chapters small and at times infinitesimal separate cells exist, just as musical reminders or *daccapo* are given in the form of flashes which may become flashbacks. The stereophonic narration shifts imperceptibly back and forth, backtracking from one character's late afternoon to another's early afternoon. Naturally, the counterpoint technique, not new, although never so blatantly declared, is an asymptote, and in the long term the novel is a sequence of fragments, a musical fragmentation that is more Viennese, like that of Webern and Berg, rather than classical-romantic.[56]

§ 34. *Huxley III: 'Brave New World'. God ousted by Ford*
Brave New World (1932), which imagines the state of the world in 2540, is a *saltus* in terms of genre, and precisely a *saltus* into Wells's science fiction.[57] This particular *saltus* is, however, as I mentioned, not so long and blatant if we consider the general or secondary theme of the four previous novels, which come into collision with the unknowns of history and the trend of the world, both concerning morals and the overwhelming rhythm of scientific research, including forecasts of genetic engineering, alarming even then. In addition to the leap into the future, and to the motif of time travel, Huxley took into account the suggestion of *The Island of Doctor Moreau*. The construction of the future model of the world is exorcistic, aimed in other words at persuading readers of the goodness of the old human and humanistic model, anthropocentric and ultimately Illuminist as well as Christian. *Brave New World* is a counter-manifesto targeting certain modern tendencies, therefore also sceptical and ultraconservative. At the same time, it creates a *trait d'union* with Orwell's two utopias, forming with them a classic triptych, even if it tends towards the moral repercussions

---

56   Some musical reviews written by Huxley for the *Weekly Westminster Gazette* were
      dedicated to the musicians of the Vienna Circle, as well as to Schönberg and Stravinsky,
      and can now be read in the edition of Huxley's collected essays (cf. *TLS*, 9 March 2001,
      4–5). There has been a heated critical debate on the precision, or rather the vagueness
      if not the amateurishness and therefore the ultimate effect, of the musical metaphor:
      a short summary of the positions can be found in Manferlotti 1987, 60–1 and n. 29.
57   Huxley undertook it as such, with parodic aims (Atkins 1967, xiii, and Bowering
      1968, 15).

and implications of the new order – and those related to civilization *tout court* – and it is by no means a political nightmare of intolerance and of a police regime.[58] Orwell accused Huxley of having plagiarized Zamyatin;[59] but he himself was to derive several suggestions from this book, even if the student was unquestionably to surpass the master.[60] The fame and fortune of *Brave New World* has been huge since its appearance, mainly in virtue of the abstract and essayistic diatribes that it raised. The novel is in itself modest in terms of pure invention or the development of ideas into plot, once again revealing Huxley's insuperable shortcomings as narrator. The canon of science fiction attracts readers by its variety and the imaginative range with which the utopians and dystopians have divined the future by 'reconstructing it' from the present according to trends which are identified

58 Orwell deemed it 'a good caricature of the hedonistic Utopia, the kind of thing that seemed possible and even imminent before Hitler' (OCE, vol. II, 32–3, and, for a similar, colourful and limiting judgement, 46 and 172).

59 OCE, vol. IV, 96–7, where Orwell notes the weakness of the political, psychological and economic motivations of the class in power.

60 However, in the dazzling 'revisitation' of the novel, *Brave New World Revisited* (1958), Huxley deemed his dystopia more prophetic than Orwell's. This codicil to *Brave New World*, full of statistics and projections which are even exact by default, and up-to-date sociological observations on the propaganda strategies, defends the paradoxical thesis that it is a more prudent policy not to develop scientific research against fatal diseases, since this would lead to death by starvation and also to dictatorial regimes, above all communist ones. Another paradoxical thesis is the denial of the socializing impulse in man, and the disapproval of every super-organization. These positions are of a nineteenth-century, Mill-style humanist liberalism, applied to the scientific techniques of dictatorships used to manipulate the masses and coerce the intellectual independence of individuals. Accordingly, the heart of the pamphlet is a paraphrase of Orwell's torture of Winston Smith. The exhaustive dissertation on drugs and their moderate approval – since 'on some occasions [one] must be directed', and in others 'an excess of tranquillity is completely out of place' – were felt at the time to be a natural viaticum for the 'flower children' and the beat culture. Huxley was among the first writers to confess to drug use, and his experiments with mescaline, similar to LSD, with which he obtained the 'transfiguration of things', are described at length in his book *The Doors of Perception* (1954). Huxley would go on to take drugs 'about ten times all told' (cf. Manferlotti 1987, 37, who denies that Huxley is one of the putative fathers of drug addiction).

in a sort of induction. For Huxley, who was not much politicized,[61] the world was going to become a mono-state whose motto, or ternary commandment, would be 'community, identity, stability'; in practice, the regulating fetish is the last of the three terms. From the first paragraph of the novel it is clear that, as Orwell would be quick to learn, totalitarian regimes, as was shown by the techniques of persuasion that had been launched by the dictatorships already established in Europe, rely, though not solely, on the manipulation and the synthetic resources of language. The dictatorships already established in Europe showed that the techniques of persuasion used by totalitarian regimes exploit the manipulation and synthetic resources of language, among other things. This was something Orwell would quickly learn, and what is made clear in the first paragraph of *Brave New World*. Huxley is equidistant from all types of fascisms and communisms, above all because his new world regiments its subjects with slogans, better still if rhyming. In other words, he demonstrates the ancient, shamanic power of the word and of the magic formula. To judge from the first scene and from the development of *Brave New World* until almost midway through, its first target is not the coercion and trampling of the individual, but the systems of procreation and the mental conditioning of those born, designed to ensure stability and wellbeing for the regime. So this, too, is a political measure, since the great majority of those born will be so incapable of thinking that they will also be unable to react and rebel. Stability is also ensured by an exponential growth of twins from a single ovary, hence all the same and all non-thinking. Huxley's genetic planning smacks of Wells, but by 1932 Wells had become proactive and utopian. Huxley foreshadows Orwell to a greater extent, even if the social classes of

61   *Brave New World* still has a nineteenth-century framework because it foresees an evolution of the world in a prevalently biological sense, and because it is conceived without that urgency and sense of danger and *political* catastrophe that instead make Orwell and Koestler so up to date. For Huxley, freedom counted, but a freedom that was purely biological and psychic. This too, all in all, is the position of T. Adorno, 'Aldous Huxley and Utopia', collected in English translation in *Prisms*, Cambridge, MA 1981. *Grey Eminence* (1941), Huxley's biography of Père Joseph, Richelieu's secretary, was also written to illustrate the 'pernicious [...] marriage between religion and politics' (Manferlotti 1987, 34).

the new future regime are five with subclasses, and identified by letters of the Greek alphabet, from the lowest which is only brutalized workforce, up and up to the pure intellectuals and the controllers. The system is oligarchic, like the one imagined by Orwell.

2. Huxley chooses to present the coordinates of his new world through a slightly disorienting narrative process, in that it is gradual and indirect, instead of providing a descriptive overview as an introduction. This is the illustrative, maieutic lesson that the Director of the Incubation Centre gives his students. In his relaxed confidence, the Director presents a summary of the many foolish scientific revolutions of history, thought of or actually put into practice, with words that seem to echo those of the English factual scientist by definition in English letters, Dickens's Gradgrind.[62] These genetic activities, precisely because of their terrifying prophecies, hark back to the more sinister practices of Wells's Moreau. But this collective opprobrium is a state one, not a prohibited experiment on an island. The students are made fully acquainted with the rigidly planned scientific exploitation of new-borns for productivity and stability. Apart from the difficulty of following him in this initial scene, overly bristling with schematic and pseudo-scientific references, Huxley ingeniously identifies the future order as the systematic inversion and semantic overturning of the past one. The imaginary historical hypothesis is that the new era began on the death of a Ford, and that the novel's facts happen in the year 632 after the death of this founder. A technical revolution could not have its Jesus, its prophet and messiah and its sacrificial god, except in Ford, the name proverbially associated with the advent of the car. Needing to dismantle and partially remedy the 'breakdowns' of the first Creator, the directors of the new state are busy overturning the evolutionary process and evolution itself, in order to return the human workforce to the same state of 'normality' as that of dogs and cows.[63] Every regime therefore needs its own mythology – even

---

62   This comparison is not in the text, where a 'Podsnap technique' is mentioned, in order to accelerate the 'process of maturation'.

63   In practice the rub being resolved is the abbreviation of the 'useless' maturation time in which the epsilon, the last step in the scale of beings, cannot yet work, unlike animals, which can be used almost immediately.

when it is based on the elimination of all mythologies – and therefore of its own counter-religion; the 'community songs' are a ritual to substitute the Mass, similar to Orwell's 'Two Minutes Hate'. During this liturgy, the consecrated host is substituted by a tablet of a drug, *soma*, whose ingestion favours the hallucination of a miraculous epiphany of the defunct god. It is also used every time the subjects and also the directors are assailed by attacks of dissidence or dissatisfaction. 'Ford' now stands in every possible locution in place of 'God'; and the symbol of the cross has been replaced by that of a T.[64] The mental and behavioural programming of the epsilon, the lowest caste, is carefully supervised since it ensures the wellbeing and subsistence of the State. The first operation performed on them is abolition of memory. Orwell himself was to start from here in creating the 'proles'. And memory is naturally codified in and confined to books, as well as orally transmitted traditions: the epsilon must grow to hate books, and their psyche is moulded by conditioning processes of a 'neo-Pavlovian' type and through 'hypnopaedia', that is, electric shock during sleep. The alpha hypnopaedically take lessons on sex and class-consciousness, and therefore no harmony subsists between the classes, only profound, rigid barriers. Management of the sexual and procreative impulse is itself the implementation of a precise theory. Eros survives, but is regulated by contraceptives; women are denied pregnancy and maternity, and when they feel depressed they can take a 'pregnancy substitute'. Prophylactics are always on hand for women, who carry them like cartridges inserted into a type of bandoleer, while babies are taught erotic games. Males are mere fertilizers, and conception is no longer viviparous but in a test tube. On this way of managing sex depends the abolition of the family as the basic cell of human co-existence; wittily enough, the god Ford is also known as the god Freud, who was 'the first to reveal the appalling dangers of family life'. Among the things overturned is monogamy, transformed into promiscuity. The repercussions on the standard of living are the abolition of poverty as the fruit of a planned economy, which coerces choices, and the apparent generalized happiness, the aim of Bentham's old utilitarianism. With this

64   An evident allusion to the Model T, the first utilitarian vehicle. Needless to say, Ford
      Motors introduced standardized labour and the assembly line.

eugenic, aseptic model,[65] western civilization – Christian, democratic, individualist, identitarian, liberalistically competitive – has been wiped out of the picture. Why do many of the characters identified by name and surname bear those of some of the greatest figures of political history, of culture, of the social philosophy of the earlier world? Why is a nurse called Polly Trotsky, and why is an official of the regime called Benito? And why is the main character a Bernard Marx? Why is his companion on the trip to the 'savage reservation' called Lenina? Huxley pessimistically taunts twentieth-century utopias and revolutions, condemning them to inanity. It is equally true that depersonalization is symbolized precisely by the fact that 'the two thousand million inhabitants of the planet had only ten thousand names between them'.

3. The narrative really gets going when it moves down from relative anonymity to the more individual actors of a parable. In order for the story to really take off, it was necessary to switch from a general reconnaissance to a credible plot of potentially real characters. The grammatical cornerstone of science and dystopian fiction is naturally the presence, in the unifying and depersonalizing political system, of one exception: of a defector, a fly in the ointment, one or two people who can think for themselves and are potential or real subverters of the regime, and who embody the supposition, or conviction, that people lived better under the old dispensation. These two mutinous internal critics are Bernard Marx and Lenina Crowne. Bernard's alien quality is that he is an alpha, though scandalous rumours say that he is actually a gamma, and that some alcohol was mixed into the 'blood surrogate' when he was conceived.[66] Various other alphas need to drug themselves to forget, or better, not to remember,

---

65   The eulogy of dirt as authentically human is often linked to Mexico in Huxley. During their failed Mexican expedition to support an insurrection, Mark Staithes declares to the hero Anthony Beavis in the last pages of *Eyeless in Gaza*: 'The world's too damned sanitary these days'. Professor Cacciaguida in *Time Must Have a Stop* echoes him: 'dirt is the necessary condition of beauty [...] hygiene and art can never be bedfellows'.

66   See the distinctly Orwellian (§ 29.8) 'vaporization of *soma*' that Bernard undergoes when he protests against being exiled as punishment to Iceland, once his collusion with the 'savage' has been discovered.

never again desiring to be, to return to being, thinking individuals. The pair carry out the most serious transgression. The novel suddenly enters the exotic dimension of a romantic Mexican adventure, during which the two travellers encounter an obscene, filthy old woman from the new world. She had become lost in the equatorial forest decades earlier and, due to distraction when using a contraceptive, she had given birth to a son – as we will discover – by the Director who is introduced in the opening scene.[67] But, from this moment on, *Brave New World* becomes summary, hasty and clumsy, and does not improve until the end. What matters more to Huxley is to take up, and close as soon as possible, the purely abstract and historical-philosophical dispute between conservation and unlimited progress. Basically, the reason why the 'savage reservation' is maintained escapes us, though it might be that nothing is perfect even in the best of imaginable worlds.[68] But the most obvious failure is the figure of the 'savage', who usurps Bernard's role as the main character, and that of the critic – from his alleged savage state – of this alleged present civilization. As is frequently the case in science fiction, the journey is that of a latter-day Gulliver, since the two travellers cross a barrier, and presume to follow a route that goes from civilization to barbarism. The thesis is the opposite; that is, it is barbarism that unconsciously moves towards the remains of civilization. The first scene that the two travellers see is a pagan-Christian dance in a fertility rite performed by the indigenous population, which apes a similar one in Lawrence's *The Plumed Serpent* without any glint of its grandiose visionary inspiration.[69] John, the son of the last Eve, so to speak – and an Eve who, by antiphrasis, in her filthiness is called Linda – is in turn a purely mental construction. The 'uncivil' education of the *enfant sauvage*

67   Thanks to the revelation of this skeleton in the closet, the official, who is supposed to be hard-and-fast in obeying the system's laws, falls into disgrace. With this, together with the recourse to doses of *soma*, a snaking internal dissidence is pointed out; so the model is in depth anything but stable.
68   Further on, a tentative, weak explanation is aired, that the environmental conditions of New Mexico are so unproductive that the region has been left to its own devices.
69   According to Meckier 1971, 81–2, the fact that the savage cannot live when removed from his primitive milieu constitutes a denial of the governing idea of *The Plumed Serpent*.

begins by his learning the alphabet and with his first attempts at reading; later his human and humanistic education is rounded off with Shakespeare, a bible and lay epitome of western knowledge.[70] The echo of Swift is now combined with one from Shakespeare, ingenious in its implications but too fragmentary. John is in fact both a Caliban and a Hamlet and above all a male Miranda. When taken back with his mother as a scientific find to the new world, he expects to discover its true wonder, and is disappointed with it. The return journey is therefore an inversion of the symbolic trajectory of Shakespeare's *Tempest*;[71] however, the closing mark is that of Othello, and of the madness that is Shakespearian and Elizabethan sanity, in arms against promiscuity and in favour of the individual's self-determination. One day, in the name of these values, he exhorts some credulous workers. His confrontation with the Controller expands the recognition of a regime dedicated to demolishing everything that smacks of the 'old', a term including not only art and religion (a god is no longer a necessary opiate, since pain and sin have been abolished), but also science itself, all in the name of stability.[72] However, with this white-hot dialogue the most Huxleyan novel of ideas re-emerges, with foil-contests and academic-style disquisitions.

§ 35. *Huxley IV: Ataraxic detachment from the world and history*

Is there a link between *Brave New World* and *Eyeless in Gaza* (1936)?[73] Through his *alter ego* Anthony Beavis, Huxley is still obsessed with the idea of individual freedom, and meditates on Pavlov's theories of conditioning. The novel's therapeutic meaning is precisely the achievement or recovery of self-mastery by fleeing from any form of prison, a therapy that is also collective for a historical period suffering from general stupefaction.

70　A 'great theological *Summa*', this is what Shakespeare's dramas are called in one of Sebastian's aphorisms in *Time Must Have a Stop*.

71　The 'savage' draws back horrified from promiscuity and extra-marital sex, while repeatedly citing Shakespeare.

72　The Controller affirms what Huxley partially agrees with, admonishing the scientist as if with the words of Dante, 'perché non corra che virtù nol guidi' ['lest he run / Where virtue guides not'].

73　A quotation from Milton, and Samson's attribute in *Samson Agonistes*.

Affirming a principle in direct antithesis to the hypothesis of the future regime in *Brave New World*, where everyone is expressly conditioned from birth, the hero of *Eyeless in Gaza* no longer has any family ties or economic constraints. He pursues freedom, and only needs to seek a centre and a meaning in life. He finds it in an expanded consciousness through discipline, a discipline that is as much erotic as it is in a certain sense altruistic, even if freedom itself is always egotistical. Thus Beavis, abstract and solitary, is Huxley himself, just as Quarles is in *Point Counter Point*. The contemporary ideological background is that of the war action, on the eve of an involvement *en masse* of young British intellectuals in the Spanish Civil War. This is not, however, the goal of the protagonists of this novel.[74] On the contrary, from the heart of Mexico a new commandment is launched, that of inaction in the form of the hybrid gospel – Christian, Buddhist, Taoist, Hinduistic, gnostic and esoteric all at once – of a pacifist saint and ascetic who is the asymptote by which Huxley's heroes often let themselves be infected.[75] The genre of this novel is that of the hero's *éducation*, both 'sentimental' and intellectual, gathered over a period of thirty years, from 1902 until 1935–1936, but summarized in retrospect in its peaks, which roughly correspond to the childhood, adolescence, adulthood and the present time of the writing. The counterpointing of the plots is abandoned, as is the choral construction. At the same time, as in classic autobiographies, Huxley provides a biographical chapter he had always glossed over, that of the hero's childhood and adolescence, as extravagant and bawdy as in Kipling. This is, then, Huxley's first authentically lyrical novel, and one that may bring to mind Proust, and therefore also Pater, for the intensity of the hero's noxious affection for his dead mother, the sense of the homely, and the poetry of places. However, the essayistic and argumentative intrusiveness

74   The most celebrated scene in the novel is that of a dead dog that falls from an airplane, and on crashing to the ground sprays blood over the embrace of the hero and his lover. It symbolizes, surreally as so often in the early Huxley, the outside world breaking into the inner world.

75   Doctor Miller, this ascetic, is the double of the mystic Gerald Heard (Bowering 1968, 135). A syncretic anthology of spiritualist and mystical thought is Huxley's *The Perennial Philosophy*, from 1946.

is that of the late, prolix and monotonous masked autobiographies of Wells, especially that of William Clissold. Huxley probably thought he had invented a funambulist variant, all his own, of formal experimentalism and modernist psychology. Only Virginia Woolf with *The Years* brings to mind a similar temporal arrangement,[76] with chapters entitled with dates, even if in Woolf the progress is linear and the internal divisions coincide with years, without the indications of the month and the day. Purely Huxleyan, however, is the temporal dislocation and the chronological counterpoint, with time leaping back and forth, and the discontinuity in the voice, the authorial one alternating with that of the diary. This is a form of attempted rebellion against the tyranny of diegetic linearity, therefore it also represents Huxley's rejection of time as such, with the aim of seeking, as a scientist, a mimesis of Einstein's relativity or Bergson's *durée* – in other words, to bring back the authentic epiphanies of the psyche, and also to distinguish between wasted time and other times having a higher psychic and emotional content.[77] An artifice, a mannerist puzzle?[78]

2. After *Eyeless in Gaza*, every other novel by Huxley presents the figure of a guru, into whom the blabbermouth and the loquacious host of the novel-symposium or circle of the early novels metamorphose. The attention now shifts to the meditation on time, a time that is no longer merely past, but also present and future, replete with the unknowns of politics, but also of science, that is, of the threatening scenarios expected from a scientific research released from every human and humanistic project. The author camouflages himself both in these figures, to whom he attributes his own weakness for aphorisms, and in those of

76 Brooke 1972, 24, notes, however, the precedent of Isherwood's *The Memorial* (§ 13.2).
77 See also R. Lalou (CRHE, 298), who specifies the nature of the divergence from Proust. Naturally, critics have found many other motivations for the method used by Huxley: Sparrow (CRHE, 247), for instance, oddly asserts that the form of the novel stands for the lack of a goal and a meaning in a life that 'Doctor Miller did not sanctify with his objectives'.
78 For Daiches (CRHE, 314) these are precisely expedients devised to 'keep up with contemporary innovators of technique'.

young people who become their followers. *After Many a Summer*[79] (1939) initially conceals its nature as a polemical novel of ideas in a satirical farce on the American way of life. Pordage, an English historian, over the hill and also physically repelling, arrives in California to sort boxes of books and sixteenth-century manuscripts on behalf of an oil magnate, and serves as an observer of a humanity that lives off purely material needs, the invasion of advertising that aims to swell the need for wellbeing, and landscape and architectural follies. All around him, in vivid demonstrative flashes he also sees the triumph of kitsch and vulgarity. This Californian superficiality contrasts strangely with the flourishing of different faiths, and therefore of sects and confessions – Protestant, Church of Christ, Mormon, and Catholic. At the same time, the most blatant exhibition of wealth clashes with the poverty of the plantation workers. But soon the vision shrinks to the confined space of Huxley's first novels, and a choral and above all verbal action comes to life among a small circle of characters. The symbolism of this coterie, cannily prepared and arranged, is played out on various contiguous planes that are closely interwoven, that is, placed in counterpoint. It hinges above all on fat old Stoyte, who surrounds himself with youth in the form of the buxom blonde bimbo Virginia, whose ingenuous contradiction lies in the fact that, although a devotee of the Madonna, she often ends up under the bedclothes with men. While the English academic from Cambridge revives and brings back to life dusty old manuscripts, a scientist has been specially employed by the magnate to treat him against old age. This 'Faustian' scientist, a Gothic parody, is also a jokey exhumation of Wells's Moreau, since he carries out sinister vivisection experiments on rats and gorillas in his laboratory; and he is finally the allegory of pure sensualism devoid of moral qualms, and thus a degeneration of that depicted in *Point Counter Point*, because by his side is a young assistant who sympathizes with socialism, and is a former combatant in the Spanish Civil War. The symposium of ideas is eventually staged

79   A title cleverly borrowed from Tennyson's dramatic monologue 'Tithonus', the mythological character who asks to be able to die because he may be immortal, but remains subject to the law of ageing. Curiously, the idea for the novel was used in a Laurel and Hardy film of 1932 (as Thomas Merton notes in CRHE, 323).

with the ill-timed entrance of a Professor Propter who embodies critical conscience, and who, without advancing a proper constructive proposal, warns his disciples about the claim staked by evil on any form of activism, and the necessity to evade time to enter eternity: 'time is potential evil', 'actual good is outside time', and eternity is God, or god, and a god that for Huxley is always something different from the first transcendent principle of a particular revealed faith.[80] His battle ironically takes aim, therefore, at those who, worried about prolonging their life, live totally within time. The sole concrete message is the commitment to peace and the cessation of every war, and the person left disappointed is Stoyte's acolyte, who burns with love for his neighbour and for populations oppressed by dictatorships. The repudiation of science and progress is symbolized by a machine for the exploitation of solar energy that the professor has built; and since he demonstrates, as a carpenter, that progress must prudently observe artisan limitations, Propter is a Christological figure of whom the assistant scientist becomes a disciple. The novel idles for the most part, lacking in events, and limiting itself to subdividing the saintly man's message into many small 'sermons on the mount'; then all of a sudden it becomes dynamic again when the magnate guns down the assistant scientist in a fit of jealousy. The epilogue in England is a leap into an authentically Wellsian fantasy and into a misanthropy that is even more Swiftian: the demonstrative visit to a couple of 'immortals', who instead of having achieved the gift of a better life only present the disgustingness of a rooting-around, animalesque existence. With this, undisciplined progress really does threaten to verify Darwin's hypothesis and, above all, that of Huxley's own ancestor, his grandfather Thomas Henry.[81]

80   At the same time: 'Good manifests itself only on the animal level and on the level of eternity'.

81   The farcical short novel *The Genius and the Goddess* (1955) returns to the portrait of the scientist as the 'psychological equivalent of a foetus', who, ever since *Point Counter Point*, had formed a duo with a likeable, more human and concrete assistant. It therefore hinges on the combination, frequent in Huxley, of intellectual greatness and puerile incapacity to tackle the emotional demands of life. An eminent physicist is married to a very beautiful woman who sees to everything for him. The bitter,

3. In the fatuous, pretentious plot of *Time Must Have a Stop* (1944), and into its chain of diaphanous events, Huxley aimed to insinuate an unlikely philosophical and salvific proposal: outlining a spiritualist parable in which ethereal spectres drift around in an aura of impalpability, all bearers of a forced symbolic import. Measured with the criteria of fictional realism, this is a return to Meredith's weird early manner, with the odd fixations, the whims and eccentricities of his cold and absurd 'humours'. The main counterpoint is that between Eustace Barnack, a mature Don Juan, connoisseur of pictures, amateur epicurean and taster of the pleasures of the palate and the flesh, and his nephew Sebastian, an ironic *nomen omen*[82] for a young man who is green and bashful but highly sensual. The arena is Florence in 1929, by that time under fascism, but a notably stereotyped Florence, bogus and second-hand, as if the author had never visited it or lived there.[83] The uncle dies practically in the arms of a half-dressed Mimì, a Florentine prostitute; and the nephew, who timidly loves an English cousin, falls in love with a more adult Florentine lady-in-waiting, in whom he sees incarnate his dream of the feminine. An orphan, he is also a 'Joycean' son in search of a mother and of a father who does not love him or take care of him; he finds a vicarious mother in the figure of a woman who has lost a son – both ghost-seekers, he the ghost of the maternal woman, she the ghost of her son. The survival of the soul after the death of the body is a motif dealt with in the semi-serious setting of a séance, and also in some experimental chapters in which the freed soul of the defunct uncle wanders ethereally through the spaces of

----

    tragic irony of the story is that the nemesis strikes and eliminates the latter, not the parasite.

82   Right from the first page, Sebastian the martyr, an angelic and seraphic young man, wishes timidly and tormentingly to find an 'evening suit' for a party, and resorts to vain and also comical stratagems to obtain it. The 'arrows' of his iconographic double are expressly those of cupidity, vanity, smugness, and in fact Sebastian will be raped at least twice, once by the ambiguous, spiritual-carnal lady-in-waiting of his old Anglo-Florentine relative; but – as is predicted to him – these will also be beneficial 'arrows' fired around him. At the end of the novel Sebastian collects the spiritual heritage of the Florentine saint Bruno Rontini.

83   I agree with Manferlotti 1987, 25.

eternity, and the sensations of his otherworldly journey are imagined.[84] Another involution is that of erudite dialogues invariably conducted on the thread of sophisms and allusive and strangely knowing winks. The *deus ex machina* of the story is a Florentine antiquarian who distils wisdom through arcane statements, and on the purely realistic plane is arrested one day by the fascist police.[85] Mindful of his experiments in the treatment of time, in the epilogue Huxley takes a *saltus* of fifteen years to check on the maturation of the young intellectual, who is 'shoring' up the 'fragments' of the world war, and responds to the threats looming over humanity with the distillation of the antiquarian's knowledge, transcribed into his aphorisms. The Florentine sage teaches a synthetic religion that places at the summit a 'gaseous vertebrate' who is no longer a god revealed; his are open, indefinite teachings, a perpetual research avoiding dogma, which pillages all the spiritualistic and esoteric faiths, but weds none of them. One of his aphorisms echoes Eliot's dictum in *Four Quartets*, asserting that 'time must have a stop' and that 'It is only by taking the fact of eternity into account that we can deliver thought from its slavery to life'.

§ 36. *Huxley V: Dystopian fantasies*

Ape and Essence (1948), which Orwell found 'awful' without explaining why,[86] is the first of a couple of writings lying close to the formal limit of the novelistic, and that revert to the module of the journey into a future world that considerably worsens the hypotheses of *Brave New World*. An apocalyptic, deliberately inconclusive farce mercilessly blamed by critics in the wake of Orwell, *Ape and Essence*, is, however, remarkably ingenious as an idea. For the first time Huxley purports to be writing a text within a text following the famous expedient of the rediscovered manuscript; the

---

84   According to Bowering 1968, 160–80, these animistic experiences cannot be understood without knowing the source that inspired them, viz. the *Tibetan Book of the Dead*.

85   A distant echo of the catalysing function that Ezra Cohen has for Daniel Deronda in George Eliot's eponymous novel.

86   OCE, vol. IV, 539.

latter is a cinema script embedded in a short prelude featuring two film-makers who are reading one of the many scripts by semi-unknown authors that Hollywood incinerates without filming; this could itself be a script for a film even today, by a Greenaway or one of Kubrick's disciples. The manuscript is found on the day Gandhi dies, Gandhi being defined as a dreamer of mankind's potential to change the order of existing things: by contrast, the script imagines the foundering of western civilization in the year 2108. The formal novelty is that the main body of the text must be imagined as being visually screened; by its nature the changes of front are frequent, rapid and sketchy, separated by cinematographic fades, while the actions are introduced and described by a narrator off screen. On this imaginary screen jumbled visions of an upside-down world come to life, a world dominated by the devil. As a result, this imbricated text also shares the structure of a drama of the absurd with its disconnections and unexpected visual changes, in a historical moment when that form of theatre was incubating. As a text it is still spuriously preparatory; it is a rehearsal of a final text, or perhaps just the script. While the opening titles are rolling, so to speak, a pantomime brings on stage Einsteinian scientists led on a leash by baboons. In short, this is the total defeat of science. In the fantastic, crazy and occasionally grotesque picaresque of the New Zealand ship reaching the Californian coast to rediscover America (this distant island was spared from a third world war and atomic radiation), Poole, a professor of botany, is both the witness of the new world and its hypothetical saviour. Sucked into this future society like every time traveller, after miraculously escaping the danger of elimination, he is the inductive tool of knowledge in the life of a world that is still suffering the consequences of atomic radioactivity. In reality, as in *Brave New World* the new god is Ford – the symbol of technology – intensified pessimism always uses antitheses but acknowledges the Devil as the symbolic lord. Ultimately, humanity is not even culpable, because Huxley – and it is here that, for all his rationalism, he may resemble Ruskin, whom he detested[87] – postulates, as a Manichaean, mankind's impotence in the face of a struggle

87   Atkins 1967, 21.

between the powers of Light and Darkness.[88] The fabric of the scenes, some with an exceptional visual impact, includes propitiatory rites that a caste of sinister priests imposes on their subjects to the chant of rhythmic 'satanic verses', rites including the sacrifice of the deformed, and a sexual orgy only allowed at rigidly set times, since sex has become 'seasonal'. Huxley proposes a cyclical salvation, if it is true that 'whenever evil is carried to the limit, it always destroys itself'. And the professor leaves for a kind of new 'savage reservation', with only one brave woman defector, to re-establish the 'Order of Things'.

2. *Island*[89] (1962), which attracted even more injurious criticism,[90] begins with a utopia, the usual utopia of a traveller landing on a paradise island; except that the utopia is only apparent, on the brink of capitulating in the face of internal and especially external forces that are threatening the island's immunity and autonomy, and its isolation from the rest of the world; so that this too ends up becoming a dystopia. Huxley is conscious that this is an overused story, and lets his traveller, and therefore also us readers, know that such a macrotext is age-old and glorious, and turns him into a conscious descendant of Gulliver and into Butler's explorer from *Erewhon*. The grammar of the genre is, however, varied by the fact that the traveller does not leap forward in time, but is shipwrecked on the island precisely at the time of the writing. Pala, the imaginary island, is found *now*, or we can at least think so, in the very real southern seas of Conrad and Stevenson. Having closed the frame, which must naturally postulate the marital and erotic unhappiness as well as the existential frustration of Will Farnaby, the typical common man, the heart of the tale is a series of didactic sessions made possible by the convalescence of the castaway, who finds himself in the area to collaborate in granting rights to exploit Pala's

88   More precisely this is the 'the Grace of Belial, which, of course, is always forthcoming – that is, for anyone who's prepared to co-operate with it'. The novel inevitably becomes a 'symposium' in which Satan's arch-vicar presents the 'history of the world' to the professor, including the consequence that mankind no longer has the strength to rebel, and humours Satan – as if throwing food 'to a roaring tiger' – to survive.

89   Its demonstrative scheme was lifted from *Brave New World Reconsidered* (cf. n. 60 above).

90   Cf. that by Kermode in CRHE, 453.

oilfields on behalf of certain multinationals. Will gives in to his trainers and engages in a Buddhist initiation to expand his awareness and reach Nirvana. He also becomes an honorary citizen of the island just as the curtain is falling on the inexorable arrival of the forces of modernity.[91] *Island* repeats *Brave New World* with the overturning of accepted terms and values, since the authentically civil world is the primitive, or slightly and judgementally modernized one, of the island;[92] that of the 'civilized' world is uncivil, or better, inhuman. The model that Huxley is now approving aims at a reform of associated life, of the economy, pedagogy and the human persona, with respect to how they are understood in the world outside. Meanwhile, Huxley has slightly revised his vision of sex and of the management of Eros. In the society dreamed of, the family has not been abolished, but on the one hand use is made of contraceptives to help birth control (resolving the scourge of overpopulation which is the ruin of the inhabited world), while, on the other, artificial insemination is used for eugenic aims. Husbands are perfectly happy if their wives are inseminated by other men to vary or improve the genetic legacy.[93] Equal attention is paid to the correct education of young children. At this point in time, Huxley was no longer disposed to salvage anything worthwhile of the west's pedagogical and educational models, or to forge a wider theology or theosophy, all of which he had jettisoned. The Christian

91   This is the conspiracy of the new raja manoeuvred by the mother, agreed in secret with emissaries from the multinationals. Because of its pacifist and Buddhist principles, the island has no real power to stand up against the symbolic invasion: it can only 'try to keep them in order, try to change their mind, hope for a happy outcome, and be prepared for the worst'.

92   The parable is symbolic and above all symbiotic, and the founders of the island's society were a Scottish Calvinist doctor who became atheist and a pious Buddhist raja. The replacement of the Christian God by the Buddha is above all motivated by fact that for Huxley God is the Calvinist god who punishes and scourges, where the Buddha lets people live in peace.

93   The 'Yoga of Eros' is *pour cause* that liberating sex for the realization of the whole human personality which represented for D. H. Lawrence, too, the salvation of western civilization; equally indebted to Lawrence is the pedagogical goal of making the children 'fully human'.

basis, which earlier coexisted with other foundations of being, is recast to seek and find in Buddhist religion a more commensurate foundation for the full and harmonious development of the person. Finally, in political terms, the island has miraculously been able to stand apart from every attempt at supremacy, both domestically and internationally: it lives self-sufficiently,[94] lacking even defensive armaments,[95] while economically it is a cooperative, and rejects every extreme form of industrialization. The weakness of this island society is that, while its objective is to completely free mankind and the state community from any sort of conditioning, in practice its members are know-it-all exhibitors of Buddhist religiosity, and too conscious of being model figures; as a result they revert to being victims of a new imprisonment.

§ 37. Bowen* I: Irish enchantments

The majority of the critics and of the reviewers, followed by the historians of literature, and various contemporary professional writers, bestowed prestigious recognition on Elizabeth Bowen (1899–1973) when her novels first appeared in the late 1920s, and soon placed her among the top British writers of the twentieth century, on a par with Jane Austen, Henry James and Chekhov, and, *ipso facto*, close to, if not above, the female writers most in vogue at the time, Virginia Woolf and Katherine Mansfield. These ballpark

94   Also racially, since the island has no ports and its race is thus kept relatively pure from contamination due to emigration. This is another of Huxley's conservative and xenophobic views.

95   The islanders point out that Buddhism is the only historical religion in which 'there was never any blood'.

*   J. Brooke, *Elizabeth Bowen*, London 1952; W. Heath, *E. Bowen: An Introduction to Her Novels*, Madison, WI 1961; A. E. Austin, *Elizabeth Bowen*, New York 1971; R. Coles, 'Youth: Elizabeth Bowen's *The Death of the Heart*', in *Irony in the Mind's Life: Essays on Novels by James Agee, Elizabeth Bowen, and George Eliot*, Charlottesville, VA 1974, 107–53; E. K. Kenney Jr, *Elizabeth Bowen*, Lewisburg, PA 1975; V. Glendinning, *Elizabeth Bowen: Portrait of a Writer*, London 1977; H. Lee, *Elizabeth Bowen: An Estimation*, London 1981; D. Gauthier, *L'image du réel dans les romans d'Elizabeth Bowen*, Paris 1985; P. Craig, *Elizabeth Bowen*, Harmondsworth 1986; *Elizabeth*

blood relationships were due to the eminently stylistic qualities of these novels, and to their diaphanous, narrowly differentiated plots with little action and prevalently based on the study of moods and sensations, and without strong social messages. They had been written by her as a poet and a painter, their patterns of visual and perceptive miniatures finely chiselled, sober and elliptical, with dialogues and scenes sketched by an impressionist of the word with a marked taste for the exquisite and the sophisticated. Similar esteem, albeit with a few dissenting voices, lasted for two decades, and was accorded to 'one of the most important modern writers', capable even of winning at least *ex aequo* the contest as the greatest British writer between the death of Woolf and the advent of Beckett. However, over the last half of the century it plummeted vertically, and Bowen's primacy and even her canonical status are now not only disputed but in real danger. The classic textbooks included and treated her with respect, citing her novels and often discussing them point by point; more recently, some have erased her name to the point that it is not even to be found in the index.[1] Bowen is a submerged, blurred, forgotten figure, the object of a small residual cult of initiates. The span of her biography almost coincides with that of Beckett, both of them of Protestant Irish extraction; more prudentially,

---

Bowen, ed. H. Bloom, New York 1987; P. Lassner, *Elizabeth Bowen: A Study of the Short Fiction*, London 1990; H. B. Jordan, *How Will the Heart Endure?: Elizabeth Bowen and the Landscape of War*, Ann Arbor, MI 1992; R. C. Hoogland, *Elizabeth Bowen: A Reputation in Writing*, New York and London 1994; A. Bennett and N. Royle, *Elizabeth Bowen and the Dissolution of the Novel: Still Lives*, Houndmills 1995; J. D. Coates, *Social Discontinuity in the Novels of Elizabeth Bowen: The Conservative Quest*, Lewiston, N. Y. 1998; M. Ellmann, *Elizabeth Bowen*, Plymouth 1998, and *Elizabeth Bowen: The Shadow Across the Page*, Edinburgh 2003; N. Corcoran, *Elizabeth Bowen: The Enforced Return*, Oxford 2004; *Elizabeth Bowen: New Critical Perspectives*, ed. S. Osborn, Cork 2009; N. Darwood, *A World of Lost Innocence: The Fiction of Elizabeth Bowen*, Newcastle 2012.

1   In other terms, the more distant the observation time becomes from the historical moment when Bowen was writing, the more the rate of attention diminishes, until it disappears. Precisely because of this, the most flagrant omission, amongst other cases, is that of BAUGH, vol. IV, which, usually so exhaustive, inexplicably excludes this writer.

she may be said to be the greatest female Irish writer after Lady Gregory and Katherine Tynan, and before Iris Murdoch.

2. Bowen's main, and virtually only, theme is adolescent innocence pitched into the brutal world of corruption and moral and sentimental opportunism. It faces adulthood shuddering and trembling in its heart of hearts, and presents itself at the threshold of love, the young female protagonist remaining disappointed and seared in her dreams and longings. This theme used to evoke the name of Henry James in many of her critics, forgetting Edith Wharton. There is in fact very little of James in these novels, with the possible exception of some later ones; sullied innocence is more an obsession of Christina Rossetti and the Victorian female novelists. Seeing that Bowen wrote a mass of delicate, sensitive stories along these lines,[2] we can also include Katherine Mansfield among her forerunners or sisters in spirit.[3] Rather, Bowen is a private and solitary writer, anachronistic or perhaps even achronic, who has often been compared to the wrong writers,

2	Angus Wilson, the editor of *The Collected Stories of Elizabeth Bowen*, London 1980, is implicitly one of the few who deemed this edifice of tales, numbering several dozens, powerful enough to surpass her novels in aesthetic duration. In his introduction, he defines Bowen's several tales set during the London Blitz, which surround the novel *The Heat of the Day*, as the most classic memory for posterity together with Green's *Caught* (§ 42.4). The purely naturalistic and descriptive spectacles are often mixed with studies of the psychic effects of the bombing and of the state of alarm in the city (dreams, disorientation, nightmares, hallucinations, like that of the woman who believes she has lived in a family 100 years earlier). Bowen's first two collections (1923 and 1927) had preceded her first novel, and they are mainly short sketches with thin, wan and clichéd plots, of an out-of-the-ordinary anecdotal nature, and strange devices and glimpses of marginal life (a teacher welcoming to her home pupils who deride her; a rather unfeeling milliner entertaining in her shop two customers who do not want to spend anything, until another mysterious customer arrives). Accompanying these are tales of young children caught in various moods and situations of almost imperceptible but serious affective disorder, or even of a snarling reaction to adult insensitivity.

3	To both may be applied the fitting metaphor of being chased from an infantile Eden: Bowen wrote that 'it is not only our fate but our business to lose innocence, and once we have lost that, it is futile to attempt a picnic in Eden' (*Collected Impressions*, quoted in Coles 1974, 115).

only because by a sheer fluke they were the contemporaries who held court at that moment, such as Green, Greene and Waugh. Bowen cannot be associated with Modernism, even though her novels of the 1920s, at least four of them, are marked by a recognizable need to identify and perform experiments that are not an exact copy of Joyce's and above all Woolf's novels; they do, however, follow in their wake and are close to them chronologically.[4] The temporal tripartition – the encapsulation of the present, the past and the present again, a construction to be found in two of her novels – is a variation on Bergson's *durée* and harks back to *To the Lighthouse*. On the other hand, the obsession with the immaculately finished artwork – the idea and essence of form, affirmed by Bowen also as a theory – results in a chain of calibrated novels, never hasty or published without breaks; those of her second phase were separated one from another by up to five years or so. The author's voice is omniscient but not invasive; the narrative pace is regular, with scenes of description and dialogues devoid of pomp or splendour; but never lacking are the beautiful cameos of scenery and atmosphere in carefully painted, sophisticated words, and the purple passage in impressionistic style. The scenic inserts and colour studies are authentic word paintings by a post-Impressionist: Bowen had in fact studied art and did paint.[5] Until the signs of some dissolution, towards the end of her career, almost every novel is modelled on the previous one, according to a carefully pondered construction and an asphyxial repetitiveness. Hers is a tidy, well-ordered, classical procedure of action, description, setting and dialogue, in chapters clustered into distinct parts. She identifies with her characters, especially the youngest ones, and with open empathy filters the psychologies starting from her own: she is an off-scene director using her acute, susceptible, impressionable perceptiveness. Bowen's interludes are

---

4   Having lived for several years in London, Bowen frequented the Bloomsbury Group but without becoming a real friend of Virginia Woolf, for whom Bowen was but another of her numerous rivals. Bowen's 'exile' was also her self-exclusion from an established literary current, and from a recognized circle frequented by established authors.

5   Bowen studied at an all-girls school in Kent, then at an art school in London until 1919.

famous and are always a pleasure to reread: not generic, or routine, they grasp the odd, the marginal and the curious, and they do so with *ad hoc*, rare and imaginative adjectives and daring matchings, to make a sensation or a scene more exquisite and precise, something that had only been done before by the Metaphysical poets. The lexical range of the English novel grows disproportionately with her, with the occurrence of words that are designated 'low frequency'. These takeaway pieces are countless, like the cameos in a book of English fiction from every epoch, where they have often appeared. That these are detached and smug mechanical *appliqués* is the other side of the coin. At times, Bowen is aware of her empathetic excesses, and lets a letter or a diary of her young main character take the stage; in these cases a new voice resounds, more silvery, disarmed, with fewer literary echoes.

3. In a certain sense, Bowen the novelist of the female condition ends where Angela Carter begins, even if the two writers, who by age could have been mother and daughter, never met and would probably have glowered at one another. Bowen's last novel is just a little later than Carter's first; in its surreal strangeness and its more unscrupulous and accepted *sui generis* feminism, it could have been dreamed up or written by the younger writer not entirely differently. It is entitled *pour cause* after an Eve, who is in part a new Eve seeking a re-foundation and re-creation of herself, alternatives to a system of values, which in part she finds.[6] This relationship between Bowen and Carter is not strange or fanciful; it can be suggested and discussed starting from the fable-like plots of both writers, central to whose works is the adolescent who crosses a threshold and becomes lost, and is often also left disgusted. Carter's *The Magic Toyshop* presents the same enchantment found in many adventures or romances of Bowen's male and female orphans caught in a symbolic progress. This sense of ontological solitude is common to both writers, although in Bowen it has a different affective origin. Nonetheless, as strange as it may seem, Bowen and Carter perhaps do not have a different idea of sexuality and its role in a woman's life; the question is moot since Bowen kept

6   § 179.3.

silent on it. It is self-evident that her adolescents live love but not yet the sexual impulse, or at least not openly; they are sexless girls, fleshless and without desire, having sublimated sex into romance. Their sexuality is extinguished or has not yet matured, but Bowen perpetuates this immaturity.[7] This reticence is part of her aristocratic personality, her innate sense of decorum, her observance of respectability; Carter was to react to all of this in a clamorously iconoclastic way. Carter leant on feminist and poststructuralist ideology and theory, to the extent of being overburdened and overloaded with it; Bowen was delightfully ignorant of such matters – all instinct, sheer and primitive sensibility. In short, Bowen's art is one of reticence and ellipsis, the art of a deliberate restriction of the focus. Her novels can be read in a flash, they are so brief, polished, and without superfluity; she intentionally avoided the large-scale novel, her more congenial dimension being the short story, so that her novels are really expanded short stories. She is a classical writer, if not for the fact that she classically tells a series of romantic *Sehnsuchten*. Hence the accusation made against her, of being a superficial writer, almost timorous in breaking the crust that would open up the horrible abyss spinning beneath the gaze. Her limit, or her patented merit, is having looked at only one side of existence, that of the surface, and the surface of one section of English society. The list of absences also includes that of the intellectual, possibly feisty, character, endowed with an idea of society or even of a utopia. Bowen represents only emotional or sentient characters, not intellectuals; and has no need to satirize the pedant either. She was self-taught, educated in her father's library and at girls' schools without attending university; hence a novel of sensibility devoid of ideological disputes and discussion. When Bowen ventures into theorizing, it is not surprising that she should sound simplistic and clichéd.

---

7   Usually Bowen is not even sexually allusive, even if one story, 'The Parrot', is singularly rich in sexual suggestions, with the maid of an elderly lady who one day lets a parrot escape and wander through the streets and gardens, until it is found and captured in that of a writer who tries to detain it by offering it fruit. Rachel, from the story 'The Jungle', 'towards the end of a summer term discovered the Jungle', and ventures into it.

4. Only the Irish nationalists and groups of left-wing politicized writers felt no liking or esteem for Bowen. Yeats, dying in 1939, managed to follow her beginnings and rise to fame, but did not take her into serious consideration nor did he ever mention her name. Indeed, the fact that Bowen had little sensitivity when it came to her ethnic and national legacy, and had no evident political and public conscience, was little discussed, or perhaps silently stigmatized by the Irish. But her writing style and its innate gifts, linked to a national stereotype, is perhaps a sufficient ethnic mark in itself. Yeats was in fact showing that it was possible to produce an art that is absolute and at the same time politically committed, and fuse the two spheres. Bowen does not speak, nor does she have her characters speak, of politics; untouched by nationalism, she never descends into the political arena. She had grown up in a kind of soundproofed bell, and non-engagement in politics was the kind of pride and joy of those Anglo-Irish to whom she belonged and from whom she was descended. In Bowen, exile is a political and ethnic condition transferred to the private sphere and a psychic dimension, that of the displaced, the stateless, and the orphan. Her southern Ireland emerging in some of her stories of the 'grand residences' in ruin, was an atmospheric Ireland of a mysterious nature, not very different from Yeats's demonic one. Ultimately, in her own way, Bowen exudes Irish and Yeatsian eeriness in the shimmering light and foggy indistinct settings that envelop her novels' plots. Familiarity with enchantment came from her double origin and genealogy, since her Irish ancestors were originally from Celtic Wales.[8] Another index of elision in Bowen is the neutrality over – or, more precisely, the complete silence on – religion. The religious simply does not fall into her sphere or visual range, nor is it an object of thought in her secular, primordial characters. Religion is confined to routine, without anyone's pouring acrimony on Protestants or still less on Catholics. She may have been an agnostic.[9] Overwhelming in Yeats,

8   Brooke 1952, 10.

9   She had certainly been one ever since she was young, as can be read in Glendinning 1977, 19, and 234–5, concerning Bowen's later ideas on religion.

her interest in autochthonous myth is equally slight or non-existent.[10] To return to the second point raised above, Bowen is a writer who may be vaguely defined as right-wing, and the rather circumscribed radius from which her characters are taken – the wealthy middle-class Londoners who live off their inheritance, or the Irish landowners – may be why Orwell, who was Bowen's almost exact contemporary up to 1950, is equally silent on her, even if Bowen could have brought grist to the mill of his theory, or polemic, about escapist literature. The title of Bowen's poetic manifesto, from 1948, 'Why Do I Write?',[11] recalls that of Orwell, but traces a genesis and objectives of literary writing which are the opposite.[12] Later critics disagreed over the hierarchies within Bowen's oeuvre, established according to alternations of fleeting tastes leading to often unacceptable or plainly weird judgements that today need to be completely revised. Deconstruction, quite as much as extreme feminism, which believed it had identified Bowen's 'subversive potential' in a feminist lesbian perspective,[13] seems to have been studying the fiction of a completely different author, making it unrecognizable.

§ 38. *Bowen II: Covert dramas of dreaming adolescence*

The emotional reservoir that Bowen needed was filled in the first twenty years of her life. Her two most precocious *alter egos* are the children Leopold and Henrietta, nine and eleven years old, in *The House in Paris* (1935). In that span, Bowen had accumulated affective experiences that are fictionally worth double and triple, and were to be split into instalments and mixed into her novels. In those twenty years, Bowen had been an adolescent tossed to and fro over the Irish Sea; as a writer she had quietly began self-mythologizing, to soon objectivize herself (it has been rightly said that any immediate,

---

10   On the autobiographical implications and the Irish legacy, cf. the interesting pages in Kenney 1975, 17–39.

11   § 21.2.

12   Orwell's implicit criticism becomes explicit with Raymond Williams, as Coates, 1998, 133, notes.

13   Hoogland 1994. I share the perplexities expressed on this book by Coates 1998, 241–5.

unseemly *cri de cœur* was foreign to her) as an adopted daughter. Her father, a well-to-do lawyer and victim to incurable psychic disturbances, soon had to undergo treatment for long periods far from his family; her mother, with whom she formed a close-knit symbiosis, she was to lose early. An orphan, she grew up with relatives and aunts, in seaside and coastal areas of southern Britain, and in all-girls schools. The affective lack was aggravated by the loss of her ethnic identity, and thus also by her search for it, usual in one of double race and class. Bowen's classic main character is therefore a wanderer, symbolically about to depart for an indefinite destination (a fact and a state often reflected in the titles of her novels, or of the parts inside them). *The Hotel* (1927) has a clichéd layout and assortment of themes as compared with contemporary novels, since it is played out in the claustrophobia of a hotel on the Italian Riviera,[14] and grows around Sydney Warren, a young English girl who seems reborn into a new life thanks to the affection of an older woman who, however, ceases her attention when her own son arrives at the hotel. Sydney's need for affection is then redirected onto another clumsy, not very masculine, guest, a not-so-young vicar on holiday. She receives a declaration from the mature Anglican minister, but initially refuses him; she accepts him *in extremis* but as a way out of that other unrequited love. The story of this flirtation, entirely platonic and obedient to etiquette, is interspersed with episodes of frequently suave humour; the awakening of the senses is set in motion by the none too passionate kisses of another couple at the hotel, only slightly more unbridled. At the end, all the doors leading to love close. The narrative pace is slow, without peaks, obedient to a series of clear rules, including that of providing a space-time vignette at pre-set deadlines; the exteriors are deliberately left hazy, in fact mannered, without a shadow of Italian colour. A similar narrative plan confirms the frequency with which British novels were set in hotels before and at the turn of the century.[15] In Bowen, the surreal nature of the setting evokes other names besides that of Arnold Bennett, and the subgenre of the boarding-house novel, whose context meant interrelations, caricatures, sketches, wisecracks at breakfast and lunch, picnics and outings. This setting was often chosen

14   The background autobiographical experience was a winter spent in Bordighera.
15   Cf. Volume 7, § 22.5 and n. 62, for this vogue.

to stage a rite of passage for immature and slightly neurotic maidens, as in Forster's classic Italian novel, *A Room with a View*, or in the collection of stories at a German *pension* by Katherine Mansfield. Even more unmistakably, however, behind *The Hotel* is Virginia Woolf's *The Voyage Out*. In Bowen, the diegetic immobility and the stasis of subplots reach almost intolerable, Chekhov-like levels.

2. *The Last September* (1929), one of Bowen's most enchanted and diaphanous novels, also takes place inside a closed perimeter, an Irish farmhouse that ends up being destroyed by a fire at the time of the 1920 uprisings.[16] A nineteen-year-old orphan girl falls in love with a British soldier who dies in an ambush set by republican rebels. These imploded, buried dramas help round out the characters. Lois is, of course, the young, hopeful, feisty, courageous girl who impulsively throws herself into life without a qualm; as often or always in Bowen from this point on, she has also lost both her parents, and has been entrusted to an insensitive uncle and an aunt (the uncle a former fiancé of her mother). This Irish farmstead is a miniature Eldorado before the destroying tempest arrives (Iris Murdoch, too, was to return, much later, to the crucial events of 1916 and 1921).[17] In the farmstead, a well-off Anglophile bourgeoisie spend their time lazing around on pastimes like tennis. It must be repeated that the characters are human phantasms, fragile, spineless, transparent butterflies from an imaginary, reborn Chekhovian theatre. The murmurings of the uprising become gradually more audible, and the Black and Tans create an incumbent and increasingly weighty menace, which transmits to the novel a much greater and more thrilling fictional tension. A certain, glamorous Marda Norton reaches the farm, gazed upon with admiration and enigma by Lois. At the dance she is anxious for the British soldier who is predestined to fall. However, the aunt, with her rigidly bourgeois

---

16   The farmhouse, which was not burnt down during the uprisings, unlike many other patrician houses, is obviously Bowen's Court, and was situated in County Cork, an environment always treated and portrayed with nostalgia and humour. On her father's death, Bowen inherited Bowen's Court and went to live there, but she had to sell it, being unable to meet the upkeep.

17   § 148.2–4.

prejudices, nips the idyll in the bud. This is Bowen's most impressionistic, fragmented, and cryptic novel to date; it is also marked by a melancholy, sorrowful and elegiac vein that rests on an elliptical and splintered style. The dialogues are often irrelevant, not in tone, scarcely intelligible, allusive, and they are interrupted by ellipsis points – in other words, Woolf's inspiration is even more marked. The smooth, dozing and uneventful plot, with its small storms in a teacup, but with a hidden eventfulness, is a form of *avant la lettre* minimalism.

3. *Friends and Relations* (1931) reflects its title and remains faithful to it, having the form of a thematic relay and of a chain of characters, friends or relatives, and, as a result, also of stories and events linked in a string. This can make it seem like an ongoing search for a main character who, once found, gives way to another, as in a choral novel. The theme has not changed, nor has the setting, an affluent society of professions and of the ruling classes. The plot is again set in the 1920s, but now entirely in England. Two pairs of sisters tie the knot with a ritual jollity that denies the none too propitious omens (the wedding day smacks of 'Sorel's execution' in Stendhal); one of the two couples must face the scandal of a much-maligned relative of the husband. Bowen's *alter ego* is a champing, ardent, eccentric fifteen-year-old girl, whose imagined ardours and marauding desires must be cooled off at a boarding-school where some proverbial but unusually pungent episodes open up. This girl, Theodora, repeating that she is 'homeless', exhibits evident symptoms of pubescent distress. The scene later shifts, with a leap similar to Woolf's in *To the Lighthouse*, to ten years later, to follow the destinies of the two couples now with children. In this case, too, we cannot expect full-blown action from a chorus of wimpy distracted characters dreamily or amiably floating at the mercy of events. The scenes of daily life, rich in exquisite and curious psychological details, are agreeable enough, until we start to suffer slight boredom due to the total absence of exceptional events. The novel seems like the palette of a documentary painter, or a documentary focused on marginal, insignificant detail, however curious. It gradually resembles a Carlingford saga[18] rewritten

18   Volume 5, § 147.3–4.

in a more academic, splintered, perceptive, and calligraphic style. The minimal vicissitudes, followed with an assiduous stream of consciousness, capture the doubled and multiplied ailments of the two couples, with the usual phase difference between the words said and the thoughts, embellished upon but not said, or their counterpoint. A subtle melancholy and a subtle unrest are covered by deafening chatter on everyday matters. And so the novel is a concealed satire against the post-war Georgian middle class.

4. In *To the North* (1932) Bowen embarks upon a change of route: from shared, sympathetically suffered pathos to a more objectified comedy, with a sting in the tail.[19] This is a step backwards towards the manner of Jane Austen and the humorous-sentimental eighteenth-century novel. The visible variant is also that the habitual *alter ego*, the pure, young and naïve orphan with her emotional hardships, is relegated to a minor and accessory role,[20] while another *alter ego* comes to the fore. She is in this novel an apparently confident, independent twenty-nine-year-old English widow who cannot decide whether to undertake a new marriage. The first fifty pages of the novel establish this new tone, which also arises from a brand new scenario, and are incalculably more nimble and natural than anything Bowen had written up to this point. On a closer look, however, the initial scene is not new; in fact it is a classic of the fiction of every age. On a train taking her home from Milan and a highly sentimental stay in Umbria, Cecilia cannot afford a sleeping car; in the restaurant car she meets a dandy, Markie; she flirts with him, but for the rest of the journey keeps her due distance from him. However, the impression that the typically Austenian and Victorian plot of the astute widow searching for a good party is being repeated, instantly vanishes, because Cecilia is torn over her future and even thinks of joining her mother in America; she does not ensnare her easy prey. The second and most secret reason is that this overused plot is worn

---

19 Markie is one of Bowen's many distracted males, and Emmeline, who gradually takes over the novel, succumbs to a frustration that the reader and she herself had believed to be extinguished or to be under control. She provokes a fatal accident in a mad car race.

20 This is her niece Pauline, whose suffering, albeit tolerated, is as always that of the school, with many, and often fresh, incidental episodes.

thin, comes apart, slackens, and gradually serves as a pretext to pluck from the hat increasingly fresh and also increasingly humorous or humorously pathetic scenes which exist independently, filling and diversifying the stasis of the plot. The incidental, the digressive and the sparklingly humorous end up prevailing over the guiding thread. Cecilia shares the limelight as main character, since she 'cedes' Markie to her sister-in-law Emmeline. But both women are an integral part of the entourage of their relative, Lady Waters, who presides over the community rites as a classic matchmaker. She organizes convivial opportunities and excursions in which the novel artfully apes, that is, wittily imitates, an old nineteenth-century conversation piece, in which a chorus of classic humours act in deliciously airy and irrelevant dialogues, and in theatrical, Restoration fencing matches. A bona fide parody of the multifocal is celebrated in the scenes at Emmeline's tourist office, with the typist's little ordeal.

5. *The House in Paris* is generally reputed to be a masterpiece, if not *the* masterpiece, of Bowen, thanks to its tragic power that reflected, less sedately and in fact rather more wildly than usual, a subsequent personal trauma of the author. It transfigured and dissimulated the chilling coldness of Bowen's conjugal relationship with an insignificant husband, and even imaginatively probed into a presumed and perhaps even consummated adultery.[21] The second reason for the favourable assessments it received lies in a belated and mostly forced modernistic attempt to update and therefore also upset a technique that had always worked quite well. The outset is brilliant and conquers and captivates the reader; it harks back to the story of the orphan children, and presents two of them, welcomed by a hearty generous English spinster who keeps a 'house' in Paris for guests and friends that becomes in this phase a nursery. We feel we hear again, in Henrietta and Leopold, the solemn common sense, the wise and mature observations of Dickens's precociously aged children,[22] or certain witty and shrewd ripostes of Carroll's Alice. The two young children are to

---

21   Behind the novel lay Bowen's still recent infatuation, albeit concealed and retouched here, with the critic Humphry House, whose name, suppressed by Glendinning in 1977, was revealed by Craig in 1986.

22   On this house, with its Dickensian surreality, cf. Kenney 1975, 47.

all effects orphans, entrusted to either their grandmothers or adoptive parents; Leopold's mother is far away, and for some mysterious reason she cannot love him and cannot live with him. Bowen focuses once again on the affective rift between innocent, unaware children and irresponsible adults. Never actually too convincing, and just passable, this long initial scene stretches out with dialogues and quips that echo in their brevity the style of Compton-Burnett's novels, especially those featuring children as the lead characters. The experimental nature emerges in a breakdown of the diegetic continuum and therefore in the non-linear treatment of time, as in the modernistic masterpieces. The first and the final parts are separated by a lengthy flashback that casts light on the mystery of the two children – or, rather, properly speaking, on that of Leopold alone.[23] Almost slipping into the perspective of her two young characters, Bowen becomes omniscient, and tells us how Leopold is the fruit of a pre-marriage relationship that his mother had with the fiancé of her then best friend. This second part stages a melodrama with long summarizing inserts and the feeling of the sensational, as in Wilkie Collins's later novels on adulterous liaisons.[24] The almost imperceptible passage from the third to the first person, and to a fragmentary stream of consciousness – with the mother who can hear and almost speak to the creature moving in her womb – is clumsy. As in the nineteenth-century sensational novel, which required a catharsis, the closure of the affair is the suicide of the lover after confessing his betrayal to his fiancée, who nonetheless covers the stain with exemplary abnegation. The past is made known to young Leopold, who then understands why his mother lacked the courage to come and see him, although her husband becomes an adoptive father for him.

§ 39. *Bowen III: Chill and hallucination before and during the war*
An even greater, unanimous, and steady consensus was won by Bowen's next two novels, acclaimed immediately before and after the Second World

---

23   The novel's structural failure lies in Henrietta who, although a successful portrait, remains extraneous to the drama of Leopold, the rejected baby.

24   Brooke 1952, 20, finds analogies with the atmospheres of Le Fanu, one of whose novels was prefaced by Bowen in a reissue, even if he calls Henrietta 'Harriet' by mistake.

War. In both cases this was an over-estimation.[25] *The Death of the Heart* (1938), which is in fact currently esteemed as the peak of Bowen's art, is in reality, and for the first time, a targeted novel that adopts successful established formulae. It unquestionably features more plot and it enriched the author with a mountain of sold copies, making a previously only esoteric writer known to the wider public. The warning light is the overly pompous, explicit title, which even bears a surplus of meaning in a novelist who is usually allusive and given to ellipsis and understatement. The very internal contrasts and symbolic clashes are markedly and immediately didactic and play rather less on the nuance. Like many other novels by Bowen, it tells the story of an adolescent orphan in crisis and affective disillusionment. The initial phases are already rather intricate in their episodic telling of the backstory of the loves of a certain Quayne, who had a son Thomas by his lately divorced first wife, and a daughter Portia by his second. With these three dead, Portia now lives in London with her stepbrother, an industrialist married to Anna, a superficial and frivolous woman. *The Death of the Heart* rivalled in its year of publication with a novel by Orwell, but is much more similar to those on the English middle classes written by Waugh and Huxley, although it does not possess, does not seek to possess, their vigour. There are no excursions outside the perimeter of a corrupt and bored class; there is no flicker of desire for social and sociological analysis; nor is there humour. Portia is observed down to her heartbeats and imperceptible alienations; she cultivates small myths, holds on tight to substitutive amulets, seeks to communicate outside the circle of her relatives; she lives her alienation and spiritual exile with an affective chill cloaked in apparent benevolence.[26] The immature girl seeks love and understanding and is let down by a seducer; she then falls but recovers and seemingly follows her path again, however bitter and disillusioned she has become. During the long interlude of a holiday in

25   Bowen, indeed, deemed *The Death of the Heart*, perhaps with *sprezzatura*, her least
      successful novel (Glendinning 1977, 125).
26   The title is in any case bivalent and could almost be applied more appropriately to
      Portia's relatives. The inspired, insistent opening on the frozen lake in Regent's Park
      is an unmistakable prolepsis.

Seale,[27] Portia is tossed into a tangle of juvenile friendships that are rather more unscrupulous and sexually more uninhibited; then one weekend Eddie, a vulgar opportunistic womanizer, grabs the hand of a girl and easily and brazenly explains away the innocence of this flirtation to Portia. In her passion, she believes Eddie, and it is she who flings herself round his neck and kisses him. She ends up enmeshed in Eddie's lack of authenticity and inconclusive sleights of hand, and takes refuge in the only other kind soul in the novel, a major who is often the author of unpardonable gaffes, and is secretly in love with Portia's sister-in-law, though having given Portia exquisite but useless presents. This fellowship of kind souls recalls similar episodes in Forster's novels, especially in the oppositions between sentimental opportunism and purity without personal profit. The finale is left somewhat open, since, out of protest, Portia has no wish to leave the hotel where Major Brutt, the other kind soul, is hosting her temporarily; and it is unclear whether the Forster-style 'rescue party', consisting of the Quaynes' housemaid, will have any effect, since the curtain falls abruptly while she is entering the hotel. Bowen's pen is far from scathing here, nor do we feel Woolf's and Mansfield's sense of torment and secret tension. The novel's surface fails to ripple, always sounding a little bogged down in the category of the uneventful. The only formal surprise, and a questionable stratagem, is the passage from the covert, unnoticeable omniscience to the diary extract and the transcription of some of Portia's letters, which also lack any really introspective interest.

2. *The Heat of the Day* (1949), another alleged masterpiece, nowadays much disputed, is the war novel that many writers felt called upon and encouraged to produce.[28] This is a request that surprises, or rather, forces the hand of a writer like Bowen, who usually auscultates the intimate and denies herself to the diktats of the market or public expectations. A similar desuetude, or lack of conviction, can be perceived in the frayed, anonymous, even inert plot, which is almost a frame for a series of descriptive scenes

---

27   In reality, Hythe, in Kent, where Bowen spent most of her youth.
28   On the analogies with and resemblances to that by Green, cf. ATD, 195, and n. 2 above. Bowen had occasionally worked as a nurse as well as an official in the Intelligence Service during the war.

provided to highlight the weird unreality of London being bombed.[29] This sense of estrangement is a widespread common denominator in such literature. Set in 1942, when peace 'was more far away' than at the start of the war, it alternates on a double track destined to become one. Louie is a naïve worker whose husband is at war; Stella is forty, divorced, and lives with Robert, a soldier back from the front where he almost lost the use of one leg; her son, Roderick, is still fighting. However, a certain mysterious, Mephistophelian Harrison,[30] whom she is unable to shake off, keeps insinuating that Robert is a German spy. The novel slackens considerably in following the excessively precise deals regarding an Irish property inherited by Stella's son, who discovers some skeletons in the cupboard regarding the love affairs of the father he has never met; and others relating to the lover's relatives. The internal time extends until the end of the war. The results are largely not up to expectations: the plot is flimsy and never really manages to take off; the dialogues are cerebral or tortuous as never before in Bowen – they admittedly smack of Henry James, or belong to an inexistent language, removed from every real objective of communication; the psychological introspections turn in on themselves. Some successful scenes worthy of a born novelist like Bowen save the day, scenes in which we breathe the surreal aura of a disoriented wartime London, as well as others that portray the genuine candour of Louie at work.

§ 40. *Bowen IV: Childhood: memories and nostalgia*

Each time Bowen returns to focus on – and sympathize with – the young female dreamer, and, through memory, to use her fog-shrouded native Ireland as a setting, the freshness of the inspiration is ensured and sounds natural. *A World of Love* (1955), which looks back to *The Last*

---

29   What has often been appreciated and admired in this novel is the correspondence between signifier and signified, or rather the breakdown of language and its ungrammatical nature which reflects the fragmentary context of the war; some critics (cf. Glendinning 1977, 153) have evoked audacious analogies with the sprung rhythm and syntactic dislocations of Hopkins; however, the end result on the page is very different.

30   Critics have often found this character Kafkaesque.

September, begins on the wavelength of the enchanted and the rhapsodic, and cannot avoid being a slightly retro-dated or rather atemporal novel. It is Bowen's novel that best bears witness to that 'poetic prose' which she thought was her personal and distinctive mark. Its first half is poetically impalpable, since recollection is instantaneous, and results in a series of moods that do not necessarily bring a story to life, and are evocative of a stasis or at best of a backstory. It slowly flags and runs aground precisely when it should be moving forward, only surviving thanks to collateral circumstantial scenes involving minor characters. The Danbys' estate looks like all the others in Bowen's fiction, and retraces that of her ancestors; the internal time is a certain recent summer; the dense fog, slow to dissipate, and the dampness of the landscape muffle a place that is not only physically but also symbolically and psychically claustrophobic: a delimited perimeter from which seep ancient, falsely dozing backstories, and consequently frictions between the few characters who live together on the estate. This explains the virtual absence of references to contemporary history, almost as if the plot were taking place in a surreal vacuum. Not only does everything occur within the restricted parameters of what is actually a short story; the module is that of a dream-like drama which, from the outset, once again shares Chekhov's moods of worn-out extenuation, and along the way those of Shaw and Barrie and of their dramas *Heartbreak House* and *Dear Brutus*; or of the Ibsen of the *revenants* and of *When We Dead Awaken*. Within the narrative space, the psychic and even visionary presence of a deceased man acts and impends; the buried past impinges on the present, provoking symptoms of distress in the living. The start of *A World of Love* is, as I mentioned, as inspired and memorable as no other in Bowen. We see the twenty-year-old Jane who, not by coincidence, bears the name of Jane Eyre;[31] in a chest in the attic of the family's run-down estate, she finds a pack of old letters from Guy, her mother's fiancé, written before he left for the front of the Great War to die there. Bowen develops and exploits to implausible heights the ambiguous, arcane talismanic power and the romantic aura unleashed by these letters, even without transcribing any of

---

31   The chest from which the pack of letters is taken, is, on the other hand, in the classic 'attic' of an ancient residence.

their contents, the letters being undated and without an address. After this discovery, Jane drifts around dressed in an old, long Edwardian ball gown, and hides the letters under a stone.[32] It is a deceptive impression, however, that Bowen has reduced the radius of her objective by returning to this single focus of consciousness.[33] The reappearance of the letters, which are eventually burnt, reawakens her mother's trauma: on Guy's departure for the front, she had discovered that he was actually engaged to someone else. After the midpoint, a less winning series of scenes follows the reactions within the family context to the finding of this pack of letters,[34] which, in Pirandellian mode, were not addressed to any of the many women who believed they were the addressees.[35] A minor *Bildung* concerns the visionary young Jane, who chases the ghost of the dead soldier with whom she had eventually fallen in love as if he were alive. She finally falls for a man in flesh and blood.

2. At the time of publication, *The Little Girls*[36] (1964) came as a confirmation, were it still needed, of Bowen's eminently anachronistic writing. She had continued to wallow unperturbed in her private world of memories, while the new recruits to the British novel took up their positions on questions of domestic policies, changes in the social scene, and the new design of national geographies. In *The Little Girls*, as in her previous books, Bowen returns to a curious, whimsical starting point, choosing as a pivot a sophisticated imaginary invention that verges on the improbable. Instead of a pack of letters as a fulcrum, there is here a very similar treasure trove:

---

32   In the story 'The Happy Autumn Fields' there is another discovery of a box of old letters. The more memorable precedent is in George Eliot's 'Brother Jacob', with the burying of a wad of banknotes under a tree.

33   Some intermezzos are collateral and not well integrated, like that of Jane at a wealthy chatelaine's, when, after drinking too much, Jane sees Guy enter the party as the consequence of a hallucination.

34   Cf. the highly informative and balanced information on this novel in IZZO, vol. II, 766–7.

35   The universe of this novel, it has often been noted, is formed almost entirely of women.

36   Among the many parodies, one targets, almost a century later, the celebrated educational novel *Little Women* by Louisa May Alcott.

one that three eleven-year-old girls, pupils at an imaginary school in Kent, filled with knick-knacks and also, each of them, an object kept secret, and then buried it in the school garden in 1912, to 'leave a sign for posterity' (hence a veiled, amusing, tongue-in-cheek apocalypticism on the eve of a devastating war). These girls, having become mature women some fifty years later, meet to dig up their treasure chest, only to find it mysteriously empty. The temporal construction, too, is taken from a previous novel, *The House in Paris*, with a tripartite form of a present from which the action goes back to the past only to return to the present again. Thus Bowen's nostalgic fondness for a sequence of separate yet united moments is revealed – united because it is a chance association, an act of unconscious repetition, that reawakens in the three women the desire to bring the buried treasure to light. But it would be erroneous to define the novel as being purely and empathetically nostalgic. Indeed, after such a lyrical and rhapsodic novel as *A World of Love*, Bowen seems to have modestly withdrawn, and offsets it with a dry, objective and detached one. There is no lack of the usual descriptive interludes, but nature is not now foggy and misty and an objective correlative of the nebulous psychologies of Bowen's Irish novels; and the action is now wholly set in southern Kent. This new objectivity is realized through a prevalently dialogic form – a crackling dialogue, thick with unexplained allusions, where spare or absent captions act as a guarantee against any sentimentalism. *The Little Girls* has precisely that façade and flavour of the early and late Henry Green, and the school setting, in itself so recurrent, echoes in particular that of Green's *Concluding*. Both novels hinge on a daydream and on the fruit of a humorous caprice, that is, the mischief and pranks of three smartly terrible young girls, and eventually of three almost elderly women. Both are filled with a wealth of crazy goings-on of an old-fashioned flavour. This vein is enjoyable provided it is not over-exploited; most of all, the peak is reached too soon, and the reader's interest wanes and the novel drags to a stalling close. *Eva Trout* (1968) is a semi-fantasy work marked by improbability and paradoxes in which Bowen, always stubbornly clinging to her narrative model, timidly shows her willingness to update and modernize. It is still a static and concentric novel, but, as in a kind of metamorphosis, the poles and peaks of the plot are now Britain, Europe and America, reached by frenetic air journeys. A novel still calligraphic and miniaturized is transformed along the way into one richer in lively descriptions and a smaller number of purple cameos. Especially notable is the distancing of the author's *alter ego*, now masked if not actually unrecognizable in the totally new creature of an Eva, again an orphan, but now awaiting an imminent, fabulous inheritance. In the first of the two parts we learn of her difficult childhood in a repressive all-girls school, her strongly felt friendships (even homosexual, as she was eyed up by a woman teacher), the loss of her mother, dead in incredible circumstances, and of a well-to-do father. When the novel opens she is living with that former teacher and the teacher's husband in southern England. At just twenty-five she is a 'natural' woman, a little odd and eccentric, rather neurotic; she runs around in a Jaguar and an ocelot fur, escapes to a villa on the Channel coast and then to America to adopt a deaf and dumb baby. One minor feminist decision is this untypical woman's skipping the conventions of marriage and also of maternity. Attempts to integrate her into life are all in vain. Her adopted son Jeremy one day believes that a pistol is a toy and inadvertently kills her. The tragedy occurs on the last page – to tell the truth in the last lines of the novel, a fact not only unannounced and unprepared, not only summarily described, but also uncommented. The curtain falls inexorably, as rapidly as an axe. The general tone is not gloomy or tragic, however, but humorous and veiledly satirical; a metafictional mannerism is the insertion of letters, some of them even lengthy, and almost all virtuoso exercises in style; one, though completely irrelevant, is from an American professor of a non-existent American university, who took a shine to the beautiful Eva on an airplane.

§ 41. *Green* I: Idiosyncrasies of an auxiliary modernist*
Henry Green (1905–1973), the pseudonym of Henry Vincent Yorke, is two- and three-faced, as we can infer from an empirical reading of his

---

*   Green's novels were first published by Dent (*Blindness*) and the Hogarth Press (the others). *Surviving: The Uncollected Writings of Henry Green*, London 1992, is a posthumous collection of minor writings, interviews, and short stories. G. Melchiori, 'L'arte astratta di Henry Green' (1952), in MEF, 243–70 (see below, § 41.5); E. Stokes, *The Novels of Henry Green*, London 1959 (a non-sequential reading, formalistic before

novels, which are of a visibly dissimilar type, and constitute the denial of
the cyclical novel, so fashionable among other contemporaries, such as
Dorothy Richardson and Powell. The three genres of Green's nine books
are, in chronological order, the realist or neo-realist one; the modernist
and even postmodern one with touches of camp; the fantastic, but with
marked propensities towards the surreal and the burlesque. Green passes
from one to the other with a chameleon-like facility for transformation.
A slightly residual cyclicism can only be traced in the rhythm with which
these genres are re-presented: his work can be subdivided into couplets and
triplets of novels, not always, in fact almost never, consecutive. While each
of them seems the brainchild of a different writer from its predecessors,
they do show a moderate reciprocal affinity. Only *Living* is a standalone
novel, though it may be linked to *Caught* and to *Back*; those that do not
fit are the first, a *sui generis* coming-of-age novel which owes something
to Maugham, George Moore and Galsworthy, and his autobiography *Pack
My Bag*. In terms of actual influences, and other experiences of writing that
lie behind or close to him, Green is a Thirties writer belonging in spirit to
Auden's group, but also to Orwell, Compton-Burnett and Firbank, naturally brought up to date. Hence the nervous discontinuity of his novels;
except for the first and last two, their sole relationship is that they are all
novels about the Second World War. Green's oeuvre is deeply marked by

---

its time, with charts of character types, tabulations of the narrative functions, the
treatment of time, the diegetic symmetries, and statistics of stylistic occurrences);
J. D. Russell, *Henry Green: Nine Novels and an Unpacked Bag*, New Brunswick, NJ
1960; A. K. Weatherhead, *A Reading of Henry Green*, Seattle, WA 1961 (with an existentialist bias); R. S. Ryf, *Henry Green*, New York 1967; B. Bassoff, *Toward Loving:
The Poetics of the Novel and the Practice of Henry Green*, Columbia, SC 1975; K. C.
Odom, *Henry Green*, Boston, MA 1978; R. Mengham, *The Idiom of the Time: The
Writings of Henry Green*, Cambridge 1982; M. North, *Henry Green and the Writing
of His Generation*, Charlottesville, VA 1984; M. Stella, 'La scrittura di Henry Green:
dalla cecità dello scrittore all'ipoacusia del lettore', in *La Performance del testo*, ed. F.
Marucci and A. Bruttini, Siena 1984, 253–59; O. Holmesland, *A Critical Introduction
to H. Green's Novels: The Living Vision*, London 1985; R. Bonadei, 'Prologhi ed
epiloghi modernisti nella narrativa di H. Green', in CMM, 531–43; J. Treglown,
Romancing: The Life and Work of Henry Green, London 2000.

this experience. He depicts systematically psychic devastation, the ruining of the affective life, the trauma of the shell-shocked; even his last two novels were influenced by its aftermath. In his own way, and in a more reduced span, he is a historian of Britain, of the splitting up of the nation between rich and poor, without any possibility of union and collaboration; also of the crisis provoked by the Great Depression, and the threat and first rumblings of the second world conflict.

2. *Pack My Bag* (1940) traces Green's story from his infant years spent at home and later at primary and grammar schools, up to his stint at Oxford University, closing in 1929 with his first novel being accepted, and the decision to leave his studies out of sheer intolerance, and to become a worker and later a manager at his father's factory. What is strange about this autobiography is that it was the work of a thirty-five-year-old. Its justification is that Green felt, at times anxiously, at times less so, the sense of an incumbent end, that same one which he was describing in a totally imaginary and visionary way in the contemporary novel *Party Going*. The whole of *Pack My Bag*, and in particular its first quarter, constitutes not an instrumental text and a source of pure documentation, but an essay of intimate existentialist writing that has few parallels in England at the time. It is no coincidence that it recalls the work of Katherine Mansfield. It forms part of an inflational genre in literature – the autobiography – and yet we breathe a sense of a memorial flow that is not designed and tailored deliberately for a reader: a monologue dictated to himself, without the smallest signs of its public destination. Nipping in the bud every impulse to spew forth caricatures, destructive humour, every successful sketch and every authorial pandering, it has little that is English about it and much that looks at European models of autobiographical writing. It is a clinical report of infantile alienation that can even be compared to Kafka's diaries. The first pages are written by a writer who identifies with himself as the child who lived sullenly shut up within the family, and looked at the spectacles around him with that hallucination that alters hierarchies, letting himself be struck by the insignificant detail and losing sight of the macroscopic ones. This is a morbid, sick, even feminine mimesis. A similar mimetic re-creation, full of surprises, odours, sensations, makes of Green in this book the one and only English Proust, to evoke another

name.[1] Mimesis also means reduction of punctuation marks, anacolutha, swings in logic, sudden digressions, suspensions, even ungrammatical sentences. It means that the writing – and here is its supreme literary quality – has the air, but only the air, of not being addressed to anyone, but of addressing the writer himself. It has therefore the art of the artless. The voice tends to an idiolect. From a young age, Green was introverted in every environment; too lonely, he had ardently longed to go to school, but at school had immediately craved that solitude from which he had wished to escape: he was always, and always defined himself as, a 'prisoner' of solitude. In *Pack My Bag*, the 75 pupils are 'escaped prisoners', an oxymoron. The two chapters on home and school describe brief careers of disaffection, restlessness, incomprehension, or more precisely, inadaptability. The undeclared rebel felt the headmaster to be a tyrant, an expressly 'fascist' tyrant. Green's school experiences continued to resonate inside him, without any interpersonal relationships or rapport leaving a mark. The most solitary pastime was for him fishing, followed by riding and hunting, two occupations and passions about which little new could be said yet which instead receive oblique and startling observations, as well as seldom found technical disquisitions. As I mentioned, the opening of *Pack My Bag* is memorable; however, gradually the narrative becomes more predictable, in fact packed with episodes of derring-do, bravura, camaraderie, sport, but also occasional larger-than-life characters and sketches which, for instance, are not so different from those found in the first chapter of Powell's first novel of *A Dance*. Remembering Oxford, Green, who was part of that same 'brilliant' youth with its whimsical and neo-aesthetic tastes as described by Waugh, tells us how he arrived at the decision to leave university and go to work in a factory: he felt ashamed when speaking to a worker; he had discovered his privileges because he enjoyed benefits that others, combatants in war, had obtained for him. That sudden *trahison*, that defection from the circles of Oxfordian intelligentsia, also implied that his language needed to get closer to reality. At the end, anecdotes, jokes, wisecracks, and little stories that seek to avoid

---

1   As it appeared to MEF, 255, too.

the 'deadening effect print has' are recounted in popular dialect. The unexplained reason why Green closed *Pack My Bag* in 1929 is perhaps the fact that by this date the curtain had fallen on the ephemeral interlude of a juvenile Eden. Auden, too, had written an intense poem on the temporal demarcation represented by this date for an entire generation. In Green, each single mnemonic flash is interrupted by the reminder of the moment in which he is writing, and by a real death knell, with the counterpoint of 'what stretches at our feet now forever unredeemed'. Green first got to know the Great War as a boy, when his family's country residence was transformed into a hospital where, he noted with sarcasm, the wounded were treated only to be sent back to the carnage. Ideologically, and in its public value, *Pack My Bag* is a strenuously pacifist document. Green begins by taking pains to counterbalance, even to mask, the narcissism of an ego-oriented writing with a diffuse collective feeling, the imminent sense of a cosmic catastrophe. The underlying aesthetic is that the threat awakens 'what is left of things remembered', and makes them become 'things to die with': that is, death, as the Romantic agnostics ultimately maintained, is more tolerable and more painless if comforted by some pleasant memories. Green recognizes that he shared a widespread mood, that of those born just after 1900. He regretted being born both late and early, exactly three years after the Boer War and nine before the First World War. He was therefore one of those deprived of an experience which was fabled to be so electrifying. These were wars in which, for the final time, one could be a hero, and at least one of them had been a just war. However, Green added that in 1940 he would be 'not too late' for a new war looming on the horizon. *Pack My Bag* begins and continues under the imminent cataclysm from which no one would escape alive. It had been some time since such an apocalyptic and terrifying threat had been heard in English literature. This diary is written in a similar end-of-the-world emergency, and, Green feels, will be a priceless document of the final witness; or rather, that was the time to deliver the memories of the old world to the few survivors after the cosmic holocaust.

3. Thus, at first blush, Green shares the identikit of those born in his year or thereabouts; then his path deviates. He was in fact a *real* defector from Eton and Oxford. Even more precocious than Waugh, Greene and

Powell, he slipped out of their wake. At those schools Green kept himself aloof, sick with melancholy, shyness, solitude and vague alienation. When his character finally settled, it was not long before his diversity again emerged. At Oxford he formed no bonds with those peers, who were destined for fame; but by the age of twenty-one he had written his first novel and had it published. The biographical turning point loomed. He gave up his studies to assist his father in managing a metalwork factory in Birmingham. Those peers and others could afford the luxury – or satisfy the imperious demand – of writing while working as publishing executives or reviewers; then they might go on to become famous and live off their royalties; others married a noblewoman, or received an inheritance. Green started writing as the son of an owner, and he could never conceal the air of a late aesthete who stood aloof from the melee by dreaming up fantasies. He was and acted as an industrialist, and he was a part-time writer in his free time, though he was highly productive. But he was not the enlightened owner who had crossed the barricade: he was not the social novelist in cahoots with the working class, like Orwell, and simply the mirror of reality. This was not the case even in his first novel, generously sympathizing with daily factory life, but transfiguring it into a sophisticated form of literariness. At the time, this double-faced identity was rare – the clandestine, nocturnal writer, who during the day[2] managed the Pontifex company producing equipment for distilleries and piping for baths. Significantly, Green would always remain a ghost-like writer. He shunned the limelight, and in his case there is no author's substantial information available on his aesthetic; nor did he provide manifestos, *artes poeticae* or other suchlike material of great significance. Bashful of popularity, he did not want to be photographed, and even when he did accept, he would turn his back to the lens, as in certain pictures by Magritte. As in the great fantasts, there is little of autobiographical in his novels, whose main characters are seldom writers.[3] Not practised by any other contemporary,

2   More exactly, according to his son, Green would write at lunchtime (Mengham 1982, vii).
3   Stokes 1959, 28.

such *cupio occultari* was strictly linked to the pseudonym he wrote under and is no affectation, as in the female writers of the nineteenth century, nor was it a necessary cover, given that the prudential reasons dictating it had ceased. In view of what has been said and owing to the genuine difficulty of finding any relevant information, it is not so odd that a complete and accurate biography was not written on Green until a quarter of a century after his death. Nor is it strange that this biography proves even more useless than we might have expected, since there was nothing in that life of that *gâté* son of a multifaceted aristocratic banker and industrialist, philologist and explorer, that we did not already know from the life of other alumni of Eton and Oxford, including the periods of unrestrained folly of the bright young things in the 1920s, brought to a close by the war.

4. However, not even this biography (by Jeremy Treglown) has solved the enigma of Green's sudden cessation of activity after 1952, and his silence until his death. The answer may be the exhaustion, from his standpoint, of all the forms and formulae of the experimental novel. Along with Huxley, Waugh, Greene, and early Powell, Green shared the minimalist and *destruens* Modernism hinging on the rejection of narrative redundancy and on the reduction of descriptive captions, hence on the consequent primacy of dialogue, thus leaving it up to the characters to reveal themselves. No single novel by Green – save for his second one, which was practically his real start – is strictly revolutionary, at least in the sense and to the extent that *Ulysses* or *Mrs Dalloway* were; and Green uses the stream of consciousness so sparingly, except in his first novel, that its adoption is almost imperceptible. It is his canon as a whole that is astonishing, since every single item exemplifies an aesthetic proposal that modifies and even reverses the previous ones; more precisely, those three moments or examples of genre, as mentioned above, reappear like an oscillating pendulum. Hence there is a fluctuation of register to be measured against the overall development. We might say he was an eccentric modernist who not only enjoyed creating virtual human universes in which his subjective idiosyncrasies are evident in the theatrical and melodramatic dialogue and the stylistic counterfeiting, but also indulged in small, whimsically playful Sterne-like eccentricities. Green's aesthetic is one of non-representation, and for him the novel is not a form of realism. In the first, premonitory novel, 'blindness is the formalization

of a doubt concerning the possibility of writing to represent, portray or imitate an outside model'.[4] The British novelists of the 1920s and 1930s rival each other in the originality of their titling, but Green surpassed them merely by the ambiguity and polyvalence of his gerundial titles. The titles of only two of his novels do not end in -ing, that is, a gerund or present participle. It has often been said that this idiosyncrasy imitates or translates an ever inconclusive movement – not a state, but motion. The wit and humour that dictated them may be caught in the *gradatio* or climax between *Loving* and *Doting*;[5] or in the distanced and reciprocal pun occurring between *Living* and *Loving*. *Back* does not end in -ing and is not a gerund or a participle: it is, however, a kind of past participle, or might be interpreted and translated as such. On the plane of internal construction, paragraphs in round brackets mark prolepsis in one case; and after the first novel the others no longer present chapter numbers, but only short narrative blocks separated by large spacings; while divisions between the parts are indicated by blank pages.

5. Over the course of his career, Green did not have an easy life either with his publishers, reviewers, scholars, or the other novelists active at the time. He was admired with reserve, because while the more open, progressive critics, favourable to experimentalism, admiringly delved into his modernistic novelties, the wing of committed Marxists asked themselves the basic question on the ultimate purpose of all of Green's experimenting. Although acknowledging certain secondary qualities in it (such as humour and comedy), they denounced its overly circumscribed readership and accused his novels of being a bourgeois entertainment for the bourgeoisie.[6] This was a criticism that went to the very heart of Green's aesthetic project: it targeted his disengagement, his distancing from the

4   Stella 1984, 256.
5   As the main character of *Doting* explains, 'love must include adoration, but if you just dote on a girl you don't necessarily go so far as to love her'.
6   Cf. KET, 175–7, for a marked expression of worried deafness. Green was attacked by Kettle, who hoped for a different novel in the future, due to his perverse wish to remain on the margins of the most serious problems of post-war British society, and for his comfortable joining of a 'minority culture'.

great transformative utopias of the world, the moral indolence of a novelist who was content with representing frivolous and empty beings without feeling excessive repugnance for them. He was contrasted with committed social novelists lacking avant-garde velleities, such as C. P. Snow, who in turn attacked Green's 'diffident', that is, socially pessimistic, and 'decadent' art.[7] To be sure, not even Graham Greene was socially and politically much committed, but he was preferred to Green as a concrete, 'virile' narrator, while Green was a mannerist.[8] This diagnosis – of a 'tightrope walker', tending to bend prose to the forms of poetry, and not the neutral descriptive kind of poetry, but the Metaphysical, Baroque and mannerist – was later developed, without derogatory ends but instead as typical of the sensibility of an epoch, by Praz and Melchiori. Frequently discussed as a benchmark, the latter's authoritative essay pointed to Green's reminiscences of T. S. Eliot, listed the borrowings, analysed Green's 'poetic' use of language and placed the novelist in the contemporary aesthetics of abstract art.

§ 42. Green II: Early experiments in the documentary and fantastic genres
Green beat in precocity many of the novelists of his times, whom he had met without exactly frequenting them at Eton and Oxford. *Blindness* (1926), which has its ardent supporters,[9] was accepted by the publisher Dent when Green was still a university student. It lies in fact on the margins of Green's main canon if not beyond, just as *Dolores* does in Compton-Burnett's. In a rare later theoretical piece – 'The English Novel of the Future' (1950) – Green attempted to argue the difficult suture of that novel with the oeuvre to come. In the story and in the metaphor of the hero who accidentally loses his sight, his intention had been to discuss both the extreme temptations of Decadent pessimistic solipsism, contrasted by the call of and re-adaptation to life, and the aesthetic and epistemological question of the impossible objectivity of the real external world. Reality is reduced to a summation of points of view, and therefore Green was also questioning the univocal nature of the work of art. *Blindness* is thus a kind of portrait

---

7 Stokes 1959, 8; and, for another slating, 66.
8 Stokes 1959, 186–7.
9 A sweeping, dense critical interpretation in Italian is that by Stella 1984.

of the budding artist, also in affective terms, and the only one of Green's novels that is predominantly autobiographical.[10] *Living* (1929), his second novel, was published when Green was only twenty-four. To confine ourselves to the 'great tradition', and with the possible but relative exception of D. H. Lawrence,[11] in order to point out its novelty we need to go back to *Hard Times* and *Mary Barton* to find a factory novel foreshadowing it.[12] It is set in what by definition is called the old off-centre English industrial area, and describes with insight and humour the daily life of the workers in a steelworks, tipping the hat to a role already venerated by the Victorians, and duly updated in a domestic situation not dissimilar to the Victorian 'hungry Forties':[13] namely, that of the 'intelligent artisan'. This figure stands out for his gifts of integrity and efficiency at work while inevitably fantasizing about better worlds, and in the cleanliness of the homes where the wives and daughters take care of the household. The only important contemporary pendant one can think of is the reportage *The Road to Wigan Pier* by Orwell, only initially fictional then gradually documentary. Orwell, however, was not interested in fictional experimentalism but aimed to highlight the example of the socialist intellectual obtaining first-hand experience, on behalf of others as well as of himself, of the wretched living conditions of mineworkers, condemning intellectuals who denounced those conditions from their ivory tower without sharing them. Green's novel is substantially about the working routine; save for the minor haggling of the unionized workers to obtain more humane working conditions and eliminate patent wrongs or injustices, all deals are made with the management with the aid of the typical, scathing proletarian presence of mind. A Gaskellian, restive dreamer of a girl flirts with two workers, and even has an aunt who is the old type of 'fallen woman', while there is no lack of the usual jokers, such as the old worker close to retirement who continually listens to the radio with rudimentary headphones. In one scene which, exceptionally, is

10   Treglown 2000, 7–9.

11   Whose influence was admitted by Green (Mengham 1982, 24).

12   Stokes 1959, 12, notes that this was in fact the first of a 'multitude' of novels of this type that followed in the 1930s.

13   The mirage is emigration to Australia, as one of the characters constantly repeats.

described rather than being dialogic, the dying owner of the firm, with no more stimuli, unexcitedly receives the visit of a prostitute, a decision which has been taken by his own wife. Green had just joined his own father in the running of the company, and Dick Dupret is Green himself playing one of Evelyn Waugh's 'brilliant' manikins in London, courting the beauties in the salons and brooding over his unrequited loves. His entrance into the world of work takes place under the dazzle of Ruskin's and Morris's gospels – that the factory should produce objects that are both beautiful and useful. Every way out for the working class seems effectually blocked as the restless dreamer, Lily Gates, wishes to flee to Canada; her endeavour fizzles out in Liverpool.[14] A kind of parallel action arises when the flirt, the self-same Lily, falls in love with a good-for-nothing, often suspended from work for poor results, instead of marrying the industrious Jim; and Dupret himself loves Hanna, who is more attracted by a soldier on leave from India. The old community wisdom tries in vain to dissuade Lily Gates. The dream of a reckless getaway is taken from the Victorians, and from Christina Rossetti in particular; however, Lily is above all reminiscent of Mary Barton, with her psychically unstable drunkard father. On the social plane, the historical moment is reflected in the reduction in manpower and working hours, imposed by a fall in demand, that is, by a crisis. While Lily's escape is under way, the ever-spare narration acquires a faster and denser pace, and the pitter-patter alternates between the scenes of the journey to Liverpool and the workers' club, where those present perplexedly wonder about the fugitive. In Liverpool, the dodgy dark streets are even haunted by the shadows of Dickensian Gothic.

2. In reality, the most significant aspect of Green's debut novel lies in the attempted foundation of a new literary language and a new concept of the novel. This experimentalism even reduces the innovative qualities, and questions the right of primogeniture, of Auden and Isherwood's *Paid on Both Sides*, which, dating from 1930, may have been inspired and stimulated

---

14   Of a proleptic value is the initial scene, in which three workers attempt to free a bird
      crushed by a window, in the first appearance in Green of birds, including pigeons and
      peacocks, often lyrically symbolic of the purity of nature threatened by mankind's
      homicidal madness.

by it rather than the reverse.[15] Green's first innovation concerns the cutting of dead moments. Tired, one might say, of long and laborious introductions, psychosomatic portraits, interlinear descriptions, Green does not eliminate them altogether, but makes them telegraphic; there was in progress in Green a systematic process of rejection of the traditional novel's very scaffoldings, more advanced and extreme than in Compton-Burnett. Indeed, this is an attempt to go forward by returning to language's primitive level, as in the suppression of verb subjects or articles.[16] Right from the first line, *Living* seems to have been written economizing on ink, since it begins with a contracted description of place: 'Bridesley, Birmingham'. The reader is disoriented, demands a guide, information, a series of coordinates.[17] Instead, facts and backstories gradually materialize from dialogue, and from this type of description, but only when inevitable. The second fact that substantiates the analogy with Auden is that *Living*, mainly consisting of dialogues, comes close to being a play or, more exactly, a string of overlapping short scenes, initially alternating between the factory and the owners' London office. The editing of the novel was indebted to cinema techniques – as Green himself admitted: 'A kind of very disconnected cinema film'[18] – and the speed with which the images follow one another is mimetic of that of life, something with which the Futurists tried to match art.

3. Less experimental in its technique and narrative language, to the extent that it seems almost traditional, is *Party Going* (1939), Green's first masterpiece. Here it is the atmosphere of a surreal and apocalyptic fantasy

15   Cf. MEF, 247–8, for a similar observation, and Stokes 1959, 200, for Green's primogeniture. Stokes is inclined to see the first stimulus of Green's linguistic experimentalism in Hopkins and in Anglo-Saxon poetry. Russell 1960, 44–9, stresses the analogies with the style of the Victorian memorialist C. M. Doughty, recalling that Green's only literary essay was written about this writer.
16   Weatherhead 1961, 33, suggests, with regard to the suppression of the definite article 'the', the realistic motivation that in the Birmingham pronunciation it became the apocope 't''. However, Mengham 1982, 17, objects that the same telegraphic style was used to describe scenes involving the middle classes.
17   Also the first person to read the novel in manuscript, Edward Garnett, felt this lack (Treglown 2000, 97).
18   Quoted in Treglown 2000, 72.

that is revolutionary. The asphyxial narrative layout, in which a meeting of acquaintances and secondary characters dialogue to while away the time, is akin to those of Firbank and also of Waugh;[19] but if that is the case, then this is a Firbank injected with livid visions bringing to mind other masters of the surreal and apocalyptic genres. In fact, at the outset, we may be induced to believe that Green, following in the wake of Woolf, and describing the walk of a thoughtful young female aristocrat through the streets of Central London, may have simply intended to portray a cross-section of middle-class holidaymakers, frivolous, licentious and superficial layabouts in perfectly uninterrupted unity of time. No stream of consciousness is used; like a bodyguard, the narrator picks up and meticulously registers what secretly passes through the mind of the various characters from the inane chatter he can hear. However, *Party Going* slowly fades into a mysterious and arcane enchantment, and rises to a metaphor of the threat of war and of the guilt that weighs upon an unredeemed society. It even verges on a visionary delirium, so potent that *Party Going* can claim the title of the most Kafkaesque, or if we wish, the most Camus-like novel[20] ever written in Britain. Because of the thick fog that has halted their train, which should be taking them to Paris and a holiday on the Riviera, the 'party' of the young rich folk are forced to stay at a hotel beside Victoria Station – in their imagination, in fact, inside its sinister 'huge vault of glass'. As frequently in Green, the roll call of characters making up this group of travellers is disorienting because of the absence of description and backstories, which are only provided incidentally. However, immediately on the novel opening, and without any sort of preamble, one preliminary still stands out, that of an elderly lady traveller who picks up a dead pigeon from the ground near the station, and secretly and lovingly washes it and keeps it wrapped in brown paper throughout the novel. This character, Miss Fellowes, is almost the only one to be uncommunicative, mute, meteoric, and then immediately struck by

19   The lady-killer Max Adey had a teddy bear as a mascot at university, like Waugh's Sebastian (§ 47.3).

20   Kafka preceded Green, but *La Peste* came later (1947). The station hotel can be compared in its visionary aspects and surreal effects with that of *Amerika*; Weatherhead 1961, 42–3, instead mentions Kafka's *The Castle* and Meursault's prison in *L'Étranger*.

an ailment which is premonitory of healing; she is indeed the only one
of the 'party' open to the dimension of the symbolic and the transcendent. The pigeon is clearly reminiscent of Coleridge's albatross, a symbol
of what is pure and airy, of what is redeemed or promises to be so, and of
sacrifice; when it is washed, it is baptized.[21] At the same time, in a series of
vivid flashes that only glimmer for a fraction of a second, and only to some
characters, Victoria Station appears a kind of bank of the Acheron, with
the train transformed into a grotesque, spectral surrogate of Charon's ferry
that is supposed to take the party to Dover and from there to France, hence
crossing the sea. The party stays at the hotel, unaware of the symbolic rite
to which it has been summoned, except for the ailing Miss Fellowes, who is
in a room struggling between life and death. The counterpoint of the frivolous, overflowing, fatuous exchange of words is a dark and dirty dampness
in which those leaving wander like 'ghosts driving through streets of the
living' – bolts or flashes that are reverberations of all the visions of London
as a 'city of the dreadful night'. At the same time, the enchanted, crazy sea
scenes of Coleridge's ballad seem to be cited to the letter. *Party Going* is then
at one in its inspiration with *Pack My Bag*; and, in fact, the station becomes
a kind of Valley of Josaphat gathering the hyperbolic and symbolic figure of
40,000 people awaiting the end and the Day of Judgement.[22] Step by step
the visionary element mounts to unprecedented heights. The hotel lobby
where the wealthy holidaymakers have taken refuge is shuttered by steel
plates, like a kind of bunker, to avoid the dense crowd outside entering; more
precisely, this hall becomes a sinister parody of Noah's ark, from which no
one can leave for fear of strangers entering. The crowd of other passengers

21   Weatherhead 1961, 52, limits himself to noting the similarity of the group of travel-
     lers to the sailors of Coleridge's ballad. Mengham 1982, 32ff., grasps this equivalence
     and discusses it at length, as well as the motif of guilt, but believes the pigeon to
     be a 'negative counterpart' of the albatross, since, in his opinion, every redemptive
     Christian scheme is rejected in the novel, and what remains in the end is a climate
     of crisis and doubt.
22   Cf. this Dantesque, and at the same time Eliotian, echo: 'I didn't know there were so
     many people in the world'. At a certain point 'a million' people are gathered outside
     the station. Other Eliotian echoes are identified in Melchiori's essay in MEF, and by
     many other subsequent critics.

begins to chorus asking for the rail traffic to start up again regularly. As this substantially jammed situation evolves, Miss Fellowes is increasingly a Christological figure who takes the cross of the unredeemed world upon herself, and whose malaise is a form of Passion.[23] Inside the hotel, the numerous travellers who are her acquaintances make her the object of gossip and suppositions, like the Roman soldiers at the foot of the Cross. The wait for the blanket of fog to lift is whiled away by the sinful pagan rites of whimsical flirting and seduction. These interludes are often spicy and vapid, like the really impressive, simultaneously Firbank- and Beardsley-inspired one of the beautiful, naïve Amabel taking a bath, every phase of which is detailed and performed in front of one of her beaus. In the claustrophobic space of the vault of glass, obscenely enticing frolics are enacted, while on the other side of the wall the death throes of the sick woman slowly proceed. Green's amazing ability is that of divisionistically passing from an allusive, priapic, voyeuristic atmosphere to another of dark and sinister scenarios, of palls of visions and hallucinations depicted in a completely different register, that of the cemetery and mortuary scenes of Thomson B. V.'s poem. Green decided not to close the Apocalypse here, and even later he would demonstrate a strange indulgent propensity for happy endings. The fog in fact miraculously clears, the trains are ready to leave again, and Miss Fellowes has recovered. However, this is a highly ironic, or sibylline happy ending.

4. *Caught* (1943) is not visionary but realistic, freely based on Green's experience during the wartime blitz, when he was a member of the Fire Brigade. The volunteer Roe, a widower, has a sensitive and imaginative son Christopher, whom he has entrusted to relatives in the country; the young boy had developed a fixation for sailing boats and suffered the trauma of being kidnapped from a toyshop. Arguably, Ian McEwan recalled this episode in one of his first novels, *The Child in Time*. In the London under the bombs the fire fighters flirt with the female cooks in the improvised barracks; and a second trauma is that of the fire fighter who discovers that he raped his own sister in his youth. The latter had been the kidnapper of Roe's son; on discovering this, the fire-fighter commits suicide. The novel

---

23   From the beginning to the end two nameless 'nannies', kinds of Marys at the foot of the Cross, wander around unidentified, without their true nature ever being fathomed.

is a *défaillance*, and in my opinion the lowest point of Green's oeuvre. With the partial exception of the tales of the fire-fighters' heroism, Green is unable, or does not wish, to be a war narrator; the numerous little scenes of barrack life following one another are insipid, weary, verveless, and the various comrades in arms are indistinguishable from one another, nor do they leap from the page in virtue of the anecdotes they feature in. This attention to the ordinary, with a tired, hackneyed dialogue that is always dragged out, may have been due to the contagion of Hemingway's novels.[24]

§ 43. *Green III: Satires, parodies and burlesques in enclosed microcosms*
In *Loving* (1945), the second of his three masterpieces, Green set himself the task of portraying the angst and storms of war contrariwise, so to speak, by setting the novel in a protected oasis that hears only muffled echoes of the war, or acknowledges it by hearsay, and thus is a 'promised land', anachronistic and superseded, and the remains of a jurisdiction and of a history that are no more. Instead of tackling war head-on, Green anaesthetizes it. The warning lies in its framework, which copies the formulae of the opening and closing of fables, and provides the estrangement: 'Once upon a day ...', and 'they were married and lived happily ever after'. In Eire – herein lies the sense of an isolation that is, shall we say, squared, since the Irish Republic was neutral during the war – in a god-forsaken mansion belonging to well-off British absentee landlords who had possessed it for centuries in a regime that was still feudal, little demonstrations and small case studies of the wielding of power follow one another, both among the ruling caste and the servants. With the total exclusion of descriptions and backstories, which survive indirectly and are provided gradually and elliptically, the dialogue-based module once again brings Compton-Burnett to mind. Burnett-like are the atmospheres and events, the various hierarchical positions of the servants, the subtle and devious interpersonal relationships, the rebellions, acts of spite, shrewd little moves, tricks, stratagems, intrigues and bouts of mischief, the large and small scenes of embarrassment and surprise (the lady owner's daughter-in-law, whose husband is at the front, is surprised in bed with a captain). The common

---

24   The father's incidental and proleptic thoughts, reflecting on his son, are enclosed in brackets, one of the few modernistic eccentricities. Only occasional paragraphs make no sense, above all due to the lack of a verb.

denominator might seem the tranquil then turbulent then again tranquil everyday life of Jane Austen's households. However, the space-time element is postdated to Ireland in an exactly contemporary historical period; and the characters' speeches, albeit grammatically correct and accurate in their lexicon, witty and scathing in their argumentations, are steeped in dialect and cockney pronunciations, unlike that impeccable English which, for instance, even the servants speak in Compton-Burnett. There is nothing from Burnett or Austen in the air of absurdity, of *divertissement*, of Mozartian or Straussian melodrama, with a whiff of the dry quip and the repartee of the illiterate manservant dating back to the Restoration playwrights, and even bringing to mind Molière, or, to Italian readers, Goldoni. The novel is also implicitly a return to Firbank. Highly formalized and totally unrealistic, the dialogues are in fact interwoven with recitatives, arias, chirrupings, duets and the concertato choruses of operatic librettos, as in *The Marriage of Figaro*, for example. Green has erected a *papier maché* world through which puppets move, puppets which, in some cases, become more flesh-and-blood characters disposed to inspire more serious reflection. The action, often stagnating into vain chatter and allusive verbal fencing, is animated by verbal skirmishes and minor domestic storms in a kind of parody of the war, the real one, which is rumbling so far away. In itself, this delightful dialogic tale rests on the career ambitions of a manservant, already 'in possession' of a completely dependent scullion, who manages to have himself promoted to butler, inheriting the arts and tactics of his recently deceased predecessor. He is to wed the smartest of the housemaids. However, this is but one of the intrigues with which this crackling multihued comedy is interwoven in its situations and skits. Some of these keep alive a sliver of suspense: the park's peacock – one of the many that are there, and counted like Yeats's swans at Coole – is slain by a young manservant, plucked, stored away in the larder and goes rotten; and the lost ring of the lady is found and given back after infinite sly manoeuvrings by the servants to keep it. This happens after an insurance inspector,[25] who lisps after having a tooth out, has alerted the whole castle, mainly because the pusillanimous servants misunderstand his firm's initials, IRA, thinking of the terrorist organization.

---

25   He is in fact the only outside character to enter among the castle's fixed entourage.

2. *Back* (1946) is a prompt reversal, and the change to the dialogic register – consistent, unspectacular, free of embellishments, of a brutally and drily functional type – is conspicuous. *Back* therefore belongs to Green's neo-realist vein. Charley Summers is a war veteran bruised in body and mind. He has a wooden leg, and at the opening of the novel he is visiting a cemetery that is the resting place of a lover, Rose, from before his departure for the front; she may have given him a son. There he meets the woman's bereaved husband, and pays a visit to her parents, giving rise to an embarrassing dialogue with his lover's elderly mother, afflicted by memory lapses, and the widower, garrulous, welcoming, kind even, due to Summers's noble proof of affection come what may. The central focus is once again the human psyche lacerated and confused by war and the affective ruin of the mutilated, sex-starved survivors. However, episodes of grotesque and surreal comedy emerge from the basic realism, resulting in estranged farce. Obsessed by his memories, Summers, assigned a menial office job, stubbornly believes that he recognizes his Rose in a prostitute, Nancy, only to end up learning that she is her stepsister.[26] The development is mostly dedicated to the survivor's clumsy attempts to unravel the mystery, including a graphology test; these attempts bring to the surface various skeletons in the cupboard for the poor and deluded man. The venerated, angelic Rose turns out to be a vulgar, undeserving woman.[27] Green leaves the possibility open that the prostitute Nancy and the beloved Rose are one and the same person, and by superimposing them he has Summers marry the former.

3. *Concluding*[28] (1948) represents another return, after a realist novel, to a surreal one. The writing appears finely chiselled, florid and 'purple' as in

26   There may be here a strident citation of Tennyson's *Maud* in Summers's delirium over Rose's name, which is that of a rose but is also the past of the verb 'to rise', which often raises in the text chains of variations on the 'name of the rose'. The psychic disablement of the two heroes, in Tennyson and Green, is almost the same, even if Tennyson's heals going to the war, while Green's falls ill on returning from it. *Maud* was the name of Green's mother. On the other hand, Summers's fixation, believing he sees Rose in Nancy, is a distant reminiscence of Collins's plot in *The Woman in White*.

27   On the effects of this bathos, cf. Treglown 2000, 187.

28   Perhaps Green's least convincing title, which seems to allude to the fact that nothing came of the investigations into the pupils who ran away from school. This title was decided at the last moment, replacing *Dying* (Mengham 1982, 187).

the protocols of aestheticism, but in a parodic and therefore Firbankian vein, thanks also to the estranging, odd, paradoxical, 'metaphysical'[29] comparisons scattered throughout. Green, who had debuted by systematically eroding captions, turns round and provides many sophisticatedly written, for example in the form of impressionistic tableaux describing the atmospheric background at various times of the day. The signs of a modernist text are more evident than ever in the classic temporal device of an action limited to twenty-four hours, or from dawn to dusk, and in the narrator's ironic attention to the friction and non-correspondence between what is said and what is thought. Green is still visibly imitating and citing Compton-Burnett, especially since the action takes place within a closed community, a girls' school where some of Compton-Burnett's novels are also set, while bringing to the fore the same secret emotional tensions and minor struggles for power.[30] Like *Loving*, which it resembles, this is a theatrical *divertissement* where anything can happen and where at any moment the rules of reality may be violated. As a result, it is also a choral and polyphonic novel, without being exactly operatic and libretto-like: a chain of solos, or duets of two at a time among the few main characters that enter the stage. Its episodes are tenuously linked in a scenario of mystery that is only nominal, and broadly one of convenience, precisely because it is expressly designed to contain those scenes. It is that of the flight of two pupils from the school, on which light is to be thrown, but without attracting undue attention for fear of phantom provisions from school authorities. The atmosphere is the illusionist one of actions that respond to a dream-like logic, or more often to one which is agreeably and playfully absurd; not by coincidence will the dance hall be adorned with freshly sawn pines whose fronds will be sprinkled with salt to make them appear snow-covered. This, then, after a long delay, is Green's first novel in which the temporal link, whether implied or given as a background in his other novels, is not apparent but rather left vague: the first novel that is genuinely atemporal, if not temporally and spatially

29   A splendid comparison is, for instance, that of the sun that cleaves through the fog 'like a woman letting down her mass of hair from a white towel in which she had bound it'.

30   Typically Burnett-like is the breakfast on which the novel opens.

disjointed.[31] It could certainly be maintained that *Concluding* imagines an age-old social model having reached the point of explosion, namely, that of the Victorian-age public school, of the girls' boarding-school in point of fact; but by 1948 this was an anachronistic attempt. Or it could be taken for a metaphor of repression in institutions or of endogenous desire; in this case it should be noted that the pupils, all at the age of puberty up to the threshold of adulthood, quiver with an ill-hidden itch, while one of them, more enterprising than the others, teases the very mature, not to say elderly, scientist, Mr Rock.[32] At the evening ball, no outsiders take part, and the girls must dance with one another without male partners. And so what does the escape of the two pupils from the boarding-school represent? A flight towards freedom and liberation, unconscious and impulsive. The internal clash, so typical of the surreal, is in fact between characters of the more classic British fictional tradition – stock ones like the couple of directors, with the overused phenomenologies of eccentricity, or like Mr Rock, the odd scientist, who lovingly ministers to his motley seraglio of pets –[33] and an outside, phantom authority often designated with the term 'the State'. We might again evoke the Kafkaesque metaphor of the metaphysical trial in the 'Grand Inquisition of a State Enquiry', with all the 'horror of Reports' that the school feels burdened with on the discovery that two pupils have escaped; or more reasonably interpret the novel as a playful condemnation of bureaucracy and formalism, or a rite of passage, and a farewell of a hypocritical and hence neurotic generation in favour of a healthier younger class. The lack of proportion between this allegorical scheme and the actual plot, despite its unreal and suggested gestures and quivers of self-liberation, remains evident, however.

31   To Melchiori it appeared to take place in a 'near future' (MEF, 241); for Mengham 1982, 181, it takes place in the year 2000.

32   The old man, during the dance in honour of the school's 'Founder', is taken down to the basement, that is, the Freudian 'cellar of the Institute', where, scandalized, he is subjected to the pupils' uninhibited attentions.

33   It is difficult to imagine in realistic terms a public school age in which Mr Rock might be living, and in particular in a small villa separate from the main building, thanks to unspecified services rendered to the nation. One of the internal disputes that keep the novel lively is the attempt of the two headmistresses to approve the transfer of the old man to an old folk's home, in order to turn the villa over to school use.

4. Green's last two novels are not by any means derivative or involutional, and they mysteriously lopped off the career of a novelist who was not yet fifty, and could have embraced a different new direction. They resemble once again others by Compton-Burnett, forming their updated counterpart, since they, too, air the dirty linen, though not that of the affluent late Victorian society, but the squalid, cynical one of half a century later. They thus share a common denominator and remind one of the theatre of the Restoration, from which they take the brilliant dialogic verve and the cold, geometric scenographic and dramatic schemes. At the same time, the reduction of events to pure routine, and the deliberate sloppiness and hastiness of the settings, accentuate the analogies with the theatre of the absurd. *Nothing* (1950), which sounds like a title by Beckett, seeks to challenge narrative conventions by abolishing authorial links or reducing them to a minimum. Its plot is based on grotesque and improbable combinations,[34] mere verbal fencing between widowers and sons of widowers in London high society. The title, as in some novels by Waugh and in early Powell, is the sole moral clue that escapes the impassive author, who counters the frivolous and scheming generation of the elderly with the more candid, fresher one of the young. No insistence strikes the malaise of a well-to-do post-war society, frivolous and bored, the same one that was about to be violently targeted by the Angries. The fathers' egoism harms their children's affections, who must break off their engagements.[35] *Doting*[36] (1952) forms a thematic diptych, and is a more pungent variation on the motif of the generational conflict in its combinations. A father falls in love with a female friend of his son's, and in a well-devised sketch, straight out of the comedy-of-errors genre, he is surprised by his wife in an amorous tryst[37] when she unexpectedly arrives home to announce that their son has

---

34   A six-year-old girl, who appears infrequently, is famous as a 'little saint', and believes to be really married to the father of her sister's future husband, in a wedding celebrated as a game.

35   Mary and Philip are probably siblings, the fruit of a youthful adventure of her father and his mother, who, as widow and widower, tie the knot at the end of the novel.

36   For this title cf. n. 5 above.

37   Arthur, the husband, is caught kneeling in front of his lover, cleaning coffee stains off her skirt, with her 'large legs' in full sight.

had an accident. In answer – or out of 'revenge' – she launches herself into an affair with a friend of her husband's, with a final adjustment dictated by lucid cynicism. The title, as I observed above, alludes to the difference between this silly senile infatuation and true love.

§ 44. *Hartley*[*]

It is fashionable nowadays to discredit certain mid-twentieth-century writers who were avowedly traditionalist, nostalgic, enemies of experimentation, reticent and slightly bloodless,[1] and therefore to target them with satire and even dismissive ridicule, using the same yardstick and accusations with which the Edwardians of the early twentieth century had treated their grandparents.[2] Such is the exemplary case of Leslie Poles Hartley (1895–1972), who struck and even enchanted,[3] at least in some of his pages, illustrious contemporary critics such as Lord David Cecil. There is a touch of the feminine, of the diaphanous, of the enervated and slothful, not only in the boys and men who are his usual main characters, but in the very empathy used to portray them. There is a lack of vigour, of any imperious sense of drama and tragedy; everything is watered down and elegantly, even too elegantly, rearranged; the furious fire of passion never rages, only spent ashes flit forth. Hartley is a narrator of exquisitely feminine sensibility, and one wonders, at first glance, whether his name may be one of the many pseudonyms chosen by prim elderly ladies who, at this late stage, did not wish to reveal their true identity. We deduce that he is a narrator of sensations and moods from a very simple fact: his plots can be summed up in a few lines, and are elementary; they start from the preparation of a fact that eventually

---

[*]	P. Bloomfield, *L. P. Hartley*, London 1962 and 1970; P. Bien, *L. P. Hartley*, London 1963; A. Mulkeen, *Wild Thyme, Winter Lightning: The Symbolic Novels of L. P. Hartley*, London 1974; E. T. Jones, *L. P. Hartley*, Boston, MA 1978; G. Pissarello, *L'esorcizzazione del male: 'The Go-Between' di L. P. Hartley*, Pisa 1984; A. Wright, *Foreign Country: The Life of L. P. Hartley*, London 1996.

1	This belatedness was accentuated by his debut at a good fifty years old; and Hartley formed part of that group of writers whom Praz called 'seròtini' ['late-flowering'].
2	Cf. S. Manferlotti in MAR, 627–8.
3	Cf. for example Bloomfield 1970, 14.

takes place with all the ensuing consequences; but the tragic outcome is only vaguely alluded to, not seen or described directly, owing to a sort of blinding or psychophysical collapse of the witness. The distance between the writer and his *alter egos* was vainly camouflaged for a long time. From a good family, a student of Oxford, a graduate in history, a friend of Huxley and frequenter of the renowned salon of Lady Ottoline Morrell, Hartley was conscripted during the First World War without reaching the front; never married, he held various positions in the world of publishing and spent a great deal of his life in Venice suffering from a nervous complaint.

2. Hartley's minor art, made up of finesse, delicacy, incision and fine design, was put to use in two recurring themes. The school he belongs to is very easy to define, that of the elegiac singers of the lost innocence of childhood and of the still calm of late Victorian and Edwardian times. The British novel of the mid-twentieth century revolves around the main character of a young, degenerate, often eroticized when not erotomaniac university student, politically committed or indifferent. Like Bowen and Mansfield, Hartley returns instead to an interest for infants, young children and adolescents, and immerses himself in their dreaming, introverted psychology. The other theme is the benevolently satirical observation of class differences.[4] The Hilda and Eustace trilogy, the transfiguration of an autobiographical relationship of the novelist with an authoritarian sister, was launched in 1944 with *The Shrimp and the Anemone*, set in a bathing resort on the eastern English coast at the end of the century. Eustace is a Hartleyan baby boy, hence dreamy and indolent, but also suffering from forms of submission and control, both psychological and religious, from which he wishes to escape, both symbolically and physically; but he is overwhelmed by a sense of guilt and the need for expiation. Hartley's children always love older women, yearning for the role of a *preux chevalier*; they are also subtly and unconsciously panderers, favouring meetings of the wrong people, therefore provoking tragic misunderstandings. *The Shrimp and the Anemone* opens abruptly with an uncommon, dream-like scene: a marine anemone seizes a shrimp and swallows it; the dilemma of the child on the

---

4   In *The Hireling* (1957) a rich widow venerates the memory of her husband by going
     to visit historic cathedrals and becoming familiar with her driver.

beach, who spies this scene in the shallows, is whether to defend the shrimp and free it, or to consider the anemone's hunger; and the swallowed shrimp is a symbol of himself, in the first of the mnemic cells destined to reappear, reoriented. The intervention of his sister results in the death of both molluscs. This is the prolepsis of the plot of the entire novel, and at the same time a representational evocation of those symbols of sexual non-differentiation, in fact of the almost Siamese indissolubility of siblings, found in the Brontës' 'sagas' ('I am Heathcliff', and the love-hate between Katherine and Hindley), and in the epilogue of George Eliot's *The Mill on the Floss*, with its funerary epigraph, 'In death they were not divided'.[5] But, compared to this novel, the roles are reversed: in Hartley, the Puritan is the elder sister, and the one seeking to free himself is the younger brother, though Hilda is really a Maggie Tulliver in the end, when she is seduced, abandoned and left suffering. At the same time, the boy's reveries on the sea in Norfolk mirror the beginning and the development of Woolf's *Jacob's Room*, with the additions of its sordid rivalries, its repressed world, sibling jealousies, the clash between the actual and the yearning to escape from it. The reconstruction of the childhood world is almost enchanting in the beginning of *The Shrimp and the Anemone*, and perhaps constitutes the most inspired moment in all of Hartley's fiction. In a subsequent scene, full of echoes from the Victorian tradition, a paralysed old lady roams about in a wheelchair, without the reader knowing that this is a foreshadowing of the end of Hilda, and that, for a second time, Eustace will have to push a paralysed woman around and take care of her, namely, his own sister. Something of a Dickensian fable springs from this scene, as the old lady invites her grotesque knight, Eustace, to take tea with her, and because of his kindness leaves him an inheritance that will allow him to attend university. The struggle against the oppressive world of grown-ups is vented in an escape that Eustace organizes with a female friend who is as indomitable as he is. From this moment on, instead of becoming, or remaining, impressionistic, and moving on to new peaks, *The Shrimp*

---

5   The reversal and complication of the morbid relationship between the siblings in George Eliot's novel *The Mill on the Floss*, which is rarely recalled by critics, are made explicit in chapter IX of the second novel of the trilogy, *The Sixth Heaven*. Citations from lyric poems by Emily Brontë are also everywhere in Hartley, and denote a profound knowledge of and esteem for this writer, who was another expert in childhood worlds.

and the Anemone slows down and loses momentum, also owing to a lack of scene shifting and an overly rigid temporal unity. This will be Hartley's typical manner, too tidy, too diligent, too scholastic and exhaustive, and in the long run wearing, in the ensuing novels. In *The Sixth Heaven* (1946), from an infantile and almost prenatal undividedness we pass to temporary separation. The lethargic Eustace spends the time of *Eustace and Hilda* (1947) almost wholly in Venice. By now, the cycle has slowly lapsed into normality never to rise again, in spite of Hartley's high linguistic competence in Italian, although it is used for a long chattering of local colour, until Eustace is compelled to run back to his sister to be her saviour. He is obliged by his moral code to expiate for having encouraged a disastrous, and psychically destructive, meeting between her and a seducer.

3. *The Go-Between* (1953), Hartley's only international success, and his only consistently lasting work thanks also to the success of a fortunate and much-admired film version, encloses various distinguishing marks of *déjà vu*, as has often been noted. It is part of the 'loss of innocence' novelistic archetype, and at first sight recalls Bowen, and further back Henry James's *What Maisie Knew*.[6] But it is also possible, indeed essential, to trace in it a more veiled and sweetened re-visitation of the prohibited erotic passion – not adulterous, but premarital – of a Lawrencian aristocratic woman for a farmer. This scandal, this infraction of etiquette and of class morals, is in fact situated in a time that is contiguous with the internal one of *Lady Chatterley's Lover*. It is therefore superfluous to note that the action of the novel is almost entirely contained in the setting of a rural English residence. These institutional places all resembled one another from the eighteenth century onwards, and constituted a chronotope that had been inaugurated by Fielding. The temporal category in *The Go-Between* is misleading, however: time stopped, stagnated and did not exist; the family meals, pastimes, readings, hobbies like croquet and cricket, the balls, with the counterpart of servants and tenant farmers, repeated themselves as if in an atemporal ritual. On the Brandham estate, all of this takes place with the clock hands

---

6   Hartley's first novel, *Simonetta Perkins* (1925), features a girl who, like James's American debutantes, descends upon Europe, and Italy, and becomes 'contaminated'; more precisely, the girl has an imaginary adventure with a gondolier under the false name given in the title.

imperceptibly moved forward. Consequently, *The Go-Between* is a novel that reanimates a small wax museum – more precisely, it is a gesture of loving nostalgia, albeit divided and ambiguous. The poles of the memorial excursion are exactly half a century apart: a mature man, Leo, re-opens and rereads his diary and relives the memory of a fortnight's holiday spent on the estate of a school friend's parents when he was twelve;[7] there he was at the time an unknowing messenger of love between his friend's sister, Marian, and a farmer with whom she had secret trysts. Found out, the girl had been forced to marry her fiancé, a viscount and therefore a member of her own class; however, she gave birth to the fruit of her sin; soon after the farmer committed suicide. At sixty, Leo reveals this scandal to the grandson of the couple of sinners. In itself, this melodramatic plot might evoke Fowles's *The French Lieutenant's Woman* (but postdated to Edwardian times; in reality, the year of the story is 1900, therefore still Victorian by a hair's breath), also and above all because of the swinging back and forth between past and present. Hartley recreates a *fin-de-siècle* awareness of vicinity to a series of anxiously awaited crossroads, subsequently opening onto a season of bitterness and disappointments, which were to bear the scars of two dehumanizing, catastrophic wars that changed creation out of all recognition.[8] It might then have been better for Hartley to stay on this side of these crossroads, in the psychically unaware protection of the nineteenth century. The crossroads *par excellence* is that of puberty, and the first golden world is that of the British public school era. The prologue presents a still intact, pristine school world, even enlivened by a healthy bawdy spirit, described without either biting satire (for instance against headmasters) or sexual and homosexual reticence. The boys wanted first and foremost to joke, perform

---

7   On the precision of the internal calendar, which recalls that of *Wuthering Heights*, cf. Pissarello 1984, 10 and n. 7.

8   In 1953, Marian surprised readers with this explicit bitter remark: 'this hideous century we live in, which has denatured humanity and planted death and hate where love and living were'. She maliciously gifts Leo a bicycle, green of course, for his thirteenth birthday, so that his services as a 'postman' will be quicker; but at the end of the novel, in reminiscing mood, she announces that she had been Ted's lover but 'not in the vulgar sense': 'Our love was a beautiful thing', an experience of total and mutual dedication.

tricks, and play at possessing power. They lived in a kind of enchanted, and therefore separate, self-enclosed world. Hence the interest in magic and astrology which turns Leo into a junior wizard who believes he can hex his schoolmates. With these powers he brags of, he manages to overcome his inferiority complex, which is also one of ignorance, stupefaction and awkwardness. The temporal crossroad of 1900 therefore lies between the world of myth and magic and reality itself, and Leo's holiday at Brandham Court terminates at the crucial point, even if he is late in discovering his own rite of passage. This watershed between innocence and experience was legendarily mobile, and every British nostalgic or apocalyptic fixed it as he or she wished; just before 1900, in his *Idylls*, Tennyson too regretted the decline of the chivalrous code. On the Brandham estate, Leo senses that reality is knocking at the door but in the form of magic and enchantment. He becomes a kind of chivalrous Robin Hood for Marian, his friend's sister, paying her exquisite, indeed, gallant attentions; but while he is acting unconsciously in the reign of myth, a myth of chivalry and courtly love, Marian and the farmer Ted belong to the order of residual romantic love, if not that of carnal passion. Leo is jokingly but repeatedly called Mercury, the messenger of the gods: and also, with a pun, the 'god between', that is, the minor god who stands midway between the real deities to whom he must deliver their love letters. The abrupt leap into reality is also symbolized by the scar of a wound which Hugh, Marian's betrothed, received during the Anglo-Boer War, a scar which was to have a much deeper effect fifteen years later, even if this Boer war, unbeknown to the people then, is almost a game of pretend compared to the Great War. Leo's platonic passion for Marian,[9] who is no cynical opportunist but repays him with delicate promiscuity, is evinced in exquisite gestures: at the river he offers her his bathing-suit to dry her hair, and she accompanies him to buy a green Robin-Hood-style outfit in town.[10] A rudimentary, almost anthropomorphic thermometer

9   Marian is also a zodiacal Virgo, with a symbolism that appears bloated (as, for example, in Leo who is a Leo).

10   The dialogue is irresistibly malicious in stretches, but stale effects of reiterated comedy are obtained from the near homophony between the name 'Hugh' and the pronoun 'you', a misunderstanding that recurs right up to the final page, that of the meeting

records higher and higher summer temperatures, cleverly measuring the platonic passion that is soaring. Leo's crossroads therefore also lies between chivalrous devotion and sexual awakening. In other terms, he is not sexually aware, and he wishes to learn, from Ted in particular whose muscular body he has espied after a swim, how it is that foals are born out of the horses' 'spooning'.[11] The explanation is not given to him until he obtains it for real, as a witness of a flagrant congress that causes in him a symbolic blinding and a loss of memory. As I hinted, Ted is a less bitter and less protesting version of Lawrence's Mellors; as a fiancée, rather than a married woman, Marian rejects the cold, well-mannered and limp love of a second war-wounded veteran like Clifford Chatterley (Hugh, with his scar), and experiences challenging uninhibited sex with a partner representing nature and the primacy of the body and the pleasure of the senses. But in Hartley all of this remains shyly hinted at, outlined, merely alluded to.[12]

4. Until 1953 Hartley was then a narrator of coordinated novels, as he had debuted straight away, or almost, with a trilogy followed by a standalone novel, though thematically similar. This thematic continuity ended in numerous later, sometimes even contemporary novels, which accepted much more disparate and haphazard promptings, even including even science and horror fiction. With the curtain down on the world of childhood, Hartley fumbled around in a vain search for another theme to identify with. *The Boat* (1949), lengthy and rather disconcerting, takes place in a village where a dreamer wants to launch a boat into the waters of a river against the advice of local fishermen. In *My Fellow Devils* (1951) he attempted a Greene-style Catholic novel, but without the latter's conviction and efficacy, featuring a woman who marries a Catholic who turns out to be a good-for-nothing, after abandoning everything for love of him. In 1960 came the dystopian, Golding-like *Facial*

---

between Leo and Marian as a mature man and woman. One example of this semi-serious humour is the quip that Ted 'has a woman' only once a week, but that this is the cleaning lady, not a lover as Leo secretly suspects.

11   Bloomfield 1970, 17, already at that date deemed the term antiquated.

12   In Joseph Losey's film (1971), based on the novel, Ted's role is assigned to Alan Bates, who, with his podgy, hirsute and bearded physique, was often chosen by film directors to play the role of the virile, muscular, and effortlessly erotic farmer, as for example in Polanski's *Far From the Madding Crowd*.

Justice, which imagines a post-atomic England in which Jael, who like all other women has undergone a 'diminution' of her beauty, rebels at the mere sight of Ely Cathedral. This sense of the worsening and inevitable regression of history and civilization is, of course, indebted to Orwell.

§ 45. *Waugh** *I: Farces of an unredeemed world*

Published before 1930, *Decline and Fall* and *Vile Bodies*, the first two novels by Evelyn Arthur Waugh (1903–1966),[1] were hailed in England with unanimous favour and a sense of expectancy, if not with the satisfaction accompanying the appearance of an unsurpassed achievement. After various

---

*   *Diaries*, ed. M. Davie, London 1976; *Letters*, ed. M. Amory, London 1980; first volume of the autobiography, hence incomplete, *A Little Learning*, London 1964.

Life. C. Sykes, *Evelyn Waugh*, London 1975 and Harmondsworth 1985; M. Stannard, *Evelyn Waugh: The Early Years 1903–1939*, London 1986, and *Evelyn Waugh: No Abiding City 1939–1966*, London 1992; H. Carpenter, *The Brideshead Generation: Evelyn Waugh and his Friends*, London 1989; S. Hastings, *Evelyn Waugh: A Biography*, London 1994; J. H. Wilson, *Evelyn Waugh: A Literary Biography 1903–1924* and *1924–1966*, Madison, WI 1996 and 2001; D. L. Patey, *The Life of Evelyn Waugh: A Critical Biography*, Oxford 1998; D. Wykes, *Evelyn Waugh: A Literary Life*, Basingstoke 1999; P. Eade, *Evelyn Waugh: A Biography*, London 2015.

Criticism. C. Hollis, *Evelyn Waugh*, London 1954 and 1971; A. A. De Vitis, *Roman Holiday: The Catholic Novels of Evelyn Waugh*, London 1958; F. J. Stopp, *Evelyn Waugh: Portrait of an Artist*, London 1958; M. Bradbury, *Evelyn Waugh*, Edinburgh and London 1964; S. Greenblatt, 'Waugh', in *Waugh, Orwell, and Huxley*, New Haven, CT 1965; J. F. Carens, *The Satiric Art of Evelyn Waugh*, Seattle, WA 1966; L. Del Zanna, 'Fede e tradizione nella satira amara di Evelyn Waugh', *LET*, XXI (1966), 739–60; D. Lodge, *Evelyn Waugh*, New York and London 1971; R. M. Davis, *Evelyn Waugh: Writer*, Oklahoma 1981; C. W. Lane, *Evelyn Waugh*, New York 1981; J. M. Heath, *The Picturesque Prison: Evelyn Waugh and His Writing*, Montreal 1982; I. Littlewood, *The Writings of Evelyn Waugh*, Oxford 1983; M. Morriss and D. J. Dooley, *Evelyn Waugh: A Reference Guide*, Boston, MA 1984; CRHE, ed. M. Stannard, London and Boston, MA 1984; G. McCartney, *Confused Roaring: Evelyn Waugh and the Modernist Tradition*, Bloomington, IN 1987; F. L. Beaty, *The Ironic World of Evelyn Waugh: A Study of Eight Novels*, DeKalb 1992; *Evelyn Waugh: New Directions*, ed. A. Blayac, Houndmills 1992.

1   His Christian name Evelyn can be unisex in English, and it is a curious fact that the writer's first wife was also called Evelyn (Gardner). The writer was called 'Miss Waugh' in the reviews of his first book, a monograph on Rossetti.

decades of decline, they marked the resurgence of the British comical and humorous tradition in its most sophisticated and modernized version, without the stylistic intemperance and the authorial interferences typical of most eighteenth- and nineteenth-century fiction. Waugh was therefore appreciated and even extolled because there was less distance between him and Fielding than between him and Joyce, and also because he was a non-experimental anti-modernist in both his forms and genres, even if his subdued ideological scenario remained T. S. Eliot's decay of the west. Contemporary reviewers praised to the stars the revival of the comical and the funny, of pure entertainment, 'savage satire', extravagance and fantasy. This light, playful vein for a long time induced Leavis's *Scrutiny* group to leapfrog every mention of the writer and to turn a deaf ear to him. However, humour is not ideological, and as a result Waugh soon managed to get everyone to agree on the basis of this distinguishing feature. As a writer Waugh was in fact almost self-made and instinctive; with few masters, he belonged to a sound autochthonous genealogy. Having left Oxford without taking a degree, he originally wanted to be a painter, a decorator, an illuminator, an architect, in short a visual artist. The aristocratic family of his first wife did not like their daughter marrying a 'cabinetmaker', if we are to believe his version; as a consequence, Waugh began to write gathering disparate cues from Carroll, Firbank, Hemingway, Compton-Burnett, and Henry Green. His first two novels, mentioned above, paved the way to a career that is not easy to summarize and seemingly offers no sure leitmotifs, fazing anyone who seeks coherence. Each new novel by Waugh, like those of Green, varies and revolutionizes the previous one, despite the fact that Waugh's is a circular and vaguely cyclical world, in which the same characters reappear in turn – a Basil Seal, a Guy Crouchback – with the same secondary characters (and in this he differs from Green).

2. We might then suppose, as a constant, that Waugh almost never opened the modernists, while he scoured the Victorian satirical novelists, Dickens and Thackeray, until he almost knew them off by heart.[2] He imitates their organization and adopts their centres of gravity. This Victorian

---

2   Sykes 1985, 332. Dickens was the author associated by definition with the publisher Chapman and Hall, of which Waugh's father, a critic, poet and man of letters, had

inheritance was, however, actually limited to the sketch, the short story or novel, with repudiation of the long form and of its deliberately sweeping architecture. Waugh's novels are, with one exception, slight, short, singularly lacking in any purple sections of atmospheric setting. One does wonder whether Waugh ever gave a description of nature as a prelude to a chapter. His plots are split into short and very short scenes and even circumscribed and self-standing splinters, often having minimal mutual links. The dialogue too is of the kind preferred in his time, of monosyllables or single lines. Waugh's early subgenre is that of the 'public school age' novel, always a trump card. It varies the Victorian module, however, by premeditatedly catapulting the main characters into a series of surreal burlesque vicissitudes. Until 1945 and *Brideshead Revisited*, Waugh took two steps along the tracks of playful realism, but the third derails towards the fantastic. His characters were found to be mad and absurd marionettes in a performance of which he was the puppet master; his detractors criticized him for his utter lack of love for them, and for scrutinizing them like a disgusted anthropologist. They pinned a label of *enfant terrible* on him for his cold and destructive satire devoid of tenderness. The radius of observation, focused on the aristocracy of the upper class London neighbourhoods, brings Huxley into play. With respect to Huxley, the Huxley of *Antic Hay*, Waugh was a late starter, by five years or so; but his first two novels, above all the second, show clear signs of emulation. Like Huxley, Waugh likes describing parties and evenings out at nightclubs, and gatherings of people whose every possible idiosyncrasy he studies. The affectation that manifestly unites the two writers is the titling of their novels by using literary quotations; yet, as I shall explain, the intention is different. However, Waugh seems to have immediately realized that Huxley's vision did not completely tally with his own. Waugh is not tempted by the novel of ideas; nor do we find in his novels the guru or know-it-all holding court. The relevant point of contact with Huxley is the stereophonic, counterpoint plan, or that of the circle of young characters who vainly meander around seeking authenticity, but remain unredeemed. This unifying pattern is merely added to, hinted at,

---

become director in 1902. It is no coincidence that Tony Last, at the end of *A Handful of Dust* (§ 46.4), must interminably read Dickens's novels to Mr Todd.

and is also and above all double-edged. Waugh forbids himself from entering the fray in the first person, and the few times he does so it is difficult to understand exactly what his position is. His messages are paradoxically limited to the titles of his novels, titles that are at times inapplicable to the content, save for remote associations; his plots ironically and allusively concern people named Adam or dreamers called Last. This conceptual planning is to be interpreted in detail or even by a sort of counter-demonstration. Waugh always remains noncommittal, and lets himself be overwhelmed by the purely comical situations he himself has invented. Waugh, or at least pre-1945 Waugh, was rightly regarded a comically immoral writer, or one uninterested in morals:[3] a writer who tends to inflate the crazy anarchy of the world, and a chaos irreducible to any order.

3. After 1930, Waugh began to be judged as less agreeable, became more controversial, and his esteem started to vacillate. From his African journeys came not merely acclaimed books and documentaries, but at least two novels that reverse and mock *Heart of Darkness* by presenting colonialism in a rather more cynical and realistic way, not only as a conflict of the great powers aimed towards the exploitation of internal resources – and this is pure Conrad – but also dispelling every arcane symbolism, since comic and indeed exhilarating sketches that are an end in themselves take centre stage. These African novels were a politically apathetic satire against modernization, and pilloried the world of international politics from an evidently right-wing bias, for example by upholding the benefits of the Italian invasion of Abyssinia. When it came to that classic crossroads for British intellectuals, the Spanish Civil War, Waugh became a sympathizer of Franco. The first historical attack against Waugh came, therefore, from the social-communist intelligentsia; the second, after Waugh's unequivocal adhesion to an old-style form of Catholicism, from the ranks of non-confessional humanist liberalism. Orwell, who probably had the idea of writing a scathing essay on Waugh around 1949, but only began it (his notes remain), was usually far from kind to him; he judged him inferior, as a picaresque writer,

---

3   This is quite evident in the rejected and rather cynical ending of *A Handful of Dust*, with Tony Last who, having returned to Brenda, uses the London flat for *his* erotic escapades (Bradbury 1964, 67).

to Smollett and Fielding, and as a comic writer to Dickens. In particular, he criticized Waugh's equidistance from communism and fascism,[4] and included him, albeit without mentioning Ford Madox Ford, among the neo-Tories, who were as much anti-Russian as anti-American, and trusted in the survival of the British power model. This neo-Toryism infected the disillusioned ex-communists who from being Anglophobes became pro-British, like C. S. Lewis, Kingsmill and Muggeridge.[5] Consequently, Orwell placed no great weight on the fact that Waugh had at least fought in the war, and on the right side, albeit for a pseudo-ideal he did not share. Waugh and other writers and fellow-believers of his time were not pacifists and deserters like those of Auden's generation.[6] The diversity of Waugh and Greene, and to a certain extent Snow, with respect to Auden and his entourage, is not only that of novelists against poets, or Catholics and none too politicized conservatives against progressives, and of hetero- against homosexuals;[7] it is a sense of belonging to actual history versus Christian and Vedantic mysticism; it is the faith in the restoration of a lost ancient order, that of pre-Reformist European Christianity and of the Catholic Counter-Reformation. This Catholicism is an old British acquaintance: it is the same Catholicism which saw in the Reformation the breaking up of the granitic compactness of Christian Europe (and, *ipso facto*, of Britain); it is, to a certain extent, Hopkins's Catholicism. Significantly, Waugh's conversion to Catholicism in 1930 was synchronous with the publication of the second edition of Hopkins's poems,[8] and Waugh's conversion germinated and was guided

4   CRHE, 294–6.
5   OCE, vol. III, 422, and vol. IV, 496.
6   Stopp 1958, 51, speaks of a decades-old 'private argument' with this group of progressive writers headed by Auden.
7   Waugh's first two novels were vaguely parallel to those dramatic experiments on which Auden and Isherwood worked, and which they usually set in a large hotel, and in the same symbolic area of the school and the factory. Centred on farce and entertainment, Waugh's two novels were also dramatic tales translatable into a theatre script. Homosexuality, like atheism, had been a 'phase' in Waugh as a young pupil and university student (cf. Sykes 1985, 78, 109).
8   This, without mentioning Hopkins, is the interpretation of Waugh's Catholicism given by Kermode in a valuable essay in *Encounter* (1960), reproduced partially in

by the Campion Hall Jesuits. Hopkins, too, planned to write an ode on the Elizabethan Jesuit, Campion. However, Waugh did not wish in the least to proselytize, and he shrank from any collusion with Catholic rhetoric. From atheistic, non-politicized and therefore non-socialist nihilism, he transitioned to Catholicism as a tool to read and re-order the contemporary world.[9] From a certain point on, his novels invariably feature Catholics, and this marks them for life; this is something binding for the writer himself, who differentiates them from non-Catholics, and makes them increasingly detached from their surroundings.

4. Orwell interpreted the phenomenon of the conversions to Catholicism of writers in the 1930s, including that of Waugh, as the need for an Eliot-style 'stronghold' or even a 'rock': 'the need for something to believe in'. But Orwell called it a 'false dawn'.[10] Those writers, like Waugh, were looking for a framework, a form of discipline, and for prestige. This was no pious and devout Catholicism, one of philanthropic action, or popular and superstitious yet alien from the subtleties of every existentialism, rather it was aristocratic and even snobbish – a Catholicism of pomp and triumph. It was, in Britain, as always, a bearer and resuscitator of division and discussion. Waugh's ability lies in the fact that his early farces can be taken at face value, and their author as a cynical accomplice in an insensate world, he himself part and parcel of the inane movement he describes: such is the absence of denunciation and persuasion. The first reviewers fell into this trap, adducing that he took nothing seriously, least of all himself;[11] but they were justified by their ignorance of Waugh's secret teleology. He had been on the brink of both affective and existential collapse, and his diary reveals that he had contemplated suicide.[12] For a start, this emotional tangle is disguised in farce, and in characters whose

----

CRHE, 279–87. Kermode also traces in Waugh the Augustinian opposition, equally active in Hopkins, between the City of God and the city of man.

9   His first marriage was annulled by the Roman Sacra Rota, and Waugh married Laura Herbert, with whom he had six children.

10   OCE, vol. I, 564.

11   Cf. for example CRHE, 89, 104 (by R. Aldington), 129.

12   Sykes 1985, 99.

journey is a decomposition of the archetype. They camouflage the author, since all of them make such a quest more naïve, irresponsible and unconscious. The opposition between farce and moral tale, which may also be that between levity and seriousness, was to increasingly amaze readers and critics because of the abysmal distance between its poles. It was in fact inexplicable that someone could breezily pass from a critical study of Rossetti to the frolics of *Decline and Fall*; or, later in Waugh's career, from caprices like *Black Mischief* to a devout biography of the Jesuit Thomas Campion, who taught the necessity of sacrifice in order to be reborn and to show the infallibility of the Church; or to the fictionalized story of St Helena, Constantine's mother, a legendarily British saint and princess who found the remains of the True Cross. Among Waugh's abandoned or merely planned projects is also a book on the Crusades.[13] All of them are restoration rites and celebrations. Waugh's monograph on Rossetti, and a more general interest in Decadentism, were a first muffled, clandestine step towards Rome, and instances of a curiosity about an aestheticizing religion that nonetheless venerated everything ancient, even if past its prime. The scandalized amazement of certain sections of British Catholicism towards Waugh was ultimately due both to an audacious 'Dantesque' strategy (to condemn decadence and aberration by describing them), and to the fact that his novels unfold in a kind of expectancy or delay of the moment of conversion, almost as if the writer were yet weighing whether or not to take this step. Discrepancies are never solved in Waugh, and remain visible until the end.[14] Unquestionably, however, Britain was in general, as ever, too preoccupied to welcome or criticize, as the case may be, a committed proselytizing Catholicism in Catholic converts, and critics either lamented Waugh's apologetic about-face or its absence, as if every Catholic novel should illustrate the duel of the faiths or that between faith and unbelief. And of course a Catholic novel would have been somewhat sectorial and narrow if it had only portrayed principled Catholics, with their problems

---

13   Hollis 1971, 39.
14   The passage from the ironic detached manner to the serious committed one, and
      regarding the biography of Campion, was clearly noted by Rose Macaulay (CRHE,
      173).

of conscience breezily resolved. Waugh wrote hagiographies of saints and martyrs, but he walks a knife-edge in many of his novels – in almost all of them, if we ignore the war trilogy. Like a latter-day Boccaccio he amusedly follows the career of the scoundrel or the opportunist. Any apology seems foreign to him. This hazardous plan was not ascribed to the desire to condemn age-old practices; but it was assumed by certain Catholic circles, those for instance of the periodical *The Tablet*, as approval or sacrilege, and a long controversy followed.

§ 46. *Waugh II: The explosion of comedy*

Twenty-five-year-old Waugh decided to go for a safe bet. *Decline and Fall*[15] (1928) is not a morbid and predictable autobiographical novel; or it may be, but if it is, it objectifies and transfigures its author's recent life only a short time later. It was as if *Ulysses* and Virginia Woolf's novels had never been written, or Waugh had soared and leapfrogged over them.[16] In fact, he took the side of the soundest autochthonous national tradition, starting from the successes of the eighteenth-century picaresque of Fielding and Smollett.[17] We can read a form of silent indifference towards, and a conservative distance from, the experimentation of foreign novelists who had corrupted and polluted this tradition – Irish, half-Germans and New Zealanders (Joyce, Ford Madox Ford, Mansfield), or aestheticizing cosmopolitans like those of the Bloomsbury set.[18] The price Waugh was forced to pay for this choice was a return to the modules of the scholastic farce, which covered a vast slice of Victorian fiction and was omnipresent in early Thackeray and Dickens. The success of Waugh's novel depends on its possible novelties with respect to those predecessors, and on the

15   A Gibbonian title, and one, as I mentioned, contradicting its contents; it is in fact a clamorous antiphrasis, and yet a remote interpretative key. After all, we cannot ignore that Paul is a student of theology.

16   Sykes 1985, 120.

17   Bradbury 1964, 42, 45, compares Waugh to Fielding in this novel.

18   At the beginning Paul is cycling back to college preparing himself to read a chapter of the *Forsyte Saga*; in prison he refuses to read Virginia Woolf's latest novel, 'published just two days earlier'.

options and expedients still available to renew that glorious scenario. On a closer look, *Decline and Fall* is the commemoration of a centenary, or very nearly. Paul Pennyfeather's story had been told first by Dickens in *Nicholas Nickleby* in the 1830s. In search of work, Nicholas, in that rather more complex and multiplot novel, joins a school where all is cheating and turmoil. Waugh's Paul, expelled from university for 'indecent behaviour', is taken on as a teacher in a Welsh school that wallows in a similar state of pitiable dysfunction. Like Nicholas, he exploits one of the few openings in the intellectual work market, applying to an employment agency. The space-time element of this novel, which is supposed to take place in 1928, is in reality backdated, as satire almost always is. Waugh digs up surpassed scenarios, like that of the prep school that could attract adventurers without scruples with the mirage of lucre, given that education was still left to free initiative; or that of the orphan who has lost his parents in India and has been entrusted to an absent-minded tutor. Paul must then resign himself to being a *trait d'union*, not as a fully sculpted main character. Vicissitude and the verbal exploit are the units of measurement; the other characters are typecast. Paul is the insipid, naïve and slightly dreamy hero, always a little backward, and therefore far from rich in initiative; it must be so because his function is that of lending a shoulder to others who cross his path and helping to sharpen their eccentricities. In the Welsh school of Llanabba, the best episode does not imitate the chapter of the burnt porridge and of the gloomy condemnation of the educational system, as in *Jane Eyre*, rather the absurdity and ineptitude reigning in Dickens's Dotheboys school. In self-closed scenes, introduced and punctuated by short captions, Waugh manages to provoke a smile or even a burst of resounding laughter through the caricatures of the headmaster and the two teachers with an adventurous past, with their unmistakable oratorical styles and their dress and behavioural eccentricities.[19] A janitor holds court with his bragging,

---

19 Captain Grimes, who has a wooden leg, is himself an old acquaintance from nine-teenth-century comedy, for his ignoble past, his pragmatic cynicism, and above all the ability with which, as a bigamist, he dupes one of the headmaster's daughters. Immediately disilluded, he fakes suicide by drowning, but is destined to reappear in prison, from which he escapes.

while at the inn we hear the occasional speeches of a stationmaster who is also a band leader, and who, when he speaks, translates from Welsh into English, coming out with picturesquely inconclusive phrases, such as only a brilliant disciple of Dickens could cook up. Given that this is a farce, many vicissitudes have a surreal flavour. The climaxes are the student athletic contests, an occasion to show the amateurish lack of school equipment, the clumsiness of the teachers who are unable to do anything right while directing the contests, and the quarrels and vagaries of the pupils' parents invited to the contest.[20] The second part is undistinguished and less sparkling. On finishing the year, Paul becomes the private tutor of a pupil and gets engaged to his young mother, the wealthy owner of a manor house, and a widow who appears vacuous, carefree and just a little rash. She is a Shavian Mrs Warren who is running a shady prostitution racket.[21] On the morning of the much publicized wedding, Paul, the *ingénu* who cannot begin to imagine what has happened, is arrested for a crime he has not committed and taken to prison, an episode which Waugh, mindful of Reade and other nineteenth-century novelists, exploits to satirize prison reformism inspired by hazy psychoanalytical theories. Other larger-than-life characters come out of the hat, but are less well wrought, duller, or too fulsome. Paul is able to turn over a new leaf in Oxford in disguise, thanks to an incredible impersonation.[22]

2. *Vile Bodies*[23] (1930) follows the vicissitudes of a group of rich young Londoners (it has been observed that their movements do not extend beyond Park Lane and Bond Street), condemned to stasis and moral decline, though it also extends to the spheres of public administration, politics, the Church, high finance and the land-owning aristocracy after the end of the

---

20   *En passant* in the parents' discourses traces of racism against blacks and the Welsh
      emerge.
21   In the following novel, *Vile Bodies*, the widow, who has become a lady who gives parties that fill a good part of the novel, again lures girls to send them to South America to prostitute themselves. Auden, too, makes use of this piece of news (§ 4.6), which evidently constituted a scandal at the time.
22   This device is reminiscent of Wilkie Collins.
23   Title taken from a passage by St Paul (Sykes 1985, 148).

Great War.[24] It intermittently belongs to the surreal subgenre as well, thanks to the rapidity with which grotesque and dream-like episodes are attributed to bizarre, oblivious characters, and to the constant metamorphosis of the narrative pace. Chapters or sections may be long and almost traditional, alternating with other, impressionistic passages; one chapter consists of monosyllabic scraps of dialogue,[25] and longer sub-chapters are followed by entries that are sometimes of one line only. Waugh had perfected a style that is to say the least succinct, telegraphic even. The plot, too, is a superseded concept, since the narrative procedure consists in the addition of incidental episodes of a bitter comedy that is sometimes absurd, at other times genuine. These snapshots, thanks to their swiftness and transitoriness, are also flashes separated from one another by asterisks. One might find an analogy with Larry Semon's short silent comedies. With this kind of technique Waugh aims to avoid any involvement and to deny himself any appearance from behind the scenes; and by refraining from any description, he also avoids any explicit moralizing. Condemnation must only be triggered by objective and phenomenological representation; this is the *regard* of an ice-cold, pitiless, sadistic observer, who abruptly alternates his stills in an impenetrable sequence. Thus, fluttering about the stage – because the fabric is precisely that of a string of sketches – are manikins without depth, or dancers without soul, not tragic protagonists.[26] Waugh summons his emblematic representative pool of well-heeled, cultured society from London's upper-class neighbourhoods, concocting situations or pretexts to bring them together, disperse and unite them again in a web of intersections. He launches the novel by having them all embark on a ferry from the French coast for Dover; he then turns to the expedient of the party, several parties, to have them meet and interact. Summarized

24   In fact, on Armistice Day. The Prime Minister who resigned 'the other day' is an index of the extreme precariousness of political life.
25   The triumph of the deadpan manner – impassive dialogue without inflection, popularized by the American writer Damon Runyon – was noticed by reviewers (Stopp 1958, 64).
26   The names, together with other plausible ones, are those pidgin ones of Lady Tangent, Lady Circumference, Lord Monomark, and Lady Metroland.

thus, the novel distinctly recalls those of Huxley's debut. It is not exactly a counterpoint, the kind of musical analogy presiding over *Point Counter Point*; instead, the novel that springs to mind is *Antic Hay*.[27] By reducing the comments between one scene and another, a structure of splinters is built up; indeed, Waugh has his youngsters dance an 'antic hay', the satirical dance.[28] They are confused, fazed, have lost their moral compass; the flesh is weak, and like Huxley's characters, they throw themselves into the arena of bodies and senses. They are the 'bright young things' in action. From the novel come no words of life. A Jesuit priest, back from the east apparently without having acquired wisdom, possesses wide-ranging but useless erudition, and in his suitcase there is also a false beard.[29] He reappears in a salon, where he plots a far from clear plan with the visible powers. Perhaps he is in the novel only because of the association of his name – Rothschild – and as an emblem of a Church that colludes with economic power.[30] A disillusioned American revivalist and itinerant missionary is followed by twelve apostles or 'angelic' virgins who vainly mask the tremors of the flesh. Religion, symbolized by these two figures, is incapable of redeeming, and inadequate to its messianic duty. The novel's limit is that, without any prior story being given, the actions of the various characters have no really complete meaning, though this may have been Waugh's objective: to

27   This novel is read by Anthony Blanche, the Oxfordian aesthete in Waugh's *Brideshead Revisited*.

28   Without evoking Huxley, the recourse to the image of dance and ballet is also discussed in a valuable review of the novel by Rose Macaulay (CRHE, 109–112).

29   This fake beard may be a flagrant filching from Huxley (§ 33.5), but it is useful for the journalist Belcair not in order to seem a virile male to women, but to take part in disguise in a reception he was not invited to, where he wants to pick up titillating gossip for the newspaper he works for. Waugh wrote his most ferocious and precocious satire of tabloid journalism in *Scoop* (1938), sparkling with vicissitudes, quid pro quos, sensational events and turnarounds, in an imaginary Abyssinian context where the frequent prototype of the unprepared simpleton is sent as a civil war correspondent. This was and is still considered a work that inspired *Night and Day* by Tom Stoppard (§ 203.2).

30   A cross between Chesterton's candid Father Brown and the wild Father Scapinelli of Kuehnelt-Leddihn, for Del Zanna 1966, 750.

make actions appear senseless, absurd, improvised, mechanical and casual. It is also true that many irreverent and scandalous allusions, such as that to the orgy taking place one night at Number 10 Downing Street, have by now lost their incendiary charge. The second part is less discontinuous; in a mish-mash of comical and grotesque situations that burst forth and topple at the drop of a hat, it follows the career of an Adam, a journalist working for an imaginary newspaper. He runs an avidly read gossip column, creating made-up characters and fashions.[31] Adam belatedly functions as a *trait d'union* and launches a sentimental-picaresque story that brings some order to the plot. He is a new figure of the *ingénu* repeatedly conned by the wily. The reader has the impression that Waugh would have achieved a better result if he had cut all or many of the hanging and lateral threads and had gone deeper into this plot about Adam – this picaresque plot, featuring an innocent man who is cheated several times by a 'drunken major', and is always on the point of tying the knot with his fiancée but continually has to put it off. Adam is then a second Paul from the previous novel, and is not all negative, despite being so vulnerable. The peak of the surreal, or surreal science fiction novel, is reached in the end, with the outbreak of a phantom war that calls Adam to the front. Varying the ending of T. S. Eliot's poem on the 'hollow men' – an alternative definition of Waugh's characters, who are moving across a similar stage – the novel closes with a 'bang', instead of with a 'whimper'.

3. Adam is symbolically the first man, while Tony Last, the main character in *A Handful of Dust*[32] (1934), is equally symbolically the last one; one is a filiation of the other under the mark of the meagre possession of surviving values of integrity, or simply of average, fallacious human nature, in a civilization of deadbeats and of moral compromises. Should we believe in the allusiveness of names, in this novel the woman-hunter John Beaver shares that epithet which, in the jargon of the intellectual youth of the time, was a synonym for a roué and a Don Juan.[33] The very title opens and closes

---

31 Another journalist commits suicide using gas because of the number of law suits.
32 The plot rewrites with obvious detachment the flirt of Waugh's first wife with a mutual friend (Sykes 1985, 138–9).
33 In this sense Gumbril in Huxley's *Antic Hay* is a 'beaver' (§ 33.5).

the moral fable: like *Vile Bodies* it refers to the ultimate corruptibility of the body, Eliot's 'handful of dust' prefiguring the Day of Judgement. In *A Handful of Dust* Waugh, however, seems to abandon the surreal tale and to take a step back towards documentary realism, thereby reducing the overall number of characters, but also the purely comical ones that people the previous novels. He starts again from *Decline and Fall*, but without isolating the larger-than-life characters centre stage, or giving room to polished or anecdotal speeches. The diegetic fabric is neat, soberly and agreeably factual; and the dialogue is often monosyllabic. Without picaresque concessions, a middle-class erotic triangle of the classic type is set up. Brenda is a well-off wife, not wicked but dissatisfied, bored and unfulfilled, partly because she is forced to live in a Victorian Gothic mansion off the beaten track to please her traditionalist husband. She has an affair with a young scrounger, the mediocre John Beaver, an unemployed layabout who is proverbial at the club for his constantly empty pockets.[34] Her husband, Tony Last, is nothing more than a prosaic being, too methodical and predictable in his mediocrity. The affair that blooms is followed closely, only punctuated by the intermezzos of the couple's young son with a passion for horses and who shows a certain youthful brazenness in defusing the adults' white lies. Beaver spends a weekend at the Lasts' on the strength of a carelessly offhand invitation, without picking up the subtle signals warning him that he is an unwelcome guest. However, Brenda passes from indifference to imperceptible curiosity, and in fact a slight air of complicity is established between the two. In this situation, Waugh does not turn to an orthodox form of stream of consciousness, but perversely puts his finger on the discrepancy between what is said and what is thought, namely, the little fibs of the host who cannot wait for the guest to leave, but openly tells him otherwise. Brenda adds that Beaver is 'quite like us in some ways'. She is looking for her own space, her own life, a Woolfian 'room of her own'; she asks around, semi-serious and semi-casual, what Beaver's 'sex-life' is like. Theirs is a cold adultery, he clumsy and intellectual, she maternal

34   Waugh, whose title cites Eliot and *The Waste Land*, also parodies Proust by entitling the first chapter *Du côté de chez Beaver*. In Beaver's passion for Brenda there is no spasmodic romanticism, only opportunism.

and only seeking a little flutter. Beaver is coarse, and Brenda is aware of it. It is a temporary caprice, or a tool to win independence; and the small apartment she rents in London, with the excuse of studying economics, is not an alcove. Just before it is midway through, the affair gains the complicity, if not the approval, of high society; Tony, as in a play by Pirandello, is the only one in the dark. Brenda and her friends try to console him by bringing him some beautiful women, with a chorus of acquaintances who declare: 'You've done more than most wives would to cheer the old boy up'. And yet he does suspect something, subliminally. He gets drunk at nightclubs,[35] and is on the point of succumbing to the flatteries of an *entraîneuse*, undecided whether to make a surprise visit to his wife who is in Beaver's company.[36] This digressive scene begins to introduce a number of secondary characters, once more demonstrating Waugh's skill in setting up incidental episodes out of the blue.

4. With the accidental death of Last's young son, and the letter with which Brenda suavely informs her husband that she is leaving him for Beaver, *A Handful of Dust* is practically finished, even though it has just reached its mid-point. The opening section is Waugh's finest to date: the looming of a conjugal crisis narrated without concessions and digressions, and with tyrannical sobriety. However, the night-club scene shows that Waugh is always interested in creating episodes that are curious, bizarre, and as a result, caricatures that are an end in themselves. From this point on, another novel begins. The deviation is immediately evident in the farce of unfaithfulness staged by Tony in order to obtain a divorce. A trip to Brighton, rich in grotesquely alienated details, introduces a capricious know-it-all young girl, the daughter of the prostitute who takes part in the staged scene. Waugh feels he must end the story by pointing to the aberration towards which the two spouses move, without explicit moralizing on his part. Brenda falls out of love with Beaver, who disappears from the

35   At this club, called 'The Old Hundredth', an extended scene takes place in *Brideshead Revisited*, from which Sebastian Flyte's moral degradation practically dates.

36   There is an example of exquisitely cinematographic cross fading in this fictional situation, when, during a phone call Tony receives at the club, the scene passes to the two lovers, hinging on an answer.

scene demanding an exaggerated sum for his maintenance; Tony, in turn, enters a phase of lethargy and serious malaise, not a night of the soul that is a harbinger of the dawn. Waugh devises a surreal and therefore barely credible epilogue to condemn the ruin and dissolution of western civilization and the burning need for a regeneration that seems far-off, given the irony of the solution. Tony refuses to agree to the divorce and sails for South America in search of a buried city,[37] and after the archaeologist accompanying him disappears he ends up being captured by a kind of odd, Conradian Kurtz. This man oppresses the local populations and stops Tony from returning home, obliging him to read him Dickens's novels *in perpetuum*.[38] Back home, he is presumed dead and his funeral is celebrated. In all of this exotic part, which sounds like a parody of a combination of *Westward Ho!* and *The Plumed Serpent*, the fictionalized travel diary, with its vicissitudes, perils, and goings-on of an involuntarily humorous effect, plus the local colour of the natives, relegates to second place any serious focus on the drama of the abandoned husband.[39]

37   Tony leaves England in search of another city, but finds only an image of death, as noted by Kermode (CRHE, 283–4) and Bradbury 1964. This is the supplementary sense of the 'handful of dust'.

38   *Black Mischief* (1932), the first novel inspired by Waugh's transoceanic journeys, documented an anthropological interest in primitive peoples and the third world, and for their remaining tribal beliefs, together with an interest in the hasty modernizations imposed by British colonizers. Basil Seal, the Englishman who becomes Minister of Modernity on the African island of Azania, is the third metamorphosis of the footloose Oxford graduate of the late 1930s. Waugh's rather muddled novel loses hands-down to Orwell's almost contemporary *Burmese Days*, and, as a piece of political fiction, to *Animal Farm*. However, what does remain memorable for the reader is the shocking particular of the hero who accidentally helps to eat the body of his lover during a cannibalistic ritual. The novel was considered distasteful and incoherent, because of certain irreverent and desecrating details, by a section of the more rigidly orthodox Catholic intelligentsia, and especially by the weekly *The Tablet*. If this is a Catholic novel, as Waugh proclaimed, it remains objectively difficult to understand and justify the oblique acrobatic apologetics it contains. This debate is well documented in CRHE, 132–40.

39   In the first version of the novel, published as a serial, Waugh has Tony return home from Brazil.

§ 47. Waugh III: 'Brideshead Revisited'. The twitch upon the thread
With *Brideshead Revisited*[40] (1945) Waugh became a convert in more
than one sense. He went from the episodic novel of a vaguely *destruens*,
comical-satirical stamp, to one that is epic, tragic, elegiac, and thus also
purely romantic and sensational, full *coups de théâtre*; but not without
insinuating into this largely popular module a subtle, ideological, impartial
and paradoxical apologetic proposal.[41] He in fact discusses the meaning
of life, the value and prospects of faith, and the paths of redemption. The
tragic epic is tempered, objectified, and distanced by an internal memorialist
who, in a first-person narrative, formally allows the real writer to keep the
whole material at a due distance.[42] If this is autobiography, Waugh splits
into at least two of the male characters, the two friends Sebastian Flyte and
Charles Ryder. The first-person memorial was in the minority among the
Victorians, from the Brontë sisters to Dickens and Collins, but not so the
multifocal one; and in *Brideshead Revisited*, as in these models, the entry
of the minor characters, the small digressions, and the textual loops are
virtually infinite. *Brideshead Revisited* is neatly divided into four parts, a
prologue and an epilogue enclosing two 'books' divided into several chapters. Its setting is not contemporary but historical. It is more precisely a
family saga that stands out against the background of the inter-war years,
and as a *mise en abyme* of British society and the well-off middle classes
of the time. This saga is updated yet in line with those by Galsworthy and

40   Subtitled *The Sacred and Profane Memories of Captain Charles Ryder*. It was 'drasti-
     cally revised' (Sykes 1985, 335) in 1959.
41   Waugh's conversion to Catholicism followed some intimate discussions which he
     had in 1930 with the Jesuit, Father D'Arcy, which may have been mimicked by those,
     rather comical ones in the novel (as we shall see below) between Mottram and his
     spiritual guide.
42   The initial chapters resort to a Jamesian technique in the biased presentation of the
     Flytes from the different points of view of many acquaintances, which bewilders
     Ryder and leaves him shocked and curious. This is also a return to the testimonial
     fiction of a Wilkie Collins. The backstories about Julia starting from 1923, and the
     meeting at the station with Ryder just arrived on a visit to Sebastian, are referred to
     in flashbacks, as is a story Julia herself tells to Ryder, ten years later, during a storm
     on the Atlantic Ocean, therefore in 1935.

Bennett of a few decades earlier. It shares with them the nostalgia, although more masked in Waugh's case, for ancient spiritual values and waning traditions. The Flytes' London home is soon to be destroyed to make way for a block of flats, but Ryder, the internal narrator, is commissioned to make some paintings of it so that it will survive in some vicarious form. It is no coincidence that Ryder will become an 'architectural' painter, who paints 'buildings that grew silently with the centuries, catching and keeping the best of each generation'. Rex Mottram, Julia Flyte's husband, is superficial like Forster's Henry Wilcox, and unable to enact a Forsterian 'connection'. Waugh's characters have become rounded, deeper, and sculpted. The observer and witness Charles Ryder is an Oxfordian who at the time of writing is thirty-nine and is waiting to be sent to the front in the Second World War. His recollection is not disjointed like those of Ford Madox Ford but is equally mimetic, interspersed with temporal overlaps, memories within memories, returns to an internal present that is always a past. On the border between aseptic observation and prejudice, his task is to trace the twenty-year story of the Flyte family, of ancient even if by now shaky Catholic traditions,[43] focusing on the life of Lord and Lady Marchmain's children. However, we must not forget that it is not Waugh who is writing directly: the voice is that of his remembering *alter ego*. This voice helps create a novel that is luxuriant, slower, more descriptive than the previous ones, not nervous and dissonant, and no longer surreal.

2. *Brideshead Revisited* is a multifocal novel because it follows the destinies of its characters, which cross and diverge and cross again; however, its iconic pattern is radial, with faith as the centre of gravity and a point of intersection or invariable asymptote. On closer inspection, the Catholicism of the Flyte family is a historically plausible fact, but one that is, for the objectives of the novel's ideological discourse, irrelevant. For the former aspect, we might define *Brideshead Revisited* as the last great

---

43   Looking back, Disraeli, Wilkie Collins, Kingsley's brother and Gissing are among the few Victorians to have written sagas of Catholic families. Ford Madox Ford's tetralogy focuses on unions between Protestants and Catholics, but is not really of and about Catholic families. Sykes 1985, 338, cites as precedents the lesser-known brothers Robert Hugh and Arthur Benson (Volume 7, § 88.2 n. 7).

English novel of Oxford life. Just under 100 years after Newman's arrival in Oxford and the official birth of the Oxford Movement, Waugh concedes one last instant of life to the Anglo-Catholicism, Tractarianism and then orthodox Catholicism that Newman had brought back to life; we have seen it surviving up to Wilde and the very last aesthetes, including its belated twentieth-century representatives. And yet Waugh does not rewrite *Loss and Gain* or *The Nemesis of Faith*, and is not interested in resuscitating the Victorian controversy over Catholicism and Protestantism. The Flytes have no direct interlocutors and adversaries, and there is no religiously motivated Protestant figure in the novel. The ongoing conflict is between faith and agnosticism, or faith and the 'disappearance of God'. Waugh had by then refounded his theology and made it more orthodox, but this is not a novel that is 'finally' apologetic and takes religion, Waugh's adopted religion, seriously. Instead, it shows at work Hopkins's and Francis Thompson's idea of a God who hunts down Man, God as a 'hound of heaven' who drives out the lukewarm believer and also the agnostic. Waugh lays a symbolic case history of human positions in front of transcendence, convinced, as a British convert, of the legacy of original sin, the stain, the weakness, the laziness, of the primal satanic rebellion. This act of assent to the designs of providence is welcomed in the form of flagrant conversions *in articulo mortis*, or even of sudden decisions to emigrate towards virgin, distant countries, or to Palestine. Waugh does not describe the perfection of sanctity, but rather the reconquest of faith after a life of sin or disorientation: his theme is the 'twitch upon the thread'. One sentence from the novel defines Waugh's Catholics from this point on, namely, 'The worse I am, the more I need God'. The paths towards faith are many, and it is possible either to approach it or stray from it. As in Browning, Waugh's discretion and cunning lie in gradually bringing an agnostic like Ryder closer to Catholicism, although he has before his eyes examples such as Sebastian and his Don Juan father, and his little sister Cordelia, whose faith is problematic, rebarbative, and delights in ecclesiastical jokes.

3. The curtain rises on the war, but through an optical illusion it is not the First but the Second, which is imminent and has indeed already begun; however, nothing has changed or seems to have changed. Waugh underlines the stupidity of this war and all wars, and the incomprehensible

movements of Ryder's small military unit recall the surreal aura of stasis of Ford Madox Ford's epic. Waugh evokes an era of affective, moral and temporal muddle, and tries to envisage how one may be saved from this ruin.[44] The prologue must therefore be understood as the end, but what this end means can only be clarified by starting again from the beginning. 1923, this beginning, is the year after the one in which *The Waste Land* had been published, and the fervent and fanatical students of Oxford were declaiming it from the balconies. Ryder's task is to reveal himself and, step by step, also the family of his rather particular friend at the time, Sebastian Flyte. Waugh's ability consists in not immediately tossing all the members of the Flyte family in front of the spectator at the same time, and having them enter one by one to better define them. Sebastian seems torn and troubled, aloof and apathetic in 1923, but he is quite the opposite. His feminine immaturity is symbolized by his inseparable fluffy teddy bear; or by the bunch of roses he gave Ryder as a mark of apology for a small accident. These are symptoms of a rapt and not totally conscious affective need. At one and the same time, Sebastian had wanted Ryder both to meet his family and to hide them from his friend, ashamed of his father who was living with a lover far from the family home. In the episode recalled Sebastian admits that he did not want his brothers to 'steal' his friend; and he took him to Brideshead because he knew that none of his family were there at that moment; he is keen that Ryder should meet his wet nurse, only and at least his wet nurse. It was at that time that Sebastian eventually had to clarify his religious position in front of the agnostic Ryder, who believed religion to be merely a myth or a repertoire of ethical maxims, and refused to believe in transcendence. After the visit to the chapel, Sebastian quoted a motto that seems inspired by Browning: 'Oh dear, it's very difficult being a Catholic'.[45] As for Sebastian, Waugh summarizes his religious path by having him experience the need for faith, albeit not rewarding him with its possession. A part of him believes in a

44   When, in 1926, Ryder returns from Paris throbbing with a bout of patriotism, and determined to defend his homeland against the revolutionaries, he soon realizes that all is as it was: in other terms, it is not political faith that can change the world.

45   See Volume 4, § 119.2, on *Easter-Day*.

silvery childlike faith, in miracles and in the prayer that pleads for them, and in the tales of the Gospel; another part rejects it. His moral decline had begun from his family's morbid desire, his mother's above all, to spy on him, force him, protect him, and lead him back to normality. Only in this sense can one explain the otherwise unjustifiable sadism of Ryder, who at the time always handed him drink money. Or perhaps Ryder actually resented Sebastian's attempts to convert him. Or he gave Sebastian drink money – but this is frankly too much – to get Sebastian to develop his own free will, the moral strength and the incentive to rise up by his own efforts. Sebastian represents the conditioning power of religious education, and his mother's responsibility in his moral weakness. But another warning signal obscurely points to the conflict between hereditary determinism and free will. Sebastian takes after his father, whom he resembles physically; and against inheritance and atavistic inclinations, and inclinations towards good and evil, little can be done. Waugh confesses his impotence against a kind of Darwinian, or more precisely Calvinistic predestination: 'It was odd, I thought, how the same ingredients, differently dispensed, could produce Brideshead [Sebastian's elder brother], Sebastian, Julia and [Cordelia]'.[46] Sebastian eventually fades away from faith and news of him becomes fragmentary for a long time. He re-emerges in Africa embroiled with a new 'friend', and when Ryder travels to join him to inform him that his mother is dying, he is found at the local hospital. Meanwhile, the chapel at Brideshead has been deconsecrated, and Sebastian goes to live with a community of monks, a prey to destructive thoughts, recalling many nineteenth-century atoners, such as Mrs Gaskell's Hepburn.

4. A second aspect of the controversy over Catholicism is that the novel's presumed apology is triggered by a destructive irony on Catholicism itself. In other words, Waugh plays the devil's advocate. It is frankly enigmatic that *Brideshead Revisited*, anything but explicit and clear in its ideological and theological design, was not appreciated by those, such as Edmund Wilson in a scathing review,[47] who had hailed the moral ambiguity

46   This reflection is of course attributed to Ryder.
47   CRHE, 245–8.

of early Waugh. The definition given by Waugh from behind the scenes – that his objective was, paraphrasing Milton, 'to describe the operations of divine providence in a pagan world, in the lives of an English Catholic family that was itself paganised, in the world between 1923 and 1939' – does not really tally with the evidence of the text. The comic conversion and catechizing of Rex Mottram, Julia Flyte's husband, is a successful episode because Mottram is so pragmatic and concrete that he seems immune to any form of spirituality, and more obtuse and bungling than the average.[48] The apology of Catholicism arises from burlesque skits like this one. Or the champion of Catholicism must be a malicious and mischievous scamp like Cordelia. Julia even confesses, were she to have a baby girl, and speaking of the prospect of her baptism and religious education: 'That's one thing I can give her. It doesn't seem to have done much good, but my child shall have it'. The whole of the second part of the novel is fuelled by a remark that Cordelia makes to Ryder, the 'poor agnostic': God does not leave his creatures in peace, but gives them some slack, leaves them unbridled, so that in the end He can give a tug and win them back. This is a quotation from Chesterton, which complements those, more secret, by Hopkins and Thompson. Ryder, who had become an adept of a Paterian 'aesthetic education' after admiring the composite architecture of the Brideshead residence, is on the loose, but only until the cord is reeled in for him, too. His period of freedom lasts for ten years, during which we find him the painter of 'Browning's Renaissance', and an earthly hater of transcendent reality, but tired and forgetful of the things and people he left behind in Europe. Back home, faith poses an obstacle to the adulterous relations between him and Julia Flyte. After the dispersal, all the characters, save one (Sebastian), reunite. The last chapter coincides with the return to Brideshead, and the death and conversion on the point of death, of Lord Marchmain, Sebastian's father. Ryder is most adamantine when it comes to

---

48 A Jesuit priest gives in to the total absence of intellectual stimuli from Rex. A dramatic turn of events, typical of a grand Victorian novel, is the discovery that Rex is already married, as he candidly confesses. A church wedding is impossible, and one is celebrated in an anonymous Protestant chapel for marriages between divorced parties.

refusing a visit by the priest, which looks like a trick to him, as he finds no meaning but only superstition in the last rites. Julia, instead, is surprisingly open-minded, in fact, annoyed with Ryder for his anti-Catholic animosity. In front of her dying father, Julia reconquers her faith and understands that to return to God she must give up Ryder. But it is precisely from the breakup with Julia that Ryder receives a push, and he kneels, though doubtfully, at the lord's bedside. Ryder's possible conversion, or the assurance that something is stirring within him, is conveyed by the image of the snows melting on the mountains and the avalanche or landslide descending into the valley. From the epilogue we also learn that Julia and Cordelia Flyte have left for Palestine.

§ 48. *Waugh IV: The war trilogy*

The short, macabre, far-fetched caprice *The Loved One* (1947) is a chapter of the anti-Americanism harboured by the old Continent and by the jealous and scandalized motherland. It is, at least in part, a sociological novel, since it deals tragicomically with post-war emigration towards the Hollywood Eldorado of phalanxes of semi-failed writers recycled as screenwriters, hence a host of disappointed and frustrated people. Waugh, too, had been invited to America to write the screenplay for *Brideshead*, and to this we owe the birth of this fantasy. Mention is often made of Huxley and *After Many a Summer* being behind *The Loved One*; the parallel work is, however, *Ape and Essence* with its huge stockpiles of scripts that Hollywood was unable to film at the zenith and boom of cinema. In the late 1940s the cultural and formative background of the Englishman had become inevitably unsuitable for the tasks to which the new exploitative industry and the 'competitive system' bent him. Sir Francis Hinsley is one of those British emigrants, and his suicide is not merely the tragic gesture of someone who feels useless, but it also represents the desperation of the old, humanistic intellectual aristocracy in the face of the progress of opportunistic modernity. The second paradox is that a promising English poet, Dennis Barlow, must scratch a living by working at a funeral parlour for pets. Shortly afterwards, and even more paradoxically, Dennis gets to know the Hollywood industry of burial cosmetics. American civilization is pre-eminently one in which cultural tradition is dead or cannot find its lifeblood.[49] In other terms, what struck Waugh was the imitative devaluation of Old England. America is the world of the sham and the copycat; names and terms are supposed to keep cultural links alive – like the cemetery island, called Innisfree – but are instead cut out in this dispensation of the superficial, that is, of a veritable absence of depth and memory. No American perceives the literary citations and cultured nuances of the English; and it is always symptomatic that every time a word derived from Latin is used, it is not understood. *The Loved One* becomes the metaphor of a world of living dead, the metaphor, more exactly, of a *trompe l'œil*, of America itself as a fiction, life-in-death, or of the illusionistic reanimation of a corpse: a civilization that is apparently throbbing with life but is actually cadaverous, 'comatose' according to an adjective that often recurs in Waugh (as well as in Auden). To be exact, *The Loved One* becomes an eschatological fantasy, since it imagines how it is possible to misunderstand death and avoid questions of a spiritual order. The cosmetic practices are in fact an attempt to keep people alive artificially, forgetting that there is a death that restores life even better. By denying death, life too is denied. *The Loved One* is then the reflection of and on a buried civilization. The whole central scene, illustrating the cosmetic practices of the 'farewell to the deceased' on behalf of the living, is a diligent, absurd catechism and a bout of funereal humour, and is the heart and acme of the story. The burlesque romance of the mawkish, unprepared and immature cosmetologist assistant of the cemetery and of the English poet – a cultural marriage doomed to fail – is rather less successful, albeit equally overflowing with novelties, unexpected events and satirical swipes.[50]

2. The trilogy *Sword of Honour*,[51] which includes the novels *Men at Arms* (1952), *Officers and Gentlemen* (1955) and *Unconditional Surrender*

---

49   With a pun, Dennis is a 'poet and pets' mortician', with only one letter less between 'poet' and 'pet'.

50   On the derivations of this finale from *Miss Lonelyhearts* by Nathanael West, cf. Sykes 1985, 419.

51   A preview and a harbinger of this war trilogy was the already bland and sluggish novel from 1942, *Put Out More Flags*, whose main character is a Basil Seal made more of a scoundrel, in a series of training sessions which already verge on the burlesque. The

(1961), was assembled from Waugh's war memories, and is, therefore, ostensibly about military life and action. Warmly received by contemporary critics almost as masterpieces and a highpoint in Waugh's overall production, these novels suffered a dramatic decline in interest and appreciation as the temporal distance from the war and its epic gradually increased. By now they have been inevitably put in perspective. Mostly taking place far from the front, they deny the general title – they are not, that is, an epic at all – and do not meet the expectations. War loses its glamour, heroism lapses into parody, tomfoolery or absurdity, with generous concessions to the picaresque. Guy Crouchback is a hero of the spent, mediocre and pedestrian kind, therefore an antihero. Waugh's trilogy ultimately seems to hark back to the absurd and the farcical in Waugh's beginnings. Sub-narrating is always a risk for any novelist, and here it results in a slow monotonous chain of events. This is certainly deliberate, but the three novels never manage to come to life and sprinkle brio on the page; it is as if Waugh had not lived these experiences and was writing from hearsay or pure imagination. At the same time, he reverts to the saga or at least the cyclical novel or the cycle of novels, adapting an easy, popular, successful formula. Confirmation is provided by the 'synopsis' to the third novel, which does, however, clarify its nature, that of a crusade of ancient ideals against modernity, while bowing to the old, waning British aristocracy as a bastion of the nation. If war by definition means action, of this element there is no trace in these overly analytical novels, which with their slowed rhythm present themselves on their own as ready-made scripts for a TV series or serial. All of these characteristics automatically and instinctively suggested, at the time of their publication, a comparison between this trilogy and Ford's 'Tietjens' tetralogy. There is a real thematic agreement between the two cycles, arising from a common nostalgic ideal, though without the two works sharing any formal experimentalism. Waugh is here indeed experimental, but in a different, less obvious way, that is, for his peculiar view of the war and a

---

novel is enlivened, however, by the vicissitudes of a trio of rather spirited orphans whom Seal slyly farms out among various well-off families, as well as by the escape of an official suspected of fascism, disguised as an Irish Jesuit.

new, irreverent approach. Ford's tetralogy is, ultimately, something else. In *Men at Arms*,[52] which is largely about training in view of a continually postponed action, Guy Crouchback is introduced as the type of a non-assertive hero who puts up with things and stores them up.[53] The very first pages play the card of exotic colour with an array of larger-than-life Italian characters and the legends and superstitions of the Catholic cult of relics, including the sword of an English canonized saint who never managed to go to the Crusades, and who is a kind of conscious preview of the hero of this novel.[54] His Catholicism is subdued, reserved, largely romantic. He feels the call to arms in defence of the threatened national community after having lived in exile in a castle on the Genoese coast. He still has some ideals, he wants to enlist, and he feels the need for a voluntary sacrifice even though he is a Musilian 'man without qualities'.[55] His background is that of a voluntary exile in Kenya as a farmer, and of a failed marriage with a frivolous socialite whom he has divorced; like all of the numerous Catholics in contemporary British novels he is obliged not to remarry.[56] At the barracks where his training is taking place, in page after page describing the unadulterated routine of military life, unexceptional caricatures take centre stage along with sketches of the ordinary variety.

52   So titled, but with the irony and impropriety I have just mentioned.

53   His own definition: 'the lonely and ineffective man [...] past his first youth, cuckold, wastrel, prig'.

54   An internal and ironic link is that the general title of the trilogy refers to the giving of a sword destined to commemorate the battle of Stalingrad, commissioned by George VI and donated to Russia as a sign of homage, first put on show in Westminster Abbey, but without Guy joining the crowd queuing to see it. This episode opens *Unconditional Surrender*.

55   One of the reasons why, for one reviewer, he was 'a 1914 rather than a 1939 figure' (CRHE, 366).

56   While on leave, he tries in vain to explain his carnal needs to his wife, who by now has various marriages and divorces behind her. In one of the most malicious scenes of *Unconditional Surrender*, Virginia, Guy's wife, teases his uncle, a bachelor and fervent Catholic, by asking him whether he is homosexual. The uncle replies in the negative, and that he has twice had sexual intercourse with a woman, but without particularly enjoying it. From this moment on, Virginia begins to like the uncle, and decides to convert.

The *miles* Apthorpe deserves the specification of *gloriosus* for his innocuous blustering; an old patched-up ruin of many campaigns, Brigadier Ben Ritchie-Hook is a dog that barks but never bites. The whole episode of the portable chemical closet belongs to the glorious genre of the military absurd. The Royal Corps of Halberdiers is tossed to and fro, for example to the coast of Limerick to repel or stop a phantom German landing. The time frame of the war extends to the Dakar expedition of 1940, in which Apthorpe contracts a tropical disease that causes his death. Having imprudently brought him a bottle of whisky while visiting him in hospital, thereby accelerating his death, Guy is sent home at the end of the novel. *Officers and Gentlemen*, as often in war novels and those of Ford Madox Ford from some decades earlier, is replete with badly digested military material, in the form of dialogues or even informative sections unconnected with one another, or in the guise of a diary or bulletin drafted by an almost impassive writer; as such, it has nowadays a very limited appeal. In the same vein as the previous one, *Officers and Gentlemen* narrates the confused preparations of a commando unit on a Scottish island, then a crossing to Egypt and the ignominious evacuation of Crete in the winter of 1940–1941. After being rescued, Guy promptly returns to Britain. The telegraphic style, which some reviewers found inspired by Hemingway's,[57] is a strategy chosen here to avoid any rhetoric or false poetry about war. The regretful Guy is the only bearer of memories, of a sense of honour, and of devotion to the real man, like Ford's Tietjens; both are anachronistic dreamers of a Europe reunited under the banner of an *ancien régime* Christianity, able to look at things *sub specie aeternitatis*.[58] Thus around him an out-of-sync militarism is moving, abstracted from the objectives of the war action, à la Doctor Strangelove. In *Unconditional Surrender* what is by now definitively missing is the invoked shock, and what follow one another are unconnected and preliminary negotiations after 1943 and the concentric allied attack on Germany. Guy, still a loser,

---

57   *The Old Man and the Sea* is from 1952, and was often reviewed simultaneously, with a similar style being noted (as in a review in CRHE, 338).

58   Ivor Claire, a military companion of Guy, is the flower of the British cavalry, Ford's theme (cf. also CRHE, 370–1), at least until he sullies himself irreparably by cowardice.

and a survivor, cashes in on the victory of the conversion to Catholicism of his wife, who later gives birth to a son not his own, before dying in the London blitz. Guy, meanwhile, has spent all of his humanity in a collateral war operation, protecting a group of Jewish refugees in Croatia. His unfailing faithfulness to his credo subsequently rewards him, because, as a widower, he can finally remarry.

3. *The Ordeal of Gilbert Pinfold* (1957), which appeared between the second and the third novels of the war trilogy, is no doubt one of the most enjoyable and creative works ever written by Waugh. It shocks the reader with its blaze of comic and humorous inventions, quite as much as the war trilogy placates and appeases him or her; it is also one of his richest in sophisticated intertextual references and implications. Ostensibly, the narrative proceeds on the borderlines of the serious, the facetious and the surreal, with an initial glut of sketches from the late Victorian repertoire. Along the way we understand that Pinfold is prey to visions and hallucinations due to the sleeping pills he swallows during a sea crossing towards the island of Ceylon. His cabin resounds with the voices of people who do not exist; his days on board become filled with embarrassing encounters and inexplicable happenings, until a delirium of visions breaks up and 'an ingenious, old-fashioned detective novel' begins. In a nutshell, he believes he is on a warship transformed into a tourist vessel, and precisely in the control cabin from which the secret connections with the rest of the ship have not been turned off. During the crossing, he quickly loses his sense of time, fazed as he is by the sea. He witnesses painful and bloody events, and the grotesque climax is his obviously imaginary, self-gratifying seduction, by someone disguised as a Don Juan, of a chaste maiden. Near Gibraltar, two Spanish generals board the ship to avenge the maiden, and Pinfold has to impersonate a secret agent of whom he has the *physique du rôle*, and he prepares, or so he believes, to be handed over to the Spanish as a hostage. At the end of a series of countless vicissitudes, into which Waugh pours all his reborn verve, Pinfold is forced to admit that the journey was purely visionary. Beneath its surface value, with its series of inebriating goings-on, *Pinfold* unleashes a sophisticated and broad-ranging satire. It is a bad-tempered retort to his critics by a Waugh who hides, and as a result is also revealed, in his *alter ego*: he is now a much

more facile, mediocre, conventional, but also weird novelist,[59] working in a historical moment of declining genius, and super-productive but only thanks to his opportunism. He lives a middle-class anonymous life, even if his Catholicism is deep-rooted, not merely an accessory, as it isolates him and represents an alternative to 1930s communism; it is, however, a niche faith, not socializing but separating. This is reflected in his traditionalist artistic tastes and in his considering even the smallest hint of the avant-garde and modernity as so much eyewash. The choice of this *alter ego* on Waugh's part is a stratagem of the same type as that used by Browning identifying with Fra Lippo Lippi and Pacchiarotto, and therefore one suited to remove, add and deform the *alter ego* himself in order to hit the target more freely. In Pinfold, Waugh burdens himself with all the despicable marks of the everyman, with a heap of ailments and a susceptibility to visions and persecution complexes; he is made the object of all possible accusations – homosexual, impotent, maniacal, anti-Semitic, Jewish, fascist, communist – all of these being opposite and thus mutually exclusive labels. Right from the start, a hilarious broad satire on psychoanalysis also rockets forward. As we see happening in Barrie's *Dear Brutus* and in Shaw's *Heartbreak House*, Freudian day's residues re-emerge and take life before departure.[60] However, *Pinfold* is first and foremost a metanarrative novel owing to its highly skilful parodic pastiche. The title loudly parodies that of Meredith's famous novel, *The Ordeal of Richard Feverel*, but the weird voyage resounds above all like a kaleidoscope of the great marine archetypes of Shakespeare, Coleridge and Conrad. The ship is called *Caliban*, and is commanded by an ambiguous and truculent captain – or so he seems to Pinfold – who bears the inauspicious surname of Steerforth, the villain in *David Copperfield*. The various and

59   Waugh also has Pinfold listen to the radio on the ship, and hear interviews and broadcasts that talk about him, and in which he is criticized as commercial and second-rate. Waugh makes Pinfold even more reactionary in his artistic tastes: like Waugh, he detests jazz and Picasso (Sykes 1985, 19, 43, 123, 445).

60   Psychoanalysis had been Waugh's *bête noire* ever since *Black Mischief*, in which Basil Seal tries to keep Seth, who wishes to modernize his small empire, in the dark about it.

successive atmospheres, dream-like and delirious, are, however, mainly Conradian, and reminiscent in particular of *Lord Jim* and of *The Nigger of the 'Narcissus'* (a black sailor is sacrificed and his sick body is dropped into the sea). Pinfold superimposes on his delirium, unaware, a scenario that is a complete muddle. Captain Steerforth's imaginary collaborator in his wicked deeds is a woman rechristened Goneril. This is therefore also the metaphor of the fiction writer who, short of subjects, creates a surreal tale, and also a kind of sadistic-erotic fantasy, using hallucinogenic drugs. The targets multiply along the way, and the sense that Pinfold experiences, of being 'kept on continual observation', makes us think for a moment of Beckett's *Film*. We then gradually discover in *Pinfold* a prose script of the absurd genre, with Beckettian and also Pinteresque moods, occasionally smacking even of Pirandello. The accumulation of visions, among others of malignant male and female persecutors, and of vague, ethereal, unreachable, angelic female benefactors, is a lethal parody of Kafka.[61] With his last word, Pinfold melts into Waugh, since he begins to draft exactly the first chapter of this 'ordeal'.

§ 49. *Greene* I: The tussle with God*
A controversial author, praised to the hilt by some, belittled and torn apart by others, and therefore often misunderstood, is Graham Greene

---

61   I agree with the authoritative opinion of Angus Wilson (CRHE, 49).

*   Twenty-two novels approved by Greene, save for the last one, are included in the Collected Edition, London 1970–1982; *Collected Essays*, Harmondsworth 1970. K. Allott and M. Farris, *The Art of Graham Greene*, New York 1951; F. Wyndham, *Graham Greene*, London 1955; J. Atkins, *Graham Greene*, London 1957, 1966 (an often debatable and partisan anti-Catholic evaluation, but with two fine chapters on dreams and namesakes); D. Pryce-Jones, *Graham Greene*, Edinburgh and London 1963, 1966; A. A. DeVitis, *Graham Greene*, New York 1964; P. Stratford, *Faith and Fiction: Creative Process in Greene and Mauriac*, Notre Dame, IN 1964; D. Lodge, *Graham Greene*, New York and London 1966 (the best short introduction); G. R. Boardman, *Greene: The Aesthetic of Exploration*, Gainesville, FL 1971; *Graham Greene: A Collection of Critical Essays*, ed. S. Hynes, Englewood Cliffs, NJ 1973, 1987; U. Böker,

(1904–1991). One section of critics espoused his cause very early on, and with skilful gauging of restrictive adjectives and specifications, already consecrated him as the greatest living British novelist by 1948. This was the date of publication of the third of a trio of novels that turned out to be his most representative and lasting. This appraisal was confirmed in 1966, after a series of books by Greene that were, however, already more mixed and somewhat below par. No other novelist had appeared on the horizon in the meantime to dispute that primacy. Foreseeing that Greene's later production – by 1966 he was over sixty – could not invalidate that judgement or lead to a reassessment, such appraisal in practice amounted to defining him as the greatest of all British fiction writers of either sex after D. H. Lawrence,

Loyale Illoyalität. Politische Elemente im Werk Graham Greenes, Munich 1982; K. C. J. Kurismmootil, *Heaven and Hell on Earth: An Appreciation of Five Novels of Graham Greene*, Chicago 1982; J. Spurling, *Graham Greene*, London and New York 1983; R. M. Kelly, *Graham Greene*, New York 1984; R. Sharrock, *Saints, Sinners and Comedians: The Novels of Graham Greene*, Notre Dame, IN 1984; G. Smith, *The Achievement of Graham Greene*, Brighton 1986 (extended to almost all of his production, but with odd recurrent mistakes in the characters' names); *Graham Greene*, ed. H. Bloom, New York and Philadelphia, PA 1987; M. Couto, *Graham Greene: On the Frontier: Politics and Religion in the Novels*, New York 1988 (very attentive to Greene's criticism of imperialism and to multiculturalism, and accompanied [206–21] by a useful interview with the author); P. O'Prey, *A Reader's Guide to Graham Greene*, London 1988; B. Thomas, *An Underground Fate: The Idiom of Romance in the Later Novels of Graham Greene*, Athens, GA 1988; N. Sherry, *The Life of Graham Greene*, 3 vols (vol. I, 1904–1939; vol. II, 1939–1955, vol. III, 1955–1991), respectively London 1989, 1995, 2003; J. Adamson, *Graham Greene: The Dangerous Edge*, New York 1990; *Effetto Greene*, ed. P. Bertinetti and P. Volpi, Roma 1990; C. Comellini, *Graham Greene: le forme del narrare*, Abano 1990, and *Invito alla lettura di Graham Greene*, Milan 1996 (the latter flawed by mistakes and inaccuracies); *Graham Greene in Perspective: A Critical Symposium*, ed. P. Erlebach and T. M. Stein, Frankfurt am Main and New York 1991; R. M. Kelly, *Graham Greene: A Study of the Short Fiction*, New York 1992; M. Shelden, *Graham Greene: The Man Within*, London 1994; P. Mudford, *Graham Greene*, Plymouth 1996; C. Watts, *A Preface to Greene*, London 1997; W. J. West, *The Quest for Graham Greene*, London 1997; C. Baldridge, *Graham Greene's Fictions: The Virtues of Extremity*, Columbia, MO and London 2000; B. Bergonzi, *A Study in Greene*, Oxford 2006; M. G. Brennan, *Graham Greene: Fiction, Faith and Authorship*, London 2010.

and of the last sixty or seventy years of the twentieth century.[1] The mass of critical studies on Greene, which was already considerable in the immediate post-war years, responded to the haste to catalogue and pigeonhole a writer overwhelmingly affirmed. However, critics were at that time at a disadvantage from an inevitably short-range perspective, being unable to guess or imagine further developments in Greene's fiction. Meanwhile, voices of dissent had already arisen from a different vantage point, masking an anti-Catholic bias behind apparent ideological neutrality. They distanced themselves from Greene with often nitpicking arguments, quibbling over his novels' schematisms, his melodramatic plots, his ability to be just an entertainer at however high a level, and his concept of character and even his post-Baroque linguistic mannerisms. Orwell, Hoggart, Kermode, Waugh in some of his reviews, and more recently, Harold Bloom, belong to this small but authoritative phalanx of perplexed or less enthusiastic readers.[2] Basically, Greene had conjured up once again the old bogeyman of British Catholicism. The critical reaction to Hopkins's first poetic edition had been a case in point half a century earlier, though the two writers can hardly be compared. Greene was a very loose and unscrupulous Catholic in his life – a courageous, heterodox, even semi-heretical one – and anything other than an echo of the Vatican when it came to doctrinal matters in his works. A second accusation was more objective and anodyne, and of a strictly literary and aesthetic nature. Greene was in fact accused of having written consumerist literature, that is, of having enacted a crafty marriage of theology and espionage, a formula of compromise suited to all palates. Greene himself anticipated this, and threw readers and critics off the track when he distinguished in his fiction novels of entertainment from serious novels: a distinction that is too neat, since his ability lies in striking a balance between the two genres, if not at times even in reversing these labels. In reality, the equidistance or proximity of the two faiths, often antithetic by definition – and antithetic for the young intellectuals of the 1920s and

1   His primacy may be contested, as I shall argue, by Powell.
2   By Bloom, cf. the frank, not unexpected condemnation of Greene's 'theological tendencies' (Bloom 1987, 7). The positions of the other critics hostile to Greene will be discussed in the following pages.

1930s: Catholicism and communism, about which Greene too was to joke in one of his last novels –[3] made him a writer who immediately appealed to both the Right and the Left. He took in fact for granted the weakness and foolishness of politicians, criticized the Americans and capitalism, and even favoured a rank-and-file religion active on the side of the poor and genuinely missionary in countries suffering under dictatorships.[4] And all of this was said by Greene without the irritating interferences of nineteenth-century fiction writers. His formula was only unpleasant or suspect to the higher echelons of criticism, where he was classified as a lesser Dickens of the twentieth century – and popularity continued to be, on principle, as in the early nineteenth-century, inversely proportional to aesthetic worth.[5]

2. If Greene is to a certain extent an entertainer, this term need not be derogatory, since any art or, at any rate, a potential form of art, is entertainment, too. Greene uniquely manages to transform, elevate and refine crime news and espionage plots, and the literature of mass consumption and consumerist 'penny dreadfuls'. He is unsurpassed as an architect of tense electrifying plots; these plots are often kaleidoscopic, being partly derived from his tireless globetrotting journeys rich in vicissitudes that never appear forced or bookish but give the impression of the lived experience. He had read avidly and he had obviously sat at a desk within four walls, but he had also been on the move, an eyewitness of two world wars. Thanks to his longevity these wars had also been the 'Cold War' and the 'Hot War', fought at the most crucial points of the globe, in Indochina, Cuba and other arenas of decolonization. It is no coincidence that just before Greene himself debuted, the thriller had been rehabilitated by T. S. Eliot with an essay on Dickens and Collins.[6] Greene is, in various ways, the direct descendant of these two

3   § 55.3.
4   Green presented himself as equidistant in an interview with M. Couto (Couto 1988), and therefore not as a political writer. He had been unbiased politically above all at the time of the Spanish Civil War.
5   It is, however, true that of Greene's twenty-five novels a good half, some of them written at the beginning of his career and some later ones, are ephemeral and may be ignored, while the other half is his best and deserves a more accurate analysis.
6   Volume 5, § 168.2.

novelists,[7] as I shall go on to explain in some detail; but he brought them back to life and borrowed from them updating their technique and modifying some of their perspectives. For this very reason, he is also the heir of the sensational novel of Braddon, Reade and the Victorian detective-story writers. His predecessors also include Hope, Buchan, Haggard, and even one Marjorie Bowen, an obscure neo-Gothic author of a novel entitled *The Viper of Milan*, the 'viper' being the colourful nickname of a ringleader who betrays his followers. These predilections extended to the American writers of the 1920s such as Dos Passos, Hemingway, Faulkner, and Scott Fitzgerald, and to their novels marked by a sense of actual life recorded factually, with spare, dense dialogues and essential plot lines. If there is a British novelist showing a marked 'cinematic quality', it is Greene, who learned this skill by working as a cinema critic.[8] But he was also a distant relative of Stevenson, and as a young man he had thought of writing a biography of him; and he

7   A whole Wilkie Collins edition is in the library of Greene's *alter ego*, Pulling, in *Travels with My Aunt*, though the Collins preferred here is the non-detective story writer. The wealth of allusions to *Little Dorrit* in Greene's novels, and especially in *The Ministry of Fear*, is investigated by Smith 1986, 46–7. My discussion will try to bring out this intertextual dialogue.

8   Almost all of Greene's major novels have been, in turn, filmed, and Greene wrote at least two memorable screenplays. *The Third Man* (1950) was modestly considered by the author as an instrumental script, but it became a highly successful film directed by Carol Reed, and starring Orson Welles, Joseph Cotten and Alida Valli, and one which was an improvement on the novel according to Greene. The glamour of the script lies in a surreal Vienna divided into four zones in 1948 immediately after the war; it lies in the opening scene at the freezing cemetery where an alleged burial takes place, that of Harry Lime, the criminal who has adulterated penicillin and is even responsible for the death of innocent children, and in his pursuit through the city's sewers. The first-person narration is made by an English policeman who in turn reports the search for the criminal from the point of view of a third-rate and somewhat impecunious novelist who, in a drawn-out humorous episode, also gives a rather unscrupulous interview on the recent glories of English literature (and behind him is Greene who derides Woolf and Joyce with venomous insouciance). While one of the band of criminals in *The Third Man* has the blatantly Conradian name of Kurtz, Lime is the Catholic caught in flagrant mortal sin who declares he is still a believer, and who dies uttering the words 'damned idiot', which can also be interpreted – the narrator adds – as an 'act of contrition'.

had read Henry James with passionate intensity, having learned from him not only his alchemical mastery in the use of the point of view, but also and above all, as he said, an awareness of the 'sense of evil', which came from his 'spasmodic lack of faith in mankind'. James was also acknowledged by Greene as the first painter of a world 'of treachery and deceit'.[9] As a result, Greene presents a series of original settings never before attempted in the British novel, firmly set in the small middle-class house or the London maze, or at best in the countryside. His novels, although beginning in England, increasingly involve trips to the remotest parts of the globe, to Africa, Asia and the two Americas. However, Greene's authentically distinctive trait lies in the use of the detective and exotic plots not as ends in themselves, but as points of departure for a discussion – therefore partially allegorical – of moral dilemmas. Greene is unanimously recognized as having revived and re-investigated human conflicts that date back to Greek tragedy or medieval dramaturgy: the struggle between divine and free will; predestination, above all to evil; compassion for the guilty; Milton's justification of the ways of God to men and of men to God, and, lastly, the ontology of sin. One further reason for his following is his universality. His theatre is the world and his characters are of various nationalities (even if an Italian protagonist is noticeably absent). In this globalized universe Greene studies the 'heart of the matter', which on a smaller scale is that of Dante and Shakespeare. Like these two major writers, he operates within the genres of the tragic, the tragicomic, the comical and the romantic.[10] In particular, like Dante, he visits the three earthly and underground realms with a marked preference for hell and purgatory; like Shakespeare, he composes exhilarating comedies, as much as accounts of the agon between the human and the divine.[11]

9   Connoisseurs of James have vigorously protested against this 'misreading', and Harold Bloom was surprised to hear him defined by Greene – in his essay 'Henry James: The Religious Aspect' – as a novelist who is not only religious but also 'close in spirit [...] to the Catholic Church' (Bloom 1987, 2–3).

10   This leaning towards romance is the object of Thomas 1988, which traces various parallels between Greene's novels and Shakespeare's romances.

11   Cf. Bloom 1987, 3–4, for the family likeness with the Jacobean and in particular Websterian tragedy.

3. Having fallen in love with a nineteen-year-old Catholic girl, Vivienne Dayrell-Browning, twenty-four-year-old Greene suddenly thought of converting. At least initially, this conversion was dictated in Greene by a desire to marry his betrothed. They had become acquainted because in one of his articles Greene had committed a theological impropriety, by stating that Catholics 'adore' the Virgin: he should have said 'venerate'. He was received into the Catholic Church in Nottingham, where he was working as a journalist, after being prepared by a secular priest who had earlier been an actor and had a biographical background similar to Greene's own. At almost the same time Waugh had converted, becoming a more observant, orthodox and conservative Catholic.[12] What is unquestionable is that Greene's Catholicism remained of the head and not of the heart, rational and intellectual rather than emotional. It was also instrumental in deepening an investigation into the awareness of evil: 'one began to believe in heaven because one believed in hell'. In other terms, we can surmise that Catholicism offered Greene the chance to better cushion his life as a hardened sinner, being a religion that in the opinion of all Britons was historically more pardoning. Catholicism offered him a way to explore impossible adventures of the spirit, to deal face to face with the Father as if transfusing oneself into a number of new satanic hypostases: to negotiate with him, to play the damned man in search of atonement. Orwell noticed in Greene the aloofness of the British Catholic, and a sense of exclusive membership of a 'club', but he ultimately saw only one side of the coin. The whole debate over Greene's Catholicism takes on a different light if we stop reducing Greene to the role of the orthodox Catholic apologist. Let us consider him instead a novelist who made use of Catholic material, and put on stage Catholic characters who are afflicted by their dilemmas, and let us see what happens on the page and the artistic result this produces. He had defined himself up to a certain moment not as a Catholic novelist, but as a Catholic who was also a novelist; over the years his faith was

12   Couto 1988, 26. In the interview in the appendix, Greene stated: 'I'd rather romanticise the Left than romanticise the Right as Evelyn Waugh did' (212). Greene also considered himself superior to Waugh as an author of travel books.

to wane, and he eventually came to call himself an 'agnostic Catholic'.[13] It was a Catholicism that was in any case contradictory, schizophrenic, illogical, as is proved by his strange veneration for Padre Pio, a saint who performed miracles.[14] Greene's aesthetic was not that of edification[15] but of objective and impartial reflection of the chiaroscuro of life – according to Browning's image, of the black and white squares of the draughtboard; and Greene stood on the black ones.

4. Greene dedicated a youthful biography of a prescient type to the libertine Restoration poet John Wilmot, Earl of Rochester. Rochester was a sexual sinner who repented at death's door, but Greene appreciated his 'total lack of admiration for the act of repentance'.[16] From this approval he drew the image of God as a 'thief' who manages to hunt down and capture the sinner's soul after a long pursuit. Greene visibly shifts the focus from the detective to the criminal. Ever since Elizabethan drama, there had emerged in England a literature of the villain, the scoundrel, the rotter and the murderer, with the author's sympathies going unconditionally to human justice, deemed an infallible tool to ascertain the truth, and with evil being embodied in that reprehensible figure without a shadow of hesitation. This iconography had cracked in the mid-nineteenth century, with Dickens's ambivalence on Fagin and other murderers and wrongdoers; then with the thief and criminal in yellow gloves of the 'Newgate novel', then with Browning's apologies of the charlatan and the unresolved aporias between human and divine justice, and the investigation into the relativism of truth and into its own, ultimate inscrutability.[17] On the other hand, the early Greene links back to a family of writers who had not been ashamed

---

13   This confession is echoed in the interview with Couto (Couto 1988, 212), and from it we can understand that his faith was reduced to a flicker, taking also the form of theological doubts on the Church's stances at that time, for example on Latin America, advised by the then Cardinal Ratzinger.

14   Shelden 1994, 372.

15   In a short aesthetic manifesto with a title very similar to that of Orwell, but not with matching contents, 'Why Do I Write'.

16   Shelden 1994, 2.

17   Greene made no mystery of this link, and used to cite a relevant passage from Browning's Bishop Blougram monologue.

to approve of and admire crime as a work of art – Wilde was no stranger
to this apology – and for whom the guilty party is as much an artist as the
detective. In this respect, Greene's novels may be placed in the wake of the
refined and shrewd thrillers of Conan Doyle, whose Sherlock Holmes uses
in his investigations the argumentative tools of scholastic theology and of
Newman's 'grammar' of assent and of the authentication of truth. Greene's
plots are dictated by inexorable fatalism, being arranged by an invisible
providence that puts the human being to the test. They often rest on the
classic one case in a thousand, making Greene appear, as I mentioned, a
twentieth-century Wilkie Collins, or the heir of the more metaphysical,
more allegorical, more theological Dickens of the last three novels. To
both Collins and Dickens, as will be remembered, I ascribed metaphysical
investigations resting on the overused scenarios of the sensational. Before
Greene, the former especially had had the fame of a sheer entertainer, but as
I showed, his *Armadale*, for example, hinges on the possibility of defeating
predestination. Comparing Greene with these two great Victorians suggests
that Greene, too, challenges and gets rid of the Calvinist legacy – that of
the curse of predestination, of the power of evil and of the paralysis of free
will – in favour of Catholic redemptive possibilism.[18] The early Greene's plot
is invariably that of a man pursued for a crime of betrayal or for another,
often violent one he has committed, such as a murder. The first theological or metaphysical move Greene makes in these scenarios is justification.
Even in the most abject delinquent he sees the image of God, and reads
the enactment of the same miraculous metamorphosis announced with a
trumpet blast in Hopkins's Heraclitean sonnet – that man is a 'worm' but
the worm is 'all at once what Christ is'. An atavistic determinism makes
a criminal innocent or less guilty up to a certain point. Even more decisively he takes the side of the guilty party, turning to Browning's relativism and empathy, when he examines his or her motives. In each of these
'everymen', Greene brings to light a difficult and troubled childhood, or
the incidence of infantile traumas: his protagonist is often an orphan, was
brutalized by his father, has suffered disappointment in love, or experienced

18   Puritan ascendancies are noted particularly by Atkins 1957, 20, 22, and 198 (who sees
      them gradually overcome and crushed).

an oppressive religious education. The fact remains, however, that he has robbed, betrayed, or killed. But to this archetypical figure Greene applies a form of irenism that is reinforced by the paradoxical situations that concretely drove the criminal to act. The criminal, at any rate, often commits a crime against someone who is an even greater sinner than himself, and is thus a benefactor of humanity who has taken a short cut and initiated a violent revolution, too rapid certainly, but with the end justifying the means. As a result, in Greene the canonical stages are the following: betraying, sinning, justifying. Every criminal indirectly does good by doing evil, a lesser evil with respect to another greater one of which his victim is guilty. In the end, one detects in Greene a familiar, recurrent mechanism of nineteenth-century fiction: Catholicism deposes Manichean Calvinism and its doctrine of predestination, a fearful, obscure and menacing predestination to evil; it deposes, at the same time, the icon of a God who does not respond to those who implore him but merely vents his rage. Countless are the times that the comparison recurs in Greene between Judas and the sinning man, so emotionally and rationally personal to him. Judas is the arch-traitor in *A Gun for Sale*, 'just someone who unsheathed a dagger to come to his aid when the soldiers arrived in the garden looking for him'. Christ, Peter, and above all Judas are the three figures mirrored in the main characters of Greene's early fiction.[19] His 'Catholic trilogy' represents a leap forward, founded on the 'heretical' Catholic theology of Bernanos, Mauriac, Daniel-Rops and Teilhard de Chardin.

§ 50. *Greene II: Siding with Judas*

One cannot be the son of a headmaster with impunity, as Matthew Arnold proves; and for Greene, too, this was a traumatic adolescent experience. As a backlash, and this is another vague analogy with Arnold, he grew up cultivating the myth of transgression. This led to a life of movement, restlessness, endless journeying, intrigues and missions of espionage pursued as ends in themselves, merely to give existence a good shake, conquer boredom, and challenge danger. Travelling came to represent the thrill of a

---

19 Greene's reading of the Passion turns on the question of who loved Christ more, Judas or Peter.

face-to-face meeting with death, the same thrill of the moth 'attracted by the flame', which 'wants to come closer' but 'does not want to die'.[20] This attitude also found an outlet in continual challenges to ethics and to the religion to which he had converted: in the modern up-to-date career of the libertine, the womanizer, the Don Giovanni; in the collections of simultaneous lovers strewn, like those of sailors, in every port of call, and in the electrifying experience he was unable to resist, even if by now hoary, of the visit to the brothel; and in the utterly Catholic veneration of the prostitute. On this Greene *maudit*, implacably brought to light by recent biographers, Matthew Arnold could have pronounced the same disgusted disapproval as he gave on the life of Shelley and the early Romantics. Greene's myth of the fugitive, in the form of the truant from school, germinated at the Berkhamsted public school run by his father. In this troubled period he ran away from home, and therefore also from school, and amateurishly attempted suicide several times. To cure him, his parents sent him to a London psychoanalyst at just sixteen years of age. In his work and in his views on life, disloyalty was to become an indispensable ethical code, a civil and spiritual duty; every progressive human being is for Greene, by definition, a dissident, unstained by any kind of collusion with power. Later in life he took the side of the Russian dissidents Sinyavsky and Daniel, protested against the American war in Vietnam, championed the utopia of a united Central America removed from the aegis of the USA; and constantly supported every revolt against dictatorships. *The Captain and the Enemy*, Greene's last novel from 1988, is a singular, partial rewriting of his first, *The Man Within*, and as such can be briefly examined here. Hurriedly read by critics, then filed away owing to the imperious and hasty necessity of the general necrology of an author who would die only two years later, *The Captain and the Enemy* is divided into two parts that are rather dissimilar. A British adventurer tries to aid the Nicaraguan Sandinistas planning an attack on Somoza, who was supported by the Americans, and perishes in the attempt. This 'captain', a romantic and fearless dreamer with his constantly changing names and his thousand lives and resources,

20   From the interview with M. Couto, in Couto 1988, 216.

revives *déjà vu* types of British fiction in the wealth of his ever-imaginative initiatives, like Edward's uncle in Wells's *Tono Bungay*. At the same time, Greene looked back to his ancestor Stevenson with a plot about a 'kidnapped' boy. The first part of *The Captain and the Enemy* is something different, however, and surprises us because, without Greene being able to foresee it of course, it closes his career confirming its perfect circularity in terms of inspiration, theme and tone. Not only does the blurry sense of the initial picaresque phases bring to mind Greene's first work, *The Man Within*, but there is also a surreal and dreamy autobiographical evocation of two vicarious father and mother figures in pages bursting with lyrical inspiration and deliberately set in a spatial and temporal vacuum.[21] Here Greene stages once again the struggle of a son against a father, a struggle that the elderly novelist is still able to recall and transfigure, yet not forget or eliminate. One day, the pupil Victor Baxter is taken from school by a mysterious and picturesque 'captain' who has 'won' him in a game of backgammon. The getaway disguises the sense of scholastic unrest with which Greene's biography opened. His real father receives the expressionistic nickname of 'the Devil'. This adoptive son, who has also lost his real mother, is welcomed by a vicarious mother of the same name, in the form of a diminutive of Elizabeth, the name of the maternal figure in the Sussex hut in *The Man Within*. The settling of the twelve-year-old into his new affective habitat is immediate and wholly natural.

2. *The Man Within* (1929, but written when Greene was only twenty-one) is not often quoted among connoisseurs of Greene, perhaps because it

---

21 The internal chronology is also contradictory and conflictual, to be reconstructed from the clues: in the beginning the main character Victor is twelve, and being a double of the author, the period is the late 1920s or early 1930s, as is proved by the reference to the film *King Kong*, which is from 1933. However, given that the second part shifts to the late 1970s and mentions the 1979 revolution in Nicaragua, this gap, of more than forty years, seems excessive. It is equally impossible to think that the second *King Kong* film from 1976 is meant. The initial date of 1933 also fits another cinematic reference, one *Tarzan's Daughter*, a title that is probably inexistent in a filmography of this myth, a myth that was established by Johnny Weissmuller in 1932.

is typical and preparatory in some ways but not at all in others.[22] What still fascinates are the lowly, suffuse atmospheres, the misty hillside scenes, the surreal moors identified through the sketchiest of signs. It is a novel filled with a relentless series of morbid situations of suspense, gloom and faint lights and eternal fog, a fixity that lends it a dimension that is constantly dazed and dream-like. This atmosphere generates a stifling, obsessive and even exasperating narration, with few occurrences in long chapters in slow motion. At the age of twenty-one Greene already hit the invariable situation, if not the narrative style at least in some passages, of his most typical kind of novel, that of the fugitive, the mentally oppressed, the psychopathic and the visionary, along with the phenomenology of flight, terror, panic and angst of someone being hunted by real and imaginary enemies. This is why the interpretative suggestions in the background are so numerous. The melodramatic, overblown dilemmas seen under the microscope, and the psychomachia, are those of Conrad and certain Slav novelists; the problem of cowardice is from Stephen Crane; the moods are Browning's dream-like ones of 'Childe Roland'; the double nature of the main character and his interior division, and his 'two voices', are an unmistakable backward glance at the nineteenth-century macrotext of the doppelganger and at Stevenson's novels in particular.[23] At the same time, the plight of the psychopath in oneiric, closed places looks ahead to the second wave of the theatre of the absurd, that of a Pinter. Ultimately, however, the metaphysically 'wanted man', along with the dialectics of courage and guilt and the action of an invisible divine providence, and with the existential metaphor of the trial, are Kafka's. *The Man Within* is just that, a first, unmistakeable 'remake' of Kafka in England; and it is thus already a 'religious' novel of a kind. A smuggler, Andrews, cowed by the outright scoundrelly but dominating figure of his father, whose mettle he lacks, venerates his successor, one Carlyon, and takes part in some smuggling expeditions on the Sussex coast. He believes in Carlyon's romantic and chivalrous stature, but

22　　Aldous Huxley, with insight, judged it 'highly remarkable', and preferred it to Virginia Woolf's *To the Lighthouse*, praising its close physical contact with reality.

23　　On this link, cf. Allott and Farris 1951, 36–7.

succumbs to a momentary *défaillance* and informs the police. Carlyon and two of his henchmen avoid the ambush, and from that moment Andrews wanders around the land terrorized by the possibility that the three could do away with him at any moment. Andrews's disturbed consciousness is visited by infantile and adolescent traumas. Among these are the loss of his mother and an Oedipal hatred for his father. Hence his spasmodic search for dens, folds and warm hearths where figures of gentle female saints can put him up. One of these is Elizabeth. This mysterious inhabitant of a cottage, wise, lucid in spirit, instils in him the courage to testify at a trial against the smugglers. Needing to be adored, and yet also to be dominated by a friendly and protective presence older than himself, Andrews had idealized Carlyon in the same way. In *The Man Within* Greene's theological frame is announced. Its main elements are linked in an isotopy but without forming a complete allegory, rather a fragmentary symbolism. Andrews is not a believer, nor does he challenge God to show Himself. The macabre detail of a dead man found in the cottage brings into play a priest, religion, and liturgical rites; albeit through hasty formulae, short prayers and biblical verses filched here and there, it also presents Andrews with the future reward for the rightful, and induces in him a minimal doubt. What is paradigmatic is that Andrews should 'kill' a father who is too exacting and brutal, inhuman in his demands and too distant, and place his trust in mild, Christological Carlyon, whom he betrays anyway. Greene expressly compares Andrews to Judas, the betrayer of the master whom he does love, and who experiences the tremendous moment following the betrayal, the moment of anguish. However, Andrews is also a Peter, Christ's disciple, who disowns the saviour in the Sanhedrin. At a certain point, the cock crows. In Gethsemane, even in the act of pardoning Christ complains that the flesh is weak, and Andrews probes the dilemma between flesh and spirit in his hesitations. The flesh is weak and becomes soiled, and Andrews succumbs to the seduction of a Lucy at an inn before the trial, disowning pure spirit, that is Elizabeth. Here, Greene's human being is already at the mercy of the 'lowly man' or of the merely human; he is always ready, after a gesture of altruism, courage and obedience to duty, to slip back into Hopkins's 'man's first slime'. And yet the redemption of the coward, and the redemption of Judas himself, is possible, since

Elizabeth earlier induced him to come forward and become a witness at the trial in order to re-establish justice. Unconsciously, Andrews is then not Andrew, like his name, but John the prophet of Christ, or a Peter who fearlessly gives evidence and testifies. He unconsciously sets out towards faith and testimony, and from time to time he instinctively prays. Having betrayed Elizabeth, but only bodily and not spiritually, after the trial he returns to her. She pardons him, and their love would end in marriage if Elizabeth were not killed by one of the smugglers, on the loose during Andrews's absence. Andrews eventually gives himself up as the murderer, as a tribute to her, and sacrifices himself with an unexpected act of courage.

3. After two repudiated novels imitating the manner of Conrad, *The Name of Action* (1930) and *Rumour at Nightfall* (1932), *Stamboul Train* (1932), republished in America as *Orient Express* (the title by which it is best known), is one of adventure and camouflaged entertainment. The type is very different: the metaphysical or allegorical background seems to be absent or latent; and yet it gradually emerges. From now on Greene was to be a specialist in extracting the metaphysical from the physical or from the everyday and the lightweight; he was also becoming a specialist in the neo-sensational and flamboyant novel, a novel devouring distances without even one let-up in the suspense, and astonishing as much with its rhythm as with its huge natural wealth of incidental finds, even more remarkable given the concision and relative brevity. The metaphor of the journey is certainly nothing new, whether close or distant in time. Eighteenth- and nineteenth-century novelists and sketch artists exploited the stagecoach or the ship, the inn or the hotel, as a place of forced coexistence of various characters. But Greene's scenario is no longer Britain or the Ocean, and in *Stamboul Train* a fast-puffing train ploughs its way across Europe bringing the cardinal points closer. From the transatlantic to the train, what survives and smoulders is an identical sense of stupefaction and loss of coordinates: 'noise was so regular that it was the equivalent of silence, movement was so continuous that after a while the mind accepted it as stillness'. At the beginning, the entertainment is triggered when the train is boarded at intermediate stops by new travellers with their caricatured idiosyncrasies. Greene opts for an impressionistic, stereoscopic procedure, limiting himself to outlining and suggesting the background of the numerous characters,

carrying forward each of their personal stories in turn. As in Dickens's 'omnibus' novels,[24] having completed his supply of characters, Greene then makes them interact. However, this is a metaphysical train, as I mentioned: no one is there by chance but they are all there and have boarded the train for a good reason, because they play a role in Greene's vision of life. Beneath the surface and all the whirling is a metaphor of western secularization; so this is also in its way one of Greene's farces of the unredeemed world, a world 'in chaos', 'old' and 'full of injustice and muddle'. The 'vileness' of the bodies portrayed in this allegorical novel – as in Waugh's second one – is that of the degeneration of western faith. The journey of this human delegation is backwards: a pilgrimage that is by now pagan and secular from west to east, towards the faint star of Nazareth. An Anglican priest alights before midway, and his head is elsewhere. In particular, a young Jew, Myatt, is retracing the footsteps of his race, but is a slave of the flesh, of short-lived sex, sought and obtained thanks to the sparkle of his jewels and banknotes. Like Eliot's Mr Eugenides, the 'Smyrna merchant', he pawns the raisins that made him rich to underline the decadence of the noble Jewish ideal and the conversion of spiritual Judaism to profit. In this novel, Greene's hunted man is a communist agitator travelling incognito, wanted by the Serbian police. Alighting at Belgrade, he is supposed to ignite an uprising against the reactionary government; however, he is slightly but fatally late, and is intercepted by the police at the border. Greene's sympathies lie with him, but they are lukewarm: the man still dreams of shaking up the crowds, 'full of magniloquent phrases and socialist rhetoric'. As an adolescent he felt he had certain duties towards God, in fact 'to a god'. But he soon adhered to the Marxist vision of a religion as an opiate of the masses, 'a fiction invented by the rich to keep the poor content'. The spiritual believer's abjuration and his passage across the barricade will be a constant from this novel on. Here the agitator is not totally convincing because he is not a Judas but a Christ, and Greene always proves more sympathetic to the Judases rather than to the Christ-figures: 'I think I shall be of more use dead'. Myatt is policeman's widow and the detainee's wife fraternize. England Coral, a ballerina,

---

24   Volume 5, § 37.2.

agreeing to sleep on his feet in the corridor; however, this exquisite gesture of altruism is counterbalanced by the pure carnality of his love and by his casual infidelity with another passenger. At Vienna, the train picks up a murderer and thief, on the run because he had broken into the house of a woman he seduced, a more abject pendant to the erotic consummation between the Jew and the ballerina. The murderer becomes a second wanted man after the Serbian agitator, but in this case no redemptive halo descends on him, since his behaviour has no justification whatsoever, and he carries out one act of dishonesty after another. He does, however, remain a foil of blind, clouded and foolish human justice, since he is arrested by the railway police at the Serbian border for the illegal possession of a firearm, and not for the murder he has committed.

4. Greene revealed[25] that he had been profoundly moved by the hunger marches and the 1926 General Strike in the United Kingdom, and *It's a Battlefield* (1934) was judged subversive, and Greene a supporter of the class struggle and of the need to overthrow the current order, to the extent that the Marxist intelligentsia greeted him as a fellow communist.[26] The wind that is blowing in *It's a Battlefield* is that of a *Lehrstück*, given that an intransigent and fanatical communism demands that Jim, the unintentional murderer of a policeman during a political rally, must die as a martyr for the Red cause, clashing with the reasons for compassion upheld by those who identify with the drama of the wife and the detainee himself, and who get up a petition for the commutation of the death penalty, which in the end is accepted. However, the workers' movement lacked unity, and the sense of fragmentation is announced by an epigraph taken from the historian and travel writer Kinglake, referring to small groups who are fighting with no mutual coordination, because of a dense fog that cloaks the battlefield. The point of view is variable, and *It's a Battlefield* is, mimetically, a constant juxtaposition of settings, groups and scenarios. Policemen and protesters are on the same side but do not know it. The best scene of this mediocre novel is when the policeman's widow and the detainee's wife fraternize.

25   See the interview with Couto, in Couto 1988, 207–8.
26   HYN, 138–9, who shows the internal nuances that relativize the truth of both the law and communism.

England Made Me[27] (1935), it too anything but a masterpiece, is Greene's only moderately experimental and therefore modernistic novel, in some sections that improvidently play the stream of consciousness card. However, others empty the detective story and transform the novel into humorous parody. An Englishman, Farrant,[28] is the totally harmless and even careless bodyguard of a Swedish financial speculator;[29] but Stockholm is an acknowledged fake,[30] thus this is a weaker *Orient Express* which tests out, a good twenty years earlier, the spirit of Greene's fantastic and humorous novel about the various Brits scattered across the Caribbean and Latin America. Instead, the murderer Raven in *A Gun for Sale* (1936) has a name that gives us a first hint of a conflictual and disturbed inner life.[31] As often in nineteenth-century novels and in Dickens's work, this is due to a difficult childhood, albeit reconstructed in an overly schematic and hasty way in its traumas and determinisms, such as the delinquent father hanged, the mother who cut her own throat, the orphanage. The harelip which Raven is trying in vain, in one surreal scene, to have sewn up – and therefore mask – by a dentist who needs to anaesthetize him, is a symbolic mark reminiscent of the purple birthmark in Dickens's *David Copperfield* and other facial signs in nineteenth-century fiction. It is the mark of his exclusion from life and from a normal affective life, the mark of his diversity and repression. It is also a mark that, when he becomes a fugitive, he must try to hide using the most varied stratagems. The novel's device, as frequently in Greene, is the meeting of the characters involved, a meeting that may appear fortuitous

27 Conceivably a Dantesque echo.

28 Farrant is the first 'resignee', that is, unattached, free, footloose, in Greene's canon, and precedes Querry and Pulling in the role (§§ 54.2 and 54.3). He also has an ominous scar below his left eye. However, the real Conradian Englishman caught in a prolonged breakdown, even if not in a South American or Asian setting, is the waster of a journalist, Minty.

29 Who also anticipates Querry, since he is irritated by the media's violation of his privacy.

30 Greene had never been to Sweden, in fact, nor would he visit it later.

31 Poe's celebrated poem, 'The Raven', was familiar to Greene, who refers to it to describe the timbre of voice of Milly, the daughter of Wormold, in the first pages of *Our Man in Havana* (§ 54.1).

as it involves the action of Wilkie Collins's fate.[32] So in his escape from justice and the police, which forms the fulcrum of *A Gun for Sale*, Raven benefits from the unwitting assistance of the fiancée of the policeman who is looking for him. His anamnesis outlines his composite justification: in a Europe on the brink of conflict, Raven is commissioned to assassinate the pacifist Minister of War of a phantom foreign power in London; but this results in a long hunt for him for having used stolen banknotes, the ones received as pay for the killing. Raven the criminal is in any case less guilty than the band of criminals who imperil European and world peace by trying to provoke war and make a financial profit from the arms race. The guilty man is thus culpable for a crime which is, all in all, minor, and he must be pitied since he is victim of a much more colossal confidence trick which he has tried to thwart. He has been betrayed, paradoxically cheated; he is a cosmic scapegoat, and in his criminality applies a code of ethics and honour.[33] Greene's skill in thriller writing lies in making Raven, a wanted man, in turn the pursuer of those who have conned him, and thus in devising two parallel hunts. Except that, in this novel, the Judas role is assigned to Anne, the policeman's fiancée. She is in fact his betrayer, after Raven, exploiting a gas warfare drill, and having to don a gas mask like everyone else, has tracked down the conman and done away with him. Raven thus impersonates the Christ of Gethsemane who challenges God to let him see Anna again, a figure who inspires his redemption. However, God is for the moment a 'disappeared' God, and He will not let him find her.

§ 51. *Greene III: 'Brighton Rock'. The satanic saint*
With *Brighton Rock*[34] (1938), the first of his three 'Catholic' novels, Greene explicitly switches from Judas to the icon of the satanic. *Oliver*

---

32   Cf. the *mise en abyme* of one of the pantomime actresses in the imaginary Nottwich (in reality Nottingham, where Greene had worked in 1926 as an editor): she 'believed in invisible powers that set up meetings, and guided people down roads they never intended to take'.

33   This is also justified by the burden of the criminal act, which, with a reference to Coleridge and Baudelaire, was 'like a dead albatross round his neck'.

34   The title contains a word play on the other meaning of 'rock', namely 'stick candy'.

Twist had been the unparalleled plot of a band of picturesque, romantic yet shady thieves and pickpockets in early nineteenth-century London. *Brighton Rock* is a kind of postdated *Oliver Twist* that reconstructs the story from within, with truthfulness and inflexibility and yet also occasionally caricatured objectivity: the tragicomic vicissitudes of a fanciful horseracing gang. This flavour, of a distant and free remake, is suggested by the fact that Brighton is here a kind of London in miniature, with a more oppressive and asphyxiant topography, almost circular and whirling, and that together with the characters the reader incessantly scours its *maelstrom* of seaside alleys and passageways. He sits in luxury restaurants, in hotel foyers in *belle époque* style, and in popular inns and pubs; he strolls along the promenades where the attractions clatter and the multicoloured sideshows spin. Greene shows himself to be an authentic disciple of Dickens in bringing a city atmosphere alive, the very civilization and epic of the aristocratic and working-class holiday, as well as a historical era and a sub-community. If that is the case, he reinterprets that Dickens novel as one of escape, which is what *Oliver Twist* also is. The flight and capture of Dickens's Sikes are mirrored in Greene, with the same imperious and inexorable suspense, in that of Pinkie, the seventeen-year-old gangster; and in both cases, the flight is actual, existential and metaphysical at the same time. And Rose, Pinkie's girlfriend and wife, descends distantly from Dickens's Nancy. Dickens's compassion for the criminal, though never unmindful of retributive justice, is, however, a slightly different and more simplistic feeling than Greene's metaphysical and theological background scheme. With respect to *Oliver Twist*, Greene cuts away Dickens's picaresque prelude, and merely skims over Pinkie's past.[35]

2. According to an internal constructive law that had become by now established in Greene's fiction, *Brighton Rock* cannot but begin with a pursuit and therefore with a pursued man and a pursuer, and with a presentiment of death and a murder. For Praz, this scene had 'a power of execution' which gave the novel, or at least its first chapter, 'the stamp of

---

35   To find a distant precedent for Pinkie, an adolescent criminal with a lucidity that is, to say the least, adult, we may have to go back to Tappertit, the pretentious mob leader in *Barnaby Rudge*.

the masterpiece': a fatal and eminently visual, cinematographic stamp, and one of inexorability. The fictional eye sticks to Hale, a poor devil who is desperately trying to flee from capture through the byways and along the promenades of Brighton among a Sunday afternoon holiday crowd; dry and uninformative circumstantial captions never allow or force the reader or spectator to lose sight of the looming threat. These first pages are a successful example of a narration given by a narrator purporting to know less about the characters than the characters themselves; the air of enigma, of suspense, of a private game, is strengthened by internal hints offered as if everyone knew what was happening: by the silence over the background events, by the dialogues that brim with unexplained slang and by the double names and nicknames. The reader is immersed in a conspiratorial aura and for long he does not understand what is really at stake. In this opening scene Pinkie's murder of the *réclame* man Hale is not described, except in its consequences and reconstructions. It is never completely clear exactly what the criminal activity of Pinkie's gang is, except that there is an ongoing feud between the one now led by Pinkie and another, rather more powerful and organized, headed by a shady Jew, Colleoni. The novel's first sentence, 'Hale knew, before he had been in Brighton three hours, that they meant to murder him', does not immediately relate to what follows and to Hale's innocuous operation of handing out leaflets, while being shadowed by Pinkie. Hale is Greene's traitor, the one who has broken a code of honour.[36] Once Pinkie has killed him, Greene's fatal, or by now providential, combinations mean that it is the waitress Rose, Pinkie's fiancée and later wife, who obtains proof of his guilt and is the only one who can prove that his alibi is false. The narrative registers alternate, and are four in number. The naturalistic register recurs in the movements of the gang members, in the phenomenology of dialogues stuffed with interjections and jargon, but without vernacular inflections. It seems to have been caught live, but it is far from rudimentary; it is often an estranged and alienated phenomenology, as if inanimate nature were taking part in the tragic and enigmatic actions it is witnessing. The expressionist register is in captions, in frequently

36   It transpires that Hale had betrayed the former leader of the gang now headed by Pinkie, by revealing in a newspaper a racket for which the gang was responsible.

unrelated and disconnected impressions and flashes, pointing to an impossible synthesis in created reality, to disunion and abandonment that reign in the phenomenological, and to an absent or aberrant teleology. Greene often inserts weird, twisted, violently incongruous comparisons between unrelated elements, or astoundingly acute remarks that are not directly pertinent, and yet are not bursts of pure ostentation. He is also lavish in descriptions of painstaking verbal care and in flashes of rhythmic prose, at times rhyming or alliterative. An alternative comic-grotesque register follows the actions of a lay Nemesis in the person of Ida Arnold.[37] The epic or more precisely biblical register fits the metaphysical parable of Pinkie, echoing with the solemn cadences of *Paradise Lost*.[38]

3. The scenes of violence in *Brighton Rock* belong to a detective story anthology. Such a scene is for instance that at the horse race, both for the scorching, impressionistic and at the same time expressionistic visual representation of the various frames, and for the chilling and wholly elliptical description of the brawl with the razors, followed by Pinkie's frantic sprint to escape his attackers, the blood running from his neck and slashed hands. Tragic necessity obliges Pinkie to rid himself of all the witnesses of Hale's murder and of his further crimes by killing them, including his young bride.[39] The climax, Pinkie's simultaneously Luciferian, satanic and Faustian

37   One of the novel's few flaws is the visibly unnecessary inclusion of this cheery character, Ida Arnold, who harbours a purely lay sense of justice that is rather conflictual with her outward behaviour. Her intermittent, talkative and exuberant appearances never manage to convince. She is a secular Nemesis for her hearty, raucous guffaws and above all her abundant breasts, the latter a detail that is mentioned at every opportunity. Her spiritual counterpart is the pale, slim and floral Rose.

38   'It was as if they were shut out from an Eden of ignorance. On this side there was nothing to look forward to but experience'. This corroborates the satanic symbolism of the postlapsarian couple wandering after being chased from the Earthly Paradise. 'Paradise Piece' is, not by coincidence, the name of the school where Pinkie received his religious education; Peacehaven, actually a real place, is where the novel ends in tragedy.

39   Pinkie deceives Rose, who has sworn eternal faithfulness to him even in evil, and he convinces her to commit suicide with him, given that every escape route is now blocked; but he accidentally blinds himself with the vitriol and plummets from Brighton Rock.

challenge[40] with God, is necessarily dealt with in the magniloquent tones of the epic, mixed with neo-Gothic solutions, such as the vial of vitriol, a contrivance that Pinkie always has at hand and with which he destroys himself in the end. Pinkie is above all, by definition, 'the Boy', with a capital B, to signify his epic status. The theological skeleton gradually comes to the surface in the deliberately abstract planning and development of the plot in the guise of a pure theorem. Pinkie's internal morphology is so exceptional that it would be unthinkable in real life. He is a criminal mastermind despite his tender years. He possesses a lucid vision of things, naturally of criminal things. He always instinctively knows what to do, he takes instant and courageous decisions and never acts by proxy; he is steadfast and fearless; he does not give in to compromises, when it would be easy and convenient for him to accept the blandishments of the more expert rival gang.[41] He openly accepts challenges, and is loyal to the others in his gang. It is no exaggeration to call him a mystic of criminality. He is, in other terms, a kind of saint in reverse.[42] The fact is that he has no vices, apart from operating with criminal intent and killing to do so, but killing just for breaches of honour, as in the inflexible codes of the Mafia. There is a religion and a dogmatics of crime, just as there is a bona fide theological dogmatics. The criminal underworld has, too, a series of commandments that must not be transgressed, along with an apostolic succession. Pinkie is a young master half Christ's age, whose disciples are always a little degenerate, absent-minded and sissy. He does not swear, smoke or drink, nor does he have promiscuous relations with women; he is indeed a virgin and feels no attraction for female flesh other than weakly and exceptionally: 'his virginity straightened in him like sex'. His still young life is totally and abstractly devoted to the criminal cause, and he kills through a deduction of which

40   Greene's characters are Faustian heroes for E. Sewell, quoted in F. Kermode, 'Mr Greene's Eggs and Crosses' (1961), included in Bloom 1987, 33–42.

41   Colleoni, who has the gaze of one who 'possesses the whole world', also radiates satanic flashes.

42   R. W. B. Lewis, 'The "Trilogy"', in Hynes 1973, 56–7, finds that the seven sections of the book represent an inversion of the seven sacraments, which therefore become the 'seven mortal sacraments'.

he is only faintly aware, that to keep his gang going he must sacrifice the life of some of its members: the survival of his 'church' is more important than the life of its individuals. Thus Pinkie radically varies Greene's cliché of the traitorous man; or at least he is traitorous in a very remote meaning of the term. If he is no traitor he is no longer a Judas. Instead, his acolytes are small Judases. Faint-hearted and ultimately losers, one of them in particular yields to the flatteries of the stronger rival gang.[43] So is Pinkie a Christ, then? In certain respects he is, and this is because he gradually becomes a Satan, or more exactly, a Lucifer. This double identity is revealed by Greene in such an intermittent and flickering way that it comes across as a schematic anamnesis. Pinkie's childhood was spoiled by traumas: pregnant young girls who killed themselves, and his disgust in spying on his parents making love. But he was pious, and he confesses that he wanted to become a priest. The waitress Rose is also from a Catholic family, and both are believers, albeit tepid and no longer practising. Rose carries a rosary in her purse and occasionally prays and goes to Mass; Pinkie has a past as an altar boy and a chorister, and believes in the doctrine of reward and eternal damnation, but abstractly; and events prove him wrong.

4. In the first scenes Pinkie wins a doll at a funfair shooting gallery, and this doll reminds him of a strange Madonna; his Calvary lies in the fact that he presumes he has forgotten and subdued God, and that God has in fact left him unbridled, though He can at any moment, and anyhow at the supreme moment of the *redde rationem*, 'twitch upon the thread', in Waugh's expression. This is precisely why Pinkie the pursuer becomes the pursued, and the pursuit is both physical and metaphysical, since, in Greene's fatal or providential vision, purely occasional instruments, and agents however casual, may become divine instigators. Pinkie is hunted first by his conscience, which he tries to silence; then he falls into the crossfire between his fiancée and Ida Arnold, whom Hale met just before being killed in Brighton, and who also wishes to shed light on the murder. In a purely literary genealogy, Pinkie is one of many appearances of the

---

43   This instance of betrayal – but the betrayal of a Peter – is evident when Cubbitt, denying to Ida that he is one of Pinkie's gang, is recognized as such with the comment: 'a courtyard, a sewing wench beside the fire, the cock crowing'.

Decadent *maudit*, of an inert Ernest Dowson lacking in willpower but craving redemption, unable to redeem himself although desiring to do so, and sinking deeper and deeper into damnation; and meanwhile turning to blackmail, the satanic blackmail.[44] The Decadent, eternally on the brink between good and evil, could 'turn the tables' from one moment to the next, and change his life. A similar satanism is heightened with Pinkie's sacrilegious marriage to Rose, and the sexual act performed outside the sanction of the Church. He knows that a registry office wedding means opting for an 'eternity of suffering' in exchange for 'personal safety'; and precisely herein lies Pinkie's blackmail or exchange. He knows of the reality of Heaven and Hell, knows that he cannot think of eternity 'except in terms of suffering'. But 'there is no need to think of it, at least until one dies'. He postpones his repentance and understands that the infernal flames await him[45] in the perception and confused intuition of Rose's warning: 'You might die all of a sudden'. As an agent of providence, Rose echoes the warning: 'you don't know the day or the time'. A first trial, which could lead to conversion, so to speak, *in articulo mortis*, is the ambush he avoids by praying, but in the end he manages to feel no remorse and discovers that he does not have 'the courage to repent'. The murder at the races of his second-in-command by the rival gang could be the 'providential' disappearance of an inconvenient witness; however, it is yet more providential that the man is alive, a risen Lazarus, whom Pinkie must now inexorably eliminate. In this way he once again rejects and distances redemption and repentance, further fuelling the hellfire that awaits him. The arm-wrestling with God is won or lost according to the point of view. By a human yardstick, Pinkie is irrevocably damned, and in this case *Brighton Rock* might more appropriately be defined as an 'anti-Catholic' rather than as a 'non-Catholic' novel, as it is often presented as being. The desire for damnation has struck and infected Rose herself, kneeling at the confessional in the last scene; but the priest recalls that a Catholic is more capable of evil than anyone else, since the

44   Brighton is of course the birthplace and theatre of operations of Aubrey Beardsley.
45   A clever ironic presage is that the horse taking part in the races is called *Memento Mori*: asked by one of his mobsters what the name means, Pinkie is evasive in his reply.

God of the Catholics is much more merciful. Greene's paradoxical and acrobatic theology leaves a door open, or at least a chink, to the unfathomable intervention of divine mercy, since Pinkie may be redeemed in virtue of his love for Rose. Rose herself believes in this prospect, only because she is unaware that Pinkie's love for her is a falsehood.[46]

§ 52. *Greene IV: 'The Power and the Glory'. The theology of the repentant thief*

The Power and the Glory[47] (1940) is played out with the soft pedal, has less raw and seething action, and is less *fauve* in its colouring. The reasons for its immense international notoriety, even for its fame as Greene's masterpiece, lie in its drunken or 'whisky' priest, a sinner against priestly chastity, and Green was therefore risking heresy and scandal. This, in point of fact, cost the novel a condemnation by the Catholic hierarchies of the day, but it is a condemnation that, as I shall conclude, in the post-Vatican II age might unanimously be commuted into the recognition of the priest's most perfect orthodoxy, considering the other side of the argument. Greene's underlying theological scheme is again very subtle, but, let us say this straight off, the novel that is supposed to embody it, is, *qua* novel, rather undistinguished. Its successive frames parody a liturgical and sacrificial action, a Stations of the Cross, but never manage to set this epic background ablaze. *The Power and the Glory* is a picaresque that in large swathes is colourless and tame, and lacks definition. Its 'whisky priest', who however always drinks brandy and mostly seeks wine for Mass, preserves this

46   This particular is entrusted to a parody of the Catholic confession, the words that Pinkie records on a disc at the funfair on the prom, saying: 'God damn you, you little bitch, why can't you go home for ever and let me be?'.

47   Written at the same time as the much more superficial *The Confidential Agent* (1939), which is a pretend detective story, and whose masked intertextual variations on *Don Quixote* and the *Chanson de Roland* announce Greene's penultimate novel. In *The Confidential Agent* a classical philologist, lacking any heroic stature, is in fact charged by his government (probably republican, in the theatre of the Spanish Civil War) to negotiate an order for coal in England; but he faces the competition of an agent of the Franco faction. This duel is interspersed with humorous skits and the agent's chivalrous courting of the coal magnate's daughter.

antonomasia and his anonymity until the end, but never achieves a really mythical stature. Greene is spare and factual, which was what he aimed at, and never attempts an illusionist and expressionist reconstruction of reality as in *Brighton Rock*.[48] The painstaking topographic exactness of that novel fades into a haziness of symbolic movements in a space without real coordinates. The theological frame is arranged and played out within a fictional framework that dialogues with D. H. Lawrence, Conrad and Orwell. At least two post-war British writers were infected by the imaginary opportunities offered by the 1911 Mexican revolution, and by that sort of *Kulturkampf* which instigated not only the modernization of the country but also the defenestration of Catholicism and the establishment of a secular state.[49] In *The Plumed Serpent* Lawrence had launched a more daring hypothesis, that of a civilization and a regime that also wiped the slate of Catholicism clean, but instigated a religion that was allegedly even more sacred, and whose fulcrum is the phallus. Greene responded in *The Power and the Glory* by staging not the exit procession and funeral cortege of the Catholic God, and the settling in of the ancient Mexican divinity Quetzalcoatl, but the resistance and therefore the spiritual comeback, and the hold, of the Old Faith.

2. *The Power and the Glory* is religiously and even sexually traditionalist, and does not argue the pros and cons of Catholicism from the point of view of the individual's sexual liberation. The motif of the English witness of the Mexican revolution is borrowed from Lawrence and Conrad, but it is distorted. Not even Conrad could have thought of the isotopy of the teeth that runs through the novel,[50] which is part of a farcical symptomatology and a counterpoint of the Mexican malaise. It is no coincidence

48   The stylistic mannerisms of this novel were lambasted with no half measures in an essay by R. Hoggart, 'The Force of Caricature', included in Hynes 1973, 79–92.

49   Greene had visited Mexico in 1938 witnessing an ongoing persecution of the Catholic Church that was particularly severe in the province of Tabasco; this experience is reflected in his non-fiction book *The Lawless Roads* (1939). The whisky priest conflates Catholic martyrs whom Greene had actually met or that Mexican people had told him about.

50   It opens with the English dentist Tench and closes, in the penultimate scene, with the same dentist treating the police commissioner's toothache.

that Conrad has been mentioned, both because Greene confessed that
he was his model, and because Greene's Mexico reminds us of a Conrad-
style 'outpost of the empire', or a Malaysian station where the British economic and commercial protectorate has established itself. The obsessive
atmosphere à la Conrad is heightened by the ubiquitous and indefatigable
action of rapacious and revolting insects and birds that include beetles,
ants, crickets, mosquitoes and vultures. The Illuminist project of the new
Mexican dictators systematically demands a purge, indeed a 'massacre':
'first the church then the foreigners and then the politicians'. To build the
new regime it is necessary to proceed to the destruction of memory – and
memory is destroyed, in this as in Orwell's 1984 regime, by burning books,
expressly devout books. Right from the first paragraph, Mexico, which can
also be taken for a synecdoche of the world, is not actually close to a new
beginning, but sinking into an apocalypse. In the overriding mugginess,
an English dentist leaves home in search of a 'canister of ether', that is, of
by now spent spirituality and creative breath, but he only spots vultures
spying on the carcasses and ravenous dogfish in the waters of the river and
the sea. This dentist, Tench, is one of Conrad's human wrecks left in trading
stations along rivers, without a Lingard arriving to cheer them along. He is
a drifter, without any remaining desires or prospects, and with a ruined life
behind him. Greene goes on to describe many other jaded and frustrated
English men and women, some with families, who live in this Mexico for
business reasons. At the same time, then, *The Power and the Glory* can be
seen as a *Nineteen Eighty-Four* with a change of sign and accent: as the
dystopia of a slightly future or slightly past world, or rather, in this case, of
a universe in which Catholicism is in extinction or threatened at its very
roots, sucked back into a lay apocalypse, and with a single survivor who
successfully struggles, sacrificing himself, to keep the flame alive. The target
is twofold. The dentist who keeps up with the times, and tries to obtain the
latest findings in dental care, and the country's political organs busy with
renewal, may create the impression of a satire of modernity and modernization. Waugh, too, was travelling around the world at that time like Greene,
and by making Abyssinia its epicentre he ridiculed other attempts to ape
Europe, and other obsessed dictators. Orwell's last survivor of the democratic state is replaced by the last exponent of an abolished faith, namely,

the last Mexican priest in activity, albeit with all his anguish and cowardly acts. More precisely, he anticipates Orwell's powerful dilemma between remembering and forgetting: 'The new children would have new memories: nothing would ever be as it was'. Here is the reason for the parallel plot of a pious woman who reads to her children a hagiographic work that celebrates a local martyr. Greene's conservatism is not dissimilar to that of Waugh, and, agreeing with Waugh, this may be an ideological gesture of Greene's, one of those striking exterior ones implying a clear-cut choice of field, that is, the celebration of the Catholic Church's stabilizing and civilizing power. It is therefore an apology explicitly contrasting Marxism or even the compromises invoked by certain Catholic fringes, such as the marriage of priests, or priests' collaboration with totalitarian regimes. The partisans who rant and rage against obscurantist Catholicism in the Mexican desert are in fact called 'red shirts'. This Mexico, or part of Latin America, is a synecdoche of the deconsecrated world, merely the physical remains of the erstwhile civilization. Winston Smith and Greene's priest are two dissidents, therefore, even if the former is fighting in favour of libertarian humanism and the latter for the survival of a religious confession. In Greene, the distance between reality and imagination is unquestionably less than in Orwell, indeed almost zero, since recent political history is substantially reflected; and yet the time seems lost in the mists of the past, and the old believers continue to yearn for the 'days when there were still churches'.

3. Since the last of the then distant Victorian decades, a Catholic priest had no longer been the main character of a major British novel, and that priest was at any rate fighting doctrinal issues different from the ones Greene attributes to his protagonist. In 1940, an alcoholic priest who had fathered a daughter could cause a scandal, but measured against the more tolerant and enlightened codes of the third millennium it almost becomes the norm. At the end of the day, what is so 'abnormal' and depraved about him? He is neither a paedophile nor a homosexual, he does not collude with capitalistic power; he is a simple priest and does not belong to the Church's high spheres. His flesh may be weak but the duration of his sin, which he fears will damn him for eternity, was just five minutes, enough to impregnate a woman and cause the birth of a daughter. He is no chronic

alcoholic, but keeps his spirits up in a desperate mission with a few drops. The martyr is a man subject to fear and to the rejection of martyrdom itself, and is no martyr until the moment when he becomes one. There are no very distinct narrative registers in the novel, rather counterpoints. The priest moves around the Mexican geography following the cardinal points; the time is that of the drought and the rains, and the Indian villages present no differences. In his movements and arrivals at stations he chances upon an English dentist who welcomes and helps him, as well as the family of a banana exporter, whose thirteen-year-old daughter hides him in a barn. These two incidental episodes occasion a separate but uninspired comedy (Greene is not Waugh, and never excels in pure caricature). The opening is ingenious because the dentist encounters the priest and the priest hears an exclamation in which God is named in vain, and this is assumed by the priest, who is circulating incognito, as proof that he is a believer, which in fact he is not. The priest is finally Greene's new version of the man pursued and wanted, though this time not for a crime, but for a residual courageous uprightness. The ideological struggle that arises is between the priest and the Mexican lieutenant, who are complementary characters, the same and opposite: in the lieutenant 'there was something of a priest [...] a theologian going back over the errors of the past to destroy them again'. The lieutenant is defined as 'mystic', but a mystic experiencing a vacuum of God. The schematism of the progress towards the Cross is traced in the ship which the priest misses, but only temporarily, on his way to the 'True Cross' – Vera Cruz – in order to help a dying woman; later he will head for Monte Cristo, while his final destination is Las Casas. The term 'power' has a range of meanings, the first being that it is not within '*his* power' – that is within the priest's power – to be a priest no longer, because one is a priest for eternity, even in a state of mortal sin, which would exclude the sinner from grace. In reality, the agon is wholly internal, between weakness and desperation on the one hand, and the lasting ministry of God even on the part of the weak and the sinners, on the other. The second meaning of 'power' is the satanic. In the priest there reappears an antagonist of God, a demonic double devoured by the ambition for power, which is not the power of the Church that subjects, but the magnification of his personal ego. He explicitly compares himself to the fallen Lucifer. Greene's first two

Catholics, Pinkie and the priest in *The Power and the Glory*, are therefore very close, in their polar excursion; in fact, one is the double of the other.

4. However, the leitmotif of Judas insinuates itself anyway. The biblical Lucifer could have been a kind of Christ, and this poor Christ, the priest, is betrayed by another priest who is a Judas, namely the humble and ever-fearful Padre José, who is a faint-hearted defeatist and quietist. In the intense prison scene, overflowing with revolting details, the whisky priest bares his soul, puts himself on the same level as the wrongdoers and confesses that he is even more abject. The theological point is here that the priest realizes that he loves the fruit of his sin; he believes therefore that he cannot be pardoned, and eternal damnation awaits him. This casuistry question may be solved by subjoining that he repents having given in to the flesh, but having done so he, as a priest, cannot avoid loving a human being, even if she is his carnal daughter.[51] After committing a sin that has a tangible sinful result, it is necessary to take note of the irreversible outcome and begin again from the new situation. It is from mortal sin that one rises more efficiently towards redemption, since venial sins keep man further from God. He emerges more cheerful from this 'night of the soul', with the desire to do more and not less for his faith. After leaving the prison he begins a peregrination across the desert, full of symbolic encounters shrouded in the surreal: he competes with a dog over a piece of meat, finds a dead baby in a shed and buries it in a spectral graveyard. This is a preparatory exodus, after wallowing in luxury and a sensation of being hungry and exhausted. Conscious of the weariness of the flight and of the need to attain peace, he is ready to embrace martyrdom. The epilogue adumbrates a further theological point. It highlights the theology of the thief pardoned by Jesus on the Cross, which becomes the predominant image instead of that of the Judas complex. According to Catholic doctrine, it is always possible to be saved on the point of death by repenting of one's sin, even for a whole life sunk in sin. And yet the lieutenant has the priest shot for betrayal, after a

---

51   In 1940 Greene already seemed to have taken a stance regarding the question of priests marrying: he denied priests the right to marry, and marriage meant for him the end of priesthood; however, he did concede that they could repent for the weaknesses of the flesh.

spectral Sanhedrin in which he, an atheist, is forced to play the paradoxical role of an ecclesiastical tribunal and impersonate the icon of a judging, severe, inflexible, and vindictive God. The lieutenant's voice becomes secular, if not altogether Marxist, when he reproaches the Church for its (economic) power and the backing of capitalist regimes, together with its inertia and social absenteeism. The most dramatic counterpoint is, however, that based on Padre José, the pusillanimous antagonist of the whisky priest. Padre José is a married ex-priest who failed to understand that one is a priest for eternity and that God has already pardoned his sin; because of this presumed unworthiness and self-suspension *a divinis*, he refuses to confess and absolve the other priest before his execution. The execution is followed by spiritual and curative miracles that the sacrifice induces for the benefit of the unbelievers. In the small collateral tale in instalments – the hagiographic one told by the mother to her children, mentioned above – which comes to an end, and closes the novel, her sceptical and distracted son hears a new priest knock on the front door, as if in a dream. This conclusive piece of the reading creates an overlapping between the priest with no name and Juan, the John of the book, who is heading for martyrdom and who bears the name of the Baptist as well as of John the evangelist, who witnessed Christ's crucifixion.

§ 53. Greene V: 'The Heart of the Matter'. The judge judged

The Ministry of Fear (1943) is in Greene an open bridge towards *The Heart of the Matter* (1948). Arthur Rowe, a middle-aged journalist just a touch worn-out and absent-minded, feels like a criminal hounded by his conscience; out of sheer compassion, he let his wife die of an incurable disease to avoid causing her further suffering. However, this private drama, which in a Freudian sense is never repressed, blends, though somewhat unnaturally, with the public one in a London being bombed by the Germans. The confused sense of danger and emergency of the Blitz is the novel's almost sole positive point. Rowe heralds Orwell's Winston Smith when he is admitted to a psychiatric clinic after accidentally discovering a British philo-Nazi group of spies and losing his memory. Not yet recovered, and still in a state of amnesia, he flees to freedom and helps the police to stop the dangerous plot. Deriving from Greene's service in Sierra Leone during the war, *The Heart of the Matter*[52] begins blandly, without clamour, with the lights off, as a colonial novel similar to Orwell's *Burmese Days*.[53] The small British community there meet at the club where home-grown snobbishness is reproduced, certain outsiders are unwelcome, the members abandon themselves to nostalgia, romantic and aesthetic desires are cultivated, books and newspapers from incoming ships are awaited, and mute frustration prevails. Around are the sea views, the local population of servants, petty delinquents, prostitutes, shady diamond traffickers who are suspected of spying for the Germans. Greene deliberately sub-narrates and for a while simply reflects the normal everyday life of the colony from the point of view of a policeman, as Orwell himself had been in Burma. In reality, the novel towers over Greene's other ones for the gradual but inexorable timing with which its moral and religious drama explodes, starting from the apparently innocuous occurrences of the petty transgressions and weaknesses of the upright man and his collusion with evil. Here, Greene's man is in the grip of a chain of determinisms that lead to the accumulation

52   The title can also ironically be read as 'the matter of the heart', given that the main character Scobie dies from a presumed angina.

53   This comparison is expanded upon in Couto 1988, 121–6. Orwell's review of this novel (OCE, vol. IV, 497–501) is in turn a short, anything but benevolent, essay on Greene's Catholic trilogy. Orwell's evaluation of Greene's novels is as follows: the best is *The Power and the Glory*, less successful is *Brighton Rock*, only in third place is *The Heart of the Matter*, which is for him 'mechanically constructed' and spoilt by many improbabilities and shortcomings, the first being that this African novel does not quite render a sense of Africa, and that the plot could also have taken place in London. But can it really be true that, as Orwell maintains, Scobie does not care about work? Orwell's target was above all what he believed to be a tenet of Greene's Catholicism, that it is better to be 'a Catholic sinner than a virtuous pagan', therefore, a snobbish and presumptuously exclusive Catholicism which did not prevent Greene from depicting sinning and unworthy priests in his novels. For Orwell, Greene was the opposite of the Chesterton of the Father Brown stories. Orwell would never retract the criticism that Greene's characters were implausible: Pinkie cannot be a satanic criminal and at the same time be aware of the conflict between good and evil; nor can Scobie be a theological policeman. And yet Orwell is singularly insensitive to problems of conscience, and convinced that man never lives with contradictions. Waugh, too, severely criticized the novel's theology as inhuman.

and geometric progression of his shortcomings, as if, theologically, a sum of venial sins could determine a mortal sin.[54]

2. For the first time, in Greene's Catholic trilogy, Scobie, the deputy-commissioner of the colony's British police force, is Musil's 'man without qualities'. Neither a gangster nor a priest, middle-aged, with fifteen years' service, by now the colony has become his habitat, and he has a recognized role and a public function. He is the guardian of order, upright in his operations; he is also an affectionate husband, even if his wife is fatuous, gives herself airs as an intellectual, reads and recites poetry, and poses. Scobie is the very spirit of responsibility, the social sense of aid and respect for one's neighbour personified. He does not drink, smoke or fornicate – unlike the whisky priest, but not Pinkie in *Brighton Rock*. He is a kind of biblical justice of the peace, who sorts out small conflicts in the local community, and exudes a priestly and Solomonic aura. He is Scobie the Just; others call him a Daniel, or the Good Samaritan: a lay saint, therefore, detached, capable of self-control, unromantic. Precisely because of this, he harbours no dreams of glory, chases after no career, and can humbly take a back seat. However, he is no simpleton, and always gives fitting answers in line with his ethics. The novel deliberately languishes in its first half because there is no threatening ripple in the professional and affective life of the Scobie couple. The only previous event worthy of note is the loss of a little daughter at a tender age many years earlier;[55] the only fact that makes us think is that the Scobie couple are Catholic, she by birth, he by conversion. While Louise Scobie's Catholic faith is mostly aestheticizing and therefore flexible, Scobie practises little but shows his pragmatic creed in his works and daily behaviour. That his Catholicism is merely superficial – as his wife reproaches him – is a tragic, lethal irony, since he will die at the behest of intransigent Catholicism. A premonitory warning is a rumour that he, the chastest of husbands, has

---

54 Even in the extremely spare scene of the kiss between Wilson, the cheap suitor, and Louise – a paragraph which is a small masterpiece – the narrator is able to comment that 'an act had been committed that would change the whole world'.

55 Lodge 1966, 30, explains that the injury due to this loss caused Scobie's unlikely attraction for a nineteen-year-old widow. At another point in the novel Scobie denies believing literally in hellfire, and defines it merely as a sensation of great loss.

had sexual relations with the colony's black women: it is a slander, like the other rumour that he receives backhanders from a rich Syrian to encourage the smuggling of diamonds. The theological novel really gets going when this lay saint begins descending a slide that eventually turns him into a sinner, in line with Greene's ever-ephemeral borderline between virtue and sin.[56] The epigraph from Péguy is proleptic, and announces the investigation of sin and its function in faith, and posits the polarity and perhaps also the equivalence between sinner and saint. Equally proleptic is the episode of a letter sequestered from a Portuguese captain, which Scobie does not report but burns, and which certifies, if not an awareness, at least the possibility that the law and even the Law could be interpreted by man, and that, in Gospel fashion, the Sabbath is for mankind and not the reverse. This fact is also the first link in the literally fatal chain, Scobie's first step on the slippery slide. He has committed the first innocent violation of the law, and will later be so righteous that only he will believe to be and want to be the first victim of the very inflexibility of the law. Another presage is the suicide – an unpardonable sin – of another policeman, which Scobie witnesses.

3. Hence a small cluster of presages thickens around Scobie, who cannot for the moment register and decode them. The tension rises due to a flirtation by Louise that could threaten the couple's conjugal life; but everything is dispelled and buried by the holiday that Louise takes, being exhausted and in need of a change of air. During her absence the inflexible and incorruptible judge begins to lose his impartiality to those being judged, for example when he takes out a loan with interest, and above all when he is mixed up in a series of tip-offs that turn out to be false. The destructive dilemma originates in a shipwreck from which a young widow, Helen, escapes alive, almost by a miracle – a perverse miracle, if it is one. Like that of Hopkins's *Deutschland*, this is a shipwreck that seems to point to the mystery of a God who kills and saves his creatures on a whim, and one that nevertheless makes Scobie exclaim that God is instead human, and as such must love all his creatures. The first theological question therefore

---

56   This is visible in one of Greene's many theologically shocking similitudes: 'Virtue, the good life, tempted him in the dark like a sin'. On this borderline Greene wrote: 'The greatest saints were men of a more than normal capacity for evil, and the greatest sinners sometimes touched holiness closely' (quoted in DeVitis 1964, 90).

regards God's inhuman inflexibility, which recalls Hopkins's distant, basic query, in 'The Wreck of the Deutschland'. The judge falls not because he is guilty before the world of breaches of honesty, but only through petty foolish acts; nor, on a closer look, does he fall merely owing to the flesh, that is for a sin of incontinence or the resurgence of desire, by cultivating his affair with the widow, who experiences everything superficially. Scobie cares for her out of sheer compassion, out of a spirit of disinterested aid; but he ends up heedlessly precipitating into adultery. His good action has ruinous consequences. In his diary he must mentally agree that the God he judged human is instead capricious and cruel: of the two desperate cases after the shipwreck, and despite so much praying, why has God let an innocent baby die and the widow, who will end up damning him, survive? The dilemma becomes insoluble on the return of Scobie's wife. She induces him to make his confession and take Holy Communion feigning she has no suspicions, though she knows of his infidelity, as does the entire colony. Scobie, who does not have the courage to confess his adultery either to her or his confessor, believes he has committed an unpardonable sin, adultery, and believing this he commits two or three more, because he must take Communion having committed a mortal sin without absolution, and because the only way out of the impasse is suicide, an act of desperation, unpardonable in Catholic doctrine. Meanwhile, he masks his fearfulness and falsehood with a counter-theology that rests on the cornerstone that 'love, any type of love, deserves a little mercy'. However, it is also true that, faint-hearted though he is, he knows he cannot deceive, because he cannot promise in confession that he will not fall into sin again, and also that he cannot bring himself to renounce that adulterous love. The confessor, who does not absolve him, recalls that God pardons seventy times seven, but each time there must be a desire on the sinner's part not to sin again, and Scobie is sincere with himself. It is the overriding sense of his unworthiness, his rottenness, the filth of his heart, too much for the Lord, which pushes him to commit suicide.[57] Shortly before his death, he talks to God, certain

---

57   The ways of the Lord are mysterious and above all contrary to those of man, if it is true that at this moment Scobie receives the news that he has been promoted to police commissioner. But Scobie is prostrate and has by now decided on self-annulment, and refuses the post.

of being damned for eternity, and of having ensured peace not only for the two women but also of having ceased importuning and above all sullying the Creator. In this sense, he has carried through a paradoxical martyrdom. Greene comments lucidly on the less lucid, merely brooding Scobie, that the doctrine of the Church is one thing, while quite another is the law of Christ who 'killed himself on the Cross', so that God can 'extend a hand that pardons' over the suicide. Committing suicide while facing an insoluble dilemma is not sin, or is not an unpardonable sin, and God may have pardoned Scobie in his immense compassion; he is not an inflexible and cruel judge. Greene closes the novel with a sort of Goethian 'er ist gerettet', instead of 'gerichtet'.

4. In *The End of the Affair*[58] (1951) an agnostic novelist, Bendrix, bears rancour against his erstwhile lover, Sarah, who, though married to a diplomat, had a passionate extra-marital relationship with him. This relationship ended for a reason which is revealed to him only on reading her diary and learning that she left him after taking a vow to believe in God if he, Bendrix, were to survive the London Blitz in 1944. The miracle happened. Greene's scenario is thus no longer of a man, but a woman who must tackle and justify adultery, having lived a double life for some time, like Scobie.[59] It soon becomes clear, however, that the conceptual, religious and moral variation is substantial. Sarah devises a battle of will with God, as Scobie partially does; but she wins, forcing the salvation of her lover from Him. Despite the detour, the result is the same: a sacrifice, except that Scobie's self-sacrifice is reversed and transmuted into the sacrifice of unfaithful love. Eternal damnation, should it exist, is avoided, and redemption smiles on Sarah. Theologically, the protest is addressed to God, with a return to Greene's initial theme of a God who hunts down and drives out reluctant humans. This is paradoxically a God who is ill-treated and offended because he insists on saving humans from sin, and has let them transgress only to steal the agreeably delicious fruit of sin from them. The challenge having been won, or in reality having been lost, the reconstruction of faith from

58   A subtly bivalent title, since it also alludes to the spiritual affair of recognizing God.
59   The private detective Parkis is one of the very few larger-than-life characters in Greene's canon, and is not out of place in a novel that, as I notice, looks like a Victorian remake.

zero begins, with Sarah finding her own way to a revealed Catholic God. The remaining doubt is whether the victory for Sarah is permanent, since she continues to love Bendrix despite giving him up, or if the flesh would induce her to fall and break her vow: death has saved her and allowed her to escape the ordeal. By now, however, Greene has crossed a border; rather more orthodox and apologetic, he makes divine proof triumph along with the natural or, so to speak, Voltairean emergence of the faith in God. The module is the tried and tested one of the nineteenth-century memoir, and is split into three time frames that are deliberately jumbled up to create continual illusionism. Told in the first person by Bendrix himself, it presents the most classic imbrications of a polymorphous text, with overlappings and temporal zigzagging as in Huxley's *Eyeless in Gaza*.[60] Sarah's diary, albeit the most melodramatic and least convincing part of the novel,[61] is intertwined with Bendrix's recollections, and from its own point of view repeats the narration of past events. Greene mischievously camouflages himself in the passionate lover who deals with religious affairs impatiently and with light-hearted derision, and ends up scorched by them. The plot is reminiscent of Wilkie Collins in its arcane coincidences and denouements, and the last of its *coups de théâtre* is that Sarah was predestined, but towards good and salvation, because she had been baptized as a Catholic, even if she herself was unaware of this.[62]

§ 54. Greene VI: Novels of espionage and exoticism

For many years after 1950, in several of his novels Greene re-entered the category of the sheer entertainer, and his fiction underwent a process of secularization which was watched with perplexity and dismay by those who

60 As is also recalled, with a somewhat perplexed judgement, by Atkins 1957, 58.

61 O'Prey 1988, 90.

62 Lodge 1966, 37–9, notes that the destructive dilemmas caused by the firm coherence with the dictates of the faith reverberate in the two not totally successful plays by Greene, *The Living Room* (1953) and *The Potting Shed* (1957). In the second, in particular, a deceased man comes back to life thanks to a miracle similar to that invoked by Sarah in *The End of the Affair*. And yet, in the play *The Complaisant Lover* (1959), Greene surprised, and still surprises, readers for his 'bland acceptance of a *ménage à trois*'.

had believed in, and even hoped for, the persistence of his investigation of conflicts between the dogmas of abstract religion and the phenomenology of the purely human. It is difficult to believe one's eyes, and admit that this later Greene is the writer who had penned the masterpieces of the 1940s. An overview of this long, 'lightweight' and on the whole disorganized production points to a writer who feels annoyance over the labels attached to him, and gets rid of the previous spiritual and theological burden by overturning, contradicting or simply downplaying it. The Catholic phase petered out in 1948 with the transition to novels focused on the great issues of international politics or their effects, in the scenarios of Cuba, Haiti and South Africa. As a character in *Our Man in Havana* says, 'We live in an atomic age, Mr Wormold. Push a button – piff bang – where are we? Another Scotch, please'. Greene's post-1950 novels are indeed classifiable as being of the 'atomic age', though this label does not imply a sense or an aura of imminent and even more weighty and frightening tragedy, rather a cheerful, comical, disenchanted exorcism of the Apocalypse. The historical background of the Second World War, the repeated arena of the fictional events until then, suddenly disappears with the anonymous and semi-serious *The Quiet American* (1955) set at the time of the Indochina conflict.[63] The Catholic question does emerge, but in a descriptive and illustrative form, as one of the peninsula's faiths in contention. Greene took advantage of his four visits to that part of Asia to disguise an inventive story and come out with a political stance behind the screen of a war reportage.[64] The plot revolves around the conflict between the American correspondent Pyle and the Englishman Fowler, who is the internal narrator of a story wholly told in retrospect. The two friends/enemies have loved the same Vietnamese girl, and have loyally competed for her like two medieval knights. The conflict is also of a moral nature, between the innocent American – a historical and racial innocence – and the guilty Englishman, guilty of connivance in

63   I agree with the restrictive judgement of Smith 1986, 129–37.

64   The condemnation of American imperialist politics in Indochina was prophetic in 1955, while the contrast of American innocence with European experience was a common cliché of American fiction, particularly in the late nineteenth century (Lodge 1966, 37).

eliminating him, and thus, right to the end, haunted by this sense of guilt. The happiness which smiles on Fowler is always somewhat spoilt. *Our Man in Havana* (1958) seemingly resuscitates the Conrad and Conrad-Greene type of the desperado left to vegetate by the western economic system in the outposts of the empire, with the supplementary burden of a failed marriage. It is played out in the burlesque, improbable, iconoclastic vein of Waugh's African stories; hence there is a kind of comeback of a genre that was very popular in British fiction of the 1950s, applied here to a different geopolitical context.[65] Wormold, who paradoxically sells vacuum cleaners in a Cuba still in the grip of a dictatorship, and therefore does not know how to make ends meet, is offered a job as a secret agent for the British anti-communist Secret Intelligence Service. After some initial hitches, he starts spreading falsehoods that are in turn part of a whole castle of falsehoods or unreal situations, namely the espionage system. This 'inventor' of lies often applies to his own case the metaphor of the novelist with his box of tricks, that is with his made-up stories and figments of the imagination.[66] However, his marvellous box merely contains repeated comic skits, especially when London appoints a 'secretary' for him, and one who would like to take things seriously and whose zeal unconsciously provokes further misunderstandings and a flurry of unsustainable situations of an unadulterated theatrical and farcical nature. If Wormold's secret relations are to be decoded with the key of Lamb's *Tales from Shakespeare*, Wormold is ultimately a Prospero who breaks his wand and confesses his castle of imaginings.

2. Greene had been a Conradian pilgrim, withered and almost 'burnt-out', and hopeless, in his expeditions to the Belgian Congo in the late 1950s. *A Burnt-Out Case*[67] (1960) descended, exceptionally, from an umpteenth

---

65   The idea of the purely imaginary relations of the secret agent Wormold comes from the gossip columns in *Vile Bodies*. Greene had no *vis comica*, and the contrast in scenes and dialogue between Milly the devout daughter and her atheist father remains a potential occasion not realized, and therefore ultimately a superfluous episode. The petulant Milly recalls Waugh's Cordelia Flyte, without improving on her.

66   By no coincidence, the novel is contemporary to Waugh's *Pinfold*.

67   As Kermode remarks in his essay, quoted above in n. 40, this is a medical term that indicates 'an illness treated too late, that has reached its terminal stage' (this essay is particularly scathing in its appraisal of the novel).

investigation into the essence of religious faith in the wake of personal experience. Greene disguises himself in one Querry, a highly acclaimed architect and a lapsed Catholic who escapes from the world and fame, from promiscuous, purely carnal love affairs, and above all from the indiscreet gossip of the mass media about his private life. Up to a point he is a double of Conrad's Marlow, for the additional reason, as the author admits, that the Congo was a 'region of the mind' or, rather, a heart of darkness where a light had begun to glimmer. Conrad therefore shows up even more obsessively in the second and late Greene than in the early one, more precisely in this ranging over the cardinal points and in these diametric movements in colonial geography. At the same time, *A Burnt-Out Case* is a Camus-style novel turning on the macro-symbol of leprosy, just as Camus's *La Peste* hinged on that of the plague. The metaphor of leprosy reverberates throughout a range of suggestions. At the Congolese Catholic mission run by monks of an unspecified religious order, poor, sick and infected natives are 'cured', even if their hands and feet remain mutilated. Querry has just arrived there as someone apparently 'cured', cured in his case from deception and from the myth of religious faith, as he himself announces, but unaware that he is sick, or more precisely convalescent. Greene in fact hints at and supports an even more paradoxical perspective, namely, that Querry is perfectly healthy. The theological demonstration that slowly takes shape is the novel itself. There is no doubt that the first phases mark the need for an operative practical faith in the contemporary world in the grip of materialism and indifference to the suffering of the planet. The garrulous and imaginative journalist Parkinson hits the mark when he comments that 'the atomic age needs saints'. In the surreal and estranged context of the leper colony, there are not only monks attempting to heal, perhaps first and foremost the body and not so much the spirit, but also a humanitarian, albeit atheist doctor, Colin,[68] and the Ryckers, a white couple who are plantation owners. Rycker's young wife is the slave of a husband who is a Catholic beset because he did not embrace the priesthood when he was

---

68   Greene makes him an atheist counterpart, in reality unconsciously a believer and a Catholic, of Dr Schweitzer, a much talked-about legendary figure at the time of the novel, recalled several times but not in nice terms.

young, and vents his frustration in fanatical and morbid blabbering on the mystical fusion of body and spirit. An antagonist or fellow traveller of Querry, Doctor Colin tries to heal and restore some degree of functionality to a body that is destroyed, mutilated, and withered. He refuses to admit it, but this is the or a first step, a *sine qua non* of religious faith, which he believes irreconcilable with a secular evolutionism and humanitarianism that is not at bottom very different from truly Christian dedication.[69] In the rather nebulous struggle between the various forms of faith and lack of belief in this microcosm, Querry wishes explicitly to embody atheism, but he is an unconscious believer. He has reached the end, the end of carnal desire and of worldly ambitions, without achieving any result: he has made the Conradian journey to the end of existence, beyond which there is no other stop; in short, he has touched the bottom of the abyss. And so it is he who is the 'burnt-out case' and the image of a spiritual desert. He is also a demonstration of the splendid contradictions of mankind. His penetration is not into darkness but into self-knowledge; and his ever-unconditional nihilism is contradicted by spontaneous, unconscious acts of altruism and compassion. His stasis is varied by insignificant tasks offered 'to be of some use', and these are small flames that are lit, or more exactly re-lit. Having faith is shown through works, and this is the pure, orthodox anti-Protestant Catholic doctrine. Querry the architect cries out his condemnation or the palinode of abstract art intent only on solving purely formal problems – spatial and proportional ones in his case – of light and volume: an art which is dissociated from its goal, or directly made a goal. Even a verbal, literary art may be dissociated. An architect will not build cathedrals where houses are lacking and there are only uninhabitable shacks. Querry announces that he has 'retired' from everything: but can one have 'retired' from faith? Is faith not a link from which one cannot be untied, since one fine day God will give the thread a twitch?[70] Querry is someone who *quaerit*,[71] who seeks

---

69   On the influence of Teilhard de Chardin's thought, admitted by Greene, cf. Lodge 1966, 41.

70   'If we really believe in something we have no choice'.

71   The name also contains 'query'. Lodge 1966, 40–1, interprets the character as a 'mystery', thus making the novel's suggestion more open-minded and elusive, with, in the

and finds or has already found. Those who seek are already redeemed and already believe. *A Burnt-Out Case*, which begins by citing Conrad and Camus, eventually finds its true theological foundation in Pascal, since, as the mission's Superior warns at the end, 'a man who has begun to seek God has already found Him'. The key point is the Grace of God, which must be regained, if not purely recognized, in its incessant intervention in human life.[72] God never denies mankind His Grace; it is mankind that removes Grace from itself. Querry's actions proclaim that he is in a state of grace, and 'they speak alone'. Greene is unwilling to stage extreme or paradoxical situations and is satisfied with making his unknown believer die almost a martyr, some believing he is and others believing he is not, and therefore seeing him as saved or damned, as with Scobie at the end of *The Heart of the Matter*. The duel between the positions is left without a winner and gives way to the small comedies of the community of monks, with their idiosyncrasies and short-sightedness, and to the rowdy entrances of a vulgar journalist in search of scoops, who tracks down the taciturn Querry, and even makes him talkative. The epilogue falls into the sensationalist novel, with Querry's wild yet chaste night with the plantation owner Rycker's wife, which ignites the husband's jealousy, mainly because, unexpectedly, Marie Rycker does not deny the accusations against Querry and reveals that he is the father of the baby she is carrying.

3. Nonetheless, many of Greene's numerous later novels until his death, some told in the first person, share a marked sign of decompression and entertainment, at times coolly mimicking the novel of adventure, intrigue and espionage which was fashionable and successful in the sphere of escapist and mass consumption literature. Some even have the pace of the first-class 'penny dreadful', fluent, detached, even cynical in simplifying and trivializing moral questions. As a result, they are mostly

---

end, each of the secondary characters assigning Querry with a different role and different motivations. In Lodge's reading – inspired by some off the record declarations by Greene, which testify to his impassibility, impartiality and abstention in the face of a debate on abstract positions – the novel is tinged with 'absurd'.

72   Querry's manservant is called Deo Gratias, and the term 'grace' arises very frequently in the theological debates between the characters.

set in small or even large dictatorial states, prevalently in the Caribbean and South American countries, where in the 1960s the communists were trying to uproot the dictatorships protected by the Americans. This narrating first person is by now a double of the restless, anguished Catholic of the previous novels, and can now play coldly with their incandescent material, or at least dilute it into comedy and even farce.[73] The narrator of *The Comedians* (1966) is an Olympianly immoral Catholic educated by French Jesuits called Brown; every now and again he actually remembers he *is* a Catholic, although he is the owner of a hotel in the Haiti of 'Papa Doc' Duvalier, and without too many scruples of conscience cultivates a relationship with a woman who is the wife of an ambassador and daughter of a Nazi criminal. This plot, or subplot, brings to mind the eccentric vein of a Waugh,[74] also because a form of internal estrangement makes the attacks and the conspiracies – and the policemen, who wear dark glasses day and night – seem like pawns of an unreal game. The title is spot on, and provides a key to the interpretation. *Travels with My Aunt*[75] (1969) is no whimsical travel book, but a picaresque story concerning two main characters, a wizened London banker[76] and a still exuberant and feisty lady over seventy whom he believes to be his aunt, but who is actually his mother, as is revealed in an unexpected denouement. Greene revives his most marvellous scenario, the kaleidoscope of

73   One case in point is, in *The Comedians*, the apology of suicide that a doctor who also dabbles in theology, of a Buñuel variety, pronounces over a minister's corpse, defining it as a lucid 'courageous act', as of a mathematician who has weighed up the possibilities of the death and survival instinct. Brown replies to him objecting that suicide is an unpardonable act for a Catholic, and one of 'theological desperation'.

74   The second of the trio of main characters, who vaguely look back to the three protagonists of Stevenson's *The Ebb-Tide*, is a former American presidential candidate whose losing card is vegetarianism; the third is a shady army major who has come to Haiti for unspecified financial activities, and who is more of a thespian than the others.

75   The aunt is modelled on Norman Douglas's 'doctor' on Capri in *South Wind*, Elizabeth Moor (Shelden 1994, 82).

76   Like Querry, Henry Pulling is 'retired', but in his case without the metaphysical and existential values implied in the term.

the Istanbul train from thirty years earlier, with long-haul trips across even more distant geographic quadrants. But, on a par with Greene himself, the Orient Express of the 1960s is no longer the same train: it has changed route, suppressed the restaurant car and lost its pre-war glamour. On the railway route between Paris and Istanbul a mini-skirted American girl boards the train, whose task is to represent degenerate youth in a perennial flight from middle-class life, even if it is not devoid of a confused human sensitivity. She smokes marijuana,[77] exhibits complete sexual freedom, and shamelessly embellishes her speech with swearwords. The basic theme is the nostalgic realization of the passing of time and of the waning of an age; with changing customs and the confrontation between an idealistic, vital and even anarchic romanticism and the sense of emptiness and lack of intelligibility that modernity provokes. The constructive principle is that of revisitation and association. The train journey is for the 'aunt' an illusionistic reliving of her turbulent, daring and scandalous past. Every station touched on the journey – Paris, Milan, Venice, Istanbul – brings to her memory a scene, an episode, a slice of unrestrained life. The novel could indeed be defined as the memoirs of a female Casanova,[78] since the formal and official narrator, the nephew, is in turn the listener and tran-scriber of the inexhaustible storytelling and memorial vein of the aunt. In these overlappings sketches come to life that always hover between the real and the imaginary, between what has actually happened and mere bragging. In British literature, this riot of adventurous, comical and pathetic episodes evokes the eighteenth-century picaresques of Sterne and Smollett; not without reason Thackeray, their imitator, is liberally mentioned. In fact, the aunt's tales have, according to a *boutade*, 'more immediacy' than Thackeray's.

77   One of the distinguishing marks of 1960s civilization and culture was drugs, and the main character receives a visit from the police due to the suspicion that drugs are hidden inside her mother's cinerary urn. This investigation forms an external frame for the novel.

78   And *pour cause* Catholic, of a Catholicism usually and cheerfully contradictory, dissociated from life, only passive or abstract or unrealistic, as so often in Greene's mainly comic characters.

§ 55. *Greene VII: The human factor*

The Honorary Consul (1973) seemingly offers nothing new, and there are many elements and stereotypes which are re-adapted or which had been exploited in previous novels. It is set in turbulent South America and in a city on the border between Argentina and Paraguay on the Paraná River. It tells of a mixed-race British doctor who has settled in that area of the world and is implicated in a political intrigue which sees some Paraguayan guerrillas trying to overturn the fascist dictatorship, and in the meantime threatening and blackmailing it by kidnapping a VIP.[79] It reuses the ingredient of the colourful South American Catholicism with a former priest, Léon Rivas, leading the rebels. The interweaving is ingenious, but unable to fulfil its promise, just as the conflict of interests at stake is prescient, so to speak. The doctor, Plarr, is the son of an English political prisoner in a Paraguayan jail. Plarr believes him to be still alive and that he can be freed by the revolutionaries in exchange for his collaboration. The kidnapped VIP is not, however, the American Ambassador, but by mistake the Honorary British Consul, who married a former prostitute, María, who is also Plarr's lover and is about to give him a son, unbeknown to her husband. In the end, the State Police, who have not given in to the ransom request, attack the revolutionaries' den and the only one to emerge unscathed from the carnage is the Honorary Consul. This synopsis may give the erroneous idea of a novel full of movement; it is, on the contrary, one of illustration and discussion. Pure action prevails at the beginning and the end, while the heart of *The Honorary Consul* is occupied by the reconstruction of the environment and of previous events, with some frank comedy and pathos, a small gallery of humours with their sketch-style Victorian idiosyncrasies. Consul Fortnum has two lives, one when drunk and one when sober; Saavedra is the autobiographical writer who goes to the brothel for inspiration, and from whose mouth falls a non-stop barrage of aphorisms on the art of narrative detachment. Fantastic realism and topical adherence exploit the distant trace of *Nostromo*, in a morally nonchalant climate that the author does not moralize on, abhor or condemn,

---

79　A British Ambassador really was kidnapped at Montevideo in those years.

but merely observes. The signs of the times are disseminated without being burdensome, such as the incipient theology of liberation, the popularity of the Perry Mason TV series, the vogue for Borges, the proclamations of 'el Che', or the advertising and consumption of Coca Cola. South American Catholicism is always one that is sleepy, contradictory, dampened but not dead once and for all, indeed merely suspended. From first to last, the characters are those typical of Greene, Catholics by birth or education, lapsed but so to speak on trial, who know that they will re-enter the fold in some form and that a reckoning will come sooner or later. From *The Power and the Glory* a priest reappears, although not defrocked, sharing with Léon Rivas a project to reform local society and to fight the rich and the powerful. Léon's reverse ethic is that in a wrong society criminals are honest, which corresponds to his exact faith as a priest, but in the negative. During long discussions between the Consul held hostage and the revolutionary priest, a climate of sympathy and familiarity is born, and the kidnapping is merely a necessary means or evil. Thus, from outside, Greene now seems to be throwing down the gauntlet in front of a Church that leaves the poor to their own devices and props up dictatorships. But he loses no chance to underline the indelible nature of a vocation and of every vocation, and therefore also of the lifetime consecration of the priest.

2. The titles of Greene's novels (I say this now deliberately, but it will have already been noticed) are very often sagacious *mises en abyme* of their allegorical plot and internal symbolism, and reveal themselves very happily chosen as one reads.[80] *The Human Factor*[81] (1978) may well be considered a summarizing title; it is certainly the most pregnant and evocative in his canon. The implicit conceptual axis is that of the human and the divine, but in this case with a surprising outcome that may represent a turning point. In this variant lies the reason why *The Human Factor* is the

---

80   As also Smith 1986, 123, notes

81   The protagonist is modelled on Kim Philby, an Englishman who spied for the Soviets and fled to Russia before being found out, and was the author of a book of memoirs, *My Silent War* (1968), with a preface by Greene. Greene was writing *ex professo*, having been a British Intelligence official during the war, an experience with far from clear implications and brought to an end in 1944 with his resignation.

most remarkable of Greene's late novels. At first blush the plot may seem a pallid, unsuccessful copy of the spy stories of Fleming and Le Carré. In reality, this is a deliberately domesticized spy story, carried through with the lights dimmed, without special effects and without the whirl of breathtaking adventures. The narrative is precise, polished and controlled as at few other times. The two secret agents, Castle and Davis, are sedentary and glamourless James Bonds, and the action progresses smoothly right up to the last scene in and around London. Maurice Castle is a secret agent who, to enable his black wife to escape from a South African prison camp, has revealed confidential information to the Russians and has become a spy for them; the enquiry into the information leak leads, however, to the elimination of an innocent person. The finale sees him in perpetual isolation in Moscow, far from the affections of his family. The prior events in South Africa come up as a flashback midway through the novel, evoked by Castle.[82] The tragicomic human factor is at this first level the weakness, superficiality and fallibility of the judgement of the high functionaries of the Secret Service; it is the gross error through which, on realizing the information leak, and due to miscalculation of probability, of the two agents – Castle pleasant, painstaking and responsible, Davis bumbling, slovenly and suspect – the innocent person is mistaken for the guilty party. However, if the human factor emerges, Greene means or implies above all that the divine one has vanished. In the ping-ponging of the revamps in Greene's last phase, Maurice Castle is once more someone haunted by his conscience and by his past. Sooner or later his petty dishonesty will come out, and his existence is perennially on the alert. So Castle is a repeat of Scobie from *The Heart of the Matter*, but shifting the dilemmas from the religious terrain to the purely moral one, if that is ever possible. He is the upstanding, incorruptible agent above any suspicion, obliged to recur to small ethical infractions which are dictated not by duplicity but by a superior value, love, compassion, the need to avoid causing suffering, in fact

---

82 It is a clumsy expedient, unworthy of Greene, that after seven years from his South African experience, the cruel racist who forced Castle to collaborate in exchange for the escape of his future black wife, receives a posting to London, and works shoulder to shoulder with Castle, reopening the inquest and becoming his main accuser.

to make sure others are well, therefore to save,[83] even if saving in a purely earthly sense. What he did was, in other terms, ensuring a person his or her purely physical protection, and the enjoyment of essential human rights in a society that infringes them. But in this way Castle has offered himself to an irreversible chain of acts which, to avoid others suffering, have condemned him to suffer. In trouble, he does not opt for suicide, but goes into exile far from his affections, and therefore choosing a kind of secular, unpretentious martyrdom. This is the comical, grotesque or even pathetic declassing of this theme (and when Castle has to escape he does not know where to leave his beloved dog). What is changing, then, is not the form or the assortment of characters or the evocative espionage context; but the controversy and the demonstration. We face now an engagé novel, almost one *à thèse*, and this thesis is that religion, and Catholicism, is latent and without influence, and replaced by a largely 'horizontal' faith of a pragmatic and political type. No one in the novel – and this is the surprise – has a Catholic education as a background or investigates questions of religious faith;[84] the eschatology has become lay and immanent. In short, Greene has no further need for defrocked priests in order to condemn with a counter-demonstration the Church's renunciation of every palingenetic role and every project for transforming this unjust world. The ongoing international disputes invoked a solution and a series of weapons of a different type. *The Human Factor* is not about the inefficiencies of the British Secret Service, but about condemning the South African regime and apartheid, and on the other hand about one of support for communism 'with a human face'.[85] The tanks in Budapest and the Prague Spring of Dubček had been the germinating and

83   The power of human love, Greene said, makes man like an 'anarchist carrying a bomb', with a clear reference to Conrad's *The Secret Agent*.

84   With only one exception, when Castle one day, by this time in the grip of the nemesis of his past, feels the need to come clean about his secret, and enters a Catholic church to confess.

85   The recognition of the signs of the times is imperceptible but omnipresent: those were the days when the first computers began to appear and be mentioned, when a certain brand of chocolate – 'Maltesers' – was bought in a shop on the Strand, when the discotheque was all the rage, when the Beatles' records began to be listened to.

provocative cell for Greene, and the trigger of his imagination. The communist faith is the equivalent of a progressive Christianity on the side of the just, which in the 1970s was shirking its responsibilities. Just as there had been incognito Catholics in Greene's novels, Castle is a communist who claims he is not one.

3. In *Doctor Fischer of Geneva or The Bomb Party* (1980), the most colourless and most forgettable thing ever written by Greene, the poor translator Jones, a language expert, is working as a secretary in a chocolate company that creates tooth decay and infections, which the toothpaste invented by his future father-in-law prevents. The paradox of this absurd and glacial farce, narrated in the first person by Jones himself, is also that of a father who hates his peers, and in particular his own daughter. Not really knowing what to do with his millions, he forces a small group of unctuous comedians to come periodically to dinner to be victims of his humiliation in exchange for expensive gifts. Dr Fischer, in a visionary twist that makes this a disquieting theological parable, is also a father who has ceased to love his progeny, and sinisterly displays its rapacious pettiness: a God who avidly humiliates mankind and annuls free will, and demands too much of his creatures. Though he has inexplicably generated a daughter who is capable of love, a perverse predestination kills this pure unaware flower in a skiing accident that is the most vivid and dense episode in the dull story. Theology, however, fails to permeate the concrete event, and the prevailing flavour is that of a remake of a Dickensian Christmas story. Dr Fischer's banquet evokes Miss Havisham's wedding dinner (and Jones has 'great expectations', being the son-in-law), or the tale of a Scrooge who has fathered (we do not know how) disinterested love, and attracts the boomerang of his egoism by committing suicide. In a completely different mood, *Monsignor Quixote* (1982) takes up the picaresque plot of the journey, so familiar to Greene, only to adapt it to a parodic scenario, the one irresistibly evoked by the title. But there is at the same time an amused play on memories and citations from Greene's novels themselves. The result is a refined metaliterary *divertissement* in which the novelist proves his skills by devising ingenious, brilliant and sometimes amusing adaptations and updates, such as the horse Ronzinante replaced by a shabby Seat 600 that often shows no desire to climb slopes. In this remake of Cervantes's novel,

Don Quixote is a naïve priest who chances to be nominated Monsignor because of an act of courtesy to a prelate, while Sancho is the communist ex-mayor of the village who has just failed to be re-elected. The two picaros form a wandering couple who travel contemporary Spain far and wide. The journey is a flagrant pretext to hype a humorous dialogic match between Catholicism and communism, an old expedient which, to an Italian reader, may evoke the name of Giovanni Guareschi, whom Greene did not know, or more plausibly that of Buñuel for the interminable duelling over theological topics in the convivial discussions along the way. For these two wayfarers there is nothing human and divine which they think unfamiliar, so that there is a cheery 'banquet' of digressions ranging from the sacred to the profane, from faith to science, from Marx to Christ, with trespassings into indiscreet, salacious[86] and contemporary topics, such as contraception or genetic engineering and other burning issues of both Marxism and Catholicism. Obviously, there were readers and critics who disapproved of this cynical trivialization of issues of the greatest import, and of the amused and irenic nonchalance with which Greene has the Monsignor and the mayor discuss them, always jovially ending their jousting in a draw. From time to time Greene emphasizes once again, in *Monsignor Quixote*, the pre-eminence of the human factor, of personal values, of a lay ethic of freedom and peaceful coexistence.

§ 56. *Snow*I: Humanism and science join forces*

Of humble origins in central England, Charles Percy Snow (1905–1980) was to die a baronet. Proverbially stubborn, and having an unceasing desire to make it big, after studying at the future University of Leicester he

---

86   In one of the many vicissitudes, the pair go to a red light cinema, to see a film which seems to the priest utterly chaste, entitled *The Virgin's Prayer*.

*   W. Cooper, *C. P. Snow*, London 1959; F. R. Karl, *C. P. Snow: The Politics of Conscience*, Carbondale, IL 1963; J. Thale, *C. P. Snow*, Edinburgh and London 1964; R. G. Davis, *C. P. Snow*, New York and London 1965; P. De Logu, 'Il noviziato di C. P. Snow e il realismo dialettico di *The Light and the Dark*', in *Critical Dimensions: English, German and Comparative Literature Essays in Honour of Aurelio Zanco*, ed. M. Curreli

became a fellow at Christ's College Cambridge in 1930, and was an official at the Ministry of Labour from 1940 to 1944 and at the Civil Service from 1945 to 1960. Later on, he was secretary to the Minister of Technology from 1964 to 1966, and held other political positions under the Wilson administration. So he was a university man, but not a humanist by training; rather, a scientist and technocrat with an incurable 'vice' for creative writing. This hunger he satisfied with a remarkable flow, impressive from any standpoint, of eleven novels linked in a saga, supplemented by a short provocative essay on the 'two cultures' – humanistic and scientific – which remains his best-known work for the general public, and is still cited and discussed today. To stay with his out-and-out skill as a novelist and essayist, the only thing we are substantially concerned with here, Snow forms part of that increasingly large group of writers, some of whom are now ignored and others treated hastily in handbooks and anthologies. In Snow's case this is a small misjudgement that I shall try to rectify in part. His decrease in popularity was intrinsic to his very nature, that of a scientist-writer or a writer-scientist, even if the mix produced, submitted to the reading test, questionable but certainly not disastrous results. He forged a novel and a form of fiction – a scientific fiction, in effect an oxymoron – which had no points of contact with tradition and current practices throughout his career. He belongs by choice to the family of objectifying writers without a trace of romanticism; but, as a writer-scientist who must systematically limit his figurative language,[1] he gradually acquired a style of writing that is elegant, refined, and rich in precious nuances. Having transferred himself into a subtle and almost anonymous *alter ego*, he kept all the fictional material he dreamed up at a due distance.[2]

2. His generation was that of the writers born in 1905, one that was to become a real throng of ultra-talented writers of the first rank if we consider

---

and A. Martino, Pisa 1978, 513–28; P. Snow, *Stranger and Brother: A Portrait of C. P. Snow*, London 1982; J. Halperin, *C. P. Snow: An Oral Biography*, Brighton 1983; J. De la Mothe, *C. P. Snow and the Struggle of Modernity*, Austin, TX 1992.

1   This tropic poverty is one of the main charges brought against Snow.
2   Lewis Eliot, his *alter ego*, is a barrister, however, while Snow was a physicist.

the five-year period lasting from immediately before to immediately after this date: Powell, Waugh, Green, and Greene, to name but the main ones. Snow may be considered the last 'among so learned a band', but not in the sense of a tail end. He stood to one side and kept himself to himself because he was neither a formal experimentalist nor an experimenter *tout court*; he was instead a follower of the old school of realism, stylistically polished but faithful to the old instrumentation. In short, he lacked those distinguishing marks of modernity that propelled his peers outside the norm. He was not much younger than Orwell, but he was never really touched by the socialist infatuation, and it is a pity or a mystery that Orwell never picked him up on his radar. This was perhaps because Snow was politically a reformist and a reformer, not a revolutionary, as will become apparent immediately below when we examine the essential cornerstones of his political philosophy. It is above all essential to stress that Snow was an exact peer of Powell, and that his saga *Strangers and Brothers* came out at almost the same time as Powell's. Their common objective was to offer a cross-section of British society in the three decades 1940–1970, therefore focusing on the rich middle class, the university intelligentsia, and the circles of politics and economics. This sweeping temporal tapestry is filtered in both cases by a narrator/witness who steps aside or lives more quietly than the characters he is observing. Powell was sharper in his satire, Snow more objective and descriptive; his front-man Lewis Eliot[3] is more properly that 'camera eye' which Isherwood, another peer, attributed to himself, a camera which, however, in Isherwood's case photographed above all humorous, sparkling sketches of Berliners. The good fortune that smiled on Snow is explained by the lofty imaginative journalism with which he recounted, almost in real time, the story of the 'corridors of power'. Nowadays, however, one cannot help but share the reserve that almost immediately began to follow the applause, since his novels are flat, lacking in intensity, incapable of vividly rendering the real throb of passions; to be frank, they quickly become tedious. Snow did not really know about or possess a sense of closure. His plots are far from dense, symmetrical and inexorable, and, in the absence of

---

3   The conjectures of those who have interpreted this name as a tribute to Lewis Carroll and George Eliot seem to me rather far-fetched.

a real structural design, are dragged forward to the rhythm of non-inevitable events.[4] In an era monopolized by the stream of consciousness, and therefore by an elephantiasis of the psychic life and by psychologism, or, on the contrary, of uncontrolled passions and Freudianism, the unpopular Snow conceived of people as beings who are active decision-makers, socialized and lucidly aware of their public role; and the task of the fiction writer is to transcribe a chain of events and a plot of negotiations for the public good. However, to accuse Snow of having had beings act who are bloodless, a little obtuse, and merely functionaries without intuition, would be to do him an injustice. In his essay on the two cultures, Snow began from a presupposition for which he was severely criticized, namely, that 'each of us dies alone'; and he recalled that his saga was entitled *Strangers and Brothers* and depicted the 'ultimate tragedy, at the core of each individual life'.[5] Hence, he too was an existentialist, and a distinction can be made in his novels between self-controlled characters and an early rebel youth without hopes. However, like Matthew Arnold who from being a desperate poet had become a constructive essayist, Snow overcame the tragedy of living in an individual being by making him embrace public responsibility. This distinction was imperative, 'unless we are going to sink into the facile social pessimism [and] to settle into our own egocentric chill'. In other terms, Snow was able to resist the temptation of purely destructive existentialism.

3. On 7 May 1959 Snow gave a lecture in Cambridge entitled 'The Two Cultures', which discussed the by-then secular gulf that existed between science and the humanities. This was therefore an attempt to rediscover a middle position between the two 'poles' and the role of an all-round intellectual on the Renaissance model. However, Snow's most scathing criticism targeted a certain literature, rather than pure science, to the extent that the essay sounded like self-criticism, at least for the part where

4   Snow's style, its mark and its narrative pace, as has often been noted, did not change substantially over a period of forty years; in other words, his manner never came to be updated.

5   The sense of an integrated, organic community after and despite everything, of foreigners who are also brothers, instead of a constellation of isolated beings, is what distinguishes him in the end.

Snow deemed himself a man of letters. Orwell had already remarked, over two decades earlier, that a certain kind of literature was narcissistically existentialist, and that it wallowed in the cultivation of the ego, protected from any awareness of concrete history and exiled from the human consortium, as if living in a void. However, Orwell had never discussed the extent to which this privileged position might be offset, and put into perspective, by science. For Snow, science was more interested and implicated in social life, more constructive and more optimistic, by definition and by easily documented historical practices. By 1959, he no longer had one of his natural interlocutors – namely, Orwell himself, who had believed he was founding a constructive literature, and execrated defeatism – to respond to the accusation of being one of those literary humanists who, desperate and downtrodden, wished that the future did not exist. However, T. S. Eliot was still alive, and Snow attacked Modernism, any kind of Modernism and also Eliotism, that of a proud opposition to science and the apocalyptic perspective of the world ending 'not with a bang but a whimper'.[6] However, when Snow goes on to the *construens* phase, his discourse inclines towards a new unrealizable utopia, and, what is worse, towards a vintage Arnold-like vein of thought.[7] On closer examination, almost 100 years after Arnold's *Culture and Anarchy*, Snow identifies a historical planetary emergence, conscious of the new role for a downsized Britain, now become a buffer state between the two new superpowers, America and Russia, with China looming on the horizon. The recipes are approximate and summary in an Arnoldian way. Equally Arnoldian – vaguely resembling, or even citing without saying so, the second American lecture on literature and science –[8] is the proposal of newly unified knowledge as a cure-all, and the consequent reform of the educational system in view of this objective. Anyone entering the pedagogical arena at that stage could not ignore Arnold's writings on

6   This citation from Eliot's 'The Hollow Men' was labelled by Snow as 'one of the least likely scientific prophecies ever made'.

7   Above all, in his additional considerations from 1963, Snow occupied himself, with a procedure that was itself Arnoldian, with carefully defining the term 'culture'; but oddly enough, Matthew Arnold, unlike Coleridge, was never mentioned by Snow.

8   Volume 6, § 32.3.

the topic; and Snow echoed his predecessor by making public education the point of departure to solve problems on a global scale, vetoing specialization, at least the overly precocious kind of British higher education institutes, and every elitist system. Is Snow's lengthy discussion of 'fossilization' and the required mental 'elasticity' not literally Arnoldian? And does Snow not come out with other precepts similar to Arnold's *porro unum est necessarium*? Certainly, the confident and indiscriminate support that Snow gave to progress and to the further encouragement of applied science went well beyond Arnold's precautions, as did his view of the industrial revolution and industrialization itself as a fulcrum of and turning point in history. Here, Snow is no longer Victorian, and in fact with his unflinching, resounding scientism he criticizes the paranoid anti-scientism of a Ruskin from a distance, sounding more like a convinced disciple of Wells,[9] and therefore also of Orwell, with the common trait of an action designed to dismantle and demolish taboos, idols, and bogeymen of the old dispensation.[10] In his opinion, only a scientific approach could solve problems of underdevelopment and hunger in the world and the discrepancy between the rich and the poor – this too a problem that had tormented the Victorians – and therefore constitute an antidote to anarchy. The intellectuals felt stung to the quick, and Leavis retorted crossly in the *Spectator* of 9 March 1962.[11] In reality, the many-sided debate that was triggered, and which inspired a subsequent retort from Snow, sounds more Victorian and more exhilarating and humorous than one could imagine. It is an Arnoldian parody,

9   Wells had arrived on the scene from nowhere, and was born into a poor, ill educated family. Snow's youthful, anonymously published *New Lives for Old* (1933), on the discovery of a hormone that restores youth, is indebted to Wells's science-fiction novels.

10   Snow's 1963 rejoinder insists more explicitly on the disavowal of ancient times as a pre-industrial Eden, thus going to the heart of the mythical assumptions of Victorian medievalism, that of Ruskin, Pater, above all Morris: 'One can teach a myth: but when the myth is seen as fact, and when the fact is disproved, the myth becomes a lie'.

11   Other celebrated intellectuals who stuck their oar in were Lionel Trilling and Aldous Huxley.

since, as we saw,[12] some later books by Arnold were, in turn, collections of detailed and very precise answers – hammer blows and footnotes that were often also quibbling – to the objections of his critics and detractors: exactly as in this piece by Snow.

4. The would-be saga *Strangers and Brothers*, or 'of Lewis Eliot', is, as I mentioned, a series of eleven novels whose main characters are fixed figures who encounter other more meteoric ones, and whose private and public careers are followed stereophonically from 1914 to 1968, and in a more concentrated form during the three decades extending from the outbreak of the Second World War. Its basic ideal and geographical triangle has its points in Snow's native Leicester in the East Midlands, in a nameless Cambridge college, and in London administrative and civil service offices. The point of synthesis, observation and reference is the ably dissimulated figure of the novelist's *alter ego*, who recounts events in the first person while managing to modestly annul himself, that is, hide the implicit satisfaction and self-celebration of a promotion to the higher echelons from the most humble of origins. In 1940, when Snow's novels began to appear, sagas had been for some time a reordering operation and a close reading of history or even of news stories. The simple constituent act of such an edifice is a hint of recognition, and launches a plan that creates the expectation of a masterpiece or an aspiration towards that dimension, and dialogues and competes with Trollope,[13] and later on with Galsworthy. At the same time, *Strangers and Brothers* could be dismissed as a copy, or even a duplicate – less unsuccessful and even less symmetrical,[14] and, above all, not chronological but with parallel episodes – of Powell's saga of the 'music of time'. As hinted above, Powell is more ambitious, more brilliant, more cultured, more of an artist, capable of creating and developing an engaging plot, also denser in episodes and sculpted characters with more cultural life-blood. Prudentially, Snow had no strong theses to demonstrate,[15] beyond

---

12   Volume 6, § 25.1.
13   In fact, Snow authored a biography of this novelist.
14   Snow had always spoken of *eleven* novels right from the first planning of the cycle.
15   As implicitly noted by ATD, 250, and – without excessive malevolence, blatantly preferring Snow to Beckett – by KPE, 161–3.

the vague approval of a healthy or fairly healthy clerisy who had guided the country rather well, all things considered, in the dramatic emergencies during and just after the war. Tolerance of human grief, innate piety, or a sense of limit, almost never push Snow to scathing satire or partisan debate; and he describes rather than explains. Only in the Cambridge mini-cycle the university fellows are not heroes but capricious, voluble and bizarre marionettes that indulge in power games. The increasingly lukewarm judgement concerning *Strangers and Brothers* was largely due to the narrative tone of a neutral, tidy transcriber, we might almost say a minute taker who permits himself only rarely poetic licence. Trollope's scrupulous care can also be evinced in the dimensions of Snow's novels. All of them have the same size, and this is the fruit of an evident, precise *a priori* programming, recalling the operations of a chemist in front of an alembic. Snow speculates and economizes on contents, and spins them out by applying that same apotheosis of the insignificant that Chesterton attributed to Browning. There is no doubt that *Strangers and Brothers* attracted and seduced many over the course of its publication as a saga *tout court*, and as the purveyor of small myths for enthralled readers; and Snow's might become popular again one day thanks to its scent of yesteryear, of stories of surpassed customs, rosewater intrigues, or the exemplary self-control of a class with its age-old rituals. Lewis Eliot himself is serene and controlled, reflective and dominated, a tad too bloodless. He acts not only like Melville's Bartleby, but also as a referee, peacemaker, arbitrator and moderator. Snow, who reconstructs in a novel the autobiographical youth of this *alter ego*, decides to keep his personal affairs in the shadows and firmly under control. Lewis Eliot acts *ad extra* with the unfailing strong sense of a public man who is a guarantor of institutions. His private life is atrophic. Hence the total impropriety of any link between him and Proust's *alter ego*, a usurped and improbable comparison. The dominant opposition is between the controlled and the defeated. If we take, for example, George Passant, or Roy and Charles, Snow sets out to represent and develop his own version of the British universities' cultured youth and intelligentsia of the years before the Second World War: and the result is a series of portraits or sketches of the weak-chinned, obscurely undermined by a *cupio dissolvi* and self-destructive fury.

§ 57. *Snow II: 'Strangers and Brothers'. Intrigues of politics and academic life*

Reading each of the eleven novels of the saga as a monad, and therefore a self-sufficient novel, can be enjoyable; reading them one after another in an uninterrupted sequence reveals irritating repetitions and overlaps. The treatment of time is not linear either, but at times takes some leaps backwards. Precisely because these novels are for the most part not a sequence but a stereophony, Snow was able to rearrange them in a different order from the chronology of publication in the so-called 'omnibus' edition. In this reshuffled version, *Strangers and Brothers* (1940) is actually positioned as the second novel in line with the internal chronology, although it was the first to be written, and shows it.[16] Snow was an able and professional writer, but this novel remains immature and clumsy, is the least satisfying of all eleven,[17] and can be assigned to his apprenticeship. In some unspecified suburban area, but in any case in the anonymous grey

16   In my reading I shall stay with the chronology of writing and first publication.

17   Far superior is the first novel Snow wrote outside the saga, an enthralling and elegant detective story entitled *Death Under Sail* (1932), recalled by the author in later years as due to 'a current vogue at that time', yet gradually diluted with extraneous elements, almost denying its original genre. On a yacht on a leisure cruise just off the Norfolk coast, the skipper, an established London doctor, is found at the helm one morning dead from a gunshot wound, and there is no doubt that the suspects must be limited to the six passengers, all acquaintances, friends and even rivals. The device is due at first sight to Agatha Christie and in particular to *And Then There Were None*, but with hints of Conan Doyle and Chesterton. The murder takes place too early, however, and the search for the guilty party is entrusted to a rather myopic policeman and to an amateur who is instead ingenious, wayward, and eccentric, and who reconstructs the event with the maniacal aid of graphs, maps and diagrams. The anticipation of the climax is not in itself an infraction of the rules of a whodunit; but the intervening deferment is, allowing the insertion of comic episodes and fluvial entertainments that can evoke the mock-heroic saga of a J. K. Jerome; as a result, as a thriller the novel lacks the snap solution and the suspense itself becomes watered down. The denouement arrives after the emergence of complex and implausible circumstances and motivations, and of a diabolical plan behind the murder: essentially there was no murder as suspected, but the captain had committed suicide, masked as a murder. As in some of Chesterton's Father Brown stories, the most obvious solution of the crime, the one that seems to satisfy everyone, is not the right one, and is undermined *in extremis* thanks to the sagacity of a non-professional detective. On the novel

region of the Midlands, somewhere between Nottingham and Lancashire, a group of twenty or so friends amateurishly seek to educate and promote themselves and stand out from the crowd. One of these friends, Jack, who works for a newspaper, one day receives the gift of a silver cigarette case from the owner's son Roy, fifteen years old and still at school. This might be an incipient homosexual infatuation, but about this we are kept in the dark; at any rate, Jack is fired and also loses his grant at a local evening school. The case shakes the community of young people, above all the influential George Passant, who, as a teacher and only a little older, champions his friend's cause and seeks to act as his protector. He works at a law firm, whose partners' names evoke Dickens's proverbial and cheating ones; except that one of them, Martineau, as a tribute to his richly resonant name,[18] becomes embroiled in an anachronistic case of fanaticism or religious folly, and leaves the firm to become a wandering preacher. In this way, Snow immediately displays the original contrast on which the entire saga is based: on the one hand, in Passant, balanced reasoning characters, on the other, in Martineau, the yielding of will-power or even fanatical disruptive passion. The two characters are parallel and complementary in their own way. Returning to the question of form and of the apparent provisional nature of the writing, this could be the conscious inauguration of a poetics of meditated and deliberate experiment. Snow might, in other words, have wished to found or try out the technique of a kind of a notarial novel of negotiations and minutes. This is suggested above all by the voice of a first-person narrator who has a name but lacks a life story, is simply an eye that watches, and one whose biography is reduced to a minimum. The singularity of Snow's novel was to be from then on the absence of descriptions, or their compression, and the undisputed prevalence of dialogue. Contextual information is sketchy or telegraphic, and there is no descriptive framework as such; but wearying dialogues that end up devoid of interest are often given in their entirety. These are not, in other

---

Strangers and Brothers, cf. the appraisal of Cooper 1959, 18, diametrically opposite to mine.

18 Cf., on the siblings James and Harriet Martineau and their Huguenot origins, Volume 5, § 103.

words, the dialogues of Green or Compton-Burnett, though they are not even the factual, practical or even dramatic ones of other writers of fiction. They supply intact daily conversation without filters, and even the titles of the chapters read as telegrams that summarize the plot and preannounce its twists and turns. Snow also recreated the novel about the community of suburban youths, who dream, verbally fence, and fight over small-scale local power. Apart from the fact that they do not speak of art, and are not the victims of class difference and social climbing, they might seem like brothers of the young main characters in Lawrence's *The White Peacock*. On the page, the outcome of this mini-epic is colourless and dull. The second part is wholly dedicated to the trial of Passant, who has been accused of embezzlement. In the end he is acquitted; but these are legal proceedings presented in an almost raw state.

2. *The Light and the Dark* (1947), an emblematic title that refers to the chiaroscuro dimension of the main character, projects onto centre stage the career of a skilful linguist from Cambridge, Roy. Roy, who appears as a young pupil in the first novel, now goes through a short infatuation with Nazism and dies during the war as an airman. The social cross-section is that of the academic world often described in British novels of the time; the climate is only a little less fictionalized than in Angus Wilson's *Anglo-Saxon Attitudes*, another novel on university life.[19] Roy is necessarily an expert on relics, which he finds and studies, and is narrowly elected a fellow at Cambridge. With him Snow tried to create for the reader a kind of Dostoevskyan character, torn, lethargic, cyclothymic, misunderstood by his more circumspect and practical friends;[20] however, he remains predictably distant from the model. The short-range events inside Cambridge evolve against the European background of the 1930s, from the Spanish Civil War onwards; on the eve of the outbreak of the war not everyone at Cambridge agrees with Chamberlain's policy of appeasement. Roy himself, having settled in Berlin, is pro-Semite, and a series of love affairs have

19   § 138.4.
20   Snow confessed that he greatly admired *The Brothers Karamazov*, 'the greatest novel ever written'.

gone wrong for him. At the end of the novel he is prematurely aged and worn out. *Time of Hope* (1949) bears a title that sounds like a paraphrase or periphrasis of *Great Expectations*. Up to a late point in its development it follows the education of a boy in the central English district; from poor and humble origins he rises up the scale of promotions and becomes an important person, with an evident update of a typical situation in Dickens or George Eliot. This is, in fact, an autobiography with a vaguely Victorian flavour, hinging on such classic situations as the father's bankruptcy, the incurably snobbish mother – the best portrait – and the interfering aunt. It is the one and only case in which Snow tried, in the whole saga, to be a humorous writer and made an attempt at pastoral comedy and even satire. In an uncommonly impressive scene the pupil, who has scraped together ten shillings from his mother to aid the soldiers at war, is hurt and stung to the quick when his teacher, along with his classmates, allude to his father's bankruptcy. The second part is rather less effective; it tells of Lewis Eliot's falling in love with the neurotic Sheila, who becomes his first wife, and of her paralysing seduction. This rapid decline is also due to the long series of reduplications and reshapings of material from novel to novel that begins here. *The Masters* (1951) completes the study of power in a symbolic microcosm that is again the University of Cambridge: namely, the egotistical and opportunistic impulses that hinder the interests of the community. On the other hand, this novel illustrates Snow's procedure, which is only partially chronological as in Powell, and is instead organized in parallel stories, each set within one another. In the previous novel, the master was suffering from cancer and in the end he died, and this plot, which simply formed the background there, now becomes primary. At the same time, this is also patently a Trollope-style parody of the 'life, death and succession' of a directorial figure. The story has in fact the sober and factual pace of the first novels of the Barsetshire cycle, and even improves on the defamiliarizing nature of grotesque namesakes: two of the election candidates are called, impossibly, or almost, Jago and Chrystal. Lewis Eliot mediates and acts as an impartial judge above the melee. Occasionally, the novel is revived by some bouts of mild academic satire (the profes-sors' envy of each other's fame, and the sense of their own importance). However, Snow ends up being hoisted by his own petard and by letting the novel suffer from its concentric nature. Too slow, it does no more than carry forward the open and secret election deals, while watching how the two parties carry out their electoral campaign; what emerges is a second, pronouncedly minutes-style example, as in the first novel of the saga. The result is asphyxiant and static. Then, artfully, the master does not die until two-thirds of the way through. The candidatures embody a conflict of cultures, of Snow's two cultures, since one of the two rivals is a humanist and the other a scientist. The party of humanistic moderates, who support Jago, lose by just one vote.

  3. In *The New Men* (1954) a side issue is introduced, relating to a brother of the narrator, a physicist who takes part in a British nuclear fission scheme to produce the atomic bomb that will put an end to the war.[21] The operations of the imaginary laboratory are interwoven with the private stories and government intrigues of unscrupulous officials and ministers. The scientist, who has just had a son and upholds life, is in reality working on a weapon to destroy it. Snow, always a champion and supporter of science as a means to improve and foster life, applauds Britain *ex post* for having renounced the 'abuse of science', that is, for having refrained from scientific research that would have produced a lethal weapon. The time frame of the novel is the whole war period, from the harbingers of war until the dropping of the US bombs on Japan. *Homecomings* (1956) is a parallel sequence that covers Snow's favourite time span, 1938–1951, and lists a quantity of private circumstances of his front-man Lewis Eliot: the illness and suicide of his first wife, his second marriage and the happy birth of his son. In the saga, this is one of three cases where Eliot is not an anonymous observer, or merely a filter of the facts, but a main character. This separation is fundamental in Snow, and shows Eliot's skill and self-control, his ability to separate the private from the public, even when this private side could affect the public one, while instead remaining outside; in other words, it goes to the root of the type and the moral stature of this *alter ego*. In *The Conscience of the Rich* (1958), which goes back in time, Lewis Eliot is the largely heterodiegetic witness of a saga within the saga, that of a rich family

---

21 As Cooper notices (1959, 24 n. 1), this British laboratory set up for nuclear fission is
   a complete invention of Snow the fiction writer.

of Jewish origin in the heart of London and in the pre-war decade until 1937. In the summer of 1927, March becomes a friend of Lewis after the final university exams, and keeps mum about his origins for a good while. He had never guessed or intuited them, since March is tall and blond. The story, which sees the narrator confined to the background, revolves around the gradual collapse of a weak personality. March gives up law and becomes a doctor, at the same time fighting a hard battle with his father in order to marry an attractive communist agitator whose newspaper is on the point of sullying the reputation of her husband's uncle. The novel is vaguely reminiscent, in its first phases, of those by Maugham, except for the analysis of the noxious and tortuous female fascination. At the same time it breaks up in intrigues and by-now forgettable wheeling and dealing that recall Trollope's political saga. Waugh's *Brideshead Revisited* also comes to mind since it relates a parallel case of psychic plagiarism of a family over a weakling, there Catholic, here Jewish. However, the ethnic mark is vague and superficial, and chiefly the source of a humorous and picturesque tale that never veers towards the tragic as in Dickens's or Trollope's Jewish novels. So this not a real, authentic tragedy of ethnic diversity, nor is there an authentic sense of threat, in a moment when European and German anti-Semitism had become more violent. March's dilemma is resolved as much in the tussle to marry Ann as in defending and supporting his wife, whose political activity ends up damaging the image of the family itself. In *The Affair*[22] (1959), set in the post-war period and in the year 1954, a scientist is unjustly accused of scientific fraud, and as an arbitrator Eliot decides to become a detective and discover the intricate truth. This is a largely repetitive novel that re-exhibits further cases of cliques and guerrilla bands inside an unnamed Cambridge college, and whose sole point of symbolic interest is the figure of the simpleton scientist, a kind of passive chump. It is ultimately correct that he should have been accused of fraud, and he does not remember and does not know what happened. With him Snow wishes to uphold the notion of the negativity of out-of-context science, and the

---

22 By Snow's own admission, the impulse had been the distant Dreyfus 'case', even if the scientific fraud was based on the 'Rupp case', today as 'picturesque' as it is indeterminable.

necessity of one that is applied and above all committed, rooted in social relations. The whole of the first third is in reality a contemporary study of a clinical case, that of Lewis Eliot's wife Sheila, of her nervous breakdown, of her attempts to become a writer, of her passion for a third-rate novelist, and of her symptoms of intolerance towards the ultra-patient Lewis. After her suicide, we leap forward two years to his relationship with the very normal Margaret. This new love does not alter the distinctive traits of Lewis, who remains cold and methodical in the sexual sphere, too. This sentimental plot is anything but primary, since he always remains active in his professional sphere.

4. *Corridors of Power* (1963) is an openly political novel, and since its time span is 1955–1958, its material was particularly pressing. The imagination enters here a short circuit with reality, a reality that was rather close at hand and still vivid in the memory. Snow is always a lesser Trollope, and this is in many ways Snow's novel of the 'Prime Minister' or of an imaginary Prime Minister, one who, however, was not even minimally a double of the real Macmillan or other political figures. Presented by Snow as an embroidery on a series of probable political figures, *Corridors of Power* is a sort of parallel history whose fulcrum lies in a question 'that had not openly emerged in politics at that time'. The minister, Quaife, who has risen through the ranks and been appointed, is placed under observation with the usual artifice: Lewis Eliot is taken on to serve him as a councillor, and the burning question of the moment is nuclear armaments. In the preparatory phases we are shown the positions of the statesmen, steadfast in keeping the nation's international prestige intact, as well as the variegated opinions of the scientists, some of them in favour, some against a nuclear armament policy. Quaife takes the side of renunciation. But Snow is interested in what goes on backstage, and spices up or integrates the specifically political palimpsest with behind-the-scenes manoeuvres and sensational *coups de scène*. A follower of Trollope's lesson, he stages the actions set up by the hooligans of one or other party, and has Quaife dragged through the mud by a scientist in favour of rearmament, by discovering a private skeleton in the closet; even the staunchest supporter of nuclear disarmament is paralysed by the discovery of an affair his daughter is having. Snow remains firmly patriotic and raises his

main character onto the pedestal of honour and almost martyrdom, in that he has him remain consistent in front of the mirages of power, compromise and even personal profit, and has him prefer political defeat, and therefore resignation, to the renunciation of principles. This is a distantly Orwellian scheme at the time, because it imagines the imminent dangers and a new scenario, a USA-USSR stalemate and what role other powers would be entitled to play. *The Sleep of Reason*[23] (1968) seemingly celebrates the wise old age of the 'elder statesman', since Lewis Eliot, who has now retired from his duties at Whitehall and Cambridge, has gone back to his roots and is now living peacefully in his home village. But he feels forced to testify again, over a regrettable sensational event that is neither academic nor political, but a piece of crime news (this was an event that had actually occurred two years earlier and was widely gossiped about and fictionalized by the press). Is this a forced, opportunistic, studied novel? It returns in fact to the point of departure, and, Proust-style, the hero revisits places, figures and associations from the first novel; and after visiting his father he goes to the art and technical college where his first friendships were born. This school is by now a university where Lewis is a board member. He wastes no time, instead of exhibiting his intimate life, to claim the usual functions and lavish his gifts of tact, wisdom, balance and good sense on the public good. As a result, this seems for some time a pure operation of updating the stories of the numerous characters in the group, without any winding up of a fictional spring that could at a certain point be released. The novel proceeds instead by additions and cunning reintroductions of previous characters who, by now aged, update one another. At that time, this sounded as the countless representation of the generational turnover by a class on the point of being surpassed, the one that from the beginning of the century had lived through two wars, and was by now obliged to pass the baton to an unscrupulous youth with more open sexual habits. This is a gap periodically demonstrated by fathers and sons that do not understand each other, with symbolic events such as the sudden retinal

---

23   A title from an aphorism – 'The sleep of reason produces monsters' – applied by Goya to one of his 'capricios'.

rupture that threatens to blind Lewis. However, Snow paints, we gradually discover, a suburban community that was by then shocked and disoriented as a consequence of the lack of the old reference points. George Passant, the youngsters' mentor, whom he kept in a grip through his charisma, is by now mentally marked, and the local malaise is shown in the gratuitous murder of a helpless eight-year-old boy by Passant's niece, abetted by a female friend; a psychiatric examination ascertains the mental infirmity of the murderers. Almost half of the novel, the finale, is dedicated to the phases of the trial, followed painstakingly as if in the form of a stenographic summary. This event is extraneous and strident, and Snow has recourse to it to shake up a plot that is too inert, and to instil it with a late dose of suspense. *Last Things* (1970) shifts the hands of time even further forward to when Eliot, a baronet, is sixty. This seems like an inevitable and predicted fictional act that carries out a series of verifications and updates or gives previously missing news; except that the plot is extended without necessity, losing itself in incidental episodes and verging on the prolixity of Iris Murdoch's last novels. Upright and responsible, Eliot refuses a post as minister and suffers a near-death experience that reconfirms his atheism and his absence of faith in an afterlife perspective;[24] and he again crosses swords with a youthful generation whom he fails to understand. One by one many of his travelling companions predictably die. The novel radiates a sense of finality preannounced by the title, which materializes in presentiments that have no particular causes. Snow speaks expressly of a belated age of anxiety or angst; and this translates in the novel into a smouldering feeling of existential precariousness, indeed the sense of the approach of a pressing confrontation, always however courageously firm, from a stance of stoic lay materialism.[25]

24 A situation similar to Lazarus' experience, often spasmodically revisited by the Victorian poets.
25 Cf. what I said above on Snow's axiom or aphorism, that 'each of us dies alone'.

§ 58. *Powell* I: Farces on impotence and power*

Almost no one openly says and writes it,[1] and if anything everyone denies it,[2] but if there is a novelist who can compete with any other for the accolade of the greatest British writer in the second half of the twentieth century – and whose death coincides symbolically with the falling of the curtain on the whole century – it is Anthony Powell (1905–2000). This recognition, based on the twelve novels of his *magnum opus* entitled *A Dance to the Music of Time*, can be measured in terms of an emblematic summary of British history from 1921 to the closing date, 1975, of his last novel. This is inevitably a selective and intermittent history, identified, however, with the destinies of the British white-collar class *par excellence*, the intellectual bourgeoisie which provided cadres to politics, fought two wars as a bastion of freedom against continental dictatorships, and represented British culture, for better or worse, over a fifty-year span, from immediately after

---

*   The standard edition of *A Dance to the Music of Time* is the revised one in 4 vols, published in England by Heinemann (London 1969–1975), and in America by Little, Brown and Company (Boston, MA and Toronto 1969–1975). B. Bergonzi, *Anthony Powell*, London 1962, and, ed. I. Scott-Kilvert, 1971; R. K. Morris, *The Novels of Anthony Powell*, Pittsburgh, PA 1968; J. Russell, *Anthony Powell: A Quintet, Sextet and War*, Bloomington, IN and London 1970; N. Brennan, *Anthony Powell*, New York 1974, and, rev., 1995; J. Tucker, *The Novels of Anthony Powell*, London 1976; D. Davin, *Snow Upon Fire: 'A Dance to the Music of Time', Anthony Powell*, Swansea 1977; H. Spurling, *Handbook to 'Dance to the Music of Time'*, London 1977 (with a one-page introduction by Powell himself), and, with the title *Invitation to the Dance: A Handbook to Anthony Powell's 'Dance to the Music of Time'*, London 1992; R. Bader, *Anthony Powell's 'Music of Time' as a Cyclic Novel of Generations*, Bern 1980; L. A. Frost, *Reminiscent Scrutinies: Memory in Anthony Powell's 'A Dance to the Music of Time'*, Troy 1990; N. McEwan, *Anthony Powell*, Houndmills 1991; R. L. Selig, *Time and Anthony Powell: A Critical Study*, Rutherford, NJ, London and Cranbury, NJ 1991; I. Joyau, *Investigating Powell's 'A Dance to the Music of Time'*, Houndmills 1994; M. Barber, *Anthony Powell: A Life*, London 2004; N. Birns, *Understanding Anthony Powell*, Columbia, SC 2004. An unsympathetic review by Praz, 'Un romanzo militare' (1972), is in SSI, vol. II, 377–81.

1   Except C. Pagetti, in MAR, vol. IV, 125.
2   A. N. Wilson, *TLS*, 9 July 2004, still defined him at that date as an 'extraordinarily underestimated novelist'.

the First World War to the first thirty years of peace, and from the Second World War to the second peace, which was also and above all a war, albeit 'cold'. Consequently, Powell offered a nation the chance to look at itself retrospectively in the mirror and discover that it was not wholly wicked. He did this ultimately using the representative art of the last great writer of the satirical, comical-humorous and Gothic-visionary British tradition. He is the last living equation of the writer as entertainer, first embodied by Dickens, but a writer-entertainer endowed with a strong, understandably more up-to-date and shrewd aesthetic than the reductive and rudimentary one of this nineteenth-century predecessor ('Let them laugh, let them cry, let them wait'). Certainly, taken singly, each masterpiece of Graham Greene – a competitor,[3] and not all of his novels were masterpieces – can beat every single one of Powell's novels. Greene was more inventive, more of a tightrope walker, more metaphysical, more gripping, but less unified; Powell deliberately scorned and neglected tension and interweaving, adopting instead a concentric analytical rhythm; however, he did command, design, ponder and gauge his narrative edifice like no one else in England during his half-century. His rich material is governed and tamed through a *persona*, the mask of an intra- and homo-diegetic but mainly extra-diegetic narrator, a strategy which allows Powell Olympian detachment and rigorous narrative control; which is also why his *opus* is a retrospective whose act of birth came a good thirty years from the original autobiographical experiences that give it substance, and that he could thus objectify and put in perspective. Powell, however, really does seem to be able to objectify the immediate, too. He is an illustrator who is supremely able to insert as filter a personal, smooth, painstaking style, one even at times calligraphic and convoluted as only Henry James's could be. Ultimately, one gift is his alone, that of the most cultured and scholarly fiction writer among his peers, and that of a prose that abounds in continual, detailed references to the literary, mythological and anthropological canon, as well as to the visual arts and music. Powell's pigeonhole is among the essayistic novelists, and that *persona* and that voice are, or mimic, those of the university professor

3   § 49.1.

and the art critic. He has been classified as a cyclical narrator of sagas, in a mould that dates back to Galsworthy and before; as a dialogic writer, according to another widespread fashion, and a comical and satirical one of the youthful *belle époque* in the moneyed London neighbourhoods; as a conservative writer, along the lines of Waugh, who drew his lifeblood from the epic of the Second World War. He is above all a late defector from the universities, with remarkable links with the historical progeny of Oxford and Cambridge defectors from just under a century earlier. Powell is indeed a product of the English universities, not a spontaneous fiction writer who has risen through the ranks; the imaginary genesis of his fiction remains his school and university experience. An incalculable amount of material for his major novels is of academic derivation, and many of the figures who pack its scenes are budding novelists, reviewers, screenwriters and artists. Only Huxley was to rival Powell in his work on the 'thresholds' of the text and in the art of titling. Almost all of his novels reproduce in their titles quotations and hemistichs of celebrated but also uncommon literary works, whose pertinence is often recalled in the novel in the most far-fetched way. From this identikit arises a preliminary consideration, that Powell's actual biography, emotional and intellectual, is to be found in his works, and that that of pure external occurrences is of no interest, since it is non-specific.[4] Suffice it to recall that Powell was the son of an army officer, studied at Eton and Oxford and then worked in London in publishing and as a screenwriter. A frequenter of avant-garde artistic circles, before he was thirty he had befriended Waugh, the painters Nina Hamnett and Adrian Daintrey, and the composer Constant Lambert.[5] A reviewer for mostly right-wing dailies and periodicals, he was called up during the war as a liaison officer without fighting at the front. At the end of the conflict he wrote as a literary critic on the seventeenth-century biographer John Aubrey, Robert Burton, and Stendhal. These were the eccentric and anachronistic interests of a retired and methodical country gentleman, as Powell was to become in the last

---

4   As A. N. Wilson recalled in an article in *TLS* quoted above in n. 2, which is a review of Barber 2004.

5   A possible prototype for the musician Moreland in *A Dance*, something, however, denied by Powell (cf. Tucker 1976, 153).

decades of his life, quietly spent in an estate in Somerset which he bought thanks to an inheritance, and interspersed with journeys to various continents. I shall be explaining below how much this lately discovered identity, after his youthful pre-war wild oats, aligned with the ideological design of his grand oeuvre. Powell's activity was rounded off by frequently limpid and perspicacious introductions to minor British classics.[6]

2. An internal division is evident: five novels were written by Powell before the war, dating from the 1930s, then a forced silence followed, lasting twelve years, which were in reality years of fertile incubation and which led to the second or real birth of the mature novelist in 1951. The long-lived Powell was not an early twentieth-century writer who dragged himself jadedly into our own times, but a bona fide post-war writer. The five early novels are, due to the accumulation of neutral elements and others that are decidedly contrary, a version of anti-Modernism; however, the anti-experimental novel is experimental, too. Powell, for instance, enlarged that group of novelists who rejected the stream of consciousness, polystylism, parody, and the practice of the novel as wordplay, and he remained faithful to linear time. On the other hand, a timid assent to Modernism is revealed in the by then pacific renunciation of nineteenth-century omniscience: the descriptions, the fine introductions, the lengthy interludes and the natural settings are reduced or eliminated, letting the characters speak; but dialogue is functional, and more selective than that of Compton-Burnett, for instance, and less disconnected and schizoid than that of early Waugh. Powell's unit of measurement is short and spare, far from the multifocal and the overlapping plots, and with a unified focus. In these five novels Powell still believed that there was and must be a story to be told, and that a novel hinges on a main character or a group of characters; he believed that life is tragicomic and therefore also comical. However, the comic sketch, or even the gag, is an element inherited from the nineteenth-century comical-satirical novel.

6   One should at least recall those to Firbank (Volume 7, § 88.1 bibl.) and to a triptych of 'high-society' Victorian novels, *Henrietta Temple* by Disraeli, *Guy Livingstone* by G. A. Lawrence, and *Moths* by Ouida (London 1947). His memories, entitled *To Keep the Ball Rolling*, were published between 1976 and 1982 in four volumes, along with *A Writer's Notebook*, posthumously in 2000.

3. Powell's early novels, a far from negligible productive effort, attended to and completed in less than a decade, are immature and minor, but not without a certain, nervous experimental aim; as a result, they are visibly uneven, and strongly unrelated as regards setting, characters and plot. They strike various targets without being coordinated with one another. The ideal and ideological link only rests on the acrobatics of the titles, which ring together in a thoughtful condemnation that is muffled in the internal variety, above all farcical, of each one.[7] The frame, the external construction and reciprocal link between the single novels of *A Dance* were to challenge and react against this dispersion and lack of organization. *Afternoon Men*[8] (1931), for some a small comic masterpiece and the best of Powell's novels before *A Dance*, hinges on the amorous adventures and disappointments of one William Atwater, a young museum clerk who is attempting to realize himself, above all sentimentally, in the London of the 1920s. He is part of a rather degenerate circle of friends and acquaintances, above all amateur painters and writers who could be placed as a class in between the true bohemians and the fringes of the aristocratic life. Their common trait is affective malaise, erotic misapprehension, and the faux pas. The girls are ready to flirt, promiscuously and opportunistically, and are therefore also ready to give themselves sexually, but their partners remain unsatisfied. The resulting comedy is at times extremely controlled and therefore a little lugubrious,[9] with an added sense of uselessness, emptiness, dissipation, and of an existential prison. New York and America form the illusory romance that is cultivated and coveted; while a certain Undershaft is a kind of Godot, a ghost continually evoked, whom everyone recalls as the one who had the

7   Cf. McEwan 1991, 22, on the novel's 'concealment of the intention'. Powell was astonished that the reviewers found in it a savage attack on contemporary customs.

8   A title taken from Burton's *Anatomy of Melancholy*, since the novel itself insists, with Burton, on the necessity to smile at human caprice.

9   An incompetent but determined painter discovers a rival, whom he has invited together with others to his house in the country, in bed with his fiancée, and decides to commit suicide by drowning; but he repents and, safe and sound, returns dressed as a fisherman. However, the comedy lies in the long, 'absurd' debate on the sum with which he will recompense the fisherman, who asks for his clothes back, and the incomprehensible monosyllable with which he receives it.

courage to leave, breaking the spell chaining all the others, and achieving success. The reader, however, thinks he is merely pretence, until he actually appears in flesh and blood to snatch the woman from a naïve fellow. Among the whole group, there is no really triumphant character: they are all poor devils. The initial impression is not so much, as is often suggested by critics, that of Waugh in *Decline and Fall* – Powell's characters are much less 'brilliant' – but that of Huxley. Powell was repeating, in a lesser format, *Antic Hay*. The prevalent dialogic form, joined with the suppression or rather the drastic restriction of authorial comment, also makes us think of Compton-Burnett. Powell comes close here to the zero degree of literary language, and thus to one of the many possible experiments with the phenomenological novel.[10]

4. *Venusberg* (1932), less successful, is wholly or partially about espionage and petty international or simply continental intrigue. A British journalist who aspires to be a theatre critic, and is therefore frustrated, is forced to accept a post as foreign correspondent in an unspecified Baltic republic that has recently ceased to be a Soviet protectorate. In the love plot he loves a woman who ambiguously prefers a fellow student. The two rivals face one another in a forced life together in that distant scenario. Meanwhile, what seems to be clear is a little misogyny on Powell's part, because the women are loved hopelessly but remain unattainable and out of reach, like Hardy's females.[11] This is contradicted, however, by the fact that on the ship the Englishman falls in love with an Austrian woman and seduces her with great ease, continuing this clandestine relationship once they have reached their destination. A particularly successful portrait is that of the elderly psychology professor, the husband cuckolded under his nose or pretending not to notice; indeed, he even favours the trysts and the affair and is (probably, because it never comes out into the open) the instigator of a punitive attack that eliminates his wife but also the wrong lover. The

---

10   Hemingway interested Powell at that time (McEwan 1991, 16).
11   A sophisticated, but ultimately false thread, in reality Wagnerian, runs through the novel, right from the title which alludes in reverse to *Tannhäuser* (and the manservant is called Pope); the receptionist of the Baltic hotel where the main character stays has the name of a 'daughter of the Rhine', Flosshilde.

sensational interweaving has a cold-war mood as a background, with communist saboteurs and a repressive army; in the imaginary republic the pitiful human larvae of Russian refugees from Bolshevism vent their nostalgia in an entourage of consuls and officials working for the ambassadors. But the foreigners have a good time at nightclubs and receptions, at balls and other socialite occasions. Powell lets himself be carried away by a series of comic skits, and sets up a far-fetched burlesque plot that in some situations can loudly evoke the atmospheres of a Firbank. The psychological profiles are deliberately flat and always hazy, and the caricatures multiply and many capricious and funny events verge on the improbable and audacious, or on the genre of the detective romance in the manner of Greene, and thus on political fiction.[12] *From a View to a Death*[13] (1933), a plot made of blurred events that follow one another in slow motion and a lengthy set of static scenes, character studies and petty wars of position, returns to the themes of claustrophobia, of the lack of a future, of existential immobility, but transposed to a rural setting. The case study of frustration and of unheroic times is exemplified in a climate of still late Victorian eccentricity. In one of three families of village notables, a daughter has had a baby girl and her husband has left her; in another an old, odd and nutty man retires to the attic to read wearing an old dress; and in a third a still young spinster thinks of nothing but lovingly ministering to some dogs. As in Trollope, whose novels *From a View to a Death* sometimes seems to parody, a gossip has an Italian husband and is formally a duchess.[14] The whole of this small community is shaken and thrilled by a theatrical show to be put on at the parish church. In short, it is a small saga of the old, provincial well-to-do middle class, and of the epic, overblown village quarrels; such is its retro flavour. The marks of the characters are imperceptibly revealed, preferably by the dialogue, and these are the irascible, gossiping, malignant, hypochondriac types. It was spontaneous for Powell the novelist to portray some amateur painters, as in his first novel. One of these, Zouch, a social climber and

---

12   One of Greene's first novels, *England Made Me* (§ 50.4), had been set in a reinvented
      Sweden, against the background of an intrigue.
13   A citation from a popular hunting song.
14   One scene is the proverbially and undeniably Trollope-like one of the foxhunt.

profiteer who behaves like a superman,[15] is in part a repeat of the village scoundrel and heart-breaker;[16] he brings lustre to the community which he willingly comes to visit as a guest. It is a satirical portrait, but at the same time a pretext, and a *trait d'union*, for a 'view to a death' or vegetative life, as the title suggests.

5. *Agents and Patients*[17] (1936) is the most experimental of Powell's novels, and in fact offers an evident contrast to the static scenario of the previous one, since it dives into the insensate vortex of contemporary life. It also turns out to be more didactic, and goes beyond the bare illustration of human oddities, idiosyncrasies and stupidity. It describes a formative process, namely, the result of experience after innocence. The first quarter is the freshest and tautest thing Powell ever wrote before the war, with its pair of ignoble profiteers, the amateur film-maker (replacing the painter) and the sly psychoanalyst who tracks down the victim, Blore-Smith. Thackeray, too, based his early sketches on the relationship between the plucker and the chicken, or cockerel. Blore-Smith is a fresh university graduate, and in London he aspires to the forensic profession; he has money to burn and little to do, and is sexually and intellectually a virgin, timid and clumsy in discovering and forging an identity. A natural prey, in short. A much sharper pen delineates the surrounding context, but ultimately Powell does not overplay his hand on the petty, up-to-date allegory of the job market crisis of the 1930s, and the struggle to live that cynically obliges a low-life confused youth to use its ingenuity. As a result, the plot is more structured, and the preparatory moves implacable in their reciprocal and almost fatal convergence; an *ante litteram* Greene-style force of gravity – as

15   In Nietzsche's precise sense, of a 'will to power', the *Wille zur Macht* which drives him towards his goals. Passenger, too, who is putting Zouch up so that he can paint a portrait of his daughter, is a second self-styled superman. A similar ideological frame is coldly applied from the outside, and supports the plot in an extremely improbable way. The duel of wills is in any case, as I shall explain, the ideological architrave of *A Dance*.

16   Huxleyan, that is, extremely sensual (cf. § 33.5), is the fluent beard constantly noted by the villagers.

17   With the opposition, apparent in the novel, between acting in first person and being manipulated.

in the masterly scene of the pursuit of Hale in *Brighton Rock* – brings about the meeting – or more precisely the dovetailing – of the three characters. Maltravers is an ambitious amateur film-maker; all he wants is to make psycho-phenomenological cinema, and he leans on his accomplice Chipchase who is more of a huckster than a bona fide scientist. The two penniless rascals draw the sucker into the trap, and from being a fugitive he becomes their pursuer. Once Blore-Smith has been duped, Powell adjusts his module, making it lean decidedly on the register of the comical and farcical; from a tidy pattern it rises to an overwhelming, when not frantic, rhythm. In Paris, the rash Blore-Smith finds himself caught in low company, faux pas, cheating, and ruinous sexual initiations. The episodes follow one another, with an absurdly surreal air, as far as the film studios in Berlin, a section arranged in the style of a chaotic riot. From the symmetrical spare tale of the gradual convergence of three characters, possibly and above all ironically fatal, the novel tumbles into a kaleidoscopic, bloated container of meteoric appearances, and visibly looks back to the experimentalism of Waugh's *Vile Bodies*. The pyrotechnic explosions are at times priceless, above all when the wanderers return to England, the film is shot, and it films life itself, demonstrating the inexistence of the boundary between reality and make-believe: in other terms, the camera limits itself to capturing a real quarrel, unbeknown to the 'agents and patients', as the title preannounced. The final result is a rather excessive and untidy satire of psychoanalysis and cinema, or of psychoanalytical cinema, since the two adventurers confusingly carry on the project of a modern-day *Oedipus Rex* that should photograph and categorize human behaviour through the eye of psychoanalysis. In the concluding scene, Blore-Smith has mended his ways, and is surprisingly firm in showing the door to his two accomplices, who have again squared up to him to recapture him.

6. *What's Become of Waring*[18] (1939) objectifies and re-imagines Powell's recent activity as an executive in a publishing company, again surrounding the main character – a first-person narrator who tends to be eclipsed, to be

---

18   The title conflates a series of astute and pertinent literary allusions. Waring is the title
     of a poem by Browning on a friend who has disappeared or run away; as I explain,
     Browning himself is implicated.

undefined, to be just an open objective and a camera – with a community that Powell has no intention of describing in any depth, but grasps in its surface ripples, comical, farcical and estranged as these might be. This plan produces an agreeable plot, full of surprises, twists, dramatic events, and peppered with the consequences of the sentimental life of one sector of the population. The novel's metaliterary nature lies in the search for the true identity and even existence in life of an established travel writer, which is at the same time an existential pre-Antonioni-style cinema thriller plot. In literary history, it hinges in turn on a theme used dozens of times by Browning – that dichotomy between public author and private personality which the early critics of that poet tended to emphasize, like Henry James in a famous story.[19] At the same time, Powell's Waring playfully foreshadows the split personality of later ghostly writers preferring to hide themselves, and not to appear in public, like Salinger and Pynchon. The 'jocoserious' vein is exploited in view of a destructive and desecrating satire on the conventions of publishing and literature itself. As an absurd comment on the biography industry, *What's Become of Waring* is extraordinarily similar to Maugham's *Cakes and Ale*,[20] reconstructing as it does, more linearly and with different pretexts and alternative incidental scenes of entertainment, the phases of preparation of a biography of an imaginary writer, who may have had a real counterpart, like Maugham's Driffield. The celebrity who reaps success is unmasked as a plagiarist here, too; but the internal narrator, who is interested in Stendhal, is forced to agree that plagiarism is intrinsic to literature, if even the top French novelist copied his masterpiece from an obscure Italian book.

§ 59. *Powell II: 'A Dance to the Music of Time' I. Refined entertainments for a relaxed intelligentsia*

At the end of the war the cultured Powell studied seventeenth-century biographic literature in his book *John Aubrey and His Friends* (1948). He

---

19   Volume 4, § 105.2.
20   And yet, or *pour cause*, it is Maugham's story 'Rain' (Volume 7, § 58.2) which is cited, during an interview between the editor Judkins and a female journalist he tries to seduce.

himself was to state in an interview that the plan of the book had arisen by chance and extemporaneously, as a *divertissement*. However, the study of the seventeenth-century antiquarian Aubrey suggested to him a new method, that of an anecdotal tale that was at the same time a picture or polyptych focused on human idiosyncrasies.[21] An emulator of Dickens, Powell immediately had the audacious idea, wagering on the survival of his strength, to organize a work into twelve units distributed in four trilogies; in other terms, he already had its complete plan in mind, and eventually concluded his enterprise within a twenty-five-year time span. A revolution in his method was silently planned and implemented: from the splintered, disconnected, lightning-quick, somewhat confused story, to a methodical succession of linked episodes and anecdotes within a fixed frame and against the background of public history; stylistically, from the asyndetic sentence to a spiralling and Baroque-style construction. Starting from its literary context, *A Dance to the Music of Time* induces us to seek the reasons for the unusually high statistical frequency of sagas, as well as coordinated cyclical novels, over the course of the twentieth century. At first sight, they descend from the need to explain, with an obviously personal point of view, a tumultuous and confused period that has just passed; secondly, they enclose an aesthetic proposal: the narcissism of an author who, hidden behind a first person, elects to be a privileged observation point; a criterion and pragmatics of the reading; a formula, in the end, of facilitated literature. *A Dance to the Music of Time* immediately invites comparison with Galsworthy's *Forsyte Saga*, a generation and a half earlier. The two universes are populated by hundreds of characters of varying importance. In a few episodes and situations Powell descends to the level of a Galsworthy: a more stylistically refined, more allusive, enormously more cultured Galsworthy, but equally anonymous.[22] If anything, his saga differs from Galsworthy's in its patterning (that of Ford Madox Ford is

21   Cf. Bergonzi 1971, 11, for the interview and the point discussed here.
22   Galsworthy, too, worked on the parallels between life and art, above all painterly
      art, though in a more amateurish way, when compared to Powell. Nick's uncle in
      Powell, Giles, quotes a Galsworthy-style sentence, not from the *Forsyte Saga*, which
      nonetheless shows the influence of this model on Powell.

too limited in the number of single novels to lend itself to a comparison). Galsworthy introduces three generations in the time span of his saga; Powell has the same characters remain on stage until the end, with a few defections. The ill-concealed Galsworthian panegyric of the white-collar middle class, risen from nothing and strayed in the descendants, might seem the exact opposite of Powell's idea; however, we shall see that this is not quite the case. More similar is Waugh's *Brideshead Revisited*, which resorts to the same spectator-narrator, to the friendships over time between classmates, to the affective breakdowns and the sentimental reversals – but, in Powell, without a religious and metaphysical design forming a frame.[23] These earlier sagas were in part nostalgic and melancholic behind a patina of virulent rejection and satire. They were also temporally older and they began earlier: from the tail end of Victorianism, or Edwardian and in part Georgian. Powell's saga is set in the period *entre les deux guerres*, and can only dialogue with Waugh's. However, Powell, who seems to have no faith, is an objective, impassive, placid observer. He presents a counter-epic for modern times.[24]

2. Powell denied that he set out to show the decline of the middle class – even if, strictly speaking, he spoke of 'civilization' and not of the 'middle class'.[25] So what was it that he wished to show? The basic supreme struggle is that of residual humanism, capable of 'connecting' and associating sensibility, against the pragmatic and atomizing culture that was establishing itself and in fact rapidly spreading in his time. Powell never cites T. S. Eliot or Spinoza or the Metaphysical poets (he does however cite Vaughan), or Baldassar Castiglione, though he refers to late sixteenth-century or seventeenth-century models of a similar 'associated' culture, such as Aubrey, Browne and above all Burton; his was the ancient ideal of Sidney's humanist soldier. This struggle is played out, even if not wholly, on the capacity

---

23   Although he admired him, Waugh expressly noticed Powell's lack of a 'solid' religious faith (McEwan 1991, 53).

24   In *A Question of Upbringing*, the guest Dubuisson speaks of the petty quarrels at the French *pension* as 'the problems of Europe in miniature', and of an 'international allegory'.

25   McEwan 1991, 14.

of certain residual humanists to capture the echoes of the arts in life, and hence on an exquisite gift of sensibility. The others are deaf. Supremely deaf is Widmerpool (who proclaims confidently that reading too much distorts one's way of looking at life). One ultimately demonstrative scene focuses on Nick Jenkins, an excellent wartime translator, ironically deemed hopeless, but the translator, in any case, of a manual that makes no sense. Powell has no intention of opposing this course of events: Widmerpool is a winner until the sudden final whisk of the tail, of an above all visionary kind; and Jenkins prefers to neatly withdraw. The life that awaits Jenkins, after the end of the novel, is the one chosen by Powell himself late in his career, that of a detached observer of the wheel of human cases, spun by time. Some critics and readers have even caught a glimmer of positivity in Widmerpool, and the hint of a healthy, proactive, tenacious resistance to an enervated, libertine middle class who continued to *piétiner sur place* and never concluded anything good. The entire cycle can, in theory, be ambiguously deconstructed, if not as the secret panegyric of Widmerpool's gifts of ductile and elastic resistance, at least as the resigned acceptance of the fact that the humanistic ideal, that of Sidney's courtier, has waned; and that in its place the times reward the *homo oeconomicus* or the Machiavellian. The fall of Widmerpool, which is largely visionary as I have just said, is also decidedly utopian: namely, that *homo* was still firmly straddling the times. Ultimately, Powell could not place the blame too heavily on that middle class to which he belonged. One index of his intentions is the ideal shifting of the times towards the world of 'intermediation'. Widmerpool and others speculate daringly, repeating in short what Melmotte had already done in Trollope's *The Way of the World*. Penniless, they both skim off the foreign contracts, until a ripple in the exchange rate causes the collapse of transactions all of which were made without money. In practice the British display the same defect that Dickens denounced: avarice, personal profit, a thirst for wealth, position, and 'getting on' come what may, indifferent to values; or even Italian *trasformismo*. The morally reduced, almost universal, dimension stands forth in an unintelligible emotional life, subject to the most unexpected variations and sudden changes of partner. As a result, it is not easy to understand the intention behind Powell's objectivity. He reveals rather little through his *alter ego* Nick Jenkins. The occasions on which

Powell comes out, having already reflected himself in an *alter ego*, are not many. He is a sibylline, or simply non-committal illustrator, too undecided and cynical ever to be a moralist. This grand succession of epiphanic illuminations of the half-century he describes is not read through any strong and distinct ideology. By dint of his apathetic *alter ego*, Powell never fully reveals himself; he is merely an observer, and his only ideological decision is the trimming of the material.

3. Powell's man lives to get ahead with some difficulty in his career, and loves and flirts in the recognized instability and volubility of affections; he has ultimately no high ideals. It is true that some writers from the pool of characters are politicized, but the internal narrator pays little heed to them. Nor is Powell an analyst of passion, much less of the furious erotic impulse. He glides over erotic inebriation, the kindling of passion and its aetiology, to concentrate on its visible effects; what interests him in the passion that arises is the later anecdotes or even scandal. He is a phenomenologist of Eros, like Stendhal, or de Sade.[26] Nor do the horrors of war touch him, the sole exception being the central scene of *The Soldier's Art*, when Nick Jenkins hears, rather than actually seeing first-hand, that bombs have fallen on various areas in London, and receives news of the hardships that have struck his acquaintances. Based on all of this, Powell can ultimately be defined as an Apollonian writer who spreads a veil of detached, refined elegance over the fictional and memorial material; or an Olympian who never breaks down or loses his patience, never exudes sarcasm and scorn, and harmoniously distils the whole of reality. Whether or not he is Nick, this Nick is able at every moment, like Tennyson for Verlaine, to recall and introduce a literary and more often painterly citation when he should be moved. Powell possessed no sense of the tragic, only that of the funny, the comical, the discreet, the vivid, the eccentric and the unforeseen. He is a neo-aesthete, not naturally in the sense that he prizes beauty over truth, or recreates the library of Des Esseintes: he is one, if anything, in seeing life *sub specie aesthetica*, through the filter of art, be it literary, painterly, or mythological. He claimed to be a naturalistic writer who simply described

---

26   'Most people's sex life is a mystery, especially that of individuals who seem to make most parade of it'.

'nothing that could not have occurred in everyday life'.[27] However, it cannot be denied that he creates a void around the circle of his characters, or leaves in the dark everything that lies out of its spotlight. His only partial realism eclipses the seamy side of life from an ill-concealed snobbish position, and for example the poverty of the working classes. Lastly, one must underline Powell's total indifference to religious or spiritual matters, and his impartial equidistance from the contemporary debate between Bolshevism and Catholicism. He is neither against nor in favour of the religious and transcendent dimension; he is purely an agnostic.[28]

4. The twelve constituent acts of *A Dance* are novels of equal length and almost the same number of chapters, like Snow's (four is the norm, five or six the exception, but never less than three). To use a metaphor that never appears in the text, they are, like a poem by T. S. Eliot, quartets, quintets and sextets, at times even septets (a group of artists, smaller than that of the writers, and of that of the painters, is of musicians, while the whole beginning of *The Military Philosophers* takes place under the banner of a musical parallelism, with a soldier polishing his equipment and recalling Wagner's Mime). And so every 'act', which also corresponds to a year or a group of years or a period of time extracted from the continuum, and therefore epiphanic in its own way, is felt as quadripartite. But every other musical analogy of 'movements' becomes problematic. A different metaphor may be evoked,[29] a military one (Powell was the son of a soldier and was destined for that career): the novels are in fact arrayed on an imaginary map like a company of four or more platoons, marching in perfect battle order and obeying their commands. The unit of measurement is the long sequence, possibly subdivided into micro-sequences, and narrated with microscopic attention to every kind of detail. Powell is never implausible in packaging informative descriptions and then initiating a dialogue that he enriches with acute psychological captions attributed to his internal narrator. As each character is gradually introduced, he is also adept at

27   Interview given in 1961 to W. J. Wetherby, quoted in Tucker 1976, 161.
28   On the absence of any transcendental hypostasis inherent in one's acting in the dimension of time, cf. Tucker 1976, 79.
29   As McEwan 1991, 12, too, notes.

drawing up a curious chart of his past as a lavish biographer, ever attentive to the physical-somatic and psychological traits, and always skilled in using erudite filters. The form is that of a detailed memoir interrupted by digressions, suspensions and embroideries of the most varied nature, provided by a narrator who ranges smoothly and elegantly over select anecdotes referring to a group of characters who are interrelated starting from their early school life, but with additions gradually deriving from their later vicissitudes. Each novel focuses on a closed caste dedicated to intermarriage. The historical landmarks are the Versailles Peace Conference, the 1926 General Strike, the rumblings of Nazism, the war in Spain, the abdication of Edward VIII, the declaration of war, the atom bomb. Nick Jenkins absorbs, arranges, subdivides and organizes this past. Events and people re-emerge changed and repetitive; often a new character recalls and seems to resemble an old and already known one, and Nick glimpses symmetries and reincarnations. Powell is not interested in tense action *per se* or suspense. He plans his novels as sequences of encounters, of two or more people; therefore his chapters result in meetings of individuals who exchange dialogues; the most usual occasion is a private party, or a tea, or a drink at some meeting place. Here Powell, through his *persona*, reports or has his new characters report their past vicissitudes, or revises their identikits. Thus he is not so distant from Henry James's practice of presenting characters, almost every character, from the point of view of the other characters. At times, the narration seems to be protracted for the sole objective of arriving at the next denouement, that is, the encounter of two friends who have not seen one another for a while and recognize one another. The chronological progress is inexorable and linear; except for the fact that sparse temporal overlaps, and therefore recollections of previous moments, appear. Every long chapter constitutes a temporal unit, but the three, four or five chapters of a novel are not always chronologically aligned, and may move backward and forward. In such a way – with its prelude to or harbinger of the First World War, relived in the idyllic English countryside – *The Kindly Ones* opens. Normally, at the end of every chapter, the curtain drops, and the action described does not continue into the next one, which is taken up with a temporal gap and, in many cases, a change of scene. It may not be possible to place the twelve novels on a rating scale. Each one includes anecdotal peaks and impressive scenes in the midst of deliberately below-par management and a rhythm of routine fiction. Powell also possesses the art of being able to carry the plot forward without saying much that is new. Such an internal updating of the many biographical and career threads takes place at every opportunity, so that everything is represented indefinitely and nothing is destroyed. But this is also a linking ploy, whose objective is to remind the reader of events and passages that may have slipped the mind, being so many. The formula of the *Dance* novel is gradually adjusted and lubricated, and, in the end, one may pronounce the same judgement that is passed on those of Compton-Burnett, whose oeuvre is for different reasons equally homogeneous, and made up of single works that are similar to one another: that there is no marked difference between the one and the other. They are, in other words, elegant, skilful, well executed, glossy even, but mixed with that smidgeon of high-level gossip of the highbrow set that can always appeal to and attract a various public. *A Dance* encloses an insidious aesthetic proposal: it is no banal serial novel, trashy and for all palates, superficial and preposterous; it is instead a dish for committed intellectuals who would like to occasionally permit themselves a moment of weakness, to distract themselves and relax. Powell packaged a product destined to be likeable and which was indeed liked, to judge from the tacit consensus and the esteem that surround it. In particular, it has managed to satisfy the British passion for all things grand and monumental, for cadastral constructions, for the arresting, Gibbonian summaries, for the works of a lifetime, or the admiration for methodical collecting. It is still a paradox or a misconception that this saga with its slow pace, tedious and static in too many segments, and a cult work as the saying goes, has been widely judged to be appealing; and that inevitably, given its unprecedented length and unwieldy import, reductions and summaries have flourished, as have reasoned, exhaustive catalogues of its characters, places, and literary allusions.[30] Its disfiguration came in the TV productions that Powell had accurately prognosticated in the novels themselves. These guides or synopses ware authorized by Powell himself,

---

30   The most useful being that of Spurling 1977, with the distinction I am mentioning.

sympathetic to his reader, who might have forgotten the links and the prior events. In reality, they are the utter, pitiful distortion of the novel's aesthetic project, and also a second-rate surrogate of the reading experience. They transform into brutal telegraphic syntagmas, and Morse-code characters separated by dashes, a flow that is uninterrupted in the text, or also a musical wave that checks the transformation of the language into a pragmatic and recapitulative instrument.

5. The driving element of *A Dance*'s vast layout is mental and cultural association. Powell's last novel before the twelve-part saga already bears an associative title, even if the trigger of the plot is a reminiscence that is not painterly but literary. And yet this title, *What's Become of Waring*, sounds rather similar to the genesis of the tale – in fact an 'imaginary portrait' – of another writer who loved being inspired by the visual arts, Pater. Pater and Powell are to some degree comparable, not least because they possess and constantly employ a kind of radar in order to capture the painterly detail underlying the phenomenal world, and as a result, believe that reality imitates art, one of the basic dogmas of aestheticism.[31] Powell opens the saga with a modern, contemporary image, apparently drained of any reminiscence, that of workers warming themselves at a brazier in the snow – which could also be the title of a seventeenth-century painting, a so-called genre painting. These workers evoke classical icons, such as the ancestral rites of legionnaires in sheepskin. Immediately afterwards the associationist memorial sense is inverted, and it is the classical reminiscence – Poussin's painting of the same name, on the theme of the rhythmic dance of time – that evokes contemporary plots. This is the icon of the movement of swinging figures reappearing in historical time – hence the post-Paterian concept of a novel as a packed canvas of figures, or a grand composition of pictures with panels containing the same characters. The informing artistic metaphor is painterly; however, the underlying concept is inter-artistic (and Huxley, in various ways Powell's master, turned to the analogy of musical counterpoint in a shorter, albeit rather contrived,

31   Cf., merely to become aware of this frequency, the Index of references to painting in Spurling 1977, 259–84.

novel).[32] The motif or basic symbol of the dance is transformed over the course of the twelve books: it is a dance that loses its rhythm and even its dancers; it also loses its universal association, that of freedom, since historical time is revealed as constrictive. Losing its very sense the dance becomes insensate. Significantly, the evocation of and from Poussin reverses Yeats's theory of the gyres, since the dancers lose their step or no longer have a handle on the music. In the second chapter of Powell's last novel, time in Poussin's scene is contrasted with the rather more agitated one of Ariosto's Astolfo on the moon. This passage is played out, in a half page, with a really Proustian sophistication: Ariosto's *ottava* recalling Astolfo's descent to the earth, with a reference to the term 'magician', leads to the awakening of the memory in a modern well-known scientist, alchemist or holy man with a train of disciples. Powell does not leave this humorous variation, and Widmerpool the widower seems to him an Orlando gone crazy over the loss of his Angelica; but the narrator himself admits that the parallel 'might not be exact at every point'. The target of the basic struggle is the chaos of history in order to affirm a pattern, a pattern that is however imposed by the mere exhaustion of the combinations; or it responds to every single capricious turn of the wheel. Something neurotically Hardyan emerges in the fact that fascinating women (such as Matilda or Pamela) feel gnawed by the desire for extramarital adventure, and commit adultery with tame, unattractive, meek men, prefiguring the absence of any hope for emotional stability. The fascination exerted by a woman as ugly as Audrey Maclintick is equally inexplicable. The law of the 'eternal return' – that nothing is lost, everything comes back, and old acquaintances reappear periodically – is recalled from Nietzsche: 'We parted company, agreeing that Nietzschean Eternal Recurrences must bring us together soon again' (*The Soldier's Art*). The supreme challenge is played out against Proust, with whom Powell has been frequently associated in an overly ennobling comparison.[33] If this is the case, he is a lesser Proust, of a visibly British stamp. *A Dance* is not an uninterrupted memorial flow, even if it is occasionally studded by many

---

32   § 33.8–10.

33   Powell humorously foresaw this. Oblivious of the bombs, during the war Nick reads the books of the *Recherche*, and various extracts are transcribed in translation.

Proustian 'madeleines'; and Nick Jenkins is an *alter ego* who falls in love with various women at the same time, suffers failures, searing disappointments and brutal cold showers.[34] Powell's aesthetic is dissimilar to Proust's because from a continuum of five decades certain moments are chosen and not others, and at times these are not moments of glory but a chain of epiphanies that are also anti-epiphanic. There is no real lyrical rapture in Powell's remembering, nor can there be; rather, an intellectualizing, rational reordering and an objectifying representation. The narrator effaces, rather than aggrandizing, himself; he leaves the melee and turns colourless, without centralist longings; he also has the stance and stuff of an editor, almost of a literary critic who warns of the decisions he will take on the page, and reveals his procedures. This also explains why Powell, weak on the plane of speculation, philosophizing, reflecting, the *esprit de finesse*, manages brilliantly sketches, jokes, tricks, flashes of humour, and especially the short dialogic scenes.

§ 60. *Powell III: 'A Dance to the Music of Time' II. Splendours and miseries of the bourgeoisie*

The module of *A Question of Upbringing* (1951) verges on *déjà vu*. It is the time-worn, rehashed novel about boarding-school and university life, Eton and Oxford, a glorious epic tradition which dated back to the Dickens of *David Copperfield*, Thackeray, and more recently Wells and Kipling, with the taunting, the camaraderie tricks and stunts of the boarders, and the caricatures of the heads and masters. The main thread of the entire group of novels can be identified as generated in the friendships, professional destinies and emotional vicissitudes of a quartet of upper middle-class students from 1921 on. They will remain fixed characters throughout. Stringham is brilliant and self-confident, but secretly undermined by weakness of will:

---

34   In *At Lady Molly's*, a title in which no one has failed to notice a possible, witty transliteration of *Du côté de chez Madame Molly*, the visit to a general's house in wartime (First World War) creates 'a vivid impression' in the mind, while the facts are 'stored away, apparently forgotten, in the distant background of memory. Only subsequent events revived them in strong colours'. This page and the following one review and paraphrase Proust's grammar of memory.

he will become an alcoholic. Equally doomed to a tragic end is Templer, an exhibitionist and womanizer; clumsy, ungainly Widmerpool is the target of the tricks, but also has a passion for sports, athletics in particular, and relentlessly trains to compete in races. This an eccentric, casual fact, but one to be carefully borne in mind, in view of a retaliation that will fully come to light, and will be astutely brought to a close, on the last page of the last trilogy. The fourth character is the narrator Nick Jenkins, the double of Powell himself. The backbone is the slow but untimely dispersion of the four members of the quartet, replaced by the entry of other secondary characters who thereby create a closed network of interpersonal relations. At the end of *A Question of Upbringing*, Templer temporarily leaves the spotlight working in the City, and Stringham becomes secretary to an influential politician; the roads diverge and the student epic is over. In the public and historical background, the German reparations, suspected pro-German sympathies, the fall of the Deutschmark, and in particular the 1926 General Strike, dominate the discussions. The string of events has its own independent worth, since it consists of humorous and signally comical skits of the school repertoire, and is therefore notable purely from the point of view of a successful representation.[35] In reality, some antagonistic dualisms are immediately established, with the aim of the conquest of influence and power at both personal and public levels, and therefore originate both in a narcissistic thirst and in an aspiration to bend the national pathways to a certain outcome or design. The entire series of Powell's *Dance* novels may be taken as representing the 'career' of the social climber in a precisely eighteenth-century and above all Hogarthian sense,[36] or as a neo-picaresque twentieth-century tale of adventures and vicissitudes that range from the realistic to the quixotic. Widmerpool's entrances are at least in

35 After the tricks of the boarders, in the chapter on the French *pensionnat* (where Nick perfects his language, and is initiated into his first calf love, which is not without its amusing disappointments), a myriad of strange eccentric caricatures are presented, well delineated in the most essential manner of Thackeray, polished and never over the top, and with additional echoes from Meredith.

36 On Powell's admiration of this painter, cf. Spurling's observations in her article 'Painting Time', *TLS*, 28 October 2005, 12.

this case truly epiphanic, and they coincide with real tableaux of striking evidence, emblematic of the progress of his career. He is the laughingstock of the students, and remains by definition the man of the banana smashed in his face, of the ill-fitting overcoat, above all of the sugar bowl thrown at his head at a dance by a girl he wooed too insistently. This character, the most cyclical of the entire lot, has been added, not without reason, to the Olympus of immortal monuments to stupidity in the British comical and satirical tradition. But his is a two-pronged stupidity, with subtle resources which no one suspects: he studies to dominate, yet with the appearance of being submissive.[37] He exercises power by creeping, and so, continuing the parallel with Dickens, he may be seen as a Uriah Heep, recalling like him a slippery fish. Striving to climb up the command posts, Widmerpool also has an affective and carnal career that is a collection of affronts and failures. *A Buyer's Market* (1952) launches the four friends, discharged from university, into the public life of London and the entourage of the well-heeled party-going middle class. This is the first novel almost wholly consisting of parties, in order to contrast Nick, Powell's *ingénu* who would timidly adhere to genuine values, with the practices of cynical social climbing and moral wretchedness wrapped in noble words. On reappearing, Widmerpool turns out to have left a radical pacifist activist pregnant, and to have then paid for the abortion. Many odd marriages are dictated by rules that are not love, and are due only to caprice or vested interest. *The Acceptance World*[38] (1955) serenely observes the sentimental whims and therefore the wheel of

37 The leitmotiv of the submission, more precisely of psychic plagiarism, reverberates throughout the cycle in the sporadic subplot – one of the many threads never tied up – of the holy man, Trelawny, who had intrigued Nick Jenkins since he was young; or in that of the palm reader and clairvoyant Mrs Erdleigh, who at a certain moment seems to be on the point of marrying Giles, the equally meteoric uncle of the main character Nick. One of the four chapters takes place in the university chambers of Sillery, the don, whose oily, Baroque ramblings exemplify another case of ideological, veiledly homosexual plagiarism. This party, like so many others later on, has the fictional function of aggregating other characters to the basic quartet, expanding the confines of the interpersonal network.

38 The title alludes to speculating on favourable exchange rates. The meaning of the term 'acceptance', strictly economic, is not at all clear to Nick Jenkins, who receives

marriages spinning crazily as in roulette. With a maelstrom of wives leaving their husbands and husbands leaving their wives, it brings to life, as in a *coup des dés*, a series of comical rematches, while also providing Powell's version – perplexed, if not negative – of the committed, politicized British literature of the 1930s, when the writers shifted *en masse* to the Left. Here, former conservatives or anti-revolutionaries take part in a protest march on the streets of London. It is somewhat ironical that the famous writer of the moment, in reality populist and trashy, has just converted to Trotskyism. In politics, too, everything was in a fluid state, in a climate of perpetual opportunistic or capricious instability.

2. In *At Lady Molly's* (1957), the first book of the second trilogy, the upper middle classes live the high life in drawing rooms, genuinely gilded and sheltered, although this masks an empty purse after the Depression; while the young intelligentsia are even more down and devise the most varied temporary trades for themselves, for example as editors and screen-writers.[39] Networks are forged everywhere simply for flirting and courting, for seducing, therefore; and even for marrying, but for opportunistic ends. Powell writes in complete agreement with Huxley's novels from the 1930s. The counterpoint is Widmerpool's many erotic adventures, which form a jarring note since his affective aims are always strictly connected to his social climbing. However, none of his matrimonial arrangements will ever end well; indeed, all will end in monumental wreckage. The widespread cultural and political temptations of the aristocracy are now to be a communist in kid gloves. One pitiful utopian figure is that of Erridge, namely, the Earl of Warminster, the courageous aristocratic tramp who one day

---

and records this answer from Widmerpool, who has left politics for finance, just after the beginning of the second chapter.

39   Almost imperceptible, and blurred incidental allusions indicate the internal chronology: the talk, on the international chequerboard, is of the imminent *Anschluss*; one discussion introduces the topic of Virginia Woolf's *Orlando*, on which the narrator Nick, and Powell behind him, pronounce perplexed judgements, without contradicting them.

decides to visit China.[40] *Casanova's Chinese Restaurant*[41] (1960) shifts the period forward to the mid-1930s, because Erridge is thinking of leaving for Spain with the anti-Franco brigade, while various forms of fascism are looming in Europe. The bohemian musicians with their conjugal vicissitudes, in dinners and soirées filled with *badinage*, come into the limelight. The main narrative event is still the party, where everyone meets everyone else only to discover buried and secret skeletons in the closet and previous stories. In this way a twisted network is established from which no one is really excluded. Those who are married come from previous marriages and other passions, or cultivate open flirting. The whole group of artists live in a precarious affective situation that can and does change from one moment to the next, but in an absolutely temporary way. During one of the musicians' parties, Stringham suffers a psychophysical breakdown masked by a flow of verbal delirium. He has become the poor lapdog of the governess who has looked after him since he was a child. Few die, many end up footloose; however, the novel closes on two deaths, that of the second-rate left-wing writer who aspires to a Nobel Prize but is floundering, and the suicide of an upright Scottish musician because his wife has left him. In *The Kindly Ones*[42] (1962) the war years arrive, but from the start under a form of associative parallelism between the harbingers of the First World War as experienced by the boy narrator, and those of the Second World War; the two events placed in parallel are the Sarajevo assassination and the German-Soviet Pact of 1939. The whole first chapter, with its agreeable old Victorian atmosphere, records the arrival of clouds over the peaceful country location where the last Victorian and Edwardian pompous rituals are being enacted before the announcement of the assassination. This pre-war

40   This is what Auden did with Isherwood, without either of them being a lord. On the likely, veiled dig at Orwell, and Powell's respectful relationship with him, cf. McEwan 1991, 7–8.

41   Previously belonging to an Italian, it now serves Chinese food. In the first chapter, and occasionally in the ensuing ones (hence the title), the *bohème* of artists discusses the psychology of Casanova compared to that of Don Giovanni, and illustrates the art of seduction in practice.

42   I.e. the Eumenides, as becomes immediately clear at the beginning of the novel.

chapter, which is therefore a leap backwards in memory, ultimately lingers lovingly over a varied community of household servants in the country residence of the by-now captain Nick Jenkins. Dickensian neuroses emerge as tics and surprise acts in sketches of cunning and petty and grim hypocrisies. The memory closed, in a 'Wagnerian' castle and in the fury of the threats of war, seven of the main characters act out a tableau of the seven deadly sins, a spectacle interrupted by the sinister appearance of Widmerpool in his military uniform. The counterpoint of the winds of war is the death of Nick's uncle in a seaside hotel. Nick has to take care of the deceased's personal effects and comes across a distant friend, discovering that he has been the lover of his ex-wife. Anecdotes of this kind are the daily bread of Powell's saga, where scurvy and unexpected tricks of destiny are catalogued with sinister enjoyment. The war immediately begins to decimate the units of the cast. Some dear friends and acquaintances die in the Blitz. Stringham dies as a prisoner of the Japanese, sent on a mission by his commanding officer, Widmerpool, and therefore as a result of a kind of retaliation for the tricks played on Widmerpool at boarding-school. Templer, too, disappears in mysterious circumstances during a secret mission in Europe. Nick rises through the military ranks and becomes a father, and the curtain falls on a thanksgiving in St Paul's Cathedral in 1945, at the cessation of hostilities.

3. *The Valley of Bones* (1964), a title taken from Ezekiel, consists entirely of chapters about barrack life, and follows the training of the hero narrator stationed in various locations, where he meets comrades-in-arms who are almost all, he discovers, linked to old acquaintances, with the result that no one is really a stranger to him. These are enjoyable anecdotal and dialogic chapters, aimed at and avidly expected by the reading public of the time, but by now slightly long-winded. In succession, they remove the protective veil from the petty miseries, the acts of cowardice and ignobility, the misunderstandings and envies of the military life and caste. This account is interwoven with affairs of the heart. As often occurs in contemporary war novels, with some exceptions, the narrative focus is not on the war action itself, but on its preparation or recollection. Not even in these three novels about war is Powell willing or able to talk about action. Nick is the prototype of the British university graduate, a descendant of the educated middle class and the intelligentsia, both extraneous to the

melee, and he democratically becomes familiar with other soldiers of other ranks, mainly professionals. Dialogues promptly end up touching literary topics and authors that Nick knows so well, and that the comrades-in-arms instead only remember vaguely, such as Kipling, Vigny, or Stendhal (Vigny had said that military life is tedious, rather than glamorous). A company captain is removed from office, and has the additional disappointment of surprising a female bartender, with whom he conceived a romantic infatuation, in the arms of another. The last throw of the dice is that the no longer young Nick is assigned to the Secret Service, and finds himself assisting Widmerpool, who has climbed the career ladder, and is now division head: Nick is, in short, in his power. It has often been observed that *The Soldier's Art*[43] (1966) is a self-standing novel and a small independent masterpiece for its realism and, at long last, the felt, or remembered emotion, in the face of the slaughter and pointlessness of war. For a start, there is an explicit, important internal link to the poet Sidney, since the British army was largely formed by humanist soldiers and educated 'courtiers' lent to the defence of the homeland.[44] It is equally true that the war was unjustly rewarding social climbers to the detriment of the honest. Stringham reappears, reduced to being a waiter at the officers' mess; Nick suffers humiliation when he is taken into consideration as a possible liaison officer, and his French translation of an absurd manual is deemed a mediocre fake. On leave in London, he takes part in one of those out-of-sync episodes verging on the surreal to be found frequently in Powell: in the midst of chatter, memories, hamming and courting, a bomb in a nearby café wipes out the lives of other acquaintances. Back from his leave, Nick witnesses a new trial of strength of Widmerpool, who punishes a drunken officer because he discovers that Stringham was helping him, among other reasons. Nick, too, is without prospects, while Widmerpool, promoted to higher ranks, exhibits complete absence of human sympathy, and only cynical and brutal selfishness. *The Military Philosophers* (1968) makes a virtue of

---

43   This title is one again a quotation, from Browning's 'Childe Roland to the Dark Tower Came', which is Stringham's favourite poem, and is read to Nick just before the fatal departure of the army's 'mobile laundry' for the Far East.

44   Sidney is evoked close to the theatre war of Zutphen in *The Military Philosophers*, as the humanist soldier who is also the model of Vigny's unswerving monk.

necessity and simply reorganizes the pawns on the board after they have been knocked down. The background is now the victorious Normandy landings, the launching of the German V1 and V2, up to the first atom bomb. Widmerpool is a big fish in the army, entrusted with vital government consultancy duties.

§ 61. *Powell IV: 'A Dance to the Music of Time' III. Rise and fall of the arriviste*

Powell's last trilogy maintains the immutable, constant, unvaried tone of voice, the stylistic approach and narrative pace of the others, and is therefore without evolutions and involutions; this is even more miraculous twenty years after the birth of the saga. It also reveals a clumsy attempt to correlate the central nucleus of characters with a cultural climate that no longer has the same hierarchies of values and interests, the same mores and the same public values as before the war. Roles previously unknown had also entered social life.[45] By 1970, Powell was a has-been with no wish to pretend to deny that the world had radically changed after the 1945 watershed. The repertory of characters, after many defections, had to be refreshed with others who were equally representatives of the times, but Powell errs now exceptionally on the side of excess, with new over-the-top creations.[46] In that closed world of a promiscuous intelligentsia Powell finds it always easy to evoke a character who lives for a few pages, or to bring back another minor one, with an ever stylish update. *Books Do Furnish a Room*[47] (1971), a novel that is more like an essay, its events often ironically commented on in the key of Burton's psycho-mythology, begins with Nick's return to university, *his* university, on a study visit to draft a book on the seventeenth-century philosopher and theoretician of melancholy.

45   This decline, together with a more obvious search for consensus, was noticed by John Bayley in a review cited by Tucker 1976, 183–4. Waugh found evident signs of 'stagnation' as far back as the fifth novel (McEwan 1991, 53).
46   I am referring above all to the character of Pamela Flitton, disagreeing with Tucker 1976, 122, who deems her 'the most ambitious example of female characterization', and who nonetheless alters his judgement just a few pages later (124).
47   This title is a stock phrase used to designate one of the founders of the *Fission* magazine.

Meanwhile, Widmerpool is an influential left-wing politician on the up who has stumbled upon yet another bad relationship, coupling himself to the neurotic and kooky Pamela Flitton, a patent case of Burton's love melancholy. He is also the promoter of an avant-garde magazine, *Fission*, where many of the intellectuals who are still alive and active work. Pages that are by this time long-winded thicken around the figure of Trapnel, the most promising post-war writer. And yet Trapnel plays one of many pranks on Widmerpool, when he steals his wife Pamela and runs away with her. Widmerpool never becomes resigned to this, and the marriage is precariously mended. *Temporary Kings* (1973) is also a case study on contemporary literature, three-quarters of it set in Venice at an imaginary writers' convention. Powell imitates Henry James by gathering a circle of writers, publishing agents and intellectuals in a patrician Venetian house, whose ceiling features a magnificent Tiepolo fresco – imaginary, naturally – depicting the story of Candaules and Gyges. Widmerpool is still tenaciously exercising his power, but Pamela, who is desired by an American cinema producer, resists him.[48] Symptomatic of the times, Pamela dies of an overdose, putting an end to a burnt-out existence. *Hearing Secret Harmonies* (1975), exceptionally in seven chapters, suffers even more from the need for an update. We are invited to perceive the passing of time, and the background of the evolution of customs, with some hippies encamped in the garden of Nick's residence. A further signal is that mediocre writers should write novels that are pillaged to become cinema scripts. Widmerpool, accused of spying for an eastern bloc country, feels the blow of his wife's death; but shrewd as he always is, he is now chancellor of a new 'red-brick' university. So what is indirectly and humorously reflected in this final novel is the age of protest, or also, as is expressly defined in a cliché that was then fashionable, of permissiveness. The stink bomb that two students throw at him during a speech is the last of the by-now legendary affronts; but Widmerpool misreads it as a form of approval for his passionate wish for a cultural regeneration. Powell attempts, re-exhumes in reality from his early novels, the card of the fantastic with a *noir* vein, and here he loses out in any possible parallel with Proust. To the question concerning the structural necessity and the

48   Who has 'something of the old American, Jamesian stamp'.

appropriateness of introducing a hippie who traffics in magical arts, the answer is that this necromancer is the reincarnation of a previous 'magician' who made meteoric appearances in the first novels of *A Dance*. He is also the leader of a protest group who, with vaguely Lawrencian aspirations, hail a total revolution of customs and the shedding of inhibitions of the body and mind. With him Widmerpool has discovered the 'ritual side of sex', that people must develop both their male and female sides, and that, à la Carlyle, 'nakedness removes impediments of all sorts'. Between the hippie and Widmerpool a 'duel of wills' develops, and the law of retaliation requires that the greatest supporter of the desire for power shall be subjugated by someone who is more powerful. In itself, this episode is not wholly successful, and is indeed somewhat strident; however, Powell does not forget to round off *A Dance*, since Widmerpool dies in circumstances that are an almost unrecognizable variation of Poussin's painting, whose elements are 'suggested in a perverted form'. Widmerpool's death occurs in fact during a frantic community run, with naked bodies crossing the fields, in homage to an occult ritual. This is a parody of the race of life, the competition of life; and we are reminded that Widmerpool had been an athlete and a long-distance runner at school; hence the retaliation. This is also a group vendetta, because Widmerpool, who sent so many to their deaths, is now made to die. The last page is imprinted with the circular stamp to be expected from such an architectural writer as Powell. The acrid odour of wood burning in the fireplace evokes the brazier of the men at work with whom the cycle opened; and the allusive density receives its apotheosis when, with the image of Poussin's seasons dancing to the sound of the lyre of Time, a passage from Burton follows, lamenting the chaotic alternation of things – 'a vast confusion' – in human time.

2. On concluding *A Dance*, Powell could appear to be, above all to himself, a writer who had by now given what he had to give, and the next twenty-five years until his death were practically empty. However, he did publish another two novels that were related to one another, in fact both centring on the 'funny mystery' of the writer.[49] *O, How the Wheel*

---

49   Together with two plays, not so distant in their theme, *The Garden God*, and *The Rest I'll Whistle* (1971), a title taken from a speech by Kent in *King Lear* (II.2.152).

Becomes It![50] (1983), a satire on the publishing world, portrays a writer with affective situations that are once again devastated and precarious, and who may therefore seem like a role that had been rejected or left unused in the final novels of *A Dance*. The writer has to edit the diary of a financial agent he has known since school, and in doing so he discovers various skeletons in the closet of his private life, and also, to his surprise, his own involvement. He is thus forced to change his opinion regarding both the writer's stature and his ambiguous sexuality (he had known him as a homosexual, then as a philanderer). This short novel abounds in comical vicissitudes, dramatic turns of events and embarrassing situations recounted with economy of means and singular effectiveness. In one episode, in which the main character receives a visit from a former lover, who has come to ask him to introduce her memoirs, Powell takes a shot at the modern mania of writers of delivering up their diaries to the public (Powell would go on to have four autobiographical volumes published). Powell's imperturbable honesty also lies in parodying himself. However, there are also distant or perhaps tangible analogies with Waugh's *Pinfold*.[51] The shoddier *The Fisher King* (1986), which, like *Pinfold*, takes place almost wholly on a ship cruising around the British Isles, is the work of a writer whose head is crammed with literary memories and overlaps these with reality, telling his story in the manner of a free and amusing game. The slow plot revolves around this author of detective stories who tells the other passengers about the past of a strange couple among the passengers, consisting of an attractive ballerina and an old photographer with a limp. This is in itself a version of the fascination for the horrid or the revisitation of the theme of Beauty and the Beast. The writer thinks of the old man as a reincarnation of the Fisher King, harking back to Eliot and taken from medieval myths and the Arthurian sagas, whom Parsifal cannot heal because he is unable to ask him the right question, which could restore his virility. But the quantity of humorous and literary allusions, exploiting the similarities between the names (Saul, Barberina

---

50   Another Shakespearean quotation, a line spoken Ophelia in *Hamlet* (IV.5.171).
51   The scene of the TV troupe who turn up at Shadbold, where he is visited by an old flame, and which he believes to be a concerted interview, is particularly reminiscent of that novel.

and others), is excessive. This minor literary pastiche is only intermittently successful, with increasingly free and specious digressions favoured by the claustrophobic setting of the cruise ship. The effect is that of a Peacock-style conversation piece in naval surroundings. Powell's fixation is now gender, and that of avidly bringing to the surface sexual ambiguity and stories of seduction, and gossip on who was whose lover (and indeed, whereas before the war people spoke of love, now they speak of sex).

§ 62. *Cary* *

Lively, exciting, ultimately always tragicomic is the fictional art of Joyce Cary (1888–1957), whose self-declared poetics is that of a skewer of adventures that initially seem to jumble his novel writing with second-rate sensationalist fiction, resolved in a frenetic chain of exploits. This accelerated pace, when not downright frantic, drew its lifeblood and nourishment from Cary's own life, but according to an objectifying transfer and an ironic and humorous distillation that apparently leaves not even a hint of a slavishly followed autobiographical basis. *The Horse's Mouth* is his masterpiece by almost unanimous consent;[1] and, a masterpiece, albeit minor, it surely is also in absolute terms. In fact, it is a misunderstood novel that merits

---

*   Novels republished in the Carfax Edition in 17 vols, London from 1951. W. Allen, *Joyce Cary*, London 1953; A. Wright, *Joyce Cary: A Preface to His Novels*, London 1958; R. Bloom, *The Indeterminate World: a Study of the Novels of Joyce Cary*, Philadelphia, PA 1962; C. G. Hoffmann, *Joyce Cary: The Comedy of Freedom*, Pittsburgh, PA 1964; W. V. O'Connor, *Joyce Cary*, New York and London 1966; M. Foster, *Joyce Cary: A Biography*, Boston, MA 1968; J. Wolkenfeld, *Joyce Cary: The Developing Style*, New York 1968; M. Echeruo, *Cary and the Novel of Africa*, London 1973, and *Joyce Cary and the Dimensions of Order*, London 1979; C. Cook, *Joyce Cary: Liberal Principles*, London 1981; A. Cozza, 'Joyce Cary', in CAB, vol. I, 531–46 (a brilliant, painstaking overview); H. Adams, *Joyce Cary's Trilogies: Pursuit of the Particular Ideal*, London 1983; D. Hall, *Joyce Cary: A Reappraisal*, London 1983; E. Christian, *Joyce Cary's Creative Imagination*, New York 1988; A. Nirmala, *Joyce Cary: A Critical Study*, New Delhi 2001.

1   Naturally, the British admirers of this writer, such as Allen 1953, sometimes draw up different hierarchies, and place other novels of his alongside it, in some cases deeming them superior, and making them the fulcrum of their discussion.

being reassessed, re-evaluated and repositioned close to the heart of the twentieth-century 'great tradition'. Cary is a kind of literary Bizet, who left us a masterpiece that was clearly conceived in an exceptional, never-to-be-repeated compositional fit in the midst of many or various chunks of dross, or at least other works of a vastly inferior weight.[2] Hugely entertaining, ebullient, ever varied and unpredictable, *The Horse's Mouth* is a sequence of interior and also public monologues derived from or inspired by Browning and Joyce, and therefore a ventriloquist feat. In fact, it presents the odyssey of an artist who is not integrated and cannot by definition be integrated, a kind of upbeat tramp in the moral wretchedness and restricted horizons of British society *entre les deux guerres*. In particular, its fantastic and creative battle against low philistine run-of-the-mill literature translates into streams of surreal flashes that posit it as the intermediate link – with even a smidgeon of camp – between Firbank and Angela Carter. He deserves such recognition for the non-stop pyrotechnics of scenic invention and evocative episodes that recall, in particular, the final two novels of the younger writer. But we can even perceive echoes of the absurd sketches and nonsense dialogue that are the trademark of another Irishman, Beckett, from whom Cary is not so distant in terms of ribald, scathing, irreverent humour. Hence, Cary's novel form is polymorphous and metamorphic. If he needs then to be reread and reappraised it is not (only) as a novelist of contents and of social realism, but, and above all, as a novelist of style and of voice. Each novel by this chameleon has a different, indeed profoundly different voice, and the range of these voices stretches from the most impalpable lyricism to its resounding mockery. There is a further affinity with Browning because Cary can impersonate and slip into different identities, and consequently often writes in the first person. It is no coincidence that Browning fore-shadowed the modernists, Joyce and Eliot, who were almost the same age as Cary, even though Cary entered the fray a good two decades later than their first modernist masterpieces – as an ironic, sardonic postmodernist, we might hazard, who appeared to denigrate Modernism itself. It is then true that his polystylism supports an anarchic and incendiary vision of the world; however, this is an approximate, visceral, and ideologically baseless and jejune attack. If there is an aspect of Modernism that Cary targets, it is

2   KRG, 146–7, instead compares him to Rachmaninoff, a failed composer.

negative existentialism.[3] His untamed and untameable vitalists are not the hypostases of those who have no wish to live. Browning comes back into play for the exuberance of some of his charlatans often also emptily and unjustifiably optimistic, more precisely with seven lives, and for the irenic and profoundly positive philosophy, echoing Pippa's execrated, heavily criticized aphorism, 'God's in his Heaven / All's right with the world!', which is a variant of a saying by Blake, a poet who was also dear to Cary, to the effect that 'everything that lives is holy'. What does remain true is that after so many hesitant thinking heroes, Cary revolutionized the current repertoire of characters and situations, inventing and launching characters who were combative, energetic, and ready to throw themselves into the fray.[4] His literary ancestry is that deep-rooted Anglo-Saxon one of those who 'call a spade a spade', mainly because he represents, more than preaches, the basic and century-long conflict between sincerity, perhaps with some pardonable moral stain, and sanctimonious hypocrisy, the target of all British satirists. He therefore resumes the tenacious, solitary battle of the innocents against the forces and instances of order.[5] Nor should it surprise us that Cary resorted to the old trick of writing in trilogies, tetralogies, pentalogies or novels in series up to the symbolic figure of twelve.[6] In the oblique forms that I have indicated, Cary too felt the urge to summarize and review the complex, chaotic British history of the previous half-century up to the present. His standing as a great minor eccentric can be found fixed and clearly evident in the literary surveys compiled just after the Second World War: he was found to be the only one, or one of the very few, to 'ring true', to have brought a whiff of freshness to the British novel between the wars, and to have silenced self-complacency. And even if he remained a controversial author, often criticized for being ideologically weak, the very fact that he was discussed

3   Cf. the very succinct but searching paragraph by Praz in PSL, 717.

4   Contemporary Marxist criticism dedicated unusual space and consideration to him, such as KET, 159–65, pointing to him as an antidote to middle-class 'sensitivity' (of Woolf, even if not said so explicitly). This was for Kettle a sensitivity that by being too sensitive becomes insensitive, and ends in a 'bog of *false* sensitivity'.

5   The English saying that can be applied to many of his main characters is 'more sinned against than sinning'.

6   A third trilogy never reached beyond the planning stage, with the novel *The Captive and the Free*, which came out posthumously in 1959.

was a sign of lasting and intact vitality. Slippage and finally total ejection arrived inexorably; and today Cary shines above all for his absence from critical surveys of twentieth-century English literature.

2. The son of Irish landowners in County Donegal, his family lost their property after the 1882 Land Act, and his parents emigrated to England when Cary was twelve years old. He was to recall his Irish childhood in some autobiographical novels.[7] Having transplanted himself to England, he was one of the Irish in exile, albeit without cultivating a mawkish and manneristic nostalgia. His childhood was poor; he suffered from asthma, lost his mother early, and only a small inheritance allowed him to live until his forties. Cary's first artistic vocation was painting, and to cultivate it he moved to Paris when he was eighteen. On his return he studied art in Edinburgh, and privately published a short book of poetry. His university education at Oxford was completed in two stages, because after two years of study he left for the war in the Balkans to support the Montenegrin population against the Turks, not as a combatant, however, but as an observer (finding material for a book of vivid memories) and a cook. In 1913, he won a competition to become a magistrate in Nigeria. Excluding periods of leave, he was to remain in Nigeria uninterruptedly for seven years. During one of these periods of leave he took a degree with mediocre marks, became engaged, and later married. With a wife and offspring under his wing, and resident in Oxford, after 1920 Cary was forced to embrace the life of a writer to maintain himself and his family. His debut with *Aissa Saved*[8] (1932) came, however, at the far from young age of forty-four; his oeuvre would grow to a total of seventeen fictional units in twenty-five years. The autobiographical material is spread in Cary over four subgroups arranged in chronological order: one African, one on childhood, one on adulthood, and one about contemporary British political life. His debut novel was followed by another two with an African setting; they were coldly received albeit they do not

7   Including *A House of Children* (1941), which some have found resembling Joyce's *Portrait*. A collection of scenes and dreamy memories without a plot, this is also Cary's novel that most closely approaches the atmospheres of Elizabeth Bowen.

8   An African woman is persuaded to sacrifice herself and her child to put an end to the scourge of a drought; hence the first study of colonial contradictions. The title may therefore be ironic or perhaps sarcastic (O'Connor 1966, 17–18).

lack some interest.[9] Some critics even prefer *Mister Johnson* (1939), which was reviewed favourably by Orwell, to *The Horse's Mouth*, recklessly making it Cary's top novel. Like Kipling, Orwell, and Waugh,[10] and later Greene in Scobie of *The Heart of the Matter*, Cary describes in *Mister Johnson* a conflict of cultures. The natives wish to civilize themselves by adopting, when not mimicking, the mindsets of white civilization, but with tragicomic results. Two characters are focused on in particular, the road-builder Rudbeck, a pompous white Englishman, and the plagiarized black employee Johnson, who has an equal number of dreams of glory and self-celebration, and thus is the forerunner of Cary's loquacious vitalists, full of initiatives that often go unrealized because they are so puerilely and fanatically utopian. *Mister Johnson* belongs to the colonial canon and in it we can recognize the updated atmosphere of that 'outpost of the Empire' of Conradian and even Orwellian memory, though Johnson is not the Conradian 'outcast of the islands',[11] and the analysis of African colonialism remains summary and picturesque, without plumbing any 'heart of darkness'.[12] The novel lacks Cary's sparkle and effervescence, although it is already the timid example of a 'vocal' novel. It is not written in the first person but employs the idiosyncrasy of a grammatical tense that is always in the present;[13] less successful is the attempt to standardize the various ways of speaking and dialects of the African Fada ethnic groups into a black English that smacks too much of *Uncle Tom's Cabin*. With the first novel of the first trilogy, *Herself Surprised* (1941), Cary

9 Both *An American Visitor* (1933) and *The African Witch* (1936) carry on the investigation into the real benefits of colonization and the clashes between the two cultures.

10 § 46.4 n. 38.

11 One reappearance is the bazaar manager, Gollop, a violent, persistently drunk Englishman, of whose accidental death Johnson is accused, being then condemned to death. Because of this incident, the novel, in some ways, sparks the event around which another debut novel dealing with Africa revolves, Doris Lessing's *The Grass is Singing*.

12 In fact, for KET, 165, and many other scholars of colonial literature in British novels, Cary ends up being an accomplice of Rudbeck's imperialistic paternalism, thereby revealing an overly broad liberalism. The Nigerian writer Chinua Achebe also wrote against Cary and this novel. Cary's political writings are nonetheless clearly on the side of self-determination for colonized populations (cf. O'Connor 1966, 15).

13 A device that O'Connor 1966, 6, believes to be inspired by Faulkner. Also written in the present is *Charley is My Darling* (1940), a colourful study of delinquency and juvenile psychology.

slipped into the right gear – or, as already said, his most felicitous formula – dedicating himself to the creation of three verbal scene-stealers of unbridled vitality and inimitable salience. The cook Sara Monday is writing her memoirs from prison after committing a theft, but with the aim of dissuasion à la Moll Flanders; a spontaneous naïve believer, she introduces Cary's theme of creative imagination and also erotic promiscuity as a guarantee and valorization of full-blown humanity. She therefore belongs to the family of maternal and telluric deities like Molly Bloom. *To Be a Pilgrim* (1942) centres around Sara's old husband, Thomas Wilcher, a cold, pernickety, faint-hearted fellow, with his hobby-horses, who is only intent on keeping intact his family legacy following the dictates of Protestant capitalism and Bunyan's dissenting evangelicalism against the background of Britain at the beginning of the century.

  3. One should not ask *The Horse's Mouth*[14] (1944) for what it cannot give, and what Cary had no wish to give. The reader that comes to it unprepared, from reading experiences of other intimist novels, sweetened, desperate, diaphanous, and sexually correct for their time,[15] remains appalled, astonished, but also disappointed by the completely alien aesthetics of the novel. One first unusual fact is the absence of any psychological depth. The initial discomfort, to anyone who is not tuned into the required wavelength, is then caused by a writer who wishes to overdo it, has no clear organizational plan and indulges in excessive oral mimesis. The novel unravels in front of us as a collection of grotesque sketches told off-hand, in the rickety, frank and unpolished way of a self-styled painter who thinks he is a genius, is a megalomaniac and has no idea of how to make ends meet. The unit of measurement is then the verbal exploit, the rodomontade; and the main character is the ancient comedian, charlatan, and chatterbox. Writing, or rather, speaking, *ex post*, his is a disordered flow of recent memories, on the thread of a sensationalistic, intemperate, excessive, even at times surreal and absurd humour, which, conceivably nostalgic as we are for the refined ways of academic writers, may leave us cold and even quickly sickened. The fluctuation of memory in

14 The title derives from the expression 'straight from the horse's mouth', which in the language of horserace betting indicates a sure-fire prediction.

15 In short what KET, 160, called 'the polite tradition'.

the evoking voice may at any moment swing toward episodes of the past
in themselves concluded, and then get back to the point, certainly in a
more regular grammatical form. From Browning, Cary apes the 'asides',
the invectives, the recurrent digressions with a particular focus (such as
those against the government, or the parallel between religion and artistic
reputation in terms of a growing tree), all inflated and repetitive. Cary's
transgression is therefore exercised against the omniscient psychological
novel; none of the onstage characters is well-sculpted, not even the main
one, Gulley Jimson, who speaks of himself and makes a fine candid show
of his inner being for 400 pages. There is deliberately no psychological
study; and the various idiosyncrasies – and all the characters are idiosyncratic – only emerge from dialogue and behavioural skits. The scene
is populated by extras, actors, puppets, more exactly 'humours', all with
something bizarre and abnormal about them. Played out in the slums of
London, among idlers and loafers, and in pubs with women of easy virtue
but a good heart, there is also a cosmos of foolish sentimental events. A
generous bartender is left pregnant by a man who leaves her for 'a blonde';
Sara is a faded, plump model, a namesake of a character in the previous
novel in the trilogy. Gulley Jimson tries to steal an ancient portrait of her
taking a bath, kept at the bottom of a chest of drawers, thinking he can
make some money. Among a handful of Beckett-style oddballs, a cobbler
and fan of Spinoza ends up in a dorm, or public shelter, after infecting
his finger.[16] Despite everything, *The Horse's Mouth* begins to please more
and more, and even become irresistible, when we understand the deal
and accept its formula, which can also be the parody of an ancient one;
especially when we discover that this is a pastiche, and that an ideological objective only emerges within this dispensation.[17] With the Irish we
can never neglect this vocal component. Gulley Jimson – who after all
is a painter, but more than literally a painter in words and in any case in

16   This section of the novel is uncommonly hilarious, and shows unmatched verve
      reminiscent of Dickens and foreshadowing Beckett (there are only three pans for
      fried fish, and the patients fight over them, but there is only one cooker).
17   Precisely what is not understood and accepted by KRG, 131–47, for example, in his
      chilly, harsh, perplexed presentation of the novelist, based on incorrect and precon-
      ceived aesthetics. The critic prefers C. P. Snow to Cary.

prose, and a memorial writer – is a continuous analogical and metaphorical barrage. I defined Bowen as a writer devising subtle, sharp, sophisticated comparisons worthy of the Metaphysical poets, but these are comparisons in the domain of the delicate and the fineness of sensitivity; Cary, through Gulley, pinpoints the shocking image, with scorching, brutal, uncomfortable unpredictability,[18] he too an adept of the association of sensibility. A second linguistic idiosyncrasy is ekphrasis. At the start of each chapter, or almost, Gulley describes the vault of the sky in striking flashes, as if he were a Constable or a Turner whose eyes are veiled or bedazzled by foggy or opalescent colours. But, as a painter, Gulley is a post-Blakean or a reincarnation of this romantic visionary poet and painter. A second habit is to infiltrate into the narrative, by acrobatic associations, extracts from visionary lyrics and other poems, increasingly by Blake, with the friction and contradiction that exists between the sacred and the profane. This staggering, shaky pace, with marked and violent excursions of tone, register and theme, is an incontrovertible foretaste of the postmodern. Gulley is the emblem of Cary's philosophy of life, the artist exiled and marginalized, but far from raving in self-pity; Rabelaisian[19] and quixotic, and hungering for experience with the indomitable ability to never give in and to rise again always.[20] Cary, who had actually tried to be a painter, has only one concept which he reiterates: that the artist is ontologically incompatible with middle-class society, and is therefore condemned to poverty and social exclusion; the alternative is the eternally homeless, the spiritually stateless man. This is an axiom, it should be noted, which is not preached,

18   Of the type: 'Lolie's changed a lot in the year. [...] When I used to know her she looked like a pig, but now she looks like a dog-faced baboon'.

19   Rabelaisian because of the drunken comedy, with its resounding laughter, rather than cold humour.

20   Gulley, who is as 'gullible' as Don Quixote, finds a travelling companion in the young art student Nosy, who acts as an echo to the painter's speeches. But in their wandering across the lush and mysterious landscape of Sussex, hunted by the police, chattering Gulley and his young companion verge on a parody of *King Lear*. The metamorphic iridescence of the narration is exemplified in Cary by this scene, which ends in purest Beckett-style absurd when the two vagabonds buy some postcards of the place and start selling them for inflated prices as pornographic pictures, until a dapper young man arrives who has exclusive rights over that trade!

rather described and represented. Gulley has in fact his own vision of social history and art in the hundred years from 1850 to 1950, but he expounds it rhapsodically, succinctly, imaginatively; he mostly uses full-blown self-irony. For him, British art had been ruined by the Pre-Raphaelites. His father had broken away from them; in the beginning, Gulley had fought against every artistic Modernism; he had accepted Impressionism, adored Cézanne, but also said No to Cubism and the avant-garde. His pictorial ideal remains Blake, the heir of Michelangelo.[21] His art is not a whit Raphaelite and much more Michelangiolesque, but such in that it enlarges the human figure and sometimes even makes it gigantic, and thus pays homage to the human body and the greatness of man created, as did his disciple Blake. His humanity is deformed and as if viewed by a surrealist painter. His caricature would appear Dickensian had it not responded to a sublime idea of humanity. Gulley has no wish to remark on Beckett-style degradation, nor on the Kafkaesque reification and animalization of the human, or not only. He refuses the metamorphosis of beauty into horror, the breakdown of the fibres, the degeneration of swollen or lanky bodies, with faun-like likenesses; what is rather at work in him is a fantasy that sees and transfigures the unity of creation, without dissociating the domains of the beast and of the human.[22] Gulley Jimson weaves, in the first person, a story that is a real, bubbling and disorderly fresco, wherein the sublime spills over into the humble in the blink of an eye. His pictorial themes are in fact a recapitulation of Creation, passing via the Fall but prefiguring the Resurrection through Redemption: essentially the subject of the sizeable canvases and frescoes that he plans and begins painting, without ever concluding them. The artist, the only authentic being, can in all conscience only defraud a society that ignores him, puts him on the sidelines,

21   But Blake was also the idol and mentor of Rossetti. The name of Rossetti does not arise in vain if we consider, in certain episodes of this novel, those farcical, grotesque and hypothetical stories of real and invented painters, narrated in the two prose tales by Dante Gabriel, and especially in Christina's *The Lost Titian* (on which cf. IDM, 83–94).

22   Gulley's mural painting is basically of naïve inspiration, and reminds Italians of Antonio Ligabue. The subject of his fresco at the wealthy Sir William's house is of tigers against very mixed and composite backgrounds – totally heterogeneous.

exploits him and finds no place in its hierarchies, by reason of his creative imagination.[23] In so doing, Cary sketches a criticism of the bourgeoisie and of the world of politics, points the finger at the inauspicious link between the affirmation of the artist's ego and superficial and unwise patrons who also, by means of their wealth, feed art without intimately understanding it, buying it merely as a decorative object or furnishing item. Art is inevitably commodified, translated into hard currency, assessed, when instead it has an incalculable spiritual value.[24] Of course this artist, by virtue of his imagination and his pseudo-divine inspiration, belongs to the forgiven.

4. The second trilogy was written, or more precisely dictated, when Cary, by now widowed, had been diagnosed with an irreversible muscular atrophy.[25] It centres on social and political life in contemporary Britain, and especially on the rise of the Labour Party. The three novels retain the device of a retrospective narrative in the first person while remaining, to a certain extent, novels of voice.[26] At the same time, they are also novels with a thesis, and a thesis that is too abstract, reductive or generic to work properly. It is that of the close and fruitful relations between religious history and the political vocation or profession. Their vein is one that had always been latent in Cary, one that was optimistically based on the rejection of the Calvinist doctrine of justification by faith. *Prisoner of Grace*[27] (1952) is the story of Nina and her passive subjection to her husband, the politician Chester Nimmo, many years older than her, despite loving another man

23   Gulley's moral justification is therefore very similar to that of Browning's Sludge; in fact, he often makes ventriloquist calls in which he pretends to be a variety of imaginary people, in order to obtain payment for paintings auctioned off in his time, given away or stolen from him.

24   See the Dickensian satire of the biography industry in Professor Alabaster, a confused, muddled and completely absent-minded scholar who is planning a biography of Jimson. Still more Dickensian is the episode of the ignorant, vague, slapdash Beeder couple, she an unvoiced artist, he a millionaire who understands not an iota of art; in their home, in their temporary absence, Gulley sketches a risen Lazarus on the immense wall of the living room.

25   Cary's decline was caused by these impairments according to ATD, 247.

26   The last novel, the monologue of a policeman, is written in a telegraphic, detached style that befits a soldier.

27   'Grace' understood in the sense of a famous homiletic work of Bunyan.

and having had a son with him. She recites the apologia of the work of her husband, who has been accused of a financial scandal. *Except the Lord* (1953) performs once again a Browning-style operation, since it is not the sequel of the previous novel, but its restatement from the point of view of the politician Nimmo himself, in a lengthy confession of sin, pain, atonement and reconciliation. Cary emphasizes the derivation of Labour from evangelicalism, as Charles Kingsley had done in *Alton Locke* for nineteenth-century radicalism. In *Not Honour More* (1955) the focus shifts to Nina's lover; in this case, too, a Browning-style, risky apology is carried out, that of the jealous murderer who dictates his version of events to a warder.

§ 63. Lowry*

Under the Volcano[1] (1947) by Malcolm Lowry (1909–1957) is a novel by an excessively, madly ambitious Icarus, and therefore an elective member of a family of writers who, at that date, already seemed extinct. Like Icarus, Lowry ended up burning his wings, because the proclaimed *magnum opus* gradually becomes a failed and foundering masterpiece, wordy and repetitive, and burdensome to read. This of course does not mean that flashes of great inspiration and blinding evocation are lacking; but they are insufficient to overturn, in my opinion, the verdict I have given.[2] In it, Lowry

---

*   *Under the volcano* is available in an edition with a remarkable preface by Stephen Spender, New York 1965. *Collected Letters*, ed. S. E. Grace, 2 vols, London 1995–1997. *Malcolm Lowry: The Man and His Work*, ed. G. Woodcock, Vancouver 1971; D. Day, *Lowry: A Biography*, Oxford 1973; M. C. Bradbury, *Malcolm Lowry: His Art and Early Life*, London 1974; *The Art of Malcolm Lowry*, ed. A. Smith, London 1978; *Malcolm Lowry: The Writer and His Critics*, ed. B. Wood, Ottawa 1980; E. Linguanti, *L'itinerario del senso nella narrativa di Malcolm Lowry*, Bari 1984; *Malcolm Lowry Remembered*, ed. G. Bowker, London 1985, also author of *Pursued by Furies: A Life of Malcolm Lowry*, London 1993; T. Bareham, *Malcolm Lowry*, Basingstoke 1989; J. Gabrial, *Inside the Volcano: My Life with Malcolm Lowry*, New York 2000.

1   With this work in progress the writer is unanimously identified. It had germinated since 1937 in a tale of the same name.

2   In other words, I can recognize myself in the slating, so painful to Lowry, by the American critic Jacques Barzun, summarized by F. Binni, 'Malcolm Lowry', in CAB, vol. II, 323–69 (cf. 337, and the discussion in the pages that follow).

remodelled and objectified his biography of a Cambridge 'defector' and a restless and tormented nomad. He died from alcoholism at just forty-eight years old. *Under the Volcano* is, apart from his youthful novel *Ultramarine* (1933), his only finished product in a disorganized jumble of fragmentary works from which there have resurfaced, edited by the writer's second wife, some reconstructed novels, a few other stories and a handful of poems. Lowry, as the spitting image of a *maudit*, long impressed the collective imagination of the British in the years immediately after this controversial cult work – by some overrated and defined as the supreme English novel of the 1940s – also thanks to the happy cinematic transposition supported by the exceptionally empathetic performance of Albert Finney in the leading role. *Under the Volcano*, in itself and judged strictly, is an attempted epigonic masterpiece, a 'novelists' novel' – to adapt a nineteenth-century tag – which was conceived and grew in the shade of other previous literary works of a more consolidated tradition: a novel of echoes and citations, of unsifted references to myth, stacked up as in a sort of prose *Waste Land*; a *sui generis* modernist work, polluted and multifaceted, into which multiple promptings flow.[3] Looking at the twentieth-century macrotext, *Under the Volcano* at first sight slots into the tradition of the exotic novel and the odyssey of the rootless British traveller, exiled voluntarily or in protest and intolerant of the middle-class society left behind. Spasmodically in search of an identity in far-off lands, his freedom often founders in a drifting, bitter and debauched existence. What is foreign to Lowry is the picturesque, sensationalist variation of the South American template, pleasing in its humorous, sardonic or even fantastic details, which – for example in *The Honorary Consul* – Graham Greene was playing out almost in the same years or a little later. Nor is *Under the Volcano* a colonial novel, because the historical situation of post-revolutionary Mexico in 1938 is not analysed in depth, and serves only as a hazy backcloth.[4] That cultured Brit, homeless,

3   Unlike some critics, I cannot find any echo here of Sterne's novel, the work of anything but a 'hothouse' writer like Lowry.

4   It is true that the day on which the novel takes place is that of All Souls' Day, 1938, but the allegory of the 'time of humanity's universal drunkenness' on the eve of the outbreak of the Second World War remains only a declaration of intent by the

at loggerheads with the motherland, and deep down a spiritual exile, is therefore a recurring character in the fiction of the beginning of the last century and beyond. It is impossible not to mention that two decades earlier D. H. Lawrence had written, with rather different and highly inspired results, *The Plumed Serpent*,[5] and that exactly one decade later Durrell would work on a reversal of the compass needle, exiling his *alter ego* in another exotic bewitchment, Alexandria and the Mediterranean. But let it be clear that the first of the influences in order of importance is Conrad. *Under the Volcano* is a pastiche of Conrad, even if it does not resolve itself entirely into one, and its ingredients are *Lord Jim*, *Heart of Darkness*, *Nostromo* with other novels by Conrad, definable as being of the type of the 'outcast of the islands' fleeing from an identity imposed on him by societal models and incapable of finding an *ubi consistam*. A disillusioned idealist, Lowry's Geoffrey Firmin, like Lord Jim,[6] stages the descent with no return into the maelstrom of his ego and therefore into his own 'heart of darkness'. But the novel imitates even more *Nostromo*, because despite being centred on the 'consul' Firmin, it also follows other drifters and hollow characters in succession.

2. Lowry's constant theme is the existential crisis, cowardice, the escape from private and public responsibilities; a crisis experienced as a nightmare that grips without respite. The three main characters are fugitives: Firmin's stepbrother, Hugh, fled from political responsibility and cannot forgive himself for not rushing to Spain to fight for the republicans; and inhabiting a world of eccentric dreams, dressing as a cowboy, formerly a guitarist, a ship's cabin boy and a journalist, he too has splashed down into this *finisterre*. Firmin's wife, Yvonne, flees but is a returnee, and dissuades herself from divorce and with noble altruism runs to help her husband, she too

---

    author. Lowry's letters abound in similar *ex post* authorial interpretations, which do not always coincide with the evidence of the text, though several critics follow them indiscriminately.

5   The 'bullthrowing', the special Mexican bullfight, occurs almost at the end, and cites the opening episode of *The Plumed Serpent*.

6   The comparison with a 'pseudo Lord Jim more tearful, living in self-imposed exile' is made by the narrator himself.

in a crisis of will.[7] The narrative procedure is borrowed from *Nostromo*,[8] but the question that arises is whether it is worthwhile to imitate Conrad's model of a story that proceeds like a piston, a little forward and a little backward, and which deliberately deranges a linear presentation of the facts and prior events by opting for inductive, incidental, fragmentary information, instead of neatly expounding it once and for all. This was a method that in Conrad had a function, but is merely artificial in Lowry, and confuses the reader with dialogues that hint at facts and events that will be known only gradually, or even remain only suggested. Glimpses of the Mexican landscape aim to be radiant and pictorial sketches in words, are striking for their purple charm, for a magniloquent and bombastic use of adjectives, and hence a rhetoric that is an end in itself, and purely atmospheric, Conrad's own bad habit.[9] The plot is a pretext for setting up a dramatic stage from where dialogues evolve that do not follow a logical thread but only an associative one; they lack a real communicative purpose, and are more often tormented psychic struggles, surveys of the ego, confused memorial outcrops, pure broodings without head nor tail.[10] Soon the novel becomes a frenzied spiritual battle. With its stream of consciousness, Lowry tries to emulate *Ulysses*, especially in the nocturnal parts; his own 'odyssey' is significantly written in the number of chapters of the short classic epics, and its development takes place within twelve hours. Its allegorical

7   Firmin and Hugh are doubles of the same biographical person, having among their attributes experiences that were Lowry's (such as that of musician, ukulele player and jazz buff: cf. Binni, essay quoted in n. 2, 326). After graduating, Lowry frequented the environs of the *maudits* in London (and Dylan Thomas, inevitably), and left the country for France where he contracted a stormy marriage. On arriving in America in 1936, he tried unsuccessfully to work as a scriptwriter, a facet attributed in the novel to the character of the film director, Laruelle.

8   As though from Conrad's imaginary Costaguana to Quauhnahuac, which conceals Cuernavaca.

9   See for instance this example: 'The shadow of an immense weariness stole over him'.

10   The concluded and linear anecdotes are very few; among them, and far from outstanding in itself, one concerns the affairs of Firmin's seafaring stepbrother Hugh in Conrad's southern seas; another vividly describes a horse ride during which Yvonne and Hugh stumble upon a girl playing with an armadillo, who is almost bought by the couple for fifty *centavos*.

design is that of atavistic guilt and of a spiritual itinerary that always dithers between self-destructive and redemptive intentions; as in Joyce it tests, in an analogical and not exactly spiritualist perspective, atonement,[11] that is, expiation. The consul dies like a Dostoevskyan innocent, because of a tragic misunderstanding, as he is mistaken for a Jew by a Mexican band that perfunctorily shoots him at the end of his earthly Stations of the Cross. Homer is, however, as compared to Joyce, overtaken by Dante, and in the surplus of mythical allusions Lowry makes no mystery about connoting Firmin as an imperfect Dantesque pilgrim, anything but 'firm', who will instead fail 'to see the stars again', in a world that is an inferno; and a pilgrim that in fact falls, in this Mexican Hell, into the circle of Malebolge.[12] However, Lowry's final parody is that of resurrecting the timeless archetype of the Titan devoured by the demon of wild associativism. The inner voice that tempts Firmin, not to carnal love or the divine challenge, but to alcohol, and which deceives him with its euphoric potion, looks back in particular to Marlowe's *Faustus*. By virtue of this second voice, Firmin is precisely a spitting image of a Faust thrust into today's world; he belongs to the family of belated titans or romantic and post-romantic giants.[13] Certainly, every so often, Firmin also echoes Hamlet, the dilemmatic hero, the existentialist, the great niggler paralysed in his will-power: 'The will of man is unconquerable', as he repeats to himself.[14]

11   Yvonne is not Molly Bloom, but Firmin often invokes a son that the couple have not had, and the novel is therefore also the father's failure to meet his son, or the longing of a father for a son.

12   It is perhaps a further creative flash that beside him, trying to staunch his drinking habit, is a Mexican doctor called Vigil, a name that has one consonant less then Virgil. Among Lowry's unfulfilled projects, *Under the Volcano* was supposed to be one of eight parts, Hell, of a Dantesque saga.

13   Which is why this antiphonal contrast of internal voices may bring to mind Clough's *Dipsychus*. At the same time Firmin is also Arnold's Empedocles who is metaphorically on the edge of a volcano. In itself, Firmin is a name already used for its ironic nuances, and its paradoxical semantics, by Thackeray in a minor novel (cf. Volume 5, § 83.2).

14   A distant heir of Lowry, but also of George Borrow, in the restlessness that took him to the remotest corners of the world in response to the frustrations of sedentary life, was Bruce Chatwin (1940–1989). Publishers sensed that *In Patagonia* (1976) could

§ 64. *Durrell* I: The mythographer of ageless cities*

A pathway all his own of cultural and existential education was that followed by Lawrence Durrell (1912–1990). Its main literary result was three series of novels linked together in pairs, quartets and quintets, the work equally *sui generis* of a writer who was isolated, independent from any

---

repeat the nineteenth-century success of travel books. Journeys were made by Chatwin with the usual means of locomotion but also on foot, like those of the 'gypsy' novelist Borrow. In the early 1980s, Chatwin aped another popular nineteenth-century author of exotic novels, Rider Haggard, or even García Márquez, with a saga set in equatorial America (*The Viceroy of Ouidah*, 1980); but also Hardy, with another story that celebrates the estrangement of two brothers from history and civilization, against the motionless background of the English countryside (*On the Black Hill*, 1982). In his last work, Chatwin returned to the travel notebook to describe the customs and habits of the Australian aborigines. These borrowings are only some of the numerous ones that critics have found (as further proof of the richness and sophistication of his prose); just as many are the historical doubles (Rimbaud, Lawrence of Arabia, etc.) that have been attributed to him. Lowry died from an overdose of sleeping pills; Chatwin's death was from infection by the HIV virus.

*   Durrell's poetry was published for the first time in an anthology in 1964, and in a complete edition (*Collected Poems 1931–1974*, ed. J. A. Brigham) in 1980 and 2006. Previous collections include *Ten Poems* (1932), *Transition: Poems* (1934), *A Private Country* (1943), *Cities, Plains and People* (1946), *On Seeming to Presume* (1948), *The Ikons* (1966); *The Suchness of the Old Boy* (1972). *Lawrence Durrell and Henry Miller: A Private Correspondence*, ed. G. Wickes, London 1963; *Spirit of Place: Letters and Essays on Travel*, ed. A. G. Thomas, New York 1969; *Literary Lifelines: The Richard Aldington-Lawrence Durrell Correspondence*, ed. I. S. MacNiven and H. T. Moore, New York 1981; *The Durrell-Miller Letters: 1935–1980*, ed. I. S. MacNiven, London 1988. *The World of Lawrence Durrell*, ed. H. T. Moore, Carbondale, IL 1962; J. Unterecker, *Lawrence Durrell*, New York and London 1964; J. A. Weigel, *Lawrence Durrell*, New York 1965; G. Sertoli, *Lawrence Durrell*, Milano 1967 (unfortunately never updated after the Alexandria Quartet); G. S. Fraser, *Lawrence Durrell: A Study*, London 1968 and, rev., 1973, and *Lawrence Durrell*, London 1970; H. Isernhagen, *Sensation, Vision and Imagination: The Problem of Unity in Lawrence Durrell's Novels*, Bamberg 1969; A. W. Friedman, *Lawrence Durrell and 'The Alexandria Quartet': Art for Love's Sake*, Norman 1970; W. H. Ruprecht, *Durrells Alexandria Quartet: Struktur als Bezugssystem. Sichtung und Analyse*, Bern 1972; G. Lampert, *Symbolik und Leitmotivik in Lawrence Durrells Alexandria Quartet*, Bamberg 1974; J. Pelletier,

school, seemingly unclassifiable. Some British writers of his and the previous generation were emigrants and expatriates; Durrell himself was never a fully-fledged British citizen. He was born in India to parents employed in the colonial service, and, like Kipling before the end of the previous century, he only lived in England for a few years, those of his adolescence and early adulthood. As for Kipling, Durrell's scholastic experience was an unhappy one, and extremely short. On completing his secondary school studies, Durrell failed his entry exam to university; thereafter he would live almost permanently in the sensual and sunny places he wrote of, the Mediterranean basin and the Middle East, Greece, Rhodes, Corfu and Alexandria. His oeuvre is also a superior and sublime form of travel literature. For Durrell, England and London were like a rotten and unhealthy land, the centre of paralysis and of living death. They were left behind with the bitter rancour of the unloved son against sham standardizing respectability. Expatriation was a gesture of concrete good sense, because his family was needy, and at the

---

Le Quatuor d'Alexandrie de Lawrence Durrell, Paris 1975; K. Sajavaara, *Imagery in Lawrence Durrell's Prose*, Helsinki 1975; W. Hoops, *Die Antinomie von Theorie und Praxis in Lawrence Durrells Alexandria Quartet: Eine Strukturuntersuchung*, Frankfurt 1976; M.-R. Cornu, *La dynamique du quatuor d'Alexandrie de Lawrence Durrell. Trois Études*, Montréal 1979; C. Alexandre-Garner, *Le Quatuor d'Alexandrie, Fragmentation et Écriture: Étude sur l'amour, la femme et l'écriture dans le roman de Lawrence Durrell*, New York 1985, and, as editor, *Lawrence Durrell Revisited: Lawrence Durrell revisité*, Nanterre 2002; *Critical Essays on Lawrence Durrell*, ed. A. Friedman, Boston, MA 1987; *On Miracle Ground: Essays on the Fiction of Lawrence Durrell*, ed. M. H. Begnal, Lewisburg, PA 1990; R. Rook, *Lawrence Durrell's Double Concerto*, Birmingham 1990; R. Pine, *Lawrence Durrell: The Mindscape*, New York 1994; *Lawrence Durrell: Comprehending the Whole*, ed. J. R. Raper, Columbia, MO 1995; G. Bowker, *Through the Dark Labyrinth: A Biography of Lawrence Durrell*, New York 1997; D. P. Kaczvinsky, *Lawrence Durrell's Major Novels, or The Kingdom of the Imagination*, Selinsgrove and London 1997; I. S. MacNiven, *Lawrence Durrell: A Biography*, London 1998; S. Herbrechter, *Lawrence Durrell, Postmodernism and the Ethics of Alterity*, Amsterdam 1999; *Lawrence Durrell and the Greek World*, ed. A. Lillios, Selingsgrove, PA 2004; R. Morrison, *A Smile in His Mind's Eye: A Study of the Early Works of Lawrence Durrell*, Toronto 2005; L. S. Rashidi, *(Re)constructing Reality: Complexity in Lawrence Durrell's Alexandria Quartet*, New York 2005. Pages of fanciful and sometimes acute criticism are those by Praz, scattered *passim* in vol. IV of CLA.

same time of satanic abjuration, reminiscent of Joyce. Durrell's diversity did stand out and scandalize because he revived the stereotypes of post-romantic and Decadent European sensibility. His most typical prose is lyrical, flowing in violent chiaroscuros, with patches and clumps of colour, alternating with a tortuous, pseudo-scientific, esoteric psychologism, sounding much like a parody of Burton's convolution.[1] With his Alexandria Quartet, Durrell wrote a type of 'African' novel, rendering in all its density the local colour and a sensuality and sexuality that are perverse and perverted, anything but bracing, rather, turbid and impotent, and a residual, barbaric primitiveness issuing into violence and homicidal fits of madness. Durrell's lover, with many misleading false bottoms, is the survivor at the centre of the works of the Decadents; he knows that '*après lui le déluge*', or the end of the world. All these chords had echoed through many predecessors. The African novel *par excellence* in English literature had been written by Conrad. Durrell is aware of this, but his Africa is first and foremost less Caravaggesque, and his prose less Miltonian; the numerous cameos and atmospheric preludes that make the unspoiled beauty of Durrell's Alexandria Quartet are quick sketches and elliptical flashes never too full of adjectives, unlike Conrad. It is true that Durrell's Africa is a place where the plotting goes on behind the scenes; it is also true that the topic of love is the appearance, but behind the substance is the struggle for power and conspiracy. It is also true that the various European writers, diplomats and consular officials in his novels are of the same breed as Conrad's operatives left to rot in the outposts of the Empire, and equally rootless. The difference is that Durrell elects not the heart of Africa as his theatre, that is a land that was still virgin and colonizable; but, if not the geographical periphery, another heart, that

---

1   As an 'anatomy of love' the quartet is defined by Kermode, 'Durrell and Others', in KPE, 216 (however, this priceless essay, 214–27, includes the disconcerting judgement that *Mountolive* is the 'best novel of the series'). From a very young age, Durrell had loved the Elizabethan playwrights, and intended to devote a book to them that was never written. From Marlowe came the Faustian scenario in *An Irish Faustus* (1963), the best of Durrell's three plays, and an example of the remaking of the Faustian myth in the twentieth century. The medical knowledge of which Durrell provides evidence in *The Black Book* induced Fraser 1973, 22, to conjecture that Durrell intended to study medicine.

Egyptian Alexandria where an atavistic barbarism was in a state of mysterious fusion with the residual roots of universal civilization, at the epicentre of western culture.[2] It is an easy step to call Durrell the twentieth-century 'Alexandrian' writer *par excellence*, with all the implications and nuances of this qualification, and the standard-bearer of a chorus that includes Kavafy, Forster and Ungaretti. Behind him is the Pound of the *Cantos*, in the counterpoint between past and present and in the awareness of the continuity, and ruin, of history. Then there is a trio of Frenchmen, Sade, Baudelaire and Flaubert, with the arguable addition of Stendhal.[3] The philosophy of love, of promiscuity, of unbridled voluptuousness, is drafted with the conscious, epigraphic and interlinear guide of the 'Divine Marquis'. Baudelaire presides over Durrell's *mauditism*; Flaubert had written the African novel *Salammbô*, an early history of murderous, sensual perversion and violence in a nearby geographical setting. However, Durrell immediately proceeds to estrange and relativize his stance as a post-romantic Decadent, after having smugly transfused himself into one.

2. Durrell may be observed and judged by extrapolating the Alexandria Quartet out of his copious oeuvre; and we will obtain an idea of him, which is however partial because this tetralogy slots into a before and an after, and at least seven other novels accompany it. From the moment when – having launched, written and published *Justine* – Durrell discovered his entelechy as a novelist, his novelistic edifice became unitary and interrelated. Critical discussions started quite early to appear, too soon thinking this construction completed, considering at most the further diptych of the 1970s, and ignoring or not foreseeing that that edifice was still incomplete, and that Durrell would expand it with another five titles. Nine of Durrell's eleven major novels lie under the symbolic aegis of a city, and each of them has a title referring to the main character in it; the two remaining ones immediately exhibit their association by means of a pair of temporal adverbs in their titles. Such a preliminary overview makes it

2   Sertoli 1967, 115, suggests that Alexandria is the 'antithesis of Greece', and notes that, for Durrell, Alexandria is still 'Europe' and 'the capital of Asian Europe'.

3   To some critics (cf. Sertoli 1967, 121), it evokes the 'emotional and colourful exoticism' of Pierre Loti.

clear that Durrell remains the conjurer of mythical, anthropomorphic cities with which he had lived in a regime of passionate, identifying relationship; they made their story resonate inside him, along with their historical and legendary suggestions. Not just any city would do, but only those with ancient roots. Durrell's literary fortune was that he had inhabited them. In succession, his novels are about Alexandria, Athens, Istanbul, Avignon and Geneva. Following Georg Groddeck, Durrell postulates the atrophy of the subject's will; he is acted upon by the city he is immersed in, and which exerts a destructive function on him. Durrell's main characters are adrift, amorphous or unconscious, 'fatal' in fact, moving about in a lethargic and contagious atmosphere.[4] His ideal place is with the great mythographers of historical-imaginary cities: with Ruskin of the stones of Venice,[5] with Yeats of 'Sailing to Byzantium', with Joyce the Dubliner, if we like. All of them had been creators and historian of mythical cities, at the same time real and imaginary. Slowly, but unmistakably, Durrell emerges first and foremost as a kind of Ruskin of our own times. He turns to one or more anthropomorphic and feminine cities revisited as in so many *Stones*, not in prose essays but in lyrical novels; or as a Pater obsessed by the *genius loci*.[6] At the beginning of the 1960s, the Alexandria Quartet proclaimed Durrell the writer of the moment. However, his own admirers were quick to notice an immediate abuse of the formula, and the author's self-plagiarism. The fulcrum of the Quartet was shifted back to the first movement, *Justine*. The third novel is anonymous, and the fourth a finale in a minor key. Praz, a secret admirer of all post-Decadents, admired the Quartet, even if the only novel he fully praised was, again, the first; perhaps, had he written on them, he couldn't have refrained to voice his disappointment at the two novels following the Quartet. The Avignon Quintet came too late for him, and would have been further slated, we may be sure, with no half measures. Even Durrell's previous admirers fell silent. As always, a late work sheds light on and re-orientates an earlier one, and the total image of Durrell's corpus is

---

4   This Groddeck-style aesthetics is intrinsic to Durrell's *A Key to Modern British Poetry*.
5   The resemblance of Venice to Avignon, both decadent cities and 'risen from the water', is recalled by Rook 1990, 11.
6   Some of Durrell's virtuoso and euphuistic prose is Paterian for Fraser 1973, 49.

redefined by means of further integrations. In other words, the Avignon Quintet reopens and modifies the critical discourse on Durrell. The fire of passion, sex dissociated from love and seen as an itchy and often random game, the dissolution of the narrative in ornate and aestheticizing warps of words:[7] these are the *défaillances* of which the novelist was accused since the times of Leavis, who notably missed in Durrell D. H. Lawrence's passionate and committed realism. Durrell will probably become popular again and return in vogue in an age such as our own, characterized by the waning of the aegis of literature as a moral, even if not moralistic message.

§ 65. *Durrell II: Prospero's flight*

Durrell's first personal myth, which reverberates throughout his mature works, is that of a Prospero who abandons his palace and seeks exile on a Mediterranean island fashioning an imaginary court in order to be able to freely attend to art. This was also by and large the myth of the early, precociously Decadent Victorians, and a temptation reflected in Tennyson's 'The Palace of Art'. A similar trail emerges in that loose autobiography entitled *Prospero's Cell* (1945). However, the analogy is questioned, because Durrell does not break the magic wand at the end, nor does he head homewards reconciled, because he is aware of the unsustainable nature of his golden exile, and therefore of the vanity of the wrangling with time. He must witness its comeback, and his 'fatal' hero is thrown inexorably into everyday life and history. Born in India, as I mentioned, to a father who was a railway engineer, and educated there in a college run by Belgian Jesuits (even though he was from a Protestant family), Durrell was taken back home at eleven and studied in two English public schools of average renown. Above all else self-taught, and having left university, at twenty he frequented the circles of bohemian Londoners, distinguishing himself as a poet. With his first wife Nancy Isobel Myers, who was a photographer and painter, and with his mother and his brother Gerald, who also became a popular scientific writer, in 1935 Durrell settled in Corfu. There he made the decisive

7   Cf. Sertoli 1967, 66–7 and 76, for accusations of artificiality and academicism. The bluff of Durrell's poetry is still denounced in a review of *Selected Poems* in *TLS*, 28 July 2006, 27.

discovery of Henry Miller's *Tropic of Cancer*, which marked the beginning of a long friendship between the two writers and, according Orwell[8] – who liked Miller and, we can surmise, could and should also have liked Durrell if he had been able to read his masterpiece[9] – the founding of a literary current. Durrell's *Panic Spring* (1937) was influenced by the American writer and by Huxley's conversation novels. In *The Black Book*[10] (1938) Durrell, wallowing yet again in an obsolete *mauditism*, is a Lawrencian Lucifer fleeing from the spiritual sterility of England, an England which is now dying, towards the warm fertility of Greece. In it, Durrell devised a meeting place for the coexistence of a youth community of drifters, *bohémiens* or *déracinés*, responding to the typical main character of British fiction of the 1920s and 1930s, whose odysseys recur in Waugh, Powell, Huxley, and Iris Murdoch. Durrell said that this was the first novel in which he had recognized a voice, his own voice, and his identity as a writer; and in

8   OCE, vol. I, 577. On the specific assessments of Miller by Orwell see § 22.4 and nn. 53 and 54. One easily conjectures that both *Panic Spring* and *The Black Book* are in their titles a contamination of Miller's *Black Spring*.

9   Miller's *Tropic of Cancer* also focuses on the microcosm of a dying civilization, expressly devoured by cancer and in the arms of the looming apocalypse ('The world is a cancer eating itself away'), but avoiding the solemn fatalism of *Justine*. Like Durrell's quartet, Miller's novel is therefore of and on a city, Paris, and an anthropomorphic Paris at that, a great sick organism, and, at the same time, a stage from which the exile can watch the ruination as a non-participant witness. *Tropic of Cancer* is then in its own way an image of the European 'crisis' after the First World War. Miller's novel, without numbered sections, is structured in memorial cameos or anecdotes often focused on the protagonist's encounter with a Parisian prostitute; writers and prostitutes alternate on the scene, and every prostitute is described in the variety of her copulative idiosyncrasies along with the oddities or exaggerations of her desire. This is the reason for the predominance of bluster, of the unexpected 'circus-show', of the large or lewd anatomical detail. Miller said he was interested in recording 'all that which is omitted in books'. Miller's *alter ego* has touched bottom, he no longer has any illusions, but is not destroyed; on the contrary, he quivers with the desire to live and survive, even if he has no great values to cling to: 'I [...] hold on nothing [...] I would live as an animal, a beast of prey, a rover, a plunderer'. He has reached the apex of the spiritual life and finds himself as naked as a savage. Neither Miller nor Durrell had any real sense of political responsibility.

10   Published in Paris, and only in the 1960s in America.

which he had been an innovator, and had not imitated. The only models he confessed to were D. H. Lawrence, Joyce and Henry Miller. Planned as a memoir, it reveals an interest that would prove to be long lasting in the imbricated narrative. It introduces a first and then a second narrator, a previous lodger or tenant of a *pension*. In his diary he tells of his unhappy love for a streetwalker who came to live with him. The first voice, foretelling the Quartet, is that, *ex post*, of an exile on a Greek island. Thus two narratives are formed, one inside the other, with two distinct narrative time frames. The resonance is multiplied in a magmatic flow of two narrators who are the redoubling of one and the same person. On a formal level, what is equally important is the announcement of a synchronic narrative, and of a 'chronology' that 'has nothing to do with time'. The novel's success lies in the frank and bitter anecdotes of characters who are eccentric, unhinged and confused. One of them is trying to complete a map of Peru (such is his way of coveting escapism). This flight remains frustrated, and the novel, with little or no development, is a sequence of squalid stories of an underclass or precarious community in London, in which physicality and sexual hunger have gained the upper hand. *The Black Book* exhibits and gives vent to Durrell's genital or rather, vaginal obsession, taken from Henry Miller. The intelligible plot gradually becomes more opaque, giving rise to free evolutions and deranged meditations, and a rather inconsistent, even if at times suggestive logorrhoea. The *mise en abyme* is that of a 'strange procession of symbols across consciousness', and symbols that 'I do not know any more what they mean'. The first of the two narrators eventually takes the reins, only to topple into a confused mental delirium that, of the three models mentioned above, is now indebted especially to Joyce and to Molly Bloom's monologue. Yet this is also a digressive vein that thematically, and for its obsessions, is strangely similar to and premonitory of the far more effective monologues in *Malone Dies* by Beckett.[11]

---

11   Some have seen in the novel an extension of the theme of *The Waste Land*. The soliloquizing rather echoes Gerontion together with Prufrock: 'I am a little ageing man, gone bald on top'. The intrusive refrain quotes Shakespeare's London winter of 'our discontent', now replaced by the Mediterranean sun.

2. In August 1937, Durrell met Anaïs Nin in Paris. From this trio, Durrell, Miller and Nin, a new school was born, with a new literary programme. The school was to be based at the Villa Seurat, but the geographic poles of the potential founders were too far apart. *The Dark Labyrinth*[12] (1947) is the only other novel by Durrell before the Quartet. Lighter, quicker, brisker and more relaxing, it is surprisingly devoid of any ideological or pseudo-ideological ballast and therefore the least 'Durrellian'.[13] The whole of the first half is dedicated to portraying and identifying a coterie of British people in the various cultural circles of London, and who, for a variety of needs, are just about to embark for Crete.[14] The background and preparation for departure bear no marks of fatality, and if anything they are narrated in a semi-serious register, reminiscent of the Victorian exotic escapism of a Rider Haggard.[15] Once together, the painter, the poet, the archaeologist, the pair of tourists, even a missionary, unleash a colourful chain of events. Once the party is in Crete, the highlight is a visit to a labyrinth where stories are told of a voracious Minotaur that still wanders around, and indeed its roar is heard by the visitors who end up trapped, all except one. The legend, as in 'rational' Gothic novels, bursts like a soap bubble, because within the labyrinth only a harmless cow is found; the hoax is due to the business resourcefulness of a Greek travel agency. Two prisoners plunge into the sea and escape, but, in an ending that recalls Wells's fantasy novels, the two tourists encounter an American woman who has lived isolated on the slopes of the out-of-the-way labyrinth ever since the First World War. The early poetry of Durrell had been inspired by the myth of the intrepid Ulyssean adventurer, of the relentless wanderer and unfulfilled romantic, along the distant lines of Byron,[16] and has now

12   The title of the novel in its second edition, replacing *Cefalù*.

13   A potboiler to pay for the divorce from his first wife Nancy, as it was defined by Durrell himself (MacNiven 1998, 299).

14   In the psychoanalyst, Hogarth, who is treating some of these tourists, Groddeck is portrayed (MacNiven 1998, 317). According to a psychoanalytical approach, the labyrinth is the unconscious that each of the tourists is going to explore.

15   As noted also by Sertoli 1967, 102.

16   On whom there is a poem (cf. *Collected Poems*, 122), commented by MacNiven 1998, 273–4.

and then a solemn and magniloquent mark. The initial tone is the intimist arpeggio still partially in the nineteenth-century manner, Victorian and rather too lyrical, that is, the ejaculation of the titanic, gloomy and saddened soul. A metrical freedom is followed by a stanzaic closure that adopts rhyme and even the form of the sonnet; for its stylization, concettism and convolution it is reminiscent of Dante Gabriel Rossetti.[17] Exceptionally, a ballad is included in Durrell's poetic book, and it tells the story of a certain general; but it seems to be a mock-heroic joke. There is also a Shakespearean pastiche. The memorial vein expands in parallel with Durrell's travels across the Greek seas; and premonitions of the Quartet therefore emerge. In the poems of the 1940s we detect a thrust towards exorbitant verbal clusters with a wealth of abstract syntactic twists and turns and conceptual associations without perceptible links, alongside a poetry evoking places and of mythological resuscitation. Consistently, in these poems, Durrell offers anecdotal evocations of as many *genii loci*.

§ 66. *Durrell III: The Alexandria Quartet*

At the outbreak of the war, Durrell's relatives, except for his wife, returned to their homeland; and on the fall of Greece the couple were forced to repair to Alexandria via Crete. Durrell was appointed press attaché to the British Embassies in Cairo and Alexandria. His diplomatic career continued after the war until he became a schoolteacher. Eve (Yvette) Cohen, whom he met in Alexandria, became the model for Justine in the Quartet.[18] Having separated from his wife, Durrell married Eve in 1947, and they had a daughter they named Sappho.[19] *Justine* is from 1957; *Balthazar*

17		Graecian, the poet of *The Dark Labyrinth*, is an *alter ego* of Durrell, as the author of verses 'that are neither experimental nor very attractive', and even 'slightly mannered, and a little outdated'.

18		This however is doubted by MacNiven 1998, 432.

19		In the same year, 1947, he was appointed Director of the British Council in Córdoba, Argentina; he was in London in 1948 only to be redirected immediately to Belgrade to follow Tito breaking away from Stalin. He remained there until 1952 (collecting material for his espionage novel *White Eagles over Serbia*, from 1957). In 1952 he moved to Cyprus where he taught English and became a government official, an experience reflected in *Bitter Lemons*. Durrell had two other wives after separating

from 1958, *Mountolive* from 1958, *Clea* from 1960. In his general preface, Durrell specifies the kind and type of writing in the Quartet, those of a verbal continuum. But it is aesthetically more important to stress that the first three novels are 'synoptic', the fourth diachronic. This is tantamount to saying that the first three narrate or re-narrate the same events in different keys, illuminations and behind-the-scene stories; it is also a kind of Browning-style[20] judiciary novel.[21] Durrell sees himself as a post-aesthete or epigonic aesthete by using the paraphernalia of the liturgy and biblical writing. He is his own evangelist, the author of a text that embraces four lay gospels of his passage on the earth, in an area of crossovers of sects, faiths and beliefs, as Palestine was in the time of Jesus. At the same time, this memorial novel, which could aspire to be compared with Proust and with the *romans-fleuves* of years or decades earlier, refuses to accept time, or the times, as its organizing principle. Only the fourth novel is sequential, while the development of the first three is synchronous or concentric, more exactly stratified. We cannot fail to mention an illustrious precedent, Wyndham Lewis's historical diatribe against the tyranny of time and the novelists who succumbed to it, and against Bergson, their philosophical inspirer.[22] The attack on the 'time-saturated novel of the day' even seems a prompt from Lewis without expressly naming him. If the river is not the icon that presides over the novel, it is that of irradiation; but, with a logically difficult passage, from the 'axis of the work', Durrell says, 'it should be possible to radiate from it in any direction without losing the strictness and congruity of its relation to "a continuum"'. Durrell adds the he will be narrating not in a chronological order, but according to psychic significance. The right metaphor is rather that of novels which are '"siblings" of each other'; but his aim was also parodic, that of imitating a rhapsodic musical structure: a quartet, more exactly, on a quartet of characters – with each

---

from Yvette. In the 1960s, he was living in Sommières, a small village in Occitanie, which he left for some time in 1974 to teach at the California Institute of Technology.

20   As Sertoli also notes, 1967, 147–8.

21   Durrell was rather amateurishly drawn to Einstein, and intended to give shape to a relativistic novel of the modern era.

22   This precedent was admitted by Durrell (Unterecker 1964, 22–3).

novel representing a 'movement', and the series as a composition of musical movements that are each a variation on another.[23] From this type of re-evocation it is vain to expect anything linear. Human history merges with the landscape and is an emanation of it. Darley, the protagonist and first narrator, writes from a kind of Johannine apocalyptic Patmos, an island where he has only a few books with him, and a little girl.[24] This is the Decadent stance of the double of the disciple, with a liturgical and sacred imagery destitute of authenticity, and therefore a posture. The re-imagined city 'begins and ends in us', with the apocalyptic sense of an ending and at the same time of a solitary survival. The Alexandria Quartet evokes and conjures up an age, and its characters play the role of later reincarnations of archetypes. Its meaning is that of the consciously degraded repetition of ancient scenes of seduction and Alexandrian enchantment; of successive reincarnations provoked by a demiurgic city-goddess (at the start Melissa, delirious at a party, and drunk, is stolen away like Cleopatra in a carpet). The individual episode is part of the history of Alexandria in the precise meaning that the city is like a historiated wall, or a scroll of episodes that are repeated cyclically, and therefore exist synchronously; and Alexandria is defined as the city of memory. The two main characters, reincarnations of Antony and Cleopatra, are themselves fused with this memory. They are two 'fatal' characters, the only ones. Others belong to a purely realistic regime. But, at the same time, Durrell gives a hearing to the stories, the fabulous anecdotes of past and present, like that of the segregated girl who is yearning to go out, and goes to the carnival masked, and it turns out that she has no nose. The counterpoint of modernized myth is invariably the incidental skit which Durrell often illuminates in an inspired way, a domain within which we meet for instance Pombal, the barber, or Scobie, the grotesque

---

23   Behind them is of course the example of Eliot's *Four Quartets*, which are also a struggle against time.

24   Spiritually from and on Patmos, Durrell wrote some lyric poems that evoke figures of prophets or sages linked to them. In 'Logos' (*Collected Poems*, 64–5), Durrell elaborates on a metaphorical analogy between him and the figure of the saint, to conclude with the cruel torture of unfulfilled Eros, expressed, as in Dylan Thomas, by images of the Passion. For the influence of Thomas, cf. MacNiven 1998, 210.

policeman, whose name is the same as that of another policeman, he too Catholic, namely, that of Graham Greene.[25] This counterpoint is also that of demoted archetypes. Durrell's the *alter ego*, initially without a name, is one Darley, also the namesake of an eccentric Irish Victorian poet who succumbed to the magnetic fascination of dramatic Elizabethan models, as Durrell himself did; and a John Keats, *ahi quam mutatus*, must write much later the biography of a self-styled famous novelist, he too exiled to Alexandria.[26] The characters are petty and mean, but they know how to pose and how to act; they feel they are on a stage and produce torrents of words. Alexandria is a grand spinning theatre, and anthropomorphic, and connective, it ensures the unity of the cycle. It is 'the city which used us as its flora – precipitated in us conflicts which were hers and which we mistook for our own: beloved Alexandria!'. Crammed with resurfacing memories, it is a 'princess and whore. The royal city and the *anus mundi*',[27] a kaleidoscopic and updated 'splendours and miseries', with its evanescence, its wealth of facets, and its relativity.

2. *Justine* is divided into marked parts, but internally it is fragmented into large and small blocks of about half a page or a page each, in the form of lyrical and memorial flashes separated by asterisks. A writer or diarist writes and recalls in the first person a story that is over, now that he is staying on an island of the Cyclades. He is a jaded monologist, surprised in a waning

25   § 53. In this case, Greene's Catholic policeman would be violently desecrated.
26   Ever since *The Black Book*, Durrell had loved doubling, not just disguising, himself in a single *alter ego*, and some novelists are alternatives and self-projections, like Justine's first husband, a novelist who has written about her from a psychoanalytical standpoint; or like Pursewarden, the 'great' novelist who is a barrage of elliptical, witty, philosophical quips, transcendental even, but who does nothing to demonstrate his greatness. Durrell is always a writer in front of side mirrors that reflect and multiply his image.
27   This ambivalence is very frequent in the symbolism of Durrell's cities. At the end of *Livia*, in the Avignon cycle, a surprising, surreal flash is that of the sewer-cleaning truck, humanized as Marius, which sucks out 'the intellectual excrement of the twentieth century in a town which was once Rome'. In fact, this metaphor evokes another, used by the writer Blanford: that of St Augustine in *De Civitate Dei*, 'Inter faesces et urinam nascimur'.

moment, who relives flashes of his three loves spent in a climate of sleepy heat, fabulous scenarios exuding millennial stories, where the history of humanity began. Every so often a clear description arises; most often it is blurred, and pretends to be a private reordering of experience, and betrays no desire to inform an unknowing reader or listener. The novel is punctuated by the entries of a diary and of a defamatory novel of a third *alter ego*, the first husband of Justine, one Nessim, a rich and refined, but somewhat scarred Egyptian Coptic banker who studied at Oxford. Messianic for his race, he is in cahoots with the local Jews for this utopia. The mechanism, the idea and the plot cannot be and are not new: they are only transposed to an exotic scenario, with only a change of the background, which smells and indeed often stinks of the east. This is the story already seen of American and British expatriates in the post-war years; it is therefore a tardy chronotope, the story of the rootless bohemian who obviously studied art in Paris and there met and experienced, as in Henry Miller's novel, the gnawing of Eros and hunger.[28] Paris was already exotic for British puritans before Durrell, and Maugham had recently revisited it; transposed to Alexandria, the city of dreams and transgressions becomes charged with the historical weight of the crossroads of civilization, races and sects. The typical *déraciné* is now the British globetrotter who had often been a spy during the wars. Everything revolves around sexual promiscuity and a man who has three women. One is the devout, passive, obliging Melissa; the other the aggressive Justine, a Cleopatra despite being Jewish;[29] the third is the spiritual Clea. Durrell saddles Justine with a pathological case, erotic dissatisfaction caused by infantile traumas, and the pathology of a dissatisfied Eros. In the first novel she is a mysterious object of desire, enigmatic and pursued; an aggressive panther with many faces, a disappointed nymphomaniac interrogated by her lovers.[30] All the pleasures of Eros, this seeking and finding and having sex, is not love, but the ultimate impotence of love,

---

28   As noted by Sertoli 1967, 18–19.
29   For Durrell, Eve Cohen had the 'flavour' of Cleopatra (MacNiven 1998, 282).
30   The scene in the brothel with the ten-year-old girls is *pro tem* a mystery: we discover that Justine was looking there for her daughter from her first marriage, who had disappeared.

an unreachable goal. The evocation of turbid, dark, contorted loves, often obscure in their psychic developments, with the odd psycho-fantastic explanations that are given, recall Baudelaire. *Justine* inevitably celebrates, or laments, the bitterness of sex and the flesh, and the dissatisfaction left by Eros. Flaubert also reverberates in it for the sensual revisiting of the African world and for the mixture of Eros and violence, cunning and primitivism; and for the cult of the right word as an end in itself, and hence of the purple passage. Durrell falls prey to the anecdotal magic and becomes the first of his readers: subdued, curious, thirsty, he is willing to put an end to the tired lucubrations of philosophy and psychology of the *boudoir*. Narouz, Nessim's brother, telluric and primordial, brings to life the most amazing exotic mythologies among the internal stories. However, the last quarter of *Justine* proceeds unusually clearly and briskly, with the hunting of wild ducks in the Mareotid and the romantic and then sexual encounter of Melissa and Nessim, two jealous beings, down to earth and insensitive to the sublime. Justine eventually flees to a Jewish communist kibbutz, having rid herself of her rapist, who died during the hunt, in a Freudian fashion. Only in the next novel will we learn that she repaired to a place where she could more easily avoid being arrested.

3. *Justine* is a masterpiece whose aesthetic and ideological foundations and intentions are immediately contradicted. In the second novel, *Balthazar*, a so-called 'interlinear version' of the first, is provided; what emerges distinctly is the idea of a palimpsest of several narrative layers and bands, and a composite text. Darley rereads the past from the Greek island where he is exiled from Alexandria, and has adopted and brought there, charitably, the daughter born from the casual love affair of Nessim and Melissa, who are now both dead. The synoptic plan reproduces from afar that relativism which the fiction writers and poets of the nineteenth century knew, and gives the events already narrated an air of false mystery. Clea will speak of the 'whole of Alexandria unrolling once more', in its scenes and colours. The same plot is repeated, pausing on stories previously skipped over and with leaps even further back in time. The enchantment is slightly reduced, and the narrative or even caricatural passage gains ground: Scobie with his parrot, his nursery rhymes, his dressing in drag 'with a Dolly Varden hat', and his tragicomic end, as he dies being stoned while joking. Fatalism

weakens under the blows of a much less enigmatic reality of brutal shocks. Justine loved the painter Clea, who one day fetishistically kissed her wrist, or rather the heart of white flesh formed near the buttoning of the glove; and Darley, who discovers that Justine has had a tryst with the novelist Pursewarden, also finds out that he was a mere cover to distract Nessim's jealousy. Justine is equally thirsting, but Pursewarden cannot love, and he insults her repeatedly and refuses her, in scenes of Durrellian contortion and masochistic suffering. This is all to say that Durrell gives his best in the incidental rather than in the substantial. The atmospheric preludes are the repeated exploits of an authentic painter of words; none of them is ever routine, but they are all written in the most suggestive, surprising and de-familiarizing of terms.[31] Lengthy chapters are dedicated for instance to hunting at the salt lake; or to awkward Nessim who visits his mother to inform her of his decision to marry Justine, a retroactive episode in which each single step and each single sentence are analysed in slow motion, and which brings a secondary character to the forefront, Nessim's brother. The latter, Narouz, is again at the centre of a matchless cameo when he visits a holy man to have information on Justine's lost daughter, and wanders through the sultry city in the night, ending up at the kiosk of a prostitute, whom he confuses with the unattainable Clea.

4. *Mountolive* is far less agile, especially when Durrell introduces into the narration a quantity of political fiction with the story of the diplomat and ambassador Mountolive who, dreamy and immature, on the day of his arrival in Alexandria meets – in another flashback – the Egyptian Leila, thirsty, sensual and Cleopatra-like (in an especially sensual scene, perhaps a reminiscence of Eliot's *Prufrock*, a crumb left in his mouth is licked as if with the tongue of a cat). The visual focus has shifted decisively onto Nessim's family, with the vivid and quick-paced evocation of the growing love between Leila and Mountolive. Narouz is still brutal and animal-like, and lops off the ear of a servant who has lied to him. In the spy story, Mountolive comes to check the truth of a conspiracy of the

---

31   A pictorial representation that descends from Durrell's poetry, which, for Sertoli 1967, 79, 'remains [...], substantially, in the shadow of Imagism'.

Copts, marginalized even though they are and feel like 'real Egyptians', to overthrow the Muslim regime. He must then determine whether the son of the woman for whom he came to Egypt is a spy. With this the spell of the voluptuous and fatal story between Darley and Justine is definitively at an end. Pursewarden is not the odd and inconclusive writer he seemed, and Darley, in turn seen by him, is a poor devil. With his allegations, Pursewarden acquires the function of a fulcrum; he will mysteriously kill himself after learning that Nessim has been trafficking in weapons in Palestine to plot against the British.[32] The fertility of Justine and Nessim's marriage is the support given to the creation of a Jewish state; and Justine's erotic adventures acquire now an altogether different meaning. The demise of the fatal pops up everywhere. However, the naturalistic incidental story, such as the penetration of a disillusioned and disguised man into the Arab quarters, louche and full of mystery, is always gripping. Also the scene in which Mountolive ends up in a brothel of sullied angels, or angelic prostitutes who seduce him, as in a nightmare, looks back to Boccaccio: he has been misled by a false holy sheikh. The romantic Narouz dies longing to see Clea, who, out of mercy, although she does not love him, rushes to his side, but arrives when he is already dead. *Clea* energizes the hero's *nostos* to the dreamed-of city, scarred by war, with the young girl in tow. The intact archetypical quality of the city is denied by the showy trademarks of physical decay, engraved by the time that has finally passed, no longer immobile. But the fatal repeats itself with Darley and Clea who isolate themselves, like Donne's lovers, from the rest of the world, namely, from the bombings. *Clea*, which seems to move forward, is in fact always backward looking, being played out in a succession of meetings whose aim is to focus on, or even discover for the first time, events, implications, and traces of the past. Its structure is hybrid and often becomes that of a pastiche. A further contribution comes from an excerpt, hazy, meandering and inconsistent, of Pursewarden's diary. The plot, made up of recollections without new

---

32   In reality, this is the first version later denied: it is not a suicide of honour but a filthier and murkier gesture, dictated by a letter to his blind sister who, in love with the diplomat Mountolive, has announced the impossibility of continuing their incestuous love.

entries, is, however, immediately quickened by the miracle of the rescue of Clea, who is accidentally hit underwater by an aquatic rifle that pierces her right hand with which she paints, and almost kills her. She is saved, but the two lovers, who have always loved one another with a diaphanous and faded passion, separate.

§ 67. *Durrell IV: The Avignon postlude*

The magic of the Alexandria Quartet fades away in every later work by Durrell; all are forced elaborations on a theme or a confused and nebulous thesis that does not sustain the plot, which is diffused and smothered, and, in most cases, runs aground. In *Tunc*[33] (1968), the first part of a diptych on the rebellious scientist Felix Charlock, the linear development and the orderly clarity of facts and prior events are lost in outcrops of fanciful and pedantic erudition. The opening is a constellation of sensational, grotesque and hybrid variations of a Priapic mould, and a real string of Sadian adventures happen, in the double arena of Athens and Istanbul, to larval, ethereal and somewhat off-the-cuff characters. A genetic fantasy sermon is pronounced on the Acropolis by a drunk and sexually fixated Welsh professor, and it will prove to be proleptic. The underlying intrigue consists in the activities of a mysterious 'Merlin Corporation' that acts in a Mafia-like way for profit and market saturation, and which finds it convenient to hire spies to keep local conspiracies at bay, and inventors and scientists to perfect their discoveries. Stripped of all fatalism, the *alter ego* that was Darley is now the only normal person among a host of deranged psychopaths. His vicissitudes in the Turkish and Greek scenario all ooze erotic fixations reminiscent in spirit of those of Byron's Don Juan. An evocative novel of a city? No longer. The *genius loci*, of which Durrell had been a lyrical master, does not waft here. The scenes set in Athens and then Istanbul exhibit a notable absence of atmospheric preludes or glimpses of landscape, previously so spellbinding. The male protagonist must still face two female icons: the good redeemed prostitute, Iolanthe, who becomes a

---

33   As is made clear in the next novel, the title is not only 'cunt' written as an anagram, but the name of a Malaysian fertility god that it is believed can curb an epidemic that causes the almost total atrophy of the penis.

cinema diva, and the thirsty and bewitching seductress, the fatal Benedicta, who radiates sinister flashes of Gothic horror in her foot with two little toes. However, from this novel of scientific intrigue flashes of the fantastic are occasionally released. The madam of the Athenian brothel reappears as the secretary of the diva, who was one of her prostitutes; and the latter, as godmother, officially opens a strange exhibition of Impressionist painters at the airport. Benedicta marries Charlock and then leaves him, but not before giving him a son, Mark. On closing the book, the reader is disappointed and remains with the idea that much of it is lacking in interest. The sequel, *Nunquam* (1970), is a parable on the delirious aims of science and the hubris of a small amateurish demiurge.[34] The core, stripped of many Sternian digressions, parodistically pedantic and satirizing the scientific jargon, and enriched with irrelevant technicalities, takes place in a British laboratory where some scientists are trying, with science-fiction-like preposterous operations of genetic engineering, to resuscitate or revivify the corpse of the former prostitute Iolanthe. It is a very topical utopia, which no doubt parodies the Frankenstein myth and the reconstruction in a laboratory of a living being with the lifeless limbs of a corpse, or of Stevenson's story of the body snatchers; or seems to cite from a distance Wells's *The Island of Doctor Moreau*. Durrell fails to infuse life into this fiction, only coming up with verbose and sardonic humour, and it clearly does not stand comparison with recent scientific satires such as Huxley's *After Many a Summer* and especially Waugh's *The Loved One*. In the latter novel dead bodies are not resurrected, but cosmetic science is applied to the dead to make them more beautiful before burial, and thus make them at least *seem* alive.[35] The final pages, however, recover speed, culminating in the killing of the creature revived or re-created by the creator. This is a gesture of pure humanity, since it is intended to restore freedom to the manikin manufactured in the

34   Benedicta loses her satanic or enchantress's halo and confesses: like Justine she has been sent to dupe the scientist. The two brothers, Jocas and Julian, so different in temperament, are a variation on the pair of Nessim and Narouz from the Alexandria Quartet. Julian embodies the sadistic, if not Sadian character, because, punished by his father for his incestuous love for his sister, he punishes those who love her in turn.

35   § 48.1.

laboratory. The knife that is stuck into its neck represents the repentance of science, which admits and accepts its limitations.

2. A distinctly esoteric fictional effort, *The Avignon Quintet*, which entirely occupied the last decade of Durrell's career, has four points of interest: the structural plan, once again one of a non-progressive narrative, and thus of individual plots that are integrated into a synchronic perspective; experimentation with metafiction, with the doubling and tripling of internal narrators, and the parallel and intertwining narratives; the revisitation of themes, actions and interlacements with a Gothic and therefore also postmodern flair; fascination with gnosis, just as the previous diptych addressed the question of science. The emblem of the quintet is to be found in the far-fetched image of the *quincunx*.[36] It must be reiterated that almost all five novels are interlacements of characters and events intended as precise emanations of the cities exuding their history, and cities that are again like a palimpsest or a series of layers bound together. Avignon is yet another basin of the imagination stimulated by history – by its river and by the river port, and by the city as a copy of Rome owing to the exile of the Popes. Old legends and fantasies seem still to be heard and resonating. Synchrony is relative, and does not prevent but indeed favours the return of the past. So this quintet, which is not entirely detached from the Alexandria Quartet, along with the scientific diptych we have just seen, forms a series of eleven novels that can be virtually considered a saga of British history of the last sixty years until the date of the final novel, in some ways like that of Powell. The same characters appear and reappear in it with minor losses and new entries. Durrell is therefore the author of a single cyclical novel in eleven acts. The variant is that, as a cycle, it is not exactly or entirely realistic, but fantastic. It unleashes a suggestion very much active today, vaguely that of the Arthurian cycle and the medieval legends revisited without suspension of disbelief: this is the hypothesis of gnosis that in turn undermines the orthodoxy of the ancient Order of the Knights Templar. This hypothesis is played out in phases that occasionally display the hammy style, and raise the same halo of impishness, of the popular Indiana Jones films.

---

36   On whose meaning and on whose implications, see n. 40 below.

3. *Monsieur, or, the Prince of Darkness* (1974) unfolds as a retrospective plot about the presumptive suicide of Piers, an eccentric owner of a manor house in Provence. His lifeless body is found in a hotel room with the head severed. The inquiry is entrusted to the law and followed by an English relative of the deceased, who writes the novel in the first person. His name is Bruce, a diplomat who is Piers's brother-in-law having married his sister Sylvie, who was institutionalized in the local asylum of Verfeuille after becoming insane. The 'dark' ingredient is the suspected membership of the suicide victim, he too a diplomat, to a sect of Egyptian anti-Christian gnostics, in turn the modern descendants of the Templars, whose secret object was not that of Christian chivalry but the extermination of the divine word. They were therefore a demoniacal sect. The preliminary question is: is Durrell able to be a credible Gothic writer? And is this a remake of the Gothic horror story, and therefore a parody, or did Durrell truly give credit to this legend? The narrative is flowing enough but perfunctory, without any peaks of real suspense. Unconvincing, if not unnatural and confused, is especially the choice of playing on the virtual nature of the main plot, which in turn is the content of a novel that a second writer is producing. Durrell resorts in fact to the acrobatics of metafiction with Blanford, the novelist writing a novel which is a kind of Pirandellian refraction or game of mirrors, which is what Durrell always delights in doing: a protracted game, that is, of ambiguous perspectives, of narrative and optical effects, including the multiplication of the internal voices.[37] At the end we discover that the cause of Piers's death is due to the rules of the Egyptian gnostics, each of whose affiliates knows that on a certain day a messenger will inexorably come to announce his imminent death to him. *Livia: Or, Buried Alive* (1978) in turn revolves around the attempts of some fanatics stationed in Avignon to locate and dig up the legendary treasure of the Templars, stolen when the Order was suppressed by the Inquisition for heresy. The characters have been almost totally replaced,

---

37   A character in search of an author, and a research so fruitful that the character is incarnate and lives a life of its own, is his *alter ego* Sutcliffe, whose odysseys are mainly of fornications.

but gravitate towards the same area as in the first novel, that is, Avignon. The eponymous protagonist, Livia, is Durrell's elusive seductress, of the family of dark women, spellbinding and sexually ambiguous; her Nazi inclinations and sympathies identify the internal time as that of Hitler's rise to power in the 1930s. If Durrell is sometimes a Paterian writer in allowing himself to be inspired by the *genius loci*, here the glimpses of Avignon invite comparison with those of the French towns in which some enchanting imaginary portraits by Pater are set. In the neighbourhood of Avignon, gypsies have lifted the foundation stones and dug 'to arrive at a layer of civilization much anterior to the Papal period of the town'. This symbolic excavation may be taken for the historical paradigm investigated by Pater: from the pagan and Greek state, layer and stage, to the Christian one, and from the atavistic to the civilized.

4. Of the five Avignon novels, *Livia* is by far the one with the most fluid, free and effusive narrative, and almost the fruit of the author's abandonment to the curious anecdote or to the comedy. It exudes Proustian flavours and auras, also because Durrell follows for many pages the movements of peripheral characters such as the diplomat Felix or the Egyptian Prince Hassad. The detailed story of Prince Hassad's courting of his girlfriend and then wife is completely irrelevant to the plot. Similar focal shifts serve the specious purpose of providing a local diorama, a carousel of views, and thus disguise a travel book. Incidentally, Durrell can never refrain from making his male characters visit a brothel, and this is by now an inevitable scene. An amusing farce is the visit to one of them by the hot-headed Egyptian prince; here Durrell's set of madams is enriched by the well-defined and showy figure of the procuress Riquiqui. In the first sentence of *Constance: or Solitary Practices* (1982) Avignon is presented as a 'lesser Rome', and its memories hover in the present as if they were passing 'into the minds of some dormant pope'. Geneva, too, second only to Avignon as an intermittent arena of the five novels, is an Alexandria in smaller format, 'the capital of cults and [religious] movements'; 'priests of every confession' abound there. The novel is constructed, in Avignon, Geneva, London and Egypt, as a tracking shot from one to another of the minor and major characters, while often returning to the prior stories and small updates. The pace is extremely slow and concentric, and the interest of the events not exciting;

but as usual, the monotonous plot is dotted with some off-camera scenes, often episodic or incidental, linked to Durrell's fixation, sex. Constance, a soldier's widow, is studied from this angle, and some shots in which this woman, often passive, and a Red Cross worker and later a psychiatrist, is seized by a fit of sudden satyriasis, are not easy to forget. In one of them, trippy and surreal, and at the same time expressionistic, Constance rhapsodically contemplates her genitals. In another, a high-ranking Catholic Nazi seduces a Polish maidservant in his mother's house, and seeks to unburden himself of his guilt by confessing to a priest who is a converted Jew. The journey of the novelist Blanford to Egypt, accompanying Prince Hassad, is a diversion to open a re-visitation, that of sensual and enchanting Egypt. The sentimental plot is bound to a political one because of the Nazi interest in Avignon and in the treasure of the Templars. This treasure may in fact represent the tangible myth of a blood revolution for the German people, the same one announced by Wagner and Nietzsche, that is, an instrument of consent. Livia, on the payroll of the Nazis, as soon as her sister has seen her again, commits suicide. Constance is increasingly vaginocentric, and another eminently graphic scene that lingers in the memory shows her after a bath dozing off with a towel wrapping her wet hair and awakening with the menstrual blood that has gushed over her feet to form a puddle. This scene unleashes a forward-looking parallelism, which is at the same time chiastic, with one in the next novel where her lover Affad lies stabbed between some bloodied sheets. Affad, a second Egyptian who for a trivial reason[38] finds himself in Europe under the name of Sebastian, proclaims the gospel of scientific, absolute, or phallic, sex, attributing the drifting of the west to impure semen. This epilogue sounds like a deliberate, and therefore mocking parody, of Lawrence's phallocentrism: Sebastian is not Mellors, but Constance is called by the same diminutive, Connie, as Lady Chatterley.[39]

38   A side story follows the therapy of the autistic son of Affad, entrusted to Constance's effective care in Geneva.

39   Witty similarities with another Constance, from Hitchcock's 1945 film *Spellbound*, are noted by MacNiven 1998, 643.

5. *Sebastian: or, Ruling Passions* (1983) explains the background of the love that has blossomed between Affad, the Alexandrian banker, and the Red Cross doctor Constance. Affad has transgressed the commandment of chastity to which his membership of the secret society of gnostics binds him, and the pivot of the story is a letter, never delivered, warning him that it is his turn to die. He leaves for Egypt to announce his resignation from the sect, and in the clinic in Geneva the letter is passed from hand to hand until it ends up in those of a paranoid Egyptian patient. This man one day takes possession of two knives, kills a nurse, and escapes disguised as a nun. The fugitive is the fatal, unconscious arm of gnosis that eliminates the affiliate chosen for death. He is unaware of the misunderstanding, since he wanted to kill his doctor, and instead stabs the lover who has just returned to her. In reality, the story only works because of a spicy detail that happens to be incidental, that is, a sexual stunt, or an exploit of a grotesque and blasphemous Sadian perversion involving a British diplomat. *Quinx: Or, The Ripper's Tale*[40] (1985) has a disjointed plot and marks time; it is also frequently muddled by the insipid and ostentatious inclusion of verses and aphorisms that alternate with more extensive narrative moments. The company of survivors from the previous novels meets in Provence to take part in a procession or festival, mixing religion and paganism, of gypsies who venerate 'Saint Sara'. On this occasion, the strange and hybrid gypsy Sabine reappears; the daughter of an English lord, she speaks perfect Cambridge English. A German general being treated in Avignon reveals the actual or legendary existence of a buried Templar treasure guarded by dragons or dragoons. Not even the search for the treasure, whose preparations are narrated at length, is an exciting episode; and in the end, when everything is ready, the curtain falls at the moment of greatest expectancy, closing the novel, and the entire cycle, on a suspension.

40   Literally 'the five points of the die, or the tale of the ripper', if 'quinx', a headword not recorded by the OED, is an abbreviation of 'quincunx'. The Latin term, which applied to the legal domain (five ounces or parts of an inheritance) and horticulture (the disposition of trees or poles, planted following the five points of the side of the die), refers here to the arrangement of the caves where the Templars' treasure is hidden.

§ 68. *Minor novelists between the two world wars*

The few novels of Rosamond Lehmann (1901–1990), with respect to her long life,[1] have as their inspirational centre the immaturity of feminine souls that are virtually orphaned. They metamorphose and vary their author's autobiography, also reflecting her later conjugal unhappiness in a double perspective – objective, and 'subjective', of other little girls who are actually the author herself, who refracts herself and spies on her parents. There is no escape from an affective nihilism raised to a cosmic and metaphysical dimension.[2] Lehmann's first novel, *Dusty Answer*[3] (1927), which enjoyed a huge *succès de scandale*, presents echoes, premonitions, and motifs common to the fiction of the time in a practically limitless number. All of them belong to the female macrotext that includes the best novels of Virginia Woolf and the equally recent works by Bowen and Mansfield, and in the last analysis the entire tradition of the novel of pubertal unease, rooted in the oeuvres of Gaskell, the Brontë sisters and a host of female novelists since Harriet Martineau.[4] By definition, *Dusty Answer*

1   The daughter of an American woman, and a Liberal MP, the editor for a certain time of *The Daily News*, Rosamond, whom certain scholars and critics still persist in calling Rosamund, was the sister of the established critic John Lehmann, and she had a sister who was an actress. Having studied at Girton College Cambridge when there were still very few women at university, she married a viscount and lived with him in Newcastle, divorcing in 1927; a second marriage was equally unhappy and ended when her husband, an artist, died in the Spanish Civil War. Very beautiful and alluring, she had a quantity of affairs, all unlucky, among which one with Cecil Day Lewis (§ 20.1 n. 24).

2   *The Ballad and the Source* (1944), which some compare to James's *What Maisie Knew*, is the story of a failed marriage from the point of view of the daughter. Its fragmented diegesis mirrors the social and emotional background. Of her other novels, in all not more than six, *The Echoing Grove* (1953) focuses on two sisters who argue over the same man, the husband of one and the lover of the other.

3   A title taken from a poem by Meredith, it points to a symptomatic need for new and exciting answers expected from life, instead of jaded ones.

4   The surname of the main character is Earle, recalling Marian Erle from *Aurora Leigh* by Elizabeth Barrett Browning (Volume 4, § 71.2), pure at first and then perfidiously corrupted before being finally saved. This intertextuality is reinforced by numerous echoes in the work, which show how well read the writer was. The influences are,

cannot but be a novel of the lost and ephemeral Eden of childhood, and even before opening the book the reader wonders what the novelist will invent that is new and not already seen. The comparison is predictably at her disadvantage. In the best part of the novel, the initial one, a little saga of childhood passions takes shape. These are passions that are raging but are discreetly masked; they are the unexpressed throbs of misinterpreted advances, of affective envies and violence. The war destroys the idyll and brutally scythes away the people and the blossoming affections, as in *To the Lighthouse*. However, Lehmann only rarely manages to portray directly this mute climate of *Sehnsucht* and alienation, and the intimate sense of occasions that inexorably escape. Often, she must and can only say this. 'Nothing memorable was said or done': herein lies the danger of a certain fictional rut that she never avoids, so that one cannot but underline once again, and lament, a chronic lack of narrative intensity. The female novel always shows the greater sensitivity of women and the insensitivity of males. Judith is yearning, but those whom she loves – all her cousins in turn – do not love her back and do not even notice her for the most varied of reasons: one dies in the war, one is refused, one seeks in her only a lover, and a fourth one she likes is homosexual. The second, less lively part reflects the author's university years at Cambridge, where heterosexual affairs are paired with lesbian ones – the only ones, as in Woolf's *Mrs Dalloway*, that are genuine and truly fulfilling.

2. It is undisputed and immediately evident that with Nancy Mitford (1904–1973) we face a writer who did not instil into her work a personal, lacerated and spasmodic existentialism that she barely managed to dominate. She is, on the contrary, a writer who steers clear of empathetic female writing and of the exploration of personal unease, and leans towards a classical, objective, firm and clear narrative art. A symptomatic passion for all things French meant that she learnt the language early on her own; apart from anything else, the family bedrock was eccentric and well-stocked, since, of her five sisters, daughters of a lord, one became a communist, another married

---

however, regulated by a species of *do ut des*, and the idea of a morbidly close-knit community of children, their dispersion and reunion over time, was to be reused by Virginia Woolf four years later in *The Waves*.

the fascist leader Mosley, and a third became a fan of Hitler. After emigrating
to France, Mitford worked as the Paris correspondent for the *Sunday Times*,
and as an eclectic writer and woman of letters wrote some biographies of the
great ladies of eighteenth-century Paris and of historical crowned figures;
she also translated French classics and adapted others for the theatre. As a
novelist, she revealed herself in the 1930s with flippant farces which, without
authorial interferences or moralizing, spoke eloquently of the whirl of high
society, reproducing into an open microphone the inflections, the discursive
marks and even the content of a *forma mentis* that was not excessively broad.
In other words, she painted the philistinism of the right-wing aristocracy
who had built their affluence in the imperial administration of India, and
self-parodied themselves with their anachronisms and complacencies. *Love
in a Cold Climate* (1949), a title apparently and deceptively Bowenish, is
Mitford's best-known novel. It is almost the sole surviving work of a large
production, and it is still mentioned today from time to time. It can be classified at first glance as an update of Disraeli's silver fork novels transposed
to the London of Mitford's times. It is therefore, at the same time, a late
and parallel version of the swirling of the 'bright young things' brought on
stage by Huxley, early Waugh and early Powell. Accordingly, its setting is
the smart neighbourhoods of London, and its static key scene is the party,
where the upper middle class and the aristocracy give themselves up to
chatter, persiflage, and verbal fencing. Mitford's constructive device is the
overused one of the first-person voice of a witness – Fanny, a relative – who
shadows the main character Polly and tells her story. This narrative strategy
reduces empathetic closeness, as well authorial interference, to a minimum.
There is therefore a displacement of psychological weights at work, since
the life of the witness, Fanny, is utterly smooth, flat, faded, channelled as it
is into the furrows of the tranquil ménage (marriage with an Oxford professor; the far from luxurious life of the depression years; offspring). Time
itself is left rather vague, and its computation entrusted to small, incidental
internal lapses.[5] *Love in a Cold Climate* is about a dominating mother, Lady

5   The time frame is presumably the first thirty years, and one of the clues are the
     novels of Virginia Woolf. An unravelling of the crass philistine nobility, supremely
     uncultivated, yet presumptuous, comes, for example, from a delicious page where

Montdore, who wants to force her daughter Polly into a marriage about which she has misgivings, and for which she is still not ready. This is the nineteenth-century reprise of the theme of the debut of the barely adult woman in high society to attract good matches. The paradoxical aspect is that no one proposes to Polly, despite all her simple and sober beauty, and her hand is asked for, provoking maternal ire, by an older widower who has a reputation as a dissolute with ambitions as a writer, which means that her marriage is on the miserable and grey side.[6] The novel ends with Polly becoming a mature and temperamental lady, who falls at the feet of an amateur aesthete whose nineteenth-century Dickensian linguistic tics and insubstantial vacuity are well captured by Mitford.

3. The biography of Rebecca West (1892–1983) is an odyssey, a bustling Victorian or late nineteenth-century *feuilleton* thanks to the daring exploits of its main character, ever stubborn, combative, unyielding in the face of bad luck and the numerous flipsides and hardships that persecuted her, though capable of always falling on her feet. West's mother was a pianist of Scottish origins, and Rebecca was educated in Scotland when her father, an Anglo-Irish journalist, died in 1908 after leaving the family and living for years alone and impoverished. Tuberculosis and poverty prevented Rebecca from continuing her studies, but not from moving to London to attend a drama school and join the suffragette movement. She gave the first tangible demonstration of her temper when Cicely Isabel Fairfield, her real name, rechristened herself as Rebecca West in homage to Ibsen, shortly after Joyce and many other young writers had become infatuated with the playwright, a universal and distinctive emblem of progressivism *par excellence*. From her promiscuous love affairs, genuine or alleged, was born a son certainly of Wells (Anthony West, who,

---

Lady Montdore, mother of Polly the debutante, says candidly that she does not know Virginia Woolf, and after having inferred that an intellectual should also, who knows why, speak of 'station managers', borrows a copy of *Mrs Dalloway*. However, she finds this novel boring, still preferring books on the British Administration in India and on the outdoor and drawing-room antics of the nobles.

6   In itself, the plot is also tenuously reminiscent of *Moths* by Ouida, which is cheesier and sloppier certainly, but with considerable scenic peaks.

the fruit of that union, was predictably to write an autobiography that was far from tender towards his mother, since he bore a surname that made him a 'nobody's child' in one way or another). From this summary overview, it is clear that Rebecca West began and enjoyed fame up until the war, and even afterwards, first and foremost as an intellectual who was, as the saying goes, 'inconvenient', a reporter and a journalist. Defining her as one of the first women globetrotters is no exaggeration. The magazines contended for her sharp pen as a reviewer and her travel columns and books – she wrote a highly successful one on Yugoslavia,[7] which she prophetically considered the focal and nerve centre of Europe – and her regular articles on mores and of protest became popular and proverbial on both sides of the Atlantic, especially in America. Thanks to the earnings these brought in, but also because she had married a banker, West led a life of luxury and showiness. But her ideas were radical, and flared whenever minorities were trampled on and justice overthrown, or the powerful resorted to violence. Her feminism was unprejudiced and therefore always unpredictable, her socialism dissident and therefore partly Orwellian, and with time even erratic; to the point that she did not deny her support to Mrs Thatcher's regime. Equally oblique and eclectic, and always doggedly re-discussed, was her religious faith. In certain respects West resembles Muriel Spark. She died at ninety, pen in hand, still editing, reviewing, transposing, planning, in full possession of her mental faculties. Coming to the pure fiction writer, we need to go very far back to her debut with *The Return of the Soldier* (1918), on the classic theme, which would later become overused, of the shell-shocked veteran. In the grip of total amnesia, West's returnee romantically recalls only the female worker whom, before marrying, he had loved but could not marry out of class prejudice. After recovering his memory, he returns to the front but having fatally 'forgotten' the woman who passionately loved and took care of him.[8] This novel was followed, with

7   *Black Lamb and Grey Falcon* (1941).

8   For more than evident reasons, six years later this story inspired Virginia Woolf to create Septimus Warren Smith in *Mrs Dalloway*. The title is also a veiled wink at Ford Madox Ford, even if it was in the saga of Tietjens that Ford had basically dealt with the same theme. The title, among many other reminiscences, also alludes to Hardy and *The Return of the Native*, and even the plot is vaguely Hardyan.

a bland irregular rhythm, by others above all focusing on exceptional feisty women like West herself, who vent their aggressiveness against male prejudice. To find one that makes an impression we must skip to *The Fountain Overflows* (1957), a composite tapestry of the condition of the nation at the beginning of the twentieth century, filtered through the vicissitudes of a family of London intellectuals out of step with the times – exactly the same story as that of the early years of the Fairfield family. This was the first act of a saga that continued in two further novels. *The Birds Fall Down* (1966), on the ideological conflicts of pre-revolutionary Russia, was so up-to-the-minute and appreciated in her time as to prompt from some the clearly disproportionate judgement on it as one of the most stimulating novels of the last half a century.

4. The perverse, immoral and 'diabolic' children, as was said later, captured by pirates in the sprightly *A High Wind in Jamaica* (1929) by Richard Hughes (1900–1976) were to inspire, twenty-five years later, the better known and more fortunate *Lord of the Flies* by William Golding, who from it took the destruction of the myth of childhood and pre-lapsarian innocence. In Golding's novel the female component was to be totally lacking, while in Hughes's novel an Emily, the female of five English siblings of settlers in Jamaica in 1860, appeared to Praz as 'the first literary hint of Lolita' of Nabokov.[9] Hughes had started very young at Oxford with an attack on Waugh's brother in the columns of the *Spectator*; with Graves he had edited the magazine *Oxford Poetry*, and written and staged a one-act play that was the very first to be expressly produced for the radio (1924). He became a friend of Dylan Thomas and lived with him in a castle in Laugharne that he owned, being a descendant of a rich Welsh family. He enlisted in the navy but served on land, and on the return of peacetime he began to write again with leaden feet and with incubation periods of more than ten years

---

9   PSL, 705. Here and in CLA, vol. I, 261–6, Praz contrasts with it the conventional Bernardin de Saint-Pierre. In turn, ATD, 58–9, focuses on the 'trippy' and estranged quality of the story (which makes the pirates the children's prisoners and therefore transforms the children into pirates), as well as on the unsettling nature of some scenes, though conducted with the cool aseptic gaze of the entomologist and naturalist, like that of the new-born crocodile kept as a mascot by a girl, and which slips into her nightdress, 'cool and rough against her skin'.

for each single work, due to spasmodic perfectionism. After a second novel with a marine setting, including storms and a mutiny, he too conceived the idea of a saga in three parts, a formula that was now for many fiction writers a sort of Ninth Symphony temptation for musicians, and would *ipso facto* immortalize whomever wrote one. It proved to be a stimulating suggestion in his case, designed as it was as a summary of the last thirty years closed by the war, but by placing history, and the great protagonists appearing with their real names, within an inventive frame. Of this ambitious project, whose general title, translated into the French of the existentialists, sounds like '*la condition humaine*', Hughes completed the first act, *The Fox in the Attic*[10] (1961), and the second, already less convincing, *The Wooden Shepherdess* (1973), leaving a few fragments of the third. The hero, Augustine, a landowner and recent Oxford graduate and therefore a double of the real author, enters the scene in 1923 carrying on his shoulder a dead baby girl. Suspected by the Welsh community of being her murderer, he emigrates to a German castle belonging to relatives, where the feudal past coexists with the first germs of impending failure. Here he falls in love with a cousin, Mitzi, who is not only blind, but naïvely and delightfully mystical, and is a witness of the failed Munich putsch in 1923, headed by a rampant Hitler. Some flashes reveal the thoroughbred writer, the exquisite craftsman capable of eking out words and the 'black' humorist.[11] On its appearance, *The Fox in the Attic* sparked off the enthusiasm of the authoritative critics and a sense of expectation, and it was said that it signalled the resurrection of the 'great British novel of the 1960s'. However, the next one intensifies the somewhat naïve passivity of the hero[12] and tosses him into a series of

10   A fine pun, since in the German part of the novel a German soldier called Wolff is wanted for a murder, so that a wolf literally hides in an attic.

11   It seems to me that Hughes's novels owe a certain, witty debt to Kafka: the opening is reminiscent of *Der Prozess*, with Augustine who is innocent and unjustly and passively accused; the German section takes place in part in a *Schloss*, where there is also a grotesque Kafkaesque creature, his cousin Mitzi.

12   He is an expressly aristocratic hero and one of aristocratic lineage, whose frequent physical handicaps probably conceal a symbol of the powerlessness of national aristocracy against the establishment of dictatorships (cf. in this connection the short profile of Hughes by M. D'Amico, in CAB, vol. I, 725–33).

imaginary experiences that are more blurred, although, or perhaps because, they are more sensational.

5. With the amazing ease of a clone of Wells, and an innate nonchalance that came to him from a family of theatre actors, the Englishman with Scottish ascendants, Compton Mackenzie (1883–1972), accumulated in the sixty years of his career a set of fiction works and other literature of immense proportions – he is said to be the author of a good hundred books – whose individual titles aroused enormous enthusiasm and were immediately rewarded by huge success and colossal sales. It was, however, a fleeting fame fading almost immediately, though it was refreshed by every new exploit. Since Mackenzie's peers are all dead, his name does not say much today to the common reader, and he, in bygone times an unalienable presence in the literary establishment, is by now almost 'extra-canonical'.[13] I mention him here as a recordman of popular and escapist literature. A partial exception can be made for his first novel which gained notoriety, *Sinister Street* (1913–1914, in two volumes with a total of 900 pages), belonging to the timeless educational and scholastic genre, which places the maturation of the hero at Oxford University and exploits that ever spicy seasoning of an attempted conversion to Catholicism. The novel had the good fortune of being praised by Ford Madox Ford and Henry James.[14] There was however an almost immediate suspicion that this ease and fluency might lie this side of the boundary of the paraliterary; Virginia Woolf was absolutely convinced of this. Nevertheless, there were cries of the miracle of a British Proust when the six volumes of *The Four Winds of Love*[15] (1937–1945) appeared. The five autobiographical volumes of Osbert Sitwell were exceeded quantitatively by the ten of Mackenzie's

---

13   A synchronic and paradigmatic quality well emphasized by WAR, 56, as well as by Orwell, who furtively read *Sinister Street* at St Cyprian, without knowing the meaning of the word 'Left' (OCE, vol. I, 400–1). For his merits the novelist was made a Baronet in 1952.

14   K. Young, *Compton Mackenzie*, London 1968, 6–7.

15   They follow the *alter ego* John Ogilvie in the first thirty years of the century. On the real differences, with respect to Proust, cf. Young's book quoted in n. 14, *Compton Mackenzie*, 21.

autobiography, completed only one year before his death, when he had recycled himself as a comic novelist with *Whisky Galore* (1947). By that time, his work had become polyhedral and frenetic in several spheres, some not exactly literary, but relating to practical and social life. He considered nothing Scottish *a se alienum*, and he was the exuberant promoter of the rebirth of Gaelic, Governor-General of the Royal Stuart Society (he was a fervent Jacobite, and a Catholic from 1914), and co-founder of the Scottish National Party. Because of his great love for his ancestral land he was buried on the Isle of Barra.

PART III

Poetry until the 1980s

§ 69. *Dylan Thomas* I: 'Shut in a tower of words'*
This definition – taken from the poem 'Especially When the October
Wind', and frequently echoed in his poetry and in his letters – seems to
postulate in Dylan Thomas (1914–1953) a complacent or painful passivity

*   *The Poems*, ed. D. Jones, London 1971, includes chronologically a good part of
Thomas's compositions which were excluded from the 1952 edition supervised by
the poet; the standard reference edition is now *Collected Poems*, ed. W. Davies and
R. Maud, London 1988. *Poet in the Making: The Notebooks of Dylan Thomas*, ed. R.
Maud, London 1968. *Letters to Vernon Watkins*, ed. V. Watkins, London 1957, and
Selected Letters of Dylan Thomas, ed. C. Fitzgibbon, London 1966, gathered together
in *Collected Letters of Dylan Thomas*, ed. P. Ferris, London 1985. Concordances: ed.
G. Lane, Metuchen, NJ 1976, and ed. J. M. and M. G. Farringdon, Oxford 1980.

    Life. J. Brinnin, *Dylan Thomas in America*, London 1956, 1971; C. Thomas,
Leftover Life to Kill, London 1957 (debunking biography by Thomas's wife); C.
Fitzgibbon, *The Life of Dylan Thomas*, London 1965, 1970; P. Ferris, *Dylan Thomas*,
London 1977 and, rev. and expanded, 2000; R. Gittins, *The Last Days of Dylan
Thomas*, London 1986; J. Fryer, *Dylan: The Nine Lives of Dylan Thomas*, London 1993;
A. Lycett, *Dylan Thomas: A New Life*, London 2003; W. Christie, *Dylan Thomas:
A Literary Life*, Houndmills 2014.

    Criticism. H. Treece, *Dylan Thomas: 'Dog Among the Fairies'*, London 1949;
E. Olson, *The Poetry of Dylan Thomas*, Chicago 1954; D. Stanford, *Dylan Thomas*,
London 1954; G. S. Fraser, *Dylan Thomas*, London 1957; *Dylan Thomas: The Legend
and the Poet*, ed. C. B. Cox, London 1960, also editor of *Dylan Thomas: A Collections
of Critical Essays*, Englewood Cliffs, NJ 1966; R. Sanesi, *Dylan Thomas*, Milano
1960; *Dylan Thomas: The Legend and the Poet*, ed. E. W. Tedlock, London 1960;
C. Emery, *The World of Dylan Thomas*, Coral Gables, FL 1962; W. Y. Tindall, *A
Reader's Guide* to Dylan Thomas, New York 1962 (by far the best and most useful
of the reader's guides); D. Holbrook, *Llareggub Revisited: Dylan Thomas and the
State of Modern Poetry*, London 1962, and *Dylan Thomas: The Code of Night*, London
1972; T. H. Jones, *Dylan Thomas*, Edinburgh 1963; H. H. Kleinman, *The Religious
Sonnets of Dylan Thomas: A Study in Imagery and Meaning*, Berkeley, CA 1963; R.
Maud, *Entrances to Dylan Thomas' Poetry*, Pittsburgh, PA 1963; J. Ackerman, *Dylan
Thomas: His Life and Work*, London 1964, 1996, and *A Dylan Thomas Companion:
Life, Poetry and Prose*, Basingstoke 1991; A. T. Davies, *Dylan: Druid of the Broken
Body*, London 1964; J. Korg, *Dylan Thomas*, New York 1965; V. Gentili, 'Il mondo rap-
preso di Dylan Thomas', *Paragone-Letteratura*, no. 202, 1966, 15–41; W. T. Moynihan,
The Craft and Art of Dylan Thomas, Ithaca, NY and London 1966; G. Capone, 'Il
sentimento del tempo nell'opera di Dylan Thomas', *Convivium*, no. 85, 1967, 430–64;

of a poetic 'I' possessed by the verbal demon. His work was hailed as a harbinger, indeed a portent, and as a foreshadowing of Lacan's theories of the
ego invaded by the unconscious, and an unconscious that is structured as

D. Cleverdon, *The Growth of Milk Wood*, London 1969; A. Pratt, *Dylan Thomas'*
Early Prose: A Study in Creative Mythology, Pittsburgh, PA 1970; R. K. Burdette,
The Saga of Prayer: The Poetry of Dylan Thomas, The Hague 1972; *Dylan Thomas:*
New Critical Essays, ed. W. Davies, London 1972; F. Binni, *Dylan Thomas*, Firenze
1973; F. Marucci, 'La fede capovolta di Dylan Thomas', *LET*, XXX (1975), 603–18,
Il senso interrotto. Autonomia e codificazione nella poesia di Dylan Thomas, Ravenna
1976, 'La materialità come salvezza nella poesia di Dylan Thomas', in *La materialità*
del testo. Ricerca interdisciplinare sulle pratiche significanti, Verona 1977, 206–31, and
'*A Host of Images*. Dylan Thomas e la tradizione neo-metafisica', in *Dylan Thomas*
a ottant'anni dalla nascita 1914–1994, quoted below, 25–37 (all of these are essays
that, whilst being children of their time, are not simply recycled here, but, rather,
are reworked and updated); A. Sinclair, *Dylan Thomas: Poet of his People*, London
1975, and *Dylan the Bard*, New York 1999; N. Fusini, 'Dylan Thomas: nel corpo della
poesia', *Strumenti critici*, no. 29 (February 1976), 126–45, and nos 32–3 (June 1977),
224–43; B. Gallo, *La metropoli dei pesci: la poesia di Dylan Thomas*, Bergamo 1976,
and *Linguaggio come pornotopia in Dylan Thomas*, Bergamo 1979 (introduction and
extensive anthology of Thomas's prose, wherein 'pornotopia' and sex are recognized
as 'central'); T. Kemeny, *La poesia di Dylan Thomas. Enucleazione della dinamica com-*
positiva, Milano 1976; R. B. Kershner, Jr, *Dylan Thomas*, Chicago 1976; R. S. Crivelli,
'Thomas/Sutherland: la forma e lo spino', in *Gli accordi paralleli: Letteratura e arti*
visive del Novecento, Pisa 1979, 303–44; R. L. Varshev, *The Poetry of Dylan Thomas: A*
Critical Study, Delhi 1983; W. Davies, *Dylan Thomas*, Milton Keynes 1986; B. Hardy,
Dylan Thomas's Poetic Language: The Stream That is Flowing Both Ways, Cardiff 1987,
and *Dylan Thomas: An Original Language*, Athens, GA 2000; G. Gaston, *Dylan*
Thomas: A Reference Guide, Boston, MA 1987; L. Peach, *The Prose Writings of Dylan*
Thomas, London 1988; *Dylan Thomas: Craft or Sullen Art*, ed. A. Bold, London and
New York 1990; G. Tremlett, *Dylan Thomas: In the Mercy of his Means*, London 1991;
G. Jones, *Background to Dylan Thomas and Other Explorations*, Oxford 1992; E. J.
McNees, 'Wounding Presence: The Sacrificial Poetry of Dylan Thomas', in *Eucharistic*
Poetry: The Search for Real Presence in John Donne, Gerard Manley Hopkins, Dylan
Thomas and Geoffrey Hill, Lewisburg, PA 1992, 110–46; *Dylan Thomas a ottant'anni*
dalla nascita 1914–1994, ed. L. Guerra and T. Kemeny, Udine 1994; J. A. Davies, *A*
Reference Companion to Dylan Thomas, Wesport, CT 1998; D. N. Thomas, *Dylan*
Thomas: A Farm, Two Mansions and a Bungalow, Bridgend 2000; E. Wardi, *Once*
Below a Time: Dylan Thomas, Julia Kristeva and Other Speaking Subjects, New York
2000; *Dylan Thomas*, ed. J. Goodby and C. Wigginton, New York 2001.

a language.[1] One can replace 'words' with 'images', and one has Thomas's famous definition of the genesis of poetry. Images, he said, emerged in him on their own and could only be tamed and governed with difficulty; and thus a self-generated chain began. The poet attended at their clash as an impotent witness: a constructive and destructive system, that is, a volcano expelling images which it then destroys.[2] 'I make one image', these are his exact words, but then correcting himself: 'although "make" is not the word, I let, perhaps, an image be "made" in me',[3] in a veritable state of passivity and systematizing paralysis. This definition should of course be taken with a pinch of salt, and the involuntary nature of the process is inevitably partial. The poet favours this self-proliferation, from which he claims to be excluded, with a judicious, indeed fervent, subsequent craft-work performed on the phonological, morphemic, lexical, prosodic, grammatical structures, and especially on the syntactic frames of the semantic field, imaginably gone haywire, of the images that he felt erupting in himself. The authorship, and the aesthetic responsibility for the final poetic product, are all the poet's own.[4] Once we have rectified the assertion of the alleged passivity of the self-generative nature of images, the fact remains that Thomas is clearly the most gifted and versatile poet-craftsman of pure words in the entire century. Joyce, his only rival, was mainly a prose writer. Behind Thomas only the seventeenth-century Metaphysical poets loom, with their connatural 'extended metaphor', a trope that was often applied – as also frequently in Thomas – to the indissoluble ontological nexus of

1   In another confession, Thomas called his poetry 'useful' to help him in a personal effort to emerge 'from the darkness towards some measure of light'. The images were mnestic materials that erupted from the unconscious, and his tension was in the deciphering and the explanation of the unconscious.
2   To Praz (PSI, 686) this seemed a metaphor for the musical creation. Immediately afterwards, Praz points to usual, arguable but also evocative similarities: with automatic writing, with Crashaw, with Swinburne's verbal orgies.
3   Cited in Treece 1949, 37.
4   If this is true, it undermines the hypothetical collusion of Thomas with surrealism (but see § 74.1).

life, or birth or sex, and death.[5] More precisely, Thomas is the magician of the associative chain of words along a semantic path: a magician, that is, of linguistic isotopies. However, his poetry is stereophonic – it moves on two levels, as he said in a poem, but two are too few – because only occasionally is a single semantic path formed, and more often two or more paths of intertwined images follow each other in his poems. Each poem is a continuous shifting from one to another system of images – a vortex from which double and multiple meanings, shades and allusions emerge strengthened. Such primacy has its counterpart: the extra-linguistic meaning decreases, it also shrinks drastically, and the attention of the poet is, and may be complacently drained by, the sheer play of words. Various poems by Thomas stand up for their prosodic acrobatics, for the pattern of their rhymes or for other formal devices; and it seems increasingly certain that only after devising such preconceived frames were they filled with content. This semantic reduction concerns each single poem and Thomas's poetry taken in toto. The stanzaic unit of measure, tyrannical in the first two collections, results in a chain of variations of an opposition or equivalence given in the first stanza, without there being a true outflow and a completed development of the meaning. In other terms, Thomas's word pursues linguistic absence, or areferentiality and hence self-referentiality, and explores and implements the 'thingness' and sheer physicality of language.[6] The literalness of the images predicated by Thomas is, on the one hand, one of his asymptotic, only partially true or even bewildering, assertions of poetics; on the other hand, it implies a systematic rejection of any reference of the word to extra-linguistic reality and thus to each and every kind of allegory and analogy, if not an archetypal one: the rejection, that is, of every type of message focused on public and social action, and on contingent reality. Let us turn, to confirm all this, to the often cited disagreement between him and Edith Sitwell, since it is rather revealing. It concerned a couple of lines in one of the ten sonnets of 'Altarwise by Owl-light': 'The atlas-eater

5   The question of influences, especially of that of the Metaphysicals, is amply discussed
      in Marucci 1994, to which I refer.
6   Fusini 1976 and 1977, Kemeny 1976, and Marucci 1976, converged on this phenom-
      enon, and on the 'suspended', 'deferred' and 'interrupted' sense.

with a jaw for news, / Bit out the mandrake with to-morrow's scream'. Sitwell had commented that the image referred to the 'violent speed and fanaticism of modern life, lover of sensations and of the horror'. Thomas retorted that Sitwell had not taken into account the literal meaning, and that only that should be intended, because there were no others to understand: poetry, for Thomas, was not a practice of public usefulness, and the poet remains 'irresponsible' if the metaphor of the tower means the classic withdrawal from social life and the concrete world of the living. If Thomas was locked in the babelish tower of words – if the cosmos appeared to him in phantasmagorias of sounds, morphemes, words, and images; if there was this verbal obsession in him, and if he described at the same time the genesis of language and its metamorphosis, separated from *realia*[7] – this was a poetics that already contained the germ of poetry's dissolution. At a given moment in his career, as will be seen, Thomas left the tower, his language became more referential, and he even reversed the relationship between *res* and *verba*.

2. *Collected Poems 1934–1952*, published in 1952, included eighty-nine poems plus a prologue, and Thomas may have been thinking before his death of other future compendia from which to expunge some poems. The enlarged 1988 edition includes 163 finished poems, plus two that have remained in a fragmentary state, and twenty-six *juvenilia*; the number of those that exceed 100 lines is scant. Thomas's poetry is complemented with various but not voluminous collections of critical essays and memoirs, with a short play for voices, an autobiography divided into individual self-contained chapters, other youthful stories and an unfinished novel. For different reasons, T. S. Eliot, Hopkins and Dylan Thomas at least share a slim, human-sized volume of verse in which we can, on becoming familiar with it, follow internal semantic developments, recurrent situations, the cross-references of the imagery: in a word, the transformational fields. One can even build a mnemonic concordance. We must then add that Thomas produced with a different speed compared to his contemporaries. He was

---

7   On the interpenetration and the unceasing metamorphosis of 'forms' in Thomas, see the acute observations of MPR, 199–200, which however increasingly recall Hopkins's Heraclitean 'bonfire of nature', rather than Rimbaud.

highly precocious, but quite soon he slowed down and began to experience the fatigue of writing (and he would frequently refer to poetry-writing as a metaphorical Calvary). He eventually got blocked and paralysed. The early poetry is chameleon-like since it is indebted to a quantity of mixed influences in a combination that sounded to contemporary readers as an alternative to the dry, guarded and oracular vein of Eliot. And it was not even close to that of Auden, who essentially worked on a single semantic field, that of the 'feud' and the 'enemy', and smacked more of tradition and the academy, while Thomas was not a university graduate. When he debuted there had been the recent revival of the Metaphysical poets, rediscovered by two new editions (1912, 1922) after a long period of oblivion, along with the appearance in print of the first and second editions of the poems of Hopkins (1918, 1930), and the new popularity of Blake's prophetic poems. Thomas began in the middle of the decade normally defined as that 'of Auden', which was also the decade of Eliot's later poetry, that of the *Four Quartets*. Auden was to remain without rivals until the natural closure of Thomas's career after nearly twenty years of poetic activity. Thomas may be thus defined as a third force of British poetry in those twenty years, even the first in terms of wide popularity and mythical status. His brief essay 'Welsh Poets' restricts the number of Welsh poets of the first magnitude to only six – five if we exclude the too-distant Vaughan. This estimate is, all things considered, still too generous, because only Edward Thomas, Alun Lewis and R. S. Thomas genuinely deserve a mention.[8] Thomas was not of course to Wales what Yeats was to Ireland or MacDiarmid to Scotland: a poet deserves this name without linguistic distinctions, says Thomas, and the Welsh poets he mentions made a name for themselves simply because they were great poets, not because they were great Welshmen. Some have tried to deny, or to judge an unconscious admission to the contrary, this proud and scarcely patriotic sense of not belonging, by pointing to Thomas's so-called, innate musicality, which was formed instead of its own accord and was an

---

8   Thomas forgot to mention Ronald Stuart Thomas who, one year older than him, gained the limelight too late, in 1956, for Thomas to speak of him. On this second Thomas, see § 101.

involuntary and passive legacy. For a short time, 'mimetic' Hopkins had become half a century earlier arguably more Welsh than Thomas, without being so from birth; the *cynghanedd*, or *hwyl*, engraved its deepest traces in Hopkins, and some of his poems were written in Welsh and signed with the appellative of Brân Maenefa. Not unlike Joyce, Thomas wanted to shake off his provinciality as soon as possible, as is proved by his escape from Swansea to London at the age of twenty, even though nostalgia later gained the upper hand, as it had in Joyce, in a thousand ways. The Welsh heritage emerges rather in Puritanical frames of mind assimilated *ab ovo* and surfacing constantly in echoes of the Bible, a reservoir of fabulous analogies even – and this happened very soon – when the substance of those stories was no longer credible for him. This residual Puritanism, or let us say Wesleyan Methodism, may be detected in its purely exterior aspect: in Thomas's declamations and prophetic utterances. The word 'rant' and the term 'ranter' are not used as metaphors in Thomas, and bring to mind the tradition of fanatical preachers who prophesied, often screaming and raving, in rural districts.

3. Starting from 1955, when Robert Graves offered a pound to anyone who knew how to explain a certain image from a poem by Thomas, the main academic critics were on the whole prudent and doused the blaze of enthusiasm. There were numerous defects in Thomas, they found, and the first was the meagreness and repetitiveness of his themes; the second, that meanings were reduced and atrophied, and went their own way, overwhelmed by a sheer interest in sound or rhythm or the chains of images. This hostility came especially from an established critical school, Leavis's group and the magazine *Scrutiny*. Immediately afterwards, Thomas became the number one target of another coterie in part spawned by Leavis, Conquest's Movement. The third stigma was the congestion of metaphors and images. Thomas was basically a reborn Hopkins with a series of Bridges at his heels, who reacted bewilderedly in the name of literary decorum and the classicism of taste and measure. An operation that would long fail or be incomplete, and was obstructed by Thomas himself, was the attempt to keep the legend that was all the rage, especially in America, separate from the poet, or to reconcile the poet and the legend. There was no way to stop deploring the fact that Thomas had become, or perhaps had always

been, a jester, a hammy entertainer, a third-rate *maudit*, or a braggart who nourished that legend with smug phrases, such as an all-too-familiar and repeated one: 'One: I am a Welshman; two: I am a drunkard; three: I am a lover of the human race, especially of women'. His main activity by the end of the 1940s had become that of the lecturer, or more exactly the showman with his podgy and quaint physique, who, well remunerated, recited poems, and not only his own, in theatres. During his fourth trip to America in 1953, he died from an attack of delirium tremens after a colossal binge. He had remained a child who never grew up and who suffered from an Oedipus complex, immature in his fantasies, as he was diagnosed by a hostile critic in no fewer than two books.[9] In Europe, however, over the years and in particular in the two decades following his death, there was a strange phase shift of interest. While Anglo-American criticism had devoted to him readings and interpretations of a traditional mould, abhorring any contamination of taste with formalistic taxonomies, in Italy the twenty years from 1960 to 1980 can well be said to have been those 'of Dylan Thomas', and reading and studying him became an academic *sine qua non*. There was no Italian Anglophile in the 1970s who did not tackle this ultra-modern poetry, and eager young beginners devoted themselves to him with unparalleled furore, conducting radiographic analyses down to the last material atom of his compositions. Thomas sprang forth on the horizon as a kind of divine gift offered to the most progressive literary criticism. With him, an unofficial but widely implicit axiom seemed to come true: that great literature, endowed with ontological primacy, unconsciously applies laws and mechanisms that critics later encode. Essentially, at least in Italy, Thomas was studied in depth in those years, and was on the ascendant, when in England his star had already waned and his greatness was slightly blurred or faded. These were essays and studies, even boldly factious ones, which wrote off the old authorities and paraded more or less appropriate quotations from new *maîtres*, the Russian and Prague formalists, Jakobson and Lacan, and the Parisian semiologists. But the need for reader's guides to Thomas, with slavish poem-by-poem comments, is not yet over. Aids of

9   Holbrook 1962 and 1972.

this kind take on an onerous, almost impossible task, because in Thomas everything is far from tallying and almost invariably a margin of the inexplicable remains inside his poems. At the opposite extreme, studies and short essays that aim to draw annotated illustrative maps of Thomas's cosmos have had a relatively easy task: easy because they discover and highlight incontrovertible internal paths, sketch transversal isotopies heedless of chronology, and, by putting texts of a different nature, and not always concordant, on the same plane, achieve a relatively plausible formulation, precisely because they cut out *ad hoc* portions of the poetic continuum leaving comfortably aside many other less amenable areas (and, additionally, never making an integral exegesis of a complete poetic text from top to bottom). Such are, and are often exaggeratedly commended, two essays by John Bayley and J. Hillis Miller.[10]

§ 70. *Dylan Thomas II: Hallucinations of genesis*

Thomas's poetic canon covers, as I mentioned, twenty years, and the first extant poems of the fourteen-year-old date back to 1930, while the last were completed in 1950. There is another collection that we can virtually call that of the 'twenty-five poems', and they are those written by the adolescent who was instinctively trying out his themes, including curiosity about death. This is immediately visible in a poem that was not his, however, since the female hand of the author is discovered in a story about a redeemed misanthrope who, shunned by all, fed a linnet, a fact that nobody knew. The poem is a small Biedermeier picture of village gossip and ostracism imposed on those who violate the laws of decorum. At the same time we witness in this early poetry Thomas's emerging propensity for veiled, dreaming, torpid landscapes immersed in an atmosphere of disorder, corruption or over-ripeness, typical of Swinburne or imitated from the dream-like poetry of an O'Shaughnessy. There are idylls exuding an oneiric, even more insistent and effusive, if not nauseous, sensuality,

---

10   The first is included in Cox 1966, the second contained in MPR. One of the later negative appraisals of Thomas came from T. Eagleton, *How to Read a Poem*, Oxford 2007, which does no more, however, than repeat the objections of the early detractors in a more sophisticated way.

and which show at work an intact Romantic myth of impalpability, unattainability, unquenched *Sehnsucht*. The poetic 'I', surrounded by soft and ill-defined landscapes, and assuming the pose of a languid, almost feminine poet, confesses tiredness, exhaustion, yearning. And yet, though in the absence of any rigid modular structure, a penchant for alliterative games begins to appear in words that are arranged in sound and associative chains. And sex? In 'My River', a phallic river fails to rub or smooth the stone, and this stone may refer to a woman who is feisty and prismatic. Here, we might assume, is the origin of Thomas's metaphor, or double-entendre, of 'rubbing', just as the waves of the river stand for the semen; the river looks ahead to Thomas's 'tides'. The woman is a simulacrum of frigidity and impenetrability, above all implacability: a woman who is 'fatale', humoral, subjugating and a touch Salome-like, who must be implored or otherwise violated. There is a poignant desire to reach a harmonious recovery after a laceration. But these youthful poems ultimately follow one another in the manner of a diary that is far too immediate. 'We Will Be Conscious' is surprising for its more prophetic nature, for its use of the royal 'we', for a more solemn and insistent awareness of the divinity and sacrality of poets and of the poet who is speaking, a vegetable and procreating poet, a plant with roots and branches, twigs and leaves, more precisely a pantheistic plant. Gradually on the increase is also the use of the already reversible religious adjective, referring, that is, to a pagan holiness and sacredness. A type of pagan baptism is officiated by a poet who is an *alter ego* of Christ, since a bird, not strictly a dove, descends from above and saws through the imprisoning roots and raises the poet in a lay Ascension.[11] 'The Rod Can Lift Its Twining Head' reiterates a challenge: scornful and satanic, the poet chooses the road of sin and damnation, and the Hopkinsian divine rod is a bearer of punishment and the phallic rod of a deified man who challenges death, which becomes a friend. The poetic 'I' is deified in a climate that is

11   This anticipates 'I Fellowed Sleep', in which the ascension to heaven has something
      distantly Rossettian and crepuscular. In the poem 'The Seed-At-Zero', from *Twenty-
      five Poems*, 'the rampart of the sky' recalls the 'bar of Heaven' and 'the rampart of
      God's house' in Rossetti's 'The Blessed Damozel'.

still Swinburnian; in fact, he is the rod, that is Christ the Saviour on the cross, and he is capable, like Christ, of achieving immortality.

2. Almost sixty further poems, slightly more mature, lay in handwritten form for several years after the poet's death before being made public. The boundary between the youthful poems and those seen as worthy of being included in Thomas's main corpus and therefore in the opening section of his expanded poetical book, is not so clear, neither in terms of dates that ensure and prove an acquired maturity, nor in terms of a greater definition of his themes and poetic world. Vice versa, a clear furrow separates the youthful poems, together with those written in 1930 and in the following months, and those in *Eighteen Poems*. Poem after poem, Thomas had written the contrary, or almost, of his mature poetry, spending his time in scarcely encrypted confessional verses with banal images of the squandering of vital forces, of Hamlet-like bitterness, erotic immaturity, sentimental failures, disappointments in love, and yearnings for an authenticity he did not achieve. The difference lies essentially in the fact that these poems are scarcely objectified and linguistically little formalized, or even melodramatic; in other terms, unshaped and written as if on the spur of the moment. In fact, they recall the classic beginnings of the Victorians – the notebooks and early poems of a Clough, an Arnold, or a Hopkins – who attended to an examination of conscience and found themselves lacking, lazy, limp, deficient in the commandments of duty, and would often blame themselves for sin and vice (which frequently alluded, in those typical Oxfordian poets, to homosexual love for their companions or to the carnal desire that possibly resulted in an encounter with a prostitute, or in onanism). Thomas transferred to the page, from the age of sixteen to twenty, this mood of interior failure, having perhaps lost his virginity and had his erotic initiation with prostitutes or undergone disappointments in love, and suffered bitter punishments for sentimental situations that never bloomed, or were misunderstood or had ended badly. In short, they are largely derivative poses. The leap in quality can be noticed when Thomas managed to distance this material, shifted it and put it into perspective, and started translating it into the 'host' of his images.

3. At the age of twenty-two, Dylan Thomas had basically already published half of his poetic canon excluding his early adolescent experiments,

and written what, in an overall assessment, amounts to his peak production and displays his most distinctive poetic trademark for posterity. Forty-three poems, mostly not longer than fifty-odd lines and in some cases even less, were distributed into two books at a distance of two years, in 1934 and in 1936. Thomas neutrally entitled the two collections *Eighteen Poems*[12] and *Twenty-Five Poems*. When all is said and done, why the international mobilization caused by the advent of Thomas? Linguistically and stylistically, the exploit of Hopkins's poetry was still in the air. Thomas's straining and distortion of poetic language rests on the phonological game, and hence on alliteration, musical sound-shaping, contrasts of phonemes; the lines have unequal syllabic length, the rhythm is irregular, the stanzaic measures varied and unusual. Syntax and even grammar are unorthodox, as shortly before Auden had done; while from Owen – another, almost bona fide Welshman – came encouragement not to work on full rhyme, but on an almost systematic recourse to pararhyme. From Hopkins, or inspired by Hopkins, Thomas imitated the creation of brand-new compounds; not only from Hopkins, but also from the anaphoric verses of the Bible, he learnt to use a marked stanzaic parallelism. In point of fact, parallelism is also and especially conceptual, semantic and thematic, hence representational and symbolic. With his first eighteen poems, Thomas built a compact universe of spasmodic terminological economy, presenting the obsessive recurrence of terms featuring a meaning that is essentially connotative, personal and private, and therefore an inimitable and patented idiolect. It is evident that the poet of *Eighteen Poems* had no possible need to vary the regularity of his formal and semantic patterns. Poem after poem hinges on semantic fields that are repeated and follow, mingle and intersect

12   Each of them, except one, is entitled with the words of the first line, apparently showing a lack of imagination, and following a habit that would become established. On the contrary, Thomas was a highly imaginative, born titler, as is clear from the prose sketch 'How to be a Poet', a satire of an acrid, fierce Swiftian flavour against the contemporary literary market. In it Thomas playfully invents dozens and dozens of curious and fashionable titles for poems and novels, as putative recipes for success among the public at large. This first collection of eighteen poems was published in the wake of a poetry award he had won, sponsored by the London magazine *Sunday Referee*.

with one another. The shock of this poetry, its strong and unexpected mark – which is why all great poetry appears as such on its appearance – is the annexation of terminological and semantic areas previously excluded. Few had written anatomical poetry before him, and – a fixation that seems that of a student just beginning in medicine – used terms such as seed, bone, marrow, nerves, or blood, the latter not in the sense of that spilt for noble goals and missions, but the actual fluid flowing in the veins, and pumped by the heart – save perhaps for the Metaphysical poets and Donne.[13] And nobody had used a private symbolism like his, although there is an evident debt to the Freudian interpretation of dreams and therefore a key that is also partially fixed. Italian structuralists of the 1970s may have been too hasty or drastic in declaring a reduction, or worse, an abolition of contents with respect to the pre-eminence of the signifiers. It is true, however, that Thomas succeeds in enriching signifieds and signifiers by moving, displacing more exactly, the words in the discursive chain, as if they were interchangeable pawns; a poem becomes a charade that alternates the same terms in ever new concatenations. These are also poems on the poet's visionary experiences, felt and communicated with marked solemnity. Another constant is the first person, with the cosmic and/or physiological occurrence invariably witnessed by an 'I'.[14]

13   The screenplay for *The Doctor and the Devils* (1953), derived, as late as this date, from an adolescent fascination with the morgue, which Thomas had often visited in Swansea during his apprenticeship as a news reporter. Based on the true story of a Scottish professor of anatomy in the early nineteenth century, who exploited for his research two body snatchers, it is therefore clearly inspired by the atmospheres of a tale by R. L. Stevenson (Volume 6, § 133.2).

14   The only exception seems to be the opening poem, 'I See the Boys of Summer', which, while displaying a good part of the collection of images, private symbols, and visual-conceptual oppositions, seems to be diagnostic of a widespread generational discontent and therefore a public malaise, with the poet who for some stanzas remains watching on the side-lines, but soon enters the fray, using the pronoun 'we', and includes himself among twenty-year-olds without a future in the 1930s. This poem established once and for all the female belly as a sea in which the waters are lifted and lowered in cyclical tides. It also inaugurates one of the symbols of male sperm as a pile of fruit, apples more precisely, by frequently having the archetypal memory of the Adamite pair hovering over each single sexual intercourse, and by

4. In a summary sense, Thomas describes the birth of life, and therefore the event of 'genesis' has a primary hierarchical significance. There is almost no poem in which Thomas does not describe the *fiat lux*. Consequently, each poem is an epic or saga of genesis, and being a saga, there is no paraphrasing, but transcription, re-imagining, rewriting, vision, which is why all or almost all the poems of *Eighteen Poems* could be entitled – as indeed two are – 'In the Beginning'[15] or 'I Dreamed my Genesis'.[16] This epic of the origins is more Blakean than Miltonic, because the frequent scenes of genesis, or of a genesis, are and are not literal and orthodox; rather, they are alternative geneses, myths, legends, reconstructions, analogies more precisely, with the material of the Bible enriched by kabbalistic elements drawn from other cosmologies, and from esoteric and occult texts with which Thomas was familiar, and which he compresses into his crucible without prior warning.[17] The biblical Genesis created man in a timeless dimension, and sin caused the Fall from Eden, and, to use Eliot's dictum,

---

adumbrating in every man an Adam. The strong analogical value of the biblical and evangelical stories may be seen from these data. At the same time, in 'I See the Boys of Summer' the generational sterility covers the sexual event without conception, the erotic experience devoid of procreative love and therefore a waste of seed, with the echo of the parable of the good sower in the background. Even when the seed is fruitful, the birth will return to the world a condemned and shabby humanity. A vein of pessimism has the upper hand in the dialectic of the three parts of the poem, on the faint or even stentorian encouragement to react. In the line 'I am the man your father was', Thomas exorcizes the threat of even poetic sterility, and here the father is the biographical one of the poet, a secondary-school teacher and a failed poet who had dreamed of having a poet son. 'Our Eunuch Dreams' closely echoes 'I See the Boys of Summer', with the poet still a member of a group of sterile boys, who only watch the love of cinema actors, and are called upon to awake from a lethargy that is not only that of the senses, but also a political one.

15   Precisely echoing the Johannine prologue, with an extended linguistic metaphor starting with 'in the beginning was the word'.

16   In some of its images this poem may even seem to allude to the now distant death of British servicemen in the war, with the explosive that jolts the heart and the mouth 'that ate gas'. However, the symbolic significance of the experience lies in the biblical word 'genesis', which is not a simple 'birth'.

17   Cf. the opposing opinions of Olson 1954, 8, and Tindall 1962, 12.

made historical time enter into timelessness or eternity. Life became subject to time, and for mankind time marks the end, save for the salvation consisting in his return, as a pure material element, to the vegetal kingdom and to its cycle. Therefore Thomas always describes a genesis that is interrupted or thwarted by sin; he describes a humanity without time, an Adam in bliss, but also a fallen man. The pre-lapsarian man could almost be a demigod. And anyway, Christ became a man. Mankind is – potentially, in a dream, or nostalgically – a demiurge. By virtue of this analogy, it shares or might share a creative power. Mankind and Thomas the man are a Christ and a christ, which to Thomas also means a phallus, that is, a crucified Christ and also a fertilizer. The forces of negation and destruction cannot ultimately get the better of the ephemeral or dreamed-of ones, those of an unceasing metamorphic creativity, even if the results of the struggle are each time at least oscillating.[18] The female belly is emptied after birth and becomes dry, but optimistically it will again become wet and fertilized; but sometimes not. However, beyond the principle of reality, mankind imitates God and feels a god while creating.[19] Thomas is surprised in the face of the event of the Incarnation, which is as much a theological concept as an anatomical fact. His geneses are also the union of bodies, the seeding of the womb, the conception of the foetus, the blessed Adamitic existence of the foetus

18   'The Force that through the Green Fuse Drives the Flower' is a well-known founding poem. It consists not exactly of a host of images – others will be more twisted and impenetrable – but exhibits a crystalline, strictly isocolic, syntactic and stanzaic structuring, inaugurating an anaphoric regularity and a texture of symmetrical parallelisms which are only violated in the two final stanzas. As a prolepsis of his themes, Thomas introduces time and the subjection that it imposes on history, mankind and the poetic 'I' itself. The human being is already 'green', that is, living and pulsating, and at the same time dying. It may seem that Thomas is exalting the perfect balance between creative and destructive vectors, but he especially stresses the latter. The condition of being dumb and of the impossibility to speak of the common destiny of destruction that grips man and nature, means to have lost one's voice yelling it. While the poet posits that man and nature are one, he still cannot glimpse the possible platonic salvation represented by the re-absorption of the human dissolved in nature, with a metamorphosis that ensures a form, the only form, of immortality.

19   Man is a 'double', that is, a duplication of the Father, at the beginning of 'My World Is Pyramid'.

swimming in the mother's womb, and its expulsion from it. Owing to this oscillation, human semen may be wasted, without reaching the target, while creating also means consecrating the creature to death and destruction, if the seed, as in the Gospel parable, does not germinate or is wasted by onanism or contraception.[20] In Thomas's conceptual and symbolic geography, to create is also, and especially, to compose poetry. The creative phallus is a christ, if Christ is a Trinitarian entity, and the Son is equal to the Father; but the phallus is also the pen or the hand that creates and writes, and thus poetizing mimics Christ's excruciating 'passage' in Galilee.[21]

5. *Twenty-Five Poems* does not properly mark a subsequent poetic phase, but is rather a complementary one, and, while including poems certainly written after 1934, and along the same lines as the previous ones, it adds several others which had been planned long before. The resulting collection is no doubt more discontinuous, more varied, more heterogeneous than the former, and its constituent poems uneven. Its two distinct compositional manners will be pursued in parallel for some time. Thomas is found intent on counterbalancing a vein that had begun to denote – and by now cause – signs of fatigue – in the repetitive and occluded turgidity of the same recurring images, and in the use of references to the most disparate and confused sources, resulting here in poems, if possible, even more hermetic and intricate than the average. This vein is countered, however, by slightly more direct, better honed and terser poems, placed outside the obsessive anatomical aegis and the imaginations of genesis. Certain others, decidedly mediocre, had evidently dodged that test which, as I mentioned, led to the exclusion of some poems from *Eighteen Poems*.[22] The further poetry of origins now

20   Threats of a feared impotence, and hopes therefore of a demiurgic sexual potency, which keeps the sense of sin at bay and makes men divine, Promethean challengers emerge in 'If I Were Tickled by the Rub of Love'. In Thomas, the conflict is often that between time that wears out, and turns off sexual desire and castrates, and the leaping, never torpid, phallus.

21   A combination of the crucified Christ, of the erect phallus searching as in a mock-heroic quest for the female orifice, and of the pen that writes down the poet's frustration, is the 'hero' of 'My Hero Bares His Nerves'.

22   'The Hand that Signed the Paper', a parable on tyranny cloaked in democracy, is, for instance, almost a one-off poem. The ending of 'Should Lanterns Shine' is in turn

undoubtedly registers a small turn of the screw: the parable of Christ born, dying and resurrected is and is not analogic at the same time, and examined in its real and literal salvific pledge it fails, in Thomas's imagination, to win the struggle with Time the destroyer. The 'luck' of mankind is the 'natural danger', a providential danger if it means a re-inclusion, with death, in the natural cycle.[23] The stentorian 'And Death Shall Have No Dominion' overturns one consolation – death as the reconstitution of the material, vegetal and cosmological unity of life – into a triumphal hymn. 'This Bread I Break' may be counted among the forecasts of a Thomas who imitates and almost achieves the sober and austere simplicity of a George Herbert, while differing altogether from his predecessor's message. We would expect in this poem that the breaking of bread and the consumption of wine should point to the Eucharist; instead, the continuity Thomas envisages, this side of a transcendent perspective, is only that of the purely biological cycle. Moreover, Christ is hazily depicted in this poem as an antagonist, since the destruction of the grain and the grape to obtain flour and Eucharistic wine is a violation of the joyful integrity of nature and of the very unison between man and nature. The theme of the impenetrable poem 'Today, This Insect'[24] just seems to be the assumption of the fabulous and therefore incredible character of the promise of salvation contained in the biblical story of Eden and the entire Bible; while 'Then Was My Neophyte'[25] resists until the last the prompting of the 'green myths' of Christ. The greeting echoed shortly before – to phallic, rapacious procreative capacity – combines by repercussion with the dysphoric prospect that copulating is like a 'hop in the dust'.[26] The series of ten interlocked sonnets, 'Altarwise by

----

an objective correlative that is almost *naïf*, about a ball thrown into the air and that has still not come down.

23	See 'I, in My Intricate Image'.

24	A monstrous, serpentine insect that is an image of Satan.

25	Where it would otherwise be impossible to explain the capitalizing of the pronouns 'He' and 'His'.

26	'Now', denied by 'Grief Thief of Time', whose second stanza is perhaps Thomas's longest periphrasis of the phallus that penetrates the vagina, but is ultimately the bearer of death. The most hymnographic and vibrant poem on the creative force of 'light' in its various meanings is 'Foster the Light'.

Owl-light',[27] reprises the recurrent motif of the fertilization of the womb, the gestation of the foetus and the birth of the child, resorting to systems and clusters of metamorphically superimposed multiple images, and therefore assembling unstable semantic chains. The gestation period is depicted as a journey towards the death of an Adam and even of a second Adam who is Christ; both prefigure the future and every unborn child, whom Christ rubbing on the cradle seeks to attract, with the related, analogic and real image of the wound of the Cross and the Cross itself, which also stands for the pain of poetic composition.[28] Precisely for this reason, a few of the ten sonnets, such as the eighth, taken in isolation come close to a more vivid, effective, surreal, or even genuinely surrealistic ekphrasis. Thomas's usual symbolism is enriched by an isotopy formed by astrological references;[29] however, the ten sonnets end up repeating, with variations, the usual, imaginary, and chiastically invertible path: 'December's thorn screwed in a brow of holly'.

§ 71. *Dylan Thomas III: 'The Map of Love'*

The Map of Love (1939), which also has a mixed structure, does not mask a certain paralysis or greater difficulty for the poet, and thus it justifies the metaphor of the 'Cross of composing'. It in fact consists of just sixteen poems belonging to three different thematic groups. One delves

27 Interlinked, since each incorporates one or more of the terms from the previous one, and starts by elaborating it.

28 The most balanced, essential and equable poem on the theme is 'Lie Still, Sleep Becalmed', from the collection *Death and Entrances*, with the image of the incurable throat wrapped in a salted sheet which is also the shroud of death, and salted because the career of the poet is a journey to the 'end of the wound'.

29 Or even, as in the witty fifth sonnet on the recurrent theme of the Annunciation and Birth, in a card game, though weighed down in the last few lines by too many literary, biblical and anthropological references in order to describe the peregrinations of the new-born baby in the world of experience. The analysis of 'Altarwise' by Olson 1954, 63–89 – according to six symbolic, criss-crossing and interrelated 'levels', the last three of which are based on 'events of the sun' in terms of the adventures of the solar hero Hercules, seen also as a constellation – remains historic, despite many scholars discrediting it as more impenetrable, convoluted and abstruse than the obscurity it aims to shed light on.

into the copious notebook of 1930; one is more or less the bequest of the years 1934–1936, and the third, and this would be enough to speak of the impending threat, that of the post-1936 years. The result is a composite collection, irregular in its registers and lines, and transitional. 'How Shall My Animal' is a discussion of poetics, since the wild animal to be tamed is Eros but also Chaos, verbal and representational, to be painfully contracted in the poetic form. On the whole, the poems of *The Map of Love* still residually hinge on an organization by semantic fields and concentric representational frames, with blocked diegetic chains and amplifications of little account – variations, more than anything else, in stanza after stanza. The evident difference is that, for the first time, the occasional event breaks the impermeable boundary drawn by the poet around his imagination. He had 'elbowed out time' and the 'city spectacles', but now his radar records and picks up the historical story, the here and now. At least three poems are new, since they are in the form of an epicedium, and epicedia of some real departed who had existed in flesh and bone. Thomas, sensitive to the passing of people, stops in front of the tombstones. 'After the Funeral',[30] especially, is a bright spell on the horizon, indeed the first poem, or almost, in the canon, to be inspired by a recognizable external event, thus marking, in principle, the overturning of Thomas's early poetics of the 'tower of words'. From these poems came the thrust of the meditation on death, the pivot of the poems to come. The residual foetal poems or those on genesis operate on the thread of extended, complex, often also far-fetched reference schemes, like backdrops onto which moods are projected. They may suddenly shift to a declarative register with melodramatic, solemn and rhetorical pronouncements, even with a hint of romantic neo-Titanism.[31] In the first two poems in the collection, the sadness due to the temporary abandonment of a woman is described against the background of the biblical story of Lot, and then with a metaphor already used, of the Egyptian

---

30 This poem is once again metapoetic, since a hyperbole on Thomas's defunct aunt Ann is used but immediately rejected as a 'monstrous', that is, rhetorical image, even though the poet soon resumes the voice of 'Ann's bard'.

31 'Like an approaching wave, I sprawl to ruin' ('I Make This in a Warring Absence'). The woman is 'fatal' in her 'proud absence'.

mummy that miraculously rises from the pyramid to life. 'A Saint About To Fall' is yet another euphemism of a birth in the guise of the sacred and the sacrificial and of the incarnation and the Crucifixion,[32] but elongated by parenthetic hesitations, clusters of appositions, an excess of periphrases, or even leisurely word games. Thomas was slowly discarding the analogic value of religious paraphernalia, or was in the middle of the ford. When he gets to grips with religion and is forced into literal speech he shifts decidedly to the counter-attack. 'If My Head Hurt a Hair's Foot' is a surreal dialogue between a mother experiencing the pangs of childbirth and a foetus who, full of attention, takes care not to aggravate her pain, knowing that birth is a journey towards death, and wanting to continue to enjoy the warmth and comfort of his mother's womb. The obsession with genesis has, however, been exorcized by now, almost filed away, and the evolutionary stage now focused on is adolescence, youth or even adult life. Some poems voice a veiled confession of malaise, and even nostalgia for happier moments of life; the erotic relationship is alienated and alienating and the couple cannot find harmony and end up separating. Thomas's 'anger' is the harbinger of a literary movement that will be born, but without Thomas's support.

§ 72. *Dylan Thomas IV: Faith overturned*

It is difficult to unify the tendencies, the proposals and chords of the twenty-four poems of *Deaths and Entrances* (1946). At that moment, Thomas could not avoid speaking clearly, and out of collective responsibility, like all British writers who had been eyewitnesses to a London incinerated by German bombs and the massacre of war. The previously isolated and withdrawn poet trembles and recoils sincerely, though his most famous war elegy is centred on a grand denial or an almost fideistic paradox: Thomas declares, in a stentorian voice, that we must not cry and must not despair, and pity and tears are useless in front of the death of so many innocents, even children, burned to death. We must in fact only rejoice, singing an

---

32   Of course, in Thomas who always walks on two planes, the saint is also a holy man, and a holy Child who must 'be awakened' in the poet, and must also let off his time bomb in the lethargic city, just as the advent of Christ was explosive in Herod's time. And the 'saint', with this 'descent' from heaven, that is, fall, remedies the first Fall.

unwavering, virile hymn, mindful of the unceasing renewal of human flesh in nature, and that death leads to another or the only life that exists: 'after the first death there is no other'. Hence, to pray in the traditional sense of the word is even to blaspheme.[33] The residual difficult and obscure poems are by now even off-putting, organized as they are in long, convoluted and zigzagging periphrases and turns of phrases which, once paraphrased, reduce themselves to a disconcerting and rather trivial meaning; while others, characterized on the contrary by linguistic depletion down to an asymptotic zero degree, seem to be by another poet. In 'Poem in October', Thomas becomes persuasive, anonymous, conventional as never before, and a refined exploiter of a self-mythologizing narcissism. A typical poem for the average reader is 'The Hunchback in the Park', so anonymous even though captivating and attractive, about the park underdog duped by children. An oblique, extravagant anecdote, which is improbably discovered to be an allegory of the very gestation of a poem, is that of the new inmate in an insane asylum ('Love in the Asylum'). In another group of poems, Thomas wants to impress in the first place with prosodic exploits. 'The Conversation of Prayer'[34] is built on a chiastic scheme of rhymes and internal rhymes that mimics the chiasmus of the events, those of a child and an adult who utter two prayers having contrary results to probability, one being fulfilled and the other not. The extreme case is that of 'Vision and Prayer', an example of an attempted, desired, deeper link between the iconic shape of the stanzas in the two parts of the poem and the process and experience they describe. This is one of Thomas's three longest compositions to date, the other two being ballads in florid, lush and overflowing scenarios and a surreal narrative mode, therefore with only a minimum of narrated action with respect to the atmosphere they aim to build with an exhausting profusion of detail. 'The Conversation of Prayer' announces the semantic, conceptual and insistent play hereafter focusing on the term 'prayer'. The poems with religious themes are explicit in being irreligious,

---

33 Such is the sense of 'A Refusal to Mourn the Death, by Fire, of a Child in London', the noblest and most solemn counter-elegy on the Blitz.

34 According to what I am about to mention, this is a 'conversion', that is, a reversal or an intersection.

and one of them mocks the Word of the Saviour which is now spent, or repetitive, and similar to a mechanical nursery rhyme.[35] The true Church is the metamorphic crucible of nature and the shrine of the deceased of history, transformed and resurrected under other species. Thomas's Christ had historically come, and still comes, to put an end to atavistic paganism, to violate and force the man-nature unison, to abolish the absence of care and of conscience, and freedom. He coerces, chases, promises, but does not convince or conquer. This icon comes from far afield, from Swinburne and Pater, singers of paganism cut down by the Nazarene; it comes from Hopkins and Francis Thompson and their pursuing God, even depicted as a barking 'hound', a pursuer of the willy-nilly fugitive. This is the sense of Thomas's God, a God 'who finds' and has clutched his creature who wants to escape. Eliot had hoped that God the eternal would enter transient time; Thomas complains that he has not. This turnaround is studied in the recurrent motif of the 'child going to bed', a main role in various poems. In 'The Conversation of Prayer', as in 'Fern Hill', one night a boy discovers Eliot's expiration of the timeless and the advent of time, and therefore he, too, enters death's compass. He discovers death despite having prayed that life be preserved, while the adult discovers life after having feared the death of his beloved. Growing up, one leaves the childish Eden in Thomas, but with one crucial compensation: the entrance into the precisely secular salvation of 'death by fire', in itself Eliotian, but with a quite different perspective.

2. The poet that is jealous and yet in love imagines his wife's encounters with lovers in 'Into Her Lying Down Head', and in 'Unluckily for a Death' he entrusts himself to her and ask for her support, addressing her as a sensual saint and a renewing phoenix in expectation of the bonfire of his vanities. Both poems, especially the first, are repetitive versions of the desacralization and free evocativeness of the sacred. 'A Winter's Tale', the first of the said three long ballads, opens with the exorbitant touches and details of a purely pictorial backcloth, an enchanted, snowy winter landscape, against which there flares up the fire of passion of a 'contrite and solitary' man who is consumed in a morbid yearning, crowned by the descent of a woman in the form of a bird. The three long ballads are

35   'There Was a Saviour'.

lumped together by the overused mythologizing of the poet as a Romantic outcast redeemed by a woman saviour, thus weighing up deifying human love as an alternative to death.[36] 'Ballad of the Long-legged Bait' unfolds as a parody of Coleridge's 'Rime', of *Moby Dick* and of the Gospel parable of the prodigal son, but switches to the surreal when the angler casts his woman as bait to hungry fish. The woman is possessed by the marine fauna in a chaotic bacchanal, to symbolize the exorcizing of sex and a rite of purification of the demonic fisherman. Thomas ultimately differs from Coleridge without turning him upside-down; the miraculous fishing is a procession of deceased transformed into children who proclaim the eternal renewal of the cosmos, in a phantasmagoria that skilfully blends far too many biblical and evangelical reminiscences.

3. The figure formed by the stanzas in the first part of 'Vision and Prayer' represents a rhomboidal slit or a lozenge with easy anatomical allusiveness; that of the second, more sublime Herbert-style wings. The two figures, swapping places, herald the symbolic journey of the poem, first in ascent and then in descent, representing the most memorable enactment of the oscillation between the literal and symbolic registers in Thomas's canon, and an oscillation turned into a fable that takes place both in the delivery room and in the Bethlehem grotto. The 'wild' new-born is baptized by and in Johannine obscurity, but is at the same time the Child who by being born is already crowned with thorns, and being born is the bearer of the light that dispels darkness. This revolutionizing event in history disturbs the apparent calm of man and of the father spectator, whose reaction is, however, not to rush to the cradle but to flee, terrified, from it. The lost evangelical sheep is eventually found and taken back into the fold, and is rapturously caught in the motion of creation towards Ascension and Resurrection. Thomas ends the first part of 'Vision and Prayer' with an apparent, even flagrant contradiction of his system of thought. Not only does the slit not open a tunnel towards the centre of the earth: it is the springboard for a heavenly flight; however, physical death, announced in

36 With the positions reversed, and without the furious phallic impetus, the bird-woman falls to earth onto the man with the same colouristic and iconic details as Leda's swan in Yeats.

the last lozenge of this first part, is a resurrection and a life. It is a partial, momentary perspective, however, because the iconic shape of the stanzas in the second part, which suggests a flight – the dialectic antithesis is instantly strong, and diatonic – is actually an escape to the centre of the earth and away from that perspective; it is also, therefore, the most blasphemous of Thomas's inverted prayers. For a moment, the child is the real one, of the here and now, who it is hoped will return to his mother's womb, because being born means dying; but he returns to being ever more Christ whose salvific promise is refused. Such a blasphemous wish – to be able to remain in the land of the dead, the unsaved, which is on a human scale and is the heart's desire – is sealed with an 'Amen'. The surprise after the surprise is that the prospect is suddenly reopened, and the person praying is overwhelmed in his prayer and 'found', and proclaims himself defeated. The composition is then, in a way, reminiscent, in its final balance and dialectics, of Hopkins's 'terrible' sonnets.

4. 'Fern Hill' forms a diptych of twin compositions with 'In Country Sleep', and it heralds its assumption or acrobatic proposal. It describes the wandering around the farm of a boy child who 'rides' and rushes like the girl of the later ballad. In both cases, Thomas's time is Edenic and primordial, and therefore at a standstill; the child lives outside time and his colour within nature is proverbially green. Like the young girl of 'In Country Sleep', the child is not only green but also 'carefree'. Only by connecting together all Thomas's poems alluding to the coming and advent of Christ can we associate this harmless adjective with the absence of scruples of conscience in the pagan age: the carefree childhood is a remote and veiled metaphor for it. However, this association becomes explicit when, much more fleetingly than in 'In Country Sleep', nature takes on sacral values, but sacral once again in an inverted, that is pagan sense (the 'Sabbath', for instance, resounds slowly among the pebbles of 'holy' streams). After the daytime jaunts, the child wearily lies down to his nocturnal rest, and falls asleep under threat. In this case, a first false alarm is thwarted: the fateful and symbolic moment is delayed, and the harmless owls mimic and simulate the theft of the farm, seeing that the following day, upon awakening, the farm is still there. And the timeless childish Eden is still intact. The strong link between 'Fern Hill' and 'In Country Sleep' rests on the Edenic and pagan sacredness, in

the absence of Christ or even of original sin, of this happiness. Like Eliot in his first quartet, Thomas evokes a 'first [...] place' that is analogous to Eden. However, in Thomas, this is an Eden that is still more analogic. Just as, in 'In Country Sleep', he says that before that fateful night the girl child was 'in grace', so the end of innocence and infantile unawareness coincides with a state 'out of grace'.[37] The semantic inversion is repeated, and 'in grace' means, for Thomas, out of grace, and vice versa. But for the children of the two poems, the end of that time is looming inexorably. Time personified is a thief committing a theft, and the theft of that farm and that timeless time; the thief therefore grafts existence onto the prospect of death.[38] Here, the author of the theft is above all Time, and the perspective is more easily that of the sudden shock that reveals the meaning of time.

5. The long, winding and sumptuous ballad 'In Country Sleep'[39] opens as a remake of the fairy-tale of *Little Red Riding Hood* applied to the poet's daughter, to warn the child who is about to fall asleep of the arrival of the wolf, which may be, literally, the onset of puberty, and to pray for her sleep to be peaceful. No less than half of the poem is expended in concentric circles of words to deny this parody, dispel this fear, and slowly enter another fairy-tale, that of *Sleeping Beauty*. Edith Sitwell, Thomas's talent scout, had written thirty years earlier the ballad of the threat of a witch, Laidronette, that is, a petty thief, in which there can be found a foreshadowing of Thomas's Thief coming in the night.[40] Thomas is less explicit about sex, and indeed denies that the impending threat is the loss of virginity.

---

37   The title of the poem is also the name of a farm that belonged to Thomas's aunt, Ann (see § 71 and n. 30).

38   At first sight, Thomas is still citing Yeats and the swans at Coole, that fly off one day to delight other observers elsewhere.

39   *In Country Sleep*, the title of Thomas's last collection from 1952 and of this eponymous ballad, which comes together with two other long poems, even if not exactly ballads, and a few other shorter ones, in all fewer than ten. All together they should have been part of the poem 'In Country Heaven', a kind of sublime and dreamy science fiction in which the protest of the dwellers of heaven were to resound against the end of the worlds; a project that was yet another repercussion of the atomic danger.

40   Volume 7, § 86.3 n. 11. It seems to me that this link has not been seen by commentators on the two poets.

As in Sitwell, however, the breaking of the spell is the end of eternity and of life outside time. In both poets, it is the imminent arrival of a faith that destroys another faith, or better a childlike credulity. The fact that nature is 'holy' is characteristic in Thomas, as is the status of 'grace', that is, of the immunity and protection it ensures. Thomas's Thief, with a capital T, 'as mild as the dew', can only be Christ, who carefully and inexorably snatches the girl from the 'grace' of nature and therefore transports her 'out of grace'. This is the same Christ who 'finds' a road, like the Child of 'Vision and Prayer' who 'tracked down' the fugitive believer. The last ten lines of the ballad are a tongue-twister, and an unusual syntactic babbling that does not allow us to understand exactly what the faith is that the thief comes to remove, and which is the one he will give to the girl: roughly speaking, the thief comes to divest the faith in faith; in other terms, she will complain that this thief or Thief never came, thus leaving her to face the 'ruled sun' alone, and removing her with his 'profane' love from the sacred protection of nature. In 'Poem on his Birthday', Thomas, who felt he had taken another step forward towards the grave, initially denies and affirms an afterlife, but the premature testament is telluric and pagan, and a prayer invariably prayed 'without faith in Him', with the enumeration of 'blessings' that consist in having no faith in the afterlife.[41] Pagan-style, witty and fabulous odes are 'Over Sir John's Hill' and 'In the White Giant's Thigh'. The former describes the Last Judgement seen from the point of view of birdlife, with the hawk that stands in the place of God and dives to devour the smaller birds that flock to their death. This is a joyful rite in which death does not throw sinister but friendly shadows, owing to an insensitivity to death that, by virtue of the animal legislation that envisages no mercy and forgiveness, is much cherished by Thomas, while it is so scaring for thinking beings.[42] 'In the White Giant's Thigh', which takes place at a cemetery where the names on the tombstones are worn away, deceased women still

---

41　The angry rejection of the consolation of Christian death, and the attachment to earthly life, resound in 'Do Not Go Gentle into That Good Night', a popular, roaring epicedium on the death of his father.

42　Thomas's falcon comes between Hopkins's windhover and the numerous ones of poets who were inspired by Thomas, above all Ted Hughes and Geoffrey Hill.

invoke from their dust to be seeded and impregnated, to have the pangs of childbirth and to be able to give birth, and the poet willingly does his duty and kisses, and wittily fecundates, that yearning dust. 'Lament' is a dramatic monologue in Victorian or even Browninguesque style with its coarse ballad-like marks. Thomas reinvents himself as an unrepentant old man, an eager womanizer on his deathbed, and one who, after a life of mocking challenge to religion ends up with a sanctimonious 'Sunday' wife, comforted by all the 'mortal virtues'.

§ 73. *Dylan Thomas V: 'Under Milk Wood'*

There are two manners and two distinct phases in Thomas's prose, perfectly correlated with the density and relaxation that follow one another in his poetry. The first, contemporary to the first two collections, and linked to the poetics of the 1930s, is that of the transfer of their dark symbolism, and of its mortuary and apocalyptic metaphors, together with the scenarios of creative pantheism and man-nature unison, into short sketches of a lividly oneiric mould.[43] So this handful of stories is the pendant to or the accompaniment of the poems, which they expand into a diegetic minimum. There are in these stories occasional or even frequent occurrences of Thomas's symbolically more loaded poetic terms. This bundle of sketches is not, however, a great achievement, especially because Thomas seems to be reporting pure dreams he really had, or even recurring nightmares, without reshaping them, or mimicking their magmatic and regurgitating form. He appears at least as a psychic, a visionary, a semi-lunatic with his gloomy daytime and night-time visions. Clumps of images and disconnected, random events, dictated by the aesthetics of the unpredictable, all end up resembling one another and inevitably cause a sense of monotony. It is therefore evident that these are fantasies or parables obsessively indebted to Blake and his prophetic books, and as many free embroideries on Genesis or genesis, featuring human couples in whom we rediscover the Edenic one of Adam and Eve before and after the Fall, and therefore also on the Nativity, the Bethlehem grotto, the Cross and Gethsemane. The new Adam and Eve,

---

43   Collected by Thomas in the first of the two parts of *A Prospect of the Sea* (1955, posthumous).

tormented by diabolical appearances, are also possessed. 'The Visitor' seems to be a pendant to 'The Force that through the Green Fuse' for its animate nature that bleeds and screams in the same way (the 'screaming weeds'); the child stolen by an aggressive, castrating she-fairy, redoubled in various terrifying apparitions, seems, in another story, to be descended from Yeats. 'The Lemon', Wells-like, tells the story of monstrous grafts made by a creator who is follower of Frankenstein. And macabre fantasies of dead men that are not dead, or survivors who explain the condition of death, are spasmodic imitations of Poe.[44] Thomas's Welsh Puritanism exudes from other neo-Gothic stories à la Hawthorne, with crazy vicars and rectors who commit crimes and sexual atrocities.

2. In time, this manner was completely set aside in favour of more traditional prose, with plots about more real events but not for this reason exactly realistic: grotesque rather, but more humorous, and with the daily and biographical reality deformed but more intelligible. With a wise decision, Thomas therefore very soon separated the two realms, and therefore also the registers, of poetry and prose, creating two vessels that were no longer communicating. Thus his mature and late prose is not a continuation of his poetry, nor is it a paraphrase or a derived product; it is, however, like his poetry, a further objectification of his autobiography. *Portrait of the Artist as a Young Dog* (1940) encloses ten tales mainly in the first person, and may be defined as an imaginary autobiography of the poet up to the age of twenty, even if his *alter ego* is essentially one Dylan Thomas; some of them objectify him and are in the third person. As in Joyce's *Portrait*, whose title is recalled parodistically, they follow, with natural gaps and in emblematic and salient moments, the affective, erotic and artistic growth of the child and adolescent. The prose is dry, sharp, elliptical, and almost naturalistic, the opposite of Thomas's baroque poetics. Some stories may be referred back to the modernist canon, as may certain descriptive passages, such as those, 'purple' and showing Woolf's influence, which seem as if written on the seashore. The hero's *Bildung* is seen as a strange, polar opposition between moments of barbaric wildness – with children who

---

44 Whose influence is documented by Moynihan 1966, 25.

wrestle and as soon as they meet come to blows to then become friends – and others where an instinctive talent for writing from the imagination has the upper hand. Towards the end, young Thomas is leaving for London, where he will become a journalist and – a cynical anticipation – will live off women. The growth of the child is accompanied by and melts into the evocation of an environment, rural Wales, a place where dreams and reality rub shoulders, as do faith and superstition, reason and madness. Accordingly, small, alternative self-sufficient communities of children and adolescents spring up, as opposed to others of adults, only mentioned in passing: new communities, that is, always different and always rather disappointing, owing to the innate melancholy in the main character, who remains an intimately solitary and grumpy creature. This is a veiled, indifferent criticism of the closure of an environment that would have pushed the young poet, if he had remained a prisoner of it, into a blind alley. For this precise reason, the stories of *Portrait of the Artist as a Young Dog* are indebted to the spirit of Joyce's *Dubliners*, not only of his *Portrait*, and quote that collection for the representation of a paralysis, postdated about thirty years, and in a different context.

3. In the early stories of *Portrait of the Artist as a Young Dog*, we read the small-scale epics of a lonely sensitive child from whose point of view a treacherous, deformed and enigmatic situation is confusedly documented. Since this child, whose mother is present in the background only through vague hints, is travelling to stay with relatives, his uncles and his grandfather, and explores an unknown and obscure reality by himself, the easily recognizable precedent is de la Mare.[45] Thomas cares little for the narrative speed and the number of events, but focuses on small insignificant and secondary details of wan, colourless, everyday life. The fulcrum of the first story is the discovery, only at the end, that to pay for drinks Uncle Jim has taken to a certain inn a piglet that his family have noticed is missing from the pigsty. His aunt and uncle's house in the country receives a visit from a rich schoolmate, and the uncle comes in his cart to pick Dylan up. The Welsh countryside is 'haunted', inhabited by spectres, elves, friendly and

---

45   Whose portrait is on the walls of the room of Thomas's *alter ego* in a story in *Portrait*.

hostile presences like the dwellings of Gothic memory. The uncle is in turn one of the first appearances of a diabolical or inverted religion. On the journey home from the tavern, he drunkenly sings blasphemous hymns, points out to the child a 'hangman's house' that will remain impressed on his memory, and says mysteriously that he hopes 'to have hung Mrs Jesus'. Meanwhile, the child's imagination is wide open to impressions, to the most varied visions and hallucinations, one of which is that of his uncle who, instead of selling piglets to pay for drinks, eats them, and is therefore a kind of ogre.[46] The farm of the child's aunt and uncle is therefore not a preview of Fern Hill, or, if it is, it is in an exactly inverse sense. The rural Wales of these tales remains the setting of sinister stories, ambiguous events, lives of insane individuals, the unhinged, eccentrics and the dispossessed, as often in the novels of the Powys brothers, other Welshmen.[47] The next human study, in the first story, is the extremely successful one of cousin Gwylim, an ambiguous seminarian who composes hymns and then changes God's name into those of the girls to whom they are addressed. He also plays the semi-blasphemous game of officiating mass, and in his improvised chapel, which is a barn, he takes confession from his cousin and his friend. The second is a story of daily madness, that of the grandfather who every night rides invisible horses and one day prepares to be buried. Thereafter the chapters of *Portrait of the Artist as a Young Dog* follow one another like Joycean epiphanies, sometimes lapsing into the third person. They focus, with abrupt passages commented with sharp humour, on the routine of the village with its muted phenomenology, along with the poet's epiphany, but in a climate of rodomontade, and in the assemblies of gently mocked old fogeys, or in the home of the new friend Dan, now on the threshold of fifteen years. In a trip to Rhossilli Beach, where Thomas and friends pitch a tent for a few days' holiday, one of them is a plaything, and Thomas makes a first approach to a certain Jean, but she is a coquette and flirts with another partner under the tent. In its expository style and in theme, this

46   In the inn, at the beginning of the story, there is a visual overlapping between the suckling pig, hidden inside the basket, and a newborn who is being breastfed by a woman at the door.
47   Volume 7, § 49.3.

adventure singularly predicts, or echoes, the fiction of the 'angry young men', of Sillitoe in particular. After the orgiastic moments of socialization, the chapter 'Just like Little Dogs' showcases the solitary side of the 'young dog' who stays on his own under bridges with two Joycean scatterbrains who do not want to return home to their wives. In 'Where the Taw Flows' Thomas avoids and exorcizes, *a posteriori*, the danger of becoming a scribbler in the amateur circles of Swansea, where people dreamt of a literature made of 'scenes of clerical life' proudly distinct from the writings of the neurotic Bloomsbury poets. In the penultimate story, Thomas is a newspaper reporter, but describes himself as a sort of ennobled Bloom, and follows the bustle and encounters of an average working day. Ultimately, he limits himself to listening to the various prickly and even vainglorious pieces of gossip of the village, but he has one foot inside and the other outside. Thomas attributes to himself the discovery of the simulacrum of a woman, whom he is always on the lookout for, in front of a latrine. In a pub where a dodgy get-together is taking place, and ever on the threshold of a misunderstanding, the young man, made a fool of by the other patrons, imagines a squalid scene: Lou is perhaps a prostitute, or an enchantress, or a nymphomaniac. The echoes are once again cleverly camouflaged, and refer back to T. S. Eliot's representation of a late provincial 'waste land': a pub at closing time, with a kind of Circe of the poor who entices the 'young man' home, where the washing is 'perilously' hanging. The rendezvous is delayed, and in the end it is understood that everything has been a nightmare, nothing real.

4. In *Adventures in the Skin Trade*[48] (1955, posthumous), a novel that was left unfinished after four completed chapters, we find narrative ingredients that were by now customary in Thomas. One such is the young dreamer who leaves the suburbs one day to arrive in London to become a journalist; or the journey itself described in terms of a spiritual adventure and a rite of passage that is also sexual. This is therefore a progress and a partly playful *Bildung*, parodistically and humorously imagined as the transformation of a reptile losing its skin (and the protagonist has a good seven to lose

48   On Thomas's inability to write a novel, cf. Marucci 1976, 41.

before finding his true self, only to remain naked at the end of the ordeal).[49] Samuel Bennet carries the significant surname of a writer, Arnold Bennett, who had debuted with a novel about a provincial man who moves to London with ambitions as a poet, and there enjoys various, partly also imaginary, sentimental vicissitudes. Those of Thomas's Samuel are much weirder and more grotesque, in the manner of a comic absurdism that was not yet born as an official movement at that time in England, but was already in the air. In particular, we feel hovering the atmospheres of de la Mare who, in his stories and in his novel about the 'midget' looked back to Dickens's grotesque while also foreshadowing Kafka (Thomas's Samuel may, in his naivety, be a distant or even close relative of Karl Rossmann from *Amerika*). But these are atmospheres that had been found in Beckett's first absurd story, *Murphy*[50] (and maybe, coincidentally, the name of Thomas's protagonist is also the same as Beckett's, while his surname is a further echo: from Bennet to Beckett). Thomas's Samuel is an arsonist, perhaps only oneiric, and the narrator plays mischievously with the reader by not making it clear whether what happens in the first chapter is only a dream or reality. Before departure he ransacks the house in the night and burns a photo album in a fit of madness; in fact, he is absent-minded, passive, as alienated as Murphy, and the chapters that follow describe the meetings with random pick-ups, like the four in Beckett's novel, made at the railway station buffet and at the little café where the simpleton ends up being tempted as much by a bizarre waitress who is also a nymphomaniac and an eccentric as by the mature proprietor. This rickety clique, which has also been joined by a hack poet, consists of caricatures which remind one of those found in Dickens's more grotesque and sinister sketches, and the string of adventures wobbles on the border of the naïve and the louche, of pure comedy and misapprehension. Two places exude the visionary and surreal atmosphere typical of Dickens and his descendants, and these are the house of the furniture dealer, in which hundreds of thousands of

---

49   Tindall 1962, 29, rightly mentions Auden and Isherwood's earlier *The Dog Beneath the Skin*.

50   As recalled by Tindall 1962, 14, and Binni 1973, 25, who adds that Thomas reviewed the novel 'lucidly summarizing, too, the stages of his own dilemma'.

pieces of obsolete furniture appear crammed into the miserable space; and a bathroom from the ceiling of which hang bird cages, and in the bathtub of which floats a rubber goose. An embarrassing and subtly lascivious scene – a grotesque idyll on the edge of the tub, as it were – takes place here, because Samuel has inserted his little finger into the neck of a beer bottle and a waitress fails to free it even by taking the bottle between her thighs; the waitress convinces him shortly afterwards to take a bath, giving him a bottle of *Eau de Cologne* to drink. London is not swinging in these four chapters set in 1933; it is a London of inns, dance halls, seedy quarters, rooms for rent, bric-a-brac shops, and of fools.

5. *Under Milk Wood* (1954, posthumous) was finished, or almost, and without the final honing, a few days before Thomas's death, and was broadcast by the BBC a few months later. Thomas had worked on it intermittently for almost ten years, changing his ideas on the general plan several times. It witnesses a tendency which had recently consolidated, towards works that were no longer darkly private and personal, but more public and more widely accessible; a tendency that brought him inevitably to drift towards drama or a specific form of drama.[51] The plot of *Under Milk Wood* could no doubt have been played out in undramatic prose, with dialogues entrusted to a modernist narrator. Its location is in fact a Welsh coastal town, its characters are a chorus of colourful and varied humanity, and its time is above all a twenty-four-hour window, from the deep sleep of a spring night to dusk and nightfall the next day. What, we might ask, is more paradigmatically modernistic than a narrative and scenic action that hinges on the awakening from sleep of one or more characters who slowly ready themselves for their daytime chores? At the same time, *Under Milk Wood* becomes a work that is at least semi-theatrical because, though lacking stage directions, two voices remain active behind the scenes, and are responsible for the few necessary settings and links in their roles of partially omniscient chroniclers who suture the plot and distribute the dialogues. In the history of twentieth-century drama, *Under Milk Wood* is the outpost of a dream-like, stylized theatre without action and only

---

51   There were also talks of a projected work with Stravinsky, for whom Thomas was supposed to write a libretto on 'atomic destruction' (Ackerman 1991, 265).

for voices that looks ahead to the middle and late Beckett. In the broadest sense, it is an example of a poetic theatre, both because of its care over the natural descriptions provided by the two external voices – which are anything but perfunctory, on the contrary enriched by strings of alliteration, inventive compounds and rare, local and outdated terms – and because, as in a sort of operetta like those composed by Auden for Britten, or a musical libretto, the dialogues irrepressibly break into short stanzas of doggerel and lightweight verse amiably nimbler but not dull, indeed exquisite and gently humorous. The characters alternate with one another on stage, only as voices that often and above all bring to life memories or express grudges, regrets, nostalgia for moments of well-being, or even reveal skeletons in the closet, shames, missed aspirations and unachieved joys, outcrops from the subconscious. With some delay, Thomas wrote a delightful, enjoyable, light-weight *divertissement* along Freudian lines, which significantly starts from the night, when the village community dreams, and dreams the day's residues as well as surfacings that have escaped Freudian censure, along with repressed aspirations in the daily life of its members. The repressive agents are bourgeois conventions and especially religion; but this is only hinted at, without any insistence, without muted existential dramas, without invective: everything is grace, irony, and humour. Placing the opening of the play in the night is a strictly psychoanalytical operation, since the public is invited to 'listen to the dreams' of the sleepers. And the first surfacing, from a symbolic sea, is that of drowned sailors who appear to an old blind sea captain. Thereafter the stage fills with a group of villagers who, like the many faces of a prism, confess their secret lives in short flashes of dialogue. The play rapidly becomes a whirl of fabulous, mythical and unreal figures, and a phantasmagoria reminiscent of a Dickensian Christmas story, because some of these figures are caricatures with unusual features or odd past stories, like the widow of two husbands or the faun-like barber. The night-time and even the daytime see the open or secret transgression against an oppressive system, as I mentioned. In the village, a system of matriarchy is in force that induces the husbands, with a deviation towards the grotesque, to pretend to submit to the rules laid down by their wives, or also to poison them as revenge, at least in dreams. Playfully, a small world is ready to explode, is indeed already on the point of an explosion judging from the exhaust valves that are operating. And as in the Victorian world, these valves are tics, forms of dyscrasia, carelessness or even semi-madness. Until about a third of its development, *Under Milk Wood* looks back more and more to the initial chapter of *Ulysses*, or to certain phases of *Mrs Dalloway*, with the villagers having breakfast, getting dressed, observing themselves in the mirror, or going into the city and soliloquizing in a sort of stream of consciousness. In particular, if there is a Joycean episode from which Thomas's play derives it is that of Scylla and Charybdis, with pedestrian routes that intersect, and life and thoughts that are interwoven. The daytime microcosm testifies to an attempt on the characters' part to gain ground on the repression of a Puritan milieu. There are those who preen themselves and dream of the arrival of Mr Right, who meanly lift their petticoats, who are gossiped about for shamelessly having many lovers and flirting with the cool guys in the village; those who are marginalized because they have been labelled as 'no-gooders'. As in Catholic Dublin, in the imaginary Welsh Methodist town small scandals reign and there is much gossip, and therefore at times it also seems like a kind of Mediterranean community.

§ 74. *Surrealist and New Apocalyptic poets*

This section might also be entitled 'the legacy of Dylan Thomas', since directly, indirectly, or even polemically – through direct knowledge, familiarity and friendship, or simply reading – the poets of the schools I will examine here revolved around Thomas. Surrealism proper came to England from France belatedly and in a watered-down form, and just as quickly vanished. Of the great literary figures of the 1930s it touched only Auden and his generation, in particular because of their independent interest in the Freudian unconscious, which was undoubtedly a *trait d'union* (surreal, at least in part, is *Paid on Both Sides* with its dream-like interlude),[1]

---

[1] Cf. § 4.5 and HYN, 217 and 220, on the early dissension of the communist press (such as the *Daily Worker*), which accused surrealism of being an expression of bourgeois decadence. On the articles by Auden, which he signed with a pseudonym in *New Verse* towards the end of the 1930s and which also discredited surrealism, cf. A. Pajalich, 'Dada e surrealismo in Gran Bretagna', in CMM, 447–57. On the differences in

and almost snared Dylan Thomas, an emended surrealist. As I mentioned, similarities have frequently been noticed or fantasized between Thomas's hallucinations – his jarring images without a link – and the paintings of Dalí. And one of Thomas's stories appeared in the first and only British surrealist magazine. At the 1936 surrealist exhibition at London's New Burlington Galleries, Thomas actually appeared bringing a cup of boiled twine in homage to Breton, and asking the French poet if he preferred it strong or weak.[2] But, in answer to a precise question, Thomas denied any bond and affiliation, and indeed drafted a jibe directed at Gascoyne.[3] The exhibition was visited by about 20,000 people and could therefore boast of greater success among the public than Fry's Post-Impressionist exhibition of 1910. Surrealism was not taken lightly or fought with bitterness, compared to other avant-garde movements, especially because to the British conservatives it appeared to originate from an indigenous tradition, and its beginnings were traced to the visionary poetry of Blake, the fantasies of Lewis Carroll, or Anglicized artists of the late eighteenth century such as Fuseli.[4] In reality, we could count on the fingers of one hand the British products of this art in the various literary sectors: a single novel, a single collection of poems, with a few essays on painting. Some of these essays were written by Herbert Read, who was also the author of a booklet on surrealism written in collaboration with Breton. Short-lived was the *Contemporary Poetry and Prose* magazine, which in 1936 gathered all the

---

    opinion between the surrealism of Read and Gascoyne, cf. the chapter on the latter by P. Bottalla Nordio, in CAB, vol. II, 507–18.

2   For his part, Gascoyne had to wrench Dalí free from a diver's suit the painter had worn to give his rather incomprehensible paper at the exhibition.

3   'Letter to my Aunt', a burlesque in eighteenth-century rhymed couplets that is very oddly reactionary and attacks any logical, conceptual and metric extravagance, and which therefore must not be taken seriously, least of all as self-criticism: rather, Thomas amuses himself by playfully setting the whole literary world of London in the 1930s on fire. In themselves, some early poems by Gascoyne display an imagery that is, if anything, more Thomasian than Thomas's own, such as when he describes the phenomenon of sunlight breaking over 'Arctic regions', or that of the 'planetary seed' that is fertilized while crawling across the 'desert'.

4   An exception, for reasons that are easy to understand, was Wyndham Lewis.

British supporters and members who recognized themselves in the pair of surrealism and anti-fascism. It was Read who pointed out that surrealism and Dada descended from a reaffirmation of the 'Romantic principle'.[5] Surrealism and neo-Romanticism overlapped and became muddled, or perhaps succeeded one another, and Gascoyne and Barker were to straddle both, getting involved as much in surrealism as in 'New Romantic' poetry, also labelled as 'New Apocalyptic'. From this union of forces there was ignited a further reaction both to the disciplined and dry religious poetry in the manner of Eliot, and to the politically engagé variety of the 1930s, of Auden and his circle.

2. The only charismatic British surrealist poet was thus David Gascoyne (1916–2001);[6] but this label turned out to be very limited and partial, to the extent of almost being unfitting if compared to his career as a whole. Making his debut at only sixteen, Gascoyne appeared a surrealist *in pectore* by virtue of an obsessive claustrophobic symbolism hinging on a flow of bewildered and unrelated dream-like evocations. His second collection, *Man's Life Is This Meat* (1936), while by now showing left-wing leanings, opened with a translation from Éluard and poems dedicated to Dalí, Ernst and Magritte, outwardly 'automatic' but, if read carefully, virtually ortho-dox. The year before, Gascoyne had written a short survey of surrealism and was in the front row when it came to spreading and upholding it. With expert knowledge of French, proud of presenting himself as a poet who was firstly Parisian and *ipso facto* European – an exception, if we consider the innate insularity of the British – for a short time he believed firmly in the surrealist gospel as a psychic and political weapon, while other amateurs feigned an opportunistic adhesion to the use of colourful images, finding in surrealism the opportunity to embrace a life of eccentricity. Gascoyne's greater stature lies in the fact that surrealism, which roughly meant images jarring simply for the purpose of surprise, along with meaningless juxtapo-sitions, lost this exclusive dimension and soon became in him the means of expression of a painful, deeply felt and anguished consciousness of the moral state of the world. In so doing, his surrealism was indeed also an

---

5   DES, 228, and, on the dissension with Gascoyne, CAB, vol. II, 507.
6   *Complete Poems*, ed. R. Skelton, Oxford 1979.

overcoming of surrealism itself. By 1938, Gascoyne had already reached the stage of a visionary post-Romanticism which he saw incarnate in the sacrificial figure of Hölderlin; and in the preface to a 1942 anthology, published with other poets, he stated that he was at that point stripped of every surrealistic trace. A catalyst of this visionary, but rather more mystical, turnaround, and of a poetry intended as an uninterrupted dialogue with and address to the Father, was the war. *Night Thoughts* (1956), a radio play highly lauded by some, arranged in choruses and cadences expressing aspirations and yearnings for the redemption of the Everyman mangled by the tentacles of the city, is poignant but verbose. Afflicted by frequent nervous breakdowns, Gascoyne became virtually inactive after this work until his death, although he continued to provoke a mixed and controversial reception – severe, mild or exalted – which recognized in him superior gifts of vision as much as the ravings of a questionable taste, if not pure and simple chains of nonsense.

3. When still a beginner, George Barker (1913–1991) and Dylan Thomas were as like as two peas in a pod. Barker even seemed like a younger brother and a less successful copy of Thomas for his unruly, bohemian lifestyle and a poetry that was nurtured, as he himself used to say, on words in the dictionary, alcohol and sex. Equally precocious, by the age of fourteen he had left school and had undertaken various jobs before settling down to live off the proceeds of the pen. At just twenty he was included by a dazzled Yeats in his 1936 anthology on modern English poetry (indeed he had been symbolically chosen as the last poet of that collection). T. S. Eliot himself had his poems published among the books of Faber and Faber, and helped him obtain a post as an English teacher in Japan. His second collection followed Thomas's first only one year later; the next, with the strange title of *Calamiterror*, and inspired by the war in Spain, came one year after Thomas's second. There was further proof of this consanguinity in the harping on the same recurring motif, the non-differentiation of humans and nature and the coexistence of vital and destructive impulses. In other terms, Barker was writing an equally 'archetypal' poetry. But he soon took a detour towards a frenzied and chaotic rhetoric and towards the more serious risk run by Thomas himself, the attitude of a bard who utters and above all shouts, crazily and fearlessly, anything whatsoever. His

most typical poems of the 1930s and after are phantasmagorias and oneiric visions vaguely definable as of 'genesis'. There intertwine deliberately, or perhaps accidentally, Thomas's repertoires of images of the womb and the tomb. A collection of 'holy' poems explicitly modelled on Donne's sonnets, despite consisting of thirteen lines, echo instead Thomas's 'Altarwise by Owl-light', the only variant being that Barker progressively disguises himself as St John at Patmos, St Sebastian dripping with blood, Judas, or the Apostles. Famous for the *kitsch* of some disproportionate or undisciplined images (the sea as a 'greedy bitch with sailors in her guts'), Barker, who had received a Catholic education that he came to reject, glories in an old-fashioned *mauditism* ('There is no martyrdom worse than a life, / Nor can it be granted with a sacrifice'). Precisely because of this, he may appear at the same time as one of many latecomers exploring the same Christological themes as the Decadents. The paraphernalia of the sacred and the liturgical are the metaphorical field of reference into which a tormenting and tormented need for expiation and innocence, and liberation from the grip of sin and guilt, is transfused. Until the close of the first half of a long career, Barker remained a mediocre poet; some of his lines taken in isolation are sketchy, garbled and limping, but not, it seems, for reasons of more mimetic and dramatic expressiveness. As poetry, it is rough, lacking in euphony, syntactically knotty, made of abrupt violations of the grammatical chain, with suspensions, anacolutha, still rough and as if never honed: in a word, 'rebarbative'. The historical judgement has been controversial, certainly more favourable on his middle and late periods, which saw the birth of a much more fluid confessional vein (1950 and 1964) in witty Villonian accents, and a long *Anno Domini* (1983), a series of rather bizarre and eclectic theological dicta, therefore by then outside the surrealist and apocalyptic orbit.

4. The New Apocalyptic poets got this name at the end of the 1930s with the issuing of the anthology *The New Apocalypse* (1939) edited by J. F. Hendry (1912–1986) and H. Treece (1911–1966, author of one of the first monographs on Dylan Thomas), followed by two others in 1941 and in 1944. They represented the point of confluence of at least three currents: the surrealists, who were by then on the retreat, some Scottish Renaissance poets, including at a certain moment MacCaig, and the fledgling neo-Romantics.

Minor poets, but also Dylan Thomas and Vernon Watkins, published in those anthologies. Neo-Romanticism was to have but a short life, at the most fifteen years; it was fought and finally felled by the Movement in the mid-1950s. The aesthetic disagreements between both groups were by then evident, and having assigned other poets to other literary currents we can again exemplify them in William Sydney Graham (1918–1986). Born in Scotland in 1932, Graham had embarked on scientific and technical studies, but, stubbornly wanting to live only as a poet, moved to Cornwall in 1944 and lived there virtually with no interruption until his death. Scottish publishers having already printed his poems, which had grown in the dense shadow of Thomas's verbalism, his consecration took place with *The White Threshold* (1949), especially since Eliot accepted it for the publisher Faber and Faber; later, he would also have the support and esteem of Harold Pinter. However, his meagre royalties from poetry had to be supplemented by a Crown Pension. Graham's early poetry is a demonstration of *corruptio optimi pessima*, and of how Thomas, badly imitated, could produce feeble and poorly convincing results. The 'seven letters' of the homonymous poem are symbolically addressed to a lover, and from the edge of the 'catastrophe of the world' and with turgid and spasmodic 'hothouse' rhetoric.[7] His acclaimed masterpiece, *The Nightfishing* (1955), tells of a night in a boat fishing for herring, finding in it the model for an easy existential metaphor. It is filled by nightmares as in a sort of *Bateau ivre* (Graham has been actually compared to Rimbaud), and is therefore also reminiscent of Thomas's 'Ballad of the Long-legged Bait'. Thomas also looms large in Graham's transition, probably as an answer to the criticisms of the adherents of the Movement, from the darkness – both spiritual and linguistic – to the light, that is, to an ever greater clarity placed at the service of a descriptive-anecdotal poetry of everyday life, and above all of that proletarian and workers' milieu Graham came from. However, the longest and most famous of these ballads, 'Baldy Bane', whose rhythms imitate those of popular rhymes, becomes gradually tedious. Late Graham

---

7   At times, even empty and insipid: for example, in the second letter, where Thomas's
     adjective 'burning' recurs even too frequently, with the vibrant exhortation to the
     beloved to 'Break break me from this high / Helmet of idiocy'.

is remarkably fluent but often misses the mark, and indulges in artificial extravagances such as a poem on a course of lessons given by the musician Quantz to a flute student.

5. Praz[8] likened the stories and novels of William Sansom[9] (1912–1976) 'to certain hazards of surrealist art', to the sinister hallucinations found in 'paintings by Salvador Dalí, Max Ernst, and Berman', and to the 'vein' of Magritte and Delvaux. If we accept this suggestion, Sansom would be the second major surrealist prose writer after Dylan Thomas himself, who was almost his contemporary. Indeed it is not out of place to find that a few slightly Gothic tales by Sansom[10] resemble and echo those of Thomas's youth. He also dabbled in some cases in self-complacent verbal manipulations and in a parodic prose that is 'narrative poetry thinly disguised, even metric and rhyming', not far from that of Thomas's poetry and prose.[11] As always with his favourite writers, Praz in his review never misses an opportunity to stress the importance of Sansom's obsessive and maniacal observation, as if he had the multifaceted eye of a fly, that is, a visual scan that isolates the marginal or invisible detail and obscures the rest, as well as his prodigiously ever-changing capacity to look at the real from mysterious and phantasmal angles, in line with oblique perspectives. Praz also expatiates on the plots of these novels and short stories, which are by and large forgotten today, retelling them with exquisite taste and uncontrolled amazement. He does this to highlight their madcap, bizarre and unpredictable pattern, the stupefying settings and their rare, unusual and visionary or even contrastive character, and the eccentric phobias and vicissitudes of figures that, Praz could not know, may now be seen to anticipate the

8   CLA, vol. IV, 126–34.
9   A Londoner, he was educated in Germany where he was sent to learn German, was a banker from 1930, and worked in advertising from 1935 until the outbreak of the war, when during the Blitz he was a member of the fire brigade, drawing material and inspiration for some of the stories he had begun to write.
10   *The Stories of William Sansom*, ed. E. Bowen, London 1969, which many have complained does not contain all of Sansom's stories, and which also excludes several of the finest ones.
11   MEF, 325.

novels of Angela Carter. Sansom defined himself as a painter *manqué*,[12] but it would be equally correct to say that he is a filmic writer, more exactly a screenwriter and the masterful author of highly evocative captions. The effects in which he was sometimes unparalleled are mainly the spasmodic deferment of an action and, as a consequence, the 'slow motion'. What for instance makes the story 'The Wall' so emblematic and proverbial is the scene of the collapse of a wall, whose duration occupies over four pages, and which might distantly recall the epilogue of Antonioni's film *Zabriskie Point*, with the exploding of the building and the blast that are obsessively repeated several times in the viewer's retina. Sansom's aesthetics and practice cannot therefore but be of the moment, and when he stretches the moment, as in his best novel, *The Body* (1949),[13] the result is much poorer, since transferring the epiphany of the moment intact to a long story, as Joyce knew so well, is extremely difficult. On closer inspection, the first possible objection to a surrealist Sansom is that he wrote very much later than the years when surrealism was in vogue, from the Second World War onward; but this would not in itself be decisive. Sansom is in substance the follower of too many writers, and one of his recognized traits is the variety of his narrative modes. There are other categories that may include him, essentially three in addition to the surreal: the absurd, the existentialistic, and the fantastic. Kafka and Poe were acclaimed as influences, and Sansom himself admitted they were; Praz, who had a notorious soft spot for de la Mare, strangely did not pick up on this wavelength and a consanguinity which seems to me the most apt, since Sansom is in many ways de la Mare's twin brother. Surrealism is ill-fitting for him when his stories are studies of

12   See the chapter dedicated to Sansom by F. Binni, in CAB, vol. II, 406.

13   The plot itself is obvious and repetitive, and may appear to be the surreal remake of a novel by Trollope (Volume 5, §§ 100–101): a jealous barber obsessively suspects his wife without foundation. The plot is also similar to that of Bowen's novel *The Heat of the Day*. Even among Sansom's admirers *The Body* is controversial: ATD, 268, gives a positive judgement, MEF, 240, and KRG, 286, negative; Praz, in his otherwise enthusiastic review, condemns almost all of Sansom's novels *en bloc*. His classic stories cannot help being of a tyrannical, epiphanic brevity, barely a page and a half long; only in some cases do they reach the length of a novella.

the Freudian *Unheimlichkeit* of daily life; and when his plots are not random regurgitations of dream-like material in their pure state, but instead have their own narrative logic, as alienated as this may be. I will discuss only some of Sansom's most emblematic stories to substantiate these assertions. In 'The World of Glass', Sansom opts, as he often does, for the first-person narrative of an *alter ego*. The story becomes the re-evocative monologue of a writer interned in a prison cell for a mad fit of violence; this well expresses Sansom's predilection for claustrophobic atmospheres that are in themselves naturally obsessive. The skip back in memory produces the dazzling and magical evocation of a train trip through a snow-clad Norwegian landscape. One constant in Sansom's stories is the exploratory trip of a nature that gradually exudes hostility, enigmas, and ambiguity, and from which disturbing unreal figures emerge. All of Sansom's stories could, like this one, be defined as and entitled 'An Encounter', like one by Joyce. This is an analogy enhanced by more than a literal and substantial recurrence, such as that of children who often make terrifying or threatening meetings, and with strangers who have odd handicaps or physical and perceptive deformities, or with distorted, treacherous, metamorphosing phenomena, and flee from them. In 'The World of Glass', Sansom turns to his existentialist archetype by introducing his hunted and hounded character; in fact, here the meeting is only with the sweet phantasmal figure of a blind girl, who is however gifted with an enhanced perceptiveness, albeit entirely illusory. Sansom's stories are often tragic or without a happy ending, and end with a twist that is abrupt most of the time: having returned to the ship that will take him back to his homeland, the main character of 'The World of Glass' suddenly punches another passenger, and this, too, is a surreal detail, since we cannot understand the reason for it. 'The Vertical Ladder' is in turn among the most indicative studies of spasmodic suspense in Sansom. It describes a kind of cognitive adventure into the unknown and the mysterious, and a journey within the known from the unknown, and that in the course of this process becomes alien: 'All things were suddenly alien', says the boy Flegg, climbing the ladder of the gasometer; but this is a phrase which is applicable to all the very frequent explorations in which Sansom's tales consist. 'A Saving Grace' and 'A Country Walk' are also about the animation of the inanimate, with the boy's 'I' that faces perceptual doubt and moves towards his hallucinations, and the penetration into an aggressive, threatening, often lethal nature. 'Various Temptations' seems like a parody of a horror story in that a sort of new Jack the Ripper enters at night the house of a working girl who then quiets him down. The atmosphere is that of Angela Carter's remake of Little Red Riding Hood, with the start of a ménage, plans for marriage, and the civilized wolf; and yet the murderous impulse gains the upper hand. 'A Woman Seldom Found' is the quintessence of a Sansom story, in its burning and blazing expressive economy. No longer than a page and a half, it seems like a Boccaccio-like anecdote played out in the smart streets of modern-day Rome, in fact the salacious tale of an Andreuccio seduced by a classy prostitute. Sansom's most frequent human type knows that life is illusion and that 'nothing ever happens'. However, the twist, and the cold shower, arrive abruptly, with the prostitute's hand that, shortly before intercourse, grows and stretches, and snaking across the carpet of the love nest presses the light switch. Sansom still aroused widespread curiosity, respect, admiration, and above all fervent expectations shortly before his death, and had various illustrious admirers; he died, after all, before demonstrating what he could have achieved. His work abundantly proves that the short story is at its highest levels a charismatic genre, and that its distance from the novel is greater than that between the novel, drama and poetry; which also denies the transitive property, and shows that a great short story writer may be a modest or merely passable novelist.

§ 75. *The Movement 'and after'*

Poetry, fiction and drama readjusted themselves in Britain at the end of the 1950s, and throughout the 1960s and beyond, at least on the common basis of a sensibility relieved of the weight of literary tradition. As Larkin wrote in one of his most famous witty poems, 1963 marked the advent of free sex, or even of 'sexual intercourse' *tout court*, without procreative purposes and for pure and simple physical enjoyment. That date fell 'Between the end of the *Chatterley* ban / and the Beatles' first LP'. Shifted to the field of aesthetics and prosody, anarchy manifested itself as a suspicion and dislike of fixed forms, reused if anything in a parodic way, and with attention and propensity to orality. The poetic art was to be applied and consumed, no longer exclusively destined to mental reading; and, if read, poetry was to be recited and declaimed, with the *sine qua non* of an audience listening to and participating in its performance. The very primacy of the word itself was in danger of collapsing with the advent of 'concrete' poetry, phonic poetry and the *poème trouvé*, and with the production of a multimedia, pan-artistic text, verbal, iconic and material at the same time.

2. The major British poets born around 1920 began writing, more or less, just before the outbreak of the Second World War, and tended to mature immediately afterwards, to give their best in the decades from the 1950s until the end of the century. In 1945, British poetry lived through the last fires of modernistic 'Eliotism',[1] and a current to which it was not entirely extraneous was that of the New Apocalyptic poets, as we have seen. The new poets had to either align themselves with one of these movements or find alternatives. The Movement was vigorously and polemically against Eliot's Modernism and any imitation of the Metaphysical poets, and grafted itself back onto the most indigenous strain of English poetry. It rediscovered, in particular, the ancient function of poetry as a public and social ritual and emphasized its wide-ranging popular influence, while Eliot

---

1   Neo-modernism, the neo-avant-garde and neo-experimentalism, subsequently reabsorbed in the 'Cambridge School', were reborn – and so in some sectors of the intelligentsia there was talk of a revival of British poetry – in several anthologies that plainly harped on the adjective 'new' in their title, and in books of poetry predominantly published by fringe publishers. The lifeblood and nourishment of these movements were Beat poetry, the 'Black Mountain' poets and Allen Ginsberg, who took part in 1965 in the first British poetry 'happening'. Their epistemological area of reference was that of the western crisis of *logos*. In Jeremy Prynne (born 1936), Tom Raworth (1938–2017) and Peter Reading (1946–2011), the existential condition of a disinherited world remained an invariable and repetitive mark, though at the same time it was fused with an experimentalism and ingenious intellectualism that is at times exhibitionist and an end in itself. Prynne's poetry, initially shaken by a confused messianic longing, gradually became more obscure, and it seemed that only a small esoteric sect of adepts possessed the key to it. Reading, in turn, frequented, exceptionally, the long sequence, orchestrated as an effervescent uproar of registers and idiolects. However, in the poem *Ukulele Music* (1985) he invented at least one memorable larger-than-life-character of a Dickensian genealogy, Viv the maid, with her droll ungrammatical letters.

had turned it into an esoteric and initiatory circuit. Unquestionably, the five greatest poets of the second half of the twentieth century are Larkin, Hughes, Gunn, Hill and Heaney. They are not easily rated with respect to each other. All five have had and still have their admirers and their clique of fans; and each of the five, except for Gunn, is hailed by his supporters as the greatest of the second half of the twentieth century. Hughes and Larkin have been granted this epithet repeatedly; Heaney is the heir of Yeats and this is enough; Hill is in turn the most scholarly and most difficult of the quintet. The opposite attitude – relativizing, throwing water on the fire – descends from the axiom, or prejudice, that the contemporary is always and on principle inferior to the ancient: being the greatest of the second half of the twentieth century does not imply being *tout court* great, even more so if a contemporary poet is compared with great poets from other ages. Alternatively, these overestimations can be circumvented by deeming them 'editorial propaganda': Praz used this label in an early review (1970) in which he asked himself in a nutshell, echoing Manzoni: 'Was this real glory'?[2] In these eulogies there is always the unspoken, overlooked or only empirical premise, involving a question of aesthetics or even merely of theory or history of taste: what is the criterion to measure the greatness or greater greatness of a writer? Eliot pointed out that Tennyson was a great poet according to two parameters, richness and variety, possibly adding a third, prosodic expertise. I personally do not believe it possible to rate poets, and hence these five poets, on the basis of their poetics: greatness is measured in terms of results, not of intentions and programmes, and it flows from the aesthetic achievement of a poem, undoubtedly a measurement without thermometer. Poets can be great both by virtue of their thematic variety or their monotonous concentration on a single obsessive theme; prosodic oscillation may or may not be preferred to skill in the use of a single, prevalent metre; productive wealth and poverty can cut both ways, because a writer can sin by excess, and have produced too much, or by deficiency, having produced little or too little, inducing priority being

2   SSI, vol. II, 456. The whole of the first part of the review (on 'the British literary scene', 455–61) is a takedown of Gunn and especially of Hughes.

given to another parameter. At the top of the measuring criteria we may place density of thought, no matter what this thought may be, and it may be an asset to be as profound as Hill; but so may be the absence of depth like that of Larkin, with an implicit premise that Hill ends up being too deep, dark, pedantic, pettifogging even. The final suggestion that stems from this overly hasty discussion, is that we cannot answer the question of who is the greatest *poet* of the second half of the twentieth century in Britain: we must specify who is the greatest lyrical poet *tout court*, who is the greatest narrative poet, the greatest theological or spiritualist poet, and so forth.

3. The beginnings of the Movement date back to the early 1950s, and are to be located between the walls of Oxford University colleges, and traced to the articles of the student magazine directed by John Wain, the writings of F. W. Bateson in *Essays in Criticism*, and the prior indirect support of Leavis and his entourage. It was Wain who in a 1953 BBC broadcast presented the poetry of Larkin and Amis as an example of the salutary advent of a kind of *Neue Sachlichkeit*. But there began to appear more and more frequently, in top flight magazines, essays and notes decreeing the end of symbolist, existentialist, experimental, romantic-apocalyptic poetry, or even the politicized kind, and hailing a compelling need for normality, practicality and neorealism, and the urgency of making a clean slate of the past. The thumbs-up was given especially to Eliot, Auden and Dylan Thomas. The founding event remains the publishing, in 1955 and 1956, of two anthologies of nine poets already sharing aesthetic and operational positions. All of them were no older than forty, only one was female. The anthologies were *Poets of the Fifties*, edited by D. J. Enright but published in Japan, and *New Lines*, by Robert Conquest. In his introductory declaration of intents, Conquest hailed a poetry without theoretical vassalage, a poetry which was not psychoanalytical or epistemological, but empirical, rooted in everyday occurrences, and addressing a kind of integral man; its objective was the restoration of 'healthy' values. Conquest included a programmatic poem of his own that sang the praises of an updated 'Enlightenment'; Kingsley Amis another, 'against Romanticism'. However, as for the cohesion and homogeneity of the group, the poets, on seeing themselves included in these two anthologies, immediately reacted with coldness and scepticism. Of the twentieth-century movements, ultimately only Imagism, and in

any case only for a short time, demanded and obtained total faithfulness to its prescriptions from its members; not so Georgian poetry, Vorticism or surrealism. The members of the Movement were to show a vague, personal, even heretical application of its guiding concepts. The intrinsic and absolute value of the Movement's poetry, which many praised heatedly as a 'literary cyclone', by now needs to be downsized. The only great poet of the Movement is Larkin, closely followed by Gunn. Enright, Conquest, Wain and Holloway were literary critics who sporadically wrote some trifling poetry and quickly petered out. Conquest strayed far from his intentions; Amis was primarily a novelist, and not even too illustrious at that, and I shall be dealing with him as such, together with other cases of transfusions between the Movement and the 'angry young men'. The only other poets of the Movement who had a distinctive personality were Jennings and Davie.[3]

3   One novelist and a novel unrelated to the fashions, and therefore difficult to place, are William Cooper (1910–2002), who graduated from Cambridge and taught for a long time in Leicester, and *Scenes from Provincial Life* (1950), the first novel from a short saga. Its hero, Joe Lunn, is often unadvisedly labelled as the forerunner of the 'angry young men'. In my view, this lyrical, diaphanous but also maliciously and covertly humorous novel recalls instead Larkin's first two narrative works, which I discuss below. Therefore, if anything it anticipates the aesthetics and the objectives of the Movement, seen empirically, in this case, as a tendency not towards greater complexity but greater simplicity. The title immediately creates a parodic intertextual expectation by citing George Eliot's collection of 'scenes of clerical life'. It is essential that this story should take place in an English province in which echoes of the metropolis and the world itself arrive muffled and a tad mythologized, with a slight delay in terms of history and civilization. In the nameless locality where the plot begins we breathe, slightly moved forward in time, that quiet sleepiness, that stagnation and that naïve forgetfulness that reign in the motionless provincial worlds not only of George Eliot, but also of Trollope, Mrs Gaskell and Mrs Oliphant. Not by coincidence, the plot, narrated in the first person with metanarrative devices, occasional Sternian quips and self-commiserating comments, is placed in the year 1939, with the winds of war that induce a novice writer and secondary-school teacher to dream of emigrating to America while loving and sweetly courting chaste Myrtle, who unthinkably lives a petty double life in the village. The development is concentric and the dynamism never pronounced, because of a prevailing taste for fine skits soberly but pointedly penned, for the bizarre larger-than-life-character, for the idyllic outdoor outings by bike, or the poetry and the little saga of school life. Never do we

4. Almost overnight, the Movement was not disavowed and ousted but metabolized by the manifesto that the critic Alfred Alvarez wrote as a foreword to the anthology *The New Poetry* (1962). He called for greater commitment from the poets, advised a more panoramic and attentive look at the problems on the carpet in the contemporary world, and lamented the insensitivity of poets to the yet unhealed war wounds. However, from the early 1960s, a unique line of succession was lost and a certain chaotic anarchy began to reign. There was certainly a lack of such a large and noisy group as the Movement and the new formations were sparser and more transient. The two and a half decades from 1945 to 1970 marked the appearance of unclassifiable poets, peripheral ones or deserters from the groups. They were often naturalized Britons or with dual nationality, and some of them, and this is symptomatic, were first translators and based their poetry on borrowed material. The germs and stimuli found again their natural transmission channel in magazines of varying duration. The Jewish Welsh poet and doctor Dannie Abse (1923–2014) headed an ephemeral revolt against the narrowness of the horizons and the shy, dejected composure of Larkin and his followers, advocating a Dionysian poetry in a suitably titled anthology, *Mavericks* (1957), which soon fell into oblivion. Equally sporadic, a one-day wonder, was the fame of the 'Liverpool Poets', not coincidentally from the native city of the Beatles. Their leader was Adrian Henry (1932–2000), a riveting entertainer of local crowds with readings of texts that were genuine whirlwinds of disparate borrowings from both high and mass culture. Concrete or visual poetry had its leading British practitioner in Ian Hamilton Finlay (1925–2006), whose compositions are polymorphic and composite creations where the verbal structure accompanies and integrates with a graphic counterpart and with a range of other materials, also *trouvés*. The strict impersonality of this operation is, however, indebted from the most various Modernisms. Finlay's poems appear as language

---

get the impression of anything stale and mechanical. Joe Lunn, as I mentioned, has little of the angry young man; he is instead dreamy, naïve, and despite all his skin-deep anarchism, non-political; and he is not, as the angry young men will be, a social climber hungry for sex. The other novels of the Joe Lunn saga show his full return among the ranks of respectability.

dismembered into its morphemic and phonological components, and take the form of free words within the paper space, or serial syntactic chains that do not seem unrelated to Beckett's practice. The late Finlay chose to opt for a more committed art by repeatedly juxtaposing symbolic objects of past and present civilizations to stress their cacophony.[4] The eclectic, extremely gifted Edwin Morgan (1920–2010) – the facility of his verse and the amplitude of his cultural references making him an Auden in smaller format – is to be allocated in equal parts to concrete and experimental poetry (until 1969), to the tradition of Scottish poetry and its 'Renaissance', to the so-called 'boomerang' of Calvinism and to a pungent and frank descriptivism of the new contemporary reality in Scotland. Active from 1952, Morgan surprises immediately for the ease with which he shifts from the most refined English to Scots, from the solemn word to the neologism, from the urban and everyday anecdotal to the experimental. His concrete poetry period extended from 1963 to 1969, and it takes the form of sequences of frames of words suspended and spaced at various heights on the page, or strings of lines of similar words and as if sprung from a computer, or phenomena of seriality in dissolution, with a progressive loss of alphabetic letters towards the end of the series.

4   Finlay was a composite and eclectic personality, and beyond and before being a 'concrete' poet he was a painter, graphic artist, sculptor and creator of gardens. He lived for a long time on one of his Lanarkshire holdings that he baptized 'Little Sparta', where he made, or rather invented, what are called 'poem-sculptures'. All these activities are only partially synchronic, as can be seen from the very representative anthology of his writings, *The Dancers Inherit the Party: Early Stories, Plays and Poems*, ed. K. Cockburn, Edinburgh 2004. Exactly half of this book is occupied by short stories written in a dry, bare and schematic style, and dealing with fishermen and children who live on the coast, an autobiographical element as the author spent his childhood near the fishing grounds. Finlay's earliest poems are even anecdotal, extravagant, naïve, or characterized by a simple, direct lyricism without artifice; the acrostic is rare, and more frequent is the landscape framework of three or four lines coated in an elementary imagism recalling the early MacDiarmid. The visual poems constitute, basically, only one segment, and their most abnormal feature is being written in thick Scots. These short poems form a small bestiary, and all the texts are preceded by a silhouette in ink of the animal referred to in the title.

5. The 'Group', created and coordinated in London from the mid-1950s by the poet and academic Philip Hobsbaum (co-editor of an anthology of its members in 1963, and, symptomatically, a former student of Leavis's at Cambridge), was in turn a free poetic society where poets of disparate training and varied calibre gathered together every week to read and comment on their poems, previously distributed in mimeograph. The motherhouse split into branches in Glasgow and, particularly fruitful, in Belfast, where Hobsbaum personally supervised the early stages of Heaney. The programmatic points of the 'Group' remained rather bland and indefinite, with the single aesthetic commandment of a rational control of inspiration, and with the result that its representatives ended up being somewhat dissimilar from each other. The members, leaving Ted Hughes due space, included figures of average value – such as the expatriate Australian Peter Porter (1929–2010), music-lover and music critic of the *TLS*, translator of Martial with satirical verve and an occasionally exquisite elegist – and others definitely more brilliant, such as the uneven Peter Redgrove (1932–2003), a vehement and undisciplined visionary and a fierce enemy of every established faith, which makes him at times an epigone of the surrealists and the New Apocalyptics; or George MacBeth (1932–1992). About MacBeth, it is proverbial to quote a judgement from the *TLS* that precociously lamented the waste of a sumptuous talent in a desultory, capricious, sensationalist vein aimed at easy success with the public. *the Review* (the small 't' is programmatic), later *The New Review*, ran from 1962 to 1979 as the natural seat of poetic experiments of an imagistic ancestry and spasmodic, minimalist dryness in its leading exponents, such as Ian Hamilton (1938–2001) and Hugo Williams (born 1942), authors of agonized compositions with finely honed preciousness and a magic and distilled enchantment, only sometimes sweetish, but sufficing to distinguish them from Larkin's followers.[5]

---

5   Both Williams and Craig Raine (§ 196.2) wrote a poem entitled 'The Butcher', and the comparison is in favour of Williams, whose poem is softer and tenderer, whereas that of Raine is merely artificial.

§ 76. *Larkin* I: Novels and early poems*

The two novels by Philip Larkin (1922–1985), which appeared prior to his debut in poetry, did not give rise to the particular or unmistakable impression of being the work of a future poet. However, one of the two characteristics which unite them is precisely that – gradually, and especially evident in the second – of depicting the absence of poetry in the life of dreamy heroes and heroines who yearn precisely for that. The other is the author's curious tendency to don a mask of a female or decidedly feminine sensitivity from which to probe this deficiency. Larkin's homosexuality had meanwhile 'evaporated'; he never married, but he did have contemporaneous affairs with women, and with time found himself a partner. He was then to be a poet who was also, if not more than anything else, narrative: a poet of anecdotes, from which he could draw a series of bittersweet, disconsolate and depressing reflections. *Jill* (1946) is precisely not the novel of a poet temporarily in search of his vocation, possibly abounding in descriptions of moods and detachable passages of a purple sort, studded with possibly sophisticated words, and passages carried through in elliptical syntax; on the contrary, it has a pleasant, easy, and therefore not always tense and exciting pace. It shows a penchant for comic, fantastic and finally tragic realism, with the hero growing up as he receives news of the bombardment of his native city. In John Kemp, this hero, the author is camouflaged, though Kemp lacks the physical and in part the intellectual attributes of the author, and comes from a city up north that replaces Coventry. The year 1946 was by now, for the novel, a no-man's-land. Larkin does not seem to have read and known, and therefore absorbed, any modernistic masterpiece. His storytelling even smacks of the *démodé* in its obsequious treatment of the character, in authorial omniscience, in its swinging between the flashback and the forward narrative; and the fantastic lacks the tones and leaps of other masters operating at the time. *Jill* is usually indicated as an unwitting travelling companion of the protest fiction of Amis and Wain, and one of those novels, indeed the pioneering one, centred on the university

---

*   *Collected Poems*, ed. A. Thwaite, London 1988, last reprint 2004, is the current reference edition, however questionable in its editorial choices, since it is not a truly complete edition but a selective one, and it presents the poems in chronological

life of talented youths coming from the provinces.[1] But the internal time is too early, and Kemp does not protest against anything. Not only does *Jill* precede by ten years the late and most acclaimed 'angry' novels, but its heart is Oxford, not a 'red-brick' university. However, Kemp is undoubtedly provincial, and a flashback tells how this inconspicuous diminutive boy was suddenly spotted by a sensitive secondary-school teacher and

order of composition, thereby disrupting the individual collections, of which the first is inexplicably relegated to an appendix. The edition with the same title from 2003 restores the original order of the individual collections and omits the unpublished ones (on the confusing fact of two different editions with the same title and the same editor and publisher, see S. Knight, *TLS*, 14 February 2003, 10, and A. Kirsch, *TLS*, 13 May 2005). A recent new edition is *The Complete Poems*, ed. A. Burnett, London 2014. *Early Poems and Juvenilia*, ed. A. T. Tolley, London 2005; *Selected Letters*, London 1993. D. Timms, *Philip Larkin*, Edinburgh 1973; L. Kuby, *Philip Larkin: An Uncommon Poet for the Common Man*, The Hague 1974; A. Brownjohn, *Philip Larkin*, ed. I. Scott-Kilvert, London 1975; B. K. Martin, *Philip Larkin*, Boston, MA 1978; A. Motion, *Philip Larkin*, London 1982, and *Philip Larkin: A Writer's Life*, London 1993; *Larkin at Sixty*, ed. A. Thwaite, London 1982; G. Latre, *Locking Earth to the Sky: A Structuralist Approach to Philip Larkin's Poetry*, Frankfurt am Main 1985; T. Whalen, *Philip Larkin and English Poetry*, London 1986; R. Day, *Larkin*, Milton Keynes 1987; *Philip Larkin: 1922–1985: A Tribute*, ed. G. Hartley, London 1988; *Critical Essays on Philip Larkin: The Poems*, ed. L. Cookson and B. Loughrey, London 1989; *Philip Larkin: The Man and His Work*, ed. D. Salwak, Houndmills 1989; J. Rossen, *Philip Larkin: His Life's Work*, London 1989; A. T. Tolley, *My Proper Ground: A Study of the Work of Philip Larkin*, Edinburgh 1991; J. Booth, *Philip Larkin: Writer*, New York 1992, and, as editor, *New Larkins for Old: Critical Essays*, London 2000; A. Swarbrick, *Out of Reach: The Poetry of Philip Larkin*, London 1995; W. Hope, *Philip Larkin*, London 1997; L. Lerner, *Larkin*, Plymouth 1996; *Philip Larkin*, ed. S. Regan, Basingstoke 1997; B. J. Leggett, *Larkin's Blues: Jazz, Popular Music, and Poetry*, London 1999; A. R. Falzon, *Negative Indicative: Philip Larkin in the Forties*, Pisa 2000; R. Bradford, *Philip Larkin: A Biography*, London, 2004; A. E. Soccio, *Philip Larkin. Immaginazione poetica e percorsi del quotidiano*, Roma 2008; M. W. Rowe, *Philip Larkin: Art and Self: Five Studies*, Basingstoke 2011; J. Booth, *Philip Larkin: Life, Art and Love*, New York 2014.

1   The preface to the 1975 reprint is an affectionate homage to the bawdy climate of Oxford in the second year of the war and to Kingsley Amis in particular. Some anecdotes recall Amis's extraordinary skill in imitation.

induced to swot to obtain a scholarship. The plot, which opens with a train journey from the Northern county to Oxford of the shy, simple and bashful fresher, immediately glitters with a good comic sketch: on the train, Kemp decides to go to the toilet to eat his sandwiches, not wishing to be seen doing so by other passengers, who calmly pull out their bags of food and offer it to him when he returns to the compartment. In its first, slightly flat and slow half, the novel explores the adaptation of the naïve boy to academic life: he does not drink, does not smoke, is wary of sex and is forced to witness the casualness and mischievousness of his room-mate and the rascally behaviours of the latter's friends. Unwittingly, he lives through a small chain of disappointments and surprises, with a slight nod to vice. In this initial phase, *Jill* suffers a great deal from comparison with the novel it openly imitates, and with which it has an air of obvious familiarity, namely, Waugh's *Brideshead Revisited*. It also invites comparison with certain comical scenes from Beerbohm's *Zuleika Dobson*, since sensual and sexual desire soon grows and erupts in Kemp. He needs to affirm his weak personality after having leant on the worldly wise and shrewd Chris Warner, the roommate who twists him around his little finger. The thread of totally stifled carnal stimuli passes through a beautiful girl on the train, a classmate and a friend of Chris's who one day tickles his chin while knotting his tie, and Chris's still youthful mother, who arrives at Oxford station one day to be met by Kemp (this is another reason why Larkin's novel recalls Beerbohm's).[2] Kemp celebrates his rite of passage by getting drunk for the first time, and by wasting some of those pounds he had earlier stashed away so covetously. The comic and sometimes sharp realism seems, having reached the middle of the novel, to have exhausted its drive, which had never been, however, very high. There is not the slightest thrill of the prohibited and not a shadow of homosexuality among the Oxford students, who are if anything too womanizing. Larkin, at this point, resorts to a gimmick, and through it the novel visibly changes its register. Kemp the shy one invents a romance which, though it itself somewhat stale, allows him to gain a certain advantage over Chris Warner, whose brazen and fascinating

2   Volume 7, § 41.2.

exuberance, like that of a Dickensian Steerforth, suffers and declines as a result. With much embellishing and romanticizing, Kemp spins Warner the small saga of a non-existent sister of his, Jill; not only this, but he discovers that he himself has fallen in love with this romance and develops it, suddenly causing the vein of a feminine writer of love stories to blossom. He starts writing the chapters of a feminine school novelette full of sighing and adolescent envy, and adopting a falsetto, and hence the disguise, of a teenager keeping a daily diary. This creates for some time a novel within the novel, Larkin lending his *alter ego* a ventriloquist's voice, and sharing in the delight of this counterfeit. The episode is artificial and unconvincing, and even less satisfactory is the next turn of events when, and here lies a further citation of *Zuleika*, this sister Jill materializes in a fifteen-year-old who really is called Jill, and is not his kin, and whom John becomes infatuated with and chases around Oxford despite her slipperiness. With Jill, Kemp can recite the role of the male conqueror to himself, but the seduction is always deferred. With this materialization, or actual encounter of an imaginary simulacrum, a playful parody similar to the Victorian tales 'of divination' (as, for instance, in George Eliot's 'The Lifted Veil') is enacted. The final fade-out is in soft focus, with Kemp lying sick without having satisfied and realized his dreams.

2. *A Girl in Winter* (1947) is swathed in vaguer and more suffuse, 'poetic' atmospheres, and is written in three stages, of which the central one is a flashback that tells of the holiday that the sixteen-year-old Scandinavian schoolgirl Katherine Lind[3] spends in England to learn English, on the invitation of her pen pal Robin. In the long romance that forms this part, a story builds up with shaded and opaque contours, and with predictable and indistinct scenes showing the deportments and pleasures of a wealthy post-war middle-class family. The absence of strong passions, and the only sketchy skirmishes, recall the fires under the ashes of tales by Mansfield or Bowen. Nothing in this flashback stirs, in an unreal calm that even on the page is slightly dozing, until the moderate surprise: that it was Robin's sister, Jane,

---

3   Her country of origin is never revealed, but we can deduce it approximately from her surname; in the only allusion, it is said to be thirty miles from the English coast across the water.

a neurotic and frustrated twenty-five-year-old, who urged her emotionally slumbering brother to invite Katherine to their Oxford country home. The return to the present introduces years later the 'foreigner' Katherine again in England, employed at a library, in search of the realization of that love which the cold, staid and restrained Robin never wanted to embark upon. Larkin is camouflaged in this feminine portrait that confesses a romantic need to escape which cannot be satisfied, if not too late and too fleetingly in the clumsy, non-committal kiss on the last day of that youthful idyll. For the rest, Katherine's alienation and extraneousness to the surrounding environment are exacerbated, underlined as they are by her foreign nationality. This extraneousness takes on a very clear colourful and symbolic import: Katherine is alienated like Camus's hero; but the snow and the frost in which the plot unfolds during the war form the same symbolic backdrop as in Bowen's *The Death of the Heart*, of whose heroine Katherine is a twin (moreover, the memory of that distant idyll is for Larkin's Katherine the remembrance of summer heat and warmth). This immature, naïve romantic purity is put into relief in the first and third parts, which take place within a period of a few hours on a Saturday during the war. They illustrate the remarkable narrative prowess of Larkin, who never did complete a third novel, and feature satirical and grotesque simulacra of squalor and alienation, from the colleague in the library with toothache to the grimy dentist that treats Katherine, especially the verbose head librarian and his girlfriend, who lives in a dingy, far from clean suburban apartment with an invalid mother to look after: all examples of an inability to dream, of that arid, degraded everyday reality worsened by the war from which the student John Kemp also seeks to escape. In the end, Katherine sees Robin again, but as Larkin the poet would often realize, the misery of the present can also disappoint a remembered, vibrant expectation from the past.

3. Generic and reductive, although confirmed by the poet, is a paradigmatic journey marked by a clear and peremptory watershed and ranging from Yeats ('as penetrating as garlic') to Hardy. This is a convenient, mnemonic outline, but it does not take into account other crucial reading experiences, and suggests more than it should that Larkin had an 'evolution', whereas he is instead a poet with a very quickly identified physiognomy. His documented debut took place when he was not yet twenty, in the school and

public magazines of his city, Coventry, understandably with poems with crepuscular echoes, a trademark of the post-Romantic Nineties, and with the typical syntactic inversions between noun and adjective, an excess of deliberate alliterations, the lexicon of 'poetic' tradition, the word paintings of natural scenery and shifting atmospheres, of wind, riverbanks and reeds, forests and ponds, seasonal changes and cycles. These pictures of pure, empathetic and intoxicated descriptiveness were to continue well into the 1940s. It is difficult not to get the impression of an exercise, also because the thematic leitmotif is the old and much exploited *tout passe*, occasionally intermitted by playful, humorous or even bawdy poems. Except that even these latter are, in their own way, already carved ditties, calligraphic but not artificial, bare, measured and economical like precise etchings – or at least the majority of them are. A Blakean 'sickness' soon lurks in phenomena that are no longer ends in themselves: behind the splendour of reborn nature is a forewarning of death, the skeleton, the shroud, in increasingly spectral, threatening, ominous visions. On the one hand, the density of the language mounts with its obscurity, elusiveness, and hermetic and less idiomatic lexicons; on the other, the poet defends himself ('After-Dinner Remarks'), tells of his malaise and exudes escapist longings, coining the first myths of the departing emigrant; or he even spies on apparent displays of unison between lovers, only apparent since even love falls into the regime of the transitory. Around 1941, we can feel the bitterness resonate in the poet's sarcastic remarks and confessions of pessimism, resignation, and absence of prospects, though spaced apart and estranged ('A Writer'). *The North Ship* (1945),[4] Larkin's first published collection, is only a more conscious and slightly matured elaboration of the forms and themes of the poet in his earlier work. Therein the same oneiric and apocalyptic scenarios pass and re-pass, livid with desolation and undoing, broken unisons, happiness destroyed, loves corroded, even if sudden glimmers of light illuminate the absence of hope. It is a small songbook of frustrations, occasionally compensated for by the spectacles of a euphoric nature, or by the thrill of

---

4   A diary of a dream-like marine trip, with weird images of ephemeral and illusory loves.

an adventure into the unknown, which requires preparation and awareness of the risks. This modulation is sober and deliberately not solemn, occasionally dense with colloquialisms, in the captivating and resigned 'metaphysical' or Catullian vein of the greeting to the departing beloved ('Love, we must part now'), or in the appeal to the heart that would wander alone without finding relief, or in a melancholy, controlled pathos, one step away from the sentimental ('Dawn'). What is new is Larkin's ability to associate, embroider and rhapsodize before an unusual phenomenon (such as the speech of a Polish girl). The form can even dry up, as in the isolated lapidary quatrain that closes with the epigram: 'Time is the echo of an axe / Within a wood'.

4. *XX Poems*, a collection from 1951, can be examined against an earlier one, a typewritten sheaf of poems posted by Larkin to several publishers for a poetic book that never materialized. This collection of twenty poems opens under the mark of continuity, but with the increasingly visible variants of the objective approach and of distancing irony. The poet is on the one hand still alienated, and repeats the admission of a hiatus between himself and nature; he illustrates a range of situations of heartbreak, and the indifference of one of the two lovers. Explicitly, he confesses a desire for purification from a morbid and contrite state of sin and discouragement, with liturgical images and metaphors (confession – the last resort of despair). But, as in the previous collection, there are some surprising glimmers of happiness and unity between the beloved ('Wedding-Wind', which is not Larkin's negative wind, but blows on a kind of Blakean, decontextualized couple of primeval progenitors in an elementary and primordial countryside of peasants and grooms). Happiness comes from a sense of a 'perpetual morning' that seems to have exorcized death. The poetic 'I' lives in a kind of 'evergreen' freeze frame, which he later leaves, being expelled and hunted down like an Adam. The fact is that outside the jurisdiction of the dream, growing means setting off towards death. 'At the chiming of light upon sleep' confirms that the myth of the expulsion from the Garden of Eden is the vague and unclear bedrock constantly referred to in this collection. In 'Come then to prayers', Adam and Eve purify themselves, and a sword comes 'to execute or crown', while a flood or deluge laps the rim of morning. Dreams, nightmares and terrifying insomnia (the writing on

the wall spells death)[5] are violently succeeded by dreamy visions of states of bliss and reconciliation ('To a Very Slow Air'). The confession of the aegis of death comes as early as the poem on Larkin's twenty-sixth birthday.[6] Larkin's binary point of view is announced by the poem, not included in *XX Poems*, 'Sinking like sediment through the day': life is a daily distillation of the clear and pure liquid separated from the dregs, just as at the end of the day the night is mere dissension, suffering, emptiness, and disappointment; or it is also a disgusting woman who induces, tempts and seduces the deluded man, who believes that by embracing her she will be beautiful, though he tells her: be beautiful and I will embrace you. This dialectic is resumed in 'Since the majority of me', which tells of a majority that wish to cease loving, and a minority that rise and doggedly recast the promises, without ever learning. 'If My Darling' establishes Larkin's fundamental opposition between inside and outside, but does so in a shrewd and ironic manner (citing Alice breaking through the surface of the mirror): how the beloved, that is, can penetrate the brain of the lover and see its disorder and ferment. 'Wants', which hopes for oblivion much more bitterly, disowns the cycle of procreativity, but it is merely a denegation. At the same time, the cloak of the apocalyptic absence of contextualization is gradually rent, and the thick mantle of the impending darkness is lifted. 'An April Sunday brings the snow' is now light and airy on the absence of a beloved woman, but absence caught in its objective correlatives, like those many jars of jam which are a sign of her presence-absence. Insomnia, too, is treated with mitigated and shrewd self-irony.

§ 77. Larkin II: The exquisite miniaturist

The spontaneous favour, admiration and almost ecumenical satisfaction that hailed Larkin in Britain after the war was due to many causes. His poetic range remained modest, his voice but a whisper, far from emphatic, and anything but elephantine; he was shy, secluded and virtually without

---

5   In the poem 'Träumerei'.

6   Cf. Motion's fine observation (1982, 73), on the very early obsession with ageing that unites Larkin and Eliot.

notable biographical events. Gradually, the cultured middle classes, and a large section of sensitive common readers, witnessed the birth or the emergence, from a poet who had initially been hermetic, dark, convoluted, of a limpid, frank and subtle singer of timeless and at the same time topical, late twentieth-century neuroses, in which they recognized themselves. Larkin was more precisely an exhibitor, in the language of high but approachable poetry, of the contemporary existential condition, with an apocalypticism that is gradually demolished and disarmed in forms and modes of irony, wit, lightness, and self-pity. This escalation was marked, until it ended up skimming political apathy and the facility of the popular ditty, and the coining of a poetry exquisitely suited to being recited. This gained Larkin the unthinkable acknowledgement of one of the very few authors (second only to Betjeman) of poetic best-sellers in the second half of the century. But one should think immediately after of Larkin as a model intellectual, a conscientious, 'sober and industrious' employee,[7] thirty years a librarian at the University of Hull. He was therefore not a professional poet, and not primarily a poet for poets. Nor was he the cosmopolitan and traditional drifter poet with a deadbeat life. Heading the Movement along with Amis, Davie and Gunn, what he shared with these poets, but had already adopted *ab ovo*, was a certain distance from Modernism as well as the liquidation of the orgiastic imagism of a Dylan Thomas. An anthology of twentieth-century British poetry that he later compiled (1973) reaffirmed the primacy of the indigenous tradition with blatant, revolutionary, revealing liberties in his selection criteria. With his stance against '-isms', Larkin satisfied a need for authenticity and patriotic and even chauvinistic nationalism: he was against the avant-garde and the mosaic-poem and the tapestry of citations of others' poetry. Except at the beginning, his own poetry did not teem or overflow with echoes, and he soon crafted his own language and a repertoire of themes. The British felt that he was one of them, their spokesperson:[8] someone with common, widely shared and accepted feelings, ideas and behaviour.[9] Finally, Larkin is not an esoteric poet, and does

---

7   'Poetry of Departures'.

8   It was Alvarez who called him 'the man next door' (quoted in Motion 1982, 31).

9   One of the tenderest and most delicate poems ever written by Larkin, 'The Mower', gratifies a distinctly British attribute, the love for animals: scything the grass the poet

not rely on philosophies, mythologies and ideological systems; he speaks directly and without filters, thus being accessible and with no special tolls to pay. Naturally, the coordinates of his poetics should be taken with a pinch of salt and as broad operational provisions. A poetry without symbolic halos, which, theoretically, Larkin said was his goal, is in principle impossible; and Larkin the poet reinstates obscurity, modernistic decontextualization, the imagistic flashes and much more in his poetic praxis. Subtilizing, he distinguished modernistic obscurity as an end in itself from that required by the 'complexity of the topic'.[10] The only substantial criticism levelled at him has concerned precisely that merit which has been found to be so peculiar in him: of being a natural – almost, one might say, an insular or isolated – poet in the worst sense of the word, and therefore 'provincial' and even philistine,[11] and a restorer and conservative instead of an experimenter.[12] He was deaf to civil commitment, it was said, and preoccupied solely with the sphere of his own individuality.[13]

---

has inadvertently killed a harmless hedgehog, and takes care to tell us he is sorry, having also fed it before, and regrets that the next day he will wake but the small animal will not, and he draws a very elementary homily on loving our neighbours.

10   Motion 1982, 18. We can also lay on him an excess in the coinage of new composite words, or of parentheses and interjections. Precisely by opposing the 'metaphysical' style and diction, Larkin falls into a convoluted and obscure argument, at least occasionally.

11   He felt no shame about his inability to understand and speak languages, nor did he like travelling or even leaving Britain for a single day, and he undoubtedly exaggerated in candidly admitting that he did not know the foreign writers considered to be trendy, such as Borges (as he confessed in the essay 'An Innocent at Home', in Salwak 1989, 54–8). He was also accused of supporting Thatcherism, a charge that he never denied.

12   The uncollected poem 'Fiction and the Reading Public', dating from 1954, is however, and right from the allusive title, a mocking pastiche directed against the crude aesthetic canons of Leavis, such as the truthfulness of literature, the morality of art, poetic justice and the literary aim of high-class entertainment. Larkin, who as a young boy wanted to be a drummer, was equally conservative in his musical tastes, and his antipathy to the modern jazz of Charlie Parker and Monk is testified to by his musical articles in *The Daily Telegraph*, gathered in *All What Jazz* (1970).

13   An accusation that is not entirely true: since 1941, with his poem 'Conscript', Larkin had tackled the folly of war and hailed a promising egotist who had enlisted; much

2. Larkin kept writing, but ever frugally, until his death, filtering and selecting without rushing madly into publication in series. A tireless revisionist, incredibly slow in polishing and honing, he only released finished products, and the collective edition enriched the published ones with a series, albeit not abundant, of unpublished poems. He was, as a result, an extremely elegant poet, verbally smooth, graceful and cultivated. He made his name at twenty, as we have seen, with lyrics of a perfectly objective type, or rather of correlative objectives, such as seascapes, dawns, scenes of nature with trees, woods, riverbanks, bird flights, surf. These beginnings, among which are short playful poems, *boutades* published in local rags or in the Oxford student magazine, do not have much to say. With his first collection Larkin became a subjective poet who auscultates his malaise as mirrored in daily spectacles. These are always recollected emotions and thoughts that, readjusted a short time later, do not give an impression of immediacy; they are therefore reflective, phenomenological poems; also, occasionally, convoluted arguments closed in the end by striking pithy lines. Larkin is a sort of Leopold Bloom with considerably more culture, and much more sophistication; less vulgar, he nevertheless remains an *homme moyen sensuel.* He sings – or more precisely laments – the eternal themes of lyric poetry from every epoch: ephemeral and frequently frustrated love, disputes with God over the meaning of creation, and therefore the very fallacy of creation that has no purpose, and the inevitability of death without other-worldly prospects. He is a humanistic and secular poet. This Joycean suggestion is corroborated when we realize that many of Larkin's compositions are in fact short interior monologues, where the public behaviour, and even the public utterance, are accompanied by a countermelody of reactions of thought, unspoken and only detected by the poet – such as mental comments, asides, whispers, growls even. The reality with which this intellectual clashes is that of post-war Britain, of the changing of customs, with permissiveness, the decline of the aegis of religion, and mass phenomena such as pop music and cinema. But it was

---

later he would joke about the withdrawal of British troops from a militarized area of the Far East ('Homage to a Government'). Without a doubt, attention to public affairs was not Larkin's forte.

not Larkin's ambition to draw up a comprehensive sociological framework. The data we find are individual, scattered, subtracted from the continuum of an available mass, thus small and softened emblems. Consequently, we cannot really say that Larkin's poetry is symbolic of the malaise of the intellectual in post-war Britain. This mask, this *alter ego*, is him – Larkin. Having said this, the omnipresent 'I' or its shadow are those of a lonely man, frustrated, remembering, sleepless, hung-up, his wings clipped from a very young age, obsessed with the passing of time and the imminence of death.[14] These traits are developed into poems of pure meditation with only the slightest traces of external events; more often in the form of experiences remembered, anecdotes and events experienced, which therefore become – another Joycean analogy – *epiphanies*. In his most typical poems, Larkin always tells us that at a certain time or on a certain day, when perhaps it was dawn, or when travelling by plane or train, a certain experience happened that made him think; but the occasion may even be omitted. In this way there starts to grow a memorable repertoire of small external events summarized in their occurrences, closed by the coda of the mental processes they caused, while the actual words addressed to others have stated different things. In the end, a behavioural habit, or a rather sad, resigned or disconsolate maxim is drawn. Larkin's preferred prosodic measure can only be the short, even incredibly short poem, without an obvious or apparent context, which with a play on images leads to a final, rather surprising, and far from galvanizing truth – or even, so to speak, to a cold shower. To find similar, neat little pictures of essential and economical words, we need to return to Housman and Edward Thomas, or to Emily Dickinson for the keenly elliptical procedure, for the sudden metaphorical twist, the *saltus* of the image or even of logic. We can find this in the poem 'Modesties',

---

14   The aetiology of frustration is investigated in one of Larkin's last poems, an externalization never so angry, and for once apparently mimetic: his lack of charm with women is due to a 'violence / Suffered long ago', to 'wrong awards', and 'an arrogant eternity', by which Larkin is perhaps alluding to the imperatives of religious faith. This aetiology is already elucidated, even more clearly, in the youthful poem (1939) whose first line eloquently says: 'Having grown up in shade of Church and State'. In 'A Writer', indeed, 'no actions were rewarded'.

which accentuates the reduction of language to its degree zero, without 'further embroidery', and whose words are the correlative of the 'simple' thought that remains. When Larkin rhymes, he is ingenious in avoiding the monotony of perfectly rhymed lines; even the prosody is not uniform, alternating series of stanzas of long lines with stubby tercets and quatrains. Larkin's language displays marked excursions: as a university graduate he often uses long polysyllabic words and others of Latin derivation, and so he is not an 'Anglo-Saxon' poet; yet he mixes this register with that of slang, conversation and spoken contractions, creating continual imbalances. Bathos becomes grating when Larkin, who already accepts in his poetic repertoire real events that lyrical poetry had not contemplated until then, cannot bring himself to tolerate periphrases; so that, from Larkin on, in the vocabulary of poetry we find those four-letter words that only novelists had previously sanctioned.

3. *The Less Deceived*[15] (1955), the collection that introduced Larkin to the public at large, was surrounded and preceded by poems, at the time uncollected, that captured the confrontation between the lonely intellectual, frustrated by an elephantine life of thinking, and an everyday reality with which he is out of step. He does not know what and why he is building and lays bricks one on top of another ('To put one brick upon another'); the whimpering gossips with whom he travels by train or by bus are not in mutual intercommunication with him.[16] In other terms, the minute and sparse phenomenology of daily life has leapt to the foreground, recapped and summarized in impressions that touch, even tear and burn, and in a story that becomes broken, like many individual telegraphic entries. Larkin had now matured into a relieved and elegiac poet from the macerated and conflictual one of the past; he knows of death but he awaits it lucidly and coldly. Thus, next to a still evocative voice, room is made for a poetry that is no longer dry, fractured into flashes of images, but discursive, argumentative, flowing with increasingly long

15   From a line in 'Deceptions', on the rape of a young girl, from which the title is drawn.
16   'The local snivels through the fields', with the self-irony of its 'labels' that 'shout', but which are ignored, and with the typical final contortion, because even death comes with 'All we have done not mattering'.

syntactic periods. 'Reasons for Attendance' is an early poem emblematic of all Larkin. In it he observes external life and a dance of young people in which he does not take part, and which at first seems to embody happiness for him; only to conclude that those who believe they are happy are happy, deceiving themselves; and that the dancers are happy but also anyone is happy who is watching them and stays on the side-lines. The novelty of this poem is a poetic stream of consciousness which expresses itself in asides and parentheses; it is also the perfect harmony between a reflection that seems to be true and the doubt that it is merely a mental reservation, or a form of self-consolation. The call to spy and watch is a 'bell', that of art – 'if you like' – which makes the observer aware of his individuality, and hence also of his separation; but with a pinch of self-mockery, a trimming of his pride. Ever more frequent is the epiphanic anecdote, such as that of the train journey and the unexpected stop at Coventry station (where a catalogue of coveted but missed opportunities is reawoken), an anecdote that must be told in a poetic form, that is pruned down to the essentials in drastic hypotaxis.[17] The poem that greets the birth of Amis's daughter is one of Larkin's two or three most famous in any period, for the delightful delicacy of the hopes it expresses. The existential investigation is toned down in the form of a joke, with a little of that distancing and humorous relief we sometimes find in Browning. But Larkin knows that he often recites self-deceptions to himself and he turns to pleasing oblique forms, as in the poem about the skin, which is a garment that must cover itself in wrinkles regardless of every rejuvenating treatment. 'Church Going', conceivably Larkin's most popular composition ever, is also the longest of the anecdotal ones, and the most discursive. A church always attracts visitors, he says, even those who do not recognize its ancient function and fiction; the poet's quiet and sceptical visit closes with the admission of a secular respect that remains open to religious mystery, and to the historical benefit of religion for the people. The success of the poem lies in Larkin's ability to reduce and arrange a modern subject and a recalcitrant experience, together with a complex turn of reasoning, into rhyming lines

17   'I remember, I remember'.

and regular prosodies. The argument terminates in a public query, in a dilemma of modern life, in other words in the sociological phenomenon of religious disaffection: what will we do with churches when nobody attends them anymore, in an ever more secularized present? This is a reflective coda of Arnoldian ancestry, since it deals with the relationship between religion, scepticism and *Aberglaube*. Like Arnold, Larkin does not disown religion's precious task of unifying what is divided. This is a clear echo of those nostalgic yearnings for a compact and unified cosmos that the Victorians harboured, and of which Larkin was not ashamed: a church is the symbolic shrine of great deeds and historical landmarks, the living register and the collective memory of birth, life, family, and death. In a church, everyone will be surprised to find in him- or herself, 'A hunger [...] to be more serious'.[18] In the sequence of modern epiphanies we also find Larkin's poem that reflects on the renouncing of women's maiden names when they marry, which still remains a form of survival of that 'I' and the identity they bore; in another ('Mr Bleaney') the poet rents the house of a previous tenant and falls into his persona and identifies with him, but without being able to penetrate his innermost thoughts.

4. The collection *The Whitsun Weddings*[19] (1964) hinges on the phenomena of the passing of time, on nostalgic remembrance, on speculation of what might have been; it denounces the senselessness of life and the terrifying speed with which death comes ('Ignorance', 'Afternoons'). However, Larkin's poems also began by then to touch the chord of pathos and overly easy regret, of the striking ending, of the moving anecdote (like that of two old spinsters of whom one dies, leaving the other frighteningly disorientated). The poet is skilful and consummate in repeated announcements of imminent death, in the depiction of horizons on which nothing

---

18   It is no coincidence that various poems were now about elderly people or no longer young characters who browse through photo albums or listen back to old records, reliving emotions and associations of a time more beautiful than it really was. In truth, an omen and a discomfort began to be felt, and we knew that the dreams would not entirely come true.

19   The eponymous lyric is yet another *tour de force*: married couples in archaic clothes get on a train, and at the railway stations celebrate local rites.

looms and of anecdotes of alienated actions in a broken shorthand style. In one pungent poem a buxom girl on a poster, advertising a beautiful beach, has her effigy marred by graffiti, until the poster is replaced (but with one bearing the admonition: 'Help cancer research'). Indirectly it is the thing itself that is advertised – the buxom girl – that disappears ('Sunny Prestatyn'). 'Love' pretends to examine the double absurdity, of selfishness and altruism, in love.[20] The collection *High Windows* (1974) also alternates short poems with other longer, impressionistic and anecdotal ones, with excruciating endings on the theme of the vanity of human expectations, of disappointed hopes, of the crossing of certain limits only to discover nothing behind them (as in the poem that provides the title). The theme that sexual permissiveness is a beatific conquest is discussed in the famous, already mentioned 'Annus Mirabilis', the year 1963. Previously, one was clumsy, one was fighting for goals of little account; after 1963 the stakes became higher; here Larkin does not take up the stance that one might expect, that is to say that sexual liberation and permissiveness were illusory (in fact, after 1963, 'everyone felt the same'). 'Sad Steps' ends up saying that nature is in perennial rejuvenation, where the old man becomes distressed. Rough and vulgar, Larkin snaps that life is a cyclical 'rip-off'. Disgorged, he soliloquizes on how we might refuse painful tasks and instead end up accepting them; but the whole poem in question – 'Vers de Société' – focuses on the discrepancy between public demeanour and rough inner thought, unspoken. In the end, the poet asks himself whether it is true that we are better off alone. The late Larkin complained more and more often about the end of rural Merrie England, and manifested his ecological concern for invasion by concrete.[21]

---

20 Measuring himself against a certain Arnold, a model husband ('Self's the Man'), Larkin accused himself of selfishness, more precisely of feeling 'a swine', only to immediately defend and absolve himself.
21 'Going, Going'. The last poems are short, euphoric paeans to identity and unison with the beloved; but also new warnings of the imminence of death. 'Aubade' is a morbid, almost testamentary analysis of this feeling of the end, albeit from as early as 1977.

§ 78. *Gunn* * *I: The celebration of entropy*

As will be seen below, among an abundant number of critical studies on Thom Gunn (1929–2004), some are miscellaneous or comparative books, and present him in conjunction with other poets, as though
implicitly granting him a personality that is not marked and towering,
an amorphous identity, a less burning poetic inscape, and ultimately the
stature of a minor poet. In short, Gunn was camouflaged as a defector
from the Movement, or associated with Ted Hughes as a blood brother or
doppelganger;[1] and these are attributions, obviously, which are contradictory, and mutually exclude one another while enclosing a partial truth. An
unsolved dilemma concerned whether and to what extent Gunn was close
to Conquest's parameters. It has been pointed out, in this respect, that he
was unduly appropriated by the Movement, to which he was immediately,
and later to an even greater extent, fully extraneous. A related question is
to what extent Gunn was an American or at least an Anglo-American poet

---

*   *Collected Poems*, London 1993 (which I will quote as *CP*), to which must be added
the collection, less convincing and by then repetitive, *Boss Cupid* (2000). *I miei tristi
capitani e altre poesie*, ed. C. Pennati, has a valuable introduction by A. Lombardo,
Milano 1968. G. Miglior, 'La poesia di Thom Gunn', in *Studi e ricerche di lettera-
tura inglese e americana*, 2 (December 1971), 21–51; A. Bold, *Thom Gunn and Ted
Hughes*, Edinburgh 1976; L. De Michelis, *La poesia di Thom Gunn*, Firenze 1978;
Three Contemporary Poets: Thom Gunn, Ted Hughes and R. S. Thomas, ed. A. E.
Dyson, Houndmills 1990, 13–98; S. Michelucci, *La maschera, il corpo e l'anima.
Saggio sulla poesia di Thom Gunn*, Milano 2006; *At the Barriers: On the Poetry of
Thom Gunn*, ed. J. Weiner, Chicago and London 2009 (includes much reminiscent
and documentary material, next to essays dealing with Gunn in the history of gay
writing).

1   This is done in Bold 1976's first chapter, where the critic speaks of that two-faced
monster that appeared to the first critics, a 'Ted Gunn'; in reality Bold, who carries
out a progressive and parallel reading of the poetry of both poets, ends up dissociating them and evaluating them in their autonomy and specificity. Gunn himself, in
turn, predictably reiterated that he had nothing in common with Hughes (see an
interview reported in Dyson 1990, 18), despised the Movement, and even denied its
existence and that it had been a close-knit group of poets. A joint edition of selected
poems by Hughes and Gunn was, however, published in 1962.

(as he himself wished to be defined).[2] Depending on the answer, certain critics have kept him out of surveys of contemporary British poetry. He was the son of a journalist, had a traditional middle-class adolescence, albeit disturbed by early family tragedies (his mother committed suicide after divorce); thus, it was asked, what sanity could ever be found in a renegade from the system and exile from England, as Gunn became, and in a life of protest, later of drugs and homosexuality, embraced from an early age, even if not exhibited?[3] His early poetry arose against the background of the Angry Young Men phenomenon, the urban violence of teddy-boys, rock music, and the cinema of the new teen idols such as James Dean or Marlon Brando, the star of the 1953 film *The Wild One*. Gunn, in reality, *posed* as unconventional, with a beard, jeans and long hair, and was an early wearer of bandoleers with showy buckles, leather jackets and armbands, and had himself photographed as an arrogant commander gazing into the distance, not as a poet hunched over books; or smiling astride a status symbol, the motorcycle. Taken out of context, his first poems produce the effect of exalting machismo, with characters that dictate dry military orders and proclaim the strict categorical codes of an ancient Roman warrior. The sense of his inclusion among the poets of the Movement begins to emerge when it is realized Gunn, despite having overheard the existentialist pronouncements of Sartre, Nietzsche and Camus, does not fully and thoroughly discuss in his poetry historical issues, as Geoffrey Hill does, nor does he examine epistemological questions, learnedly conduct dialogues with predecessors or dabble in political and theological theory, even though for years, like Hill, he was a university professor of literature.[4] As a poet, Gunn could sing

2   More exactly Californian.

3   The 'mark of the beast', homosexuality, as it was hypocritically deemed in academic circles of the 1950s despite being widely practised, was kept hidden by Gunn for many years, indeed decades. In his wanderings, Gunn followed not by chance, although not only for this reason, the ideal path of British homosexuals in search of free zones of tolerance, like Auden and Isherwood: England, Berlin, and then America. Recent criticism has been predictably anxious to reread Gunn's corpus following the alleged, constant and encrypted homosexual background.

4   Gunn was a very weak theoretician. Although he was a quite prolific literary critic, it would be difficult to cite anything memorable in this regard.

the fact itself of posing, and indicate its existential need, while knowing how to subtly crack it, seeing the crisis of personality and of the will. His poetry also moves from the cult of posing to the criticism of it. And as soon as he arrived in America Gunn became a pupil of the anti-modernist Yvor Winters.[5] Gunn's poetics is based on perspicuity from the outset: 'I too tried / to render obscure passages into clear English';[6] at the same time it is a poetic of totality: 'Whatever is here, / it is material for my art', adds 'Confessions of the Life Artist', devised as a series of rules that continues with Gunn stating, without acquiring speculative margins: 'The one thing clear is that I / must not lose myself in thought'. Gunn's poetry taken as a whole might be described as an 'Essay on Man', updated and revised since Pope's time. The name of the Augustan poet is often evoked when Gunn is presented, mainly in order to point out an old-fashioned devotion to strict prosodies, obedience to the rhyme, even rhyming couplets, and the rigour of form, only broken in the last phase of his poetry. In part, Gunn shared with Pope an interest in the relationships between man and nature, and to an even greater extent, the exhortation to humility and resignation. More specifically, he focuses on human energy, a need that emerges power-fully from its contrary, from the weakness of mankind itself.[7] He therefore turned to nature where energy is intact and never entropically fizzles out;

5   In the poem dedicated to this master, Gunn lauds his firm intellectual lucidity, admits his own moral weakness, by yielding to the temptations of the night that feeds a 'neurotic vision', and makes life seem unintelligible. We can note a certain similarity between this poem and the idealization of the strong masters, or a group of strong masters, in Matthew Arnold (Volume 4, § 159.4) while sailing the same dark sea, and the first of whom was his father.

6   *CP*, 381.

7   Gunn's cult of energy was often misunderstood as an apologia of force, and he was accused of secret philo-fascism. For Gunn, in homage to a principle of physics, energy is always opposed by another energy, as in the poem 'Innocence', in which a trained Nazi, due to an unfailing sense of duty, tortures a Russian partisan (on the poem and its abstract casuistry, cf. Miglior 1971, 21–7). Gunn had actually done military service for two years, had grown up in wartime, and ambiguously idealized the soldier, *par excellence*, as a being without desire, happily exempted from want, and only held to blind obedience. Gunn was subsequently in Berlin a few years after the war, and occasionally his poetry evokes the horrors of Nazism.

or he sings of the ancient, the primitive, and the barbaric. Gunn is not at all Popian when he feels the nostalgia for the ancient warlords, or even only for the fighter-poet, like Byron. A step forward and here is the theme and the crucial moment of transfusion and regeneration: of men who go back to being animals or become arboreal, fused with nature, ideally or in an oneiric trance; or the strange appearance of beings that are monstrous in that they are two-faced, with a dual nature, as for example the Centaurs.

2. Gunn's specific theme is therefore the sense of movement, often brutal, wild, not finalized – the idea of a Heraclitean cosmos in turmoil – from which a poetry of chaos and disorder is born, in a signifier that disagrees with it, and which is the elegant, polished, classic forms of pro-sodically regular verse and the obsessive normativity of rhyme, which produces strident but totally indirect effects of parody and pastiche. A soul passionately, incontinently romantic in search of classic composure; a disorder that was also moral and which he tried to sublimate: in point of fact, Gunn, from his scenes of a spiralled landscape, whirling in turmoil, as his sea often is, was able to shift to the classic composure of the Greek world in the form of a diatonic contrast. In one of his collections, he begins from the episode of the lotus-eaters and places them in an epigraph. This distant classical world thus returns. Another index is the heroism of the heroes who throw themselves into the fray, but can only be remembered now. Thus, some matrix in common does exist with Ted Hughes. Both nomadic, they watched the animate and inanimate and the humans who attempt to fuse with them and share their momentum.[8] If, however, Hughes had

8   The Aristotelian dichotomy between power and action seems a central paradigm, as does the Heraclitean one of energy consumed and not exhausted, judging by the literal occurrences throughout Gunn's poetry. I shall limit myself to a few samples. In *CP*, 231, the whirling waters evidence 'incompleteness', that is, a tension towards completeness, 'what I love'. *CP*, 235, is on a boy who had 'potential' but wasted it. A poem on the eighteenth-century naturalist Bewick, 'not separated from what he sees', indicates the degree to which the scientist was at one with nature. The wind is first and foremost 'energetic' in Gunn, and the very air we breathe often brings strength; nature is never still but is traversed by this motion. The discontented student, as Gunn was when young, sniffs this 'powerful' air (*CP*, 285), having lost everything before even having it. Gunn is then 'easily', after Shelley or perhaps Hopkins, the greatest

created and cultivated his own romantic myth, and described himself as ecstatically possessed, Gunn moves in his poetry to a demythologization. His references to Greek myths are unconvincing, and result in simpering academic poems; equally unsatisfactory are the ones that expatiate on his own narcissistic existentialism, in which he builds and stages his double by resorting to the image of the poet in front of the mirror or to the very metaphor of Narcissus. It is precisely by emerging from falsehood and the magniloquence of self-idolization that Gunn finds his finest vein in a poetry that is always capable of lampooning and laughing at himself, in the best British tradition of wit (and this is what Hughes did not possess). He matures into an old-style lyric poet who speaks of himself but more frequently looks around him. Hughes posed, and Gunn, as I mentioned, came to criticize poses even when they were his own.[9] Hughes is defeated by his myth, the myth of the titan that rivals nature; Gunn demolishes it. Hughes transfigures reality and wraps it in transcendental mythopoeic veils; Gunn anchors himself to it as a realist poet without mythologems. His secret matrix, which in the end resurfaces, is that of a poetry that is discursive, narrative and hinging on epiphanic anecdotes, with all the inevitable limitations of the anecdotal, that is, repetitiveness and super-ficiality, especially in his late collections. These are often encumbered by long pretentious ballads, but also ennobled by touching, graceful poems on humans, animals and especially a secondary humanity marginalized in the American metropolis. This evaluation, which is the fruit of an under-lying entelechy that was always latent, originates from an examination, now possible, of all of Gunn's poetry, of which there had been partial and also frequently inaccurate reviews and interpretations while the work was

British singer of the wind, of the gust that sucks away human beings anchored to the earth, and kidnaps them, instilling its creative and restoring energy into them. A late poem from the 1990s (*CP*, 443) again features a character who has eyes that 'appear to transmit energy / And hold it back undissipated too'. One of the very last poems, among the tersest ever written by Gunn, is on a nasturtium that grows from debris, 'Self-spending, never spent'.

9   *CP*, 381.

ongoing. Gunn returns, in a broad sense certainly, to being that 'healthy' poet he had been diagnosed as being in the beginning.

§ 79. *Gunn II: Stasis and motion*

Fighting Terms (1954) is already an ambiguous title. It refers to the 'quarterly' terms in a scholastic sense and also to the terms and conditions of a battle, or to the words and languages exchanged in a battle. To fight is to act, anyway to abandon inertia. The first controlling metaphor is disease, in antithesis with convalescence, and the collection opens significantly with 'The Wound',[10] a dramatic monologue in rhyming stanzas of five lines each, attributed to a Greek warrior, but a turncoat of both fields, who, shaken by the news of the death of Patroclus, takes up his weapons again. It is irresistible, in terms of genre, to see it as an echo of Browning, an imitation even. Gunn attends in fact to a poetry of impersonation, and a controlled game that seems to be indebted both to Browning and to Yeats's theory of the masks – as the author revealed – and is instead a prismatic refraction of insecurity, the consciousness of a broken personality, which is reconstituted in the sum of his poses. 'The Wound' is about a symbolic wound, in particular, and its healing. *Fighting Terms* is closed by the dream-like monologue of another wounded man from an unspecified time, a ghost that appears to the poet's hallucination, and who is one of his coveted doubles; the ghost tells of his bloody, passionate heroism, having fallen in battle 'regretting nothing'. The counterpoint to the present is represented by other, occasional Homeric frameworks, such as the abduction of Helen. When Gunn voices the elegy of the frank and healthy Elizabethan age, violent and cruel but strong, it was as if he were confessing that he wanted to relinquish the miserable lacklustre period he lived in, which he also called the Welfare State. Hence the fantasies of being able to at least resurrect the indomitable heroism of the Elizabethan knights or of the Tudor wars. From heroic Romanticism there loomed challengers of adversity, with Shelley and Byron recollected in Lerici, with Byron 'masterful to water' while Shelley was tamed by it. Fairy-tale, anecdotal or fantastic parables are dedicated to exiled heroes,

10   On the possible homosexual allusion cf. A. Corn, in Weiner 2009, 39.

misanthropes, utopians and the fallen.[11] In *Fighting Terms*, Gunn, however, soon moves away from this survey of ancient heroism towards scenes of contemporary neurosis, devastated love affairs, the aboulic motions of a subject in search of he knows not what, straining upwards to gain panoramic glances that make the real intelligible. He plays with impersonation and ventriloquism. One voice is that of worker, 'angry' like the one in Sillitoe, who goes in search of girls after work, woos them, takes them to the cinema, and makes love to them; but even sex leaves him dissatisfied and he suffers a malaise of uncertain origin. A lighthouse keeper sees everything around him as round. In 'Looking Glass' the poet idealizes himself as an estranged and naïve gardener who cultivates a bucolic Eden of his own, undisturbed, enchanted, atemporal. Gunn's confessional poems are however the most scholastic, punctuated as they are by banal images of split personality, amnesia and hallucination (in 'The Secret Sharer'[12] the poetic 'I' sees himself inside and outside the house; it only takes the wind to evoke this mirage). Others are dialogued, either in the form of silent language or in thinking aloud, and admit the poses, the doubts, the uncertainties of love and the fluctuations of desire ('a forked creature') with the grammatical mimesis of the present tense. Far-flung echoes of Marvell or of erotic Caroline poetry are to be found in a frank dialogue in reflective and gnomic formulations. 'A Kind of Ethics' focuses on the trees, that is on nature which is exempt from an inculcated ethics, is pure innocence, and a ministrant of natural rituals without intermediaries: a nature removed from the obligation to pray, adore, and regenerate. Gunn's falcon is a frequent apparition in English poetry; it protests against its taming by the falconer.[13] In the few poems on natural forces and animal nature an uncommon, imagistic sharpness of contours, and a rigorous essentiality of touch, begin to emerge.

11   The miracle of Lazarus, often at the centre of Victorian poems and monologues for its symbolic representation of the inquest into the afterlife, is revisited by Gunn in a sardonic and surreal anecdote: incited by friends and by the bystanders to rise again, 'he had chosen to stay dead', and the 'announced' miracle did not take place.
12   A deliberately Conradian title.
13   Announcing the almost Baudelairean constriction of infinite will made finite, so dear to Gunn, the hawk is 'catcher' and 'caught'.

2. In the opening poem of *The Sense of Movement* (1957), 'On the Move', Gunn now celebrates the unguided and aimless motor instinct in nature, a primordial energy therefore, and immediately afterwards in the motorcyclists described with the rapid impressionisms of a practising rider. The sense lies in the roar of the engine: 'They ride, direction where the tyres press'; and this drifting dispels or immobilizes doubt. The last two stanzas theorize laboriously, and more thoughtfully, on the philosophy of perpetual motion, which is the confused search for a goal in the dual nature of the motor-cyclist, the author of the movement and the victim of it, 'both hurler and the hurled'.[14] Gunn defines this as a compromise solution, and the movement cannot ensure *per se* the attainment of the 'absolute', even if 'One is always nearer by not keeping still'. This is the selfsame, remote idea of Leopardi, an early existentialist himself, that moving dispels irrational fears and makes one forget (in the words of the poem, 'a valueless world'). At a distance, this theme of exorcizing motion is taken up again in a poem about a motorcyclist who, like Yeats's airman,[15] foretastes the fatal crash after the thrill of the speed, ejected from a fragmented and alien ambience, and welcomed into the womb of nature that transforms him organically.[16] Didactic poems and lampoons in Augustan rhyming couplets exalt the 'hard men', to whom are added portraits of humans and even animals waiting to spring into action, feline, always on the alert. Gunn reflects on both mental and lost time, from places that are ever the same, where the subject has changed and time has inevitably passed. In so doing he glimpses a sterilely circular life without anything new, and consisting only of boredom and inanity. 'Legal Reform' voices the existentialist complaint of a condemnation to a life spent in prison, the Law and therefore also the sentence having been decreed by the 'I' itself. Momentary reflections, or others written absent-mindedly, alternate with lighter, anecdotal, curious ones in the present tense. Gunn, a non-believer, appreciates in any case a faith

---

14   As in the hendiadys of the falcon seen above.

15   Volume 6, § 261.6.

16   The exaltation of unfinalized movement continues in the long, verbose monologue 'Merlin in the Cave', which recognizes the imperious commandment of acting in any case, 'and make / The meaning in each movement that I take'.

that is not contemplative but active, such as the holiness of St Martin in a ballad with a nineteenth-century flavour. Pagan Rome was weakened by the advent of Christianity, guided as it was at the time by emperors who were faint-hearted and spiritual, whose emblem was Marcus Aurelius, and who withdrew from action in a by-now silver-streaked Roman civilization. In a somewhat Swinburnian poem, Gunn exalts Julian the Apostate, and in another Mary monologues over a humanized Jesus, not divine, and therefore also naïve.

3. The celebration of heroic masculinity was already half-hearted and undermined. In *My Sad Captains* (1961) Gunn becomes critical of the heroism he has sung, and not only lays bare the artificial protection of the group within which the member loses his identity, but dismisses his real heroes, even the authentic, public ones of history. His hero gradually becomes the anti-hero of the street and the homeless: a nobody. Formally, the collection moves towards dry phenomenological poems increasingly freed from fixed prosodic obligations, in which the poet refuses to interpret the real, or to attach messages or concluding reflections, and is satisfied simply to see. The strong, marked and in its own way bitter opening poem remains an ekphrasis of Caravaggio's painting of the Conversion of St Paul, to which, however, a small community of faithful praying raptly in the Roman church of Santa Maria del Popolo is oblivious. Attentive to the forms and manifestations of becoming, Gunn interrogates the painting, explores the painter's intentions, and identifies a Saul in the process of becoming Paul. Caravaggio, in the overly resounding and rhetorical final image, is someone who reaps nothingness but resists and opposes it, and is yet another follower of motion that, at the same time, exorcizes death. The archaic sense of risk endures, recreated from Greek myth, in 'The Book of the Dead', an anecdote of blood sacrifice that promises salvation and success, and with Gunn again identifying with the horizons of barbaric man and the ancient warrior. The hiatus between past and present is even too blatant and didactic. 'Black Jackets' spreads an indulgent irony over the portrait of a bully dressed up on a Sunday in a bar, and over the glances, gestures, and repressed motions of this man, deaf and blind to insignia on the walls illustrating bygone heroisms. 'Misanthropos', a cumbersome and rather maladroit semi-monologic poem, which some consider a masterpiece,

revolves around an *alter ego* who is a wild caveman (some hints suggest he is a combatant in a war, perhaps shell-shocked, or a survivor of an atomic war in the future), who has nonetheless been generous, friendly, human, and is even a little similar to a Beckettian tramp, a figure that had become proverbial in those years.[17] In 'A Map of the City' the poet is mirrored in the drunk, the *flâneur*, the sailor, to close on the concept of life as 'power' or potential, and a preference for the crushed, imperfect and unfinished. Romantic and Wordsworthian imitations unfold with the contemplation of the grass and the cycle of maturation in nature, which from a bud ends as a flower. 'The Book of the Dead' and other poems imply a psychic contact between the poet and the forces of the dead underground, who tremble, coerce, still live or wish to relive, symbols of an entropic force that is recharged after each consumption, distant and yet close and perceived: forces of nature, at the same time, and incandescent stars that pour and shed their energy and yet conserve it intact. The force that breaks and is dampened, the energy that is lost and weakens, and life that seems to proclaim its unity, and instead is disunity: these are the frames of 'Back to Life', the phenomenology of a small park in which natural and human elements parade in a warm dusk, the young exuding energy and the elderly reclining, so that no one can perceive that all creation grew from a single branch. There is a clear watershed occurring with the second part of the collection,[18] which includes specimens of a sort of *Neue Sachlichkeit* focusing on objects and phenomena given in their removal from the continuum, 'neutral sections' that lack 'connection' as well as unity, while being events that exhibit the absence 'even of potential meanings'. Here Gunn reveals that he is really a late Imagist who wishes to see without questioning and without going beyond the boundary of the phenomenon and in search of

---

17   The misanthrope is still the first and last Darwinian man, that is, primitive, bestial, only the senses and the mind in formation, wandering across coves and marshes, or is perhaps someone absent-minded, who has regressed through the stages of civilization.

18   A watershed that is also prosodic, with the adoption of a 'syllabic' metre: this presumptive and highly praised innovation consists mainly, if not entirely, however, in the abandonment of rhyme and in the greater frequency of *enjambement*.

noumena.[19] 'Considering the Snail' is such an observation of self-propelled movements, or obscure impulses that are not understood.[20]

4. The collection *Moly* (1971) cites Homer in its epigraph, and specifically the episode of Ulysses and Circe with the transformation of the sailors into pigs, and Hermes' gift to Ulysses of the eponymous plant. It starts therefore under the banner of metamorphosis, that of men who regress to beasts or even centaurs, taking its cue from the epigraph. Metamorphosis means the drunkenness or sinister consciousness of a consanguinity with the bestial that quakes in a being, and wishes to emerge or re-emerge. But the factitious mythical reference soon dissolves, and images of masked moods appear, or phenomena of stunning, such as in the insane yet innocent woodcutter in a Wordsworthian encounter on the road. While remaining poems that do not want to prove anything, that 'should not mean, / But be' according to MacLeish's famous motto, they gradually lose real incisiveness and relief. Marine and natural images slide under the eye of the spectator who participates in them, and quietly shares the life of nature. Describing the surfers dancing on the waves in equilibrium, Gunn exploits the theme of the desired fusion between man and nature, with the observer who watches and in the end 'becomes', that is to say, undergoes a metamorphosis ('I become what I see'). Yet this is an absorption that is only partial and fragmented, which does not attain the completeness and integrity of unison. The poem remains therefore descriptive of a restored or rediscovered virgin nature, which is Edenic, divine, but inexplicable, and untranslatable into words, so that, even when the spell vanishes, the poet knows that it will return, and feels rooted in it. Man is 'completed', indeed made angelic, by what he contemplates, modelled by the flower in front of which he is kneeling. Gunn was therefore not so much or merely a Popian poet in these poems, but a genuine

19   This allegedly documents, for De Michelis 1978, 64, 77, 102–3 and *passim*, the 'fundamental' influence of William Carlos Williams.

20   'A Crab', not reprinted in the complete edition, is one of those animals or insects that are not listed in Hughes's bestiaries, because harmless or even simply disgusting. Another intense description of two snails mating is in *CP*, 399.

and reincarnated Romantic and a disciple of Wordsworth yearning for these unisons.[21]

§ 80. *Gunn III: Gunn 'on the road'*

Jack Straw's Castle[22] (1976) is a fully 'American' collection, and abounds in its contours with landscapes, scenery and human dwellers of the American coasts and metropolis. Hybridization also concerns an incipient slackening of the diction, which becomes less literary, less and less academic, while, overall, conserving, or at any rate only occasionally rejecting, rhyme and regular prosodies. Gunn remains an observer, whose gaze swivels around and then fixes on some strange, abnormal sight often of pure and primordial vitality; at other times and more often he is attracted by outcasts, poor souls, drunks, drifters, or even the sick.[23] The poems of this collection establish a visual continuity on the less glaring aspects of the American Dream, and resemble live reportages of a poet who meets symbolic figures who, stunned and anomalous, having come to San Francisco from the south must scrape a living there. An ingrained habit often makes the poet begin his poems scholastically as an occasion experienced, with an event that really occurred, an authentic anecdote, from which reflections or discursive variations flow; and these tidy incipits bear the indication of time and place and consequently convey the flavour of direct experience. Gunn is increasingly a classical poet of nature in that he uses the old introductory frame, which is often successful and

21   The last poems in *Moly* bear the caption *LSD*, and are said to have been conceived and written after taking this drug. The magic herb donated to Ulysses, the moly, was intended by Gunn as 'similar to LSD' (quoted in De Michelis 1978, 122).

22   Also the title of a long ballad about a sensual old man, the victim of a series of rambling hallucinations and terrifying nightmares in his castle, including the apparition of the Medusa at the behest of the fanatic, Charles Manson. This is another ambitious composition, often highly praised by critics, but in my view a complete failure.

23   Photos of London taken by his brother Ander accompanied by poetic texts made up Gunn's book *Positives*, from 1966. The London slums and a marginalized humanity form a preview of the poems of and about San Francisco.

personal, touching or graceful, though at other times more tamed and banal: the horse chestnut trees that, without feelings, embrace strongly and tightly, and grow hard, or the cherry tree that is yearning to bloom, with a spasmodic sense of mimesis, almost a mother giving birth to her offspring with an effort. Once the metamorphosis is complete, Gunn offers the readers an unsuspected gentle, sentimental, almost feminine facet, coming from the bottom of a soul that adored primitive sex – D. H. Lawrence was the same. In the poems on 'orgiastic' themes, describing sudden excitations of the senses that break down barriers, as in Lawrence, the nude bodies join without inhibitions. Inflammation of the senses is an exorcism of time. However, these naturalistic and microscopic descriptions of lovemaking turn out to be virtuosic and ends in themselves, or, worse, even cynical or unjustifiably lewd, like the poem of and about a hundred masturbations.[24] Where Gunn experiments more resolutely, he fails or decidedly falters, as in the long, pretentious 'The Geysers', in which he wants to refer mimetically to an irrational, orgiastic, and mystical ecstasy, and to an inebriating loss and disintegration of his identity and conscience, and accordingly opts, instead of rhythmic and syntactic regularity, for a hiccupping, broken, fragmented verse without links. When he describes sensations and psychic visions, composes mental rhapsodies and dream-like fantasies, or wants to make his poetry a moan, a broken voice, mimicking the effects of drugs, that is, psychedelics, Gunn ends up being disastrously artificial. 'Wrestling'[25] cannot compete with Hill's poems as an evocation of the original language behind the words, and of words behind words. The poem is intermittently disconcerting also because it shamelessly leans towards another outdated form, the nursery rhyme: the collection includes several of them, such as one on the newborn who would like to return to the mother's belly, accentuating its naïve character with a lulling rhythm and rhyming couplets.

24   *CP*, 292.
25   The reflections on the relativity and fluidity of language in 'The Conversation' (*CP*, 319–20) seem rather amateurish.

2. *The Passages of Joy* (1982) opens with the story of a suicide, and hence its title is at least in part ironic. The break with tradition had already been made by Gunn, who adds stories and anecdotes which are successfully contextualized and from which various comments are extracted. He is now a phenomenologist whose grammatical tense is not the past simple of remembrance, but invariably the present simple of fact, caught *in fieri*. A small catalogue is formed, or a documentary of cases of the American metropolis, of not always very visible spectacles, but hidden ones, taken from the sphere of the underworld, poverty, marginalization, and disease.[26] The author disappears only to reappear occasionally with his neuroses, loves, cravings, breakdowns and memories. This last Gunn gains enormously in pure readability at the expense of density. The flipside is the number of flaccid poems that never soar, or of the dead anecdotes and long digressions. However, it should be stressed that this final phase is one of a poetry that has lost its 'poetic' marks, is increasingly offhand in its lexicon and forms of speech, and, shunning all rhetoric in an intentionally sloppy style, assumes the form of unrevised improvisations. The poems of *The Man with Night Sweats* (1992) celebrate homosexual ecstasies in a tone that is even devoutly chaste. The unitive impulse is described in human loves and, as always, in a humanized nature, for example in the by now countless sets of trees. The picture of an otter, an image of 'Power set in fur', can only make us think of Hughes. On the other hand, some examples of letters in verse, in playful rhyming couplets, recall Auden, the proverbial tightrope walker. A thorny section, a kind of poetry of memory for a minor holocaust, includes poems on the daily goings-on and practices of drugs and drug addicts, and scenes at the bedside of those sick with AIDS, at the end of their lives. 'Lament', like others in solemn rhyming couplets, grates prosodically with its subject matter of disintegration and death.

---

26   'Hide and Seek' is like a visual sketch or the opening scene of a film, with children playing on the pavement, the gaze swivelling to the surrounding events, and mothers calling their children to come home.

§ 81. *Jennings, Davie*

Compared, for instance, with another minor poet that I chose to shift back in time, namely Stevie Smith,[1] Elizabeth Jennings (1926–2001) appears even more remote, almost the type of a being overwhelmed by a civilization of incipient or growing secularization. Even the uninitiated reader soon intuits that Jennings at least had Anglo-Catholic sympathies, and receives confirmation of her real affiliation with the Roman credo. As we advance through her oeuvre, we encounter in fact poems expressly dedicated to saints, imaginary and not, or clergymen and nuns who 'have a vocation' and take the veil, as in the devotional poetry of the nineteenth century, of Hopkins and Christina Rossetti in particular. To Jennings, life is a daily experience of the sacred and divine and means a constant need of veneration; for her, things high and worthy of devotion still survive, and man is still surrounded by fragmentary and fragmented details that transcendently point to the universals.[2] She comes across as a Herbert of modern times; more precisely she shares the same spiritual mark as those terser and more suasive Metaphysicals such as Vaughan and Traherne; as a Keble and even more Hopkins, especially the very early and very late Hopkins. As in these predecessors, Jennings conceived poetry as a spiritual diary, a thermometer of the soul, a purgatorial therapy. Her poems are worked out, as she says in one of them, 'inside my mind',[3] and are a study, sometimes a ruthless clinical examination, of her own inner life.[4] Except that her mind gradually becomes a conflictual, fretfully conflictual, and ungovernable space, as described by Hopkins himself in his 'terrible sonnets': 'my mind is a room whose wall I can see / The top of but never completely scale'; elsewhere she speaks of a 'panic' caused by 'the perception of ourselves',

---

1   Volume 7, § 72. The two poets are intuitively antipodal, and yet 'Tea Shot', where Jennings imagines having been slain by a bullet and having a hallucination of the afterlife, is one of her rare visionary, hypothetical, and even surreal poems, and thus can even seem written by Smith.

2   See 'Kings', dealing with the symbolic function of royal power, the need to 'Construct the grandeur [a term that echoes in Hopkins throughout] from the simple thing', and revealing Jennings's implied or alluded conservative political creed, when she warns that 'Kings prevented from their proper ends / Make a deep lack in men's imaginings'.

3   'In the Night', a classic example in Jennings of a 'correlative' reading of the natural spectacle.

4   A victim of frequent nervous breakdowns, Jennings was interned in a psychiatric hospital in her forties after a suicide attempt.

a paraphrase of the fearful peaks and bottomless abysses of a Hopkins-style psyche. Hopkins's model of the 'terrible sonnets' is unmistakeable in 'In the Night', which complains about the poet's disturbed insomnia faced with the peace of the stars, which she cannot make her own and absorb into her being.[5] The meditative poet is mirrored by definition in the landscape, being a spectator who wavers or even shudders in carrying out an immediate comparison and in reading in the light of it his or her own rich and dense interiority, and also his or her own inferiority. This is a basically Romantic stance, but in the long run it turns into something else, because in Jennings there is never any empty, exclamatory exultation in front of nature, but stillness, modesty and discretion. Nature always flourishes in the cycle of its seasons, and it withers but will not be late in being agreeable the following spring. Anthropomorphic, 'it gropes in search of us', offers itself as 'solidification', says Jennings, of fleeting moods, and hence also their resolution and relief. Sooner or later we must question what in Jennings obeys the commandments of the Movement, since she was published in Conquest's 1956 anthology after having started out on her own, and is usually cited as being a member, even if minor, of the group. In the end, what did Jennings have of the Movement? Seemingly, only the rejection of the image's primacy, only the castigated, tamed, unglittering diction and the renunciation of every supremacy of the syntactic, lexical and phonological signifier. Jennings's typical poetic structure hinges on a long and sinuous sentence, often closed by a full stop within a stanza of four, five or six lines, in which there unwinds a finished and articulate argument that almost in principle banishes the image, and seeks to avoid the rhetoric of comparison and metaphor. Except for the rhyme and its concatenations, Jennings's classic poem sounds like versified prose due to the heaviness of the hypotactic chain. The initial self-prohibition to write anecdotal poetry, in favour of an abstract and moralizing one, translates into statements of just discovered truths, not into expressions of emotions in their pure state; on the

---

5   'A Fear' confesses that it brings 'inward the agony of the self alone', although laboriously hidden from the masks imposed by associated life, before closing in the third sestet, describing the awakening from a restless night (Hopkins's 'mantle of night'), visited by nightmares and yearning for a child's innocence. On the very close relationship between the two poets, and the analytical and very competent essays that Jennings dedicated to Hopkins, cf. M. Wheeler, 'Elizabeth Jennings and Gerard Manley Hopkins', in HAP, 104–6.

contrary, these emotions are always explained, paraphrased, and filtered. Hers is gnomic and sententious poetry, voided of the traditional British qualities of wit and humour; or solemn, austere, painful, drained. Thus, we find no attention paid to the anecdote, not even to the one gathered among the ranks of the everyday life of the proletariat; no satire, no irony, no preoccupation with instincts and the corporeal, no background of a milieu in change. No member of the Movement shared a similar spiritualism of a mystical mould and a dazzled, suspended, solemnizing sense of the sacredness and sacramentality of nature, or such a lofty, cognitive and heuristic concept of poetry with the complete exclusion of recreation and fun. All things considered, we must call her militancy in the Movement tangential, even misunderstood, or temporary. 'Teresa of Ávila' is surprising not only for its explicit homage to the saint and its spasmodic craving for a genuinely thirst-quenching water,[6] but also because of its unusual telegraphic and synthetic parataxis; the last stanza – and they are all prosodically irregular – even loses the outward marks of the poetic form along the way. Among the rare poems really inspired by the poetics of the Movement is the Larkin-like 'My Grandmother',[7] exhibiting for once exceptional freshness and attention to descriptive detail, streaked with pathos and even humour.

2. The theoretical framework of the Movement and its incubation had been primarily due to two critical essays by Donald Davie (1922–1995). *Purity of Diction in English Verse* (1952) launched the announcement – decisive, fearless and apodictic – of a new tradition bowing to few ancestors and building on the foundation of syntax, as proof of the rediscovered intelligibility of the world. Among those ancestors was Yeats but not Hopkins, of whom Davie was one of the frankest and bitterest historical enemies, after much covert or explicit flirting with him on the part of generations of poets up to the date of this book. It was no coincidence that Davie subsequently became a disciple and successor of Yvor Winters at Stanford. The latter was in turn the progenitor of a rationalistic *revanche* and the frank

---

6   'Fountain' is the single most famous poem by Jennings, who re-exploits the old
     religious symbolism of water. A poem on St Teresa has a counterpart in one on St
     Francis of Assisi.

7   'At a Mass' may be taken as the counterpart of Larkin's 'Church-Going', since Jennings
     admits to confusion between aesthetics and the sacrament.

denouncer *par excellence* of Hopkins's 'rhetorical vice'. Davie's *Articulate Energy* (1955) stages the crucial theoretical conflict in the practice of the poets of the Movement, that between, on the one hand, the image and the metaphor, and the victorious syntax on the other; it therefore promulgates the principle of individuation of the new poetry along with the axis on which it lies, and its Jakobsonian 'dominant'. As a poet, Davie was devoted to illustrating these theories. The metapoetic 'Remembering the Thirties' evokes the birth of the new sensibility in 1950s academic circles, which inevitably placed in perspective the major historical events that had inflamed souls in the 1930s. Of this poem's shrewd, steadfast and apathetic stance of poetics, the final invitation to prefer a 'neutral tone' has remained famous and proverbial. Davie gives his own version of the syntactic *legato* that he urged, and which is shown by the statistical frequency of the possessive 'whose' in his poems. Never properly verbal explosions, Davie's poems resemble those of Empson: sophisticated, curious, extravagant. Academic, cerebral, calculated, often also sibylline, they play with ideas rather than reporting deeply felt experiences. They are conceived in a spirit of dry wit of an eighteenth-century kind, and hinge on dense networks of antitheses and on an abundance of syntactical and lexical inversions and oppositions. The experience of teaching in America ended up, at any rate, projecting Davie out of the narrow orbit of the Movement. The petering out of that experience is also witnessed by Davie's rediscovery of a poet, Pound, who had been one of the primary targets of the Movement; at the same time, this was an oblique rehabilitation of Modernism, which had been shown the door. Davie devoted two books of criticism to Pound, and his later poetry metabolized him in the form of symptomatic references, echoes, internal dialogues and stylistic devices, and in the adoption of an open form, after the dictatorship of the Augustan quatrain of his beginnings.

§ 82. *Empson**

One of the three most influential and proverbial books of twentieth-century academic criticism in English, and *ipso facto* on the international

---

*   Empson's poetic edition of 1955 is now replaced by *The Complete Poems*, ed. J. Haffenden, Harmondsworth 2000, which exceeds 500 pages but has only 200 of

scene, is *Seven Types of Ambiguity* (1930) by William Empson (1906–1984). In homage to an elementary hierarchical principle, it is necessary to speak of his work as a critic before discussing his poetry, which, despite only having a temporary intrinsic value, was a peripheral phenomenon of the Movement. *Seven Types of Ambiguity* is certainly a legendary text, but it has proved more useful in raising and systematizing the question of literary ambiguity, rather than being truly known, attentively read and explored in depth. As Praz often said (about de Sade, for instance), *Seven Types of Ambiguity* is indeed one of the least read, but most spoken about books of critical theory. The biographical industry has recently extended its subject matter to the life of literary critics, often reconstructing their personal and circumstantial contexts, which had been previously reabsorbed into the strictly heuristic sphere. The huge official biography by John Haffenden sheds new light on the turbulent, schizoid, somewhat exhibitionist, and always unpredictable life of Empson, the same one that we find described, by and large, in the novels of Huxley and Waugh about the eccentric, bizarre and bisexual university youth of the 1920s. The book that in 1930 caused such a stir in the western world, *Seven Types of Ambiguity*, was the work – it is hard to believe this – of a twenty-four-year-old who had obviously rushed into things and spent a good part of his intellectual energies in assiduous readings informed by an unusual guiding principle: a linguistic reading of poetry, especially of the lyrical and dramatic kind. The pioneering value of *Seven Types of Ambiguity* lies in the deferment of a value judgement about a literary text, indeed in its declared secondariness. One tenet is fixed and inalienable in Empson, with twenty or more years in advance on the structuralists, and in silent agreement with the formalists: that the literary text is a tight system of relations. Thus, Empson preliminarily rejects the idea that a poem is made of separable elements and may be reduced to pure sound or simply to a series of moods. At the same time, his aesthetic raises a wall against the temptations of the ineffable: it is irritating, Empson declared, to hear that beauty cannot be analysed; his approach, as a consequence, is often self-defined as analytical. With regard to the practical and demonstrative result, things, as has been universally noticed, are much different. *Seven Types of Ambiguity* 'makes painful reading', as the saying goes, and is initiatory to the extent that

---

text. J. Haffenden, *William Empson*, 2 vols (*Among the Mandarins*, Oxford 2005, and *Against the Christians*, Oxford 2006).

it seems to have been written for the benefit of the author himself. The procedure by samplings without references to the context of the act of writing
and other introductory explanations, does not help.[1] The definitions of the
seven types of ambiguity do not shine for their clarity, and are indeed rather
broad and elastic. In the initial paragraphs defining the seven types – such as
that of the fifth – the contortion of the assertions verges on the grotesque. The
diagram of ambiguity ranges from forms of harmonious agreement of terms to
increasingly more open and strained cases of contradiction and conflict, until
the seventh type, that of unconscious Freudian 'denegation', and therefore, *ipso
facto*, of deconstruction in advance of the times. A similar phenomenology is
shown in a survey going from the Anglo-Saxon and Chaucerian beginnings
to the latest literary discovery in 1930 – Hopkins. The lion's share is taken up
by Shakespeare with his sonnets and tragedies, and rich reservoirs of examples
are the Metaphysical poets, with Herbert and Donne, Milton, the Augustans,
and contemporaries such as Yeats and Eliot. Some examples are taken from the
Romantics, but few are from the Victorians (only Swinburne is mentioned,
and intermittently Tennyson). It is particularly difficult to follow Empson's
usually warped demonstrative statements when he extracts individual lines
from contexts that he largely takes for granted. The reader, in other terms,
must subject Empson's exegesis to a second exegesis.[2] Just as there are poets'
poets, Empson is a critic for critics, and very well-read ones at that, having the
whole poetic canon at their fingertips. Empson discusses briefly two poems
by Hopkins, 'Spring and Fall' and 'The Windhover'. Regarding the first, he
shows how Hopkins may have intended to say different things depending on
the distribution of stresses. In the sonnet 'The Windhover', Empson highlights
Hopkins's contradictoriness: he says the opposite of what he thinks and thinks
the opposite of what he says, especially regarding his life of renunciation and the
windhover's self-exhibition and proud self-complacency. Empson places the
sonnet in the seventh type of ambiguity, but, substantially, it could be an

---

1   Sertoli, in a heading on *Seven Types of Ambiguity* in *Dizionario Bompiani delle opere
     e dei personaggi*, Milano 2006, 8944–5, notes negatively the drawback of a method
     that does not examine individual works in their entirety, but only titbits, cameos,
     and fragments.
2   The correct perspective is to reopen and reread the book in instalments, occasion-
     ally returning to the author and the passage being studied, in order to check what
     Empson has to say.

example of the fifth, when a poet 'discovers his idea in the act of writing'. One might find in the sonnet an even greater ambiguity if it were true and authenticated that the ever-higher flight of the windhover is also a metaphor for sexual erection.[3] From the time of his second critical work, *Some Versions of Pastoral* (1935), Empson's criticism had begun spinning in circles. This book espoused the cause of committed literature, but it left the card-holding communists flabbergasted through its choice of acrobatic sample texts such as Carroll's *Alice*, which no one thought capable of bringing grist to the mill of Bolshevism. Theoretically, Empson emptied and deconstructed contemporary proletarian art, since the writer 'never makes common cause with any audience'. But hats off to whomever manages to thoroughly understand, in the first chapter of the book ('Proletarian Literature'), in what sense the old and new pastoral literature are the only 'good proletarian art'. These assumptions receive a rather bland demonstration in the subsequent chapters.[4] Empson's remaining two critical books replace the word, as the cornerstone of the literary text, with the ideological frame. What is questionable, in the end, is Kermode's definitive verdict, of a rather journalistic flavour, to the effect that Empson is the greatest twentieth-century critic in the English language – though we cannot think of any close rivals at hand, save perhaps for T. S. Eliot.

2. A good half of Empson's poetry was written at Cambridge, thus within the first twenty-six years of his life, in the wake of Eliot's *Waste Land* and in parallel with the settling of Auden and his circle in Oxford. The voice is personal, but in it can be traced the shadow of Eliot's impassivity in its most sardonic version, and in the black humour. Thirdly, these poems witness scientific interests that date back to Empson's youthful studies in a university that had notoriously greater epistemological inclinations and credentials than Oxford, and where Wittgenstein was living and teaching. The condition of man in history, a history understood as unintelligible becoming, and man therefore in need of illusory alternative pretexts: this is Empson's ultimately Romantic and post-Romantic poetic theme, elicited by the most bizarre and far-fetched ideas and occasions, which sometimes

---

3   Cf. my own assumption in IDM, 146 n. 6.
4   On the *later* grouping of already written essays, and doubtfully rediscovered by Empson as preventive polemical discussions of Zdanovian aesthetics, cf. HYN, 172–3.

set the teeth on edge, as in certain episodes in Meredith's novels.[5] The poet reads Lucretius and Samuel Johnson, and here is a witty reflection on centaurs, half-men and half-beasts, or, mindful of Darwin, on the nature of the gap between man and animal. At the British Museum, the visitor stops in front of a statue of an ancient wooden idol and witnesses an unrelenting succession of beliefs. 'Villanelle' laments despondently a world that is an Eliotian 'waste'. Empson calls into question the ancient gods or reviews the totemic statuettes of polytheistic religions with the nihilism of a pagan poet and an existentialism veined with nonchalance. The referents he addresses are the stoics, the unbelievers, the doubters, and Wittgenstein. 'This Last Pain'[6] paraphrases the cave myth in commenting on the inscrutability of the knowable even within the sphere of religious scepticism (man looks at the eternal soul as if through a keyhole, and knows that the key to the door is lost, but that the hole will not be closed). The sense of human life was commented upon by Empson himself: 'Life involves maintaining oneself between contradictions that can't be solved by [psycho?] analysis', which sounds like a paraphrase of Kierkegaard's *Either/Or*. The single most famous line, a quintessence of Empson's poetry, is a whole programme: 'learn a style from despair'. Empson's exorcistic style is witnessed by a reflective type of poem that solidifies in prevalently paratactic structures and in an excess of ellipses that fail to clarify the unfolding of the *argumentum*, even though it undoubtedly whets and stimulates the reader's intelligence and intuitive ability. Conceptual subtlety causes friction with anachronistic and traditional formal devices, and semantic extravagance conflicts with prosodic conformity and with an inflexible rejection of *vers-librisme*. This is a poetry that agrees with that of another literary critic and poet, and more of a poet than Empson: Davie. For Empson, too, the stimulus to a poem is filtered, rather than pure emotion, most often a capricious idea, a quip, a wisecrack, a paradox, or a pun.[7] Empson illustrates, furthermore,

---

5   One telling example is the appearance of the woman brushing her teeth with lake water at the beginning of the poem 'Camping Out'.

6   The poem summarizes in its incipit the thesis of Empson's book *Milton's God* (1961), an unoriginal exaltation of Satan against God's tyranny.

7   A striking example of Empsonian ambiguity is in the lyric 'Missing Dates', a title that can refer both to dates as fruit, as it does in Carlo Izzo's Italian translation, and to 'missing appointments'.

that emblematic case of perversion in poetic communication, that is, when copious notes to a literary work make its already obscure textual meaning even more obscure, and often also amplify one which, taken alone, is very slender. The reception of Empson's poetry has been highly contentious: indeed, Empson the poet attracted, more than anything else, some very honest, and far from diplomatic, harsh comments.

§ 83. *Richards, Leavis*

In reality, behind Empson there was no vacuum, but a throng of shapers and inspirers, among whom Bertrand Russell with his epistemology and English logic, T. S. Eliot with his first critical essays and books, Graves and Riding – as Empson admitted – with their prolegomenon constituted by their *A Survey of Modernist Poetry*,[1] as well as Joyce's polystylism and Freudian psychoanalysis. Over all of them loomed I. A. Richards (1893–1979), Empson's Director of Studies at Cambridge and a paternal advisor who, with prudence and tact, attempted successfully to dampen his pupil's hot flushes. *Principles of Literary Criticism* (1924) and its pendant, *Practical Criticism* (1929), are incunabula of the 'close reading' of the literary text, and an intuitive prefiguration of the formal and linguistic, or more exactly formalistic method, especially through a concept of the text as a cohesion of levels – and, unknowingly echoing the Russians, through the demarcation of the gap between a referential language, essentially univocal, and poetic, polysemic language. However, Richards was equally conversant with a historicist and humanistic perspective that combated and tried to exorcize Macaulay's famous threat – 'As science advances, poetry almost necessarily declines' – by assigning a palingenetic anchoring role to poetry against the drifting of history towards standardization. A dissident from what was called the critical school of Cambridge was F. R. Leavis (1895–1978). In Leavis, the fulcrum of the artistic product is in fact no longer technique, but art's civilizing function, the last ditch against the advance of technological civilization, and therefore the repository

---

1   Volume 7, § 69.1.

of surviving values; or we might also say that, with Leavis, language ultimately becomes a tool rather than an end in itself. With an education and background in history, Leavis moved to literary criticism under the influence of Eliot's 1926 lectures in Cambridge on the Metaphysical poets, and in their shade were born *New Bearings of English Poetry* (1932) and *Revaluation* (1936). These two books could and can still seem to endorse a modernistic and even avant-garde approach; yet the supposed organic nature of contemporary literature, or of that just past – Pound, Eliot, and Hopkins, like that, more plausibly, of the sixteenth to eighteenth century – acted as a mirror and a secret admonishment in order to disapprove of and curb the disaggregating impulses of civilization between the two world wars. After 1945, Leavis's admiration for Henry James, on the one hand, and D. H. Lawrence, on the other, was due to the assumption that a novel must be rich in 'social and moral instances'. *The Great Tradition* was first published in 1948, although its five chapters had first appeared as essays in *Scrutiny* beginning from 1937. The authors treated, as if to imply that they alone deserved saving, were Jane Austen, George Eliot, Henry James and Joseph Conrad, the last two not properly or fully British. Dickens was given a small role, and only *Hard Times* was deemed worthy of an 'analytical note'. Leavis cared for the novelist's attitude to life rather than the stylistic vehicle; and in the novelists he studies, he draws a distinction between serious, moral and ethical fiction and one in which a confused stylistic mannerism triumphs. With surprising frankness he disapproves of late James, to conclude however that James was at the top of the tradition of the novel in English for the deep seriousness of his interest in life and the ethical and moral urgency despite and beyond his cold symbolism. *The Bostonians* is praised to the hilt for the ambiguity and variety of its representation of America versus Europe. A somewhat polemical postscript clutches at straws to support the assertion that we can hardly follow the later James 'unregretting', while James's famous prefaces were written by a mature James and with the ideas of a mature James, and are thus 'misleading' and do not repay our time and attention. Here Leavis reacts against the incompetence and superficiality of living critics whom he mentions by first and last name (and Spender emerges with broken bones). Also in James's other final novels he blames the disproportion between the technical and the ethical. Ultimately, James is transformed into a sort of Tennyson criticized by the Cambridge 'Apostles': 'So he came to live in [art]', and his was the life of a 'spiritual recluse'. Just as the post-Victorians demolished Arnold at the opening of the twentieth century, the criticism of Leavis – who deeply admired Arnold as a critic of 'culture', and developed his ideas – became over time a synonym for an intimidating dogmatism devoid of theoretical props, capable only of imposing limiting 'ideas' which were disseminated among British universities through his followers. One of those ideas was for instance the condemnation of late Joyce in 1933, before that of late James: Joyce of *Finnegans Wake*, that is, after having read the sections of this work that by then had been published.[2]

§ 84. *Tomlinson*

The timeless, although too general classical-romantic antithesis is a criterion of recognition and classification that is still useful and applicable to the twentieth-century poetry of the last fifty years, and is in any case ideal for framing the poetry and inspiration of Charles Tomlinson (1927–2015). For instant orientation, Tomlinson, Apollonian and neoclassical, or even spiritually Augustan, was the antipodes of a MacDiarmid and a Harrison, Dionysian and neo-Romantic.[1] However, and this will be my contention, in Tomlinson the two genetic moments are sutured or strike a balance between them. We must first take into account that Tomlinson was almost a contemporary of Larkin and the poets of the Movement, and debuted in 1951 against this grain, since he looked beyond the national borders, rebelled against provincialism and was instead an adept of that cosmopolitanism which was spurned by the members of the Movement.

2   On Leavis's objectively valuable insights into nineteenth-century poetry and fiction (on Dickens especially, the object of a reparative book of 1970, and on Hopkins), cf. Leavis in the Index of Names in Volumes 5 and 6.

1   The limiting judgement pronounced by Tomlinson (PGU, vol. VII, 460) on the late MacDiarmid, due to his sloppiness and lack of order, is significant.

Influenced by American Poetry, learned and multilingual, he translated from Italian,[2] Spanish and Russian (Leopardi and Ungaretti, Octavio Paz, Vasko Popa and Philippe Jaccottet). A university professor and award-winning poet, he was also active as a critic, and gave public readings of his poetry and recorded it and that of others. Last but not least, he dabbled in painting. He was therefore yet another exceptional case of British versatility. Donald Davie was his tutor at Cambridge, and this is readily apparent. Davie wrote in fact a flattering preface to the slim volume with which Tomlinson's debuted in 1955, where we can even recognize traces of Empson, in turn a disciple of Davie. Davie and Empson are indeed behind the early Tomlinson, a poet of ideas and concepts, and therefore 'conceited' or 'concettist' in the negative meaning of the term.[3] Davie observed that Tomlinson's hallmark is a poetry directed *ad extra* and not *ad intra*, and objectifying the world before our senses and investigating how we perceive it. Vigilantly, Tomlinson bans excessive emotional involvement, debars the ecstatic exclamation, cooling experience in finished verbal organisms that are accurate and unblemished, as much as they are argumentatively insidious. Strong emotions are kept in check in favour of precise analyses of perceptive mechanisms, functions and operations, and pride of place is reserved for the processes of the artist composing: the poet, the musician and especially the painter. From all this, it follows that he was a poet loaned to or stolen from philosophy, and that the philosophical school to which he belongs is post-Kant perspectivism. The recipient perceives only a façade, a phenomenon, while he is precluded the knowledge of the noumenon; however, there is no trace of Berkeley in Tomlinson, and the cups – in an exemplary poem which we will see – are and do exist, and are not just simulacra of our mind, which they invade with their 'thingness'.

2   A year-long stay in Liguria immediately after graduating long reverberated in Tomlinson's poetry, right up to the collections of the late 1980s, with short genre scenes, conspicuous skits, and sketches of the coastal and marine landscape, punctuated by a few sentences in Italian. Poems affectionately dedicated to Attilio Bertolucci are equally frequent.

3   That Davie and Empson influenced Tomlinson, an opponent of the Movement, confirms how much the two more elderly poets really were peripheral to it, rather than its orthodox theorists.

Significantly, in the poem 'The Binoculars' it is not the naked eye, or not only, what is celebrated in the 'ceremony of the eye' (and we immediately notice the silently sacral metaphor), as much as the binoculars ('the last phase of romance'), or even the microscope, which are the optical instruments fit for discovering and recognizing visible reality. Recognizing is the word *par excellence*, and the cardinal action, in Tomlinson. In reality, the eye deceives, and binoculars are truthful but intimidate; in its 'conceit' the poem turns on a synaesthesia, since without the binoculars a deceptive vision does not form, while the roar of the evening is unleashed. In terms of genre, Tomlinson in his poems composes paintings in the truest and most ekphrastic sense of the word, and most often still lifes that explore the resonances elicited in a human subject who observes them. 'Paring the Apple' describes through images that are, so to speak, imagistic, how we perceive and recognize an object. This is done by means of the blade of a knife that removes the apple's phenomenic surface to force out the flesh, and a blade which is inserted between the skin and the 'freshness', between the yellow of the outside and the white of the inside. Here lies the true amphibian character of Tomlinson's art: he is often found to be a poet – just as there are painters – of views, belonging to the category of the early nineteenth-century British landscape painters, above all Constable. Constable is predictably the dedicatee of a poem that revisits his habit of sitting in front of 'meteorological facts', and how these were observed and translated into a painting. To return to the point introduced above, one can agree on Tomlinson's hybridization of sources that are as much classical or eighteenth-century as Romantic or modernist. Tomlinson's Modernism emerges and can be glimpsed in his rejection of rhyme and in the adoption of free verse. However, his poetry remains dianoetic, performing, that is, a dense argumentation that is articulated in long sentences (with a musical analogy, critics evoke a Tomlinsonian *legato*); while no temptation from fragmentism is accepted from Pound and Eliot. And yet: did Tomlinson not wish, in the last analysis, to intellectualize emotion? Those who submit his extraneousness to the family of poet-painters, especially the visionary poets like Blake and Rossetti, are right: Tomlinson is on the side of the view but not of the vision. It is not even accurate to link him to Wordsworth, who tried out many emotions, poured them out and recollected them in tranquillity, and who above all implemented a mystical fusion between the object and the subject, like the rest of his Romantic brotherhood.

2. A poem by Tomlinson is usually a secondary and not a primary discourse, and, in the middle, there is often the buffer of the learned inspiration, the cultural opportunity that aroused it, the source from a book or the writer or thinker behind it; it is never an undifferentiated description of emotional states, or of sensations and reflections in their pure state. His poetry is more exactly essayistic in form, and, highly appreciated in America, it has left the educated public back home cold. The often heard criticism is in fact that it is as monotonous, arid and, undeniably, long-winded. Tomlinson's responses were the numerous collections published by him after 1978 and until his death, which were intermittently turned to more topical issues and even to political protest. This was however a temporary change of direction, and there is no real evolution in Tomlinson. Ultimately, he had the same curious interests as Browning, without mimetically dramatizing them, however. Browning is the only poet who brings into play as many painters, musicians and writers as Tomlinson does: a Browning speaking empathetically in the third person. But there was Modernism to curb the exuberance, and Tomlinson is entirely dissimilar to Browning. To say that he was not Romantic – to try to answer the question raised above – is instinctive but shallow, because Tomlinson, too, has his own inborn mystique of nature, and, like Wordsworth, he learns from nature. Suffice to see how he sacralizes and spiritualizes it, having for instance a stone[4] speak a language and representing it as the repository of laws and even hidden human feelings and metaphysical values: stoic stones, vigilant, precisely resistant, and tolerant. These stones are then also touchstones, points of reference, symbols of the imagination. In front of the stones, perhaps his most fundamental and recurrent symbol, the poet discovers the dynamism and the kinesis of a nature that only according to a false euphemism is 'dead', and on the contrary is never inert, rather, constantly in motion. Tomlinson's arguably best-known poem, 'A Given Grace', calls 'grace' that which spreads

4   'In Defence of Metaphysics'.

from an inert object; in reality, Tomlinson appears more Kantian or even Platonic than we might at first imagine: the cups are reflections of another entity, and they, too, are dynamic, and what lies behind or above imparts and transmits a 'force' and refines and intensifies the colour. My reference to the poetics lying behind the cups, jugs and bottles in the painting of Giorgio Morandi is not completely random, in a poet like Tomlinson who knew many things about Italy, perhaps the most Italianate of contemporary British poets. This poem is also conspicuous for the use of the rhetoric of antithesis, in the empty container that fills what is already full, and the observer discovering himself to be empty. Nature is always in movement behind the apparent tranquillity in Tomlinson. Anthropomorphic trees preserve the memory of places, and nature is read like a text, and therefore means, or even extends the distant echo of an Edenic phase of corrupt history.[5] Another crucial poem is 'Song', in that it uncovers or infers the mastermind behind the natural spectacle, or, as the poet says, the imperfect symphony covered by cacophony. Like the dissonance that becomes harmony in Schönberg's twelve-tone music, a willow first ruffled by the wind returns to quiet the next day, with other images that demonstrate the reduction of the manifold to unity: this is the theme of 'Ode to Arnold Schoenberg'. And contingent man? Defenders of Tomlinson hail poems of his in which nature is no longer inanimate, absolving him from the accusation of having no sense of history. Tomlinson meditating in Tarquinia in the eponymous poem is a kind of Gibbonian Keats who faces the disconcerting, grotesque epiphany of human transiency as opposed to the eternity of art or simple matter. Tomlinson is far less successful when he experiments with pacy narration, as in 'The Flood', a poem which, however, is on a time-worn theme, the meeting/clash between man and nature and the faithful support of the stone, which never lets us down.

5   Knowing is only undertaking, as in the sensationalism of Hume, while a barrier is erected between the leaves and us, leaves that, however, make their greenness explode ('How Far').

§ 85. *Betjeman*

John Betjeman (1906–1984) and Tomlinson, and perhaps also Davie and Empson, help to clarify, *ex post*, that the Movement was active in its free state as a reaction against Modernism and each derivation from Romanticism, even before being officially codified; and that, once encoded, it could generate the same antibodies from its bosom. A small galaxy of precursors, participants, semi-participants, dissidents, and even deserters or negotiators gyrated around its central core. Betjeman is a peripheral participant, and the eldest of the historical members of the Movement, and his poems, in some of their ideas and themes, flowed naturally into its aesthetics and programmes. But Betjeman is much more, and earns himself his small stature as an independent conservative, the author of a poetry that may captivate, or disappoint, but never leaves one indifferent. Meanwhile, it is symptomatic that he crossed the paths of T. S. Eliot, C. S. Lewis and Auden, was fascinated by them and fascinated them in turn (except for Eliot), and that from the sense of risk and adventure of the modern he withdrew into his own cocoon, suffering the ostrich complex: in reality, building himself a series of shelters and being perfectly comfortable and at ease in them. Born John Betjemann in London to a Victorian family of furniture and antique dealers of Dutch origins, he became Betjeman during the First World War to avoid seeming too German. At middle school he had among his teachers T. S. Eliot, who returned the pupil's early poems to him without comment. Nevertheless, as we shall see, there is in Betjeman a vague assonance with Eliot's Anglo-Catholic ideas and patriotic feelings. At Marlborough College a fellow-student was MacNeice, while at Oxford his peer was Auden, who was to welcome, and appreciate with detailed comments, Betjeman's sagas, rites and pseudo-epiphanies of the British petty bourgeoisie. Auden himself was the editor of his poems, but there was nothing more alien to Betjeman than the engagé poetry of the 1930s. At Oxford, his studies of ecclesiastical history were to leave an indelible mark on him, both owing to a misunderstanding with his tutor C. S. Lewis and because he repeatedly failed a theology examination, the consequence of which was that he left the university without graduating, something that was to haunt him for the rest of his life. Additionally, Oxford instilled in him an interest in and passion for Victorian, that is, neo-Gothic, architecture, and made him adopt, as it were, the motto *Victorianum nihil me alienum puto*. This infatuation had been put to fruition, in the meantime, as a journalist and collaborator of history, sociology and architecture journals. He was declared unfit at the outbreak of the Second World War, was a press attaché in Dublin during it, divorced in 1951, and by virtue of his fortunate poetry collections, which won him the appointment of Poet Laureate, became a legendary media phenomenon, first on the radio, then on television and later in the cinema. *Summoned by Bells* (1960), a blank-verse autobiography, flat and conversational like those of Pushkin and Byron, and a recreation of the epos of Pater's Oxford and therefore of a vestigial world, became a film in 1976. The first reason for Betjeman's stratospheric success was that many educated contemporaries read him as a witness of a bygone age. It was the same age of a Praz, who in his essays on Betjeman became sentimental and struck on the idea, without expressly saying so, of Betjeman as an ideal member of the group of nostalgic humorists, that of his beloved Lamb, and of Thackeray and Beerbohm.[1] Betjeman was liked by this elite for his canny blend of nostalgia and irony, and for attacking and sharing, dissociating from and associating with his targets, according to the old proviso, that the satire of satirists is *de te* and *de me satira*.[2] If his are faded, old yellowing postcards, and if he is a cartoonist and a graphic artist of scenes of a bygone time, he is not even that far from a gentle nostalgic like Arnold Bennett. Betjeman astutely got by between the two poles, and the immediate response was that his collected poems of 1958 sold 90,000 copies, while later estimates give the dizzying figure of two million. It is not uncommon to find at second-hand booksellers whole shelves of used copies, annotated by readers, of Betjeman's collected poems. This shows the popularity of the repertoire of sometimes rather pedestrian considerations that the poet offered. Betjeman provided no less than an updated handbook of offhand plausible and moralizing anecdotes, mixtures of the serious and humorous, the satirical and nostalgic, for middle-brow readers; he resuscitated a

1   CLA, vol. IV, 318.
2   Praz, deducing this from Lord Birkenhead's preface to the 1962 London edition of Betjeman's poems, makes the important observation that Betjeman lacked the cruelty and rancour needed to be a true satirist.

British civilization that had only recently become outmoded, celebrating its pastimes and entertainments, which were regulated by a rigid timetable and were followed up by other rites enjoyed and obeyed in a playful spirit, as if the whole world revolved around them. Is this not the same climate as that of a J. K. Jerome, the author of the little saga of the imperturbable men in a boat, blissfully heedless of the pressure of time? In the story in verse, 'Beside the Seaside', the middle-class family, come the holidays, sets off in their old jalopy for the sea, where they find everything still, frozen and expectant just like the year before. The sunny middle class is, however, surprised by the war, and in a poem a party is stopped by the announcement that it has actually broken out.

2. Architectural art was a testimony to the spiritual life of the nation for Betjeman, and hence the poems consisting of pure descriptions of architectural details, in the form of guided tours in words through the recesses of old English churches, where the pilgrim bows his head to recite acts of devotion and contrition. Conversely, in a dialogued poem a municipal employee expounds his modern ideas aiming to change the face of old English architectural monuments – 'A beauteous England's really on the way' – and replace them with 'concrete villas in the modern style'. This poem, 'The Town Clerk's Views', may well come across like a pendant to Larkin's 'Church Going', since among the delirious views on architectural and urban modernization is the one that churches have become 'redundant', the same assumption considered by the worried and perplexed Larkin, who, like Betjeman, ends up questioning it in his poem, and for not entirely different reasons.[3] Here is precisely what the two poets had in common: nostalgia for a dear old England about to be swept away by the so-called modern.[4] Betjeman often sings adopting the easy rhythms of the light classical

---

3   § 77.3. Larkin, who esteemed him greatly, thought that Betjeman seemed to have reduced or even eliminated the complexity and the obscurity of Modernism, and to have preceded him in the immersion in local detail: in the everyday life of the common man, far from the spotlight.

4   Praz, in PSL, 702, summarizes Betjeman in a footnote, and one, rather oddly, in his chapter on D. H. Lawrence, with whom, however, Betjeman shared the protest against the industrial civilization that had stifled Victoria's good reign.

song with its banal and slightly trite comparisons. There is no lack, in other terms, of frank lapses into doggerel, nor of conventional, inert, *déjà vus* poems, such as the one on Christmas, predictable from the first to the last word with its genre images and hackneyed wonder over the incarnation of God in the Child in a grotto. Betjeman's cult for things, especially small things, can be pointed to as confirmation of Asa Briggs's acute book, *Victorian Things*,[5] as the *mise en abyme*, that is, of a whole civilization. Among these things are bells, bicycles, tiles, saddles, tennis rackets: amulets, pawns, miniature worlds. The boundary between the pleasantly sentimental, the melancholic, the heartfelt and bittersweet remembrance, and the shoddy, or pure kitsch, is vague in Betjeman. Sometimes that cult of the object turns into that, stale and unbearable, of things that are not just antique but simply old, and Betjeman in this case sounds like the heir of their Victorian singer *par excellence*, Eliza Cook.[6] So skilfully does Betjeman imitate the nineteenth-century 'poetic diction', with its old lexicon, syntactic reversals, insistent and syncopated trochaic rhythms, that we could take it as a deliberate parody on his part, yet without it being so.

3. Betjeman's emotional and symbolic centres are first and foremost the church, with its merry, festive and gently intrusive bells calling the faithful to its services, and a landscape that always looks uniform and invariable, with rural communities who live outside time, and in any case before the crumbling of the communities themselves. But this is a 'before' that is considerably delayed. The fascination with the Anglo-Catholic liturgy may seem in itself an 'aesthetic' element, and in part it is, as Betjeman was indeed, or posed as, a belated disciple of the Oxford Movement and of Pater, Hopkins, or even Wilde. Like Beerbohm, for the benefit of the nostalgics, Betjeman recreates Oxford, especially, along with the epics of academic life with its oddities and eccentricities, with a poetry on the glamour of places that had now been made anachronistic by history. Wilde, incidentally, is at the centre of a poem recalling his arrest before the trial for sodomy; it is rich in vivid, colourful, almost inebriating satirical stabs worthy precisely

5   London 1988.
6   Volume 4, § 214.

of a Beerbohm. The fact is that Betjeman is truly devout, even though he is always detached and can also dwell on the humorous and droll sides of a religious ceremony. One of his more incisive, albeit not representative poems, and one almost self-standing, is 'In Westminster Abbey', for once a genuinely cruel and merciless attack against the mindset of the crass and materialistic middle class, shrouded in bigotry. A lady kneels and prays, and the poem transcribes this mental prayer, in which we perceive only self-righteousness and a perversion of authentic faith. It therefore recalls a dramatic Browning-style monologue, of those whose aim was to brand faith deformed for personal use. The lady asks God for what she herself wants to occur as per her national and class prejudices, and her myopic egotism. We are at war, she says, and one does not pray for peace, but for God to bomb the Germans – except for the women! It is blasphemous, she continues, to think that God could want to destroy and not love all the creatures he has created. The prayer indirectly targets the warmongering ideology of the lady and the class she represents, and passes quietly over the imperial exploitation of oppressed nationalities, which provide soldiers for the Empire, which in turn sends them to the carnage of the front. The last straw is that the blacks can die and be massacred, while the pure white cannot. In short, what flows mutely from her lips is the most sinister ideology of imperial power and of the 'white man's burden', British freedom and a civilizing, that is, straitening, religion. God is adulated in tones of blackmail that echo the monologue of Browning's Bishop at St Praxed's.

4. In this simulated and reanimated civilization, the means of locomotion *par excellence* is the bicycle. It allows one to still feel deceptively located, and as if hibernated, in a bygone time forever finished; conversely, 'No motor coach can take me back / To that Edwardian "erstwhile"'. In 'Middlesex', it is the train that goes 'Where a few surviving hedges / Keep alive our lost Elysium – rural Middlesex again'. In gradually more numerous poems we see Betjeman doing pure and simple reconnaissance of English rural areas with heartfelt recordings of how they were years earlier, and before the passing of time, and modern civilization, altered their aspect. A chord that resounds, distantly Wordsworthian or even Blakean, is that of the poet who exclaims: 'Time, bring back / The rapturous ignorance of long ago'. Certain youthful experiences were burning in Betjeman's

innermost depths – his failure to graduate, his abortive marriage, not having continued his family's business; and infantile and immature imbalances of his character re-emerged and persisted, such as keeping close a teddy bear (which inspired Waugh when he created Sebastian Flyte). The effeminate Betjeman was at Oxford the constant target of mockery by his more athletic and virile companions. But it is also true that algolagnic inclinations, of the type of Swinburne's as a young schoolboy, are reminisced over with completely different results, and his bitterness is easily sublimated. The Betjeman fixed on the architectural details of churches is also the maliciously platonic lover of a series of women; this should in itself cast light on some of his complexes and disturbing perversions. These women are, à la Swinburne, femmes fatales, but humorously so, and Betjeman the poet does feel a sadomasochistic thrill before such figments, but immediately debunks it, and glides over these side issues, softens them, tones them down, and dissolves them. Ever since the poem 'Pot Pourri from a Surrey Garden' Betjeman evokes the icon of an athletic giantess, often a tennis player or cyclist who subdues the shy and anaemic poet who yearns for her, while admiring one by one her out-of-the-ordinary features and the power with which she strikes a tennis ball, tennis being the most symbolic sport of this *belle époque*. The venerated and gently domineering woman is always 'Olympian' and therefore also Olympic, tall and mannish, and she just feels 'disgust' for an 'unhealthy worm' like the poet. And we should notice in 'The Olympic Girl' with what nonchalance the poet confesses that he himself would like to be her racquet pressed 'With hard excitement to her breast / And swished into the sunlit air' to hit the bouncing ball. One of these numerous femmes fatales is described as a panther ready to leap, but frequent comparisons are with beasts that are harmless and threaten emptily. The peak of erotic excitement turns out to be a bicycle ride along woodland paths! In 'The Licorice Fields at Pontefract', 'Her sulky lips were shaped for sin', but then no hint of Baudelairean, Swinburnian, or *maudit* raciness materializes – quite the opposite, in fact. Betjeman's poetry is not a unified novel in verse, but idylls of this type – pedestrian and bathetic – punctuate it. Ultimately, here one witnesses the exhumation of those idylls 'of the dining-room and the deanery' that Patmore had chiselled with such unattainable neatness 100 years earlier. Those of Betjeman are also idylls, with the main character going into ecstasy over small, exquisite daily pleasures, and feels but tames the stings of the flesh.

§ 86. *Ted Hughes** *I: The force of nature*

In the following presentation of Ted Hughes (1930–1998) I shall elaborate on the denotative and figurative ambivalences of this title. Hughes sings the original energy – constructive, aggressive and destructive – of animate and inanimate nature. He is a 'monographic' poet for the number of poems, if not collections, focusing on the study of the vital impulse and of the survival instinct, the instinct for evil and original oppression inherent in the animal kingdom. He is the poet of obsessions, his eyes being like tinted glasses whose colour envelops and stains everything he sees. The linchpin of his poetic imagination is the

*   *Collected Poems*, ed. P. Keegan, London 2003. *Poesie*, ed. N. Gardini and A. Ravano, Milano 2008 is an Italian, virtually complete edition of the poems with parallel text, whose rich comments I shall cite as Gardini 2008. *Letters of Ted Hughes*, ed. C. Reid, London 2007. K. M. Sagar, *Ted Hughes*, ed. I. Scott-Kilvert, London 1972, *The Art of Ted Hughes*, Cambridge 1975 and 1978, and *The Laughter of Foxes: A Study of Ted Hughes*, Liverpool 2000 (Sagar also edited *The Achievement of Ted Hughes*, Manchester 1983); A. Bold, *Thom Gunn and Ted Hughes*, Edinburgh 1976; R. Crivelli, *L'universo indifferente: miti di aggressione nella poesia di Ted Hughes*, Pisa 1978; E. Faas, *Ted Hughes: The Unaccommodated Universe*, Santa Barbara, CA 1980; T. Gifford and N. Roberts, *Ted Hughes: A Critical Study*, London 1981; S. Hirschberg, *Myth in the Poetry of Ted Hughes: A Guide to the Poems*, Portmarnock 1981; T. West, *Ted Hughes*, London and New York 1985; A. Lombardo, 'La poesia di Ted Hughes', *Lingua e letteratura*, IV, 6, Milano 1986, 88–96; D. Walder, *Ted Hughes*, Milton Keynes 1987; M. Stella, *L'inno e l'enigma. Saggio su Ted Hughes*, Roma 1988; C. Robinson, *Ted Hughes as Shepherd of Being*, London 1989; N. Bishop, *Re-Making Poetry: Ted Hughes and a New Critical Psychology*, Brighton 1991; *Critical Essays on Ted Hughes*, ed. L. M. Scigaj, New York 1992; A. Skea, *Ted Hughes: The Poetic Quest*, Armidale 1994; P. Bentley, *The Poetry of Ted Hughes: Language, Illusion, and Beyond*, London 1998; E. Feinstein, *Ted Hughes: The Life of a Poet*, London 2001, 2016; D. Middlebrook, *Her Husband: Hughes and Plath – A Marriage*, London 2003; N. Roberts, *Ted Hughes: A Literary Life*, London 2006; J. Greening, *The Poetry of Ted Hughes*, London 2007; *The Cambridge Companion to Ted Hughes*, ed. T. Gifford, Cambridge 2014, also author of *Ted Hughes*, Basingstoke 2014.

animal, and his work is an uninterrupted variation on that imagination, just as certain painters work for their whole life on the same subject and use it in continual metamorphoses. In British painting we can evoke the name of Landseer, a painter of animals which he did not catch in their sinister state – dark, demonic, and predatory – but romantically sublimated, as faithful and unfailing companions of man; but he only painted animals. Broadly speaking, Hughes is an evolutionary and still post-Darwinian poet, attentive to the distinctive mark of the aggressive, untamed, humanized animal; an animal therefore risen very close to the boundary with the purely human; however, Hughes increasingly accompanies this theme with an ancient, although updated, polemic against an absent or indifferent deity. Such a purely metaphysical stance is combined, in Hughes's middle and late poetry, with more disparate topical echoes, such as the protest against industrialism and atmospheric and river pollution, surface phenomena that enrich the image of a pagan poet, surprisingly nostalgic for an intact and virgin nature. The second, representational and metaphorical meaning of the 'force of nature' lies in a poetic voice that suddenly wells up in a powerful spurt, as if from a primordial spring. Few other poets of recent British literary history can match Hughes as an authentic 'poetic animal' and in the naturalness of his expression, an expression that proceeds as in glossolalia or in an apostle on whom the Pentecostal flame has fallen, or in divine children of history like Mozart. With Hughes, the poet comes back into possession of the primary and principal gift of the imagination; he is someone who knows, first and foremost, how to clad the history of everyday and human life in beautiful and always uncommon and surprising images. The image, as for Dylan Thomas, is the quintessential ingredient of his poetry and its driving force: an image that is always unpredictable, unprecedented, undisciplined, often also illogical.

2. Hughes's poetry is little less than immense and grandiose in its proportions. This exceptional effusiveness is itself an anomalous fact, if compared with the productions of the twentieth-century poet, who was on average and for the most part laconic, reluctant to publish, scrimp, suffering protracted expressive crises and even afflicted by aphasia, or overwhelmed sooner or later by total silence. Hughes is far from anaemic, and far from afraid

of the challenge to utter; minimalism is unknown to him. Compared to the many writers who hide, camouflage themselves and become, so to speak, the ghosts of themselves, he was the classic artist who desires to attend every social event in order to get noticed. His unit of measurement and production rate were those of the best-selling novelists, and quantitatively he is on a par with Lessing, Murdoch, Greene or Spark. The only shadow of a suspicion one might have is that, like fiction writers, Hughes sought market success, because his imperious and never-stifled need to speak also responded to a necessity, especially at the beginning, to live off the proceeds of poetry; and several collections of his were conceived and completed as double creations, collaborations with photographers, graphic artists, illustrators and painters of the moment, and published as luxury editions. Behind such operations was always however the sincere, noble, utopian and romantic attempt to bring grist to the mill of poetry, and disseminate it among the masses, the young and those who did not usually read poetry.[1] To circumscribe our radius – and to immediately suggest a brutally mnemonic classification of the two poets recognized as the greatest of the last twenty-five or even thirty to forty years of the twentieth century – Apollo was to Dionysus as Larkin was to Hughes.[2] We have just seen Larkin: an accomplished, sedentary employee, always sitting behind his librarian's desk, at most a Sunday cyclist removing the clips from his trousers to visit a deserted suburban church, or travelling by train from Hull to London. Hughes seems a ready response to a criticism of the poetics of the Movement made by the poet Charles Tomlinson, and often quoted:

1   Immediately after graduating from Cambridge, Hughes embraced various temporary jobs, firstly because he had decided to be a full-time poet; in addition, a poet, as Hughes conceived this role, could not but be a poet and only a poet in every moment of his existence. Each new collection was in the running for cash prizes that allowed him to feed the sacred fire of poetry. And he was skilful in sniffing out who counted at the BBC, in the Sunday papers, and on the juries of awards; he also knew how to sell himself to the highest bidder with prodigious commercial instinct.

2   The first collections of Hughes were judged with enigmatic favour by T. S. Eliot, and later Hughes held the position of Poet Laureate which, according to him, Larkin had refused.

the 'lack of awareness of the external *continuum*', addressed to those poets who were a part of it. By comparison, Hughes is possessed, wild, demoniacal. The absence of repose and, conversely, motoric delirium are his deepest soul; but his is an especially spiritual restlessness, the existential search for an *ubi consistam*, therefore always temporary and asymptotic, ever a run-up towards a goal, and a landing place of peace which, by definition, are never and could never be achieved. To classify Hughes in his exceptionality and uniqueness we should go back even further: for his implacable compositional furore, expressed in a fluidity and ease without equal in his time, he recalls a Browning, a Blake, or a Yeats for a similar or analogous mythopoeia. Blake and Yeats are ultimately the true literary progenitors of Hughes. A first agreement with Yeats is the voracious faith in poetry and the poetic, at any latitude and in any language. As a young man Hughes became infatuated, like Yeats, with poets of little or no value, and he let himself be dazzled by the pure sound of their verse. With Yeats, and also with Hopkins, he believed that poetry should be read, recited and declaimed, and witnesses assure us that he was a fascinating reader, capable of declaiming Dante, perhaps without fully understanding him, for the simple music of his poetry. Such an icon of a primitive poet matches the description of the mythological role of the shaman made by Mircea Eliade, a scholar whom Hughes had read, and had been deeply struck by, at university. In one of its allegorical meanings, the shaman is the poet who sees poetry as the reciting of sheer sounds, and believes in the materiality of poetry even prior to being a communicative and semantic system (Hopkins, too, insisted on the *aural* nature of poetry, before and beyond the communication of its meanings).[3] Hughes tried to put such an auditory/visceral concept of poetry into practice in *Orghast*, which remains today in the form of scattered notes and scribbles,[4] and which the poet failed to combine into a unified text: a work, therefore, that was Promethean, pioneering, yet symptomatic of a vision and practice of poetry as *Ursprache*. The instinctual meaning of poetry cannot provide a solid aesthetic theorization, and in Hughes we

3   Volume 6, § 191.4.
4   *Orghast at Persepolis*, ed. A. C. H. Smith, London 1972. The dramatic action was
      staged at Persepolis under the direction of Peter Brook.

notice accordingly the flagrant lack of a poetic theory established for its absolute value, rather than an exclusively personal one.

§ 87. *Ted Hughes II: Autobiography and self-mythologizing*

Contrary to the rule of thumb I set myself, not to include in my discussions the biographies of post-war writers, and *a fortiori* those of our contemporaries, I must make an exception for Hughes. Writing, summarizing, recapping his biography is essential, since Hughes's life is closely related to his poetry and vice versa: his life is even at a premium over his written work and stands up to it. His poetry is in turn the written translation of his personal myth: it speaks of his panic fusion with an especially savage nature, of the intuition of Nordic nature and his original landscape of Yorkshire; it speaks of his intense imaginary life and of his psychic contact with external reality: of wonder, the mystical trance, visions. Hughes utters all this in the adapted language of his region of provenance, which preserves ancient and archaic inflections and dialect stratifications. Later, this swarm of primordial intuitions merges with a magma of culturological accretions that are not precisely 'nature' any more, but 'culture', and drawn from disparate areas whose vague *trait d'union* is the same one that ultimately subtends all mythologies and theosophies. Tracing Hughes's biography amounts to discovering the way this poet has an inalienable and unbridgeable diversity compared to other British poets of the second half of the twentieth century; indeed, he leaves them all behind in a group. Hughes is a living metempsychosis of the Poet with a capital letter, a simulacrum like the vates of ancient times, who after several centuries of relative lethargy had been reincarnated in some Romantics and Decadents. He is the poet-redesigner of the cosmos, and he stands with Hesiod and Lucretius; as a 'fatal' poet, beyond good and evil, he is the contemporary doppelganger of Shelley, Byron, Wilde, Nietzsche, Yeats and Lawrence. These great predecessors each cover one face of his prismatic personality.

2. I mentioned above that Larkin's biography is unnecessary and provides no appreciable result, or almost, as regards his poetry; that of Hughes forms an engaging plot for the dense symbiosis between his life and his work. He is the last holder of a biographical myth. He is one of those artists whose life is entirely resolved in their vicissitudes, of whom D. H.

Lawrence was the closest representative in time and space. A turbulent plot, rich in twists. Impatient with working routine, Hughes exemplifies the drifter poet, wild and always on the move; in him there relives the Romantic poet and the bohemian. A northerner, with partly Celtic and Irish ancestors, he was born a few miles from Haworth, and the same spiritual life-blood as the Brontë sisters ran in his veins. On the native moors and their ashen, shaded and windy landscapes, Hughes learned early on to know nature and its immutable laws. His mother, like Lawrence's, was a small reservoir of stories, legends and fantasies that fed a galloping and unbridled imagination. He soaked up small myths, folklore, and oral tales. At the same time, he could study mental and oneiric disorder in his father, a First World War veteran who screamed at night in the grip of nightmares. Hughes's throbbing desire to immediately be a runaway, at least on the wings of fantasy, was nurtured by the oppression exerted by his family's Methodist religion. His literary education was that of the classic English nature poet: Wordsworth, Hopkins, and immediately behind him Edward Thomas, who, a decade earlier, more sedately and coldly but equally precisely had classified natural phenomena, the whirring of birds and botanical varieties. But Hughes's opening up to the sense of mystery, the enchanted, the ghostly, is a Yeatsian foreshadowing. The subsequent step of the written word was taken by Hughes when he began to avidly read the stories of fishing and hunting and the comic books that his father sold in his emporium, while his first schoolteacher made him read Kipling, Hopkins, Yeats and Lawrence. Cambridge, for which he only just managed to obtain a grant, served to root in him a rejection of the traditional methods of the teaching of literature, and to shift his interest towards astrology, esotericism, anthropology, and some authors outside the canon (at the time, Hughes would get drunk with some friends reading popular Scottish and Irish songs with a baritone voice, and was an adept of medieval poetry). If it had been vaguely possible to associate the debuting Hughes with the Movement, his repudiation of it was sanctioned with the statement that it was like an overwhelming 'maternal octopus' that strangled with its coils. His red-hot, torrid relationship with Sylvia Plath, the promising, neurotic American poet who was at Cambridge on a Fulbright scholarship, erupted at first sight as the classic lightning bolt, following the publication of some of Hughes's poems in student magazines, and the desire of both to emulate the Lawrences, a couple of decades after the death of the author of *Lady Chatterley*. This immediately furious poetic-erotic romance is documented by the letters they started to exchange, letters that are always over the top, showing apocalyptic magniloquence and exclamatory turgidity just a step away from Lawrence's ecstasies. Hughes and Plath married in secret in London, moved to America and then back to England, determined to be freelance writers. Hughes, who had already taken on various jobs to survive, and had a thousand volcanic ideas to make ends meet, in 1957 won an American poetry prize. His first collection was published in the same year on both sides of the Atlantic, in London by Faber with the approval of T. S. Eliot. All in all, it was a consecration.

3. Hughes's life would always travel on the parallel rails of a frenetic writing activity and an equally hectic rhythm of lived experiences, according to a twentieth-century association of sensibility. This was ancient and modern hubris, nothing other than the continuous search for ultimate experiences, which proved to be provisional, and the story of a parched man who never quenches his thirst, or who, after quenching it, and therefore feeling satisfied and having ended his journey, immediately discovers that he is still thirsty, and sets off again. We can count in even hundreds the people Hughes was dazzled by on meeting, or the regenerating experiences that he believed could bring some as yet undiscovered new meaning, or the whole significance *tout court*, to his life. This life became a chain of continuous electric shocks which burnt out much too soon. Reading his letters proves how much Hughes, as a new Adam, hailed everyday events with amazement – such as the visit to a place never seen, or a new house – and as a sort of re-creation or new creation, as though from that moment he had re-begun or really begun life from a kind of new year zero.[5] He was one of the most travelled poets of modern times. He brought the cardinal points closer, one day here and tomorrow there; he possessed the soul of the explorer and colonizer, in search of a primordial landscape in which

---

5   As late as 1972, on buying Moortown Farm, Hughes exclaimed: 'I feel to be waking up for the first time in my life'.

to stay far from the metropolis.[6] An ambassador of poetry, he strove and would always strive commendably to recreate a suitable space for it in the modern and contemporary era. He launched and chaired literary prizes, held courses and organized multimedia programmes to introduce children to poetry; a dreamer and megalomaniac, he was by no means insensitive to grandiose projects such as Wagnerian *Gesamtkunstwerk* productions based on plots of oriental mythology that included the use of colossal companies of singers and actors. He was a cultural entrepreneur, an unflagging and inexhaustible aggregator, the founder of a magazine of international poetry in translation, a prose and folktale writer, a playwright, translator, anthologist, screenwriter, and critical essayist.

4. Hughes's 'fatale' nature is something of which he was conscious and that clearly emerges from his letters and is verified therein: it is the cleft between the poet and the man. Hughes the man, dividing himself, judges the poet after the lived or even the written event. Hughes the man who writes letters and confessions is in temporary separation from the poet who has had his uncontainable, disruptive hubris. His letters are often intolerable for the indulgence and narcissistic complacency they exude; they make their subject melodramatic and fatal, a subject who has split into a memorialist. At a certain point, and on reading some, it seems no longer as if we are reading Hughes, but D'Annunzio or other aesthetes, so great is the prosopopeia, the absolute and magnified egotism that echoes forth, the cult of personality, in other words. At the same time, they are also a collection of exalted moods, of moments of panic fusion with the landscape, commemorated with at least one smidgeon of exhibitionist untruth. The 'fatale' element in Hughes is the same one as Yeats believed he read in his own life: a series of coincidences that cannot be the result of chance but of personal fate. Hughes listed them, a little startled but not terribly so. Several of his works were born from pure recordings of his dream life, because the dream imposed itself as reality, and was a dream that

6   In 1958 he and Sylvia Plath abandoned Boston for a tour around unknown America, sleeping in a tent.

happened to him and to him alone.[7] He borrows from Yeats, emulating him, but also from Lawrence, the vision of Eros and the function of the body. Still more Yeatsian is a ravenous curiosity about alternative mythologies to the Christian one, gathered from every corner of the globe. The relationship with Sylvia Plath mimicked that of Yeats with his wife when, at the end of the 1950s, they both dipped into hermetic philosophies and the Kabbala,[8] and even resorted to hypnosis to enhance and release their mythopoeic capacities. From Yeats also came the emphatic need to allow an outflow of the vitality of modern man, that is, to recover the hendiadys of body and spirit, which had been divided. In the 1970s Hughes sketched an astrological system of symbols, convergences, planetary oppositions and influences, cusps and houses – an amateur *A Vision*, in other words. The proof of that intellectual marriage – Yeats plus Lawrence – surfaces in the pleasantry of the name Frieda given to a daughter born in 1959. From Nietzsche, furthermore, Hughes inherited the idea that the poet is an *Übermensch* and lives his super-humanity day in day out; given his Nonconformist origins, a similar breach in the confines of good and evil is accompanied in Hughes by a sense of guilt, but always as an after-effect. The tragic end of his relationship with Sylvia Plath, and the numerous affairs with other women, cannot help evoking in the English reader the precedent of Shelley. Hughes lived through, but ultimately overcame, the drama of a possible co-responsibility in his wife's suicide out of jealousy; and he led a second wife to suicide. His consanguinity with Shelley is further suggested by his political and palingenetic utopia. No one was more democratic than Hughes, and he did not know what poetic rivalry was; he was that old Romantic poet motivated by the desire to purify the world. He was also an ecologist, and after his marriage he bought a farmhouse almost ten centuries old with a matted ceiling, a deliberate parody of Yeats's tower; there Hughes kitted out his own studio. It was an area

7   The radio play *Difficulties of a Bridegroom* (1962), about a husband who, returning home from a lover's, runs over a hare, sells it to a butcher and with the proceeds buys some roses, was dreamed by Hughes, on the word of his revelations.

8   Often unsuccessfully, because of delays by the publishers; Hughes wished his poetry collections to come out on certain astrologically favourable days.

of Devon that was mainly rural and unpolluted, rich in uncontaminated rivers full of fish, and a long way from nuclear energy facilities. These data summarize the civil battles into which the poet had launched himself and been engaged in since the early 1960s. With melodramatic romanticism, he considered himself guilty of his wife's suicide, albeit under mitigating circumstances: 'If there is an eternity, I am damned in it'. Yet he was the pecuniary and especially literary heir of Sylvia Plath, and after the tragedy he began a thirty-year atonement that had public and combative controversial aspects, especially with his first mentor, now his enemy: the *Observer* critic Alfred Alvarez. Hughes became the lambasted editor of Sylvia Plath; a progressive, he was demolished by insurgent feminism; wherever he went he was contested, whistled at, and morally lynched.

5. From a shining star after 1962 Hughes gradually became the target even of progressives in politics, who interpreted his praise, or simply his insistent analysis, of animal violence as an occult and figurative apologia of fascism. And yet that autobiography, or euthanasia of a love, *Birthday Letters* (1998), a work of 400 dense pages, was immediately translated (into Italian, for instance) and became a best-seller on the news stands. This obstinately poetic romance, an autobiography of his falling in love, marriage and its tragic end, is above all a posthumous memory of his female partner. It studies, interprets and imaginatively psychoanalyses Plath in a pastiche that combines memories and above all pages of a diary and excerpts from poems and prose of the deceased. And yet, judging by the phenomena of her malaise, by her incurable mental disorders, her destructive and especially self-destructive crises and her moments of demonic possession, Hughes, who often presents himself as a humble nurse and guardian, wrote nevertheless his own apologia. This is also the only true unitary poem written by a poet who, given his nature, could have aspired to this crowning achievement much earlier. It lacks the continuous flow typical of this genre, because Hughes remains faithful to his preferred arrangement, a series of short, titled, unrhyming self-enclosed poems in largely rhythmic and *andante* prose. Hence it is a chain or sequence of epiphanies that are not always linked, since they from a free stream of remembrances and associations that dictates the pace, in an alternance between remote, and recent, past and present. This is the vision of a

revenant and the illusion of still being able to speak to her. Plath is thus known and always invoked, as in a Spiritualist séance, with the intimate 'you' of the mute dialogue. In my opinion, this much-vaunted and much-read romance is one of Hughes's most overrated works. It is occasionally vivid and incisive, but its diction is sloppy and approximate (all too frequently incipits are in the form of questioning phrases, right from the opening poem), although perhaps deliberately so for the sake of mimesis. The biographical plot becomes long-winded and little varied as it progresses; merely ostentatious are the pathos of certain acts auscultated and relived, the insistent 'fatal' symbolism, or the search for effect, especially in lapidary closings. There is no lack of peaks, which come especially in the impressionistic vignettes of real life, in the remembrances of journeys, explorations, dangers, or in certain dazed anecdotes. Inevitably Hughes inserts his last close observations of animals, a genre in which he is nearly always infallible, including the chipmunk, the bat, the bear as aggressor, or a fox cub. A grating counterpoint is that between the daily trivia, whose description skims the poetry in prose, and the superimposed mythical transfiguration. *Birthday Letters* repeats in chiasmus the situation found in Elizabeth Barrett Browning's *Sonnets from the Portuguese*, even if these sonnets were not dedicated to a dead husband who had betrayed her. As the last act of his mythopoeia, Hughes was the director of the pageant of his own death: he asked that his body be cremated and his ashes scattered to the wind near the sources of the four rivers on Dartmoor. He wished however this place to be marked and immortalized by a block of granite, engraved with his name and his birth and death dates.

6. By his thirties Hughes was the most discussed poet of his generation, and his success had fashionable implications, of a symbiosis at the summit of a poet with a woman poet who was also on the crest of the wave, and already launched in the literary firmament. The resemblance, later denied by facts, came spontaneously: Robert and Elizabeth Browning, Katherine Mansfield and Murry, or Graves and Laura Riding. Hughes remains a poet who can seduce, bewitch, dazzle and mesmerize, if his poetics is accepted and if we are unable to withdraw far enough from the smokescreen of his images, his arcane metaphors, his mythopoeic figurations and his verbal spell. If we fall victim to this fascination, he really does seem to beat every

other contemporary. Even Larkin, by this yardstick, is outclassed. In truth, viewed more coldly, Hughes reveals his limits.[9] The first to be snared by him, if not to swallow his bait, were his critics. One may identify three dominant approaches to his poetry, and the first and most widely adopted is the mythical. It is of course possible to measure Hughes's stature on the indiscriminate wealth of his mythological and anthropological references. Hirschberg is one of the critics who has followed this option more strictly than others, by tracing an overly clear-cut triadic progression along the stations of the shaman, the trickster and the scapegoat, and particularly by vehemently affirming, like others, that Hughes's mythical skill had a 'growing and immense value in his creative work'.[10] For Hirschberg, the second step is the figure of Prometheus, assumed, in the pioneering drama *Orghast*, as a sufferer against whom there rages a vulture that embodies the myth of the mother-goddess, rather than being a challenger.[11] A benevolent way to classify a wildly eclectic operation is to call that of Hughes a composite mythography; in reality, it is an agglutination that forces him to violent shifts, from Australian myths to those of the Tibetans, the Eskimos and the Redskins, which are then joined to Indo-European ones, subsumed from the Celtic and Arthurian myths. This sinuous and labyrinthine process translates into a poetry which is prevalently meant for subtle exegetes; and in fact critics who follow Hughes along these paths must embark on acrobatic and

9   Already brutally denounced by Praz, twisting the knife in the wound (feature on 'the English literary scene', SSI, vol. II, 455–61). In this feature Praz, writing as late as 1970, stumbled upon an evident bum note in this slating of Hughes and the new poets (especially Gunn), while making some comparisons that downsized the hype that had already grown around Hughes.

10   Hirschberg 1981, 34.

11   As a complement to the drama, twenty-one short, incisive poems were written by Hughes attributed to 'Prometheus on the cliff'. I have already referred above to Mircea Eliade's influence; in turn, the simulacrum of the Goddess had persisted wearily in the background of Hughes's poetry ever since his first adolescent frequentations of Robert Graves's *The White Goddess*. The action of this memory of reading on Hughes is recapped, and necessarily trivialized, by Gardini 2008, xvii-xix, in the following way: the goddess represents the instincts and impulses of the origins, which, far from being placated, emerge as demonic powers, or at least appear to be as such for the logical man of modern society, who has done all he can to extinguish them.

tiring *tours de force*, having taken for granted that his poetry is eminently esoteric. This one-sided tendency typical of Hughes's critics was denounced by Maria Stella,[12] who, however, having criticized and refused this aegis, ended up falling victim to another, adopting an equally prearranged key, in short that – Barthesian and Lacanian – of the vicissitudes of a language initially decentred from the subject, a language that reflects its dearth of sense and is then gradually re-centred so that it eventually rediscovers its fullness. This is done in discussions that were justified, in the late 1980s, by the spread of that critical method and approach, but which sound today excessively confusing and circumlocutory. The third approach deciphers Hughes's poetry as the formal vicissitude of the *parole*, as a chapter in the history of British prosody and rhythm, a new revolution or rather involution of poetic language: more precisely as a polemical recovery of an Anglo-Saxon tradition that excludes Latinisms or Gallicisms. This approach points to the ever-constant asymptote behind and within Hughes's poetry, that of an atavistic, non-semantic and preverbal language, where pure sound, in Foucault's terms, is the icon of the referent or accompanies deixis. My own approach will tend to highlight the superiority of Hughes's first collections, not yet encumbered by myth, or some later ones, in which the poet returns to a poetics of immediacy, slenderness and essentiality. From this synthetic survey, the reader understands that the dilemma with Hughes is whether he really is an emulator of the writers he came after or merely a supreme amateur. He possesses the versifying ease of a storyteller and of the ancient *aoidos*, and could compose poetry *ad libitum* and on a given subject for hundreds of lines; his evocativeness may be sparkling, but his theoretical baggage is filled with mythologies that amalgamate, and derive without originality from, previous ones, and are confused and imprecise. Ideologically, Hughes was really little more than an eavesdropper; consequently, he cannot be presented as a *maître à penser*.

§ 88. *Ted Hughes III: The bestiaries*

Hughes's forty-year career is divided into numerous and increasingly monographic collections of short poems. He never wrote a long poem, as I

12   Stella 1988, 8–9.

mentioned, or wrote one *in extremis*, but always by splitting each continuum into individual acts or 'stations' within the theme. Having kept his beginnings hidden, he sprang forth at twenty-seven with an already accomplished, adult poetry that would never know substantial changes of theme or style. What is immediately perceptible is a decisive prosodic option, the rejection of the traditional musicality of verse: the quatrain reigns supreme, but we almost never find a trace of rhyme, or lilting rhythms, or of sought-after grace and elegance; and, gradually, every regular stanzaic division disappears in favour of a free verse that is orientated towards rhythmic prose. If anything, Hughes's verse evokes the gritty roughness, the power, and the primordial nature of an utterance; rhyme is replaced by alliteration on harsh and strong, plosive, fricative, above all guttural, phonemes. Hughes referred to his innovations, implemented for example in *Crow*, as language that was 'ugly', deliberately so, indeed 'super-ugly', 'without any music'. The most provocative thematic mark of his debut collection, *The Hawk in the Rain* (1957), is in turn constituted by a reversal of the relationship between man and nature: more precisely, a reversal of the centuries-long intuition – the *topos* itself – of nature as it had been conceived and illustrated at least since early British Romanticism. Nature, that is, the landscape, and in the broader sense the plant and animal kingdoms, had been for Wordsworth a womb in which the human personality could form and shape, and a maternal source calming every anxiety or existential irrational fear; eternal, immutable, generous in her silence, she did not disappoint those who approached her. Moreover, the Romantics had idealized birds, often the lark[13] or the nightingale, as symbols of ideality, immateriality and purification from the dross of a condemned or corrupt humanity. It is true, however, that nature for the Romantics was or could be double-faced. Blake is the previous link to Hughes because his nature harbours as much good as evil, and is a divine as much as a demonic hypostasis. Victorian Romanticism had had a binary approach to nature, too, albeit for an instantaneous fraction,

---

13   A lark is studied in 'Skylarks', from the collection *Wodwo*. However, also through the intertextual dialogue with Shelley, it is rendered unrecognizable from the Romantic models, and transformed into a gloomy and sly bird of prey, as Hughes's birds always are, especially the falcon that 'nosedives'.

since the most typical mark of Victorian nature is its immediately discovered sacramentality. Ruskin and Hopkins are also involved in Hughes. How is it possible not to think of the Ruskin of the 'storm cloud'?[14] Or of the difficulty, really paralysing at times in Ruskin, in tracing the more sinister appearances of the naturally demonic to a divine plan, and thus subduing the demonic in nature? Hopkins is in turn behind Hughes not only for the ingenuity of his verbal compounds,[15] which derive from Hopkins in a very evident way, and his abrupt rhythms and rhetorical cadences, but precisely because Hopkins too, indeed above all Hopkins, seems in some cases to subtract 'Heraclitean', convulsed and destructive atmospheric nature from the divine governance. Two eloquent examples are from the 'Wreck of the Deutschland', which is an inexplicable destructive apocalypse almost right to the end; and the windhover wheeling in the sky, supremely heedless of that symbolism – we might even say, that allegory – of Christ which, belatedly, the poetic 'I' believes and firmly declares to have discovered. There is no escaping the fact that Hughes's first collection, in its title and in the opening title poem, places itself under the banner of Hopkins, and, more precisely, of the octave of 'The Windhover'. Hughes is the foremost, systematic explorer of a rapacious nature inimical to man, and even of the hostility within the natural and animal kingdoms.

2. An offensive and aggressive instinct forms the leitmotiv of the most valuable poems on animals in *The Hawk in the Rain*. The poetic 'I' has the task either of contemplating, and if necessary fearing, this demonstration of an instinctual repressed brute force, or sharing it. Hopkins is always absorbed through Nietzsche. Hughes's man must 'sich überwinden', he too must exert a similar aggressive instinct; but more often, or conversely, Hughes shows only a weak, above all cautious, man, oppressed as in Nietzsche by petty, actualized religious faiths, and by the separation between the body and the spirit or soul. Where the beast is no longer free, but in chains in civilized society or imprisoned behind bars, it growls

---

14   Volume 6, § 48.3.

15   'The Horses' boasts a compound – 'the hour-before-dawn dark' – which seems to be precisely modelled on those found in Hopkins – and indeed Hughes's horses are archetypal, 'megalithic', horses, in fact.

and roars because it has been derided and subdued. Next to the free flight of the falcon or the exploration of the fox in search of prey, Hughes shows the jaguar in the zoo and the parrot in its cage. On the formal level, a deliberate symbiosis of signifier and signified reigns. He transcodes the bestial quiddity in lines of grating, harsh and rough sonorities, with strident and insistent alliterations whose effect is enhanced by the high recurrence of mono- or disyllabic words. The absence of melody, grace, lilting or mellow echoes is immediately evident. This disturbing and irritating sound texture is more than a compensation for the absence of rhyme: it is necessary and indispensable in collaborating with the contents; rhyme would have been not only a formal encumbrance but also a semantic weakening or a contradiction. Starting from the title poem, Hughes's poetry is a phantasmagoria of aggression and violence, followed with avid voyeurism.[16] There are gruesome anatomical scenes in opposing visual fields; strong if not excessive gestures and events, marked sensations in the poetic 'I'. The unit of measurement is the image, the cluster of images, and these are then cruel and even repellent spectacles of flowing blood, open wounds, torn limbs; animals are crying, ripping each other apart or awaiting their prey, mauling or ready to do so – scenes of suffering, mockery, and wounding. A human 'I', in the first frame, contemplates a hawk 'hanging' almost motionless in the sky,[17] which, as in Hopkins, 'rebuffs' the atmospheric elements, unleashed, and lashing like wind and rain. The 'I' has difficulty walking and is almost swallowed up by the fissured earth; the hawk has instead the sinuous ease of Hopkins's skate 'sweeping smooth', and 'makes no effort'. As in Hopkins, Hughes describes a spasmodic identification taking place between the poetic 'I' and that 'master-fulcrum' of violence. But the earth wins, and the hawk, too, is challenged, fought, chased and eventually destroyed, that is, engulfed. Thus the aggressive urge of the bird of prey is depicted, always directed in Hughes against man but equally frequently towards its kin. A small gallery is formed here, of other visions

16   A 'voyeur of violence' was the accusation against Hughes from reviewers of his first
     collection (Sagar 1978, 34).
17   But even Dylan Thomas has a hawk that 'hangs' in 'Over Sir John's Hill' (on the dif-
     ferences between the two poems see Hirschberg 1981, 217 and 218 n. 6).

or tumultuous fantasies showing the bold, Promethean vibration of caged animals yearning to break their chains.[18] The fox in the midnight forest lies in wait to catch its prey, pretending to be lame as in Aesop. The poet fills the page of this spied vision of the fox, and tells how animal-like motions form the material his poetry. *The Hawk in the Rain*, however, is not yet a monographic collection.[19] In ballads and short sibylline stanzas there are anecdotes, satirical and sarcastic remarks of and on reactionary cowardice, and therefore hymns to the arrogant and challenging heroism of the man who learns the lesson of nature. Hughes contrasts anaemia with vigour and masculinity.[20] Love is also the arrival of the falcon in a nest of doves. 'A Modest Proposal' has nothing Swiftian, if not in its anti-traditional provocative force: it analyses love as an immaterial but also destructive attraction. A similar vision and antagonistic version of the sexes is also Lawrencian: desire, in the next poem, clings but divides. Other anecdotes and monologues are composed against the background of a love that is far from always rewarding, or is varied in its phenomenology.

    3. *Lupercal* (1960) is an exact replica of the previous collection. It has the same number of poems, counts among its most valuable ones studies of animals caught in a freeze-frame, intercalated with others of a bitter ballad-like flavour, and imagistic, dream-like or memorial fantasies.[21] Those about

18   The girl who dreams the warrior for herself cossets the parrot in the cage, which recalls Dylan Thomas's approach of puberty.

19   With a considerable delay, a small section is of poems about war, which is, however, the First World War and not the Second, and whose unspeakable horrors, as I have already mentioned, had been known by the young Hughes, since his father was a veteran still traumatized by his participation in the conflict. In 'Six Young Men', Hughes seems to superimpose the 1916 Easter Rising on the war, in the descriptive terms of Yeats, since in his case, too, a 'terrible beauty' was born.

20   In the homonymous poem, the 'conversion' of Reverend Skinner is in the opposite direction, towards the veneration of evil and sin, hence a challenge. A distortion of the Immaculate Conception, with marked, blazing visionary images, is 'Complaint'. The collection is closed by the remembrance of another clergyman, far more manly and challenging in his sacrifice, Bishop Farrar (more exactly Ferrar), Hughes's ancestor, who was put to death by Bloody Mary.

21   With respect to doubles, a second poem is on Hughes's ancestors, on the great-grandson of the bishop burnt at the stake, and the founder of the community of

new beasts and birds, or even fish, and hence constituting a review of the underwater or marine world, are still snapshots or short sequences catching its subject as if with a high-definition, slow-motion camera. These static and empathetic portraits, admired, contemplated, reworked – a bull, cats and dogs, a hawk, a pig, an otter, thrushes – should be potentially, silently protesting metaphors of a world that has lost its contact with nature and with the life of the farm and the barn. They are lively, evocative thumbnails, but ends in themselves, a little 'overwritten', clearly deliberate. The wolf and the falcon express the aggressive and rapacious spirit in the pure state. But in Hughes's mental geography, horses reappear as Swiftian commonsensical animals in a state of reflective quiet. 'Hawk Roosting' is a *naïf* monologue full of flagrant swagger, therefore almost playful, attributed to a falcon on the point of flying off to go hunting. 'Relic' is perhaps the most beautiful and intense short poem of its kind, on the ruthless rivalries in the animal world; it turns on the contradiction that the jaw which serves to prey in the undersea kingdom is in turn picked clean – the phrase 'go gnawn bare' is truly effective and chilling in its pealing and rhythm – and floats to the surface among other debris, as a symbol of the renewal of the life cycle. A constant is the celebration or memory of lost vigour, of times when elementary forces decimated and defeated, a harsh law of primordial codes. Hughes lays down a dominant and an ideological frame that is a kind of Spenglerian sunset of western civilization implying the loss of important and precious values. Nature has been robbed and impoverished; the barbarian and primordial residues have been eliminated. Hughes laments this with a manly elegiac spirit. That was a wild, dangerous, but exciting world. In terms perhaps too broad, such as to appear merely sketchy and too vague, Hughes draws the evolution of history through arbitrary watersheds, such as the pernicious influence that Greek Socratic thought which was absorbed, and thus survived, by the Christian world. He attempts to do what only Yeats and sometimes not even Yeats managed to do, ideological poetry transfused into metaphors or sibylline apologues. In 'February' Hughes recalls or perhaps complains that wolves in England are an extinct

---

Little Gidding opposed by Cromwell's Puritan obscurantists. This may appear as a belated tribute to T. S. Eliot.

breed, and reviews some fairy-tale mythologies on them, from Grimm to Little Red Riding Hood. The wolf is now a pair of legs separated from a head, and only lives and moves in dreams. The area where these myths of violence and vigour were still throbbing, and from which 'the arrogance of blood and bone' arose, is Hughes's coarse, native Yorkshire, further idealized by the nostalgic poet who wrote most of these poems at a distance, from America. This is the source of stories, fables or local legends that illustrate the workings of merciless nature (the predatory ermine) or even a humanity that is intact, crude, thick-skinned, with its related anecdotes. *Lupercal* should be soaked in the first place in the spirit of the wolfish, and place itself under the mythological aegis of the wolf. An additional and unnecessary overload is instead the far-fetched reference to the Roman and pagan rite of the Lupercalia, a fertility ritual that Hughes reuses as a metaphor for the subversion of an ancient natural order. In this ritual he mirrors his religious malaise, which made him postulate God as Evil, the Son as the victim, and the Mother as redeeming love.

4. *Wodwo*[22] (1967) is a mixed book of prose and poetry, so mixed as to appear and indeed be extremely disorganic. Hughes included in it, as in a heterogeneous container, almost everything he had written from the previous collection onwards, intercalating this material with prose tales, five stories,[23] and a radio drama with poems added as a comment. Here Hughes's practice of drawing inspiration from history, from local folklore, from the most disparate mythologies, and from the daily news, reaches its peak. A syncretistic acrobat, he tries desperately, with frequently unsatisfactory results, to amalgamate them into forced syntheses. The general object of the collection is ambitious, increasingly and markedly Yeats-derived; Hughes does not use the same myths, of course, even if ultimately all myths are alike. His mythical references aim to fascinate and partially dazzle the reader,

22   As an epigraph from the Middle English text *Sir Gawain and the Green Knight* (ll. 720–4) informs the reader, the 'wodwos' are the 'woses', or ogres, that Sir Gawain fought in the Anglo-Saxon poem; here they should be construed as woodland creatures, half-men and half-beasts.

23   With additions, these stories went on to constitute the aforementioned *Difficulties of a Bridegroom* (§ 87.4 n. 7).

who in the end finds it difficult, objectively difficult, to recompose them, make them agree with one another, and not be cut off from several cryptic poems that elaborate, in an extremely summary manner, folklore legends and regional superstitions. Without this key, in itself rather artificial, they remain disconnected evocations, albeit individually powerful and arcane. The general linchpin is in *Wodwo* the drama of Sylvia Plath's suicide, which is fatalistically heralded and visibly stretches its shadow over the poems; on a symbolic plane, images of destruction and extermination prevail, for a sort of propagation, over those of reconstruction and resurrection. Hughes, at the time, had already developed a pseudo-shamanic philosophy, and repeatedly envisioned a mental journey of initiation; here he outlines and evokes it, but confesses he is unable to bring it to a conclusion. This is the additional meaning of 'wodwo' from the Arthurian poem, while Gawain, in the usual surplus of mythological ciphers evoked by Hughes, is an objective correlative in his temporary disorientation, in the existential crisis that grips him and in the final, but utopian and asymptotic, attainment of the goal. On the objective plane, nothing has changed: man surrenders, and the animals, as they did before, continue to battle cruelly and bloodily among themselves seeking mutual destruction. Theirs is therefore, if anything, wasted energy. For his part, the poet has not matured. Nature is tetchy and bloodstained as never before, in a phantasmagorical jumble that recalls the landscape of Browning's 'Childe Roland' ('Thistles'). Therefore, coarse natural scenarios predominate, ones of animated rocks and thistles, and ready to be hurt or *ab aeterno* impassive. This objective correlation is, however, intermittent. Hughes resorts to a technique of contrastive images whose evocativeness is ensured, but that strike as having an aura of mystery without reciprocal links. They are like visions that have appeared as if in a dream ('Cadenza'), or in a nightmare, rather, like the delirious invasion of the giant crabs, as terrifying as in a science fiction film, intent on possessing the world even though their fury is essentially self-destructive ('Ghost Crabs', a powerful but unconvincing, artificial apocalypse). In 'A Wind Flashes the Grass' the purely natural frame, grim and injected, is threatened in a pathetic fallacy deliberately imitating those of Ruskin. Demonic art is indignation and scorn against low existential coasting, and a secret dialogue and contact with the supernal powers, invisible to everyone. Hughes cites Shakespeare on this psychic capacity, and, with increasing frequency, musicians, Mozart and Beethoven especially. In the dialectic centre of the collection some poems introduce an 'antinomian' theological vision and therefore one with very ancient ancestry: that of a sadistic usurper god opposed by a maternal principle, a good goddess. Even the story of Eden is revisited and deformed in a series of irreverent and reductive rewritings of Genesis. 'Gog', a long disorganic phantasmagoria, opens with the voice of a Blakean Satan who soliloquizes on his condition as an outcast. This poem is continued in the adventure of a knight of the Grail, in fact Spenser's Knight of the Red Cross, for whom the Grail itself merges with the contours of the belly and with the female sexual organ. Apocalyptic compositions and rhapsodies also describe the rampant destruction that invades and has invaded the world in the form of global conflicts and historical wars. Hughes scours and sifts history to spot examples of his cosmic vision, the advent of repression and destruction. He puts religion and war, but also economy, at the top as forces of oppression: at times, he sounds as a new Pound, but one even more delirious and ranting.

§ 89. *Ted Hughes IV: 'Crow'*

Crow (1970) is a critically acclaimed masterpiece, if not *the* masterwork of Hughes. A similar evaluation is appropriate because it is his most unified work, albeit not fully and completely.[24] It creates an evocative universal mythopoeia,[25] in fact the small epic or odyssey, mock-heroic and sardonic, delirious and surreal, of the creature who rebels against its creator and remonstrates with him, to the extent of fashioning a counter-theology or simply a genuine neo-humanism. Segmented into short titled 'acts', it manages to become stitched in a diegetic, demonstrative and argumentative continuum, although, as always, this framework is at the service of the pure

---

24   *Crow* was indeed a 'project' carried out by Hughes in various parallel drafts, and formally never closed, and which is read in the version prepared by the editor of *Collected Poems*; gaps in the internal plot, occasional reduplications and some repetitive poems, can also be explained by this genesis.

25   Hughes confessed his concern 'to produce something with the minimum cultural accretions'.

virtuosity of representational association, and of the chains of stunning, spectacular images become ends in themselves. Hughes has not abandoned or modified his representational, surreal, Baroque and excessive style, but does welcome miscellaneous solutions and heterogeneous and experimental procedures, which are the first modernist borrowing we encounter in him. Occasionally his verse dries up and becomes stripped of its flesh, arranging itself in solemn, obsessive, bewitching anaphoras that echo the Bible. It often takes the form of lists, with the lines whimsically arranged on the page, even made of isolated single words, and similar exploits of the avant-garde poetry of forty years earlier. There is more: in its obvious theatricality, in its dramatic outer frame, leading to closed pieces for voice in the form of laments and litanies articulated[26] and shouted, or even of supplications, expressly designed for a stage performance, we may recognize an analogy with the diminutive dramas for a single voice by Beckett.[27]

2. Crow is a survivor of the historical apocalypse; he must begin again from its ossuary, in a world reduced to ruins, rubble and debris. Embodying the primordial essence of survival, Crow is in fact at first a stray in search of leftover food among the waste. This epic of the stray, the last and first man, has for its scenario and habitat a sort of Gethsemane of a Jesus about to be crucified. Hughes is quick to insinuate this overlapping, engrafting into Crow a Christ who protests vehemently against the mission entrusted to him by his Father. The clearest and most effective of these vignettes, or stations of a Nietzschean negative theology, are the transactions between a sleepy, nebulous, generically didactic deity, and Crow who is unable to absorb the lesson (as in 'Crow's First Lesson'). In this composition, God intends to teach him love, but the word cannot be pronounced and learned by Crow because it is abstract, just as its concept is abstract and therefore untrue when measured against the reality of a world in which hatred, oppression and destructive voracity win out. The refutation of love, that love postulated by a God who is absent in the cosmos, is witnessed by a

26   In this form is 'Amulet'.
27   See especially the section, consisting of purely anaphoric fragments, 'Life and Songs of the Crow'.

life dominated by destruction and death, decay and spitefulness; it is also witnessed by the resurgence of biological needs and primordial impulses that religion denies or sublimates. Crow sees around him the same scenarios of a predatory nature that Hughes had shown in previous collections; he sees expressly 'the horror of Creation'. In Crow who asks if 'he must stop eating' and strive to 'become light', there is summarized the message launched in the world by Christianity and by western spiritualisms. That message revolved around the renunciation of everything material and corporal. In its various metamorphoses, Crow is the serpent of Eden that altered and ruined the divine plans; he is also a Lucifer who wants to be readmitted to Paradise and is expelled for a second time. For the purposes of Hughes's neo- or counter-theology, a crucial poem is 'Crow's Theology', which is an almost literal restatement of the Victorian notion of the two gods or divine hypostases: a God of love and at the same time of hatred and destruction, who must be held responsible for the purely animal and physical impulses rooted in the world and in mankind. This theological debate is continued in apparently naïve short parables and nursery rhymes that, sometimes even sinisterly funny, trivialize and distort the biblical story of Creation and of the call and the mission of Christ on earth. They often have the freshness, the effervescence and the alienating and imaginative wit found in Nietzsche's *Zarathustra* or in Browning's *Ferishtah's Fancies*. The further, more undefined targets are a western civilization that is now detached from nature and the aegis of rationality and technology; not far off was, at the time, a real danger, that of the destruction of the globe due to a possible atomic war.

3. As a consequence, some digressions explain Crow's inability to adapt to the scientific spirit that vainly dissects and analyses the machinery of creation. The wanderings of this new Oisin are designed to bear witness to the contemporary deterioration of history under the mythical veil and the epic transposition, including the failure of linguistic referentiality and logocentrism itself (Crow often notes the emptying of words, the uselessness of corrupted words, the siege of worn and expressionless words). *Crow* is therefore written on the eve of a possible regeneration of the world, a world reborn on new bases, more properly a palingenesis. Did Hughes then manage to shape a unified alternative myth, without contaminating it with

other mythological embellishments, and without the consequent creation of his frequent mythopoeic patchworks? Crow is the arena of the clash, a point observation, a free forum to poetically discuss questions, opinions or views, fears, traumas, or theories and pseudo-theories or mythological and esoteric curiosities. *Crow*, too, often abandons the evocative moral fable resting on some ideological foundation or irrational fear but without the relevant knowledge of them being strictly necessary. It veers dangerously, in fact, towards the elaboration of secondary material.[28] The suspicion and the lesser approval originate here, as they do in the face of all the overly esoteric texts soaked in lucubrations. In other terms, it is never a good sign in poetry when it becomes necessary to explain the mythological allusions that lie behind and before the letter of the text. The poetic art ends or is undermined when the poet must explain in detail, and in prose, the thought process that lies upstream of the individual poems, trivializing it and rendering it truly far-fetched and acrobatic.

§ 90. *Ted Hughes V: Diaries of farm life*
Gaudete (1977), originally a screenplay conceived for the film director Ingmar Bergman, and written exclusively for financial gain, was later completed and published along with a set of forty-five short poems. Its plot is that of a priest, Lumb, led by the spirits of nature to the afterworld. The spirits of nature leave in his place a double of him carved from an oak log; this wooden double, having come alive, preaches love to the women parishioners, but in fact seduces them, provoking a reaction from their husbands. The sequence of poems forms the verse counterpart of Lumb's first quest. He was in fact exiled by the spirits for the precise purpose of making him seek, in a 'shamanic' initiatory journey, the morbidly evasive but desired generating goddess, the symbol of nature and the earth. They highlight Hughes's undoubted evocative talent, but reverberate once again with odd and disparate mythical references; they also now satisfy a stylistic mannerism in which all alogical associations, all perceptive irregularities,

---

28   This is the mythological model of the trickster, at which I hinted above, but fused and intertwined with many others.

all unforeseen and sophisticated combinations are possible.[29] In one of
these evocations the anonymous and diaphanous goddess fuses into and
overlaps with Sylvia Plath, and therefore the whole cycle can also serve as
a discreet, psychic evocation of the deceased.

2. At this point of his career – with the works of the late 1970s, *Cave
Birds* (1978), *Remains of Elmet* (1979), and *Moortown Diary*[30] (1979) –
Hughes had undeniably lost much of his freshness, inventiveness and personal motivation. Short on ideas and irresistible intimate stimuli, he felt
forced to resort to culturological promptings, odd and unusable plots,
insipid chronicles of the present amenable to mythical keys, and extem-
porary curiosities. The average reader is now bored if not impatient to
learn that behind insignificant details is a reference to remote codicils of
obscure mythologies, Indian, Egyptian or belonging to local folklore. The
first of the above three works hinges on a form of symbiosis between poetry
and illustration (Hughes's collaborator and inspiration was the American
Leonard Baskin). A man is condemned, having been unwittingly guilty of
the death of a woman; he is redeemed, resuscitates, in line with the motif
of the crisis of values of rationalized man who, wandering in the afterlife,
is still on trial, but corrects and alters the reality he has left behind, as in
a dream. Hughes's critics, always indulgent to him, have taken their distance because of the chaotic throng of multiple references – indeed often
mere hints – to various mythologies, and for the forced nature and lack of
conviction of some phases of the plot. Hughes's highly ambitious objective
is that of denouncing western macho rationalism embodied by the hated
Socrates, who, as well as being homosexual, is the antagonist of the goddess
whose simulacrum and whose reality Hughes's protagonist spasmodically
chases. All this obviously waters down Graves's *The White Goddess*. But
there is a palpable sense of disproportion between the highly elaborate
signifier – an undoubtedly fascinating, evocative verse, rich in shocking
images and arcane juxtapositions that are spectacularly striking – and a

29   My negative judgement is shared by Gifford and Roberts 1981, 150, against Sagar
     1978.
30   The name of a farm in Devon where Hughes had lived, helping his stepfather Jack
     Orchard, whose figure is celebrated in the last poems of this cycle.

diegetic plan that is even borrowed and second-hand, namely, the old one of life, death and resurrection, with the hero's initiation into the mysteries. What becomes clearer than ever is a shortage of human material barely compensated for by a rehashing of mythologies, skilfully embroidered as by a goldsmith or engraver. This is a frankly kitsch work, judging by all the improbable mythological implications that are enclosed in it.

3. *Remains of Elmet* is a polyptych evoking places of the county and region where Hughes was born and educated, Yorkshire. He plays this card, new for him but in reality old and overused in literature. It is a poetry of revisitation in the elegiac or even quivering vein of Villon's *où sont les neiges d'antan?* (and the titles of poems, referring to the places revisited, usually caught in their desolation, sound like a parody of Wordsworth, who drew from his wanderings in nature quite different comfort and messages).[31] Nature is sullied and wounded, deflowered by industry, also a Victorian theme. For Hughes, this is undoubtedly a poem about travelling and a journey that can sometimes also be *his* 'journey', that is, the archetype or one of the possible archetypes of the initiation of the hero and the quest for self-realization, or even the asymptotic approach to his 'goddess'.[32] This exploration soon becomes, in fact, a series of psychic and epiphanic occasions, and under the rod of the dowser the landscape conjures up familiar figures and the dear departed, and the whole horde of the deceased. It even weaves the fabric of a memory that goes back to the beginnings, but whose existence is, however, linked to the 'fineness of a hair'.[33] From a similar

31   The beginning of the poem 'Cock-crows' – 'I stood on a dark summit' – obviously cites and varies one by Keats, 'I stood tiptoe on a little hill'.

32   The archetypal and mythical journey closes, or rather, is made explicit in the concluding poem, 'The Angel', an angel that looms out of the sky in a child's vision and on which the figure of Sylvia Plath is superimposed, as is hinted by the 'enigmatic square of satin', which is the angel's halo and at the same time the veil which, on being raised, revealed to Hughes the face of his dead wife. The collection opens in the name of Hughes's mother, whom the child of this last poem asks for explanations about the celestial apparition. The angel is a synthesis of the two female figures.

33   It is automatic that the Brontë sisters are among these evoked spirits. They were born near Hughes's birthplace, and he dedicates to them various, rather conventional and banal mentions and complimentary expressions.

initial declaration there arises a sequence of fleeting and ephemeral recollections, real will-o'-the-wisps that can wane immediately. The atavistic abyss is in fact covered by the appearance of modernity, so that the poet's deaf polemic is still directed, especially directed – faithful to his design – to the advent of technology and, in the final analysis, to the modern, which erases and engulfs the vestiges of the past. Hughes is here the singer of bygone times, the survivor of a heroic age of his land, whose epic and ancient past he celebrates; he is also a sort of telegraphist who captures the magnetic waves, suspended in the air, of local ghosts, which no one else can hear.[34] The verse, while spare and rough, often even lapidary, is charged with epic resonances and arcane metaphors, and the single poems repeatedly consist of visions of ancient female deities who return to those who can see them, and gyrate in the heavens above and in the landscape. Hence the usual contradiction is created in Hughes between the daytime vision of a landscape that is completely tangible, and deaf and blind to the numinous, and the oneiric panoply of folk memories of Celtic heritage (stones, stelae, ruins, engravings, cenotaphs, signs of this past civilization to which the poet is sensitive, Elmet being the last of the Celtic kingdoms to become extinct). Every single poem is precisely the rhapsody of the singer who revivifies and reanimates episodes of a past to which the tourist, the hiker,[35] or even the textile workers of an area where this industry was the main one, are indifferent. The elegiac song arises so marked that it becomes emphatic and rhetorical, nor does Hughes always manage to represent the everyday epic[36] in a collection that is amongst his longest and fullest.

---

34 The rhetorical device applied far and wide is Ruskin's pathetic fallacy, as in the prophetic mouth of the rain, the 'hill-stone' 'conscripted / Into mills', and 'in position / Defending this slavery against all', the excommunicating tree, the smelling wind, etc. See, too, the anthropomorphizing of the villages in 'Heptonstall'.

35 'The throb of the mills and the crying of lambs / Like shouting in Flanders / Muffled away / In white curls / In memorial knuckles / Under hikers' heels' ('The Sheep Went On Being Dead').

36 As in the poem on the game of soccer, 'Football at Slack', immediately followed by another on a cricket match. In the oldest layer, autobiographical poems celebrate the carefree hunting of partridges and other birds, or the stifling attendance at the Sunday services at the Mount Zion Wesleyan Chapel.

4. *Moortown Diary* is undoubtedly a new beginning in Hughes's career, as far as technique and material are concerned, and the best work of the three dating from the end of the 1970s. He opts now for the diary form and writes individual items that are dated; this diary starts, continues and ends entirely within the ideal enclosure of a stable and therefore of a farm in Devon. It is a winter diary of a stay scourged by the unforgiving natural elements, such as snow, rain, hail and frost. Style and form have changed slightly accordingly. This is rhythmic unrhyming prose, the only poetic marks being alliteration in often monosyllabic words, contractions and ellipses and verbal compounds that reduce the links and the extension of prose. Hughes is skilful in passing from purely descriptive, short and verb-less phrasing in the form of telegraphic sentences, to spiralled periods that are broader but never really heavy. This poetic prose has a family air with all prose poems in English from Wordsworth and Whitman down to Frost; perhaps for the first time in Hughes it is dynamic and narrative and is the highest point ever reached by him in terms of discursive, fluent and leg-ible poetry, while always being punctuated by the metaphorical twist, the idiosyncratic and deviant image, the de-automatizing jolt. As a last virtue, Hughes waives all mythological schemes, or at any rate lightens them, and avoids overloading the poem, as he often does, with far-fetched references that make them clumsily pretentious. It is nature, or rather, the animal kingdom, the life of the stable, and the horizons of cattle, sheep, lambs, cows, calves and bulls, that powerfully and obsessively impose themselves[37] on Hughes's imagination. It is easy and banal to evoke the name and the world of Virgil, especially since these are no longer the wild beasts and the birds of prey, aggressive and destructive in the early poems. Hughes observes and studies meeker animals, although they are equally tough in the fight to survive.[38] His cows and sheep are now the repository of a surprising, passionate maternal feeling, and recall Jack London's wolves,

---

37   'claustrophobic' is the adjective used by Hughes (cf. Gardini 2008, 1573).

38   A symbolic castration, a secret parable of human civilization, is the cutting of the cows' horns, which must 'make up for in tits' what they have lost 'in weapons'; except that, in this way, 'they've all lost one third of their beauty'. One of the most intense poems, in its own way rich in suspense, describes moment by moment the difficult

while the men who govern them are de-humanized and mechanized and thus in part are also animal-like. The instincts of the beasts are naturally sexual, and aimed at promiscuous couplings. Hughes, as a diarist, controls himself and sticks to objectivity, but deliberately does not avoid registering spontaneous moments of tenderness and empathy,[39] which intersperse the purely analytical recording.[40]

§ 91. *Ted Hughes VI: Poems on fish and flowers*

An uneven collection, *River* (1983) is considered by some the second, if not the only true, masterpiece of Hughes. It may be regarded as the counterpart of *Moortown Diary*, with fish, and especially the salmon – the poor and violated salmon with its indomitable reproductive force – in place of cows, and without the powerful diary-style immediacy of that work. *River* is a series of partially descriptive rhapsodies of river life, the life of existing rivers and the banks of rivers visited or known or frequented and named by Hughes. But these banks are first and foremost those of an absolute river, those of all rivers in their atavistic and anthropomorphic archetype – as in T. S. Eliot's third Quartet – of river gods and of secular theatres of love and death, destruction and rebirth. Equally archetypal and paradigmatic is the subterranean life of fish, which is eternal in its phenomena. Not by coincidence, the collection is entitled to one river and not to rivers. The connective tissue of the imagination, the river is evocative to the poet who looks at it from its bank and abandons himself to its enchantment – the enchantment of stories, legends and mythologies that are not necessarily British. But Hughes could not refrain for long from reminding himself of his own metaphorical addiction and of the stimuli of his poetic imagination. Every single poem begins or may begin with a caption missing a verb, a little like a diary entry, with and like a string of annotations, and

---

birth of a cow in terms of a 'struggle'. Here the symbolism of Christ born in a stable is only alluded to, and is far from jarring.

39   A recurrent adjective is 'poor', referring to the fields, or the birds. The animal stares at the man trying to understand the world, and vice versa, in the poems on two roe-deer and in 'Surprise', where the poet 'shar[es] the cows' trance'.

40   Another metaphor used by Hughes is 'video-recording' (Gardini 2008, 1573).

may continue along these lines. Compared to the Moortown diary, the individual poems of this new work have much less real experience behind them, sometimes none at all, and at any rate each experience is transfigured and therefore made opaque. No river epic, in other terms, is formed, except in flashes. When the poet is a real witness the text profits from it, as in the undoubtedly powerful opening poem[41] and in others resolved in narration or epiphany,[42] or depicting in freeze-frames the protagonists of river life, including not only the salmon with its saga but also the eel, the dragonfly, the cormorant or the kingfisher. Elsewhere, Hughes is compelled to resort to his prodigious, lush, intact and inexhaustible ability to wrap the actual datum in specious and sumptuous curtains of words.[43] *River* falls back within the domain of the embroidery, of hyperbole, of excrescence; even within the domain of bewitching and synonymic poetry in its rich elaborations and digressions and in its series of repetitions and reformulations. These are all frames of luxuriant eloquence, verbal flares, flashes of the imagination that leave the occasions, if any, at a great distance. Where the experience is scanty, or missing altogether, the irrelevant mythological embroidery takes over, which makes many poems conceptually viscous. In *River* the actual observer full of human and vibrant reverence is too often replaced by the cold embroiderer of mythological variations.[44]

2. *Flowers and Insects: Some Birds and a Pair of Spiders* (1986) comes across as a work requested and expected from a poet who, always or mainly objective, makes the observation and intuition of nature his prerogative.

41   The salmon caught in the net are gutted of their eggs and sperm to enrich the breeders, an operation described with the same implacable accuracy and slowness as the birth of the calf in *The Moortown Diary*.

42   The ecstatic encounter of the angler with the fish in 'After Moonless Midnight' corresponds to the meeting of the two roe-deer in *The Moortown Diary*.

43   A 'baroque over-abundance' that 'beautifies again and again / every particular', is attributed by the poet to the river in spring. An example of heatedly superabundant rhetoric is provided by the opening and development of 'Salmon-Taking Times', or by the long, extended metaphor of the river as an enticing and death-bringing 'lazy woman', in 'Low Water'.

44   Cf. the opposite opinion of Gardini 2008, 1590, who locates in the 'calligraphic' this excellence and even the primacy of this work in the panorama of all modern poetry.

An investigator of fauna, of the quiddity of the beast and of the variety of birds, of the fish kingdom and of the bovine and ovine species, Hughes had so far neglected the flora (nature understood as atmosphere, an affair of the skies and the clouds and the weather, is in Hughes a fixed backdrop, whose eventualities, changing variety and turbulence are especially captured and registered in *The Moortown Diary*). The spirit of that diary is at work again in *Flowers and Insects*, in part because in a few poems – for instance one in which the author writing a letter faces the irruption of a flock of noisy starlings – he repeats its mimesis; in part, because Hughes adopts and perfects its type of gaze. Instead of providing and composing vague and intuitive visions of flowers and insects, here Hughes explicitly makes use of the microscope, the magnifying glass or binoculars. *Flowers and Insects* is then a painstaking and prolonged inspection of the phenomena of two sub-reigns: an inspection that is above all detailed, and therefore slowed down, and tending to the static. Poetry is entomology in the poem about the two spiders ('Eclipse', a *tour de force*, the most analytical poem Hughes ever wrote), and two spiders spied on while coupling, and whose erotic intercourses may be expressly visible only under the microscope. An objective and always objective poet? Hughes is no longer firmly and integrally so. Not only does he coldly file and record; he is now a scientist with the gift and talent of the never repetitive image, a scientist ready for the unexpected metaphorical twist; but not only, since he sings his sympathy and his empathy, though without clamour. The title and the subject of the collection recall Lawrence, or Wordsworth, in a poem emphatically entitled 'Daffodils'. [45] The insect and the flower are anthropomorphized

45 We have here the demonstration of Hughes's always extraordinary and considerable skill in narrating, especially in slowly decomposing certain operations (such as cutting daffodils and arranging them in bunches), always halfway between realism and transfiguration (the daffodils are like naïve young girls in ball gowns). The sale of the daffodils, which causes in the poet a profound sense of guilt that he is unable to shrug off ('I had killed them'), is another detail that works at the narrative and symbolic level, since it is linked to his dark sense of guilt over the death of Sylvia Plath, of whom Hughes is reminded by this flower (and he was to return to this poem and redo it in *Birthday Letters*). His staring at the mating insects also proves the motions of a natural instinct devoid of any moral sense; many of the flowers and

in long extended metaphors, and in poem after poem Hughes moves to a discovery of their quintessential nature, their dominant association, above all in human terms. The average result is a singularly fresh and delicate vein, more delicate and far less sharp than Hughes's poems usually are, except for the sheer entomological recording of the two spiders mating.[46]

3. *Wolfwatching* (1989) is perhaps Hughes's most disappointing collection, since a good part of it is random, not monothematic and therefore not unified, and not even relatively speaking, like many of his previous ones. It seems as if all the discarded poems, or even those that had not been worthy of inclusion in those earlier collections, have been merged or confined by the author within a kind of sketchbook. As a result, we find here inferior duplications, the last portraits of persons and roles whom we have already met, the last motionless and analytical snapshots – more discursive and duller and yet once again artificially and unnecessarily associated with esoteric motifs – of animal exemplars such as the hawk, the rhinoceros, and the irremediably mangy wolf, the laughing stock of visitors to the zoo and a dreamer of its freedom, or the dove. Further 'theological' dialogues hark back to the time of *Crow*, with the sublimating Christian God who wants to steal the soul from the body, while Adam balks and takes his revenge. In reality, what we perceive, though in an uncertain manner, is a poet whose subjectivity is rising, and who focuses increasingly, and almost reluctantly, on memory and the testamentary statement, and increasingly yielding to effusion. Hughes reminisces the times of his life as a child in poems that he had never written, or published, such as elegies to his father wounded in the war, or his mother, or recollections of infantile raids with other anecdotes somewhere between the carefree and the satirical. He dallies, utters noble aphorisms, passionately addresses his loved ones; but he is unusually awkward, because in the end this is not his most genuine art.

---

insects are expressly female flowers and insects that cheerfully and lasciviously offer their temptations. But, in some cases, feminine attractiveness is death-bringing, and the male, having impregnated the female, succumbs.

46　Indeed, the preference is for delicate, larval, mild insects, without substance and almost without existence, such as butterflies, or the 'ephemerals' that leap to their death like little kamikazes, rather than for birds of prey.

§ 92. *Hill* I: After the fall*
The opening poem of the poetic canon of Geoffrey Hill (1932–2016) bears the demanding title 'Genesis'. We cannot take this poem as a general model of the poet's technique and form, since we know that it was conceived by Hill when he was very young; it is, however, prophetic in its contents, and he quite rightly placed it as the opening poem in the collected and anthological editions of his poetry. The immaturity of this poem lies in its Blakean cadences, in its solemn Miltonian sonorities, in its adoption of conspicuous Romantic modules, as well as in the cadences of the visionary ballad arranged in stanzas that are irregular in the number of lines but have a somewhat uniform iambic heaviness, accentuated by alternate or rhyming couplets. Anaphoras lend rhythm to the story of a demiurgic 'I' in six symbolic days of creation. According to its genre, in the background

---

*   *New and Collected Poems 1952–1992*, London 1994, to be integrated with *Selected Poems*, Harmondsworth 2006, which contains, in selections, *Canaan* (1997), *The Triumph of Love* (1998) *Speech! Speech!* (2000), *The Orchard of Syon* (2002), *Scenes from Comus* (2005) and *Without Title* (2006). The volume of essays *The Lords of Limit: Essays on Literature and Ideas* (London 1984) is now included in *Collected Critical Writings*, ed. K. Haynes, Oxford 2008. M. E. Brown, *Double Lyric: Divisiveness and Communal Creativity in Recent English Poetry*, London and Henley 1980, chapters I-IV (1–72); C. Ricks, *The Force of Poetry*, Oxford 1984 and 1987, 285–355; *Geoffrey Hill*, ed. H. Bloom, New York 1986; H. Hart, *The Poetry of Geoffrey Hill*, Carbondale, IL 1986 (often far-fetched exegeses and paraphrases, with spectacular inaccuracies and oversights);[1] *Geoffrey Hill: Essays on His Work*, ed. P. Robinson, Milton Keynes 1986; V. Sherry, *The Uncommon Tongue: The Poetry and Criticism of Geoffrey Hill*, Ann Arbor, MI 1987; E. M. Knottenbelt, *Passionate Intelligence: The Poetry of Geoffrey Hill*, Amsterdam and Atlanta, GA 1990; E. J. McNees, 'Signs of Presence and Absence: Geoffrey Hill's Way of Dissent', in *Eucharistic Poetry: The Search for Real Presence in John Donne, Gerard Manley Hopkins, Dylan Thomas and Geoffrey Hill*, Lewisburg, PA 1992, 147–91; R. Pordzik, *History as Poetry: Dichtung und Geschichte im Werk von Geoffrey Hill*, Essen 1994; W. S. Milne, *An Introduction to Geoffrey Hill*, London 1998; A. M. Roberts, *Geoffrey Hill*, Tavistock 2004; J. Wainwright, *Acceptable Words: Essays on the Poetry of Geoffrey Hill*, Manchester 2005; *La poésie de Geoffrey Hill et la modernité*, ed. J. Kilgore-Caradec and R. Gallet, Paris 2007 (indispensable for a first general overview of Hill's poetry after 1983); M. Sperling, *Visionary Philology: Geoffrey Hill and the Study of Words*, Oxford 2014; A. Pestell, *Geoffrey Hill: The Drama of Reason*, Bern 2016.

1   Such as the birthplace of Campanella, given as Spain (111), or Aeneas guiding Dante in the afterlife (165).

there soon emerges Coleridge's 'Rime', and the evocation of the Leviathan is countered by that of the albatross, which, by the automatic and magnetic propagation of that literary memory and the symbolic references to which it points, attracts the image of the Cross (the sea, where 'the Capricorn and zero cross'). Published in 1959, 'Genesis' is a review of predatory animal nature. Hill may give the impression of echoing Hughes and his early work, via Hopkins, as he also introduces a hawk awaiting the prey to devour it.[2] Since 'Genesis' was very probably composed before Hughes's poem, this is sheer coincidence. In the final analysis, Hill's conceptual plan is more indebted to T. S. Eliot. This is indicated, indeed stated in advance, in the opening lines, where Hill the poet imagines the sea – the revitalizing principle – breaking 'Upon the dead weight of the land'. Hill could not quote *The Waste Land* verbatim: in this line, he interposes a filler between the adjective and the noun and replaces 'waste' with 'dead'. Later on in the poem, he diagnoses a pessimism that follows the ardour of this attempted but failed purification: 'This fierce and unregenerate clay'. It is a precisely Eliotian diagnosis, therefore, that of a symbolic land which is not regenerated, specifically not regenerated by religion.

2. Hill's poetry may indeed be described by and large as a series of variations on, or very free paraphrases, vague until they become unrecognizable, of biblical and evangelical episodes or liturgical ceremonies. The synthetic symbolic path goes from the creation of the world, from Genesis and thus from the Adamite couple who receive and lose Eden, to corruption, sin and guilt, the expulsion, and the Redemption, Crucifixion and Resurrection of Christ, right up to the Apocalypse, that is, the Second Coming. This 'progress' is used in a symbolic, analogical, and in part also literal sense. Hill elects corruption as his theme, and observes it in the domain of the ontological as well as in that of civil, political and institutional history. Corruption also means for him the corruption of language, never really secondary; he envisages it as a fluid, arbitrary and encrusted instrument. If history means decline, we need to dream of an elsewhere, and of cyclical moments of virginity and purity: Eden before

---

2   § 88.2.

the Fall, the Anglo-Saxon Middle Ages, or *tout court* the order of feudal society or the late seventeenth century in England, or the new Gothic age of the nineteenth century with its paladins.[3] A further element is Hill's interest in historical or mythical figures who yearned for redemption, their own and that of the world: political reformers, utopians, idealists, mystics, saints modelled on Christ himself; ones, in other terms, whose common destiny was to end up being imprisoned and killed by repressive agencies, or were set free by a miracle. Such obsessive and morbid worship is late Romantic or post-Decadent, but tempered by detachment, impassivity and irony. Among the many symbols and myths of the liturgy, Hill made that of the Pentecost especially his own, intended as flow and flame of Pauline metanoia and metamorphosis. Except that, ultimately, even the mystics and the mythical figures are victims of the instability of language and of the drift, decline and corruptibility of the psyche, so that Hill studies in fact the dangerous and tormenting blend of carnal and spiritual impulses, and, in short, the self-deceptions of the mystic. With Péguy, the criticism of holiness and mysticism reaches levels that are even caricatural.[4]

3. Redemption is a theme, and a metaphor, that works within a range of meanings and implications. Hill is a spiritualist and religious poet in the broadest sense, because he recalls a cosmic history that, wishing to free itself from the grip of the Creator's eschatological plan, is always laboriously caught, and said to be, in motion towards its redemption. It is both a universal and a local history, the history of the land where he was born in the geographical heart of England, and where the layers of history are perceptible for those with eyes to see. But these eyes are blind, and the continuity obscured, and the imperious need arises for a Pentecostal breath that will again descend from on high. So the analogical, correlative and symbolic value of the Pentecost is central and crucial in Hill's *Weltanschauung*, a

---

3   Hill was also nostalgic for a restored 'radical Tory' and semi-feudal, agricultural, hierarchical Britain, and for the patriarchal Southern America that had been defeated in the American Civil War.

4   § 95. Hill translated Ibsen's *Brand*, and *pour cause*, Brand being no different from his mystics, utopians, apocalyptics, dreamers, martyrs, fighters for redemption, often even crazed or possessed.

term that in his case is not unrealistic but appropriate. Hill welcomes again the possibility that death is a rebirth, and if he does not always believe this he always hopes so. His faith? 'A heretic's dream of salvation, expressed in the images of the orthodoxy from which he is excommunicate'.[5] An incipient deconstructionism paralyses, blocks, and haunts Hill, who takes too many precautions not to call himself *totally* a believer but at the same time not *totally* an agnostic either, and always admitting the flip side of the certainty of believing, the fear of believing. Reflecting himself in Péguy, and at the same time dissociating himself from him (therefore for these definitions, dictated as if on the borderline), Hill recalls the characters of Graham Greene and his whisky priest in particular,[6] excommunicated yet inside the Church. In one of his aesthetic pronouncements, Hill defines poetry and every poem as an act of 'atonement', a 'setting at one, a bringing into concord, a reconciling, a uniting in harmony'; and the poet who closes a poem as a weary creator, exhausted after the labours of the seven days of creation.[7] A similar religious paradigm is applied to the history of language: words are created, then become corrupted, like human nature, and Hill applies here the 'paradigm of the loss of the kingdom of innocence and original justice'.[8] At the end of Hill's ideological trajectory is the breaching of the referential agreement between *res* and *verba*, followed by the arbitrariness of language, whereas the language of prayer was formerly a rule that served to cement a community. Hill engages in the Lacanian, daily struggle of the poet with a language that possesses him. The use of the word is regulated by the axiom that 'etymology is history', and words are used with this premise, seen and applied in their transformational journey and with an awareness of their roots.[9] With Hill we must always keep

5   Quoted in Sherry 1987, 22.
6   § 52.1.
7   Quoted in Ricks 1987, 319.
8   Quoted in Sherry 1987, 167.
9   Often the semantic history of a word not only documents a slow and gradual change
       in its meaning, but a polar excursion: a frequently recurring word in Hill, 'seraph',
       is understood and used with the echo of its Hebrew root 'saraph' in mind, which
       denotes a fiery serpent (Sherry 1987, 186).

the etymological dictionary at hand, and reopening it leads exactly to the discovery of the diachronic corruption of language and its etymons; his or anyone's poems change, displace or even reverse their meaning depending on this etymological trajectory. The next deduction, for Hill, is the innate mendacity of language, even its Faustian, Mephistophelian, satanic nature: we use a soiled instrument or vehicle, one dipped in blood, violence, and oppression, and we must make it virgin. Hill delights in this demiurgic possibility, but also feels the guilt of his race, carries the burden – the symbolic cross of Christ – on his shoulders. Writing is like damning or at least staining oneself. The language of poetry is the same language being used, or historically used, to condemn, kill, and give orders to exterminate. Hill does not separate language from the ethical responsibilities it contains in essence, and he speaks of the 'atrocities' of language.

4. It is therefore necessary, though not sufficient, to inscribe Hill and his 'genesis' as a poet in the historical atmosphere of the incubation of deconstruction and in the philosophical climate of Cambridge in the early 1950s, where Wittgenstein had left his mark and had inspired the English epistemologist J. L. Austin, the author in 1962 of the famous book *How to Do Things with Words*. This training, translated into poetic practice, would seem to make Hill a poet apart, unrelated to poetic movements; indeed, although not only because of this, it confirms it. The point of departure is different but that of arrival is shared. Hill is not extraneous to the crisis of the uneasy intellectual who disagrees with his times. He inclines towards Hughes in the beginning because he is not a poet devoted to narrative poetry, to the daily anecdote grasped in its pungency and abnormality, albeit revelatory; and he belongs instead to visionary, imaginative, oneiric, associative, historical-mythological poetry. However, Hughes lacks the sense, taste and willingness of the impeccable structure, and occasionally wastes words in his exuberance; Hill, on the contrary, exhibits the scrupulous, rigorous, algid economy of a Larkin, without of course sharing his subject matter. The reconnaissance of forms and techniques begins in Hill from a lack of an alliterative diction, at least to the strongly marked extent of Hughes; Hill in turn accepts rhyme, pararhyme and the conventional forms of tradition. Anyone who opens one of his books of poetry is impressed, if not shocked, by a sequence of formally finished, externally balanced, smooth

and stylish poems, though with elusive semantics: polished, oracular utterances to which only the author seems to possess the key. With apparently total indifference to a wider audience, they address an elite of readers with whom the poet has long been familiar and with whom, by virtue of this familiarity, he can dialogue simply by way of allusion or implication. In Hill, the meaning arises from, or more precisely is often illuminated by, the most microscopic and infinitesimal measuring units of poetic discourse: for instance from the friction between the title and the content, from the etymologies of some terms he uses, even from the punctuation marks. To delve into the range of meanings of some individual terms in Hill, Empson's seven types of ambiguity do not suffice, and this is because, in accordance with Hill's epistemology, the poet presents himself without a defined thesis to demonstrate and as if, remembering Arnold, he were *in utrumque paratus*.[10] This indeterminacy rests on a ubiquitous polysemy, as much synchronic as diachronic. Hill's poems do not primarily communicate emotions or rely on anecdotes actually experienced, but consist of supremely mediated argumentation (and therefore their 'musicality' is far from opulent, they were never intended for recitation, but to be read and reread mentally), and the basic conceptual oppositions are not demarcated and proclaimed loudly, but are blurred. With a photographic metaphor, in them there nestles a large hermeneutic 'development' in comparison to the 'negative' of the few lines. Scrolling through the complete poetry of Hill until 1983, we realize that it consists of five meagre collections that altogether do not exceed 200 pages, although from this collective edition the author expunged his youthful production. On arriving at that date, which marks a first, indeed *the* dividing line in Hill's production, the meagreness becomes even more evident if we recall that each page contains

---

10   We owe to Brown 1980 the ingenious application to Hill of the seventh form of
     Empson's ambiguity, 'a fundamental division in the mind of the writer' (2); Hill,
     we might add, systematically puts into practice the double and contrary semantics
     embodied for instance by Hopkins in the phrase 'here / Buckle!' in ll. 9–10 of the
     sonnet 'The Windhover' (Volume 6, § 201). As Brown recalls (20–1), Hill endorsed
     Eliot's axiom concerning the separation between the 'mind that creates' and the 'man
     who suffers'.

only one poem, and that Hill's habitual measure does not exceed thirty lines. Hill gained in contraction, more exactly in condensation, what he 'lost' in sheer quantity.

5. Every aesthetic or phenomenology of obscurity hinges on mimesis, that is, on the symbiosis of form and content, and a poem is obscure because its referent is obscure. If this explanation is simplistic it is because there is no true aetiology of obscurity. Hill's obscurity, better defined as *indirectness*, is not due to syntactic dislocation, and only in one respect to grammatical irregularity. His poetic phrase is indeed often and in one way facilitated, often paratactic; it does not indulge in contortion and in the accumulation of secondary clauses, and his sentences, syntactically elementary, and made up of subject verb and object, may come across as flat, if taken individually. The difficult thing is to relate them to one another and extract a coherent *dianoia*. The rhetorical figure that predominates is ellipsis, which means both the vacuum, the apparent argumentative hiatus between the sentences, and the absence of a connecting verb, outwardly producing the effect of unrelated impressions or annotations on the page. We can take as a model a poem in four tercets, 'A Pre-Raphaelite Notebook', which demonstrates the poet's procedure starting from the title. In Hill, titles not only fail to orientate the reader by restricting the referential field, but often also throw him off the scent; or they motivate their relevance by way of remote, arcane hints well off at a tangent. In this poem, what appears before our eyes is a notebook of impressions given in a list without a verb in the first tercet, and in part in the others; the only thing that is Pre-Raphaelite is a veiled reference to a painting by Holman Hunt or to the Annunciation. Instead, there is an intertwined web of images and therefore words not arranged in a uniform or immediate isotopy, but juxtaposed and contrasted. Elsewhere, this sharp drop in internal referentiality rests on the interplay of voices: the speaking 'I' is that of the poet or other monologuers who are distinct from him. French critics have seen in Hill a *symboliste* who is an heir of Mallarmé,[11] while the British ones find in him a modernist who is a descendant of Eliot. Before Hill, Eliot had meditated, as I have amply discussed, on the sense of

---

11   Especially René Gallet, the most profound non-British connoisseur of Hill.

time, and had closed his journey on an eschatological perspective and on the final redemption of history. On the contrary, Hill's poetry ranges well beyond the threshold of the simple evocation, and he is at the same a prose writer and essayist. Like Eliot, he believed it necessary to help his readers through self-annotation. In his case this annotation is scanty, elusive, always patchy, sometimes semi-serious, even blatantly inadequate. With Hill, we are in terrible need of a 'reader's guide', of the type of the numerous ones dedicated to Eliot, in order to fully appreciate what is behind and within the poems, or even just the factual allusions and references they contain. The unmistakable personal mark of his poetry may favourably provoke the reader as much as make him impatient and irritated. If Hughes seduces, Hill makes no concessions to readability, and his austere and esoteric poetry can scare away at first sight. Historical critics have been reverential, servile and aphasic, almost dependent on Hill's self-paraphrases: it is rare to encounter a disagreement, a small or timid distance taken[12] in a choir of verbose and bizarre interpretations which necessarily refer back to oracular premises of Hill himself. Differing in this from Valéry, Hill does not wait for critics to explain his poems, but has their key in hand. Every possible disagreement has been silenced by the high respect paid to Hill by such authoritative critics as Ricks,[13] Bloom or George Steiner. However, those who are not swept away by uncritical enthusiasm can note limits in this case as well. Detractors recognize in Hill linguistic acts of supreme rarefaction and distillation, but cold and calligraphic, bloodless and passionless, and above all, Orphically sibylline. The individual poems are made up of far-fetched subtleties, of Baroque *agudezas*, of alembicated argumentations that fade into the sophistic. Hill declared that he believed in, and was implementing

12   A review by Tom Paulin (*The London Review of Books*, 1985, no. 6, 13–14), dictated by an inexplicable and rabid rancour, chilled the zeal of critics, blaming them for their 'reverential credulity'. In this review, Paulin accuses Hill of having imitated and plagiarized poems by Tennyson, Eliot and Stevens, and denounces echoes, veiled but very real, of the racist and xenophobic political views of an Enoch Powell.

13   The two very learned essays by Ricks 1987 – masterful, albeit belated examples of linguistic and structuralist close reading – follow the hidden semantic paths that can be sketched out – which says it all – from case studies, and the phenomenology, of parentheses and of the divisive/connective hyphens in English compounds.

a poetry which, in the wake of Milton, is 'simple, sensuous and passionate': sensuous is what Hill is at times, passionate almost never and simple never. By applying that simple trick which, arguably, was for Goethe the litmus test of great poetry (what remains after being translated), various poems by Hill may be reduced to elementary, banal, obvious formulations, sometimes even to the classic, brilliant but obvious solution to a problem.

§ 93. *Hill II: Reservations on the votive word*

Except for his academic curriculum, Hill's relevant biography must be limited to a few schematic facts, both because it is irrelevant for the purposes of his poetry, and because his longevity, his mere existence in life, until recently inhibited biographers. Hill was never reluctant to give interviews, however, and the posthumous biographies will presumably add very few other essential data to those we know from his own lips. Hill, in other terms, is a ghost figure, and more than anything else a thinking and poeticizing intellect. It is only necessary to know that he was a native of the West Midlands, that his parents were barely literate, his father a policeman, and his mother a worker at an ironmonger's. One constant that unites the natives of the Midlands is consciousness of their historical memory, which, thanks to the landscape, is, as if mediumistically, a centuries-long story of stratified civilizations and of clashes between races, right back to their Celtic origins. Hill revealed that, like Tennyson, when he was young he loved to stroll and walk across the rough countryside of his district, and communing with it he 'muttered to the stones and trees'.[14] He attended Oxford University, where he started writing poems, and was among the few in England to acknowledge the American poets, especially Allen Tate. Hill thought Tate capable of compressing in his poetry metaphysical and cerebral content in closed forms. By the time of his first collection, Hill loomed as a belated modernist, forty years younger than Eliot, Pound, or even David Jones. Being born between the two world wars made him yet another poet marked by a double psychic experience; hence, the archetypal denunciation of dictatorship, the pity for the fallen, the celebration of the

14   Sherry 1987, 2, and Volume 4, § 78.1.

martyrs for freedom and the utopia of freedom. On the other hand, it should not be forgotten that when he was a child, Hill sang in the parish choir, and that this musical experience, including the familiarity with the liturgy and with the stories of the Bible, remained indelible, and provided him with a reservoir of formulae, languages and rituals tirelessly retraced and re-emerging, not only in their analogic value, but also and simply as a repertoire of beautiful images. 'Genesis' is, as we have seen, a demiurgic act that certifies the birth of a poet, a poet who is similar to a god contemplating his creation, but with a desperate sense of impotence, and who, as in a poem by Dylan Thomas, is 'dumb to tell' yet tells. Nature rebels against its creator, manifests impulses contrary to the divine plan of love, and the divine doppelganger, by refusing to implement a benign plan of creation, discovers the key of Hobbes to be in force, namely that man is wolf to man.

2. In *For the Unfallen* (1959), Hill, donning several masks, repeats his stubborn ambition to regenerate the unredeemed world, reconciling especially its dark, absurd and violent impetus. He fails and tries again, but to no avail. The imaginative self-mirroring in legendary figures, and historical, biblical, Blakean, and Promethean ones – Titans, martyrs, climbers, doubles of Christ, thirsty reformers who succumb destroyed by their hubris – mainly occurs in poems not included in *Collected Poems*. The poet might embrace the example of Christ, throwing himself into the fray and emerging bloodied, but he rejects the Eucharist, returns disappointed by the burning bush, or from the hill of the Transfiguration.[15] A chain of examples shows the continuation of a brutal, alien, 'not regenerated' jurisdiction, as if Christ's redemption were yet to come, and he were a Christ who redeems humanity by the shedding of his blood, since every regeneration passes unavoidably through his Passion. This motif pours out in objective correlatives of a wait for a revelation in ambiguous ecstasies, with paraphrases of Revelation or the visions of mystics and saints, and the overturning of rapacious nature into a meek one, like that of the she-wolf (the visit to its lair is in a poem dedicated to Holy Thursday). It has been

---

15   'God's Little Mountain', where some mystical experience occurred, but the poet does not know how to report it after the return: 'Now I lack grace to tell what I have seen'.

noticed and frequently repeated that Hill's title is in this collection a nod at 'For the Fallen', a conventional poem on war victims by the Georgian poet Laurence Binyon. Nevertheless, in the general plan of the collection, the most urgent and crucial resonance is the state before the Fall, a term to be interpreted in a literal, metaphorical and eschatological sense. Here is the proof that Hill is investigating the state of decay and decline, and *ipso facto* Adam's fall and man's entry into the time of Redemption and Liberation. The title of the collection is also relevant because of the 'for', namely, 'in memory of'. The individual poems are commemorations, and one is expressly entitled 'In Piam Memoriam'; in memoriam is also a poem on a local pig-headed elderly lady who challenged death. The titles increasingly refer to liturgical terms and operations, such as 'canticle', 'requiem', or, only slightly less religious, 'elegy', and outwardly take the form of hymns and rituals, ceremonies and liturgies, though with some implied irony or lack of conviction. The development of the poem often proves to be in conflict with the title, or to undermine it. History, being a history of outrage, massacre, innocent blood spilt, is also a history of death; Hill explicitly 'wants' to 'consider the dead', who are, however, by now the 'shell' of what was once 'rich seed'. The commemorating voice is not heard by the dead, and even the kings are now, with their soul departed, merely 'the dropping-back of dust' (hence lacking any transcendent perspective). This liturgical action moves, broadly speaking, from Genesis to the Passion, since two widely separate poems take place on Holy Thursday and Good Friday, and others are sceptical of the Universal Judgement or discuss its prospect in any case. The public history polemically touched on, or alluded to, is the Conference of Versailles, when the European plenipotentiaries denigrated the Pentecost by sitting mute, prophesying and planning ruin, and ringing bells that already announced the Second World War, a war that, at such a distance, still unleashes in the poet two 'formal' elegies, and made Europe a second waste land.[16] 'In Piam Memoriam' turns on the contrast between the artifice of a stained glass window depicting an inert, mummified saint, and the Heraclitean tumult of nature. The irony lies in linguistic details that deny

16   In the four-part mini-cycle 'Of Commerce and Society'.

both the title and the expectation. This is therefore a paradigmatic poem in Hill, who avails himself of linguistic ambivalence: 'created purely from glass' implies 'pure' creations as much as the opposite, creatures 'purely' of glass, that is, unreal, incapable of living and vivifying. In another poem of similar ambiguity, the alabaster glory of the tombs of the Plantagenet kings is denied by the expression 'they lie' (reclining, but also fibbing). The possible aquatic metamorphosis is a reference to *The Tempest*. 'Picture of a Nativity' and 'Canticle for Good Friday' twist and deform the icon of the Nativity, as well as the Passion, questioning their traditional features (the Infant emerges as from a submarine seabed, and the cross is borne by a Thomas, perhaps the sceptical disciple). The infant is also a poet in the midst of indifferent, serpentine, or obtuse disciples. The first of the poets who are ideally prisoners, mental prisoners underground, but of moral temper, daring visionaries of another world, and mystics, is Hölderlin.

3. The opening poem in *King Log*[17] (1968), entitled 'Ovid in the Third Reich', laments the late disappearance of God by registering the impossibility of curbing the blood lust, distant yet always close, and of perceiving his hand on the cosmos. It principally involves the non-disjunction of ethics and aesthetics, denounced *e contrario* in a new Ovid faced with Hitler's madness. Thus, it is an appeal addressed in the first instance by the poet even to himself, in favour of the activist militancy of poetry, and against an art that is quietist, disengaged, sunk in fatalistic pessimism about its ability to change history. This is an art that is justified in the inclusion of each historical occurrence within the inscrutable plan of divine love (with the invocation to an ecumenical forgiveness of the 'damned'). But is this so? The poem is deliberately shorn of its dialectic rejoinder. In 'September Song', Hill's best-known and most commented poem, paradigmatic in order to study his polysemy and ambiguities and how they are deployed, the poet identifies with a baby Jew deported by the Germans, who has almost the same birth date as the poet. The poem discusses in the final analysis the self-gratification of art, the 'sorrowful' commemoration of misfortunes, enacted, however, after one has been an accomplice in causing them. It

17   An allusion to the sardonic Aesopian fairy-tale about Jupiter who gives the frogs a
      king in this form, a log.

indicates the enemy in the addiction to cliché, which, like metaphors that become catachreses, no longer reveals the mechanism of the message, and in this case the command of death which this message contains. As in Shakespeare, and in the funeral discourse of Mark Antony, the poet uses stereotypes ('in his time', 'as expected') to unmask precisely their nature as clichés, so that the carrying out of the hideous murder becomes common and routine.[18] The two sonnets 'on the Annunciation' discuss how language, in the historical-epistemological perspective, and the Word in a theological perspective, were launched into history, and from the original purity turn back, subsisting certainly but sullied by the mire into which they have fallen; yet all this engenders a complacent and equivocal satisfaction. God himself is the one who 'spreads corruption'.[19] 'History as Poetry' is an *ars poetica* which lays down that poetry is greeting, apostrophe, and a Pentecostal flame, hence a descent or an instigation of the Spirit, and the poet a risen Lazarus; yet he is also a 'mystified' Lazarus, a term which incorporates the significance of the mystical and the deceived, which makes him a 'common man' who may have only dreamed the leap into the afterlife. The bloody violence unleashed by fanaticism binds the Holocaust to some selected episodes of history.[20] 'Funeral Music' is an internal cycle of eight formally imperfect sonnets, dedicated to three English noblemen beheaded during the War of the Roses. The falling of the axe is a Pentecostal glow in the monologue about the three killed, who quiver with confidence and fear, and with the just repressed pride of holiness and humility, as in T. S. Eliot's Becket. Hill sharpens the morbid feelings of the prisoner, of the accused, and of the heretic who has been tried and is awaiting his sentence, with whom he identifies.[21] The War of the Roses is

18　In contrast, Hill wrote four poems on the 'resistance' and integrity of four poets who are not imaginary, Campanella, Hernández, Desnos and Mandelstam.

19　Although, with the ambiguity 'of the seventh type' typical in Hill, the term 'scatters' may be read as meaning the exact opposite of 'chasing off'.

20　The Battle of Shiloh, one of the bloodiest episodes of the American Civil War, proves for Hill that the war was not one for human rights but one of conquest.

21　Hill's note, affixed to this composition, reveals his sophisticated historical culture, and also his extravagant sense of disproportion: the poet strives to make 'a holocaust' out of the battle of Towton during the War of the Roses, as he says it has been for

seen as the end of the Edenic, active and peaceful coexistence and the first scourge of anarchy in an inexorable cyclicism. But Hill equally insinuates doubts on the motivations of the three noblemen, though finally admitting that their heroism was an exceptional fact, like the appearance of a comet in the sky. The fourth composition is exceptionally revealing, and depicts a desolate world that may be revivified by faith, and is now subjected to a 'void rule'; criticizing Averroes, Hill tries to convince himself of the need for the soul.

§ 94. *Hill III: The 'Mercian Hymns'*
The thirty *Mercian Hymns* (1971) seem the distillate of the consultation of an entire library of historical studies on the late Middle Ages in what is now England. Hill emulates Eliot with his accompanying sibylline notes, which mention with scrupulous care far-fetched data reported with surreality and impertinence, and causing a clash between the erudition in which the poet, without any kind of estrangement, is immersed, and the real benefit the reader gets from it. The poem is a *tour de force*, and it certainly ranks among the most artificial of an artificial poet; it can even aspire to a primacy within English poetry of the second half of the twentieth century, that of the most experimental, just as *The Waste Land* had been that in the first. Formally, each of the individual short pieces is in prose, except that the words are occasionally split by a hyphen for the return at the end of the line. It is in any case poetic prose, arranged in stanzas separated by gaps, wider margins, and indents after the first line; and poetic especially in the systematic use of ellipsis and in the contrast established between sentence and sentence, stanza and stanza, and between the single pieces of the thirty. Anachronism, too, relates it to the structure of *The Waste Land*. Offa, an Anglo-Saxon monarch of the eighth century, is also a king of our time and transcends time like Eliot's Tiresias or Joyce's Finnegan and HCE (the twenty-seventh stanza stages the funeral vigil over the bier of the dead mythical king). If Offa is a historical-mythical figure he is therefore also

---

the popular mentality. This and other notes to the poems are written in a bombastic, tortuous, difficult, and even pedantic style.

immortal, and his immortality means he lives through the historical epochs, and that it gives him an eternal, although metamorphic, existence. He is in fact recognized in some modern archetypes, such as public entrepreneurship, the real estate market and high finance. À la Joyce, though not à la Eliot, Hill shows a unique taste for savoury, gross humour, and a series of unexpected and sudden transitions of scenario. Some pungent, highly economical tableaux sound like limericks vivified by the inexhaustible resources of polysemic words. The Joycean, nocturnal or at least surreal syntax, and the mythical frame, destroy any diegetic linearity right from the start, with a list of appositions and of historical and imaginative duties covered by the metamorphic monarch, who contentedly hears them recited by his minstrel. Offa is seen as a primordial force of light, progress and civilization, because he is moving 'towards heaven' through the barbarian ivy; he is the bearer of civilization to wild England. His phenomenology is, however, trivialized or gently satirized in non-consequent actions having a mysterious and arcane flavour, actions of an inscrutable or even hieratic meaning, but not exactly appropriate to the character; and yet he matures and legislates, and thus curbs the anarchy. He is a Solomonic, indulgent, spiritual king (remorse is the cure of the soul) and an animal lover, eager to learn; thanks to his work people become industrious and specialize in arts and crafts. The sudden deviation toward the ludic cannot mask a work that is one of hymnography, votive and commemorative, as the title, once again, has announced. Hill also sketches the birth in England of the goldsmith's art, of upholstery, sculpture, the manufacture of coins, and the epic of the primitive Christianity of pilgrimages. Transfigured as a wanderer, or tourist or motorist of today, Offa makes an educational trip, and in Pavia takes lessons from Boethius – yet another prisoner. That distant time was one of waiting and of a life that was carefree, credulous, and enjoyed; a transitory, mixed age on the border between barbarism and civilization. That orderly age had been broken during the childhood of the poet, who, in agreement with Ruskin's utopias, 'writes this', in the time of the enunciation, 'to the memory' of his worker grandmother. The poetic 'I' remembers his childhood, and can now submerge himself, become confused in and disguise himself as Offa, without experiencing any guilty narcissism, and without reproaching the artist's self-gratification.

§ 95. *Hill IV: 'Tenebrae' and 'The Mystery of the Charity of Charles Péguy'*
Hill had earlier tested erotic frustration, enigmatically masked as a
mystical impulse, in the cycle dedicated to the imaginary Spanish poet
Sebastian Arrurruz, who bears these symbolic traits doubled in the name
of the traditionally sensual saint and in the word 'arrow', encased in his
surname. The mini-cycle 'The Pentecost Castle', which opens, not too
strangely, a collection placed under the banner of the ritual of Holy Week
('Tenebrae'), is an Arthurian ballad in linguistically essential lines as never
before, arranged in quatrains (lovers of the poem may be believers, fre-
quenters of the church and the Eucharist, and they are killed by pagans
in an ambush). These are lines which at the same time sound, in Hill, like
an imitation of Provençal poetry for their ecstatic and hyperbolic diction
of sensual passion, and therefore also Pre-Raphaelite in the mixture of
sacred and profane, sensual and ascetic.[22] The short monologues question
Christ's oxymoronic nature, and a love that is renunciation or suffering.
The night of the soul can also be the delight of the senses, and, as a masochistic necrophilic, Hill in 'The Pentecost Castle' is a Decadent with an
acute sense of the pleasure of suffering, dying, and agonizing. The ecstasy
of martyrdom shows traces of Pater and Morris, according to the sensibility that Pater defined as 'aesthetic poetry', where mysticism is tinged with,
and is one with, a form of Eros that is slightly less fleshly.[23] Therefore this
poem, from a Hill always attentive to self-mystification, is about deception and the covert and contradictory implications of mystical passion.[24]
The section 'Lachrimae', containing meditations in the mystical number of
seven, is of sonnets as if recited at the foot of the Cross, but divided if not
torn between penetration of and adherence to the mystery, and awareness

22   The suggestion comes, according to Hill, from the musician Cabezón, but the text
      is a variant of a tragedy by Lope.

23   As is also suggested by Sherry 1987, 191.

24   'Scenes with Harlequins' is a not new paraphrastic exercise, a calligraphic exploit of
      empathy and recreation inspired by the correspondence of the poet Alexander Blok.
      Two souls are again on a quest, mystically united, towards a goal in the afterlife, in a
      harlequinesque version of a contemporaneity that makes one prefer dismissive and
      sarcastic silence.

of the rejection and the incorrigibility of the human heart. At times, these are 'terrible' sonnets of hopeless resistance to the Crucified One, which therefore echo Hopkins, for example in the fourth one, in which the contrite 'I' does not know where to turn. Christ hurts and makes the faithful suffer whom he would like to save, and the dense questioning begins. These are exceptionally lively sonnets for Hill, because the veils fall away and a certain dramatic lyricism prevails, *almost* immediate, and therefore also partially masked, which Hill had never allowed to be heard. In the fifth, on the desire of martyrdom and the joys it brings, the pair of lines, 'I founder in desire for things unfound. / I stay amid the things that will not stay', is the most Hopkinsian sentence ever written by Hill. Man is a Judas who cheatingly kisses Christ in the sixth; the seventh is a passionate, equally Hopkinsian dialogue, or even complaint, suited to a true Metaphysical poet. The eponymous subsection 'Tenebrae', with eight compositions of variable length, starts from Hill's classic and symbolic epigraph, a prison and a meditative exile immersed in night. It is a series of lamentations, prayers, remembrances, invocations, even if divided, alternating with the outbursts and growls of a temporary or extreme, therefore also partly diabolical, refusal. The crucial theological point is the imperfect renunciation of *amor carnalis* in conflict with the spiritual.

2. The inspired and exceptionally passionate 'Hymns to Our Lady of Chartres' (1984) describe forms and customs of the popular cult of the homonymous sanctuary of the Virgin. They parenthetically introduce the French poet Péguy, as an example of a worship made of 'gnashing and gnawing', recalcitrant, almost sceptical, or of the nature of Pascal's wager, yet always ritual, while the people plunge into the faith without reservations or hesitation. For a moment, rational man mistakes the believers for fools, and reasons sceptically over the popular superstition with which he would not want to mix. In the end, an invocation flows forth to the Virgin herself to subdue such scepticism with her authority, to imprison unbelievers, willy-nilly as in Hopkins's 'Deutschland' (including those who greet the Madonna with closed fists). A long introduction in prose by Hill to 'The Mystery of the Charity of Charles Péguy' (1983) informs us of his admiration for this writer who fell prematurely in war. Hill had identified in Péguy one of his models, the passionate poet in search of the absolute, an idealist secretly longing

for martyrdom and the 'desire to suffer', or also the example of a sacrificial patriotism that Péguy had already manifested during the Dreyfus Affair. A contradictory personality, first and foremost a socialist, then perhaps the one who ordered the killing of the socialist Jaurès in 1914, Péguy is acquitted by Hill of every accusation of fascist and anti-Semitic fanaticism. Hill is interested in the 'mystery' of his death in the early months of the war 'in a field of beetroot': whether, that is, he died in the odour of grace and conversion, even after having received the Eucharist, since he had formally abandoned the Church and religious practice. But his devotion to Our Lady, as Hill had recalled in the immediately preceding hymns, had resulted in two pilgrimages to the Cathedral of Chartres. Hence Péguy is yet another test of the irresistible rush to sacrifice in order to accomplish a full-blown palingenetic renewal. But Hill, constantly aware of the other side of the coin, remembers him to indicate his delusions, above all to question his foolish and unrealistic attempt. This cycle in ten sections is a tribute, in Hill's own words, to a great prophetic understanding and to one of the great spirits of the century. The epigraph pays significant homage to a man who said that a world had ended, after which another would come, that of those who no longer believed in anything. The individual *in memoriam* sections retrace Péguy's biographical and spiritual journey without chronological order and with no documentary evidence, that is, in a phantasmagoria. In Péguy facing the wretched world that surrounds him, Hill wishes in fact to outline a cosmic battle; his every act is a symbolic gesture, a phase of the fight of the brave spirit and of a palingenetic utopia, and religious and reforming fanaticism in a time alien from the spiritual. Péguy's departure for the front imaginatively becomes the pilgrimage of the Magi to Bethlehem, and is also associated with the lighting of the flame of the Pentecost. Péguy does for Hill what Sister Gertrude did for Hopkins in another wreck, that of the 'Deutschland': 'Here the lost are blessed, the scarred most sacred' (with an obvious anagram).

§ 96. *Hill V: Ventriloquist digressions on unredeemed history*

Always laconic, always thrifty, always elliptically dense, Hill broke the banks and opened the floodgates after 1984. Seven poetry collections flowed forth at short distances from one another; it is easy and indeed unoriginal to speak of a stream, a gush, a Pentecostal blaze in him. With